The daughter of career diplomats, now married to the
writer and traveller Nicholas Luard, **Elisabeth Luard**
spent much of her life abroad. A lifelong student of
the history of cooking, she is the author of the much-
acclaimed *European Peasant Cookery* (now re-issued as
The Rich Tradition), *The Princess and the Pheasant* and
The Barricaded Larder. A talented wildlife painter, she
illustrates her own work. *Emerald*, her first novel, will
also be published by Bantam Press in 1994.

'Puts a breathtaking perspective on commonplace
dishes from scouse to gravad lax, porkolt to paella' −
Harpers & Queen

'Clearly the fruit of living, eating and cooking among
the peasant guardians of various culinary traditions . . .
a fine collection' − *Literary Review*

'Elisabeth Luard has broken completely new ground
. . . will be turned to many times by anyone looking
for something totally different' − *Country Life*

'History, lore and complete recipes are presented en-
tertainingly and informatively' − *Time*

'A chance to discover recipes that deserve to be more
widely known' − *Country Living*

'An excellent read, and its country-hopping, folklore
and fascinating food facts will keep you absorbed even
on the longest long-haul flight' − *Westmorland Gazette*

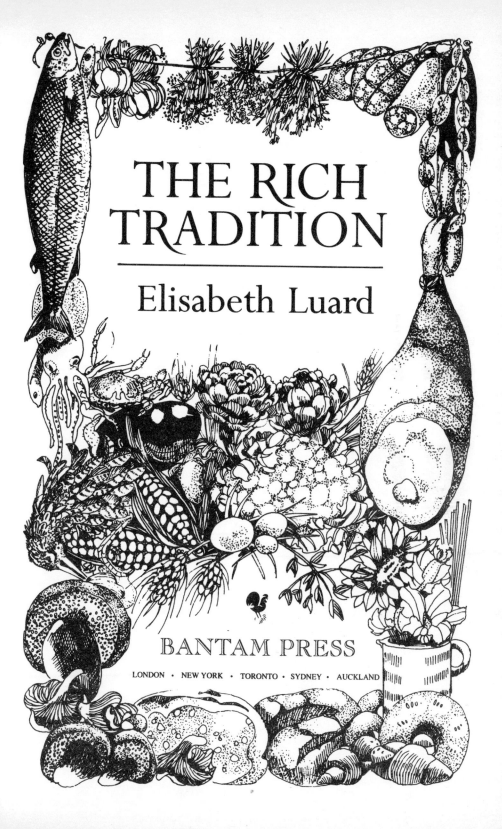

THE RICH TRADITION

Elisabeth Luard

BANTAM PRESS

LONDON · NEW YORK · TORONTO · SYDNEY · AUCKLAND

TRANSWORLD PUBLISHERS LTD
61–63 Uxbridge Road, London W5 5SA

TRANSWORLD PUBLISHERS (AUSTRALIA) PTY LTD
15–25 Helles Avenue, Moorebank, NSW 2170

TRANSWORLD PUBLISHERS (NZ) LTD
3 William Pickering Drive,
Albany, Auckland

Published 1994 by Bantam Press
a division of Transworld Publishers Ltd
Copyright © Elisabeth Luard 1986

First published in 1986 under the title *European Peasant Cookery*.

The right of Elisabeth Luard to be identified
as the author of this work has been asserted in accordance
with sections 77 and 78 of the Copyright Designs and
Patents Act 1988.

A catalogue record for this book is available
from the British Library

ISBN 0593 037944

Printed in Great Britain by
Clays Ltd, St. Ives plc.

To my children, Caspar, Francesca, Poppy and Honey, without whom there would have been no book. And to my beloved husband Nicholas, for thirty years of good companionship at table and on the road.

ACKNOWLEDGEMENTS

Over the years, many people from many countries have helped me in many ways with the preparation of this book, notably those who appear in person in the text, but also to Betty Molesworth Allen, Maurice de Ponton d'Amecourt, Bernard Auge, Elisabeth and Odbjorn Andreassen, Viviker and Richard Bernstrom, Tomas Bianchi, Mrs Vasili Frunzete, Alfred Grizel, Christian Hesketh, Vane Ivanovic, Frau Klein, Mitte Lhoest, Cecilia McEwen, Maureen McGlashan, Kiki Munchi, Ilhan and Ruya Nebioglu, May Pocock, Dr Astri Riddervold, Monica Rawlins, Erzbet Schmidl, Iolanda Tsalas, Jacqueline Weir; and for patient assistance in cultural and culinary matters to the staff of the London Library, particularly to Douglas Matthews, the Librarian. Above all, my thanks to Priscilla White, Chrissie MacDonald and Venetia Parkes, who valiantly tested the recipes.

More recently, while making the television series which was inspired by the book, I owe thanks for the energy and faith of the Australian film team who made the programmes, particularly the three who were with me all the way: cameraman-director Carmelo Musca, soundman Piercy Porter – and my polyglot daughter Poppy, art-director by trade, who was responsible for all location-work. We were on the road together for six months, sharing a camper-van, joined when necessary by expert interpreters, often not knowing what the next day might bring.

Pot-luck was the rule – and those who watch the series will not necessarily find in this book the precise instructions for each of the dishes featured in the thirteen episodes. From the northern uplands of Scandinavia to the shores of the Mediterranean; the mountains of eastern Slovakia to the western coast of Ireland, it is in the nature of peasant cookery that a dish follows no fixed recipe. Among self-sufficient communities, the daily dinner is dictated by the unpredictable: those vegetables which happen to be in glut at a particular moment, the contents of a storecupboard after a long winter, the fisherman's catch, the milk-yield of a family's flock of sheep, even the sleight of hand (and temper) of a particular cook. A further random element was provided by the domestic celebrations which we were invited to join. We were made welcome at a wedding in the Tatras mountains, danced at a spring festival in northern Italy, shared supper afloat with Sicilian fishermen, attended an eightieth birthday party in Sweden, went on a pilgrimage in Andalucia, feasted at Easter in Hungary, attended a pig-killing in the Black Forest, a christening among the Ruthenes, a ceilidh in the Western Isles.

To all those who opened their doors to us, and demonstrated their skills with patience, tolerance and justifiable pride, I owe a debt which can never be repaid.

Contents

Introduction

The market stalls in the southern Spanish port of Algeciras, among which as a young wife and new mother I found myself and my basket one bright June morning in 1965, had very little in common with the shelves of the city supermarkets where I had been accustomed to shop. I was bewildered, but also intrigued. A childhood spent in several distant parts of the world with my parents, foreign-posted diplomats, had given me an early appetite for street-corner food. This youthful enthusiasm had also left me with an unshakeable optimism that I could eat, and usually appreciate, anything that was palatable to any other human. I had discovered a single exception. Monday school dinner, at the English boarding school to which I was periodically returned, invariably consisted of mouse-grey mincemeat accompanied by wet toast. That I had never managed to stomach, not even with an appetite sharpened by outdoor swimming at seven o'clock of an English March morning.

Algeciras market could not have produced a school dinner in a month of Mondays. The vegetable stalls which formed its outer ring were piled with unfamiliar greenery: a heap of *tagarnina*, thistle stems waving tarantula-like green extremities; bundles of fresh garlic, like ice-white onions; smiling pink segments of watermelon; purple-tipped cardoons tied as rosebud bouquets. Between the stalls were little encampments of gypsy children, presiding over sacks of tiny snails with translucent bodies and inquiring pinstalk eyes, and flanked by baskets of wild mushrooms and bundles of slender wild asparagus bound with esparto grass.

The fish vendors, raised above their customers on a line of white-tiled stalls dripping sea water, were bellowing out their wares: octopus, squid, cuttlefish; monkfish, sea bream, bass, anchovies, and sardines; horse-mackerel and spiny red and blue sea creatures, whose names it took me years to memorize and pronounce correctly in the thick Andalusian dialect; crayfish, prawns, lobsters, and shrimps all alive and jumping; black and yellow eels thumping the counter; huge, pink slabs of tunny fish and thick steaks of swordfish. The poultry market was livelier still. There were bunches of chickens squawking on the ends of brawny arms, a blue-eyed goose, and a few mournful turkeys gobbling in one corner — no Andaluz housewife would trust a dead barnyard bird as far as she could chase it. The egg woman's wares were speckled with hay and feathers — there were bantam's eggs and eggs with double yolks, duck eggs and goose eggs, while behind her was balanced a tray of unlaid eggs winking like red-veined eyeballs from a Frankenstein movie.

The dry-goods stalls offered tins of corn, sacks of chickpeas, beans, lentils, maize, strings of onions and garlic, tins of oil, jars of honey, small round goat's cheeses, and loops of every imaginable dried sausage garlanding whole haunches of dried salt ham. The butchers' section was the least fathomable of all: rounds of unidentifiable meat hung on hooks from the beam which fronted each stall. It appeared the meat could be cut in one of two ways: thinly sliced for frying or in a single muscle-dictated oval chunk for adding to the stew. The offal was marginally more recognizable: hanks of tripe, loops of paprika-dark black pudding, slabs of liver and trays of kidneys, bull's testicles dangling from the last hook like forlorn stuffed string bags — the butchers took special delight in explaining them to puzzled visitors.

The spice lady must have had fifty open sacks around her: almonds, six kinds of tea, bayleaves, dried garlic and paprika, cloves and cinnamon bark, thyme, rosemary, marjoram, coriander, poppy seeds, liquorice twigs, pumpkin seeds, dozens more. Often she would be asked to make up a flavouring mix: a sugar-paper twist of the herbs to spice four kilos of snails, to prepare a side of pork in paprika lard, to provide the aromatics for ten kilos of olives. Later I learnt to rely on her expertise myself.

María, my neighbour up the valley where I and my growing family settled, was my mentor in those first years.

'Así se hace,' she would patiently explain, 'This is how it is done,' as I struggled with the ink sacs in the cuttlefish, or attempted to cook the chickpeas without soaking them first. Very often she would come by with gifts of food for my children — honey from her uncle's hives, the first figs, wrapped in one of their own leaves, from the tree in her father's garden, oil biscuits which she had made after baking day.

My family and I saw the seasons round in the valley. The children went to the local school, where they learnt along with the three Rs how to trap and skin rabbits, how to stake pastures to hold the forest's hogs, and how to mend a hand-drawn threshing sled made to a design unchanged since the Iron Age. With María's advice and under her tutelage we acquired a donkey, a kitchen garden, and a household pig — the last, I stipulated, only if María helped me at its final hour. The pig thrived mightily on the scraps from my kitchen. Finally on a late October day deemed suitable, the moon being in the right quarter and the pig having been fattened to the correct weight on acorns from the surrounding cork oaks, María's husband and brother-in-law arrived at sunrise to prepare for the dreaded event. Soon afterwards María, her cousins, and her mother appeared to help with the kitchen labour. The children were packed off to school early, and all day we worked salting hams, seasoning sausages, stuffing black puddings, spicing *chorizos*. That evening, as she prepared the traditional celebration meal of *chícharros* pork scratchings, kidneys in sherry and garlic-fried liver which follows a country *matanza* or pig-killing, María finally put the question which made me embark on this book.

'Tell me,' she said, her voice sympathetic as she leaned over the table and restored control of the sausage casing for the fifth time to my clumsy fingers, 'I have been wanting to ask you ever since you and your family arrived, but I did not wish to seem inquisitive. Please forgive me, but did your mother teach you nothing at all?'

From then on María became a surrogate mother in the old ways of the countryside to all of us. Seven years later, when we departed for the Languedoc to give the children a year's schooling in France, she came down the hill to see us on our way. As we climbed into our crammed vehicle she handed a bundle in through the window. Inside was a bag of dried sunflower seeds — the children's favourite *pipas*, to be cracked between the teeth and the shell expertly propelled through the open window — a hank of dried sausage, and a gigantic loaf pricked with the baker's initials, a bread of the size normally baked for a cork-tree stripping gang on a two-week excursion into the hills.

'There,' she said. 'I could not bear to think you might be hungry on your journey.'

Once we were established in the Languedoc, María's role in our lives was taken over by our neighbouring farmer's wife, who kept a fine old-fashioned barnyard, pigeon loft, and piggery. Her three strapping sons and burly husband bore visible witness to her culinary skills. From her I learnt how to choose a *foie gras* while it was still encased in the goose, how to pot a *confit*, and the correct way to layer a *cassoulet*, even how to bake the goose feathers to sterilize them for stuffing a feather pillow. When the time came in its turn for us to leave the Languedoc to return to England for the children to finish their schooling in a more conventional fashion, she also gave us a picnic basket for our journey. In it, wrapped up in greaseproof paper, were thick slices of her special cured ham, a cool square of sweet butter, and a big bunch of radishes from her garden. Nestling in one corner was a small bottle of *eau de vie aux cerneaux* — walnut-flavoured white brandy — which the farmer himself distilled, as of ancient hereditary right, and flavoured with leaves from his own tree. She too did not wish to see us leave hungry.

'I shall call peasants those who have, at the least, this in common: their agriculture is a livelihood and a way of life, not a business for profit.' Thus Dr Redfield neatly defined 'peasants' in his influential study, *Peasant Society and Culture* (University of Chicago Press, 1956). Certainly both my neighbours in the Andalusian valley and on the plains of the Languedoc grew or earned a cash crop to supplement their way of life. María's mother told me that her mother used to raise silkworms for money to buy supplies of salt, a little coffee, spices, and a few other things which the household needed and could not make. But the larders of both families were still filled largely from the fruits of their own labours. Even tea was grown in the garden. Today the pattern of European peasant life is changing swiftly, but throughout eastern Europe the same pockets of self-sufficiency can still be found.

Given Dr Redfield's definition, peasant cookery must of its nature depend on ingredients which can be easily obtained or grown locally. The glow of embers on the hearth, a savoury broth simmering in the cooking pot on its tripod, a flitch of bacon from last autumn's pig smoking in a hollow in the chimney — until very recently these were not nostalgic pleasures, for centuries they were the very stuff of life in Europe. Peasant cooking was always dominated by practical rather than economic factors. Peasant communities had no organized trade. Barter was the chief form of exchange, and there were no regular tradesmen to supply goods or services. Fuel in particular was precious. It needed energy to collect and was often in short supply. In consequence cooking was usually done on a single heat source.

Possessions were scarce — a medieval peasant kitchen would be equipped with a boiling pot, a frying pan, and a kettle. As late as the seventeenth and eighteenth centuries the peasant house was only one room, plus barns and storehouse. The fireplace was the focal point, whether there was a chimney to extract the smoke or not, and there would have been one large table with benches set round it, the benches also being used for sleeping. Early mattresses were of heaped straw and were replaced later by home-produced feather bedding. The whole household gathered together at mealtimes and ate from a communal bowl with wooden spoons — children often took their meals standing up. There were wooden boards for portions of bread, and a knife, often shared, for the meat. After 1800 sugar, coffee, and tea became widely available and affordable.

The limitations imposed by a single pot, a single heat source, local produce, and little or no access to imports, are all characteristic of peasant cooking and give it its particular identity. But in no sense does this mean that the ingredients were necessarily poor or inferior: salmon, oysters, crayfish, snails, excellent cheeses, superb truffles and fungi, and an abundant game larder featuring venison, partridge, wild duck, wild boar, and hare were all available to local communities. Even the most sophisticated delicacies such as *foie gras* were as likely to be found in a French peasant's larder as in the kitchen of the *Roi Soleil*.

There were no sudden influxes of foreign spices, imported delicacies, or fashionable chefs, such as those who fled to Britain after the French revolution, in the peasant kitchen. Each generation in a community might throw up perhaps one particularly inspired cook, whose innovations would be added to the repertoire of the immediate area. This has led to variations of local dishes which are peculiar to an individual neighbourhood and whose merits are fiercely contested — there are dozens of different recipes for the making of a Spanish *paella*, for instance, each dependent on the local ingredients. There is, however, an underlying philosophy which governs all the recipes for a particular dish, and an understanding of this allows the cook to experiment and adapt the recipe to local produce.

The peasant larder varied according to climate and conditions. In northern Europe, Norway, Sweden, and Finland make good use of their sea coasts: salted, sometimes smoked, and pickled fish, including salmon, were and are important items of the region's diet, as is dried meat, while barley, oats, and rye are the chief cereal crops. Central Europe is rich in wheat and dairy produce: cheese, bacon, potatoes, vegetables, and the fruit of the vine are all plentiful, and this is reflected in the peasant cookery of Germany, Austria, Romania, Hungary, Bulgaria, and northern France. The Mediterranean region, in particular Spain, Portugal, southern France, Italy, Greece, and Yugoslavia, has the advantage of olive oil, abundant vineyards and citrus fruit to add to good supplies of fish from the long coastline, as well as a temperate climate for the growing of a great many varieties of vegetables.

The ideal of peasant life is probably most nearly represented by the philosophy of Spanish anarcho-syndicalism: communal, supportive, and hardworking, yet allowing the individual enough dignity, freedom, and leisure to develop intellectually and physically. A most difficult ideal to achieve. All those who have had first-hand experience of peasant existence hark back to the fundamental issue — survival. In the peasant world, the work is perpetual and the living is hard. Yet most insist that the way of life has its own rewards in the satisfaction of tasks well completed, of responsibilities to the land properly discharged. The earth must be husbanded, coaxed, and cared for, it cannot be exploited or it will take swift revenge. The old peasant kitchen habits of frugality were part of that husbandry — making stock out of bones, pickling and salting in times of glut, stocking the larder, using diet to care for the sick and the elderly, making good food out of few and simple ingredients.

The efficacy of this regime was reflected in the life expectancy of the peasantry such as that of England in feudal times, who, having survived the dangerous childhood years, were likely to live longer and in better health than the overlord who dined daily on large quantities of meat and fine white bread. The ordinary diet of the famously long-lived Georgians, listed by F. P. Armitage in 1922, is quintessential peasant food — black bread, rice, wheat cakes, beans, raw green vegetables, cheese, milk, and fish, salted, smoked and dried. In poor communities which could not afford doctors, good health was clearly essential to survival, and country-dwellers became extremely knowledgeable about the adjustments in diet necessary for those who were ill or to combat seasonal maladies. Winter food was well balanced for the winter months. Storecupboards were stocked to restore seasonal imbalance. Traditional prejudices about what should be served with what were based on sound and practical grounds of health. If any one phrase can summarize peasant cuisine it is precisely that — good health.

European peasant cookery is immensely old. It has evolved, it has been tried and tested, over centuries, perhaps over thousands of years. Throughout its existence the patiently gathered hard-won knowledge it incorporates has been passed on orally. Like all orally transmitted traditions it is only as strong as the last link in the chain of communication. Today our predominantly urban-dwelling, industrialized population is obliged to rely on increasingly mechanized methods of food production, and is inevitably distanced from the primary products of field and barnyard, dairy, piggery, and kitchen garden — and the checks and balances of season and economy have disappeared. Most peasant meals would have been (and still are in those communities which survive) structured around a single dominant ingredient at a single moment — when the new peas were at their best, the pig had just been slaughtered, the hens were laying particularly prolifically.

For that reason I have arranged this book around ingredients rather than in the more normal soup-fish-meat-sweet divisions. This reflects the central importance of the raw materials — that in the peasant world, the 'real' world of climate and season, of mountain and plain, forest, meadow, and shoreline, with all their changing patterns and rhythms, it was not possible simply to go out and buy an ingredient if it was lacking, and that seasonal abundance was far more likely to dictate the composition of the meal than whim. Most of the recipes, therefore, include suggestions for the completion of the meal of which they are the centrepiece — the suggestions equally coming from the same ancient tradition of what was available, excellent to the taste, and nutritionally appropriate.

Apart from those leisurely foundation years spent in wild Spain and rural France, my practical research has taken me into markets and kitchens, larders and vegetable gardens, farms and vineyards, across Europe from the North Cape to the Golden Horn. I have been met everywhere with great courtesy and generosity, although sometimes with surprise that anyone should need to write down things which were so obvious. In those places where the demands of modern life have all but obliterated the traces of the old ways, even the most sophisticated of restaurant chefs still remember with nostalgic pleasure the dishes Mother used to make, and recall their own then-small fingers helping to rub suet or mould dumplings. Curnonsky, the author of the definitive *Recettes des Provinces de France* (1959), was in no doubt about the importance of the role of the peasant cook in national cuisine:

'A nation's gastronomical level should be examined by tasting both the products of the best private kitchens and restaurants and the dishes from the kitchens of the peasantry. Somewhere in between lies the true level of excellence.'

Europe's peasantry has undergone many changes in the last two hundred years. The most severely dispossessed emigrated to the New World in large numbers during the eighteenth and nineteenth centuries, taking much of their culinary expertise with them. Often early American cookbooks are considerably more accurate on European regional cooking than the Old World equivalents, which have already been through a process of gentrification. It is arguable that as soon as a recipe has been written down it has already been compromised, that the fixing of what is of necessity fluid and adaptable has already changed its nature.

Such recipes and methods are best demonstrated, as María knew well, by mothers to daughters, fathers to sons: the moment to pick the plum, the exact brining necessary for a particular ham from a particular pig fattened in a particular oak-wood. Even the ancient earthenware *toupin*, whose curve is precisely right for the beans of Soissons, is perhaps an essential part of the 'true' recipe. Yet in the course of my travels I became aware that there can be no definitive recipes, just as there are no definitive mothers and fathers. What I am sure of is that there do exist old and exemplary culinary traditions which are passed on by good cooks, working within the boundaries of their own local produce, from one generation to the next.

They are the 'mother recipes' from which all European cookery springs — whether it be bourgeois or haute cuisine, fast food or fibre diets. For most of us in the western world they are as integral a part of our past, and of what shapes and nourishes us today, as our literature and songs, our paintings and technology.

As María would say in the old Spanish greeting to those at table, '*Gracias a Dios — buen provecho*,' 'Thanks be to God — good provender.'

CHAPTER 1

Fish and Food from the Sea

Plentiful, unfenced, and free — fish is the ideal peasant food. Peasant communities with access to fishable waters have long made good use of this superb protein source, and for thousands of years, with one strange and notable exception, fishing has supplemented farming to fill the European family larder. The exception is Ireland, whose inhabitants only began to exploit fish as a resource comparatively recently — an almost inexplicable blindness to the riches of their surrounding waters which cost the Irish dear during the fearsome potato blight of the last century.

Stews, soups, and frying-pan cooking are the most common methods of preparation, and shore-dwellers throughout Europe all have their favourite recipes. During the Middle Ages many a prosperous seaside town came into being as a result of the fishing industry. Amsterdam claims to be built, both metaphorically and literally, on herring bones. Ways to preserve what was essentially a seasonal harvest evolved gradually — the methods being dictated by climate and the availability of preserving agents such as salt or wind. The Mediterranean countries pickled with vinegar or brined their glut of fish. The northerly countries salted and smoked or wind-dried theirs. The sea-going Scandinavians, last of the Europeans to be converted to Christianity and the Catholic rules of fast-day fish-eating, were the first to turn their ocean treasure into a negotiable asset as they built up their salt-cod trade throughout the Middle Ages.

BASIC PREPARATION

Scale, gut, and wipe, in that order, any fish to be cooked. Wipe inside the fish with salt to remove the blood. In the case of a large fish take care to cut round the anus and remove it. Always rinse your hands and implements in cold water after preparing the fish and there will be no trace of fishy smell on either. A fish 1 in/2·5 cm thick will take 2 minutes to cook in simmering liquid. A fish 2 in/5 cm thick will take 8 minutes to cook. A fish 3 in/7·5 cm thick will take 32 minutes — the required time increases in relation to the thickness of the fish and it is not simply a matter of doubling-up.

Fish Soup

BOUILLABAISSE
(France)

The city of Marseilles claims the *bouillabaisse* for its very own. And if the Greeks founded Marseilles, as its citizens believe, then the origin of the ambrosial soup must, they maintain, lie in the kitchens of the gods. Venus herself is credited with the first hand on the soup pot. She is alleged to have brewed up the concoction one merry evening when she had a tryst with Mars and wished to put her blacksmith husband, Vulcan, to sleep during the assignation. A key ingredient in her recipe was saffron, long held to be a soporific, and about whose powers Alexander complained, somewhat later in the human timescale, when he found his army slumbering on a crocus-carpeted Turkish hillside.

The *bouillabaisse* is fish soup carried to its ultimate. As prepared today in many restaurants of maritime Provence it has left far behind the uncertainties of the local fisherman's catch. No longer is the scented broth, a blend of soup and stew, composed of whatever was wriggling in the bottom of the net after the saleable fish and crustaceans had been auctioned off. None the less *bouillabaisse* in any of its forms remains a superb and authentic Mediterranean coastal dish, as variable as any other and depending for its flavour on what the cook's taste and the stocks of the larder embellish it with. It is named after the method of cooking — *bouillon-abaissé* being broth rapidly boiled to reduce. For those of us dependent on cold-water northern fish as the principal ingredients, *bouillabaisse* cannot be made exactly as Venus prepared it. Yet the ideal composition of the soup is not as rigidly circumscribed as

21

the Marseillais would have the rest of us believe.

Although immensely ancient as a dish, and undoubtedly prepared in other parts of coastal Europe, it was not until Victorian times that the Marseilles version was adopted in more northerly ports such as London. There it was greeted with enthusiasm. William Makepeace Thackeray, the author of *Vanity Fair*, felt the subject worthy of a ballad:

> This Bouillabaisse a noble dish is —
> A sort of soup or broth or brew
> Or hotch-potch of all sorts of fishes
> That Greenwich never could outdo:
> Green herbs, red peppers, mussels, saffron,
> Soles, onions, garlic, roach and dace;
> All these you eat at Terré's tavern
> In that one dish of Bouillabaisse.

The net to trap the ingredients is cast wide. Out there among the rockpools, the waves and tidal races, the banks and shoals and fishing grounds, who is to say what may swim in to grace the glory of coastal Provence?

Sea perch (*rascasse*)
Sea bass (*loup de mer*)
Angler fish or monkfish (*baudroie*)
Scorpion fish (*chapon*)
John Dory (*saint-pierre* — marked with the thumb-prints of St. Peter the fisherman)
Conger-eel (*congre* or *fiela*)
Red mullet (*rouget barbet, rouget de roche*)
Red gurnard (*grondin* or *galinette*)
Wrasse (*rouquier, roucaou* in the patois)
Whiting (*merlan*)
Weever fish (*vive*)
Spiny lobster, also known as *langouste*, crawfish, and rock lobster (*Palinurus vulgaris*)
Little shore crabs (*crabes verts* or *favouilles, ériphies, étrilles de sable*)
All manner of shrimp and prawns (*langoustines, squilles, cigalles, crevettes*)
(Note the absence of mussels and clams, in spite of Mr Thackeray.)

Quantity 7–8 participants is the minimum number for which to prepare a proper *bouillabaisse*, according to the great nineteenth-century authority on Provençal cooking, J.-B. Reboule. The rule of thumb is to allow ½ to ¾ lb/225 to 350 g fish per person and 1 pint/600 ml water plus 1 tablespoon olive oil per 1 lb/450 g fish. The rest of the ingredients would all be to hand in the Provençal vegetable patch, with the exception perhaps of the soporific saffron.

Time Preparation: 40–50 minutes

5 lb/2·5 kg mixed fish (including sea perch — the one species reckoned vital to the dish)

3 medium onions

3 cloves garlic

2 tomatoes

fennel, parsley, and thyme

a curl of dried orange peel

½ wineglass (around 6 tablespoons) olive oil

5 pints/3 litres water

6 strands saffron

pepper and salt

7–8 slices dry bread (In Marseilles a special bread called *marette* is available for the purpose.)

rouille (see below)

Utensils A large, deep-sided cooking pot, several plates, a perforated spoon, and a strainer

Make the *rouille* up to the point where you add the fish broth. There will not be time once you start on the fish.

Put the firm fish on one plate: on one side the spiny lobster and crustaceans, on the other the sea perch or *rascasse*, weever fish, gurnard, eel, angler fish, and anything else that feels hard to the finger. Wash, scale, and gut the fish where necessary. Cut the larger fish into pieces the size of small fish. Remove such heads and fins as are unaesthetic.

Put the soft fish on another plate: sea bass, wrasse, John Dory, whiting, and whatever else you have that looks like a member of the group. Wash, scale, and gut the fish where necessary. Again, cut the larger fish into pieces the size of small fish. Peel and chop the onions and crush the garlic with a little salt. Pour boiling water over the tomatoes to loosen the skin. Peel and chop them.

Put all the vegetables and the herbs in the base of the large cooking pot. Lay the crustaceans on this bed, and the firm fleshed fish (all those on the first plate) over them. Sprinkle over all the olive oil. Cover with the water. Add the saffron, a teaspoon of salt, and a turn or two of the peppermill. Cover the pot and bring all swiftly to the boil.

Meanwhile put a soup tureen, deep soup plates, and a large serving dish to warm in the oven, and warn your eager guests that you will be ready in exactly 10 minutes.

Allow the broth to boil rapidly for 5 minutes uncovered. Then lay in

23

the soft fish from the second plate. Bring swiftly back to the boil and continue boiling briskly, covered, for another 5 minutes.

Take the pot off the heat and gently remove the fish to the serving plate with the perforated spoon. Put the dry bread into the tureen and strain the soup over. Put both broth and fish on the table at the same time, with a warm deep soup plate and a fork and spoon for each guest. A large napkin each and a plate for the little bones would make everything go more smoothly.

Finish making the *rouille* (see below).

The bowl of pungent, scarlet *rouille* and more bread, fresh this time, to accompany. Guests eat as they please — soup with fish, soup then fish, a glass of the good white wine of the Rhône beside them.

SUGGESTIONS

● Make a fish stock first with the heads and bones if your fish are very large.

● A glass or two of white wine can replace the same volume of water.

● A leek can replace one of the onions.

● Some of the fish can be replaced or augmented by various of the northern natives: Dublin Bay prawns (*langoustines*), tunny, skate, small turbot, mackerel, bonito, and native crustaceans of a likely hue.

● Hand round a bowl of *aioli* (see page 444) as well as the *rouille*. It may be gilding the lily, but it is worth it for the sake of the dramatic contrast between the fiery scarlet of the peppers and the soft gold of the *aioli*.

LEFTOVERS

● Strain and use to make a *Bouillabaisse borgne* (see page 23).

ROUILLE
(France)

The sauce which always accompanies *bouillabaisse*. It is also very good with fish cakes and fish pie.

Quantity   Enough for 7–8
Time   Preparation: 10 minutes

3 cloves garlic
½ teaspoon salt
3 red peppers (tinned pimentos can be used instead and should be well drained)

2 slices (about 3 oz/75 g) bread
½ pint/300 ml hot fish broth

Utensils   A liquidizer or pestle and mortar

Crush the garlic with the salt. If you are using fresh peppers, burn off the skin by roasting them in a very hot oven for 15 minutes, or burning them over a direct flame. Soak the bread in a little water and then squeeze it dry. Pound all the ingredients together into a smooth paste, or blend them in the liquidizer if you like. Stir in the hot broth just before you serve the *bouillabaisse*.

ONE-EYED BOUILLABAISSE
Bouillabaisse borgne (France)

If your fisherman's catch is not all it should be, make a One-eyed *bouillabaisse* — *Bouillabaisse borgne* or *aigo-sau-d'iou* in the Provençal patois.

Quantity   Enough for 4–5
Time   Preparation: 30–40 minutes

fish trimmings and a few small fish	bayleaf, sprig thyme
1 large tomato, chopped	3 pints/2 litres water
1 leek *or* onion, chopped	4–5 large potatoes
½ teaspoon saffron	4–5 eggs
salt	4–5 slices dry bread

Utensils   A large cooking pot, a perforated spoon, and a strainer

Make the fish broth by boiling the fish trimmings, tomato, leek, saffron, salt, bayleaf, and water rapidly together for 20 minutes. Strain out the solids and bring the soup back to the boil. Turn down to simmer.

Meanwhile peel the potatoes and cut them into thick slices. Put them into the simmering broth to cook — 10 to 15 minutes should be enough. When the potatoes are done, crack each egg into a cup and slide it into the soup, allowing one egg per person. Poach the eggs gently in the broth for a few minutes. Place a slice of dry bread in each deep soup plate and ladle some broth over. Serve the potatoes and poached eggs on another dish as if they were the fish from the *bouillabaisse*. Accompany with a *rouille* (see page 24) and you will dine well.

SUGGESTIONS
● You can always go vegetarian with a *Bouillabaisse d'épinards* (see page 352).

FISH SOUP WITH AIOLI
Bourride (France)

Of all the fish soups, this is my favourite. It seems to embody the rich scents and colours of Provence: camomile meadows and clumps of reed-grass hazed with tiny blue flowers; pearly tree-trunks and the furry undersides of olive leaves; pink onion-scented flowering heads of the wild garlic, *Allium roseum*; flocks of goldfinches stripping the dry thistles; lazy swallowtail butterflies hanging on lavender flowers; and, beyond and below, the tumbling dark rocks and bright wavelets of the Mediterranean shore.

Quantity   Enough for 6
Time   30–40 minutes

3 lb/1·5 kg whole fish. Choose from monkfish (angler fish or *baudroie* — the one with the huge ugly head and flesh as firm, white, and sweet as lobster), sea bass (*loup de mer*), whiting (*merlan*), and small cod.
1 onion

bouquet thyme, fennel, bayleaf, and a curl of dried orange peel
3 pints/2 litres warm water
salt and pepper
6 slices dry bread
4 egg yolks
aioli made with 1 pint/600 ml oil (see page 444)

Utensils   A large cooking pot and a perforated spoon

Make the *aioli* first.

Cut the fish into thick, even-sized steaks, leaving the skin on if it suits you (monkfish is usually skinned). Peel and chop the onion. Put a tureen, a serving dish, and some deep soup plates to heat in a low oven — once you start cooking the soup it will be ready in no time.

Put the chopped onion and the aromatics in the large cooking pot. Lay the fish steaks over them. Cover all with the warm water. Add a teaspoon of salt and a grind of the peppermill. Bring all swiftly to the boil and cook for 10 minutes. Remove from the heat and take out the pieces of fish with the perforated spoon. Turn off the oven. Put the fish on the warm serving dish and leave them in the oven while you finish the soup.

Put the slices of dry bread in the bottom of the tureen and sprinkle them with a ladleful of the fish broth. Leave them to soak. Now put half the *aioli* into a deep bowl and whisk in the egg yolks. If the eggs are small, use one per person. Whisk in a ladleful of the hot soup. Then whisk in another ladleful. Strain the rest of the soup into the bowl and whisk it in well. (This step can be successfully achieved in a liquidizer.) Rinse out the cooking pot and pour the soup back in. Cook it over a low heat, stirring constantly with a wooden spoon, while it thickens. It is done when it masks the back of the wooden spoon. Take it off the heat. The soup must not boil or it will go grainy. Pour the beautiful velvet broth over the bread in the tureen. Call your guests to table.

Serve the soup and the fish at the same time, to be eaten simultaneously or consecutively as pleases you. Hand the rest of the *aioli* round with a plentiful supply of fresh bread. A *vin gris*, the flinty-dry pinkish wine from the salt flats of the Bouches du Rhône, to accompany. Complete the meal with a lemon tart (see page 540).

SUGGESTIONS
● This recipe is equally suitable for other mixtures of fish. I once made bastard-bourride with a brilliant black-and-yellow eel which had made its way into a fisherman's net in the Straits of Gibraltar, and subsequently into my local market in the little port of Tarifa. The extraordinary brightness of the skin colours of the fish when cooked, bathed in the sunflower-yellow broth, made a most dramatic dish.
● Use white wine instead of half the water.

BASQUE FISH SOUP
Ttoro (France/Spain)

A fish stew-soup made with one fish only, this is probably the oldest of all of this family of soups. Basque fishermen were trawling for cod in distant Atlantic waters long before Lief Erikson girded up his loins to tackle the northern ocean, and certainly centuries before Christopher Columbus acquired his first compass. The original *Ttoro* was always made with salted codheads, cut off when the fish were prepared for salting and kept as the fisherman's portion. The heads had no commercial value to the Basques' southern customers, the Spaniards. Fresh or salt, these heads made a nourishing, strong soup, boiled up with onions and garlic and poured over slices of dry bread which had been sprinkled with oil. Cod cheeks are fine and sweet and are the carver's portion of the fish — boiled cod head and shoulders was accounted a great treat on the Victorian dinner table in England.

The Basques finally wearied of the long trek across the dangerous ocean when competition from better-equipped Portuguese fishermen, who were increasingly encroaching on the ancient fishing grounds, took over their lucrative salt-cod trade. Basque fishermen then turned their attention to home waters and the cod in the *Ttoro* was replaced by its close relative, the hake. Fresh hake is the fish which is now reckoned essential to the dish, and a hake-based *Ttoro* remains the favourite supper of the Basque mariner home from the sea.

Over the years the soup has evolved and become regionalized. In recent times the Basque–New World connection was re-established when many Basque woodsmen emigrated to Canada to find employment in the prosperous forestry industry. There they found plenty of Newfoundland cod to provide them with the staple for the original *Ttoro*.

Quantity   Enough for 6–7 home from the sea
Time   Preparation: 30 minutes
             Cooking: 1 hour

4–5 lb/2–2·5 kg whole fresh cod *or* hake, scaled and gutted, but with head and bones
1 lb/500 g onions
5 pints/3 litres water
3–4 bayleaves

peppercorns and salt
½ loaf dry bread
4 tablespoons olive oil
a good handful fresh herbs: parsley, thyme, chervil
2 cloves garlic

Utensils   A large stewpot, a strainer, and a soup tureen

Wipe the fish inside and out and cut off the heads. Remove the flesh in thick fillets and put them aside. Peel and slice the onions. Put the bones and the onions into the large stewpot and cover them with the water. Add the bayleaves, a teaspoon of salt, and a dozen peppercorns. Bring all to the boil and then turn down to simmer. Cook for an hour, uncovered, by which time the bones will have enriched the soup, and the liquid will have reduced by a third (if it is not reduced enough, turn up the heat for a moment to allow evaporation).

Cut the bread into cubes, put the cubes into a soup tureen and sprinkle with oil. Chop the herbs roughly, and scatter them over the bread. Crush the garlic under the blade of a knife, mash it up with ½ teaspoon salt, and then scatter it over the bread. Lay the slices of fish in the tureen, and pour on the boiling soup. Let the soup develop for 5 to 10 minutes while you set the table and call your guests.

Serve the *Ttoro* in deep soup plates with more bread, a jug of wine, and a spoon and fork with which to tackle your soup-stew. You will need nothing else tonight, except perhaps a nugget of strong blue-veined *Cabrales*, made in the mountains behind from the goat's milk of your shepherding cousin.

SUGGESTIONS

• 3 egg yolks and ¼ pint/150 ml cream may be stirred in to thicken the soup at the end (do not let it boil, or the eggs will curdle).

Fry the bread golden in the oil with the crushed garlic before you put it in the bottom of the soup tureen. But I like the taste of uncooked olive oil myself, so you will be on your own.

AVGOLEMONO FISH SOUP
Psarosoupa avgolemono (Greece and neighbours)

Avgolemono is the favourite Greek flavouring mix: lemon juice is beaten up with eggs and a hot liquid. It is often used as a sauce for a rice pilaf, or, as here, to thicken a soup. If you have prepared a good strong stock in advance, this recipe provides a nourishing instant meal. Once you have added the *avgolemono* mixture, the soup becomes rather delicate and should not be boiled or reheated. Inland the soup is made with meat or chicken. The Turks prefer the chicken-based version (called in Turkish *terbiyeli ciorba*). I give the fish recipe here, which is very popular around the coast of Greece. To make the others, just use a good broth and proceed as for fish.

Quantity   Enough for 6
Time   Preparation: 20 minutes
Cooking: 1½ hours

For the broth
2 lb/1 kg fish heads and trimmings
2 carrots
1 onion
parsley stalks
1 small head celery (with the well-
flavoured white root piece)
3¼ pints/2·3 litres water
1 teaspoon salt
½ teaspoon peppercorns

For the garnish
3 oz/75 g long grain rice
3 eggs
juice 2 lemons

Utensils   A large stewpot, a strainer, a whisk, and a roomy bowl

To make the broth, put the fish heads and trimmings and the vegetables, roughly cut up, into the pot with the water, salt, and peppercorns. Bring to the boil and skim. Turn down the heat and simmer for an hour. Strain out the solids and return the broth to the pot.

Add the rice and bring the broth back to the boil. Cook until soft.

Meanwhile beat the eggs in the bowl with the juice of the 2 lemons until they are light and frothy. When the rice is soft, in about 20 minutes, take the pot off the heat. Add a ladleful of the hot soup to the egg mixture and whisk thoroughly. Continue to add ladlefuls of the hot soup until you have added half the full quantity. Stir this back into the rest of the hot soup, moving it constantly. Serve the soup without reheating it. A Greek salad, plenty of bread, and a jug of wine will complete the meal.

FISH SOUP
Kakavia (Greece)

The *kakavia* is the pot in which the soup is prepared. The Greeks maintain that this is the original *bouillabaisse,* and that it was their adventurous sailors who showed the world how to prepare a fish soup. The recipe, as with all fish soups, is quite rightly as varied as the catch in the fishermen's nets.

Quantity   Enough for 6
Time   Preparation: 20 minutes
        Cooking: 40 minutes

2 lb/1 kg small fish (including a
   few rock fish such as the sea
   perch)
3 pints/2 litres water
salt and peppercorns
bayleaf
1 lb/500 g onions

1 lb/500 g tomatoes
6 tablespoons olive oil
juice 1 lemon
6 slices bread

Utensils   A large stewpot or a *kakavia* if you have it, a roomy saucepan, a strainer, and a perforated spoon

Scale, gut, and wipe the fish. Remove the heads, and fillet those fish it is convenient to fillet. Put the fillets and larger pieces of fish aside. Put the trimmings and the very small bony fish in the saucepan with the water, a teaspoon of salt, 6 whole peppercorns, and the bayleaf. Bring the water to the boil, then turn down the heat and simmer for 40 minutes.

Meanwhile peel and slice the onions and chop the tomatoes. Put the oil to warm in the bottom of the stewpot. Stir in the onions and fry them gently until they are transparent. Add the tomatoes. Leave to melt together until the fish stock is ready. Strain the stock into the stewpot over the tomato mixture. Add the uncooked pieces of fish, and bring the soup to the boil. Turn the heat down and leave all to simmer for 10 to 15 minutes, until the fish is well cooked but not broken up.

Toast the bread. In Greece this would be slices of dense-textured country bread charred on one of those primitive toasters which can be placed over a flame. Set out 6 bowls and put a slice of toast in each.

Lift out the fish carefully with the perforated spoon. Divide it among the bowls. Stir the lemon juice into the soup and ladle the broth on to the fish and bread in the bowls. Put a plate of quartered lemons, a bowl of little black olives and radishes, and fresh bread on the table.

Plenty of *retsina* to drink with it, with fresh fruit and white cheese to follow. Finish with a little cup of strong Turkish coffee.

SUGGESTIONS
● This soup is meant to be flexible — embellish and add to it as you please. It is rather good with a few potatoes cooked in it before the fish is added.

LEFTOVERS
● Strain the solids out of the soup, and bring it to the boil with a handful of rice. Simmer until the rice is soft. Then stir in an *avgolemono* mixture.

FISHERMAN'S STEW
Caldeirada (Portugal)

By the mid-sixteenth century the Portuguese were making inroads in the Far East, particularly in Japan, where they introduced *tempura* cooking — a method of coating small foods (the Portuguese used shrimp) in batter for frying, which the Japanese adopted and adapted. Among the flavours that the travellers acquired a taste for was fresh coriander, the herb that not only looks like parsley, but appears in eastern recipes with quite as much frequency as parsley does in the west. It has a very distinctive flavour.

This fisherman's soup is as variable as his catch — which was usually obtained in the cold waters of the Atlantic. The ingredients are easier for Atlantic coastal-dwellers to come by than those of its cousin, the Mediterranean *bouillabaisse*. There are no rules, only guidelines. It is the dish that the fishermen would cook for themselves on their long fishing trips. After the first catch, a little charcoal-burning brazier would be set up high in the bows of the vessel where it would be sheltered from the wind and spray. The soup would be cooked over the flame in a heavy iron pot.

Quantity   Enough for 8–10
Time   Preparation: 20 minutes
        Cooking: 30–40 minutes

3 lb/1·5 kg mixed fish (ray, flounder, hake, cod, bass, eel, mullet — whatever is fresh and cheap)
1 lb/500 g squid
2 large onions
2–4 tomatoes
2 lb/1 kg potatoes
small bunch fresh coriander *or* parsley

2 cloves garlic
¼ pint/150 ml olive oil
salt and pepper
½ pint/300 ml white wine
2 bayleaves
½ pint/300 ml water
1 lb/500 g clams *or* mussels (weighed in the shell)

Utensils   A very large stewpot with a lid and a ladle

Clean the white fish and then cut them into slices if large. Cut the eel into short lengths. Clean the squid — it has a beautiful clear bone, like plastic, which must be pulled out when you separate the tentacle body from the hollow body. Rinse the squid and cut the bunch of tentacles (which you keep) from the head and innards (which you discard). Pull off the freckled mauve outer membrane from the hollow body, and pick out as many as you can of the little sharp 'toe-nails' with which the suckers of the tentacles are equipped. Slice the body into rings and the tentacles into short lengths.

Peel and slice the onions. Peel and chop the tomatoes. Peel and slice the potatoes. Chop the coriander or parsley and peel and chop the garlic. Find your largest and heaviest stewpot, and pour in a little of the oil.

Put the ingredients into the stewpot in layers, adding salt and pepper and sprinkling in the oil and wine as you go — lay half the onion rings on the base, then the potato and garlic, then half the tomatoes and a bayleaf, then the fish and squid, then the herbs, then the rest of the tomato and the other bayleaf, and finally the remaining onion. Pour over all the remaining oil, the wine, and the water. Bring to the boil, then turn the heat down. Stew very gently for 30 to 40 minutes, either in the oven or on top of the stove. Push a knife into the centre to see if all, particularly the potato, is cooked and soft.

Meanwhile rinse the clams or mussels in fresh running water. Lay them on top of the stew to open in the steam. When they have opened, it is ready.

Serve the stew with a large ladle, keeping the layers separate.

SUGGESTIONS
● Red and green peppers can be included, as can shrimps, scallops, or anything fishy and fresh.
● The potatoes are not always included — they are sometimes replaced by slices of dry bread.
● Crisp-fried anchovies or sardines, or fried bread *croûtons*, are sometimes served with this dish, laid alongside each portion.

LEFTOVERS
● Use to make *Roupa velha de peixe*, fish hash — an excellent dish and quite as good as the original stew. Warm a little olive oil in a frying pan over a gentle heat, and add the leftover stew. Bubble gently until all the liquid evaporates and the rest begins to fry. Continue frying until the base is dry and golden.

PORTUGUESE FISH SOUP
Sopa de peixe (Portugal)

This soup, as prepared in a fisherman's wife's kitchen in one of the little fishing villages which bead the Algarve coast, has something of that ancient flavour, that concentration of boiled-down essences, which makes a true *pot-au-feu* unique. The basic soup is served from a big cauldron kept, like the *pot-au-feu*, at a constant simmer on the back of the stove. Small fresh fish from the day's catch are added to it as the boats come in. The bones and heads of the fish melt during the course of the long stewing, and a really good stock is so thick and gelatinous it is almost sticky. The soup might well be as old as the pot in which it cooks.

Quantity   Enough for 6–8
Time   Preparation: 20 minutes
          Cooking: Minimum 2 hours

1 lb/500 g small fresh shrimps (preferably raw)	¼ pint/150 ml olive oil (Portuguese if you can get it)
3 lb/1·5 kg mixed small fish *or* pieces of larger ones	1 tablespoon paprika
2 large onions	4 pints/2·5 litres water
4 cloves garlic	2 bayleaves
3 red *and/or* green peppers	salt and peppercorns
	2 crusts dry bread

Utensils   A large, heavy stewpot and a wide-meshed sieve

Pick over the shrimps. Scale and gut the small fish. Leave on their heads and do not bone them. Peel and chop the onions and garlic very finely. Scorch the skins of the peppers (this makes it possible to peel them) by holding them on a knife over a gas flame, or singeing them on an electric ring (charred pepper has a spicy, pungent aroma with a splendid nostalgia value). Skin the scorched peppers and cut them into small squares.

   The Portuguese, unlike all other Mediterranean olive-growing nations, allow their olives to ferment for a week before they press them, and their olive oil has a quite distinctive flavour. Warm the oil in the stewpot — do not overheat it. Add the onions, garlic, peppers, and shrimps. Stew them in the oil for a few minutes. Mash to release the flavours. Add the paprika and then the fish. Cover with water and add the bayleaves, a few peppercorns, and a little salt. Stew gently, uncovered, on minimal heat for at least 2 hours. More water may be needed, but add sparingly. When the fish is thoroughly pulped, crumble the bread crusts, scatter them over the top, and then stir them in — they will absorb most of the paprika-tinted oil on the surface. Press the soup through the wide-meshed sieve — you aim to achieve an unctuous, dark soup clouded with fish debris, thick and smooth.

Serve the soup in deep plates, very hot, with plenty of bread and quarters of lemon to be squeezed in by those who wish. A salad, a few fried fish, fresh fruit, and a piece of *toucinho do celo* (see page 464) to complete your dinner.

LEFTOVERS
• You could pour them back into the pot, simmer, and keep on adding to the pot until your great-grandchildren are fishermen themselves, but a Portuguese friend of mine has sounded a caution — the pot would have to be kept continuously on the hob if you wished to avoid the risk of an untimely demise from the development of a salmonella culture. Better today, she suggests, to start afresh each time you make the dish.

WATERZOOTJE FISH STEW
Waterzoi (Belgium)

This is the inland version of an ancient fisherman's dish. In the days of furnaces and steam power, hungry deep-sea fishermen would keep a great iron cauldron hanging over the furnaces of the fishing boat. Every sailor suspended his own bag of potatoes in the water from a grid, and fish from the catch were thrown in virtually straight from the net. Each man took a cup of broth and selected a fish and a few shellfish or crabs to be eaten with his own potatoes. Stuff that culinary — and ocean — dreams are made of.

Quantity Enough for 4–6
Time Preparation: 20 minutes
　　　　　Cooking: 25–30 minutes

2 lb/1 kg freshwater fish (eel, pike, tench, carp)	parsley and 2–3 sage leaves
3 sticks celery	salt
3 oz/75 g butter	2–3 pints/1·5–2 litres water *or* stock made with fish trimmings

Utensils A large, heavy stewpot

Rinse and cut the fish into chunks. Rinse and slice the celery. Melt half the butter in the stewpot and lightly cook the celery in it for a few seconds. Lay the fish on top and sprinkle in the herbs and salt. Cover with the water or stock.

Bring to the boil and dot the surface with the rest of the butter. Turn the heat down and cook half-covered until the fish is ready and the liquid has reduced to a well-flavoured sauce — this will take 20 to 30 minutes. Serve with slices of buttered bread.

SUGGESTIONS
● The *waterzootje* is also sometimes prepared with a jointed chicken. Onions and/or leeks are then included, with a little lager beer in the cooking liquor. Simmer a chicken *waterzootje* for at least an hour.

White Fish

FISH PUDDING
Fiskepudding (Norway)

There are *fiskematbutikks* in most Norwegian seaside towns which sell minced fish. Very often it is all they sell and quite excellent it is too — not ground-up bits and pieces of discards from the catch, but fresh haddock, pike, or young cod. The mince is either sold raw as *fiskefarse* or cooked as *fiskeboller* (fish dumplings), *fiskepudding* (fish pudding), or *fiskekaker* (fish cakes). In any of its forms it is a delicious and interesting dish — a kind of fish hamburger-meat.

Until recently Norwegian housewives made their own *fiskepudding*, and everyone knew that *their* mother made the best in the country. She served it on feast days and holidays with her own beautiful cream-and-shrimp sauce. The dish is much like those delicate soufflés and quenelles which are the pride of the French kitchen. Simplicity and clarity of flavour are its chief delights. Unlike the French version no eggs are included — in peasant recipes eggs are rarely used in conjunction with other forms of protein. There is also an interesting similarity in

35

ingredients and method to the French salt-cod dish *brandade de morue*.

The basis of the following three recipes is minced and pounded *fiskefarse*. A Norwegian grandmother would have rolled her sleeves up her brawny arms and pounded her fish in a marble mortar so large and heavy that it stood on the floor and required a waist-high pestle. A food processor provides the perfect modern muscle. The potato or flour are not essential, but they do help the mixture stick together and remain juicy. The fish and the cream, or rich fresh milk, are the only essential ingredients — a very simple recipe indeed.

Well-to-do households with access to a merchant would use half a teaspoonful of powdered mace or nutmeg to spice the mixture. The Scandinavian seafaring nations had better access to such luxuries than most peasant communities through their active involvement in the salt-cod trade. Excellent cream, butter, and milk remain widely available today. Peasant-farmers in Scandinavia kept, and still keep, milk-cows: hay to feed the beasts is often the only crop harvested in the more northerly farms above the Arctic Circle.

Quantity   Enough for 4–5
Time   Preparation: 30 minutes
          Cooking: 1 hour

For the pudding
1 lb/500 g filleted fish (haddock *or* pike is best although cod is good too. Do not use frozen fish or you will have a watery pudding.)
1 tablespoon flour *or* 1 medium-sized potato, cooked and mashed (you can do without either if you wish)
½ teaspoon salt and pepper

1 tablespoon milk
½ pint/300 ml single cream
½ teaspoon ground mace *or* nutmeg (*optional*)

For the sauce
4 oz/100 g unsalted butter *or* ½ pint/300 ml cream (soured *or* fresh, but thick) heated with 4 oz/100 g little peeled shrimps

Utensils   A food processor, liquidizer or pestle and mortar, a small baking dish or casserole, and a skewer

Skin the fillet by gripping the tail end and running a sharp knife held at an angle away from you between the flesh and the skin. Discard the skin. Remove any remaining bones (pike in particular are full of tiny sharp filaments).

Preheat the oven to 375°F/190°C/Gas 5.

Chop the fish flesh roughly and put it in the food processor or liquidizer. (Should you possess neither, you will have to follow the Norwegian grandmother's example and use a pestle and mortar.)

Mince the fish thoroughly. Stir the flour or mashed potato with the salt and a little milk, add to the fish and continue to process as you pour in the cream, beating until you have a light doughy mixture. Add the mace or nutmeg if you are using it. You may need a little more liquid. Beat hard, either in the processor or with a wooden spoon. The more air you include, the lighter the mixture. Beat it some more.

Butter a baking dish and pour the mixture in — a *fiskefarse* should be used as fresh as possible. Cover with foil and bake the pudding in the pre-heated oven for 45 to 55 minutes.

The *fiskepudding* dish can be stood in a baking tray full of hot water to keep the pudding moist and light. Test to see if it is cooked by running a skewer into the centre. When it comes out clean, all is ready.

Run a knife round the sides and turn the pudding on to a hot plate.

Serve with a jug of melted butter and floury boiled potatoes cooked with dill, dried on the heat, and tossed with more chopped dill. Or instead of the butter with a sauce made with shrimps simmered for a few moments in the cream. If the cream is soured you will have to stabilize it by stirring half a teaspoon of flour in before you heat it.

This ancient Norwegian fisherman's dish used to cook very well on its home-fire, in a heavy iron pot suspended over the hearth, with a few coals glowing on the inverted lid. Outside the waves slapped against the grey stilts of the harbour mooring. With a salt sea breeze whistling through the cracks under the wooden door of the fisherman's hut, appetites sharpened by a long day in the fishing grounds could well appreciate such a feast.

SUGGESTIONS
● Stuff the *fiskefarse* mixture into sausage casings, tie them into lengths, and poach them in simmering water for 20 to 25 minutes. Serve with a cream sauce, perhaps on a bed of spinach.
● Use mushrooms, particularly dried wild ones, or green peppercorns, instead of shrimps in the cream sauce.
● A green vegetable to accompany — spinach, peas, or lightly cooked courgettes.
● Any fresh herb or a spoonful of chopped onion instead of dill to dress the potatoes.
● Accompany with rice instead of potatoes. The Scandinavians are very fond of imported rice and rice pudding is traditional Christmas fare.

LEFTOVERS
● Fish pudding can be sliced and reheated gently in a cream sauce. It will almost be better like this.
● Squares of it are delicious poached in a clear fish soup made with the trimmings of the fish boiled with herbs and an onion.

FISH DUMPLINGS
Fiskeboller (Norway)

Delicious little morsels of fish, very much like French quenelles. A Norwegian friend of mine remembers being given these to nibble like sweets when, as a small girl, she went shopping with her mother.

Quantity   Enough for 4–5
Time   Preparation: 30 minutes

1 lb/500 g filleted fish (as for
   fiskepudding above)
1 tablespoon flour *or* 1 potato,
   cooked and mashed
⅓ pint/200 ml single cream
salt and pepper

For the sauce
½ pint/300 ml fresh *or* soured
   cream
4 oz/100 g small shelled shrimps
   (*optional*)
salt and pepper

Utensils   A liquidizer and a large saucepan

Make the *fiskefarse* mixture as for the fish pudding. You may need a little more cream but the dough should be a little firmer this time. Meanwhile bring a large saucepan of well-salted water (1 oz/25 g salt to 1 pint/ 600 ml water) to the boil. Turn down to simmer.

Using 2 teaspoons dipped into cold water, form dumplings from the *fiskefarse* mixture. Drop them one by one into the simmering water until the whole surface is covered with the little bobbing dumplings. Simmer for 10 minutes or so (depending on the size of the dumplings).

Simmer the cream for a few minutes to thicken it (if the cream is very liquid or soured, you may need to stir in a teaspoon of flour, mixed first to a paste with a little milk), and add the small shelled shrimps right at the end. Taste and add salt and pepper.

Serve the dumplings sauced with the cream, accompanied by potatoes boiled with dill or mashed potatoes.

SUGGESTIONS
• As for the fish pudding.
• The little dumplings are also excellent cooked and served in a plain but well-seasoned fish soup. Make the soup with fish trimmings and heads, strain and then cook 1 lb/500 g peeled and sliced potatoes in the soup as you simmer the dumplings. Chopped dill or chives and a bowl of soured cream to be handed separately for stirring in.

LEFTOVERS
• Reheat in a cream sauce, perhaps with a few sliced mushrooms. Serve with fluffy boiled rice.

WHITE FISH CAKES
Fiskekaker (Norway)

These are sold hot — rather like doughnuts — in Norway's *fiske-matbutikks* (fish markets).

Quantity   Enough for 4–5
Time   Preparation: 30 minutes

1 lb/500 g filleted fish (as for
  fiskepudding)
1 tablespoon flour *or* 1 potato,
  cooked and mashed
⅓ pint/200 ml single cream
salt and pepper
2 oz/50 g butter for frying
3 oz/75 g butter for pouring
  (*optional*)

Utensils   A liquidizer or pestle and mortar and a frying pan

Pound the fish with the flour or potato and cream as for the fish pudding. Season well.

Melt the butter in the frying pan. Using a soupspoon dipped in cold water, scoop up a portion of *fiskefarse* and gently put it straight into the hot butter. Pat it lightly with the spoon to flatten it. Brown the fish cakes carefully, cover them, and turn them over halfway through the cooking time. They will take about 10 minutes and they must be cooked right through.

Heat the extra butter in the pan after you have finished frying until it turns a pale nut brown and serve in a small jug. Accompany with a bowl of plain boiled potatoes, shaken over the heat to dry them off and make them floury, dressed with soured cream and chopped dill or chives.

SUGGESTIONS
• Use bacon dripping or butter with some chopped bacon added to fry the fish cakes, and sauté the potatoes in the same pan afterwards (you will need additional fat or butter). In this case, omit the butter sauce.
• Serve with a plain green salad dressed with chopped chives.
• Serve with peas with ham (see page 370).
• Serve with a spinach purée.

LEFTOVERS
• Reheat in the oven and serve with a fresh tomato sauce (see page 293).
• Serve cold with a tomato and onion salad.

COD TAIL
Gestoofde kabeljauwstaart (Holland)

The most popular way of serving the best part of the cod. The tail-meat on a fresh cod is pure white and firm with an incomparable flavour.

Quantity Enough for 6
Time Preparation: 10 minutes
           Cooking: 30 minutes

 2 lb/1 kg cod tail
 salt and pepper
 2 lb/1 kg small potatoes
 water
 2 oz/50 g butter

Utensils A heatproof casserole with a lid

Wipe the fish and sprinkle it with salt. Scrub the potatoes and slice them. Put the potatoes in the casserole and pour in enough water barely to cover. Season with salt and pepper and bring to the boil.
   Put the cod tail on top of the potatoes so that it can cook in the steam. Scatter the butter over the fish. Cover tightly and put the casserole to cook either in the oven at 350°F/180°C/Gas 4 or on top of the stove on a gentle heat for 30 minutes. Simplicity and perfection, depending on the excellence of the raw materials.

LEFTOVERS
● Beat in an egg and some milk and chopped parsley, and fry spoonfuls as for the fish cakes.
● Or make a fish pie. Mix any leftover fish with a white sauce flavoured with parsley and chopped hard-boiled egg, season well, and put in a baking dish. Cover with the remains of the potatoes well mashed with butter and milk. Dot with butter. Cook in a moderate oven, 350°F/180°C/Gas 4, for 20 minutes to heat through and gild the top.

BASQUE TUNNY AND TOMATO STEW
Marmitako (Spain)

Tunnyfish has always been a prize catch for the Basque fishing boats. Brined and barrelled, conserved tuna is a storecupboard staple around the Mediterranean and has been so since the days of the Phoenicians. The fishermen made a stew with the tail and head pieces unsuitable for preserving. Bonito and even mackerel can substitute. The dish takes its name from the iron kettle used for the stew. About 2 lb/1 kg fish will feed 6. You will also need an onion, 2–3 cloves of garlic, 3–4 large tomatoes, a green pepper or two, all peeled and chopped as appropriate, and stewed with half a glass of olive oil as for the basic *Piperade* recipe on page 460. A chilli and a teaspoon of paprika or a dried red pepper can be included. Add 1 pint/600 ml water to the stew, plus 2 lb/1 kg potatoes, peeled and sliced. Add salt — a ladleful of sea water would do the trick. Skin, fillet, and cut the fish into chunks. When the potatoes are soft, mash them into the sauce a little, and lay the fish on top to cook in the steam — 6 to 7 minutes should be ample.

COD WITH BEER
Morue à la flamande (Belgium)

An excellent combination, and entirely proper to the seaside-dwellers of Belgium as this recipe features two of their prime ingredients.

Quantity   Enough for 4–5 good Flemish appetites
Time   Preparation: 20 minutes
           Cooking: 25 minutes

2 lb/1 kg cod fillets	½ pint/300 ml strong lager
½ teaspoon salt and pepper	bayleaf
1 lb/500 g onions	1 oz/25 g fresh breadcrumbs
2 oz/50 g butter	butter to finish

Utensils   A frying pan and a casserole

Preheat the oven to 400°F/200°C/Gas 6.

Skin the cod fillets with a sharp knife, starting from the tail end and gripping the skin firmly with one hand. Season the fillets with salt and pepper. Peel and slice the onions. Fry them in the butter in the frying pan. Pour in the beer, turn up the heat, and boil fiercely for a few minutes to evaporate the alcohol. Your nose will tell you when this is done. Pour all into a casserole, add the bayleaf, and lay the fish fillets on top. Scatter a layer of breadcrumbs (fresh, not dried — they do not give the same result) over the top. Dot with more butter.

Bake in the oven for 20 to 25 minutes, until the fish is cooked and the topping is crisp. A delicious dish with its traditional accompaniment of young hop shoots, boiled with salt and served with butter. As a substitute for hop shoots use baby green beans, blanched in boiling salted water for no more than 2 minutes.

Trout and Salmon

TROUT IN SOURED CREAM
(Norway)

Norway's many lakes and streams are well stocked with small mountain trout and rosy-flanked char. Sweet-fleshed and delicious, they are
at their best when fried in fresh butter with the blue water-bloom still on
them. Soured cream, pale and thick and brought down, in the old days,
from the upland summer farms, should be the basis of the sauce to
accompany them.

Quantity   1 fish per person
Time   Preparation: 10–15 minutes
        Cooking: 10 minutes

1 fish weighing at least 10 oz/275 g (*or*, if smaller, 2 for each person)	2 tablespoons soured cream per fish
1 oz/25 g unsalted butter per fish	2 tablespoons water per fish
	salt and pepper

Utensils   A frying pan

The fish are best if prepared as soon as they are caught. Gut them and
wipe out the cavity, but not the outside of the fish, with a little salt.

  Melt the butter. When it foams, slip in the fish. Brown swiftly,
turning once. Pour the soured cream and water round them, add salt
and freshly ground pepper, and let the fish simmer for 10 minutes.

  Particularly good served with wild mushrooms such as apricot-yellow chanterelles fried in butter and cooked with the fish. Little new potatoes boiled in their jackets, sweet as nuts (and called almond potatoes by the Norwegians), to accompany.

OATMEALED TROUT OR HERRINGS
(Scotland)

Scotland's two favourite fish. Highland burn trout, in the opinion of the Scots, are the best in the world. There are still those who practise the old art of tickling or 'guddling' to catch them. Rising early, when the first violet light streaks the sky above the moor, they go down to the stream, spot a trout lying close to the bank in the shallows, and slide their hand into the water behind its tail. With immense care and patience they move their fingers forward until they are cupping the fish's belly. Then they grip the trout and swiftly lift it out. Only the wiliest old fish knows the tickling fingers are not fronds of weed.

Quantity 1 fish per person
Time 10 minutes

   1 trout *or* herring
   1 tablespoon fine oatmeal per fish
   ½ teaspoon salt per fish
   ½ oz/12 g butter per fish

Utensils A heavy iron frying pan

If you are preparing trout, rinse and gut but do not wipe the fish, and then roll them in oatmeal. If you are cooking herrings, scale, gut, and behead the fish, split them in half down the back, and lift out the backbone. Pat dry and then roll each fish in oatmeal.

   Put the frying pan on the heat, and sprinkle in half a teaspoon of salt for each fish. You will need no extra fat to fry if you put the fish in the pan on to the *hot* salt, and keep shaking the pan so that the fish do not stick.

   You could also grill the fish, but then you would need to dot them with a few pieces of butter or bacon fat. The oatmeal coating is delicious and filling, particularly served with mustard and a hot buttered oatcake. Excellent as a light lunch or supper, or as a sturdy breakfast dish for a frosty morning.

BLUE TROUT
Forelle blau (Germany)

Germany is well served for fish — the mountain streams of the Alps yield fine trout and char while the clear waters of the Baltic provide a plentiful harvest of herring, mackerel, and flatfish. The technique of 'blue-cooking', when the fresh fish is either doused with vinegar just before cooking or is cooked in a vinegar-spiked liquor, is a major contribution to European fish cookery — there is no better way to prepare perfectly fresh trout. Whether the technique is of French or German origin is difficult to judge — across the centuries the boundaries of the two countries have ebbed and flowed as freely as the rivers which cross their modern frontiers.

The trout must be as freshly caught as possible. Best of all, it should be still alive when it reaches the cook's hand. If so, bang its head sharply against the table to stun it. Gut the fish and wipe out the cavity with salt. Do not wash the skin or wipe off its natural bloom — it is this delicate veil which brings a blue blush to the cooked trout.

Quantity   1 fish per person
Time   Preparation: 15–20 minutes

  1 medium-sized trout per person
  1 tablespoon vinegar per trout

Utensils   A large saucepan

Bring a pan of water to the boil. Douse each fish with wine vinegar before you slip it into the boiling water. If the fish is very fresh, it will stiffen and curl immediately. Bring the water back to the boil — wait for one thumping bubble, and then turn off the heat. Depending on size leave the fish in the water for 5 to 10 minutes, it will be cooked when the eyes are white and the fin pulls easily from the flesh.

Accompany with very lightly browned unsalted butter served in a sauce boat. Serve with plain boiled potatoes dressed with chopped dill or fennel.

SUGGESTIONS
• Any small or medium-sized fresh fish can be cooked in this manner. Cook mackerel 'blue' and serve with a fruit sauce — stewed gooseberries, cranberries, or redcurrants. This is a dish from the Baltic coast of Germany.
• To serve the trout cold, allow them to cool in their liquor (do not serve them refrigerated). I find trout too rich for a mayonnaise. It is much nicer with a horseradish sauce, made from whipped cream soured with

a little vinegar, into which you fold grated horseradish — proportions roughly 1 tablespoon of horseradish to $\frac{1}{4}$ pint/150 ml cream.
● Hatchery trout are often pink because they have been fed paprika which contains carotene, a substance found in shrimps, the natural prey of the sea trout. This turns their flesh the rosy hue of salmon. Carotene also provides the pigment which tints flamingoes pink — zoo birds quickly turn pale when deprived of their diet of shrimp and have to be fed paprika or carrot.

CURED SALMON
Gravlaks (Norway)

The ancient Scandinavians evolved a variety of ingenious ways to take culinary advantage of a climate where the ground is frozen for half the year. Those who lived on the seashore found wind drying, supplemented later by salting, the easiest and most satisfactory method of fish-preserving. Inland, without the benefit of the sea breezes, the country people took to burying their perishables, particularly their fish — a logical development given a landscape which is one huge potential cold-store.

Some of the more northerly groups buried cheese and the crock with the *aquavit* as well. Today a cured leg of mutton — *fenalår* — is a favourite stand-by in the larder: the mutton is put in salt and left for some weeks before it is hung up to dry in a cold room. In the old days, as still happens in some country districts, this would have been either in the outside *stabbur* or larder, or in the attic.

The most original product of Scandinavia is probably 'fermented' fish. Pike, char, perch and best of all, trout and salmon, have long been subjected to the universal deep-freeze. *Gravlaks* — buried or 'grave' salmon — is the direct modern descendant, and is now becoming increasingly popular outside Scandinavia. The *gravlaks* method is one of the most ancient and primitive of all, not even requiring a cooking fire. There is a record of its use in a manuscript of 1348, and the technique is almost certainly thousands of years older still. It evolved originally as a way of preserving the catch when the fishermen were far from home. The fish, sandwiched between two layers of birchbark and fir branches weighted down with stones, was buried in a hole dug out of the soft sandy shore. It could either be eaten after four to six days or allowed to lie for six to twelve weeks, during which time the flesh fermented.

Raw fish prepared by the *gravlaks* method rivals any Japanese delicacy. Today most fish is fermented for a relatively short time and mechanical refrigeration has replaced the natural ice-box. This recipe comes courtesy of Dr Astri Riddervold of Oslo. She adds the rider that the weighing is important as precise measurements allow you to use less salt, and that the inclusion of a small quantity of good alcohol improves the flavour without toughening the fish.

Quantity   Allow at least 4 oz/100 g prepared fish per person
Time   Start 3–4 days before
  Preparation: 40 minutes

6–7 lb/2·5 kg (or even larger) whole fresh *or* deep-frozen salmon
1 tablespoon brandy (*optional*)
¾ oz/20 g sugar

1½ oz/40 g crystallized (not dehydrated) salt
freshly ground pepper
good bunch fresh dill

Utensils   A large china plate, foil, a board, and a weight

Cut off the head and tail of the fish, and remove the intestines and the blood carefully. Remove the gutstring by cutting a circle around the anus. Take care not to press out the content. Do not wash the fish, but wipe it well with kitchen paper.

Cut out the bone, leaving 2 sides with the skin on. Sprinkle the flesh with the brandy.

Mix the sugar and the salt and a good helping of pepper. Scatter the mixture over the fillets. Put one of them skin-side down on the plate. Roughly chop the dill and spread it over. Place the other fillet on top of the first, skin-side up, head to tail, sandwiching the dill between them. Cover the salmon with foil and put a weight on top. The combined weight of a 1 lb/500 g tin on a carving board is about right.

Leave it in a cool place. The temperature is important — it should be about 37°–39°F/3°–4°C. The salad compartment of a refrigerator with the thermostat set in the middle range can be used. A clean, dry, and cool storeroom in the cellar with the right temperature is preferable. You are aiming to achieve ground temperature in the early months of a Scandinavian winter.

Turn the fillets twice a day and pour the pressed-out liquid back between the fillets. Remove the weights after 2 days. The *gravlaks* will be ready in 3 to 4 days and no further preparation is needed. Serve it cut in very thin slices, sprinkled with more pepper and chopped dill.

Accompany the *gravlaks* with rye bread and butter, and potato salad dressed with dill. Or with that other excellent product of the Scandinavian peasant kitchen, flatbread, still sometimes home-baked today and rolled as thin as brown paper (see page 508). Add a bowl of floury boiled potatoes, cubed and tossed with soured cream. Wash it down with good light beer and a swallow of *aquavit* to sharpen the tastebuds. To finish, a bowl of fresh berries — blueberries, raspberries, wild strawberries or, best of all in Scandinavia, the delicious cloud-berries (like plump golden raspberries but with a faint flavour of pine needles) which grow wild on the Arctic moors and need the midnight sun to ripen them.

Serve the berries with *seter rømme*, a thick cream which used to be home-soured at a *seter* or summer mountain farm where the cattle were, and in places still are, pastured in fields of purple cranesbill, egg-yolk yellow vetch, and sweet meadow grasses. No sugar is necessary. That is kept for the delicate syrups and wild berry jams, which are stored for the winter. For the rest of us who have no direct access to the heather and silver birch-clad uplands beyond the Arctic Circle, the Finns make a cloudberry liqueur which is exported widely. It has echoes of the real thing, and a glass of it to follow such a meal would be most appropriate.

SUGGESTIONS
- If you do not have a whole salmon, split and bone a single side and lay the raw sides together to marinate, the thin end of the wedge to lie on the thick.
- Serve with lemon wedges and buttered brown bread, as for smoked salmon.
- Serve with creamed spinach.

GRAVLAKS SAUCE
(Norway)

Modern Scandinavians often make a dill sauce (basically a mustard vinaigrette) to accompany the *gravlaks*. To visualize the combination, imagine, if you will, a dish for a tall blond Nordic fisherman who has acquired a beautiful dark-haired Mediterranean wife while trading his salt cod for her southern wine and olive oil.

Quantity   Enough for 1 lb/500 g *gravlaks* to serve 3–4
Time   10 minutes

2 tablespoons mild mustard	$\frac{1}{2}$ teaspoon freshly ground pepper
1 tablespoon wine vinegar	6 tablespoons light oil
1 tablespoon brown sugar	1 heaped tablespoon chopped dill

Mix the mustard, vinegar, sugar, and pepper together with a fork in a shallow bowl. Add the oil in a trickle, as if for a mayonnaise. Be patient and the mixture will thicken. Add the dill. Serve in a bowl alongside the salmon.

Cured or 'Buried' Fish

Several species of fish are traditionally cured in the same way as the *gravlaks* and eaten raw. It is now held advisable to freeze for 24 hours all fish to be eaten raw. This kills any parasites living in the muscles of the fish. However the process does not destroy potentially dangerous microbes, so cleanliness remains essential as a safeguard in preparing any food which is not subject to cooking.

Salt-cured trout   Prepare as for *gravlaks*. Marinate for 2 to 3 days depending on the size of the trout. Serve with a horseradish and cream sauce.

Salt-cured halibut   Prepare as for *gravlaks*. The fish will be ready after 2 to 3 days in its brine. A bowl of soured cream and a pickled cucumber (see page 410) will keep it good company.

Salt-cured mackerel   Freeze the fish for 24 hours. Prepare as for *gravlaks*. Mackerel will need 2 to 3 days in the brine. Coat with plenty of pepper, roughly crushed in a mortar.

Salt-cured herrings   Freeze the fish for 24 hours. Prepare pickle as for *gravlaks*. Scale and gut the herrings and split them by running a sharp knife between flesh and backbone. Leave the fish whole, opened out in a butterfly shape, and sandwich them together in pairs. The herring will need 2 to 3 days to take the salt. Horseradish, mustard and soured cream are good accompaniments. Serve with a bowl of potatoes boiled with salt and dill.

LEFTOVERS
- Dress for the *smörgåsbord* table as for salt herrings.
- Also excellent for a Scandinavian breakfast.

BRINED SALMON
Lenrimmad Lax (Sweden)

This is the simplest method of salting salmon, or any other good fresh fish, and uses a made-up brine instead of dry salting. The salmon is mild in flavour, and is nearly transparent when sliced. The whole process of brining requires only good fresh materials and a little patience. Pork, beef, mutton, and lamb can all be brined in the same fashion.

Quantity   Allow at least 4 oz/100 g per person
Time   Start 2 days before
          Preparation: 30 minutes

1 salmon
2 oz/50 g rough salt (not the dry kitchen variety) per 1 lb/500 g filleted fish

1 pint/600 ml water per 1 lb/500 g filleted fish

Utensils   A large, deep china dish

Prepare and fillet the salmon as for *gravlaks* (see page 45). Boil the water and dissolve the salt in it. Allow to cool. Put the fish in the china dish. Cover the fish with the brine. Leave in a cold larder or the salad compartment of the refrigerator for 2 days.

Drain and dry the fish. Slice finely against the grain and serve with rye bread and unsalted butter. A fine simple dish for a warm summer evening. A bowl of strawberries, tiny wild ones if you can get them, or fresh raspberries to complete the pleasure — most Swedish kitchen plots boast a raspberry-cane fence and a strawberry patch.

SUGGESTIONS
- You do not need a whole salmon. A nice plump tail or middle-piece will do very well.
- Serve with potatoes boiled with a teaspoon of dill seeds, or a whole head of dill.
- Serve with a potato salad dressed with soured cream and chopped dill.
- Serve with a bowl of thinly sliced cucumber dressed with yoghurt and dill.

LEFTOVERS
- If you are fortunate enough to have any left, it is a useful addition to the *smörgåsbord* table, particularly if the salmon is dressed with a *gravlaks* sauce. It can be treated as for any of the *smörgåsbord* herring recipes.

SALTED SALMON
(Finland)

Ethel Tweedie was one of the dauntless nineteenth-century English lady travellers who recorded their journeys with vigour, wit, and acute observation. Here she is in Finland:

> One of the greatest features of a high-class Finnish meal is the Smorgasbord. On a side-table in every dining room rows of little appetising dishes are arranged, and in the middle stands a large silver urn, brannvin, containing at least a couple of liqueurs or schnapps, each of which comes out of a different tap. Every man takes a small glass of brandy, which is made in Finland from corn. . . . Usually in summer the Smorgasbord contains salt graf lax, raw or smoked salmon.

Quantity   Allow at least 4 oz/100 g per person
Time   Start the day before
　　　　　Preparation: 40 minutes

1 salmon
1 oz/25 g sea salt per 2 lb/1 kg fish
1 oz/25 g sugar per 2 lb/1 kg fish

Utensils   A large china plate and foil

Clean and fillet the salmon as for *gravlaks* (see page 45). If the fish is large, cut each fillet in half across the waist. Sprinkle the fillets with salt and sugar. Sandwich the sides together flesh inwards and lay them in the china plate. Cover with foil. Keep in a cool place overnight. The next day the salmon is ready.

Finnish peasant farmers had large brick ovens built into the wall behind their fireplaces in which they baked excellent bread. Serve the salmon with a Finnish dark sourdough bread (see page 494), new potatoes, and soured cream. Berry compote (see page 565) to follow to balance the meal. To drink, a stout such as Guinness. All Finnish gardens had a hop plant or two to flavour the home-brewed beer — there is a Finnish dark beer with a strong flavour of burnt barley which is much favoured in the countryside. Include a small glass of vodka served at room temperature.

SUGGESTIONS
• Slices fried for a few minutes in butter are delicious. Serve with floury boiled potatoes cooked and tossed with dill.

LEFTOVERS
• As with *gravlaks*, salt salmon is a good candidate for the *smörgåsbord*

table. If you have a friend with some leftover smoked ham, and another with some marinated herrings, you lack only the *aquavit* and the lager for a proper *smörgåsbord* party.

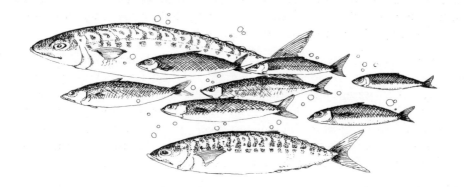

Herring and Mackerel

STOVED HERRINGS
(Scotland)

The best herrings come from Loch Fyne, and the local Clydeside method of cooking them fresh is excellent.

Quantity   2 fish per person
Time   Preparation: 15–20 minutes

2 herrings per person
½ oz/12 g butter per pair of
   herrings
salt

Utensils   A frying pan and skewers

Scale, gut, and wipe the fish inside and out. Split the herrings down the back kipper-fashion and remove the backbone. Dot the flesh with knobs of butter and sprinkle with salt. Sandwich the opened fish together, skin-side out. Skewer them in place and then grill or fry them in a lightly greased frying pan (herrings have plenty of their own fat and need no extra in the pan). Serve with more cold butter and floury boiled potatoes, well drained and shaken over the heat to dry.

BAKED HERRINGS
(Holland)

There is no scrap of doubt about the Dutchman's affection for the herring. It is his boast that Amsterdam is built, quite literally, on herring bones. The first herrings of the year, the *groene* or *niewe haringen*, are caught in late April or early May. They are gutted, boned, and lightly salted on board the fishing vessels and sold to be eaten with nothing more than this preliminary preparation. Or rather such was the practice until recently, when it was discovered that the fish contained tiny worms, nematoids, which could be killed by freezing. Today herring to be consumed raw is frozen for 24 hours before sale.

The next catch of the season is the plump *maatjes*, fished between June and August when the fish are fattening up before spawning. These highly prized virgin fish are usually pickled in salt and sugar with a small amount of saltpetre for their initial preparation. They are bought from the barrel by Dutch housewives and eaten with raw onion and bread.

This fresh herring recipe combines the Netherlander's favourite ingredients.

Quantity   Enough for 4
Time   Preparation: 30 minutes
Cooking: 40–50 minutes

4 fresh herrings	½ pint/300 ml soured cream *or* milk
2 lb/1 kg potatoes	salt and pepper
2 oz/50 g butter	4 eggs
8 oz/250 g onions	

Utensils   A saucepan, a frying pan, and a casserole

Scale and gut the herrings. Fillet them, and chop each fillet into 3 or 4 pieces. Meanwhile scrub the potatoes and put them on to boil. Cook for 20 minutes until soft.

Put half the butter to melt in the frying pan while you peel and slice the onions. Cook the onions gently in the butter until they are golden. Remove. Mix them with half the soured cream or milk and all the chopped fish. Season with salt and pepper.

Preheat the oven to 350°F/180°C/Gas 4.

Skin the cooked potatoes and mash them up with the rest of the butter and soured cream. Beat the eggs together and then beat them into the potato. Season with salt and pepper.

Put a layer of the potato-and-egg mixture into the bottom of the casserole. Cover with the fish-and-onion mixture. Put another layer of potato-and-egg on top. Dot with more butter. Cook in the oven for 40 to 50 minutes, raising the heat to brown the crust for the last 10 minutes.

There is no better herring pie.

LEFTOVERS
• Makes wonderful fish cakes. Either mix well with a raw egg and drop little patties into hot oil-and-butter. Or beat together when cold, make little cakes, and egg-and-breadcrumb them before shallow-frying in hot oil.

MACKEREL WITH BACON
Makrelen mit Speck (Germany)

The combination is perfectly logical. The fisherman's wife kept a pig and salted her flitches of bacon each autumn, so the main ingredients were always to hand to complement her husband's catch.

Quantity 1 fish per person
Time Preparation: 5 minutes per fish
Cooking: 20–30 minutes

1 mackerel per person
4 thin rashers streaky bacon per
  mackerel
pepper

Utensils A baking dish and foil

Preheat the oven to 350°F/180°C/Gas 4.

Fillet your fine fresh mackerel to give 4 fillets from each fish. Remove the rinds from the bacon and place each fillet on its own rasher. Roll up in a tight little parcel like a Swiss roll. Continue until all the fish are done. Pack the rolls into a baking dish that they fit exactly. Pepper them well — the bacon should provide enough salt. Cover the dish with its lid or foil. Bake in the oven for 20 to 30 minutes, or on top of the stove in a covered pan for 20 to 30 minutes, turning the fish once.

QUICK-CURED SALT HERRINGS
(Sweden)

The fast way to salt herrings and extremely convenient if you want them in a hurry.

Quantity Enough for 4
Time Start 3–4 hours before
Preparation: 10–15 minutes

8 herrings
2 pints/1·2 litres water
4 oz/100 g sea salt

Utensils A saucepan and a shallow china dish

Scale, behead, gut, and fillet the herrings. Make a brine by bringing the water and the salt to the boil and allowing it to cool. Lay the herring fillets in a shallow dish, pour the brine over them, and let them take the salt for 3 to 4 hours. Drain and use in salt-herring recipes.

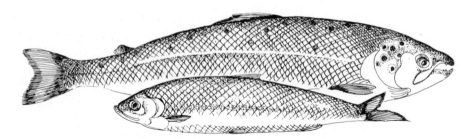

Smörgåsbord Herring Dishes

MARINATED SALT HERRING
FOR SMORGASBORD
Inlagd Sill (Sweden)

Visiting Goteburg in 1871 the French traveller, Paul du Chaillu, appreciated the Scandinavian way of dining:

> I was led to a little table, called smorgasbord, around which we all clustered and upon which I saw a display of smoked reindeer meat, cut into small thin slices; smoked salmon with poached eggs, fresh, raw sliced salmon, called graflax, upon which salt had been put about an hour before; hard-boiled eggs; caviare; fried sausage; a sort of anchovy, caught

on the western coast; raw salted Norwegian herring, exceedingly fat, cut into small pieces; sillsalat, made of pickled herring, small pieces of boiled meat, potato etc. with olive oil and vinegar; smoked goose-breast; cucumbers, soft brown and white bread, cut into small slices; knackebrod, a sort of flat, hard bread made of coarse rye flour and flavoured with aniseed; siktadt bread, very thin, and made of the finest bolted flour; butter; gammal ost, the strongest old cheese one can taste, and kummin ost, a cheese seasoned with caraway; three crystal decanters, containing different kinds of branvin [spirits]; renadt, made from rye or potatoes; pomerans, made from renadt, with the addition of oil or bitter orange and somewhat sweet, and finkelbranvin, or unpurified spirit.

The Swedish *smörgåsbord* — literally the 'bread-and-butter table' — is a full self-service meal made up of several different dishes, mostly cold and ranging from smoked meats to raw fish to berry compotes. The composition is a direct descendant of the classic peasant party meal. All guests at such a gathering, perhaps a wedding or a christening, would bring their own contributions. The Danes and Norwegians have their own variations.

It is a delightful way to eat. All the diners help themselves to the dish that best pleases them. In former times it also gave the family cook an opportunity to taste the neighbour's delicacies without the trouble and expense of full-scale entertaining — a system which adapts well to life today. The dishes can include meat specialities such as salt-cured lamb, potato dishes, ham, meatballs, head-cheese, and brawn, other seafood such as salmon, eel, and shrimp, and all the various breads and cheeses. The one essential ingredient is a varied supply of herring dishes, and these are traditionally the first to be sampled.

Salt herrings can be bought in tins, or straight from the barrel in a delicatessen. They will all need soaking to de-salt except for the variety sold as *Matjes herring* (a Dutch cure), which will not need the treatment. Although salt herrings used to be so much a staple of the Scandinavian diet that they would be eaten in simple homes without further embellishment, they are much improved by the addition of a few imported ingredients.

Quantity   Enough for 1 dish on the *smörgåsbord* table
Time   Start 2–3 days before
            Preparation: 20 minutes

6 salt herrings	2 bayleaves
½ pint/300 ml vinegar	½ teaspoon peppercorns
½ pint/300 ml water	1 medium onion
4 oz/100 g sugar	

Utensils   A medium saucepan and a large jar for the herrings

Skin and fillet the salt herrings if this has not already been done. Soak the fillets in water or water and milk for an hour if they are commercially prepared and already soaked, to remove excess saltiness. If they are home-cured or cured in an equivalent manner they will need several hours (say, overnight).

Meanwhile bring the vinegar, water, and sugar to the boil with the bayleaves and peppercorns. Allow to cool. Peel and slice the onion.

Put the filleted herrings into the large jar, tucking in the rings of raw onion. Pour in the marinade. The herrings will be ready to eat in 2 days but will keep for 2 weeks in the refrigerator, or longer if sealed. Drain and eat the herrings with boiled potatoes, soured cream, and a sprinkling of chopped chives.

With their *smörgåsbord* the Danes like to serve rye bread (see page 494), the Norwegians flatbread (see page 508), and the Swedes their thicker *knäckebröd*, plus the various Scandinavian soft breads and black breads. A Swede would serve beer and schnapps with the meal. The Danes make very good beer and the Finns particularly good *aquavit* — both drinks are excellent all over Scandinavia.

SUGGESTIONS

• Concoct your own delicious marinated herring dishes by mixing the fish with suitable vegetables. The mixer should equal the fish in volume. Allow a dressed salad to stand for half an hour before serving. Serve cool but not ice-cold. For a simple main meal, serve three or four different salads together with a pile of potato pancakes or *lompe* (see page 509), so that each person can roll and fill their own. The do-it-yourself element is an integral part of an independent and servantless community. *Aquavit* to accompany.

Salt herring with cucumber   Mix equal quantities of marinated herring, drained and chopped into bite-sized pieces, and cubed cucumber. Dress with soured cream or yoghurt and dill.

Salt herring with cooked carrots   Chop the herrings and slice the cooked carrots — equal quantities of vegetable to fish. Dress with some of the marinade and a little extra sugar.

Salt herring with potatoes   Equal quantities of cold boiled potatoes mixed with chopped marinated herring. Dress with the marinade thickened with a little mild mustard. Sprinkle with chopped dill or chives.

Salt herring with dill and beetroot   Equal quantities of chopped marinated herring and cubed beetroot, and lots of chopped dill. Dress with a few spoonfuls of the marinade.

Salt herring with potatoes and pickled cucumbers   Mix equal quantities of drained, chopped marinated herring with diced cold potatoes and slices of pickled cucumber (see page 410). Dress with soured cream or yoghurt. Sprinkle with plenty of chopped dill or chives.

LEFTOVERS
● The Scandinavians love to eat their leftover *smörgåsbord* dishes for breakfast.
● Otherwise, arrange the dressed fish on a slice of buttered bread as a *smørrebrød* or open sandwich, the Danes' favourite lunch.

ROLLMOPS OR VINEGAR-PICKLED HERRINGS
(Germany)

There are almost as many ways of preparing herring in the German kitchen as there are in the Scandinavian. Methods of pickling in these more southerly and vine-growing climes include vinegar as a preserving agent.

Quantity   Allow 1–2 herrings per person as a main dish (Baltic herrings are smaller than the Atlantic variety)
Time   Start 1 week before
Preparation: 1 hour

4 lb/2 kg herrings	1 teaspoon peppercorns
4 oz/100 g salt	4 bayleaves
2 pints/1·2 litres water	4 pickled cucumbers (*optional* —
1 pint/600 ml white wine vinegar	see page 410)
(cider vinegar is used in some	2 large onions
districts)	

Utensils   A saucepan, a large shallow dish, foil, and 2 or 3 large glass jars

Scale and gut the herrings and remove heads and tails. Remove the backbones — if the herrings are small they will pull out attached to the heads. Also remove all visible small bones. Leave the 2 fillets joined. Lay them in a large shallow dish and cover with a strong brine made from the salt dissolved in the boiling water. Cover with foil and let the fish lie in the brine for 3 to 4 hours to take the salt.

Meanwhile bring the vinegar to the boil with the peppercorns and bayleaves. Allow to cool. If you are using the cucumbers, cut them into chunks and slice the onions.

Take the herring fillets out of their brine and drain them. Roll each flat herring round a piece of cucumber and a slice of onion. Pack the cylinders into glass jars. Cover with the spiced vinegar and seal down. .

Store in the refrigerator. Rinse everything, including your hands, in cold water to get rid of the fishy smell.

The herrings will be ready to eat in a week and will keep for months. They are a major ingredient in the *Katerfrüstück*, the German hangover breakfast, when they are accompanied by beer and schnapps — a splendid start to the day although it risks leaving the eater with an even worse hangover.

PICKLED HERRINGS
Bismarckheringe (Germany)

Bismarck herrings are prepared in much the same way as in the rollmop recipe given above. The maturing is quicker.

Quantity   Enough for 10–12
Time   Start the day before
               Preparation: 45 minutes

  4 lb/2 kg herrings
  1 pint/600 ml vinegar
  2 large onions
  salt and cayenne pepper

Utensils   A large shallow dish and foil

Gut and behead the herrings and then fillet them into 4. Put them to soak in the vinegar overnight. Slice the onion into fine rings. Layer the fillets with the onion rings in the dish — seasoning each layer until all is used up. Cover with foil and put in a cold larder or in the refrigerator. Ready to eat in a day. The dish is not meant for longevity — eat within 4 to 5 days.

Small Fish

SKEWERED FISH
(Greece)

The Greeks love everything from the sea — a natural taste in one of the world's great seafaring nations. If it comes from the waves, they believe, it must be good: eels, cuttlefish, squid, octopus, sea urchins, devil fish, giant mussels as long as a man's arm — as fish-eaters the Greeks have the most catholic of tastes.

Cut the fish you have chosen into walnut-sized pieces. Thread the pieces on to fine wooden skewers. Trickle olive oil and lemon juice over them, salt and pepper and leave to marinate for half an hour. Sprinkle the fish with a little marjoram or oregano or thyme to remind you of the herbs crushed underfoot among the dry grey rocks of the Greek hillside. Make a basting liquid with 1 part lemon juice to 4 parts olive oil and put a cut garlic clove to infuse in it while the fish is marinating.

Cook the skewered fish over charcoal or under a hot grill. Baste with the mixture throughout. Serve with a sauce handed separately, either a simple oil-and-lemon mixture with the addition of a handful of finely chopped parsley, or with a bowl of *avgolemono*.

FRIED FISH
(Greece)

Quantity Enough for 3–4
Time Start about an hour before
Preparation: 20 minutes

1 lb/500 g fish	salt
4 oz/100 g flour	1 egg, separated
water	oil for frying

Utensils A bowl, a deep frying pan, a perforated spoon, and kitchen paper

Make a frying batter with the flour and enough lukewarm water to produce a liquid like pouring cream. Beat it well and add a little salt. Beat it some more. Leave for half an hour or so. When you are ready to fry, beat in the egg yolk. Beat the white well and fold it in immediately.

Heat the oil until a blue haze rises. Dip each piece of fish into the batter and drop it into the oil.

This can be used as a frying batter for fish steaks or vegetable fritters. Particularly good as used in Turkey, where street vendors in the villages on the Bosphorus make a summer living selling roasted sweetcorn and deep-fried mussels. All morning the fishermen sit out on the decks of the fishing boats shucking gunmetal-dark mussel shells 3 or 4 inches long. They yield bucketfuls of sweet, plump, orange molluscs. All afternoon and into the night the vendors thread the fat little fish on skewers, dip them in a bucketful of the batter, and fry them — waterfront streetfood. Each skewerful comes with a lemon-quarter and a slice of bread. Wonderful with a bowl of garlicky *skordalia* (see page 397).

LITTLE FRIED FISH
Boquerones fritos (Spain)

It is hard to know quite why the coastal-dwellers of Spain fry fish so perfectly, but they do. Certainly the excellence has something to do with the superb raw materials available, and the beautiful olive oil (now sadly becoming so expensive that cheaper vegetable oils are often used instead), the good rough salt, and well-tempered iron pans. But it also owes much to the housewife's unsurpassed sleight of hand in the flouring and handling of the most fragile sea creatures — a talent which echoes her skill with the crochet hook and the embroidery needle when making tiny garments for her children. Babies, fish, and donkeys are always well dressed in Spain, whatever else is not.

Quantity   Enough for 3–4 people
Time   Preparation: 20 minutes

1 lb/500 g fresh anchovies (smelts
    or any fish no longer than 4 in/
    10 cm will do too)
3 oz/75 g coarse flour
1 teaspoon rough salt

olive *or* vegetable oil for frying (a
    mixture of olive and sunflower
    is good)
lemons

Utensils   A plate, a deep frying pan, a perforated spoon, and kitchen paper

Gut the fish, and nip their heads off. Rinse them in fresh water and drain them. Mix the flour with the salt and spread it on a flat plate. Dip the damp fish in the flour and pinch the tails together to make fan-shaped groups of 3 to 5 fish. The tails fry together deliciously crisp and make the fish much easier to handle.

Heat the oil in the frying pan. When it is hazed with blue, test it by putting in a small piece of bread. If it bubbles and turns golden immediately, you may start frying.

Fry the fish in their groups quickly until golden, turning once. Put them on paper to drain. Serve piping hot with quartered lemons, a plate of chips, and a salad of cos lettuce and onion rings dressed with lemon juice, olive oil, and salt.

SUGGESTIONS

• The tiniest fish of all, *chunquetes*, no longer than a pin, are at the time of going to press declared an illegal catch in an attempt to conserve stocks, but they may reappear in the markets at some stage in the future. They are delectable and need perfect skill. They are tossed, a handful at a time, in a sieve full of salted flour, then thrown into hot oil for no more than a moment, during which they have to be constantly moved to keep them separate. They are removed just as they crisp but before they have taken colour, drained immediately, and served piping hot. Wonderful.

• Squid or *calamares* — both the large ones which have to be sliced into rings, and the tiny *chocos*, baby cuttlefish, which are fried whole — are also prepared thus, and can be dipped in milk before being fried. Do not salt squid, octopus, or cuttlefish before frying as this makes them tough. Other fish which take kindly to the treatment include tiny plaice or sole, little whiting, and any larger fish which can be cut into steaks. Very often a whole plate of mixed fish will be presented, the freshest and cheapest the market can offer or the fisherman catch.

PICKLED ANCHOVIES
Boquerones en vinagre (Spain)

Until the middle of the twentieth century, the peasants of the hill villages of the Alpujarras below Granada had fresh fish every day. The two-way trade between the coast and the hills bartered anchovies and sardines for silkworm cocoons, a cash crop common to the peasantry of the south-eastern Mediterranean. The donkey-boys would set out from the coast before dawn, as soon as the first fishing boats returned to harbour. Boy and donkey would climb the herb-scented hills swiftly racing the competition — the first salesman makes the best sales. They would reach the top villages on the ridge, five or six miles up the steep oleander-tangled ravines, by midday at the latest. In twin panniers woven from tough esparto grass slung over the grey flanks of the tough little beasts of burden, their wares glistened emerald and silver.

On the return journey the donkey-panniers would be piled high with silkworm cocoons — huge pale pyramids as light as thistledown on their way to the silk merchants in the town far below. Those were the days before nylon put the silkworm breeders out of business, and did many a poor housewife out of her pin money. Mulberry trees, on whose leaves the silk worms fattened, still shade village patios, but the fisherboys' donkeys have been replaced by vans and motorbicycles. The fish vendor only visits once or twice a week now, and only the rich can afford to have their cloth spun by the diligent little caterpillars.

Pickled anchovies are a legacy from the silk-fish trade. Thus prepared the highly perishable little fish would keep sweet and fresh in a shady larder for a week. They are still much appreciated even today, when refrigeration makes preservation unnecessary, as a favourite *tapa* dish served in little bars all over Spain.

Reminiscing about the trade, Miguel Moreno, an Andalusian fish vendor, said in 1958: 'In the villages the demand was only for the cheaper sorts of fish: sardines, *jureles*, whitebait [anchovies], sea-bream.' Miguel's record load was 107 kilos. (*The Pueblo*, Ronald Fraser, London, 1973.)

Quantity   Enough for 4
Time   Start 1–2 days before
           Preparation: 20 minutes

1 lb/500 g fresh anchovies (*or* small smelts, sardines, *or* any other small fresh fish)	½ pint/300 ml white wine *or* sherry vinegar
½ teaspoon salt	4 cloves garlic
	small bunch parsley

Utensils   A shallow china dish and foil

European anchovies, *Engraulis encrasicolus*, and smelts, *Osmerus eperlanus*, do not have to be scaled (unlike the American striped anchovy *Anchoa hepsetus*, and most other little fish).

Clean, gut, and slit the little fish down the backbone. Butterfly them out without cutting them in two. The backbone will pull out easily — sever it neatly just before the tail. Lay the fish, opened out, skin-side up in the shallow dish, sprinkle with salt, and pour over them most of the vinegar. Cover with foil and leave to marinate for a day or two in a cool place.

Drain the anchovies and turn them over, so that they are flesh-side up. Pour some more fresh vinegar over them. Peel and slice the garlic finely and scatter it over the little fish. Chop the parsley and sprinkle it over the top. Eat with chunks of fresh bread and a glass of dry sherry, or the wine of Montilla which lays claim to being the original sherry.

Pickled anchovies will keep in a cool place for at least a week.

PICKLED FISH
Peixe frita de escabeche (Portugal)

A very common way of preserving fish. Similar preparations are found in Spain and, under the Iberian influence, all over Latin America including Mexico where, as *Seviche*, the dish is prepared with raw fish marinated in lemon juice. 'Ceveach' is the English version: *The Lady's Companion* of 1733 has an almost identical recipe for pickling mackerel.

Quantity Enough for 4
Time Start the day before
            Preparation: 30 minutes

1 lb/500 g fresh fish (sardines, anchovies, mackerel, whatever is fresh)
2 cloves garlic
1 tablespoon salt
½ tablespoon ground peppercorns
2 bayleaves

few sprigs marjoram *or* parsley
4 tablespoons olive oil
juice 1 lemon
4 tablespoons seasoned flour
1 large glass white wine *or*
    ½ pint/300 ml wine vinegar
    mixed with ½ pint/100 ml water

Utensils A small pestle and mortar or a liquidizer, a frying pan, and a deep china dish

Behead, clean, scale, and gut the fish. Cut them into chunks if they are too large for one bite. Peel and chop the garlic. Make a marinade by pounding or blending together the garlic, salt, peppercorns, bayleaves, and herbs and then mixing the paste with 2 tablespoons of the olive oil and the lemon juice. Rub it well into the fish and leave to stand for an hour or two.

Pour off the marinade and save it. Roll the pieces of fish in seasoned flour. Heat the remaining 2 tablespoons of oil in the frying pan until a faint blue haze rises. Fry the chunks of fish in the oil until cooked through and golden. Put them in a deep dish. Pour the white wine or vinegar-and-water mixture into the frying pan juices and allow them to bubble for a moment. Stir in the reserved marinade and bubble that up. Pour it over the fish while it is still hot. Ready to eat in a day. Will keep in the refrigerator for a week.

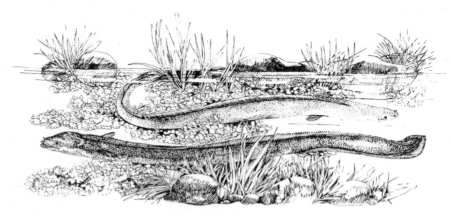

Eel

Although the moray and conger are both fished in European waters, the species most often found in the European cooking pot is *Anguilla anguilla* — the common eel. The common eel is born and dies in the sea, but spends most of its life in fresh water. Eels can survive out of their native element for a comparatively long time, and their flesh remains sweet and fresh for a considerable while after death. American and European common eels use adjacent spawning grounds in the Sargasso Sea. The tiny, transparent, pin-eyed American elvers take a year to reach their destination in the estuaries and rivers, but the Europeans must journey all of three years before they reach their feeding grounds.

If they are not caught for the Spanish and Italian tables, where they are much appreciated as elvers, the eels swim up-river, turning dark and opaque as they go, where they live for an average of between nine and twelve years. The delta of the great river Rhône, which flows into the Mediterranean to the west of Marseilles, has been a rich hunting ground for eel-fishermen for thousands of years. So much so that the Camargue is now a largely man-made landscape dominated by *digues* — great earthworks thrown up over the centuries to accommodate and trap the large eel population of the river. Rosy flamingoes and millions of seabirds have long since learnt to take full advantage of the arrangement.

GRILLED EEL
Anguille grillé (France)

Eel flesh is very rich. Although the eel-fishermen of the Camargue treat their catch as a cash crop for export, they will sometimes eat the delicacy themselves. I have eaten this dish on a bright spring day on a patio on the Marais, watched with interest by a migrating flock of bee-eaters, their blue and gold feathers dazzling in the sunlight.

The Camargais are as dark as gypsies and their food has a strong Spanish flavour. Old Sara, owner of a *Mas*, or marshy farmstead, on the crossroads near Les Saintes Maries de la Mer (and herself named after the black servant of the two Maries of blessed memory), serves a midday meal to the herdsmen of the half-wild cattle which pasture the reedbeds. The Camargais are somewhat suspicious of outsiders, but Sara can sometimes be persuaded to cook for passing strangers as well as her regulars. Her barbecue fire in the chicken-scratched backyard, fuelled by the trimmings from the vineyards which surround the *Mas*, never seems to go out. Presented with an eel Sara has no time for niceties. She stuns it with a blow to its head on the table, hangs it from a hook on a wooden post, and unceremoniously skins it.

Have your fishmonger perform this service for you.

Quantity   Enough for 4
Time   Preparation: 20–30 minutes

1 lb/500 g eel	olive oil
1 teaspoon dried thyme	lemons
pepper	

Utensils   A barbecue or a very hot grill

Sprinkle the slices of eel with thyme and pepper and brush them with olive oil. Leave them to marinate while the grill heats.

Put the slices of eel to grill. They will take 10 to 15 minutes if they are thick. Serve them with quartered lemons and salt. Sara accompanies the dish with a bottle of *vin gris*, dry, pale pink and slightly salty, plenty of home-baked bread, dense-textured and sweet, a generous plate of crisp-fried chips, and a salad of roughly chopped lettuce, tomatoes, and mild purple onions. Before the meal serve Provençal olives to take away the first pangs of hunger.

JELLIED EELS
(England)

Buy your eel alive and have the fishmonger kill it, bleed it and gut it. Have it cut into roughly 3 in/7 cm lengths. Soused eel is the preferred English way with this rich meat. Jellied eels are still a favourite racecourse and sporting snack, as well as having long been the favourite fast-food of Cockney London's East End.

Quantity   Enough for 4–6
Time   Start the day before
             Preparation: 10 minutes
             Cooking: 2–3 hours

 1½ lb/750 g eel
 parsley
 bayleaves
 onion
 vinegar
 salt and 6 peppercorns

Utensils   A saucepan and a deep casserole

If the eel is unskinned, put the pieces in a saucepan and cover them with cold water. Bring the water to the boil. Lift out the eel and you will find the skin comes off easily. Loosely pack the sections of eel vertically in a deep casserole — they should not reach more than three-quarters of the way up. Put a few herbs in between the sections: sprigs of parsley, bayleaves, and a sliced onion. Cover all with a mixture of half vinegar, half water, filling the dish right up to the brim. Sprinkle in a teaspoon of salt and the peppercorns.

   Cover the dish and put it to bake in a slow oven 250°F/130°C/Gas 1 for 2 to 3 hours (depending on the thickness of the fish). Remove the herbs and leave the dish to cool overnight. The next day the bones will have dissolved and the fish will be surrounded by a rich sharp jelly.

GREEN EEL STEW
Anguille au vert (Belgium)

As before, if possible buy your eel alive and have your fishmonger kill, bleed, clean, skin, gut, and cut it into lengths for you on the spot.

Quantity   Enough for 6–8
Time   Preparation: 40–50 minutes

2–3 lb/1–1·5 kg eel cut into
   2 in/5 cm lengths

1½ lb/750 g green herbs — sorrel is
   almost essential for its bitter
   flavour (watercress the only
   possible substitute), plus a
   selection from parsley, celery
   tops, mint, sage, chervil, and
   summer savory

1 medium onion

3–4 oz/75–100 g butter

salt

pepper (*optional*)

Utensils 2 saucepans, one heavy with a lid

Wipe the pieces of eel and put them in a saucepan with salted water to cover. Bring quickly to the boil and cook for 5 minutes. Take them off the heat and leave them in the water while you prepare the greens.

Pick over the leaves and remove any thick stalks, then shred them finely. Peel and chop the onion. Rinse the greens, leaving water clinging to them. Put them with the chopped onion into the heavy pan with half the butter. Cover tightly. Stew the greens gently, shaking the pan occasionally so that they do not stick, for 10 minutes. Then add the pieces of eel and a cupful of the cooking liquid. Cover again and continue to cook for another 10 minutes.

Remove the pieces of eel and put them on a hot plate. Stir the remaining butter into the green sauce. Adjust seasoning, adding pepper if you like. Pour the sauce over the eel pieces and serve, with thick slices of bread, well buttered.

SUGGESTIONS
● If you cannot find any sorrel, use watercress with the juice of half a lemon or a tablespoon of vinegar.

SMOKED EEL
Anguille fumé (Belgium)

Do not skin a fine fat eel, but clean it and chop its body into 6 in/15 cm lengths. Sprinkle with salt and then hot-smoke it for 30 to 40 minutes in a small home-smoker.

Fillet into its convenient square fillets. Serve with grated horseradish mixed with thick cream beaten with a little mustard, and accompany with thick slices of buttered brown bread. Quite the best way to eat eel.

Shellfish

Europe's generous larder of shore-based shellfish provided her earliest hunter-gathering inhabitants with one of their most easily obtained suppers. Excavation of prehistoric sites, such as those in Portugal's Tagus valley, have yielded quantities of emptied mollusc shells alongside wild pig and cattle bones. Dishes which include cockles in sauces for pork still survive in Portugal and Wales.

The smaller molluscs are usually full of mud and sand and should be left overnight in fresh running water if possible to spit out their grit. Check that each shell contains a live fish and discard those which are heavy with sand.

Oysters   Since prehistoric times these most succulent of shellfish have been gathered around the shores of Europe. Until the oyster beds succumbed suddenly to overfishing and pollution in the middle of the nineteenth century, they were a staple food of the poor. Wild oysters of the species *Ostrea edulis* are the best. They have a stronger sea flavour than cultivated oysters, which are fattened in river mouths where they are washed with alternate tides of sea and fresh water. Otherwise, differences depend on size and source. Portuguese oysters are the long and narrow ones. Cheaper and not as finely flavoured, they are a different species, *Crassostrea angulata*. Oysters out of season (in the months without an 'r') are perfectly edible, but will be breeding, which gives them a milky appearance that the French call *laiteuse*. They are at their most delicious eaten raw, sauced only with a squeeze of lemon, or a shake of chilli vinegar, a turn of the pepper grinder, and their own sweet liquor.

Scallops   *Pecten maximus* has been known as the pilgrim shell since the Middle Ages when religious travellers adopted it as their emblem.

The scallop, as the pilgrims had observed, is no mean traveller itself, propelling its shell great distances through the water by means of a kind of squirting action achieved with its large white adductor muscle (the white meat of the creature). Scallops do not burrow in the sandy shore. If your scallops are not opened (they are much better and will taste of the sea if they are still in the shell), leave them in a pan of cold water after you have scrubbed them. They will then open enough to allow you to get your knife in.

Cockles Beds of *Cardium edule* are to be found in the sandy mud of estuaries and sea marshes. These small rib-shelled bi-valves can be raked out from their hiding places — about 2 in/5 cm below the surface — at low tide with a shallow fork. Wash them thoroughly and plunge them into boiling water. Leave them there for 2 minutes while they open. Remove them as they do so and pick out the little fish. In England they are usually eaten cold with vinegar.

Winkles Periwinkles, *Littorina littorea*, tiny, dark smooth-shelled sea snails, were particularly popular eating in Victorian times. They are a dish tailormade for those with time on their hands. Cook them in boiling sea water or heavily salted water for 10 minutes. Drain them and eat them. There is a soothing rhythm to the ritual of winkling the little fishes out of their shells with a long sharp pin. The saltiness of the shell after its poaching in strong brine wrinkles the ends of the fingers, and seasons the meat by proximity. In Ireland winkles are sometimes served in a sauce of carragheen moss and milk.

Whelks Whelks, *Buccinum undatum*, are comparatively large rib-shelled sea snail-like creatures. Soak them in several changes of water until they stop spitting out sand, then scrub them. Steam them for an hour. Pick them out of their shells with a sharp twist from a long-pronged fork. The de-shelled mollusc looks somewhat like an illustration from a medical textbook, but it will none the less be delicious eating. Remove the delicate horn trapdoor which blocks the shell. In England they are served cool on little saucers with vinegar. Or hot with a white sauce made with 1 oz/25 g flour lightly fried in 2 oz/50 g butter, then simmered with $\frac{1}{2}$ pint/300 ml milk and a generous handful of parsley to 1 pint/600 ml whelks. Do not forget salt and pepper.

Clams A catholic selection of the *Veneridae* family is collected and eaten all round the shores of Europe. They can be cooked as for mussels or scallops. The shells of these bi-valves can have rough or smooth ribbing. The fish which inhabit them burrow in the sandy shore — hence their large 'feet'. Carpet shells and venus shells are the *palourdes* of France.

Razor shells The long, thin shells contain a long, thin and very powerful 'foot'. They are often the preferred titbit of the shell-fishermen themselves, collector's pieces which rarely come on the market. They are at their best only a few minutes out of their sandy homes, grilled swiftly for long enough to open them, and then eaten with salt — and a squeeze of lemon where lemons are grown. The meat is incomparably sweet.

OYSTERS IN GREEN JACKETS
Huitres en habit vert (France)

Quantity Enough for 2–3
Time Preparation: 20 minutes

12 oysters
¼ pint/150 ml cream
1 small bunch parsley

few drops Pernod (*optional*)
2 oz/50 g butter

Utensils A large, shallow ovenproof dish

Open the oysters by levering the shells apart. There are dagger-like instruments for the task on sale in French markets. Otherwise, a short, strong knife should be up to the job. Grip the rough shell firmly in a cloth while you work.

When the oyster is opened, leave the fish on the deeper of its two shells. Sprinkle it with cream, chopped parsley, and either finely chopped garlic or finely chopped onion. A few drops of Pernod will not go amiss as well. Dot with butter. Arrange the oysters in the large dish, and cook them under the grill for 5 minutes or in a hot oven for 7 to 8 minutes. If you prefer, instead of the butter, lay a piece of fine-cut streaky bacon over the oysters. Grill for 5 minutes. Do not try and move them from their dish, but serve them as they are with bread to mop up the juices.

BAKED OYSTERS
Huitres au four (France)

The way the oystermen of Brittany themselves like their oysters cooked.

Quantity Enough for 2–3
Time Preparation: 20 minutes

12 oysters
2 oz/50 g fresh breadcrumbs
2 tablespoons milk

2–3 shallots *or* 1 small onion
salt and pepper
4 oz/100 g grated cheese

Utensils   A shallow gratin dish

Open the oysters and leave each fish on its deeper shell. Arrange them in a shallow gratin dish in a single layer. Soak the breadcrumbs in the milk while you chop the shallots or onion finely. Top the oysters — do not stuff them, this is a crisp little hat, not a blanket — with the soaked breadcrumbs, the chopped shallot, salt and freshly ground pepper, and a sprinkle of the grated cheese.

Bake the oysters in a hot oven or under a grill for 6 to 7 minutes — just long enough to melt the cheese. Serve on the instant. Plenty of bread to accompany and a glass of cold Muscadet to sip when you have burnt your tongue on the cheese.

CLAMS
Almejas (Spain)

There are at least half a dozen different varieties of *concha* or shell that are collected and enjoyed around the coastline of Spain. The smallest and sweetest, *conchas finas* or 'delicate clams', have a pale, fine near-translucent shell with a mauve blush inside. These clams or cockles are sold raw and on the shell. They are sometimes cooked *a la plancha*, on the plank — a metal sheet laid over a fire which acts as a simple grill. Otherwise they are cooked in a wide frying pan — in my view the best way for these little molluscs to be treated. They are eaten immediately, before they have time to toughen.

Quantity   Enough for 4–6
Time   Preparation: 15–20 minutes

2 lb/1 kg clams *or* cockles *or* any small shellfish (fresh and in their shells)
2 cloves garlic
1 small bunch parsley
2 tablespoons olive oil
1 wineglass dry white wine *or* sherry

Utensils   A large frying pan or wok with a lid

Rinse the shellfish, checking over and discarding any which are broken or filled with sand. Peel and slice the garlic. Chop the parsley.

Put the oil to heat in the frying pan (a wok comes into its own here). When it is lightly hazed with blue smoke, toss in the garlic and fry for a moment. Add the parsley, quickly followed by the shellfish. Pour in the wine or sherry. Turn up the heat.

Cover with a lid, shaking the pan to redistribute the shells so that all have a chance to cook. If you have no lid, keep moving the clams with a metal drainer. It will take 3 to 4 minutes for all the shells to open. Do not cook them any longer but serve immediately. They should not be reheated, and are delicious even when cold.

SUGGESTIONS
• In Portugal these little shellfish are often cooked with diced bacon or cubed fresh pork, plus a chopped onion and chopped tomato. All the ingredients, with half a glass olive oil and the well-rinsed clams and perhaps a few slices of *chorizo*, are then put into a covered wok-like frying pan and given 20 minutes over a moderate heat.

LEFTOVERS
• Serve with a dish of rice. Using the leftover liquid in the cooking of the rice, put the fish, in or out of their shells, on the top to warm quickly in the steam, but without allowing them time to go rubbery.

MUSSEL STEW
Moules marinières (France)

Collecting mussels from the seashore is one of the most satisfying of seaside holiday amusements. There is the pleasure of spotting the beds at low tide: rockscapes clustered thickly with indigo colonies, flashing gunmetal and ink, stacked in tidepools thick as tenants in tenements, baby shells no bigger than a fingernail, small and sweet and pale-fleshed, together with plump old monsters sheltering at the base of wooden breakwaters.

Cold-water mussels are the best. Mussels thrive in mud and sand, and by the time they arrive in the kitchen they are in need of a good wash. Give it to them, overnight if possible, in a large bucket of cold water with a handful of salt sprinkled into it. The following day, rinse them again. The simplest way to prepare them, and one of the best, is as follows.

Quantity   Enough for 4–5
Time   Preparation: 15–20 minutes

   5–6 pints/3–4 litres mussels
   plenty of parsley
   1 onion
   1 pint/600 ml water

Utensils   A very large shallow pan or a wok with a lid, a small saucepan, and a perforated spoon

Pick over the mussels carefully. Discard any that are broken, or whose shells do not close when you stir them in the bucket. Any shells that are particularly heavy are probably full of sand — throw them out, they will do the broth no good at all. Scrape the barnacles and seaweed off the shells, and pull out the little black seaweed-like beards.

Put 4 to 5 deep soup plates to warm in the oven. Chop the parsley. You will need plenty — 4 to 5 tablespoons is not too much. Finely chop the onion.

Put the water in the shallow pan or wok and bring it to the boil. Throw in the mussels, turn up the heat, and let the molluscs open in their own juices. Cover the pan and shake it to distribute the heat. As soon as all the mussels are open — which will take a few minutes only — lift them out with a perforated spoon and pile them on the hot soup plates. Mussels should be eaten as soon as they are cooked. Prolonged cooking makes them like little pieces of orange rubber. Strain the broth into a smaller pan and throw in the chopped parsley and onion. Reheat this and serve it separately in a jug.

To accompany, plenty of bread, radishes, unsalted butter, and a good cheese. The Atlantic coast of France, where this recipe comes from, has rich pickings: serve a Port Salut, a Camembert, or a quarter of a wheel of Brie (from a little further inland, on the outskirts of Paris, as befits the favourite cheese of that elegant diplomat, M Talleyrand). Accompany the dish, too, with dry white wine or good Normandy cider. Follow with a big round wheel of apple tart (see page 538) together with a jug of thick yellow cream. The French slightly sour *crème fraîche* is best — stir a spoonful of soured cream or yoghurt into the thickest sweet cream you can find.

SUGGESTIONS
- Replace the water with dry white wine or dry cider.
- When the mussels have been cooked to this stage, they can be picked out of their shells and cooked in a sauce. Try them with ¼ pint/150 ml thick double cream stirred into the cooking liquor and then reheated. Simmer until it thickens a little.
- Try them as a substitute in the snail recipes (see pages 122 to 126). Particularly good heated with garlic butter — the French sell flat earthenware dishes with dimples for holding snails, with or without their shells, which are perfect for this substitution.

LEFTOVERS
Arrange the cooked mussels, each on a single shell, in a large dish which will accommodate them in one layer. Chop together finely tomatoes, peppers, and sweet onions, and dress them with oil and vinegar. Top the mussels with this mixture, so that each little shell has its share. Leave overnight to marinate. An excellent Spanish dish.

CARRAGHEEN WINKLES
(Ireland)

Quantity Enough for 4
Time Preparation: 30–40 minutes

1 pint/600 ml carragheen moss
water
1 pint/600 ml milk (cream is even
   better)

1 pint/600 ml cooked shelled
   winkles
salt and pepper

Utensils A medium saucepan

Wash the carragheen very thoroughly, cover with water, and cook for 20 to 30 minutes until tender. Drain and put it back on the heat with the milk or cream. Simmer for 10 minutes and then stir in the shelled winkles. Heat to boiling point. Taste and adjust the seasoning. Eat with a spoon and plenty of bread.

SUGGESTIONS
• On some of the little islands off the coast of Wales, the winkles are picked out of their shells and then fried in bacon fat with an egg or two scrambled in with the juices. Roughly 1 pint/600 ml shelled fish will feed 4 people.

SCALLOPS IN THEIR SHELLS
St. Jacques en coquille (France)

I have often eaten these fine shellfish, prepared in this way, in the salt marshes beside Mont St. Michel. There, where the ancient island fortress marks the border between Brittany and Normandy, the products of orchard, dairy, and ocean are all at their finest.

Quantity Enough for 4
Time Preparation: 20–25 minutes

6–10 scallops (they vary greatly in
   size)
1 large glass cider
¼ pint/150 ml thick double cream
salt and pepper

1 small bunch parsley
1 oz/25 g butter
1 tablespoon oil
1 oz/25 g fresh breadcrumbs

Utensils A shallow pan, a small saucepan, and a frying pan

Put the scallops in their shells, well scrubbed and round side down to cup the juices, in a shallow pan of boiling water or into a low oven. After a few moments they will open. Remove the frills and the little sandy sack of intestine. Slice the white adductor muscle horizontally into 3 or 4 medallions and put them aside with the coral. Scrub the 4 largest of the curved shells and put them aside.

Preheat the oven to 400°F/200°C/Gas 6.

Put the cider into the small saucepan and bring it to the boil. Slide in the scallop pieces and poach them for 3 to 4 minutes. Remove and divide them among the 4 curved shells. Boil the cooking juices until they are reduced by half. Stir in the cream. Bubble it all up again. Taste and adjust the seasoning.

Chop the parsley. Heat the butter and oil in the frying pan until foaming, and then throw in the chopped parsley and the breadcrumbs. Fry until golden, then scatter them over the scallops. Put all in the oven for a moment to heat through. Serve very hot.

COCKLE PIE
Pastai gocos (Wales)

There is an abundance of cockles around the Welsh coast. The Welsh, unlike the English, never liked their cockles doused in vinegar. This description of the Welsh cockle-wives comes from Wirt Sykes, the American consul in Cardiff towards the end of the last century:

At the little village of Penclawdd, in Glamorganshire, countless tons of cockles are gathered and despatched by rail to all parts of England. Women alone do this work; men are absent from the scene, and spectators are not wanted. But it is a unique spectacle when the sand-bank is lined with the cockle-wives, bent over with their heads near the ground and their bright-hued drapery flying in the fresh ocean breeze, 'scraping' for cockles. The tide here recedes for as much as a mile, sometimes farther, leaving exposed acres upon acres of sand in which the cockles are embedded. The great day for this business is Friday — the day when nothing is doing, Saturday; both facts accounted for by the potent influence of Saturday's market. The habits of the cockle are very similar to those of the American clam, and he is caught in much the same manner. The searcher for cockles finds the sand dotted with thousands of little holes about as large as if pierced with knitting needles; the cockle is there, embedded a couple of inches below the surface. The cockle-wife is armed with a 'scraper' made from an old reaping-hook, and a deft Penclawdd lassie will pick up the cockles as fast as a farmer can dig potatoes. Some of the women have little carts or pannier-laden donkeys, but the majority bear their baskets on their heads.

Quantity Enough for 4
Time Preparation: 25–30 minutes
Cooking: 20 minutes

1 pint/600 ml cooked shelled cockles	salt and pepper
1 oz/25 g flour	2 oz/50 g breadcrumbs
2 oz/50 g butter	1 lb/500 g potatoes — boiled,
½ pint/300 ml cockle liquor *or* milk	seasoned, and mashed with butter and milk

Utensils A medium saucepan and a baking dish

Preheat the oven to 350°F/180°C/Gas 4.

Pick over the cockles. Fry the flour in half the butter until it looks sandy, and then whisk in enough of the cockle liquor to make a creamy sauce. Adjust the seasoning. Layer the cockles, the sauce, and a handful or two of breadcrumbs into the baking dish. Finish with a layer of mashed potato. Dot with the remaining butter and bake in the oven until the pie is hot and the crust is golden — 20 minutes should see it ready. Perhaps some oat bread (see page 498) to accompany.

SUGGESTIONS

● If you have some over from the dish, make Welsh Cockle Fritters. Roll the shelled fish in seasoned oatmeal and fry them in bacon fat.

Crustaceans

BOILED CRABS
(Scotland)

The sweetest crabs I know are caught in creels off the rocky coast of the little island of Iona, sacred haunt of St. Columba and one of the most ancient of the Christian holy places. This is how the local Hebridean fishermen advise their preparation.

Quantity Enough for 4
Time Preparation: 40–50 minutes

1 large crab weighing 2½ lb/1·5 kg will give 1 lb/500 g meat	6 pints/3·5 litres water
	8 oz/250 g salt

Utensils A large saucepan

Fill the saucepan with the water and salt or ordinary sea water with 4 oz/ 100 g extra salt. Put in the crab with its claws tied while the water is still cold, and then bring it gently to the boil. Hold it under for 2 minutes so that the poor creature has an easy demise — the nearest thing to Davy Jones' locker. Keep the water just on the boil for 15 minutes for the first 1 lb/500 g and 10 minutes for each subsequent 1 lb/500 g.

Female crabs are considered the sweeter. You can tell the sex by looking at the tail flap which is tucked under the body — the male's is much narrower than the female's, which needs the extra width to protect the eggs. When cooked the crab should feel heavy for its size. Let it cool. To prepare, pull the body from the shell, remove the ring of feathery grey 'dead-man's-fingers', and snap off the mouth part. Everything else is edible. Hit the claws with a hammer to crack them.

Eat with your fingers and let the 'de'il tak' the hindmost'. A sharp instrument can be provided for picking meat out of the claws. Put a bowl of plain boiled potatoes and a dish of fresh butter on the table for those who still have a corner unfilled. Fresh raspberries to remind you of the heather and a dram of whisky to finish. St. Columba himself could not turn down such a meal.

SUGGESTIONS
● Serve the cooled crab with a home-made mayonnaise, quartered lemons, lettuce hearts with no dressing, and thin slices of brown bread and butter.

BOILED LOBSTER
Kokt hummer (Sweden)

The Scandinavians and the Scots have the best crustaceans in Europe. There is something about the cold waters of the North Atlantic which firms and sweetens the flesh of lobsters and crabs like no other.

Heligoland, a tiny island in the North Sea between Denmark and the north-west coast of Germany, used to be the most famous North Atlantic lobster fishing ground, before the gastronomes of Europe out-ate its capacities. The British bartered the island with Germany at the end of the nineteenth century, in exchange for the then more strategically useful clove-island of Zanzibar. The Scandinavians are very knowledgeable about their seafood. Providing it is fresh they feel the lily needs no gilding.

Quantity   Enough for 2
Time   20–30 minutes to cook the creature

1 medium-sized live lobster
6 pints/3·5 litres sea water *or*
  6 pints/3·5 litres fresh water and
  4 oz/100 g salt

1 crown dill (the flowering head
  with its seeds) *or* 1 teaspoon dill
  seeds

Utensils   A large saucepan

Bring the water to a rapid boil with the dill, and plunge the lobster in head-first. Cover and simmer for 12 minutes for a ½ lb/250 g lobster, 15 minutes for a 1 lb/500 g lobster, and 25 minutes for a 2 lb/1 kg lobster.

Allow the creature to cool in the water, then drain it. Split the body and remove the dark intestinal vein. Crack the claws. Give each diner a large napkin and a bowl of warm water for rinsing fingers. The sweet flesh needs no embellishment except sea salt and a slice of dark rye bread (see page 496) spread with pale unsalted butter.

GRILLED PRAWNS
Gambas a la plancha (Spain)

The Cadiz fisherman's way with his inshore catch. The grill he uses is a simple metal sheet with a charcoal fire beneath. Larger specimens of *Palaemon serratus*, so fresh they are still grey-blue and stiff, are simply salted with the grainy bay salt which has been dried since Roman times in the salt flats around Cadiz bay. The metal sheet is then wiped over with a rag dipped in olive oil, and the prawns are ready in a few minutes.

Quantity Enough for 4 — allow 6 large prawns per person
Time 5 minutes

 2 lb/1 kg prawns (the largest
    possible)
 salt
 olive oil

Utensils A metal *plancha* or a very heavy iron frying pan or griddle

Salt the prawns. Put the frying pan or griddle to heat. When it is good
and hot — a drop of water should bounce off it immediately — wipe the
surface with oil and put on the prawns. They will be done in 2 minutes a
side — depending on the thickness of the creatures.

Serve with plenty of thick-cut *pan de campo* (see page 492) and
quartered lemons. Accompany with a dry *manzanilla* sherry (well
chilled) from Sanlucar de Barrameda, the little port at the mouth of the
Guadalquivir River from where Columbus set sail on his first and most
momentous voyage. The prawns caught by the fishermen off its pine-
clad dunes are the most prized in Spain, and its wines can outrival those
of Jerez.

CRAYFISH
Kraftor (Sweden)

On the stroke of midnight on 7 August every year, freshwater crayfish
can legally be netted in Scandinavia. The season only lasts until mid-
September. Traditionally crayfish parties are held at night when the
creatures can be caught by torchlight in the chalk streams. A piece of
rotten meat trailed in a net in the water will bring them scuttling to the
bait.

Plunge your crayfish live into plenty of boiling salted water, to which
you have added a crown or two of dill or a teaspoon of dill seeds. Bring
the water back to the boil and simmer for 5 to 6 minutes. Cooked
crayfish blush a deep carmine — brighter than any other shellfish.
Leave them in their liquid until they are quite cool. Drain and serve
them piled up on your best dish. Exquisite little morsels. Crack the
claws in your teeth and suck out the juices.

Accompany the feast with rye bread (see page 496), unsalted butter,
and rough salt — and perhaps a little bowl of chopped dill. Afterwards a
generous piece of cheese to fill the gaps — crayfish are delicious, but not
very substantial. Light beer and ice-cold *brannvin* to drink under the
midnight sun.

STEWED CRAYFISH
(Romania)

D. J. Hall in his book, *Romanian Furrow*, published in 1939, visited one of the water-powered villages that spearheaded the industrial revolution in Romania. Spinning, dyeing, weaving, leatherworking, forging all were accomplished with the aid of the mill wheels.

> I do not know how many mills I saw in the first week. The stream raced between narrow banks and over it were built the mills, little, square, wooden boxes perched on piles above a massive wheel. Sometimes they were for shredding out wool, sometimes for grinding corn. The flour-mills consisted only of two immense grindstones; the upper stone had a hole in its centre and a funnel was suspended above it filled with corn from which the seeds dropped. Beneath, a bin caught the coarse, golden flour as it poured from between the stones . . . . In the clear water of the stream above the village, boys and girls searched for crayfish.

Quantity   Enough for 4
Time   Preparation: 20 minutes
          Cooking: 15 minutes

1 lb/500 g crayfish	4 strands saffron
2 medium onions	4 tablespoons oil
2 cloves garlic	1 glass white wine
2 green peppers	juice 1 lemon
½ lb/250 g tomatoes *or* 1 medium tin	salt and pepper

Utensils   A heavy casserole with a lid

Rinse the crayfish. You now either boil them swiftly for 3 to 4 minutes in salted water prior to skinning them ready for the dish, or cook them straight in the dish. The second method is messier but more rewarding.

Peel and slice the onions and the garlic. Hull, de-seed, and chop the peppers. Plunge the tomatoes into boiling water to loosen the skins, and then peel and chop them. Soak the saffron in boiling water.

Heat the oil in a casserole and then lightly fry the onions and garlic until they take colour. Add the peppers and stir them around in the oil. Put in the tomatoes, the saffron, and the wine and lemon juice. Tightly cover and simmer for 10 minutes. Take off the lid — the sauce will be rich and thick. Add salt and pepper. Throw in the crayfish — if they have not yet been cooked, they will turn as scarlet as the sauce and be ready in 5 minutes; 2 to 3 minutes if they need only to warm.

Serve with a dish of pilav rice (see page 269). Or with potatoes. In either case provide good red Bulgarian wine — the Cabernet Sauvignon grape flourishes in both Bulgaria and Romania.

CRAYFISH IN WHITE WINE
Ecrevisse à la nage (France)

Catch your own crayfish if you can. They are to be found in swift-running mountain streams. Like all their tribe they are scavengers and can easily be tempted with a piece of meat (rotten is best) on the end of a string or in a net. Being creatures of little brain, once they have found it they will hang on to the bitter end. They hide under stones and give an unwary toe a nasty nip.

Quantity   Enough for 4
Time   Preparation: 30 minutes

3 lb/1·5 kg live crayfish — they survive for a long time out of water
1 pint/600 ml water
thyme, parsley, fennel stalks, bayleaf

1 onion, sliced
peppercorns
1 teaspoon salt
1 bottle white wine (a Muscadet, dry and pale, is excellent)

Utensils   A large stewpot

Rinse the crayfish. Put the water with the herbs, sliced onion, peppercorns, and salt into the pot. Bring all to the boil and then turn down the heat to simmer for 20 minutes.

Add the wine and bring it back to the boil. Throw in the crayfish. They will jump for a moment and then all will be peaceful — humanity dictates that once again you bring the pan swiftly back to the boil. Turn down the heat a little and cook for 10 minutes. The crayfish will turn a brilliant scarlet. Serve them as they are in a deep dish with their liquor. Don't worry about the dark stripe down the back that some advise removing. It makes no difference to the flavour.

Plenty of bread and a salad to accompany. Afterwards a fruit tart with cream. Finally, as your guests may still be hungry, you have an excellent opportunity to serve a selection of really good cheeses.

LEFTOVERS
● Make a crayfish salad. Pound up the shells and heads — an easy job in a liquidizer — and press out all the deliciously flavoured juice through a sieve. Stir this into a mayonnaise. Compose a salad with the leftover crayfish meat, fresh crisp lettuce hearts, and perhaps some baby green or broad beans — blanched for no more than 2 to 3 minutes in boiling salted water and drained immediately. Don't douse them in cold water. It does them no good. Sauce with the crayfish-flavoured mayonnaise and sprinkle with chopped dill, chives, or parsley.

BOILED SHRIMPS AND POTTED SHRIMPS
(England)

The best way to cook tiny brown shrimps, *Crangon crangon*, is to plunge them live into boiling salted water (sea water is best) as soon as they are caught. Bring the water back to the boil as fast as you can. The shrimps will turn pinky-brown and opaque immediately. Drain them at once. Eat with brown bread and butter. It is a matter of individual choice whether you peel them or eat them whole.

Morecambe Bay potted shrimps can be made with these little scavengers whose European range stretches from the Dardanelles to the North Cape. To pot, peel the shrimps and warm them in enough melted butter to cover. When the butter has frothed up, pack all into pots with plenty of pepper.

SUGGESTIONS
● If they are too small to peel, put them whole in the liquidizer with melted butter and pepper. They grind up into a superb paste for spreading on toast.

GARLIC SHRIMPS
Gambas al ajillo (Spain)

This dish is known as *Gambas pil-pil* in what was for several years my local Andalusian port of Tarifa, guardian of the Pillars of Hercules and staging post of Phoenician, Greek, and Roman mariners. The legendary Spanish hero, Guzman the Good, held Tarifa's fortress against the invading Moors. His more glorious moment came when, faced with the threatened death of his hostage son, he hurled his own sword from the battlements to the invaders below as an instrument of execution.

The men of Tarifa have always been sailors and fishermen. Their little bars and waterfront cafés make the most of the local catch. The best time of year for a Tarifan feast is February and March, when the big scarlet spider crabs scuttle for cover from the storms and are caught inshore in their hundreds. The nets also yield black and yellow eels, octopus and cuttlefish, shrimp and prawns, all driven to take shelter from the rough Atlantic storms. Then the market brims over and the fish trucks trail their watery loads up into the hills, along the same roads and tracks which for centuries were used by donkey-borne vendors of the sea's harvest.

Quantity Enough for 4 as a light dish
Time Preparation: 15 minutes

1 lb/500 g raw shrimps (frozen
    ones should be de-frosted and
    drained first)
4 cloves garlic

4 small dried, de-seeded chillies *or*
    one fresh green chilli
¼ pint/150 ml olive oil
salt

Utensils   Either 4 small, shallow earthenware dishes or cocotte dishes, or a shallow gratin dish

Peel and slice the garlic. Chop the de-seeded chillies. Peel the raw shrimps. Divide all 3 ingredients among the earthenware dishes or arrange them in the gratin dish. Divide the olive oil equally among the dishes. Sprinkle with salt. Put the dishes directly on to the heat if they are flameproof, or put them under a very hot grill, until they bubble fiercely. Remove immediately — the shrimps toughen and lose their delicacy if overcooked.

Serve very hot with bread to sop up the juices.

SUGGESTIONS
- This recipe is also very good made with cooked crab meat.
- *Angulas*, tiny eel fry now largely caught in the Severn Estuary and exported to Spain, are cooked in this way and served, looking like a pile of little noodles, to be eaten with wooden forks while still sizzling hot.

LEFTOVERS
- Use the shells and heads of the shrimps to make a fish broth — add a pinch of paprika and a few strands of saffron for colour and scent, and a chopped carrot, onion, and bayleaf for flavour. Simmer for half an hour. Then strain the broth, mashing the debris well and forcing as much as possible through a sieve. Reheat the broth and poach some rice or slices of potato in it. When they are soft, drop in any leftover shrimps or a few squares of fresh fish. Serve with little piping hot *croûtons* fried in oil. All the better if you have some leftover *rouille* (see page 24) or *aioli* (see page 444) to stir in too.

SHRIMP FRITTERS
Camaroes fritos em massa (Portugal)

A most interesting recipe, not only because the dish is delicious but because it is the mother of the now universally popular Japanese dish *tempura*. The recipe was exported by Portuguese sailors and traders on their highly successful sixteenth-century travels, when their Japanese hosts, eager to flatter the unaesthetic but powerful Europeans, had the dish prepared to please their guests. The resourceful cooks of Japan adopted the technique, and expanded and refined the dish to include meats other than shrimp.

In Portugal these excellent fritters are still the shore-dweller's standard way of preparing small shrimp. They are particularly good made with the tiny krill-like creatures which jump like fleas and are sold out of salt-streaked buckets by small boys in the southern fishing villages. The shrimps are plunged into the batter live and unpeeled, and their crunchy carapaces add to the crispness of the fritter. It is, however, necessary to peel the shrimps if they are the fishmonger's larger variety.

Quantity   Enough for 4 as a light dish
Time   Preparation: 25–30 minutes

1 lb/500 g raw shrimps (frozen
   ones should be de-frosted and
   drained first)
1 egg
4 oz/100 g flour
salt
2 tablespoons olive oil
¼ pint/150 ml water
oil for frying

Utensils   A large bowl, a whisk, and a frying pan

Separate the white from the yolk of the egg. Sieve the flour, make a well in the centre and put the yolk and salt into it. Pour in the oil and most of the water, and stir until you have a smooth cream. Beat it a little. Leave it to rest for at least half an hour — or long enough for you to catch a pailful of little jumping shrimps.

Beat the egg white until it is stiff and fold it in just before you are ready to fry. Heat a pan of oil until you can see a faint blue haze rising from it.

Stir the shrimps into the batter. Drop spoonfuls of the mixture into the hot oil. Each fritter will puff up crisp and golden within a few minutes. Drain and serve without delay, with quarters of lemon.

LEFTOVERS
● Use any leftover batter to coat thin slices of courgette; sliced, salted, and drained aubergines; onions cut in rings; or thin slices of baby artichokes. In fact, make extra batter for the pleasure of these delicious fritters. Serve piled up together, shrimps, vegetables and all, in a large hot dish with plenty of lemon quarters to squeeze over and a little bottle of chilli oil (see page 340) in case someone likes their food hot.

SHRIMP CROQUETTES
Croquetas (Spain)

Spanish cookery came under Dutch influence during the sixteenth century, when Charles V, the Holy Roman Emperor, managed to unite most of Europe. Today these Flemish-originated *croquetas* are nearly as popular a dish in Spain as the *tortilla*. A certain dexterity is needed to roll the soft shapes, but it is a skill which many otherwise simple peasant cooks have mastered. Much as all Spanish women can turn out a good *tortilla*, so can most of them make a *croqueta*.

Croquetas are often served as a *tapa*, as the titbits served with wine in Spanish bars are named. *Tapas* can range from a simple dish of green olives to tiny portions of complicated *cocidos* or stews. The name seems to have come from the Spanish word *tapar* meaning 'to cover'. Little dishes of delicacies used to be balanced on top of the bar's speciality — a glass of the local red wine or one of the light dry sherries of Jerez and Montilla. There is usually one house in even the tiniest of rural communities which does duty as a bar, and everyone who can afford the price of a drink will take an evening glass or two, accompanied by its 'cover'.

Quantity   Enough for 4–6 as a light dish
Time   Start the day before if possible
        Preparation: 50–60 minutes plus 30 minutes rest period

4 oz/100 g cooked shelled shrimps *or* prawns	salt and pepper
	seasoned flour for rolling
6 oz/175 g butter *or* 6 tablespoons oil	2 eggs
6 oz/175 g flour	breadcrumbs for coating (homemade are best)
1 pint/600 ml milk *or* 1 pint/600 ml stock (*or* a mixture of both)	oil for frying

Utensils   A small saucepan, a large flat dish, several flat plates, a deep frying pan, and a perforated spoon

Chop the shrimps or prawns up finely. Put the butter or oil to warm up in the small saucepan. Stir in the flour and cook gently until the mixture turns sandy. Stir in the liquid, beating to avoid lumps — if you are nervous, heat the liquid before you add it and then there will be no question of anything but a beautifully smooth sauce. Cook gently over a medium heat, stirring until the mixture is a thick panada. This will take about 10 minutes. Add the shrimps, a teaspoon of salt, and plenty of black pepper, and boil it up again. Pour it on to the large flat dish, and leave it to cool and solidify. Overnight is best.

When you are ready to proceed, set out in front of you in a line first the now-solid *croqueta* mixture in its dish, then a plate with seasoned flour, then a plate with the eggs beaten with a little milk, then a plate with breadcrumbs, then an empty plate. You now have a conveyor-belt arrangement. Drop spoonfuls of the mixture into the seasoned flour and roll each spoonful into a small bolster with well-floured hands. Roll the bolsters in the egg and then in the breadcrumbs. Transfer the egg-and-breadcrumbed bolsters to the empty plate. Continue until all the mixture is used up.

Put the *croquetas* in the refrigerator to rest for half an hour if there is time. Put on a deep pan of oil to heat. When a fine blue haze rises and a cube of bread turns golden in a moment, drop in the *croquetas* and fry them until golden — 5 to 6 minutes should be enough. Remove the cooked *croquetas* with the perforated spoon. Do not do too many at a time or the temperature of the oil will drop too low. Continue frying until all are ready.

Best served hot from the pan. To accompany, a cos lettuce, tomato, cucumber, and onion salad, chopped roughly in the Spanish manner and dressed with olive oil, vinegar, and salt. Add a plate of thin-fleshed green peppers fried in olive oil with a few slices of garlic (the imported variety of pepper will have to be hulled, de-seeded, and sliced first). To drink, some light cold beer or a bottle of chilled dry sherry, and your meal will have been well worth the effort.

SUGGESTIONS

• Sometimes the white sauce is flavoured with chopped Serrano ham, sometimes with cheese (Dutch Gouda, called *bolla* in Spain, is the favourite), sometimes with chopped hard-boiled egg. Any little bit of cooked ham, chicken, or fish can go to flavour the mix, although it is often made innocent of any complications.

• The men of Oostduinkerke on the Belgian coast, where the last of the equestrian shrimp-fishermen ride their carthorses through the surf, prefer their catch cooked in a similar manner. The peeled shrimps are bathed in a thickened sauce made not with stock or milk, but with dark beer. The mixture is then piled into scallop shells, and the breadcrumbs are sprinkled over and dotted with butter before the whole is put under a hot grill to brown.

SEA URCHINS
(Mediterranean)

These hedgehog-prickled sea creatures are sold in every Mediterranean harbour market as a mid-morning snack. They are clipped round the middle by the deft salesman, with a special utensil called in France a *coupe-oursins*. The customer consumes the sweet orange flesh then and there without embellishment save a squeeze of lemon. Eliza Putnam Heaton went fishing for sea urchins in Sicily, in 1908:

> He [the fisherman] dipped a reed into his oil-jar and let fall on the choppy water a drop or two of oil. Then he put overboard a tangle of net, dragging it across the bottom by the hook on his cane rod, keeping within the circle of the oil mirror. After a little he lifted the net and took out of it, enmeshed by their spines, half a dozen big brown sea urchins. 'Shall we eat?' he suggested, bringing out the basket with bread and cutting the 'fruit of the sea' as one might slice off the top of a lemon.'

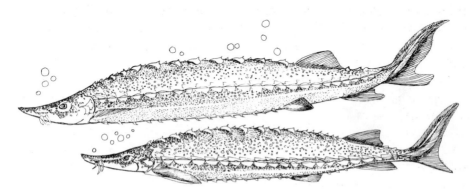

Caviar

KEEPING CAVIAR
(Finland and neighbours)

Fish eggs are the fisherman's portion. Fresh caviar is a highly perishable delicacy and was, before the advent of refrigerated transport, consumed on the spot. Excepting the mighty sturgeon, whose roe has long been the food of the emperor as well as his peasantry, lumpfish (or sucker-fish or paddle-cock, provider of those salty little black or red-dyed fish eggs familiar from delicatessen shelves) are not the only fish which bear good caviar. Excellent eating, too, are the eggs of salmon, trout, capelin (an inhabitant of the Arctic seas chiefly famous as the cod's lunch), and the two whitefish — powan and vendace — which migrate between fresh and salt northern waters. Mullet, shad, turbot, and pike can also be added to the list. All caviar is at its best eaten fresh without further fuss. Simply spoon it on to buttered black bread with a little chopped onion or a squeeze of fresh lemon.

If you need to store your caviar, prepare it as follows.

Quantity   Enough for 4–5 (minimum 2 oz/50 g per person)
Time   Start the day before
          Preparation: 10 minutes

8 oz/250 g fish eggs
1 tablespoon salt
1 tablespoon light seed oil

½ tablespoon plain *aquavit*, vodka,
   or eau-de-vie

Utensils   A bowl and 2 to 3 small jars with seals

Leaving the roe whole, salt the covering membrane thoroughly. Leave in the refrigerator overnight to firm up.

The following morning split the membrane and empty the contents into a bowl. Sprinkle on the alcohol. Pot and trickle over a thin film of oil. Seal and keep in the refrigerator. Thus prepared the caviar will be good for a week.

Serve with rye bread and unsalted butter, pepper, quartered lemons, and a bowl of chopped onion on the side. Or serve with potato *lompe* (see page 509), in which to roll up each spoonful with some soured cream. A glass of Finnish vodka will complete the pleasure.

CARP ROE PASTE
Icre negre (Romania)

A special caviar, eaten fresh and only very slightly salted. Lumpfish roe will do at a pinch in its place.

Quantity   Enough for 4
Time   Preparation: 15–20 minutes

8 oz/250 g caviar (Romanian carp
   caviar is best)
2 oz/50 g fresh breadcrumbs

2 tablespoons milk
6 tablespoons oil
juice 2 lemons

Utensils   A food processor or liquidizer, or a pestle and mortar

Make the breadcrumbs and put them to soak in the milk, and then squeeze out any excess liquid. Pound the caviar with the breadcrumbs, then add the oil slowly, as if for a mayonnaise. Stir in the lemon juice. This can be done in a liquidizer or food processor.

Serve the caviar in a bowl with quartered hard-boiled eggs, hot toasted bread, a dish of black olives and, for each diner, a little glass of *tuica* — Romania's strong dry plum brandy. Vodka will do duty in the absence of *tuica*. One of the excellent thick Romanian soups to follow — the salad soup (see page 351) or perhaps the bean soup (see page 256).

COD'S ROE SALAD-PUREE
Taramasalata (Greece)

The roe of the grey mullet, *tarama*, which is still salted, dried, and preserved in wax all around the Mediterranean, was the original ingredient for this ancient preparation. It is now so expensive that even the Greeks use cod's roe as a substitute. The best known of all the Greek salad-purées.

Quantity   Enough for 6–8
Time   Preparation: 20 minutes

12 oz/350 g *tarama or* salted
   smoked cod's roe
1 small onion

2 slices day-old bread
½ pint/300 ml olive oil
juice 1 lemon

Utensils   A food processor or liquidizer, or a pestle and mortar, and a bowl

Remove the hard bits of skin from the roe. Peel and then mince the onion very finely. If its flavour is strong, sprinkle it with salt and leave it to drain for 15 to 20 minutes. Rinse off the salt before using. Put the bread to soak in a little water. When it is soggy, squeeze it dry. Pound the roe with the bread, and then slowly beat in the oil and the lemon juice until you have a smooth, light paste.

Alternatively all the ingredients can be put into the food processor or liquidizer and pounded up together — the oil should be added in a steady stream as for a mayonnaise. This method produces a creamier mixture than the hand-made version — very good, but slightly different. Serve cool. It will keep well in the refrigerator stored in a screw-top jar or covered pot, but no longer than a week.

Decorate with a few black olives and serve with a dish of radishes and hot pitta bread. Sit in the sun and scoop the *taramasalata* up on your bread. Have a little glass of *raki* and a tumbler of fresh spring water at your elbow — the fish paste is salty. To follow serve a dish of Greek salad topped with a slice or two of well-flavoured feta cheese, and a plate of chips fried twice (once to soften them and once to crisp them) in good olive oil.

SUGGESTIONS
● You can include garlic in the *taramasalata* if you must, but this is often only done to add taste if the mixture has not sufficient fish roe and has been bulked out with bread. Save the extra stale bread for a *skordalia* (see page 397) to accompany this salad.

Storehouse Salt Fish

The Lofoten Islands, a wild and beautiful outpost off the Norwegian coast, lapped by the warmth of the Gulf Stream, have been a centre for the preparation of dried and salt cod for at least a thousand years and probably much longer. A rocky archipelago two hundred miles inside the Arctic Circle is a long journey from the hills of the Mediterranean, but the Norwegians sprang from Viking stock and their long ships went where they pleased. It is from the cod fishermen of the North Atlantic that the peasant farmers of the Spanish, French, and Italian olive groves get the raw material for many of their favourite dishes.

Recipes for salt cod are so deeply rooted in the southern kitchen that they appear as festival food — an *aioli* with *morue* is the fast-dish traditionally prepared in France for the Christmas Eve supper. Salt cod has such excellent keeping qualities that it became one of the few items for which inland peasant communities were prepared to barter — a storeroom staple which has a high nutritional value.

The traveller, Paul du Chaillu, was much interested in the salt cod on his visit to Henningsvaer on the Lofoten in 1872:

> The warehouse of my host was a sight worth seeing: long deep rows of freshly salted codfish, six feet high, were packed together, to be afterwards laid on the rocks and dried. There are three different ways of curing the cod.
>
> The first, and the most common, is to cut the fish open, flatten, and salt it, putting it afterwards on the rocks to dry. The second is to open the fish, tie them two and two, without being salted, and hang them on frames. The third is to divide each in halves, connected only by the gills; the spine is then taken out, and the fish hung upon the frames; this method is much

the quickest, as the air now operates directly on the exposed flesh of the fish, soon making it as hard as wood. It takes one to two months to dry the fish according to the season.

Every year towards the end of February, while the snow is still lying in drifts on the pebbled beaches, the cod shoals travel from the Barents Sea to spawn off the coasts of the Lofotens. From early February onwards the seaside-dwellers keep watch on the headlands and in the crows-nests of their boats for the darkening patch of troubled water, which heralds the arrival of the fish. When the news breaks, hundreds of fishing boats scramble to sea to reap the harvest. In the old days the boats were small and sturdy single-sailed smacks, painted in combinations of green and blue, and red and ochre, which the fishermen built and patched themselves during the long winter months. Today they have company on the waves and have to compete with big ocean-going trawlers supplying modern factory conveyor belts.

Most of the fishing settlements on the wind-scoured Atlantic coast of the Lofotens have long been abandoned. Today they are ghost villages of single-roomed *rorbu*, fishermen's huts, built on wooden stilts to fringe the shoreline as close as the incoming tide would allow. Their former inhabitants can afford to build new wooden dwellings and stilt-raised boat-houses on more sheltered inlets, where the gales of the long Arctic night do not beat down their doors. These modern fishing hamlets now punctuate the islands' inshore coasts, strings of pastel-painted wooden walls stretching up the long fingers of the inlets, and petrol engines have replaced the muscle power once vital to get the boats swiftly out to sea after the shoals.

The original method of preserving fish was by wind-drying — a technique admirably suited to the cold, clean northern climate and long used by Atlantic fishermen to dry their catch on board. Scots fishermen used to hang it on the yardarm, and naturally enough it became known as 'yardarm fish'. Wind-cured in the sea air the fish picks up a natural salt content — a good selling point for the traders since salt, after gold, was for centuries the world's most prized trading item. The resulting stiff planks of protein, which remained edible seemingly for ever, were eagerly bartered in every market from the Bosphorus to the Bight of Benin — even today shops in Ghana take annual deliveries from the north Atlantic.

During the Middle Ages the dried cod trade became so valuable that it came to the attention of the powerful Hanseatic League, a consortium of Lübeck burgers that dominated the European commodity markets of the time. The League took the trade over and ran it for two centuries from their base in Bergen in southern Norway.

Drying racks for *torrfisk* still dominate the fishing harbours of northern Norway — forests of pearl-grey wooden poles, triangular or rectangular stacks of slats that tower over the houses. As soon as the boats return, the villagers set to work preparing the catch. *Torrfisk* requires that the fish are cleaned, gutted, and tied together by the tails in pairs. These are then hung over the poles to dry — with the nets that fished the cod flung over the whole edifice to frustrate the ever-hungry gulls. By June the racks have been cleared, and the fish, now stiff and dry, are on their way for export.

Salt was not imported in quantity into Norway until relatively recently. This was perhaps because the natural preserving agents in the climate made it less important than elsewhere. In Sweden, however, the Hanseatic League wielded great power throughout the Middle Ages as the suppliers and controllers of the import of salt into the Baltic ports. Salt was vital for the preservation of the herring catch, the Skånesild, and Stockholm itself was originally a Hanseatic town. In Norway the Hansas traded grain for stockfish, and in Sweden salt for cured herring.

Norwegian exports of dried fish flourished even more when salt, largely produced from evaporated sea water, was added to the wind-drying process. Mediterranean countries soon came to prefer the salty flesh of these *klippfisk* — named after the rocky cliffs on which the cod was laid out to dry. The triangular kite-shaped sheets of fish, coated with coarse grey salt and layered in wooden crates, are still annually despatched to village shops around the Mediterranean. Today they also reach other more distant destinations whose immigrant communities long for the taste of home. Salt cod has a potent nostalgia value. A particularly pungent odour announces the arrival of the *klippfisk* to coincide conveniently with the year's first pressings of olive oil. The best Mediterranean salt-cod recipes marry the two ingredients — the harsh, pale flesh of the northern ocean and the rich, gold fruit of the southern hill slopes make a perfect union.

Portugal and Britain entered the trade during the Middle Ages. Today Newfoundland is the major source, and salt cod is now exported by Canada as well as Norway and Iceland.

SALT HERRINGS
Sill (Sweden and neighbours)

Barrels of salted herrings used to stock one corner of every Swedish farmhouse's winter larder from Jutland to Lapland. The fish was often simply gutted, scaled, and barrelled with salt only, as for *rakørret* (see page 95). The inclusion of the sugar and spices gives a gentler flavour. A higher proportion of salt will be needed if the sugar is omitted.

The Norwegians kept their barrels of salt herrings in the *stabbur*, a wooden hut on stilts, whose raised floor is hung beneath with heavy stones to weight it against the fierce winter gales. A carelessly tethered *stabbur* could be whipped off the hillside and its precious contents flung all over the valley in a flash. The *stabbur* is occasionally still to be found in use in country districts — it provides a cold outside larder with a temperature kept well below freezing all winter.

Time   Start the week before
Preparation: 1–2 hours

10 lb/5 kg fat fresh herrings (30 to 40 fish — no point in doing things by halves)
1½ lb/750 g sea salt

½ lb/250 g sugar
2 teaspoons juniper berries
2 teaspoons peppercorns

Utensils   A wooden tub or 1 to 2 plastic buckets and a heavy weight

Gut, scale, and wipe the herrings. Rub inside and out with salt. Starting with a layer of salt, pack the fish into the tub in layers, prettily fan shaped if you like, sprinkling more salt and the sugar and seasonings between each layer. Weight the top to keep the fish under the brine. Store below 46°F/8°C in a cold larder. Check after a day or so that the herrings are covered in their own brine (this forms naturally as the salt and herring juices mix).

The herrings will be ready to eat in a week, but will keep all winter in a cold larder. Refer to the section on Herring and Mackerel (see page 51) for recipes for salt herring.

SUGGESTIONS
● When you prepare the fish, save the roe to fry in butter and eat on toast. They have a delicate unfishy flavour, and need no embellishment apart from a sprinkle of salt and a turn of the pepper grinder.
● A small bunch of hops was sometimes included as flavouring. A hop pole had its place in the Scandinavian kitchen garden and was used to flavour and preserve home-brewed beer.

FERMENTED BALTIC HERRING
Surströmming (Sweden)

It is the fishermen of northern Sweden who are responsible for *surström-ming*. A certain dependence on geographical peculiarities makes it unsuitable for home cooking, but I include it because it is odd and original and truly peasant.

A catch of Baltic herring (a smaller species of herring than the Atlantic variety, with a lower fat content) is barrelled up with half the usual quantity of salt and left to ferment in the warm midsummer air — on double-time since the midnight sun never sets.

This method of preparation has a legend, recounted by Alan Davidson in his book *North Atlantic Seafood*. He tells how a certain group of fishermen ran low on salt to preserve their catch one year. There being no corner store for a thousand miles, they barrelled up the fish regardless — using half rations. The canny fellows, resourceful as peasants everywhere, managed to convince their clients, a local tribe of reindeerskin-trading backwoodsmen, to try the new delicacy at a special discount. The customers, to their suppliers' surprise, expressed themselves well satisfied and ordered more of the same for the following season.

The year's supply of *surströmming* is deemed ready for release each 20 August. It is then canned and shipped to supermarket cold cabinets all over Sweden. The tins bulge alarmingly and must be opened with care. Devotees eat them with a good helping of chopped onion and the new season's potatoes. Down your supplies before Christmas (it has a four-month 'eat by' date on it). Or serve it layered with whey cheese and chopped onion, and topped with breadcrumbs and butter. Bake in a hot oven for 15 minutes at 425°F/220°C/Gas 7.

SALT SPRATS
Haili (Finland)

Haili also haunted us in every peasant home. It is another species of small fish which the peasants eat raw, a little salt being its only preparation. They seem to buy or catch haili by the ton, and then keep them for months in the cellar. We were always seeing them eat these haili, which looked something like sprats. . . . On high days and holidays they partake of them accompanied with baked potatoes; but potatoes are rare, and therefore the fish on black bread alone constitutes the usual meal. Sometimes better-class folk eat haili, but then they have them grilled on coal; these are rich people, for coal is as great a luxury to them even as potatoes to the poor.

They seemed very happy, those men and women who had been up and hard at work in the fields since three or four in the morning, and would not have finished their day's labour until between eight and nine p.m. for the summer is short, and while it lasts the peasant gets little or no sleep, during the light warm days. It was the 10th of July; the hay was cut everywhere, and thrown up on the wooden palings erected for that purpose.

Ethel B. Tweedie, *Through Finland in Carts*

FERMENTED TROUT
Rakørret (Norway)

A great Norwegian delicacy and another 'buried' article. The Scandinavians themselves are in two minds about their fermented fish. Some love it, some hate it. I include the recipe to illustrate this very ancient method of fish preparation — more for interest than because it is particularly suitable for home preparation. Hands, knives, and bowls must all be as free as possible of bacteria — three months is a long haul.

Time   Start 3 months before
Preparation: 1 hour

10 lb/5 kg fish (at least)
2 oz/50 g rough salt for each 1 lb/
   500 g fish

Utensils   A wooden tub or a plastic bucket and a heavy weight

Gut the fish and wipe them thoroughly. Rub each fish inside and out with salt and pack them into the tub, bellies up, scattering more salt between the layers as you do so. Put a weight on top.

Store at below 40°F/5°C, that is in a very cold larder, failing the great frozen northern outdoors, for 3 months. Check after a couple of days that the fish is submerged in its own brine. If it is not, top up with a strong brine — 2 oz/50 g rough salt to ½ pint/300 ml water. Put back the weight to keep the fish under the surface. They must not come into contact with air.

When the 3 months is up, you will have a pungent, soft-textured salty delicacy to be served straight from the barrel, with new potatoes and plenty of unsalted butter.

SALTED ANCHOVIES
Acciughe (Italy and neighbours)

Barrels of these little fish can be found in every village shop around the Mediterranean. Pungent and salty, they add their own particular character to many Italian dishes. A taste for strong fishy flavours stretches back to Roman kitchens. Apicius, the millionaire voluptuary, was particularly fond of *liquamen*, a powerful pickle brewed from fermented mackerel intestines and used by the Romans as an all-purpose sauce. The process of salting the fish is rather lengthy, but I include it so that the method holds no mysteries. You can then buy the anchovies ready salted and prepare them according to the recipes which follow on.

Time   Start 6 months before
           Preparation: 1 hour

10 lb/5 kg anchovies
2 oz/50 g bay salt (not the dried
    kitchen salt) per 1 lb/500 g fish

Utensils   A wooden barrel or a plastic bucket and a heavy weight

Behead and gut the fish — a quick pinch between thumb and forefinger will do the trick. Sprinkle a thick layer of salt on the base of the container. Put a layer of fish on the salt in a circular fan shape, tails to middle. Sprinkle in another layer of salt. Then another of fish, and so on until the fish are all used up. Weight the top. The fish will make their own brine. If they are not submerged within 3 days, make a strong brine — 4 oz/100 g salt to 1 pint/600 ml water — and pour it over them. Ready in 6 months.

ANCHOVIES IN OIL
(Italy and neighbours)

1 lb/500 g salted anchovies from
    your own barrel or the
    delicatessen's
1 pint/600 ml milk and water
    mixed
¼ pint/150 ml good olive oil

Utensils   A large bowl and 2 to 3 glass jars

Soak the anchovies in milk and water for 10 minutes to de-salt them. Fillet them and pack them into glass jars. Cover them with the olive oil. Wonderful on pizza, on a fresh tomato salad, or on their own on good bread.

ANCHOVY PASTE
(Italy and neighbours)

1 lb/500 g salted anchovies
1 pint/600 ml milk and water
    mixed
¼ pint/150 ml good olive oil

Utensils   A large bowl, a liquidizer, and 2 to 3 small pots with seals

Soak the anchovies to de-salt them in milk and water for 10 minutes. Remove the bones — if you have bought the tinned variety, you can omit this step.

Liquidize the anchovies with the olive oil. Seal in small pots under a layer of olive oil. This paste can be used in sauces or as a spread on fresh country bread.

TO KIPPER HERRINGS
(Scotland)

It is the dampness of the British climate — it began to deteriorate around 700 BC — which led the inhabitants to look for new ways of preserving their sea harvest to augment the more widespread methods of wind-drying and salting. The last was often carried out on the seashore with no preliminary scaling or gutting. Larger fish were very heavily brined indeed, and dried stiff and hard as planks. By the fourteenth century the Dutch had introduced British fishermen to the joys of barrelling their catch with salt. Smoking was added to the culinary repertoire at about the same date — the first to benefit from this treatment being the herring catch.

Kippered herrings are cool-smoked. It is quite easy to rig up a small smoker for yourself. You will need a sheltered corner of a shed or outhouse, and an empty 40-gallon/180-litre barrel or metal drum. Check that it contains no trace of dangerous chemicals before you embark on the project. Remove the base and the top of the drum, leaving you with an oversize tube. Cut a semicircle out of the base to allow the smoke to be funnelled in. Build a channel with bricks or a piece of wide piping leading into the smokehole, leaving the other end without a cover so that you can build the smoke-fire in it. This arrangement acts like a kind of large tobacco pipe, except that the fire is at the stem end instead of in the bowl. Light the fire with kindling first. Then feed it with beech, birch, or oak sawdust. The draught will draw the smoke through the pipe, into the drum, and out either up the chimney or into the open air.

Time   Half a day

  12 fresh herrings
  1 lb/500 g salt

Equipment   A deep dish and a barrel smoker or smoking shed

Clean, split, and wipe the fresh herrings, leaving their heads on. Layer them in a deep dish with plenty of salt and leave them to take the salt for 30 minutes. Take them out and shake off the salt. This cure is very light and will not preserve the fish (even after smoking) for long — no more than a week in the refrigerator, although they will keep much longer if you freeze them.

If you need to preserve them for more than a week, leave them in the salt overnight. Hang the fish to dry for half an hour or so in a draught, until the surface is dry. Smoke the salted herrings by stringing them, tied together in pairs, looped on sticks balanced over the open end of the barrel smoker. Smoke them for 8 hours, which is sufficient to give them a wonderful flavour and turn them a deep burnished copper. Keep the fire smouldering constantly — it is not good for the cure if you allow changes in temperature.

Eat them just as they are, still warm from the smoker, with fresh oatcakes, cold butter, and hot milky tea for breakfast. Or cook them further by grilling with a little butter. Or fry them in a dry pan, sandwiched in pairs with a small pat of butter.

My Edinburgh-born grandmother used to pack her kippers into a roomy jug, so that only the tails poked up. Then she covered them with boiling water straight from the kettle. She would leave them for 5 minutes before taking them out, draining and serving them on a hot plate with a pat of cold butter to melt into them. She liked her kippers with hot buttered toast.

Bones are the trickiest part of kipper eating. The backbone of a freshly smoked kipper pulls free of the flesh and can be hooked out quite easily, bringing the smaller bones with it. There are those who put the grilled fish on the plate flesh-side downwards, tackling the problem by eating their fish from the skin or non-bone side.

TO SMOKE SALMON
(Scotland)

Time 3–4 days

> 1 salmon weighing 8–10 lb/4–5 kg
> 8 oz/250 g salt per side of salmon

Equipment A wooden board or large dish and a barrel smoker

Scale, gut, and wipe the fish carefully. Remove the head, trim the fins, and split the fish down the back.

Sprinkle salt on the board, lay the fish on it skin-side down, and spread a layer of salt about ⅛ in/3 mm thick on the flesh side of the salmon, with a thicker layer at the thick end of the fish. Leave the fish to take the salt, allowing it to drain as it does so, for 5 to 6 hours. When it is ready it will feel springy to the touch. The thicker the fish, the longer the salting. Wash thoroughly under running water to remove the surface salt. (The surface should still taste salty afterwards.) Tie a string round the top fin and the hard gill-joint. Hang the salted salmon in an airy room for about 12 hours until the outside of the fish feels dry to the touch.

Hang in the barrel smoker for 5 to 6 hours. On a windy day it will be smoked more quickly. On a calm day it can be left in overnight. Leave to settle for 2 to 3 days before eating. Slice finely and serve with brown bread and butter. Like all smoked fish, it has an affinity with scrambled eggs.

TO SMOKE HADDOCK or FINNAN HADDIE
(Scotland)

Finnan is a little fishing hamlet, six miles south of Aberdeen, which acquired a particular reputation for the excellence of its smoked haddock. The fish are smoked over peat, which gives them a highly distinctive flavour.

Time Half a day

haddocks
2 oz/50 g salt per fish

Equipment A barrel smoker

Prepare the fish as for kippered herrings, cleaning the fish thoroughly and splitting them — although in this case the heads are removed. (Note the dark prints of St. Peter the fisherman's thumb beside the gills.) The haddock, being larger than the herring, will need longer in the salt — an hour should be quite enough. Smoke the salted and dried fish over the barrel smoker, hung tied by the tails in pairs.

The haddocks will turn the colour of old ivory, pale and delicate. They are a truly delectable dish. Poach them or bake them — particularly delicious if you use milk as the cooking liquid. They are also excellent with creamy mashed potatoes — haddock has an affinity with cream and eggs, both scrambled and poached.

SALT COD SOUP-STEW
Guiso de bacalao (Spain)

Choose a clean white fish (not a yellow-tinged one) and wash it thoroughly. Soak for 24 hours in cold water, changing the water several times. If the fish is particularly large, it may need an extra day. Poke it with your finger and taste to see if it is sufficiently de-salted. If so, drain the cod. It is now ready to be cooked. Salt cod has an affinity with tomatoes and potatoes. In the peasant kitchen the most usual method of preparation is in a soup-stew — using the salt cod in place of fresh fish or meat to give substance and body.

Variations of this dish are eaten all around the Mediterranean. The soup is flavoured with the herbs of the maquis (rosemary, thyme, and fennel, which grows tall and feathery all summer), and enriched with olive oil. It cooks best in an earthenware casserole which has been tempered to withstand direct heat. An enamel pot or roomy saucepan will serve almost as well. It is homely but classic fare that has comforted many an empty-handed fisherman — and indeed a full-handed one too, since the salt cod is often preferred to the fresh.

Quantity   Enough for 6
Time   Start 24 hours before
            Preparation: 30 minutes
            Cooking: 30 minutes

1½ lb/750 g salt cod
2 large onions
3 cloves garlic
¼ pint/150 ml olive oil
1 lb/500 g tomatoes
2 lb/1 kg potatoes

1 bayleaf
sprig thyme and sprig rosemary
2 pints/1·2 litres water
1 lb/500 g greens — spinach *or*
    Swiss chard

Utensils   A large stewpot

Dry the soaked cod and chop into bite-sized pieces. Do not skin the fish, but do remove all visible bones.

Skin and slice the onions and garlic. Heat the olive oil gently in the stewpot. Put in the onions and garlic and soften them for a few minutes. They should not take colour. Add the tomatoes roughly chopped. Raise the heat and boil hard for 5 minutes more, uncovered.

Peel the potatoes and cut them into thick slices.

Turn down the heat under the pot and lay the salt cod on top of the tomato sauce mixture. Chop the herbs and sprinkle them over. Tuck in the bayleaf. Then lay on the potatoes. Pour over enough water to cover to a depth of 2 fingers. No salt yet — the cod has plenty of its own. Bring to the boil and then lower the heat to a simmer. Leave to cook gently for 25 minutes, by which time the cod and potatoes should be soft. Chop or prepare the green vegetable you have chosen. Add that at the end. Another 5 minutes will be enough to cook it. Serve in deep bowls and eat with a spoon and fork.

To mop up the soup you will need good bread, best of all a loaf of your own making. The Spanish *pan de campo* (see page 492) or a Greek country bread spiked with olives (see page 498) is ideal.

A chilled bottle of young red wine to wash the meal down. Fresh fruit and a piece of cheese to finish. A meal to enjoy at your leisure in the long shadows of a summer evening beside an olive grove.

SUGGESTIONS

• You can use fresh cod. It will be good, but will not give the same gelatinous texture to the stew. Fillet the fish and cut into squares. Add last of all so that it only cooks for 5 minutes.

• Red or green peppers can be included at the beginning — fry them in the olive oil lightly first.

LEFTOVERS

• Reheat and at the last moment stir in a tablespoon of fresh herbs chopped finely with a clove of garlic.

• Or reheat and serve with a bowl of *croûtons* fried with a little chopped bacon. They should be so hot that they sizzle when you add them to the soup.

SALT COD AND SCRAMBLED EGGS
Balcalhau e ovos (Portugal)

The Portuguese have been preserving fish since at least the first millennium BC. Prehistoric fish-salting tanks have been discovered at many sites on Portugal's coast, and the Romans' favourite condiment, *garum*, a strong fermented fish paste, was exported to Rome in enormous quantities during the days of the Empire. Later, these same salting centres provisioned the mariner-explorers, and salt cod became a major trade item — in particular with Brazil, then a Portuguese colony.

The combination of eggs and salt cod is a very popular dish in the home country. Today salt cod has become a rather expensive ingredient — the following recipe makes it go further and produces one of the best and simplest of this range of dishes.

Quantity Plenty for 6
Time Start the day before
          Preparation: 40–50 minutes

1 lb/500 g salt cod
2 lb/1 kg potatoes
1 lb/500 g onions
3 cloves garlic
4 oz/100 g ripe black olives
8 fresh eggs
pepper
½ pint/300 ml olive oil

Utensils 2 to 3 bowls and a deep frying pan

Soak the salt cod in several changes of fresh water for at least 24 hours.

Peel and chip the potatoes. Peel and slice the onions and the garlic. Stone the olives. Beat the eggs together lightly. Season with a turn or two of the peppermill — you are unlikely to need extra salt since both the salt cod and the olives will have been well brined.

When the salt cod is well soaked (poke it and lick your finger to test for saltiness — some fish need longer than others), drain it and pat it dry. Remove the skin and bones (toss them into your cauldron of fish soup) and flake it into large pieces.

Heat the olive oil in the frying pan. Fry the chips. Drain and put aside in a roomy bowl. Pour half the oil out of the pan and reserve it. In the remaining oil, fry the onions and garlic. Drain them and add them to the chipped potatoes. Drop the salt cod into the hot oil and continue to fry for 10 minutes (add some more oil if it looks too dry). Take out the salt cod and put it with the vegetables. Put back 2 tablespoons of the remaining oil and stir in the eggs. Scramble them gently until creamy, and then stir in the fish and potatoes, onions and olives.

Serve from the pan with plenty of fresh bread and a simple salad — perhaps thinly sliced raw peppers, or tomato and onion. My own favourite is made with the big juicy Mediterranean tomatoes, sliced and dressed with a trickle of olive oil, a little sugar, freshly ground pepper, and a sprinkling of chopped garlic.

SUGGESTIONS
- Use fresh cod but include a small tin of salty anchovies.
- Substitute smoked haddock for the salt cod.
- Some households bake this dish in a moderate oven, 350°F/180°C/Gas 4, without the eggs, but after the potatoes and onions have been cooked through. The eggs, hard-boiled and quartered, are added at the end as a garnish.

SALT COD FRITTERS
Bakalarios (Greece)

The much travelled salt cod, named *bakalarios* in Greece, is often prepared well soaked, drained, de-boned, and cut into bite-sized pieces which are dipped into batter and then deep fried until golden. Alternatively use this more sophisticated recipe which, as in the previous recipe, makes the expensive commodity go further.

Quantity Enough for 5–6
Time Start the day before
  Preparation: 30–40 minutes plus an hour or two rest period

1 lb/500 g salt cod	2 oz/50 g hard cheese
1 lb/500 g potatoes	2 tablespoons chopped parsley
¼ pint/150 ml milk	flour
2 eggs	breadcrumbs
pepper	oil for frying

Utensils 2 saucepans and a frying pan

Soak the cod for 24 hours in several changes of water. Put it in a saucepan and bring it to the boil in fresh water. Simmer it for 10 minutes, then drain it and mash it with a fork. Peel and then boil the potatoes until soft in salted water. Drain and mash them well with the milk.

Separate one of the eggs and reserve the white. Beat the yolk and the other egg into the fish mixture. Beat in the mashed potatoes. Add pepper — you are not likely to need extra salt. Grate the cheese and stir it in. Stir in the well-chopped parsley. Leave the mixture to firm up in the refrigerator for an hour or two.

Form the mixture into croquettes and roll them first in the flour, then in the egg white, and then in the breadcrumbs. Put the oil on to heat. When it is smoking faintly blue, slide in the croquettes and fry them crisp.

Serve with bread and a generous bowl of *skordalia* (see page 397). Proper food for the wide-ranging Greeks and one of their best loved dishes.

PUREE OF SALT COD
Brandade de morue (France)

By the early Middle Ages, salt cod was already one of the main imports of the countries of southern Europe. Much cheaper than dried or smoked meat it provided winter food for the poor, both urban and rural, and a Lenten diet for the rich. From the seventeenth century onwards *Brandade de morue* became a feast dish for all, particularly at Easter. It seems to have appeared first in the Languedoc — one of the few areas where cows rub shoulders with olive trees. However, the Norwegian cream-and-pounded-fish *fiskefarse* recipes are near enough in spirit to suggest that the Nordic purveyor of the delicacy might have given a few culinary hints to his customers, particularly on the matter of the inclusion of the cream, a Scandinavian staple. *Brandade* is eaten all over France, from Brittany to Nice, although today it is usually commercially prepared. It is basically a rich 'dip'.

This *brandade* recipe comes from the Farnoux family who live deep in olive country in the hills of Provence. M Farnoux inherited his olive mill from his father — who in turn inherited the ancient press from his own father. There has been an olive mill in the same little village for five centuries at least. There may well have been a mill there since the Romans built their amphitheatre and spa at neighbouring Vaison-la-Romaine.

M Farnoux' hometown of Nyons is famous for its olives. Groves of the ancient trees, said to take thirty years to grow, thirty years to mature, and thirty years to die, flash silver leaves on every surrounding hillside. The harvest begins in November when the Farnoux' great wooden corkscrew press works far into the night crushing green juice from ripe fruit. Speed is essential — a few hours' delay and the fruit will ferment. Then the oil will not settle into that beautiful golden *huile vierge* which is used in the family recipe for *Brandade de morue*. Mme Farnoux' neighbour makes her *brandade* without the milk — she feels this is the more truly Provençal version of the dish.

Quantity   Enough for 6–8
Time   Start the day before
　　　　　Preparation: 1 hour

2 lb/1 kg salt cod	½ pint/300 ml milk *or* cream
2 bayleaves	1–2 cloves garlic, crushed
6 peppercorns	½ teaspoon ground pepper
1 pint/600 ml olive oil	

Utensils   1 large and 2 small saucepans, a perforated spoon, and a food processor or liquidizer

Soak the cod for 24 hours, changing the water at least 4 times. The fish will smell unpleasantly, but persevere — at least the odour will be nothing like as bad as that from its Scandinavian cousin, the *lutefisk*.

Drain the softened fish and cut it into large pieces. Put the fish, the bayleaves, and the peppercorns into a pan of cold water and bring it gently to the boil. Skim the water and then turn down the heat. Poach the cod for 10 minutes only — it must not be allowed to overcook. Drain thoroughly. Remove the bones but leave the skin on. This gives more body to the dish and a rather pretty peppered appearance from the grey flecks of skin.

Put the oil into one small saucepan with the crushed garlic and the milk or cream into another. Warm the 2 liquids until the heat is only just bearable to your finger.

In the old days you would now have had to *brander* or crush the fish with the oil and milk until they formed a smooth emulsion, a time-consuming activity which would have had the advantage of sharpening your appetite and building your muscles. The liquidizer offers a welcome alternative.

Put the pieces of cooked cod, still hot, straight into the liquidizer or food processor. Using the machine on a medium speed, add the warm oil and garlic alternately with the equally warm cream or milk. Do not allow the liquids to cool or overheat — if the mixture is too hot, it will curdle, but can be revived by further beating. A last resort is the addition of a pounded boiled potato. When ready the *brandade* will be a thick creamy purée much like mashed potatoes. Season with freshly ground black pepper. More salt should not be necessary.

Serve with slices of bread, rubbed first with garlic and then fried golden in olive oil. A salad to accompany, perhaps tomatoes dressed with oil and a sprinkling of sugar and black pepper; or a plain green salad tossed with oil and vinegar and a little chopped raw onion; or a salad of baby green beans, cooked for 3 minutes only in boiling water and dressed with oil and vinegar while still hot. A bowl of black olives on the side.

If you cannot find a supply of salt cod, make the *brandade* with fresh cod, with a few salted anchovies beaten in to assist the flavour.

SUGGESTIONS
Instant Brandade   M Edouard de Pomiane, the admirable and much-esteemed broadcaster of recipes to French housewives until his death at the age of 90 in 1964, gives this simplified version of *brandade de morue* in his *Good Fare*. Polish by birth, he had a fine irreverent attitude towards culinary sacred cows (even those which rub shoulders with olive trees): 'Prepare a thick Béchamel, using olive oil instead of butter. Add to the sauce a little finely chopped garlic and its volume of flaked cod — the cod having been steeped and boiled beforehand. Mix well over the fire. Pound in a mortar until the mixture becomes a thick paste. Add the cream, mix well and serve.' Easy.

WALNUT OIL BRANDADE
Brandade à l'huile de cernaux (France)

In the hill country of inland Languedoc around Figeac, where nut plantations replace the olive groves of the south, local housewives use the wind-dried unsalted stockfish *torrfisk* — which used to be exchanged for wool by the enterprising merchants of the Middle Ages — and make use of the locally milled walnut oil.

Quantity   Enough for 6–8
Time   Start 10 days ahead

1½ lb/750 g dried stockfish (*torrfisk*), soaked for 10 days
3 lb/1·5 kg boiled potatoes
6 eggs, replacing the cream of the Languedoc *brandade*

1–2 cloves garlic, finely minced
1 pint/600 ml walnut oil

Utensils   2 saucepans

The method is similar to the *Brandade de morue*. The *torrfisk* must be split after you have soaked it for a day. After the full 10-day soaking, bone and beat the fish. Boil the potatoes and the fish separately and beat them together while hot. Stir in the eggs and the garlic. Heat the oil and add it slowly to the hot mixture. Keep it hot as you serve it. A dish for Good Friday. Drink a young red wine with it.

LEFTOVERS
● Serve the gently reheated *brandade* in deep-fried day-old bread rolls which have had their insides scooped out to make a hollow cup. If it splits and you cannot beat it back to a cream, add a hot mashed boiled potato.
● Reheat in little pre-cooked pastry cases (with care — do not overheat). Use the pastry recipe on page 530. Serve as a first course.
● Reheat and serve with *crudités* — fresh raw vegetables cut into short lengths for dipping. Raw carrots cut into sticks, baby turnips washed and quartered, raw baby beans, sticks of cucumber and celery, raw baby artichokes — any vegetables which are young, crisp, and fresh.
● Beat the leftover *brandade* into an equal quantity of mashed potato, add an egg to bind, and fry in hot oil in spoonfuls. Serve with a fresh tomato sauce (see page 293).

CHAPTER 2

Small Game

Pigeons, partridges, quail, and all manner of small birds, including larger marauders such as rooks, find their way into the peasant pot. Rabbit and hare are traditionally the poor man's portion. Snails and frogs are available equally to the poor and the rich — to anyone, in fact, with a trained eye for the ways of the countryside.

Country techniques for catching wild prey range from liming, when tree branches are smeared with glue to ensnare roosting birds, to minute and intricate twig and thread traps for ground game. Some of the ancient methods are remarkably ingenious. Writing of rural life in southern Spain, Nicholas Luard describes one which was still being used in the early 1980s:

> Toni (a peasant boy of twelve) was extraordinarily skilful with his hands. His favourite pastime was to make and fly a baited kite with which he caught darting swifts, among the fastest of all birds, on the wing. The bait was a fragment of dried grass which hung glittering like an insect from a thread below the kite. Attached to the piece of grass was the noose of a draw-string. When the kite was flown, the swifts would swoop to take the bait, the draw-string would pull tight, and Toni would haul the birds down from the clouds like a fisherman reeling in trout. When he'd caught enough, a fire would be built, the birds would be plucked, and the boys would roast and eat them.

Partridge, Quail and Pigeon

PARTRIDGES WITH SAUERKRAUT
Rebhuhner mit sauerkraut **(Germany and neighbours)**

Quantity   Enough for 4 hungry hunters
Time   Preparation: 30 minutes
Cooking: 40–60 minutes (the sauerkraut will take longer)

2 lb/1 kg sauerkraut
2 oz/50 g fat bacon *or* lard
½ teaspoon caraway seeds
3 pints/2 litres water *or* white wine and water mixed
2 partridges (old birds are fine for this dish)

1 onion
1 teaspoon juniper berries
½ teaspoon black peppercorns
2 oz/50 g smoked bacon
¼ pint/150 ml soured cream

Utensils   A roomy saucepan with a lid and a heatproof casserole with a lid

Rinse the sauerkraut in cold water. Put the fat bacon, cut into small cubes, or lard into the saucepan to melt. Add the sauerkraut and the caraway seeds, and barely cover all with about 2 pints/1·2 litres water or wine and water. Cover the saucepan. Bring to the boil and then turn down the heat to simmer gently for 1 to 1½ hours.

Meanwhile wipe the partridges. Peel the onion and chop it. Crush the juniper berries and peppercorns. Cube the smoked bacon and put it to melt in the casserole. Sauté the birds gently in the bacon fat until nicely brown. Add the onions, the juniper berries, and the peppercorns. Pour in 1 pint/600 ml water or water and wine. Cover and stew gently for 40 to 60 minutes until the birds are tender. Take out the birds and joint them. Raise the heat under the pan to reduce the liquid to ½ pint/300 ml well-flavoured juice. Stir in the soured cream.

Drain the sauerkraut and put it in a warmed serving dish. Put the partridge joints on top and bathe all with the creamy sharp gravy.

PARTRIDGE STEW
Pistache de perdreaux (France)

This rich garlicky stew is claimed equally by the Catalans and their neighbours in the Bas Languedoc. A boned rolled shoulder of mutton or lamb, proper to a shepherding community, is used when the partridges are out of season. A fine fat joint of mutton takes fifty cloves of garlic as its portion — enough to keep all the sombre devils of the Languedoc Cathars at bay.

Quantity   Enough for 6, allowing ½ partridge per person
Time   Preparation: 30 minutes (all that garlic-peeling)
       Cooking: 1 hour

3 partridges (old birds are fine)
4 oz/100 g unsmoked raw ham *or* gammon
40 cloves garlic (about 4 whole heads)
2 tablespoons goosefat *or* 3 tablespoons olive oil
1 glass white wine (not too dry — a sweetish wine complements the garlic)

1 glass water *or* stock
a bundle of herbs (thyme, rosemary, bayleaf, parsley, with a piece of dried *or* fresh orange peel tied in)
pepper

Utensils   A heavy casserole which the birds fit into snugly

Pluck and draw the birds if this has not already been done. Wipe them over and pull out any stray feathers. The birds should not be hung for this dish — the French do not like their birds 'high' in the English manner. Cube the ham. Peel the garlic cloves, leaving them whole.

Preheat the oven to 350°F/180°C/Gas 4.

Put the goosefat or oil in the casserole to warm. Add the cubes of ham and the peeled cloves of garlic, and fry them gently for a moment. Then push them aside and put in the little birds. Turn them in the hot fat. Add the wine, the water or stock, the bundle of herbs, no salt as there should be plenty in the ham, and a turn or two from the pepper grinder.

Cover the dish tightly and put it in the oven. Leave it to cook for an hour, until the birds are tender and the garlic has melted into a thick, sweet sauce.

Take the casserole out of the oven. Joint the birds (or slice up the lamb), and transfer the pieces to a warm serving dish. Mash the garlic well into the liquid to thicken it. Serve the birds bathed in their own rich gravy.

Serve with plenty of bread, and follow with a dish of lightly cooked fresh vegetables or a gratin of potatoes (see page 336) and a green salad. Accompany with the wine you have chosen to use in the *pistache*.

SUGGESTIONS
● Pigeons can well replace the partridges in the pot, as can lamb or mutton. Adjust the cooking time and garlic quantity accordingly.
● The ham must not be already cooked — a piece of lean bacon will do at a pinch. Spanish *jamón serrano*, Italian Parma ham, and French *jambon de Bayonne* and *Toulouse* are all unsmoked and raw.

BRAISED QUAIL
(Bulgaria)

These elegant little migratory game birds are a favourite huntsman's quarry in eastern Europe. Quail prefer the wide open spaces and the Thracian and Hungarian plains suit them admirably. The birds have adapted comfortably to cultivation — fields of winter wheat, early barley, and rye afford them good nesting cover. In spite of this, pressure of hunting, particularly when the flocks are on migration, has decreased their numbers in recent decades. Quail farms now supply most of the table birds in the West.

Quantity   Enough for 4 hunters
Time   Preparation: 20 minutes
         Cooking: 30 minutes

8 quail, plucked and drawn, *or* 4
   pigeons *or* 2 partridges
8 oz/250 g tomatoes *or* 1 medium
   tin
2 onions
8 oz/250 g mushrooms (the
   Romanians gather good wild
   ones for stews)

2 oz/50 g black olives
6 tablespoons sunflower oil
1 glass light red wine
1 sprig thyme and 1 bayleaf
salt and pepper
2 more tablespoons oil
8 small rounds bread

Utensils A heavy casserole and a frying pan

Pick over and wipe the quail. If you are using pigeons or partridges, split them in half. If you are using fresh tomatoes, scald them with boiling water to loosen the skins, and then peel and chop them. Peel and chop the onions. Wipe and slice the mushrooms. Stone and roughly chop the olives.

Put the oil into the heavy casserole, heat it gently, and put in the onions. Fry them for a moment and then add the birds. When they are sizzling, add the mushrooms and fry again. Then put in the tomatoes (with a teaspoon of sugar if they are sun-starved northern vegetables) and the olives. Simmer for a few moments before pouring in the wine and herbs. Sprinkle with a teaspoon of salt and a few turns of the pepper grinder. Cover and stew gently for 40 to 60 minutes, depending on the age and size of the birds, until they are tender. If there is too much juice, remove the lid to allow the liquid to evaporate for the last 10 minutes.

Put 2 tablespoons of oil in the frying pan to heat, and then toss the bread rounds in it — the oil will immediately be soaked up. Continue to dry-fry the pieces of bread in the hot pan. Don't worry if the edges blacken a little — this is how it should be. Put each bird on a round of bread with some sauce. Wonderful. Eat them with your fingers and suck the delicious juices from the bones. The bread will be best of all, so leave it until the end.

GRILLED SMALL BIRDS
Oiseaux en brochette (France)

Farmed quail must do duty in these days of dwindling wild stock. The marinade will serve to replace the incomparable flavour of a diet of herbs and berries on the maquis.

Quantity   Enough for 4–6
Time   Start the day before
Preparation: 20–25 minutes

8 quail	1 teaspoon juniper berries
2 tablespoons olive oil	½ teaspoon peppercorns
1 glass white wine	2 cloves garlic
bayleaves	2 oz/50 g piece fat bacon (*petit salé*)
small bunch thyme	

Utensils   A skewer or toasting fork and a hot grill or barbecue

Split the little birds down the back. Spread them out, flattening the breastbone, so that they look like frogs. The French call this *à la crapaudine*. Make a marinade with the olive oil, wine, bayleaves, thyme, juniper berries, peppercorns, and garlic pounded together. Leave the birds in the marinade overnight if possible.

Preheat the grill or barbecue.

Brush the marinade off the birds. Spear the piece of bacon or *petit salé* on the end of a skewer or toasting fork. Hold it under the grill until the fat runs. Lay the birds still frog-shaped on the grill or barbecue. Baste them as they cook with the melting bacon on its skewer. The birds will take 15 to 20 minutes to cook. Turn them once.

Serve with plenty of fresh bread and a salad. A light red wine from Bordeaux to accompany and a good cheese to follow.

SUGGESTIONS
Spanish quail   In southern Spain the birds are split down the back and then marinated in garlic, oil, and lemon juice overnight. The following day they are wiped, dried, and deep fried in olive oil. They are served sprinkled with rough bay salt from the Cadiz salt flats, and with thick wedges of Spanish country bread (see page 492). A salad of sliced cos lettuce dressed with oil, vinegar, and salt completes the meal.

LEFTOVERS
• Put any leftover birds to reheat in a well-flavoured sauce, as for *Pajaritos en salsa* which follows.

STEWED SMALL BIRDS
Pajaritos en salsa (Spain)

Today the tiny bird on your plate in a hill *venta*, a little roadside bar, is more likely to be a farmed quail than a plump robin. It was not always so. Robins, sparrows, blue-tits, thrushes, blackbirds, goldfinches, anything and everything feathered and foolish enough to be netted, limed, or trapped used to be reckoned the most delicate of dishes in the Mediterranean countryside. They were caught by small boys and sold, strung together in garlands, by black-clad old women at the entrance to Andalusian villages.

Happily for the cause of conservation, the increasing number of wildlife programmes on television, together with wildlife protection laws, have largely re-educated all but the most recalcitrant of hunters. When the birds are cooked with the powerful aromatics so beloved of the Mediterranean palate, there is not much difference in flavour between the farmed and the wild. This recipe can substitute beef escalopes for small birds.

Quantity   Enough for 4–6
Time   Start the day before
Preparation: 30 minutes
Cooking: 40 minutes

For the birds
8 quail *or* fine-cut escalopes of beef
   (beef-olives, called in France,
   oiseaux sans têtes) *plus* the 2
   fillets of a breast of chicken
½ teaspoon juniper berries
½ teaspoon black peppercorns
1 teaspoon salt
1 clove garlic
8 rashers fine-cut streaky bacon *or*
   petit salé
1 glass dry sherry *or* white wine

For the sauce
2 cloves garlic
2 onions
2 peppers
½ lb/250 g tomatoes *or* 1 medium
   tin
¼ pint/150 ml olive oil
2 oz/50 g *chorizo* sausage *or*
   gammon (*jamón serrano* in Spain)
bayleaf, thyme, rosemary
1 small glass *anis seco* (the Spanish
   Pernod) *or* brandy

Utensils   A pestle and mortar and a medium-sized casserole or stew-pot with a lid

If possible prepare the birds or escalopes the day before. Put the juniper berries, peppercorns, and salt in a small mortar with the peeled garlic clove, and pound all these aromatics together.

If you have quail, rub them with the pounded aromatics and sherry, and wrap each in a piece of bacon.

113

If you are using escalopes, unroll and lay them flat on the table. Lay a bacon rasher on each escalope. Cut each chicken fillet into 4 lengthways, and place a strip of white meat across the middle of each piece of dark meat, so that it can be rolled up in the middle of it. Sprinkle with the pounded aromatics and a tablespoon of sherry. Roll them up like little carpets, and tie them with thread or secure them with toothpicks.

Leave the birds, whether real or phoney, to marinate — a minimum of half an hour, overnight if possible.

Now prepare the sauce ingredients. Peel and chop the garlic and the onions. De-seed and chop the peppers. Pour boiling water over the tomatoes if you are using fresh ones, and then peel and chop them. Tinned ones go in as they are.

Put the oil to warm in the casserole. Put in the garlic and the onions. Fry for a moment until they take colour. Then push them to one side and turn the marinated birds in the oil. Chop the sausage or gammon into small pieces and add to the casserole. Add the tomatoes and the herbs. Pour in the rest of the sherry and bubble for a moment to evaporate the alcohol. Cover tightly and stew gently for 30 to 40 minutes. Stir in the glass of *anis* or brandy and bubble up the sauce again. Best if you let the dish cool and then reheat it. The birds taste more strongly of their flavourings if this is done.

Untie the strings before you serve the birds. Provide plenty of bread for mopping up. A large plate of crisp-fried chips on the side and a salad of chopped tomatoes, onions, and green peppers dressed with olive oil, salt, and vinegar.

Follow with a dish of ripe figs, purple or green and sweet as honey. This dish used to be made with plump little fruit-stealing fig-peckers. A glass of *anis dulce*, the sweet Spanish *anis*-flavoured liqueur, to finish.

SUGGESTIONS
● Treat the little birds as in this recipe, but stew them with mushrooms and cream, as in the Austrian hare recipe (see page 117).
● The Italians like their small game stewed in the same manner, but with mushrooms included in the stew, preferably wild ones such as *porcini*, sold dried in Italian delicatessens.

LEFTOVERS
● Reheat gently, stir in a tablespoon of garlic chopped up with parsley and fresh herbs, and serve with a dish of rice.

SMALL BIRD PATE
Ci-devant pâté de grives (France)

The thrush population of southern France takes a sharp upswing in the autumn when the grapes are ripening. The presence of plump small birds growing plumper on the fruits of the vine has long been irresistible to the French countryman, and the day's bag would go to make his favourite pâté. However, recent legislation has outlawed traps and lime, and new ingredients must be found.

Quantity　Enough for 6–8
Time　Preparation: 20–30 minutes
　　　　Cooking: 35–45 minutes

2 farmed quail and 1 pigeon masquerading as thrushes (the flavour will not be quite so delicate, but you can listen to the reprieved victim's serenade instead)
8 oz/250 g pig's liver
8 oz/250 g pork belly without its skin

1 tablespoon juniper berries
small bunch thyme
salt and pepper
small glass brandy
12 rashers fine-cut good streaky bacon to line the terrine
1 bayleaf

Utensils　A small earthenware terrine and a baking tray for it to rest in

Strip all the meat from the bones of the little birds, any way you can. This should yield about ½ lb/250 g meat — which is as it should be, since the weight of the 3 principal ingredients should be equal.

Chop up the bird meat, the liver, and the pork belly as finely or roughly as you like the texture of your pâté to be.

Preheat the oven to 300°F/150°C/Gas 2.

Pound up the juniper berries and strip off the thyme leaves. Mix these herbs into the meats, with a teaspoon of salt, plenty of pepper, and the brandy. Line the terrine with the bacon, leaving flaps at the side to be folded over the top, and then pack the pâté in. Put the bayleaf on the top and cover all with bacon. Do not use a lid, except for the last 10 minutes of the cooking so that the top does not burn.

Put the terrine in a baking tray full of hot water. Put the arrangement to cook in the oven for 35 to 45 minutes. The pâté should still be rosy in the centre, so push a skewer in at the end of half an hour. If the juice runs pale pink it is ready. If it runs clear, the dish is overcooked. If no juice runs at all, it is undercooked.

Leave to cool. Serve the pâté in its own terrine, with crusty hot bread, a dish of radishes, washed but still garlanded with their own green leaves. To complete the meal, a bottle of good red Graves, a green salad, and one of the beautiful little French goat's cheeses which are black as charcoal on the outside and pure snowy curd within.

SUGGESTIONS
● Try to use good bacon and not the chemically cured kind — the flavour is so pervasive that the pâté will taste of nothing else. If that is all you can find, then line the terrine with thin slices of pork fat, cut from a piece of back fat left overnight in salt. This instant *petit salé* is a most useful standby as it will keep in the salad compartment for a long time and can be used in all recipes which need fat bacon.

PIGEONS WITH BACON
Pigeonneau en compote (Belgium)

The Belgians are fond of their vegetables, of which they have a goodly repertoire. They have long been excellent gardeners, numbering the Brussels sprout and Belgian chicory (specially blanched in heaped-up furrows) among their contributions to the vegetable markets of the world. The battle between the sower of seed and those he sees as seed-stealers is very ancient: in this recipe the thieves are stewed with the gardener's vegetables. A dish for all seasons.

Quantity   Enough for 4
Time   Preparation: 30 minutes
           Cooking: 1 hour

4 young pigeons	½ lb/250 g small onions
2 oz/50 g butter	½ lb/250 g carrots
salt and pepper	1 lb/500 g small potatoes
winter savory	1 small cauliflower
4 oz/100 g fat bacon	

Utensils   A deep casserole with a tight-fitting lid

Pluck, draw and wipe the pigeons. Put a knob of butter in each, worked with salt and pepper and the savory, chopped fine. Cube the bacon and sweat it in the casserole until the fat runs.

Meanwhile peel the onions (tiny ones are best and can be used whole) and chop them. Peel and slice the carrots. Scrub the small potatoes. Divide the cauliflower into small florets.

Preheat the oven to 375°F/190°C/Gas 5.

Turn the birds in the hot fat until they sizzle. Tuck all the vegetables around them and add two tablespoons of water. Sprinkle with salt and pepper and a little more chopped savory. Bring swiftly to the boil. Cover tightly, sealing down the lid with flour and water. No steam must be allowed to escape.

Stew in the oven for an hour. Unseal the lid at the table. The gardener has his revenge. No other accompaniment but good Belgian beer.

Hare and Rabbit

SADDLE OF HARE WITH SOURED CREAM
Hasenbraten mit rahmsauce (Austria and neighbours)

Hunting is an Austrian passion. Neighbouring Germany, Hungary, and Czechoslovakia have equally itchy trigger fingers. All have access to beautiful forests, including the Vienna Woods and the Black Forest, which blaze with colour in the autumn hunting season. There can be no more beautiful shelter for deer and boar. Game is one of the major culinary pleasures of the Austrian table, and the recipes of the countryside have usually been tried and tested over many generations. The game and the mushroom seasons coincide, so there are many recipes which include both.

Game which has not been hung, as in Britain, for a relatively long time, should be marinated to develop its flavour. If this is not done, the meat can taste disappointingly ordinary. Marinating also helps break down the fibres in naturally tough meat.

Quantity   Enough for 4–8 (hares vary markedly in size — almost as much as appetites)
Time   Start 2 days before
Preparation: 20 minutes
Cooking: 60–90 minutes

1 hare
1 teaspoon peppercorns
1 teaspoon juniper berries
½ pint/300 ml wine vinegar
½ pint/300 ml red wine
½ pint/300 ml water
2 bayleaves
4 oz/100 g streaky bacon
1 onion

1 carrot
thyme and marjoram
wild mushrooms, dried *or* fresh,
   are always welcome in this dish
   (*optional*)
½ pint/300 ml thick soured cream
   — more or less, depending on
   the size of the hare

117

Utensils   A large saucepan and a deep stewpot with a lid

Game to be marinated must first be jointed and the outer membranes stripped off with a sharp knife — particularly so for hare, which has a very tough membrane indeed all over the legs and saddle.

First make the marinade. Crush the peppercorns and juniper berries. Mix the wine vinegar, red wine, and water with the peppercorns, berries, and bayleaves in the saucepan, bring to the boil, and then allow to cool. Pour the marinade over the game to cover. Leave to marinate for 2 days, depending on the size of the joints.

Take the hare out of the marinade and pat it dry. Reserve the marinade. Cube the bacon and sweat it in the stewpot until the fat runs (you may need extra fat). Push the bacon to one side and add the hare to the hot fat. Brown the meat gently.

Meanwhile peel and slice the onion and carrot. Add them to the browning meat. Add the thyme and marjoram and the mushrooms if you have them. Pour in half a cup of the marinade, including the spices. Cover tightly. Cook slowly until tender, adding more marinade sparingly when necessary. It will take between 1 and 1½ hours. When the meat is soft the dish is ready. Stir in the soured cream.

Serve with stewed cranberries, dumplings or boiled potatoes, and red cabbage.

SUGGESTIONS
● A spiced wine and vinegar marinade gives good results and, in addition, provides a cooking juice. If you use another method of marinating, then red wine and water will have to be used in the recipe instead of the marinade liquid (don't forget to include the juniper, pepper, and bayleaf). Large joints like a saddle of venison can be marinated by wrapping in a cloth soaked in vinegar for 4 to 5 days. Buttermilk is often used as a marinade — particularly for boar. A large ham will need 5 days' soaking.
● This recipe can be used for joints of boar and venison. The marinade will also do wonderful things for a tough cut of beef (see the *sauerbraten* recipe on page 216). Leg joints take longer to cook than the saddle, so bear this in mind when preparing game.
● A tablespoon of gin will enhance the juniper flavour.

RABBIT WITH GARLIC
Conejo al ajillo (Spain)

This is a favourite way with both rabbit and chicken, the meats most likely to be found, along with the products of the family porker, in the

Spanish peasant kitchen. A peasant neighbour in Spain, who lived with his goat-herding and cheese-making family down the valley from my house, used to be sent out as a child during Spain's Civil War on an unusual, but typically ingenious, form of rabbit hunt. He had to watch below a cliff where a pair of huge eagle owls nested until one of the birds returned to their young with a rabbit. He would then run to alert his father, who climbed the cliff and robbed the owlets of their supper. This is how the family liked its pirated rabbits cooked.

Quantity   Enough for 4, with plenty of bread
Time   Start the day before
              Preparation: 20 minutes
              Cooking: 25 minutes

1 rabbit	1 large head garlic
3 tablespoons white wine vinegar	¼ pint/150 ml olive oil
1 tablespoon flour	1 glass dry sherry *or* white wine
salt and pepper	

Utensils   A wide shallow pan with a lid

Skin the rabbit if this has not already been done for you. It is very simple. Paunch it by slitting the belly fur and pulling out all the insides on to a sheet of newspaper. Save the liver, the heart, and the kidneys, and throw the rest away. Be careful of the little bitter gland near the tail. Slit round the paws and up the back legs to the cut in the belly. Grip the flap of skin where the hindleg skin has been cut, and pull steadily down towards the head (easiest if you hang the back legs from a hook). The rabbit will skin as easily as pulling off a glove.

Joint the rabbit into about 16 pieces, and trim off the tough exterior membranes with a sharp knife. Sprinkle with the vinegar and leave overnight to marinate (include the inside meats, well washed). The marinade softens both flesh and flavour, and is more necessary with a rabbit than with other game.

The next day pat the joints of rabbit dry and roll them lightly in the flour seasoned with salt and pepper. Peel the garlic — there should be 10 to 12 good fat cloves — and chop it roughly.

Heat the oil gently in the shallow pan. Put in the rabbit pieces and allow them to take colour. Add the garlic and fry all together for a moment. Add the sherry or wine and allow it to bubble up and evaporate the alcohol. Cover the pan and leave all to stew on a low heat for 30 to 40 minutes, until the rabbit is tender and the liquid nearly evaporated. Serve in its own garlic-scented oil with plenty of bread to mop up the juices, and a plate of thick-cut chips fried golden in olive oil. Accompany with a salad of fresh tomatoes sliced and sprinkled with a little chopped garlic, a teaspoon of sugar, and plenty of freshly milled pepper. Finish with a summer fruit — custard apples, ivory flesh starred with ebony pips, to be cut in half and eaten with a spoon, or sweet orange-fleshed medlars.

SUGGESTIONS
● To make the dish with chicken, joint the bird into 16 pieces, and cook to the same recipe. No marinating is necessary.

RABBIT WITH BEER AND PRUNES
Konijn met pruinen (Belgium)

Rabbit is Europe's most widely distributed wild game. Considered a crop-destroying pest since the first pair escaped from the domestic warrens installed in their colonies by the Romans, rabbit meat has long been the fare of the poor. The Belgians carried on the Roman tradition and bred ever-larger rabbits for meat. Their 'Flemish Giant' now stocks commercial rabbit farms all over the world. My family's pet buck rabbit, Pila, who must have weighed ten to twelve pounds in his prime, was a powerful and fertile member of the breed. He would thump through his chicken-wire run as and when he pleased, and succeeded in increasing the size and number of wild rabbits in our Andalusian valley by at least half. My Belgian neighbour, proud of his garden and fearful for his fine young lettuces, took to patrolling his boundaries with a shot-gun. This is what he did with the victims.

Quantity   Enough for 6–8
Time   Start up to 24 hours in advance
　　　　Preparation: 20 minutes
　　　　Cooking: 1 hour

2 small wild rabbits *or* 1 Flemish Giant	1 lb/500 g onions
1 lb/500 g prunes	1 lb/500 g carrots
1 pint/600 ml water	2 oz/50 g butter *or* lard
1 teaspoon salt and pepper	1 pint/600 ml lager (*gueuze* is preferred for the dish in
1 teaspoon juniper berries	Belgium)

Utensils   A large casserole and a liquidizer if you like a smooth sauce

Put the prunes to soak in the water — overnight if they are very dry, 1 to 2 hours otherwise.
　　Skin the rabbit or rabbits, if this has not already been done, and joint

them. Chop the saddle across to give 4 to 6 joints, depending on the size of the beast, then chop each hind and fore-haunch into 2 to 3 sections each. Include the liver, heart, and the little kidneys. A peasant household would certainly include the head, split in two. Season the meat with salt, pepper, and the juniper berries, crushed.

Peel and slice the onions and the carrots. Put the butter or lard to melt in the casserole. Add the vegetables and sauté them for a moment. Push them to one side and put in the rabbit joints. Fry them until they take a little colour. Cover with the lager and bring to the boil. Add the prunes with their soaking liquid and continue to cook, either on top of the stove or in the oven at 350°F/180°C/Gas 4, for an hour. Before serving, crush the carrots, onions, and loose bits of prune into the stew to thicken the sauce — if you like your sauce smooth, purée some of the vegetables with the juices in the liquidizer.

SUGGESTIONS
● This recipe is also excellent prepared with a jointed chicken.

LEFTOVERS
● Rewarm for long enough to cook a few thin slices of potato in the sauce, into which you have stirred a small glass of strong, juniper-flavoured Dutch gin. It will be even better than the first time round.

Frogs and Snails

FRIED FROG'S LEGS
Grenouilles sautés au beurre (France)

Unfortunately the world population of frogs is not able to keep pace with the world population of humans. It is therefore probably time to call a halt to the consumption of the one species by the other, so this recipe is included for nostalgia.

The chef-proprietor of the excellent *hostellerie* in my neighbouring village in the Languedoc, St. Felix Lauragais, had bought himself a country retreat some twenty miles distant and so far off the beaten track that no anxious diner could winkle him out on his day off. There of a Monday he busied himself building dams and hollowing banks to establish a line of descending pools along the stream which watered his territory. The sole purpose was to encourage the local population of *Rana esculenta* to move in and multiply. When both he and they were

121

well established, he explained, the arrangement would benefit both parties.

The frogs were caught in the traditional way. A light cane rod is strung with fine line, weighted with a lead pellet and carries a hook baited with a scrap of red rag. A skilled fisherman can make the bait dance across the reeds in such a way that it proves irresistible to frogs. The prey must be killed immediately to put them out of their misery, the frog fisherman insisted, by tapping their heads against the rod. Only the back legs are snipped off and skinned for use. My gourmet neighbour approved only the simplest of treatments.

Quantity   Enough for 4
Time   Preparation: 20 minutes

12 pairs frog's legs	1 lemon
2 oz/50 g butter	salt and pepper
parsley	

Utensils   A frying pan and hot plates

Melt a piece of the butter in the frying pan. When it is hot, put in the frog's legs. Cook them gently, shaking the pan sometimes so that they do not stick, for 10 minutes, turning them over once. While they cook, chop a large handful of parsley finely. Quarter the lemon. When the frog's legs are done, add the rest of the butter, season them with salt and pepper, and sprinkle them with the parsley. Throw over a glass of Pernod if you have one, flame it, and serve immediately with quarters of lemon, sauced with their own butter. Bread and a bottle of dry white wine to accompany.

LITTLE SNAILS IN THEIR BROTH
Caracolitos en caldo (Spain)

In Spain two varieties of snail are eaten — the usual large Roman snail, *Helix pomata*, and its close relations, and the tiny cream and brown species, never bigger than a thumb-nail, which aestivates on the dry thistles in the summer heat of Andalusia. All the world's land snails are edible, including the giant African snail which was domesticated by the Romans and mentioned in the despatches of Apicius. The only problem is that as herbivores snails may have fed off plants which humans find toxic. They must therefore be starved before preparation to empty their digestive systems. Snails which have hibernated, and the small summer-hibernating varieties, are self-starved. Care must also be taken not to collect snails from pylons or fences which might have been painted with lead paint.

In early summer the meadows of southern Spain are brilliant with ten-foot high yellow-flowered tree thistles, *Carthamus arborescens*, and the more modest but equally beautiful blue *Cynara humilis*, whose spiny stalks are often completely covered by little gasteropods. From mid-June onwards, as soon as the spring rains are truly over, parties of women and children make day-long expeditions to favoured fields with buckets and stout sticks to gather the snail harvest. It is hard, hot, and prickly work, but the snails are so prized as a summer treat and their soup so valued for its curative powers, that there is never any shortage of helpers. At the same time the harvesters gather bundles of penny royal, a spearmint which is used to brush the foam off the simmering snails and to flavour the soup. The old spice-woman in any country market will make up a screw of snail spices to order.

Quantity Enough for a dozen portions
Time All the afternoon

4 lb/2 kg tiny snails	1 teaspoon black peppercorns
1 lb/500 g salt	2 little dried red chillies
small bunch penny royal *or* mint	1 teaspoon coriander
1 tablespoon vinegar	1 tablespoon dried fennel stalks
1 whole head garlic	

Utensils A deep roomy saucepan

Salt the snails to make them froth. Then wash them thoroughly in 5 changes of fresh water, salting in between and rubbing off the froth or *baba* as you do so.

Put the snails into the saucepan. Cover them with cold water. Bring the water gently to the boil. As the bath warms, the snails will be lulled into emerging from their shells. This makes them much easier to pick out later. When the water boils it will froth up. Brush off the foam with a bundle of penny royal. Throw in the vinegar and the foam will subside.

Singe the whole head of garlic by holding it on the point of a knife over a flame. The paper cover burns black, the garlic is lightly roasted, and this gives the broth its characteristic flavour. Put the whole head in with the snails.

Now add the spices. The peppercorns stay whole, the chillies should have their seeds removed (take care not to rub your eyes — they are very fiery), the coriander must be crushed a little to release the seeds and oil. Add the fennel stalks and a few more sprigs of penny royal or mint.

Simmer the brew gently for at least an hour. Taste and add salt if necessary. The pot can be reheated as often as you like and is almost immortal. Serve the snails in their broth in a bowl, with a toothpick or a pin to winkle them out. When you have finished, drink the delicious peppery liquid which remains, or mop it up with fresh bread.

SUGGESTIONS

• The pot with the snails is kept on the back of the stove and ladlefuls are warmed up when required — this is a great treat during the annual *fiestas*, carnivals with fairs, bullfights, and dancing until dawn, which are held in every village each year. Beer often accompanies the snails at *fiesta* time.

• The black spicy broth is drunk as a tonic by anyone who feels poorly. I find it an excellent cold cure.

LEFTOVERS

Cassolette d'escargots Migrate any leftover snails into the French peasant kitchen. Remove the gasteropods from their shells (pinch off the dark curl of intestine at the end of the body) and put them in a small shallow earthenware dish (a *cassolette*). Crush 6 large peeled cloves of garlic into a large knob of butter with 2 tablespoons of chopped parsley. Dot the snails with this butter. Season with pepper and salt, and moisten with a small glass of *marc de bourgogne* or brandy. Sprinkle a handful of fresh breadcrumbs over the top. Put to heat in the oven at 350°F/180°C/Gas 4 for 25 minutes, until all is piping hot and bubbling. Eat with a spoon and plenty of bread.

SNAILS IN SAUCE
Caracoles en salsa (Spain)

There is a different treatment in Spain for the large variety of snail — the ones so beloved by the Romans that they bred them in special *vivaria* and repopulated most of Europe, including their province of Iberia, with their favourite snack. The large snails are usually prepared in a thick well-flavoured sauce.

Quantity Enough for 3–4
Time Start a week earlier if you pick your own
Preparation: 20–30 minutes
Cooking: 1½ hours

36–48 large snails	1 lb/500 g tomatoes *or* 2 medium
salt	tins
1 tablespoon vinegar	2 tiny fiery chillies
4 tablespoons olive oil	few stalks and fronds fresh fennel
1 large onion	2 bayleaves
3 cloves garlic	small glass dry white wine (dry
½ lb/250 g green peppers	sherry is best)

Utensils A deep stewpot, a perforated spoon, and a shallow pan

As always starve your snails, if necessary and unvouched for, for a week or two. They must have plenty of air in their container, and be cleaned out regularly. When you are ready to cook them, salt them and wash them in several changes of fresh cold water, rubbing them well to scrape off the froth which is their response to the salt. Put them in the deep pot and bring them gently to the boil. When the froth rises, stir in the vinegar to cut it. Skim. Lower the heat and simmer them gently for 1½ hours. Drain and rinse them. Pick each snail out of its shell and pinch off the long dark intestine at the end. Stuff it back in its shell. Peasant cooks in Spain do not usually bother with this nicety, but those who live in the wilds can be more certain of their raw material.

If your snails are ready prepared or tinned, start the recipe here.

Put the olive oil to warm in the shallow pan. Peel and chop the onion and garlic. Sauté them lightly. Peel, de-seed, and chop the green peppers, and stir them in to fry as well. Add the tomatoes, chopped if fresh, and simmer until the pulp melts in to make a sauce. De-seed, chop, and add the chillies. Chop and add the fennel and the bayleaves. Add the wine. Stew all gently together for 20 to 30 minutes, until you have a smooth rich sauce. Put in the snails and heat them through.

Set the table with extra plates for the shells, large napkins, and toothpicks. Serve the snails very hot in their sauce. Accompany with good country bread and a glass of cold dry sherry. A salad of chopped cos lettuce, sliced raw mild onion, and chopped tomatoes dressed with thick green olive oil and salt would always accompany this dish in Spain.

SNAILS IN GARLIC BUTTER
Escargots à la bourguinonne (France)

Snails are creatures of regular habit — an ideal target for the pastoral terrorist. If you wish to raid your own natural resources, you will have to study the local landscape and take note of the habits of its gasteropod population. In the Languedoc in south-west France, just before the dew-laden dawn broke over the remote rib of upland which bore my farmhouse, a small brown army would begin their ascent of the hedgerows. They climbed for no more than twenty minutes, during which time they could be picked off the twigs like crab apples from a branch. Then, as soon as the sun rose over the horizon, down they came. Five minutes later they had all vanished into the long wet grass.

If you cannot find fresh snails in the market, be brave and go out and collect your own. Once again if you are not sure of their grazing habits, starve them for a week or two before using, to allow them to evacuate whatever they have ingested.

Quantity   Enough for 4, allowing a dozen snails apiece
Time   Start a week earlier if you pick your own
   Preparation: 30–40 minutes
   Cooking: 2 hours

For the snails
48 snails
1 tablespoon vinegar
½ bottle white wine
1 pint/600 ml water
1 carrot
1 onion
a handful fresh herbs
salt, peppercorns, and a bayleaf

For the butter
6 oz/175 g butter
3 large cloves garlic
a handful parsley
salt and pepper

Utensils   A large saucepan with a lid and, if possible, snail dishes or *escargotières* (but a baking tray will do)

Wash the snails very thoroughly in several changes of cold fresh water and salt. Blanch them in boiling water acidulated with a tablespoon of vinegar, for 5 minutes. Drain and rinse them with cold water. Pick out the snails from their shells. Pinch off the black curl at the end of the intestine. Put the unshelled snails back in the saucepan with the wine and water, the carrot scrubbed and chopped, the onion quartered, the herbs, a teaspoon of salt and one of peppercorns, and the bayleaf. Cover and simmer for 1½ hours.

Meanwhile wash the shells thoroughly. Soften the butter and mash it with a fork. Chop the garlic and parsley together very finely, and then mash them into the butter with plenty of salt and pepper. A dash of *marc de bourgogne* would do no harm.

Preheat the oven to 375°F/190°C/Gas 6.

Push a small knob of the garlic butter into the base of each snail shell. Press the snail back into its home. Fill up the entrance with another knob of garlic butter. Continue until all the snails are ready. Arrange the shells in a snail dish if you have one — if not, either prop the shells against each other with the opening pointing up so that the juices do not run out, or cut small holes out of slices of day-old bread and put them in a baking tray. The shells will stay upright and the bread will toast deliciously.

Give the snails 15 minutes. Serve them piping hot with fresh bread and a good supply of toothpicks to pluck them out of their shells.

CHAPTER 3

Poultry and Barnyard

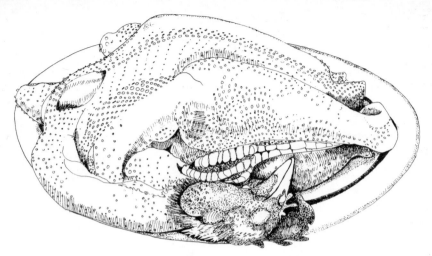

Chicken

Even the poorest European peasant households could usually support a few barnyard fowl, particularly since good egg-layers often provided the wife's cash crop. Although farm hens were primarily kept for eggs rather than meat, a few young cockerels were often fattened up for high days and holidays. Most peasant recipes concentrate on ways of dealing with elderly birds — plenty of soups, stews, and slow cooking.

The actual killing of poultry was almost invariably women's work. Grey-haired María, the baker's sturdy wife at my nearby village of Pelayo in southern Spain, was the local expert. María kept hens herself and sold the eggs. Sometimes at Christmas she would act as agent for the farmers who lived in the hills behind, and they would walk their turkeys and geese down to the little bakery beside the main road for her to sell on their behalf. The unwary purchaser, perhaps a motorist on his way home to the town below, was likely to find his Christmas dinner fully feathered and squawking on the seat beside him unless he specified in advance that he did not wish to receive it on the hoof — or, more accurately, on the claw.

When María consented to act as executioner, the good lady would make her customer secure the bird's legs and then with one swift sure movement, double over the chicken's head and sever the spine at the base of the skull. She preferred to pluck her chickens dry, sitting out on the back stoop in the sun and working from the head to the tail. It never took her more than three minutes a bird. Heads, feet, gizzards, and necks all went into the stewpot. Any of the little golden unlaid eggs she found inside would go to enrich the *puchero*. Nothing was ever wasted.

COCK-A-LEEKIE
(Scotland)

Kissing cousin to the ancient English dishes of Malachi and Gallimaw-frey, Cock-a-leekie is the best version of this soup-stew that has survived into the modern kitchen. The dish can be prepared with a good bone stock and the leeks on their own. The chicken is a luxury addition, special occasion food. The loser in a cock fight used to be recommended since its sinews would be firm and give body to the soup. Today an ordinary roasting chicken normally has to do duty instead.

Quantity   Enough for 6
Time   Preparation: 10 minutes
      Cooking: 2½ hours

1 large boiling fowl weighing 3 lb/1·5 kg at least	1 teaspoon salt
6 pints/3·5 litres water	1 teaspoon peppercorns
	5 lb/2·5 kg leeks

Utensils   A large stewpot and a perforated spoon

Wipe over the chicken and put it in the stewpot. Cover it with salted water and with the crushed peppercorns sprinkled in. Boil gently, skimming regularly, for half an hour.

Wash and cut the leeks into short lengths. After half an hour, add half the leeks to the soup. Continue simmering for another 1½ hours. Add the rest of the leeks and continue to cook for another half hour. The soup must be very thick with leeks, and the first part of them must be boiled down into the soup until they become almost liquid themselves.

Sometimes the chicken is served in the tureen with the soup. Sometimes it is served afterwards, cut in pieces and accompanied with potatoes, peeled and sliced and simmered in a little of the soup.

SUGGESTIONS
• The inclusion of prunes or raisins in the soup is a matter of contentious debate among experts on this famous dish. If you wish to do so, add a handful, well soaked, half an hour before the end of the cooking period. M Talleyrand, diplomatic as always, suggested that the prunes be cooked in the broth but not served in the soup. This would serve to colour lightly and sweeten the soup — a logical notion since all the onion tribe, to which the leek belongs, have a high sugar content. Some traditional recipes advocate the inclusion of a teaspoon of treacle or sugar.
• The soup is sometimes thickened with a handful of fine-ground oatmeal.

● Chopped spinach or chard can be added half an hour before the end
of the cooking time.

BOILED CHICKEN AND NOODLES
Suppenhuhn mit nudeln (Austria)

This is an innkeeper's dish, very popular as a second breakfast. An
elderly boiler past its egg-laying days will do as well as a spring chicken
— the flavour of an old barnyard fowl is far superior to that of a young
battery hen. Serve with noodles cooked in the broth — either noodles
you have bought or, preferably, your own.

Quantity   Enough for 6
Time   Preparation: 1 hour (if you make your own noodles)
         Cooking: 1–2 hours

For the soup
1 large chicken
bunch parsley *or* a parsley root
   and a few sprigs lovage
1 lb/500 g carrots
2 fine leeks *or* 2 onions
7 pints/4 litres water
salt and peppercorns

For the noodles
½ lb/250 g plain flour
½ teaspoon salt
2 eggs
approximately 2 tablespoons water

Utensils   A large stewpot, a perforated spoon, a strainer, and, if you
have one, a pasta roller

Wipe the chicken and put in the stewpot with the parsley and lovage,
the vegetables scrubbed but not peeled, and the water. Bring all to the
boil and then skim off the grey foam. Turn down the heat to simmer,
and add a teaspoon of salt and half a dozen whole peppercorns.
    Simmer gently for 1 to 2 hours depending on the age of the bird.
When it is soft and the soup well flavoured, take out the bird and put it
to keep warm. Strain the soup and heat it again, ready for the noodles to
be cooked in it.
    Sift the flour and salt together directly on to the kitchen table. You
need plenty of elbow room. Make a dip in the middle and crack the eggs
into it. Work them into the dough with your hand. Add water,
kneading as you go, until you have a soft pliable dough. (This can be
started in your mixer and finished by hand.)
    If you have a pasta roller, so much the better. It is the easiest way to

make noodles and if you like both them and other pastas, it is well worth acquiring one. A pasta roller is an implement which bolts on to the kitchen table like a little mangle, and operates on the same principle. When you have rolled the dough thinly enough by progressively decreasing the gaps between the rollers, you then roll it through a slot equipped with cutters — there is normally a choice of 2 or 3 ribbon widths.

If you have no roller, flour the table and roll out the dough until it is very thin — it will spring back, but persevere. Leave the flat sheet to dry out for 15 minutes. Then sprinkle it generously with flour, roll it up into a Swiss-roll cylinder, and slice it into rings — fine-cut for soup, thicker if they are to be served plain with butter or with a cream sauce spiked with chopped ham or dried mushrooms. Leave the noodles piled loosely to dry out for another half hour.

The noodles should be poached in the boiling soup, or boiling water, for 2 to 4 minutes depending on size and freshness.

Serve in deep soup plates. Very comforting on a cold day.

SUGGESTIONS
• Egg noodles store well — make double the recipe and allow one portion to dry until brittle, then keep it in an airtight jar in the larder.
• Serve either in the soup, or as a sweet after a thick vegetable soup. No German or Austrian farmhouse cook would dream of producing a main meal that did not include a noodle, dumpling, or strudel dish.

SOUR SOUP MADE FROM CHICKEN
Ciorba de pui (Romania)

A much-loved peasant staple, made usually, naturally enough, with an old hen past her useful egg-laying age. Appreciated in 1939 by the traveller D. J. Hall, taking a welcome meal with the village doctor:

> I have never eaten such a meal as I did the next day; and that is saying a good deal of a meal in a country whose people are the most prodigious eaters perhaps in the world. Though capacities might increase everywhere if food became as plentiful and cheap as it is in Romania. We had first ciorba de pui, a sour soup made from chicken, rich with butter and filled with vegetables. This was followed by a sucking pig. It came on to the table whole, half an apple in its mouth, a blue bow on its forehead. I felt sad till I began to eat it, and then my sorrow passed. That seemed to me to be enough. But then came slices of roast goose with peppers, and afterwards a cheese pancake. The wine was good too.

Quantity   Enough for 6
Time   Preparation: 20 minutes
      Cooking: 1½–2½ hours

1 chicken weighing around
   3 lb/1·5 kg
bayleaf and allspice (acquired in
   Romania from the 'foreigners'
   market')
3 medium onions
3 carrots
1 celeriac root

parsley root if you can find it
salt and pepper
½ cabbage (optional)
2 slices old bread or ¼ pint/150 ml
   single cream
1 tablespoon vinegar
3 egg yolks
dill and savory

Utensils   A large stewpot and a perforated spoon

Wipe and trim any stray feathers off the chicken. If it is an old boiler, it will take twice as long to cook as a roaster, so put it on to boil in enough water to cover with the bayleaf and allspice for an hour before you add the vegetables, trimmed, peeled, and left more or less whole.

If you have a roasting chicken, put it in the stewpot and immediately add the mixed vegetables, bayleaf, allspice, peppercorns, and a little salt. Cover with cold water. Bring to the boil 3 times, skim and add a little cold water each time to send the cloudy bits to the bottom. Simmer for 1¼ to 1½ hours, until the chicken is tender.

Slice the cabbage if you are using it and add it 15 minutes before the end of the cooking time. Mash the bread (you can upgrade the soup by replacing the bread with the cream) with a tablespoon of vinegar. Beat it into the egg yolks and add a ladleful of hot broth from the chicken to the mixture. Beat it well in. Take the pot off the fire and stir the egg-yolk mixture into the soup. Do not boil it again.

Chop up the herbs and scatter them over. Serve the soup with bread and wine. A handful of sweet grapes or plums and a glass of *tuica* plum brandy to finish the meal.

SUGGESTIONS
● Save the chicken itself for the recipe which follows, and you will have two dishes for the price of one.

CHICKEN POT ROAST
(Romania)

We ate as only Romanians know how to eat, immensely and well. First *mamaliga*, a kind of solid corn pudding, soup, a whole roast chicken, with a plate piled high with salad, and much wine.

D. J. Hall, *Romanian Furrow*

The young woman who gave me this recipe, a shepherd's wife in the Carpathians, had just bought in the market at Sibiu a special dish in which to cook it. She showed me a chicken-shaped earthenware casserole, oval and without a lid. Carpathian shepherds are exempt from modern Romanian state collectivization, and their larders are well stocked — there is no shortage of cheese from the sheep, butter and cream from the family cow, or eggs and poultry from the yard, as there is in the rest of the country.

Quantity   Enough for 4
Time   Preparation: 10 minutes
  Cooking: 30 minutes

1 boiled chicken *or* any piece of boiled meat	2 oz/50 g butter
15–20 cloves garlic	¼ pint/150 ml thick fresh *or* soured cream

Utensils   A small baking dish or casserole and greaseproof paper or foil

Preheat the oven to 350°F/180°C/Gas 4.

Peel the garlic, slice it, and scatter it over and in the chicken. Put the bird in the close-fitting baking dish, tuck the butter inside it, and pour the cream over it. Cover all with greaseproof paper or foil, and roast in the oven for half an hour. Serve with noodles, a salad, and cold white wine. Mme Frunzete, the shepherd's wife, grew beautiful grapes in her courtyard, and would serve them to finish the meal.

This treatment of a soup-meat as a roasting joint after its preliminary boiling is characteristic of the Transylvanian kitchen. The method is effective with any tough joint of meat. The roots of the technique can be found (appropriately enough to the Roman colony of Dacia) in ancient Rome: Apicius gives similar recipes in his fifth-century work *De Re Coquinaria* — ancient lessons well learnt.

CHICKEN WITH PAPRIKA
Porkolt csirke (Hungary)

Porkolt means 'singed', which indicates the culinary method that distinguishes this dish from a *gulyas* (see page 224): the meat is boiled so dry it fries for the last few moments of cooking. *Porkolt* can be made with any kind of meat or game or even fish. This is the dish served in Austria as a goulash. Like the *gulyas*, it has no cream and no flour. The Austro-Hungarian *gulyas* version uses beef. As for the chicken, there is an old Hungarian town-dwellers' joke that when a peasant kills a chicken, either the peasant is sick or the chicken. In this case, assume it a dish to fortify a poorly peasant.

Quantity   Enough for 4–5 — with noodles it can be stretched to 6
Time   Preparation: 25–30 minutes
             Cooking: 50–90 minutes

3 lb/1·5 kg chicken, young *or* old
1½ lb/750 g onions (plenty of
 onions in this recipe — more
 than in the *gulyas*)
2 cloves garlic

2 oz/50 g lard
2 tablespoons paprika (Noble Rose
 if possible)
salt and pepper
1 wine glass water

Utensils   A large stewpot

Joint the chicken into a dozen pieces, using the whole carcass. Peel the onions and slice finely. Peel and crush the garlic with salt. Put the lard to melt in the stewpot.

When the fat is well melted, add the onions and the garlic. Fry them gently until golden. Put in the pieces of chicken. Fry them gently too. The whole operation will take 10 minutes and is more like stewing than frying.

Take the pan off the heat and stir in the paprika and a good sprinkling of freshly milled pepper. Put the pot back on the heat and add the water. Bring it to the boil, then cover the pot tightly, turn down the heat and stew very gently for 50 to 60 minutes if you have a young bird, and for 1½ hours if the bird is an old boiler. Check regularly that the pot has not boiled dry, adding the minimum of liquid necessary.

Turn up the heat and take the lid off the pot at the end, and watch carefully as the liquid boils nearly clean away. Take it off just before anything burns. Paprika is a vegetable and the flavour is fugitive.

Serve the chicken *porkolt* immediately with its own minimal but wonderfully aromatic juices. There won't be any leftovers — just as well, since chicken *porkolt* is at its best on the day it is made. Accompany with flat or barley noodles. Take a glass of *palinka*, the excellent Hungarian fruit brandy which is drunk both before and after the meal. Best of all is the delicious *barakpalinka*, a dry apricot brandy so strongly flavoured with the ripe fruit that it is traditionally likened to drinking sunshine.

SUGGESTIONS

• Optional, in deference to Hungarian gardening skills, include 2 to 3 cloves of garlic crushed with salt, and a green pepper, de-seeded and cubed.

Fish porkolt   Make a *porkolt* with a large fish cut into pieces. A carp is particularly good: it was eighteenth-century French monks who originally selectively bred this naturally rather muddy-flavoured and tough-scaled fish into its present domestic excellence. The variety called mirror carp is now found all over eastern Europe, fed in ponds for a year or two until it reaches a weight of 3 to 4 lb/1·5 to 2 kg. The fish are then kept alive in tanks in the fishmarkets, to be individually chosen and scooped out in a net on demand by housewives from the Bosphorus to the Baltic. To a northern visitor enormous fish tanks, crammed with slow bodies and unwinking eyes, are one of the more exotic sights in the markets of eastern Europe.

Prepare the sauce first, as for the chicken *porkolt*. The fish will only take 5 to 10 minutes to cook, depending on the size of the pieces. If you do not fry the onions first, but only lay the pieces of fish on top and add rather more water, you will have the famous *Szeged* fish soup. A 4-lb/2-kg fish will feed 6 people.

CHICKEN AND VEGETABLE STEW
Jachnia (Bulgaria)

A recipe midway between the southern and the northern kitchen. The practice of frying food before stewing liquid is added was introduced into the European kitchen from the Middle East. Its purpose is usually explained as 'sealing in the juices of the meat'. In reality it does no such thing: it is the function of the stewing process to break down such barriers. However, the browning of meat or sugar-rich vegetables like onions gives the dish an appetizing colour and a lovely roasted flavour.

Quantity   Enough for 6 homesteaders
Time   Preparation: 25–30 minutes
      Cooking: 1 hour

1 large chicken (*or* 2 scraggy Bulgarian ones)	1 lb/500 g tomatoes *or* 2 medium tins
1 lb/500 g spring onions with their leaves	8 tablespoons sunflower oil
2 fresh garlics with leaves *or* 4 cloves mature garlic	salt and pepper
1 lb/500 g aubergines	1 tablespoon each fresh savory, mint, parsley

Utensils   A medium-sized stewpot with a lid

Wipe dry and then joint the chicken into 12 pieces. Top and tail the spring onions, leaving the green leaves on. Do the same for the fresh garlics, or peel and chop the mature garlic. Hull, wipe, and cube the aubergines. Chop the tomatoes.

Heat 2 tablespoons of the oil in the stewpot and put in the chicken pieces. Fry the joints gently until they brown. Push them to one side, and add the onions and garlic. Fry them until they soften. Add the rest

135

of the oil and lightly fry the aubergines in it. Season with salt and pepper. Add the tomatoes. Cover and simmer gently for an hour.

Chop the herbs finely and add them 5 minutes before the end of the cooking time.

Serve with rice or bread. There are some good light Bulgarian red wines which would pleasantly accompany the dish.

GARLIC CHICKEN
Poulet à l'ail (France)

A dish to be eaten in the evening. The Gallic gentleman who recommends the recipe follows it with this advice:

> Garlic eaters, assuredly wiser than lotus eaters, have to enjoy their pleasure among themselves. Either everybody eats garlic and delights in its beautiful flavour as well as in the vitamins which make it so healthy — or nobody does so. People who reek of garlic are pests to their neighbours at parties and in public places. Neither is it advisable to arrive at any love or business appointment in an aura of garlic. The results in both cases could be disappointing. Enjoy your garlic at home parties only, maybe for lunch in the country; but in town, only for supper, so that everybody has a good night's sleep ahead to eliminate the fragrance which could be unbearable to others. Garlic has to be restrained to private pleasure.

Quantity   Enough for 4–6 depending on the size of the chicken
Time   Preparation: 20 minutes
          Cooking: 1¼ hours

1 roasting chicken	branches of thyme, rosemary, and
1 wine glass olive oil	mixed herbs (bay, wild thyme,
40 cloves garlic, unpeeled (more if	savory, marjoram, chives,
the chicken is large)	hyssop, chervil, but no
salt and pepper	tarragon)

Utensils   A casserole with a lid which will accommodate the whole chicken

Preheat the oven to 400°F/200°C/Gas 6.

Pour half the oil into the casserole and then put in the unpeeled garlic cloves. Settle the neatly trussed roasting chicken on this pearly bed. Sprinkle with salt and pepper and pour on the rest of the oil. Tuck the branches of herbs all around and on top. Cover tightly, sealing the lid with a flour and water paste if it does not fit absolutely snugly.

Bake the casserole in the oven for 1¼ hours. Use the last 15 minutes waiting time to make a green salad and to cut for each diner 2 or 3 thick slices of bread. Toast the bread under a very hot grill — there are wire grid-contraptions sold in Mediterranean countries for toasting bread over a top flame. This gives a delicious singed flavour to the toast. Large napkins and water bowls for the fingers may be necessary. Call your guests to table and carry in the still-sealed casserole.

When everyone is seated, remove the lid. The scent will be heavenly — and the chicken perfectly cooked and deliciously succulent. The diners help themselves to bread, a piece of chicken, and a few of the whole cloves of garlic which are still sealed in their papery jackets. The garlic cloves are to be squeezed out on to a piece of hot toasted bread — you will find baked garlic tender and remarkably mild and sweet — and topped with a little piece of chicken. Eat it. There are those who put the cloves of garlic straight into the mouth, and then pop the skin with their teeth. Then you have only to solve the delicate problem of transferring the empty shell to the rim of your plate. Continue until all is finished up. Then you can rinse your fingers and take a big draught of cold white wine.

ROAST CHICKEN AND BREAD SAUCE
(England)

The classic English way with a bird. The same method can be used for game birds — pheasant, grouse, and partridge. Today's battery farmers produce table birds so cheaply that roast chicken has overtaken beef in popularity as the British Sunday dinner. The frugal barnyard-tending housewife would not have wasted her future laying hens on such a dish, and only the young roosters would be taken at a tender enough age for roasting. A dish this pure and simple is really only good prepared with a free-range bird. Try and buy the best you can find. The sauce is a recipe which dates back to the bread-thickened sauces of the Middle Ages. It has the peasant virtue of making the meat go further, as well as being an excellent complement to all roast birds.

Quantity Enough for 5–6 modern appetites
Time Preparation: 40 minutes
  Cooking: 1 hour

For the chicken
a 3-lb/1·5-kg roasting chicken, with
  giblets
2 oz/50 g butter
half an onion
a few fresh herbs (thyme,
  rosemary, parsley)

3–4 thin rashers smoked bacon
  (not the wet vacuum-packed
  variety — a piece of thin cut
  fresh pork belly is a better
  substitute)

For the sauce

3 cloves (a luxury for those who
could afford this expensive
spice — wartime recipes usually
instruct readers to rinse them
off and re-use them)

1 onion (*or* the other half of the
one that went into the bird)

½ pint/300 ml milk
salt and pepper
2 oz/50 g fresh breadcrumbs
1 oz/25 g butter and a little cream

Utensils A roasting tin for the chicken and 2 small saucepans for the
bread sauce

Preheat the oven to 375°F/190°C/Gas 5.

Pluck, draw, and truss the chicken if this has not already been done
for you. Spread half the butter over the bird and cover it with the bacon
or pork. Put the onion, herbs, and the rest of the butter inside. Wipe the
liver well, trim off any bitter green bits, and put it inside the bird. A
hollow bird must be stuffed, or it will dry out in the roasting oven.

Put the chicken into the roasting tin. Roast it for 1¼ hours, allowing 25
minutes per 1 lb/500 g. Start the cooking with the bird lying first on one
side and then on the other — leaving it breast-side up for the last half
hour. Baste frequently. Remove the bacon fat from the breast 10
minutes before the end of the cooking time to allow the skin to crisp.
Test by piercing the leg with a skewer — the juices should run clear. If
they run pink it is not yet done, and chickens, particularly battery
chickens, must be well cooked. If no juice runs at all, the chicken is still
raw.

While the chicken cooks, put the gizzard, the neck and heart, and
some peppercorns to simmer in a little water so that you have a stock for
the gravy.

Meanwhile prepare the sauce. Stick the cloves into the onion, and put
it with the milk and the breadcrumbs into a small saucepan to infuse
while the bird is roasting.

Heat the sauce gently 10 minutes before you are ready to serve. Allow
it one big belch and then turn down the heat. Simmer gently for 10
minutes. Stir in a few more breadcrumbs if it is not thick enough —
bread sauce should not be too runny. Add salt and plenty of pepper,
and stir in the butter and cream. Hand separately and very hot, with the
roast bird.

When the bird is cooked to a turn, transfer it to a serving dish and put
it to rest in a barely warm oven while you make a gravy. Strain ½ pint/
300 ml giblet stock into the brown juices in the roasting tin. Boil all
together fiercely, scraping all the sticky little well-flavoured bits into the
gravy. Tip in the juices which have run from the chicken meanwhile.
Taste and adjust the seasoning. Serve in a separate gravy boat.

Accompany the roast chicken with the bread sauce, roast potatoes (see page 373), and a dish of young peas, or little broad beans, or green beans, or carrots tossed with butter.

SUGGESTIONS

• Instead of the onion and herbs, stuff the chicken with a delicate forcemeat made with 2 oz/50 g breadcrumbs mixed with 1 oz/25 g melted butter, plenty of chopped herbs — shallot, parsley, thyme — and the chopped chicken liver, salt, and pepper.

• Feathered game such as pheasant, grouse, and partridge can be cooked in the same way and with the same accompaniments, but with the addition of fried breadcrumbs and a sharp, clear fruit jelly — rowan jelly is particularly good with grouse.

CHICKEN OR TURKEY WITH YOGHURT
(Bulgaria)

Quantity   Enough for 4
Time   Preparation: 30–35 minutes
    Cooking: 30 minutes

1 lb/500 g chicken *or* turkey meat, off the bone	2 leeks
	2 green peppers
1 clove garlic	½ lb/250 g tomatoes *or* 1 medium tin
salt and pepper	1 small cucumber
6 tablespoons oil	handful parsley
1 teaspoon paprika	¼ pint/150 ml thick yoghurt

Utensils   A heavy casserole with a lid

Chop the chicken or turkey meat. Crush the garlic with half a teaspoon of salt and work it into the meat along with a tablespoon of the oil and the paprika. Season with pepper and leave aside to marinate while you prepare the vegetables.

Wash and slice the leeks. Hull and de-seed the peppers, and cut them into chunks. Plunge the tomatoes into boiling water to loosen the skins, peel and chop them. Peel and chunk the cucumber. Wash and chop the parsley finely. All the solid ingredients should be more or less the same size.

Put the oil to heat in the casserole. Sauté the leeks in the hot oil, and then add the peppers. Fry for a moment. Push them to one side and add the marinated meat. Fry for a moment. Add the tomatoes and a tablespoon of water. Cover tightly and simmer for 15 minutes. Add the cucumber pieces. Simmer for 15 minutes more. Stir in the parsley.

Serve in its own casserole, or in a shallow earthenware dish, with the yoghurt poured over it. Plenty of bread, and you will be well content. Finish your meal with black Turkish coffee and a glass of *slivova*.

GRAPE-PICKERS' SOUP
Soupe des vendanges (France)

This is the *soupe* on which the grape harvesters of south-western France sup after a hard day in the fields. The scent will have been curling out of the farmhouse kitchen window all afternoon, and perfuming the soft autumn air in the vineyards below. Unbearable anticipation. The supper soup is eaten in three courses out of large deep-rimmed soup plates: first as a soup, then as a *chabrot*, finally as a boiled dinner of the meat and vegetables. It is a magnificent feast which has its own rhythm and ritual.

Find a huge earthenware pot or saucepan to hold all the meats. In France special *marmites* are sold for just these soup-stews. There is always a pottery merchant in the market who sets up his wares alongside the vegetable stalls. He lines up his stock of *marmites* along the pavement in regiments of descending size, like an army of squat brown-lipped chimney pots on a palace roof. Beside them, still half-swaddled in their skins of brown tissue paper, is his range of speckled enamelled saucepans. Behind them looms a forest of wooden spoons and ladles, peeled-twig whisks, wooden pastry wheels, round wooden boards for cheese, and all manner of odd little kitchen instruments: wire grills for making toast over flame, olive pitters, cocotte dishes, larding needles, snail tongs, skewers, pestles, mortars, mousetraps to supplement the farmyard cat's vigilance — in short all the equipment deemed essential by the French country wife.

Quantity Enough to feed a dozen hungry harvesters
Time Intermittently all afternoon

1 boiling fowl with its own liver, *plus* any unlaid eggs inside *or* 1 whole egg
3 oz/75 g breadcrumbs soaked in 2 tablespoons milk
parsley, chervil, chives, tarragon, salt, and pepper
3 lb/1·5 kg shin of beef on the bone, *plus* a few extra bones
6 fat leeks
2 heads celery
an additional bunch parsley
2 onions
6 cloves
4 cloves garlic
2 lb/1 kg knuckle of veal
2 lb/1 kg turnips
2 lb/1 kg carrots
salt and peppercorns

To accompany the meal
3 lb/1·5 kg ripe tomatoes
1 loaf dry bread
1 lb/500 g Gruyère cheese
1 jar capers
1 large jar pickled gherkins

several bottles strong red wine
(St. Emilion for preference, but
it does depend on where you
do your harvesting)

Utensils A mammoth stewpot or *marmite* — a 25-pint/15-litre monster, a perforated spoon, 1 large and 1 small saucepan, a trussing needle, a liquidizer (optional), and 2 bowls

Put the chicken and the breadcrumbs and herbs aside while you put on the broth, which will take far longer to cook than the rest.

Put the beef and bones into the stewpot or *marmite* and pour in 10 pints/6 litres cold water. Bring all to the boil, allow it one big belch, and then turn the heat down to simmer. Skim off the grey froth which rises. Trim off and add to the pot the tops of the leeks, the leaves of the celery, and the stalks of the parsley. Turn off the heat every time you add fresh meats to the broth, to allow the sediment to settle and so that the broth is as clear as you could wish. Add the onions (unpeeled so that their skins can add a little colour to the soup), stuck with the cloves. Add the garlic cloves, also unpeeled, a dozen peppercorns, and a teaspoon of salt.

Allow all to simmer for half an hour. Then add the knuckle of veal. Bring the soup back to the boil. Then skim off the foam and turn the broth down to simmer. You will be adding the chicken in half an hour.

Skim the fat off, roughly enough, soup and all, from time to time — and put it in a saucepan on the side of the stove.

Meanwhile prepare the chicken. Put the breadcrumbs to soak in the milk for a moment or two, and then squeeze them dry. Chop the chicken liver. Mix the chopped liver with the breadcrumbs and add just a pinch of salt and pepper. Wipe the chicken and pluck out any little feather stumps which have escaped attention. Feel around inside and pull out any unlaid eggs there may be in the cavity of the chicken — they can be added to the stuffing. Chop the herbs and add two tablespoons to the mix. Stuff the bird and sew it up. Turn off the heat and lower the stuffed chicken into the broth. Bring it back to the boil, allow it one big belch, skim it, and turn it down to simmer. If you are using a young bird which has not yet started laying, add an egg to the stuffing and do not put the bird in to cook until an hour before you are ready to dish up.

Simmer the meats for another hour. The soup has now been cooking for 2 hours and you are ready to add the vegetables — the leeks, celery, parsley, turnips, and carrots — rinsed and chopped into short lengths. But first take the pot off the heat, and remove the bones and vegetable debris with the perforated spoon. These leftovers will now be appreciated only by the household pig.

Bring the soup back to the boil with all its meats and vegetables. Then turn it down and simmer for a further 40 minutes.

Meanwhile prepare the accompaniments. Pour boiling water over the tomatoes to loosen the skins, and then peel and chop them. Put them into a small saucepan on a low heat to melt into a sweet fresh sauce (you can put this through the liquidizer if you wish). Cut the stale loaf into thin slices. Grate the cheese. Open the jars of capers and pickled gherkins, and decant them into separate bowls.

Turn your attention back to the stove. Take out all the meats, which should now be soft, and vegetables, which should now be cooked. Put them to keep warm in the large saucepan, which is by now half-full of the oily stock skimmings.

Turn the heat up under the soup, and boil it uncovered for 20 minutes to allow it to reduce and strengthen.

Put deep soup plates and a large serving dish to warm. Go and call the harvesters. When they are at table, remove the soup from the heat and stir in half a ladleful of cold water to send any cloudiness to the bottom. Put a slice of dry bread into each plate, and cover it with a ladleful of the broth. Allow the bread to swell for a moment before handing the plates round. Pass round the grated cheese.

While the soup is being eaten, you can prepare the meats. Take them out of the stock and put them on the serving dish. Put the fat stock back on to the heat. Slice up the beef, the veal, the chicken, and its stuffing. Arrange the vegetables around.

By now the first course has been finished. Put the bottles of red wine on the table. Fill each plate half-full with very hot fat stock. The diners now add as much red wine to their plates as they wish, stir it around, and then, to be strictly correct, drink it straight out of the plate. This process is called *faire chabrot*. No southern-born French countryman would miss it out for the world.

Either hand round fresh deep plates, or give each person a chunk of fresh bread to wipe the old one clean.

It is time for the third course, the boiled dinner. Bathe the meats with a ladleful of hot fat stock, and set the steaming dish on the table for everyone to help themselves to whatever pleases them. Accompany with a bowl of the tomato sauce, lightly seasoned and diluted with a little of the fat stock, the bowl of capers, and the bowl of pickled gherkins.

Peace descends on the company, and you can at last eat your own dinner. Set out a bowl of the year's new walnuts for those who still have a corner to fill.

You will not have to cook again tomorrow: the leftover *bouillon* will reheat to perfection with a handful of new vegetables. Perhaps the next day you might serve such of the meat as remains (tossed with a few capers and gherkins) in a sharp little vinaigrette, well spiked with mustard — but that is tomorrow's problem.

Time now to *faire chabrot* by the fire and hope the harvest will have been good enough for you to do the same for many years to come.

Guineafowl

All recipes for chicken and feathered game are suitable for this recently domesticated bird. Its flavour is somewhere between pheasant and chicken, and it is very popular in the French barnyard. Recipes which make use of wild mushrooms are particularly compatible. Remember the guineafowl if you come across a few morels in the spring or chanterelles in the autumn.

Duck and Goose

DUCK WITH CUCUMBERS
(Romania)

Rural Romanians wove strong fences to keep marauding wild animals at bay — there are still wolves and bears roaming the uplands of the Carpathians today. The poultry would wander free in the yard during the day, protected by the basketwork walls which encircled the small-holding. Romanian farmwives found the duck feathers useful for stuffing the household's bedding. Duck and goose bones weigh heavy, so there is always comparatively little meat on the birds. This is a light and delicious way with the rich flesh.

Quantity Enough for 4
Time Preparation: 30 minutes
        Cooking: 40 minutes

1 duck for roasting	1 glass water
salt and pepper	1 lb/500 g small pickling
1 tablespoon chopped marjoram	cucumbers *or* 1 large cucumber
4 tablespoons sunflower oil	2 medium onions

Utensils A heavy shallow casserole with a lid and a frying pan

Wipe and then quarter the bird. Rub it well with salt, pepper, and marjoram. Put a tablespoon of the oil to heat in the casserole. When it is lightly smoking, put in the duck pieces and turn them until they take colour. Add the glass of water and cover the casserole. Leave them to simmer for 30 to 40 minutes until they are tender.

Meanwhile grate the cucumbers and put them to drain. Peel and slice the onions and fry them gently in the frying pan with the rest of the oil. Ten minutes before the end of the cooking time of the duck, add the onions and cucumbers to the casserole. Finish cooking all together.

Serve after a dish of *mamaliga* baked with soured cream (see page 273). Cool white wine to accompany.

POTTED GOOSE OR DUCK
Confit d'oie ou de canard (France)

Anser segetum, the wild goose, is the begetter of all geese used for food in Europe. For roasting there is a breed known as the grey or farmyard goose, which attains a weight of 8 to 10 lb/4 to 5 kg before being ready for the table. The goose which is fattened for the sake of its liver and for potting is the Toulouse goose, which can grow to a net weight of 20 to 24 lb/10 to 12 kg, of which up to 4 lb/2 kg can be liver. This larger bird is really best suited to the *confit* pot — it is too rich and fatty to be roasted in the normal way.

The *confit* pot is one of the most useful storage items in the French farmhouse kitchen. The meat is succulent and wonderfully well flavoured, while the goose butter in which it is preserved can be used to make the simplest of dishes, such as plain sautéed potatoes, into food for the gods. It is used in many of the beans-and-bones dishes and the *garbures* which defy the icy winds that sweep the Languedoc plain in winter.

The household *confit* is prepared sometime between mid-October and early January, when the geese that have been fattened for the Christmas *foie gras* are sent to market. Mme Escrieu, my Languedoc neighbour, fattened her own geese: two for her family storecupboard, and perhaps three or four more birds as her small cash crop. Acorns and walnuts collected by the children, maize from a corner of the vegetable patch, and greens gathered from the neighbouring hedgerows, all went to fatten her flock. By early September the great white and grey birds had disappeared from the yard, and *la mère* Escrieu was to be seen disappearing into one of her steadings with a basket of chestnuts and acorns.

Preparing the geese for market is women's work as the care of the barnyard always has been, whether it involves the plump doves in the loft or the rooster outside the kitchen door. Any financial return from the sale of eggs or *foie gras* goes into a corner of the housewife's apron. Mme Escrieu took her crop to the Saturday market in the local town of Revel, the wicker baskets bulging inside her son's battered pick-up truck. Once there, she would lay out the carcasses plucked clean to the polished ivory skin on white cloths spread over trestle tables in the square. The women of the town prodded her wares and interrogated her carefully about their diet and habitat — the size of the unseen liver, the *foie gras*, is at the purchaser's own risk. Then, her sales made, Mme Escrieu would replace the birds from the box of new-hatched goslings under the poultry man's conveniently adjacent stall.

The cycle began again when she returned home and the fluffy little creatures were installed in the farmhouse kitchen, warm in a corner by the stove inside a shoebox lined with an old winter coat. There they were cosseted like new-born babies all through the first cold weeks of spring.

Quantity   Enough for a small family's winter supply
Time   Start two days before
Preparation intermittently: 1–2 hours

2 plump geese *or* domestic ducks — preferably those which have been fattened for *foie gras*	additional pure white pork dripping (the exact quantity depending on the fatness of the birds)
salt	
5 cloves garlic	6 cloves
small bunch thyme	1 teaspoon peppercorns

Utensils   A very heavy iron pot and a straight-sided earthenware storage jar

Quarter the birds and remove all their interior fat. The livers you will, of course, have potted for another purpose. The rest of the giblets will do very well for a giblet stew (see page 147).

Put the golden fat to render slowly in the iron pot until it has completely liquified. Save the little crisp golden nuggets which are all that remain of the solids, and salt them for the children to nibble.

Meanwhile rub the goose joints with rough salt. Leave them to cure in their own brine for at least 24 hours. Then brush off the excess salt and pat dry. Warm the goose fat — add extra dripping as you think you need it — with the peeled garlic cloves, a few sprigs of thyme, the cloves and peppercorns, and when hot, but not smoking, put in the goose joints. Cook gently for an hour. The meat must be thoroughly cooked. Test it with a skewer and when the juice runs clear rather than pink, it is done. Lay the pieces in the earthenware crock and pour the fat over them, making sure all is submerged. Next day, pour another layer of pure lard over to seal. Press a circle of greaseproof paper directly on to the solidified lard, and tie more paper over the top.

Confit can be kept for months in a cool dry place. Whenever you take a piece of goose out, make sure the remaining pieces are completely covered with fat.

SUGGESTIONS

● Apart from its use in the *cassoulet* (see page 257) and the *garbure* (see page 370), there are many delicious dishes in which the *confit* stars. These are my favourites.

Confit with potatoes   Take out a piece of *confit* and warm it in its own fat. Meanwhile peel and boil a sufficiency of potatoes — remembering that a sufficiency of this dish is never quite enough. When the potatoes are soft, slice them while they are still hot and put them to sauté in the goose fat. They are ready when they are golden brown and flecked with little crisp bits. For absolute perfection, include a few slivers of black Perigord truffle (see page 432). Even the medieval Albigensians, whose famous heresy held the world to be the domain of the devil, might be moved to call the dish heavenly.

Confit with cèpes (see page 427)   Take out a piece of *confit* and warm it in its own fat. Slice the *cèpes* and sauté them in the goose fat. Toss in as you finish the cooking a handful of chopped parsley and garlic crushed in a very little salt. There is something very compatible about geese and mushrooms.

Confit with cabbage   Geese are grazing beasts. In Hungary they crop the roadside meadows like cattle, so perhaps their affinity with green cabbage is unsurprising. Slice, wash, and cook a small cabbage in the water which dews the leaves after rinsing. Take out a piece of *confit* and warm it in its own fat in a heavy casserole. Remove the piece of goose. Keep it warm. Put the lightly cooked cabbage to fry gently in the goose fat for a few minutes. Put the *confit* back and braise all together for 20 minutes.

POTTED GOOSE LIVER
Confit de foie gras (France)

Selecting your *foie gras* is much easier if it has already been removed from its original owner. If it is still in the bird, as is normally the case in French country markets, feel the tautness of the surrounding skin and the swell of its curves. A plump skin, pearly with fat, is a fair indication that the liver will be a good one. If you can examine the liver itself, you are looking for an object which is firm to the finger, pale as ivory, and only lightly tinged with pink. There should be as few dark veins as possible. Toulouse and Strasburg are the two main centres in France. Austria, Hungary, and Czechoslovakia also produce good *foie gras*, although it never seems to achieve the creamy perfection of the farmwife's hand-reared goose of Toulouse.

Quantity   Enough for 6–8
Time   Start the day before
　　　　　Preparation: 10 minutes
　　　　　Cooking: 1–1½ hours

1 fresh *foie gras*
1 tablespoon salt
small glass brandy *(optional)*

Utensils   Preserving jars with lids, and a large saucepan or roasting tin

Detach the *foie* from the cavity of the bird with care. Check the surface for dark blood vessels or veins, and gently remove them. Look also for the dark streak of green which betrays a bitter gall-bladder stain. Sprinkle the *foie* with salt and leave overnight under a weighted plate. There are those who also sprinkle on a small glass of brandy. Mme Escrieu, whose instructions these are, preferred to drink the brandy as she contemplated the pleasure to come. The following morning, drain, pat dry, and wipe off any excess salt.

Sterilize the jars. For convenience, divide the *foie* into 1 lb/500 g pieces and pack into suitably sized jars. Clip down the lids to seal and place the jars in a pan of water. Boil steadily for 1 hour if the *foie* weighs 1 lb/500 g, 1½ hours for a 2 lb/1 kg *foie*, or bake the jars, standing in a pan of water, in a fairly hot oven, 350°F/190°C/Gas 4, for 10 minutes longer than you need for the top heat.

The *foie gras* will keep, unopened and in a cool place, for several months if need be and you can withstand the temptation. The French enjoy their *foie gras* in the company of the best sweet wine the neighbourhood can offer. Those who live near Château Yquem are doubly blessed.

STEW OF DUCK OR GOOSE GIBLETS
Alicot (Central France)

The goose is a versatile bird: there is barely one part of the creature which cannot be made into an excellent dish. This stew is designed to be made with the fresh giblets (excluding the liver, of course) of a fine, fat *foie gras* goose on the evening of market day, after you have potted the *foie gras* and put up your *confit*. The dish can also be prepared from the giblets of an ordinary roasting goose, or indeed from those of a duck. However, you will miss the pale, sweet goose fat which the Romans, who prized it more highly than butter, considered an aphrodisiac. It should be remembered that the Romans considered many curious things to be aphrodisiac — and on the flimsiest of evidence. The true aphrodisiac nature of goose fat may have been better recognized by the beauties of medieval times, who used it as the basis for complexion creams and body lotions.

Quantity　Enough for 6–8
Time　Preparation: 25–30 minutes
　　　　　Cooking: 2–3 hours

2 lb/1 kg duck *or* goose giblets (hearts, gizzards, necks, wing tips)
1 lb/500 g onions
4 cloves garlic
1 tablespoon goose dripping *or* lard
½ lb/250 g salt pork *or* bacon

3 large carrots
1 lb/500 g tomatoes *or* 2 medium tins
½ pint/300 ml stock *or* white wine and water
peppercorns
bouquet bayleaf, rosemary, thyme, and parsley

Utensils　A heavy casserole with a lid

Peel and chop the onions and the garlic. Put the dripping to melt in the casserole. Add the onions and garlic and leave them to fry gently while you cube the pork or bacon. Wipe and slice the giblets where necessary. Push the onions to one side, and add the meat and the giblets.

Preheat the oven to 300°F/150°C/Gas 2.

Leave them sizzling quietly while you scrape and slice the carrots, and peel and chop the tomatoes. (Cover the tomatoes with boiling water first to loosen the skins. Tomato skins never seem to break down however long you cook them, and end up, after 3 or 4 hours stewing, marooned in the sauce like spars from a shipwreck.)

Add the vegetables and stew all together for a moment. Pour in the liquid, with a few peppercorns and the bouquet of herbs. Cover tightly and put into the oven to simmer slowly for 2 to 3 hours.

Delicious with a dish of white haricot beans, stewed with a little garlic, herbs, and olive oil. Or served quite simply with bread and a delicate green salad.

CHAPTER 4

Pork and Storehouse Meats

The most important domestic animal in the peasant yard was always the pig. The winter larder depended on him, and the autumn pig-killing was an occasion for celebration and thanksgiving. Mlle Louise Morell, born at the turn of the century in Buis-les-Baronnies, in the hills of Provence, recalled for me the responsibilities of her childhood:

'While Grandmother was alive, our family always had a pig, or if it had been a good year, two — one to sell in the market. The pig was an important member of the household. He lived in a shed at the back of the house, and it was my special responsibility to feed him, morning, noon and evening. His morning and evening meals were the peelings and gratings from the day's vegetables. I had to wash them and boil them, and then they had to be mashed. At midday he had grain swollen in water. I was small and a little scared he might bite me, so my father cut a flap into the wooden wall for me to push the dish in and out.

'By late October the vegetables were running out and the pig was fully grown. I was always given a new baby pig in the spring, but that October pig was ripe for sausages and hams. Grandmother made wonderful hams. She had a special old wooden drawer for the salting. Her hams always took the salt better than anyone else's. It was the wooden drawer, Grandmother said — it was like an old midwife who knew her business. And she would rub just a little pepper round the bone. That's all. Nothing else. Then when the brine had finished running, when there was no more juice, the hams would be bound in special clean white cloths and hung up from the beam. And there would be ham until Pentecost.

'The rest of the meat was made into sausages. Grandmother prepared them with rosemary and thyme, with garlic, with pepper, the meat chopped sometimes large, sometimes small, the finished sausages, salted and dried and then rolled in flour to keep them fresh. I would help Grandmother wash and salt the intestines, scrubbing and bleaching them until they were as white and clean as her ham cloths. I had a child's quick little fingers and I was good at stuffing the skins. I would sit on the table pushing the mixture through the funnel into the long white tubes, while my mother made black pudding with the pig's blood. They looked like long snakes, the black pudding coiled into the enamel bucket until it was full. My sausages were salted and hung up to dry in the cold larder, and I had one more duty to perform. The *boudins* had to be cooked in salted water until they were firm — the water could not be allowed to boil or the skins would burst, so I had to watch that the bubbles in the water did not get too large.'

The tripes of the pig would be prepared for the evening meal, Mlle Morell said, stewed slowly with wine and a few carrots, a turnip or two, and a bunch of fresh herbs from the *garrigues*, and the neighbours and perhaps the curé would be invited in.

SPINACH FAGGOTS
Caillettes aux épinards (France)

'Let me tell you the best of all,' Mlle Morell finished.

'Later in the year Grandmother would make her own speciality after the pig-killing, her spinach *boudin*. Sometimes, as it was late in the year, there was not much left in the vegetable patch. Then she would chop cabbage and chard in with the mixture too, together with a handful of minced sweet pork fat, a chopped onion, and a little garlic. She cooked them with a little more pork fat and a glass of wine, in the earthenware casserole which sat on its tripod by the fire. Other people made these sausages — but they all said Grandmother's were a work of art.'

Quantity   Enough for 6 as a light meal
Time   Preparation: 45–50 minutes
Cooking: 1–1½ hours

3 lb/1·5 kg spinach
a few leaves sorrel
4 oz/100 g pork liver
8 oz/250 g pork belly (fat pork, without skin)
1 onion
3 cloves garlic

parsley
salt and pepper
8 oz/250 g pig's caul (this is not vital)
1 oz/25 g lard
1 glass dry white wine

Utensils   A saucepan, a gratin dish or a pâté dish with something to cover it, and a food processor if you have one

Wash and strip out the leaves of the spinach. Put the spinach and the sorrel to blanch in a pan of boiling water for a few minutes. When the leaves have wilted, drain them and squeeze out all the liquid. Chop up the spinach very thoroughly with the lean and fat pork (a sharp knife or a processor is better for this than a mincer), the peeled onion and garlic, the parsley, the salt, and the pepper.

Preheat the oven to 325°F/170°C/Gas 3.

Make 6 balls with the stuffing, enclose each in a caul, and place them in the gratin dish. Dot with lard, pour the wine around, cover and bake in the oven for an hour.

If your butcher cannot supply caul, you can bake the mixture as if it were a pâté — in which case include the wine in the mixture, pack it into a pâté dish, and lay thin slices of pork fat over the top. It will need 1½ hours in a moderate oven (325°F/170°C/Gas 3).

Serve with bread and a glass of chilled sweet white wine. A salad and cheese to complete a light meal.

COUNTRY PATE
Pâté de campagne (France)

Every French charcuterie worthy of the name has its own recipe, and every French country housewife has her own secret variation. The basic mix is pork, but other meats can be included, particularly poultry and game. These pâtés used to be encased in pastry, as in England they still are in pork pies.

Quantity   Makes a 3 lb/1·5 kg pâté
Time   Start the day before
Preparation: 30–40 minutes
Cooking: 2–3 hours

2 lb/1 kg lean pork
1 lb/500 g pork back fat without rind (if you are in France ask for ½ lb/250 g each *panne* and *gras dur*)
1 teaspoon salt, ½ teaspoon peppercorns, 1 teaspoon allspice and juniper berries, thyme, parsley, 1–2 cloves garlic

1 small glass brandy
6 oz/175 g fine-cut streaky bacon *or* 6 oz/175 g extra back pork
½ lb/250 g onions
2 oz/50 g butter
1 egg
2 glasses white wine
1 oz/25 g fresh breadcrumbs

Utensils   A large bowl, a small frying pan, a medium-sized pâté dish, a roasting tin, a food processor if you have one, and some foil

Mince or chop the lean pork and the pork fat, and put it in the bowl. Pound the salt, all the spices and herbs, and the peeled garlic together. Work the crushed spices well into the meat with the brandy. Leave to marinate overnight. If you are using back pork instead of bacon, rub salt in it and leave it to take the salt overnight as well.

Next day, peel and chop the onions finely. Melt the butter in a small frying pan and fry the onions gently until they soften. Add them to the marinated meat and mix them in with the egg, lightly beaten up with the wine and the breadcrumbs.

Line the pâté dish with the bacon or salted piece of pork fat sliced as finely as possible. Leave long ends hanging down at the sides to fold over and seal the top. Pack the meat mixture into the middle. Fold over the ends.

Cover with foil and put it in the roasting tin filled with water in a moderate oven, 325°F/170°C/Gas 3, for 2 to 3 hours (the depth of your tin is the determining factor). When the sides are pulled away and the juice runs clear, the pâté is done. Leave it to cool under a weight overnight. Eat within 3 days, with crusty bread, unsalted butter, and a bunch of well-washed radishes.

SUGGESTIONS
● Cook the mixture in a sealed preserving jar. Same oven time, but it will keep for far longer.

ROAST PORK AND APPLE SAUCE
(England)

A favourite roasting joint and one which was always more widely available to country households. A pig could be fattened not only on kitchen scraps, but on windfall apples in the orchards and on the edges of communal woodland. The leg, shoulder, and loin are all suitable joints for roasting. Unlike the rest of Europe, the English like to roast their pork with the skin on, to produce a delicious crisp crackling. Your butcher will score it for you with a sharp knife.

Quantity   Enough for 5–6
Time   Preparation: 15–20 minutes
        Cooking: 1¼ hours

3 lb/1·5 kg pork joint on the bone, with its skin on, scored heavily so that the skin can crisp to crackling	salt and pepper
	a few sage leaves
	1½ lb/750 g sharp apples
	½ tablespoon flour
lard *or* oil	1 glass cider

Utensils   A roasting tin and a small heatproof dish with a lid

Preheat the oven to 375°F/190°C/Gas 5.

Dry the pork very thoroughly with a clean cloth. It will not crisp properly otherwise. Rub the skin with the lard or oil, and sprinkle salt and pepper over the flesh-side. Tuck the sage leaves in near the bone.

Put the joint to cook on a grid in the oven, with a roasting tin beneath to catch the drippings. Allow 25 minutes per 1 lb/500 g, so this joint will need 1¼ hours. Baste the meat regularly. Meanwhile prepare the rest of the accompaniments to the Sunday lunch.

Peel, quarter, and core the apples, and put them in the covered dish in the oven for the last 40 minutes of the cooking time. They will melt down into a thick sauce. Hand this round separately.

Turn the oven heat up at the end of the cooking time to crisp the crackling. Take the meat out when it is thoroughly cooked — the juices should run clear when you pierce the joint with a skewer. Transfer the joint to the warm serving dish. Allow the meat to settle for 15 to 20 minutes before you carve it.

To make a gravy, pour off most of the fat from the roasting tin and stir in the flour. Fry for a moment and then stir in the cider. Boil fiercely for a few seconds to evaporate the alcohol. Dilute with half a glass of water. Boil up the gravy again, stirring to make sure it is not lumpy. You can strain it if it looks too bitty. Hand it round separately in a jug or gravy boat.

Plain boiled potatoes are the best accompaniment for the pork — it is a very rich meat. Save the delicious dripping to roast vegetables for another meal (see page 372). There are those who reckon Sunday dinner *must* include roast potatoes, so you may have to bow to pressure and cook a few, parboiled first and then roasted for 40 to 50 minutes in the dripping tray along with some stuffing balls (see Suggestions).

SUGGESTIONS
Sage and onion stuffing balls   Make these to accompany the pork with 4 oz/100 g breadcrumbs, soaked and squeezed out, bound with an egg and melted dripping, and flavoured with a finely chopped onion and a tablespoon of chopped sage. Add salt and pepper. Put the balls to roast in the tray under the meat — pour out and save any excess fat for basting the meat. They should be nicely crisp after 30 to 40 minutes.

BRAWN
(England)

Brawn or head cheese is made from the meat and skin of a pig's head (or indeed a calf's head or sheep's head), sometimes salted first, sometimes not. It can include any other trimmings: heart, trotters, and tail, or even a piece of shin of beef. Whatever the ingredients, they must be well boiled with aromatics until all is soft and gelatinous. A most excellent dish.

Quantity   Enough for 6 for breakfast or supper
Time   Best if you start it in pickle 2 days before, plus 24 hours to set
       Preparation: 30 minutes
       Cooking: 4 hours

1 pig's head, complete with ears and tongue	1 teaspoon peppercorns
	3–4 bayleaves
4 oz/100 g salt and $\frac{1}{2}$ oz/12 g saltpetre *(optional)*	1 teaspoon salt
bunch of sage	onion skins (the papery brown outside only)

Utensils   A large stewpot, a perforated spoon, and a pudding basin or mould

If you want the brawn to be a pretty pink, put it to pickle rubbed with the salt and saltpetre for 48 hours before cooking.

Have the butcher split the head in two. Put it in the stewpot which should just accommodate the meat, with the aromatics, the salt, and the onion skins (these serve to tint the jelly a pale gold, but the onion itself is not used as it would encourage the jelly to ferment). Cover with cold water. Bring all to the boil, and then turn down the heat and skim the froth off the liquid.

Simmer steadily for 4 hours, until the meat virtually drops off the bones. Take out all the solids and strain the stock back into the pan. Leave the stock to boil and reduce uncovered while you pick the meat off the bones. Chop all the pieces and pack them neatly into the pudding basin or mould.

When the stock is well reduced to about 1 pint/600 ml, taste and adjust its seasoning and pour it over the meats. Allow it to cool, and then put it in the larder or refrigerator for 24 hours for the jelly to set solid. When you are ready to eat it, unmould by pouring hot water swiftly over the outside. It will unmould instantly and elegantly. Serve on a bed of watercress or parsley.

Brawn will keep in a cool larder or refrigerator for 2 weeks, but don't store it in the deep-freeze or the jelly is likely to liquify when you defrost it.

Serve plenty of strong English mustard with the cold brawn, or a jug of white sauce vigorously flavoured with mustard. Baked potatoes to accompany.

SUGGESTIONS

• If you are going to eat the brawn straight away, stir plenty of chopped parsley and a little grated lemon rind into the jelly when it is cool but still liquid, before you pour it over the meat.

• For a sharper flavour add a tablespoon of vinegar to the stock before its final reduction.

• *Pihti* is the very similar Christmas dish of brawn prepared in Greek villages. Carrots and 2 or 3 sliced hard-boiled eggs are set in the jelly with the meat from the pig's head.

• *Disznokocsonya* is the name for the dish as prepared in Hungary. Pig's head, tongue, knuckle, feet, salt, a clove or two of garlic, and a teaspoon of peppercorns are boiled all together for 4 hours. Strip the flesh from the bones and chop the meats into squares. Pack them into a deep basin. Skim all fat from the cooking liquid and boil until reduced to about 2 pints/1·2 litres. Clarify by stirring in the beaten whites of 2 eggs, and boil them so that all the impurities are gathered in. Strain and pour over the meats. Leave to set overnight.

RAISED PORK PIE
(England)

The heir to the medieval 'coffin' pie — a solid structure in which all manner of game could be cooked and stored. The 'coffin' in turn was the heir to the ancient practice of protecting small meats, such as birds and rabbits, from the fierce heat of the fire when they were being spit-roasted over an open hearth.

The pie was designed to remain good for a long time without refrigeration, so the recipe includes nothing that will encourage it to go bad, such as onions or vegetables.

Quantity   Makes 2 pies, each of which will feed 4–5 people
Time   Preparation: 1 hour
Cooking: 2¼ hours

For the filling
3 lb/1·5 kg lean pork (weighed when off the bone — keep the bones for the stock)
1 lb/500 g fresh firm pork belly
salt
white *or* black pepper

herbs according to the district — sage and marjoram are good
2 pig's trotters, blanched and split
peppercorns
onion skins (the papery brown outside only)

For the pastry
1 teaspoon salt
2 lb/1 kg plain flour
½ pint/300 ml milk and water mixed

6 oz/175 g butter
6 oz/175 g lard
beaten egg

Utensils   A large stewpot, a perforated spoon, a fine sieve, a small saucepan, a food mixer if you have one, and a baking tray or two baking tins, preferably raised-pie tins with hinged sides

Strip the meat from its bones and chop roughly. Chop the pork fat very fine and mix it into the meat. Season well with the salt, pepper, and chopped herbs, and leave aside to absorb the flavours.

Put the bones into the large stewpot with the pig's trotters, a few peppercorns, salt, and the onion skins to give the stock colour (no onion flesh or the keeping qualities of the jelly will be impaired). Cover with cold water, bring to the boil, and skim off any grey foam which rises. Simmer gently for one or two hours, uncovered, to reduce to under 1 pint/600 ml liquid. If the hot stock is not clear, pour it over a beaten egg white, bring nearly back to the boil, and then remove it from the heat and allow to settle. Pour it through a fine sieve — you will find the egg white has collected all the impurities and it will strain out clear. Leave all to rest while you make the pastry.

Hot-water crust is the pastry used to make a hand-raised pie crust — that is, a crust which holds its shape without being held in position by a tin. Mix the salt into the flour and pour into a warm bowl. Put the milk and water, butter and lard into a saucepan and bring to the boil. Pour the hot liquid into a well in the flour, mixing hard with a wooden spoon. (You may need a little less or a little more liquid, so have a kettle of boiling water available.) This operation is important and the liquid must be poured and beaten in while still scalding — you may need an assistant to pour. You should now have a ball of slightly translucent dough. As soon as it is cool enough to handle, knead the dough thoroughly by hand. If you have a mixer, it can be beaten with the dough hook immediately. Leave the dough to develop in a warm place for half an hour. Do not allow it to get cold, or it will crumble when you work it. Too hot and it will collapse down the sides of the tin. Cut the dough in half and keep the half you are not working warm.

Take three-quarters of the dough and roll it into a ball. If you have the special raised-pie tins with hinged sides that unclip to allow the sides to brown, it will be an easy job to work the pastry over and up the sides.

If not, you will have to set about the task in the old-fashioned way: slice a quarter off the top of the half you are working and hollow the rest out by pressing and knuckling with your fist. Or mould the crust round the outside of a wooden cylinder (the instrument looks like a short, fat single-handled rolling pin). A glass preserving jar or an earthenware straight-sided pot will do as a mould. It should be floured first and the pastry allowed to cool before the mould is removed. Shape the second pie. When the pastry shapes are cold remove the moulds. Fill each pie with half the meat mixture. Pack all well in. There must be no gaps. Pour in as much reduced stock as will reach to within 1 in/2·5 cm of the top. Use the two quarters remaining from each half of the dough, press out the lids and lay them over. Damp and mark the edges with a fork to seal. Cut a hole in the middle for the steam. Decorate them as it pleases you — this dough is an excellent medium for artists. Gild with beaten egg.

Bake for 1 hour at 350°F/180°C/Gas 4. Then turn the oven down to 325°F/170°C/Gas 3 and bake the pies for another 1¼ hours. Test by running a skewer into the meat through the steam hole. When the juice runs clear, it is cooked. Reheat the reduced stock as soon as the pie is out of the oven and pour in as much as you can. Allow to cool — overnight is best to allow the jelly to set.

SUGGESTIONS
• A firm shortcrust pastry made with 2 lb/1 kg flour, 1 lb/500 g fat will do duty instead of the hot crust.

- There were many regional variations on the pie: Nottingham liked a pie made with sour gooseberries instead of meat, and glazed when cold with melted apple jelly.
- Veal, ham, and chopped fat bacon make a good pie.
- Chopped apples or berries can be included in the stuffing.
- The lean pork can be replaced by chopped and skinned boned game, in whatever proportion is liked. Don't omit the pork fat or you will have a very dry pie. Game is good spiced with juniper berries and thyme.
- A hard-boiled egg is sometimes included in the pork or veal-and-ham version.

PIG HAGGIS
(Ireland)

The pig's stomach was the gift to the helper at the pig-killing. Wash the stomach very thoroughly, and stuff it with potatoes boiled and mashed with onions and bacon fat. Roast for 2–3 hours in a medium oven.

SILESIAN PORK
Schlesische Himmelreich (Germany)

A typically northern dish which combines rich sweet pork and a sharp fruit compote, served with potato dumplings to mop up their mingled juices. Sweet and sour are very much at home together in the German kitchen.

Quantity Enough for 4
Time Start the day before if possible
          Preparation: 10 minutes
          Cooking: 35 minutes

 1 lb/500 g dried fruit (prunes,
    apricots, apples)
 4 fine pork chops *or* 1 lb/500 g lean
    pork steaks
 2 oz/50 g lard *or* butter

Utensils A medium-sized stewpot with a lid

Soak the fruit for a couple of hours, or overnight if possible, either in plain water to cover or cold tea, which will give them a darker, richer juice.

Fry the chops in the fat, turning them once, so that they take colour.

Add the fruit and the soaking liquid. Cover and simmer all together for 30 to 35 minutes, until the fruit is soft and the chops cooked through.

Meanwhile make potato dumplings (see page 330). Serve them with the pork and fruit stew.

SUGGESTIONS
- In autumn, replace the dried fruit with peeled and quartered fresh apples.
- Serve plain boiled potatoes instead of the dumplings.

LITTLE KEBABS
Pinchitos ('Little Thorns' — Spain)

A relic of the Moorish occupation when the meat used was anything but pork, this is one of the most popular snacks at the carnival *ferias*, which are held annually in every village and town, rich or poor, large or small, throughout Spain. The *pinchito* specialist travels round with the floats and amusements and circus turns, and sets up his tiny open-air kitchen beside the best-patronized local bar in whatever town has booked its *feria* for the week (in small villages it might only be for a day or two). The *pinchito*-man is an expert at spicing and marinating his meat, which he then strings on long thin skewers. These days very fine stainless steel knitting needles are the preferred instrument, and the purchaser is honour bound to return the needles. The *pinchitos* are grilled to order over a Moorish brazier — a charcoal-fuelled oblong metal box — by the vendor himself, who usually sports a Moroccan fez whatever his ethnic origin. A small piece of bread is included speared on the end.

Quantity Enough for 4–6
Time Start the day before if possible
Preparation: 20 minutes

1 lb/500 g pork (other meats such as beef or even liver can be used)	paprika (sometimes turmeric is used as well or instead)
1 teaspoon cumin seeds	½ teaspoon powdered hot chilli pepper
½ teaspoon black pepper	4 tablespoons olive oil
1 teaspoon coriander seeds *or* a small bunch fresh coriander	salt

Utensils A pestle and mortar, a bowl, a dozen fine skewers, and a grill or barbecue

Cut the meat into small cubes no more than ½ in/1 cm square — this is why the skewers have to be so thin. Pound up the spices in the mortar. Marinate the meat in the spices and the oil overnight if possible.

Heat the barbecue or grill.

Thread the meat on to skewers. Grill over charcoal, or under the hottest possible grill. As soon as the heat warms the spices, the meat begins to smell wonderful — no wonder the *pinchito*-sellers do such a good trade.

When the meat is crisply charred, sprinkle with salt and serve with a chunk of bread skewered on the end so that each piece of meat can be gripped and pulled off in it. Tankards of iced beer to wash it down. There will be plenty of time for more — during *feria* the night is always young.

BACON PANCAKES
Spekpannekoeken (Holland)

As a pig-keeping and farming community of long standing, all the ingredients for these pancakes come easily to hand in Holland.

Quantity   Makes 6 pancakes
Time   Preparation: 15 minutes
              Cooking: 30 minutes

6 oz/175 g plain flour	½ pint/300 ml milk
2 eggs	½ lb/250 g fine cut smoked bacon

Utensils   A bowl and a frying pan

Put the flour in the bowl and make a well in the centre. Stir in the eggs and the milk. Beat vigorously until the mix is smooth and airy. Allow to stand for half an hour or so.

Cut each bacon strip across the middle into 4. Heat a small frying pan and fry 4 small pieces of bacon until crisp. They should yield enough fat for no further greasing of the pan to be necessary. Leave the bacon in the pan and pour in enough of the batter to cover the bottom of the pan. Fry the pancake, flipping it over as soon as the edges curl away from the pan and the mixture looks dry on top. Repeat until batter and bacon are all used up. Serve from the pan, with honey or golden syrup on the side.

SUGGESTIONS
● The pancakes can be made on their own, without the bacon.
● There is a substantial 'farmhouse' version, too: along with the bacon, fry a few cooked, chopped carrots and potatoes and a spoonful of chopped onion or leek.

PORK AND HERRINGS
Kallalaatiko (Finland)

A very characteristic north European dish: the Finns say that pork keeps you warm and warmth keeps you loving.

Quantity   Enough for 4
Time   Preparation: 25–30 minutes
         Cooking: 1½ hours

4 pork chops	1 oz/25 g butter
2 fresh herrings	2 eggs
4 medium-sized potatoes	1 pint/600 ml milk
4 onions	salt and pepper

Utensils   A casserole

Preheat the oven to 350°F/180°C/Gas 4.

Wipe, gut, split, and bone the herrings. Cut off the heads and tails. Peel and slice the potatoes and the onions.

Butter the casserole and, seasoning as you go, put in a layer of onions, followed by a layer of potatoes, then the herrings, laid flat, then the pork, then another layer of onions. Finish with potatoes. Cook in the oven for 1 hour.

Mix the eggs with the milk. Season. Pour this custard into the dish and put it back to cook for another half hour. It cooks for 1½ hours in all. There is your warmth. You will have to find your own loving — try a glass of vodka to help you on your way.

BLACK PUDDINGS
(England)

English black puddings can be made with blood from a pig — in bygone days the blood from sheep or cattle was used as well. The fresh blood is mixed with a cereal, usually fine oatmeal or barley, and with chopped suet. In some districts liver was included in the home-made mix. The pudding was usually stuffed into casings, which in some districts were brushed with blood before baking to give them their characteristic black skin. In the south and west the mixture is sometimes cooked in metal or earthenware pans.

This recipe is an excellent light mixture from Westmoreland, which I include for anyone who has access to the necessary central ingredient. The dish is well worth making if you are wise enough to keep your own pigs.

Quantity   Makes plenty
Time   Preparation: 30 minutes
    Cooking: 1 hour

2 pints/1·2 litres fresh pig's blood	8 oz/250 g fine oatmeal
8 oz/250 g bread cut into cubes	1 teaspoon salt
2 pints/1·2 litres fresh *or* skimmed milk	2 teaspoons ground black pepper
1 lb/500 g cooked barley	2 teaspoons dried and crumbled mint
1 lb/500 g fresh beef suet	

Utensils   2 to 3 large roasting tins and a large bowl

Put the bread cubes to soak in the milk in a warm oven (do not heat the milk beyond blood temperature). Have the blood ready in a large bowl, and pour the warm milk and bread into it. Stir in the cooked barley. Grate the beef suet into the mixture and stir it up with the oatmeal. Season with the salt, pepper, and mint.

Grease the large roasting tins thoroughly. Divide the mixture between them — they should not be more than three-quarters full. Bake in a moderate oven — 350°F/180°C/Gas 4 — for about an hour, or until the pudding is well cooked through. This makes a beautifully light pudding which will keep well in a cold larder.

Cut into squares and fry till heated through and the outside is crisp, in bacon fat or butter. Delicious for breakfast, or for supper with fried apples and mashed potato.

SUGGESTIONS
● All the nations of Europe have their own black puddings. The French like theirs mixed with cream and eggs, the Spaniards flavour theirs with paprika and garlic, the Scandinavians like theirs sweet with raisins and will eat them with sugar and treacle.

SAUSAGES AND MASH
(England)

It is worth searching out a good butcher who makes his own pure meat sausages and does not bulk them out with rusk or breadcrumbs. Cumberland produces some good traditional sausages still: the long casings are not sealed off into links as they are elsewhere, and the sausage can be fried in a single snail-curled length. If you cannot find good ones, make your own. Well made, this dish is fit for king as well as peasant. A perfectly prepared sausage and mash is one of the chief glories of the English kitchen. It depends on the excellence of its ingredients — old floury potatoes are as essential as good sausages.

Quantity   Makes 4 lb/2 kg sausages — 2 lb/1 kg will feed 5–6 people as a main dish
Time   Preparation: 1½ hours

For the sausages

2 lb/1 kg lean pork
2 lb/1 kg fat belly pork (without the rind — save that to stew with dried white beans)
a hank of sausage casings
plenty of pepper

1 teaspoon salt
fresh chopped herbs of your choice (thyme, marjoram, sage, penny royal)
lard for frying

For the mash

3 lb/1·5 kg old floury potatoes
salt
4 oz/100 g butter

¼ pint/150 ml creamy milk *or* half cream and half milk
pepper

Utensils   A bowl, a mincer if you have one, a large saucepan, and a frying pan

Soak the sausage casings for an hour or two in cold water to rid them of the salt used to preserve them.

Put the other sausage ingredients once through the mincer. If you have a sausage funnel which will screw over the mincer's opening, loop the casings over the spout, pushing each length well up, like a glove on a finger, and then tie off the end loosely, so that air can escape.

Put the meat back through the mincer and ease it into the casing. Twist into sausage lengths. Tie up the end. If you have no mincer and attachment, get the butcher to mince the meat for you twice, then season it and push it into the sausage casing through a funnel (you may need to saw the narrow end off the funnel so that the opening is wide enough). A very satisfying operation.

Let the sausages dry while you prepare the potatoes for the mash. For 6 people you will only need half the quantity of sausages you have made. Freeze the rest if you do not wish to use them immediately.

Put the potatoes into the roomy saucepan, and cover them to a depth of one finger with cold water. No salt yet. Bring to the boil, turn down the heat and boil gently for 20 to 25 minutes, until they are soft all through. Drain and then put them back on the heat. Sprinkle half a teaspoon of salt over them, and shake them over the heat for a moment or two until they are dry and crumbling. Mash them with a wooden spoon or a potato masher. Beat in the butter and then the milk over a gentle heat. Add pepper, and taste to see if you need more salt.

Melt a nugget of lard in a frying pan. Prick the sausages with a fork and put them to cook in the hot fat. Let them sizzle slowly for 20 minutes if you have made thick sausages. They will need turning a few times to brown them on all sides. Serve on your best blue willow-pattern dish, prettily arranged round a pile of creamy mashed potato. Accompany with fresh young peas or, in winter, lightly cooked and well-buttered cabbage. Do not forget to put a pot of strong English mustard on the table. Cider or light ale to drink.

SUGGESTIONS

• Fry 1 lb/500 g peeled, cored, and quartered apples in the fat which runs from the sausages. Or make an apple sauce (see page 153) to serve instead. Or a rich gravy (see page 210).

• If you cannot get your butcher to supply you with sausage casings, just roll the mix into sausage shapes, flour them lightly, and cook them as they are. Or make faggots by encasing a patty of the meat in a piece of caul.

Storehouse Sausages and Ham

Mlle Morell is far from alone in remembering the autumn pig-slaughter as one of the most vivid events of her long-ago childhood. As in France so all over Europe it was an extremely important near-ceremonial occasion for those rural households who depend on its products to add flavour and protein to an otherwise somewhat dreary winter diet.

The ritual has always fascinated outside observers. Travelling through Romania towards the end of the nineteenth century, author Theresa Stratilesco observed:

Even before the beginning of Advent, a pig has been put apart in a cotet, a little pig-sty of his own to fatten . . . . The Ignat [the feast of St. Ignatius on 20 December] comes at last; the day of reckoning has come; from the early morning you may see the smoke ascending the sky, with its shadow capriciously stretched across the snow-coated hill. Under the burnt-out straw, thrown aside with the iron fork, the pig is discovered in his hard skin, turned ivory after some rubbing and scrubbing, whereupon the cutting out begins. The joints for ham, the sides for the bacon, are carried up to the loft for smoke; the rest of the meat being mostly used for the filling of the traditional carnati and chiste, the former being the thin ones, filled mostly with meat, the latter, the wider ones, filled with passat, the national rice, the seed of the millet. And on a Christmas Day there is no peasant table on which the roasted carnati will not be grilling in their own

fat, beside a golden smoking mamaliguta. . . . The beggars and gypsies will get their share.

María Avila, farmer's wife from the village of Tajo in Andalusia recalled for Ronald Fraser in 1958:

I got married in 1924 . . . . My husband's farm was good and he worked hard. So did I. We were able to eat a bit better than most, we had fish more often and every year we killed a pig. From that I cured a couple of legs of serrano ham, made sausages, mortadello, black puddings. When you slaughtered a pig it smelled good for a mile around, not like today when pigs are fattened on artificial foods and garbage and stuff of that sort. Then they were fattened on figs, sweet potatoes, groundnuts, green stuff, and they tasted delicious.

Paul du Chaillu remembers the occasion in Norway in 1872:

With the month of October comes the slaughtering time. The housewife then has a great deal to do in preparing sausages and bacon to last until the following autumn. Meat has to be salted, dried, or smoked. Molja, made of blood mixed with flour, is put up in large quantities, preserved in bladders or cakes; when used it is either boiled or fried.

The most developed repertoires of preserved pork-butchery belong to France, Germany, Italy, and Spain. I include here a brief summary of the most important items in their winter larders. Climate plays a considerable part in the matter — nordic countries could rely on natural refrigeration to preserve their stores, whereas those with damp or warm climates had to make other arrangements.

165

FRENCH CHARCUTERIE

Andouille   Salted and often smoked as pre-cooked sausage. Made from the large intestine and tripe of a pig. Usually sliced and eaten cold.

Andouillette   Small pre-cooked sausage made of tripe. Can be split and grilled or fried. Very good slashed and grilled, and served with mustard and creamy mashed potatoes.

Boudin blanc   White pudding, pre-cooked, made with minced chicken, pork, cream, and eggs. Very delicate and delicious. Prick them, baste them with butter, and grill them gently. Serve with a purée of potatoes and celeriac.

Boudin noir   Black pudding, pre-cooked. Made with blood and pork fat, onions, and cream. Cut the *boudin* into lengths and fry gently in butter. Cook peeled and quartered apples in the pan afterwards, and serve all together.

Cervelas   Large pre-cooked sausage for boiling. Often smoked. Made with minced pork and beef and flavoured with garlic. Nicest if reheated by simmering in red wine. Serve with cabbage or sauerkraut or a hot potato salad. Can be served cold.

Crepinette   Fresh sausage mixture wrapped in a caul. Sold raw or cooked for immediate consumption. Bake, fry, or grill.

Jambon de Bayonne   Salted, dried, and smoked ham. Eaten as it is. Also used chopped and in small quantities to give a wonderful distinctive flavour to local dishes. Prepared as the Spanish *jamón serrano* and the Italian *prosciutto*, with the addition of a short smoking.

Jambon de Toulouse   Ham, salted and dried. Uncooked and eaten uncooked, often with a pat of fresh butter. Also used to flavour stews and soups. Prepared as the Spanish *jamón serrano* and the Italian *prosciutto*.

Jambon de Paris   Salted, if smoked only very lightly so, and then cooked before sale.

Petit salé   Belly pork salted, with juniper, peppercorns, bayleaf, and other spices in the cure. Cooked with cabbage, and used in many soups and dried bean dishes. The favourite larder staple of the French country wife.

Rillette   Potted meat. Belly pork cooked so long and so gently that it disintegrates into shreds. Then spiced and packed into pots for storage. Eaten cold on bread.

Saucisson sec   A wide variety of regional dried salami-type sausages.

Saucisse de Toulouse   A fresh all-meat sausage made with chopped pork — rougher textured than the usual sausage. Sold uncooked. This is the sausage used in the *cassoulet* (see page 257). Use proportions of 3 to 1 lean pork to hard back fat, season with salt, pepper, and a pinch of saltpetre, and proceed as for the English pork sausages (see page 162).

Rillon Large slab of *rillette* mixture.

ITALIAN PROSCIUTTO AND SALAMI

Prosciutto crudo Raw ham, salted and dried for winter stores. Pickled in salt and sometimes garlic for a month, and then hung to dry in a current of air until the brine no longer drips. Then rubbed with pepper and hung in the larder for cutting in slices to eat raw, or cubed for cooking. A staple of the peasant winter larder. Gammon is the nearest equivalent — cooked ham does not get anywhere near the correct texture and flavour.

Prosciutto cotto Italian cooked ham, preserved in brine, and then boiled when needed.

Pancetta Salted belly of pork, rolled and dried as for *prosciutto*. Used in the same recipes and in much the same way, *pancetta* has a similar flavour, but more fat.

Cotechino A boiling sausage. Made by stuffing a sewn-up roll of pork skin with spiced, chopped meat — a mixture of pork and beef is common. Many Italian delicatessens sell *cotechino*. Cook the sausage whole, pricking it well all over and bring it to the boil in plenty of cold water. Simmer for 2 hours per 1 lb/500 g sausage. Use the broth to cook 1 lb/500 g lentils for every 4 diners, or serve with mashed potatoes moistened with some of the broth. Serve the sausage cut in slices and placed on top of the lentils or potatoes. The skin is not eaten, but imparts to the broth a strong delicious fragrance — it can then be used as a basis for good vegetable soups and stews.

Zampone A boiling sausage made with the same stuffing as the *cotechino*, but stuffed into an empty pig's foreleg complete with trotter. Use as *cotechino* — the inclusion of the trotter gives a particularly good broth.

Salami There are many different variations on this well-known spiced and dried pork and beef sausage. The mixture is stuffed into the larger intestines of cows rather than pigs. Flavourings vary: salt and pepper always, red or white wine and garlic usually, chilli pepper, paprika, and fennel seed sometimes. The Milan salami has fine-ground meat and fat, which gives a smooth pink sausage; the Tuscans like theirs more coarsely chopped — with the meat dark red and the fat in snowy lumps, the whole dotted with black peppercorns. Each region of Italy has its own particular preferences.

Budino Italian blood sausage. There is a semi-sweet Tuscan variety called *sanguinaccio*, which is mixed with breadcrumbs, pine kernels, raisins, and candied fruit, and flavoured with cinnamon, coriander, and nutmeg. This is stuffed into a large intestine, tied up and then boiled for half an hour before storage. It is eaten fried in butter, or with beaten eggs poured round it in the pan to make an Italian *frittata* or flat omelette.

Salsiccia   Fresh pork sausage, often flavoured with garlic, salt, and black pepper, and sometimes marjoram, oregano, or other aromatic herbs. Can be packed into jars and covered with oil for storage, or eaten fresh, fried, or grilled crisp.

GERMAN WURST

'*Weck, Wurst und Wein*' loaded the German peasant farmer's board, and he has always expected to partake heartily and well of all three. A jug of his own excellent wine, a thick slice of black bread — country bread, rich and dark and heavy with rye — keeps comfortable company with the best sausages in the world. A good helping of mild German mustard, a grating of fresh horseradish, and a dish of sauerkraut or pickled vegetables completes his meal. Schnapps is the preferred short drink — washed down with a *stein* or two of magnificent German beer.

Frankfurter Bratwurst   A smoked sausage for storing. The same composition as the *bratwurst* sausage, flavoured with salt, pepper, coriander seeds, and nutmeg, the whole moistened with red wine (hence the rose colour). The sausages are smoked to preserve them. To finish, bring them to the boil in a pan of water, then turn the heat down and simmer them gently for 5 minutes. If you boil them too fiercely they will split. Frankfurters are very good served with sauerkraut, accompanied by potatoes plain boiled with salt. Or with good black bread, plenty of mild German mustard, and a little pile of freshly grated horseradish.

Rindfleischwurst   A fresh sausage to be served fried. The meat is beef minced with pork fat, and flavoured with garlic and cloves. A little saltpetre is included with the salt. Sometimes called summer sausage because it lasts longer in warm weather than the pork-based version. Can be smoked and given a preliminary cooking before storage.

Leberwurst   Liver sausage, to be eaten cold. Made with pig's liver thoroughly minced with pork fat in proportions of 3 to 1. The mixture is seasoned with salt, pepper, and allspice, and cooked before storage. If you wish to make it yourself and have no sausage casing, bake it in a terrine covered with foil. Excellent as a simple hors d'oeuvre or picnic dish served with unsalted butter, black rye bread, and radishes. Beer to wash it all down.

Schwarzwurst   Black sausage, made with pig's blood, cooked to be stored. Eaten hot, fried. An awkward dish to prepare at home unless you slaughter your own pig. All German peasant farmers, in common with most of the old peasant communities, would have kept a couple of pigs for the winter larder. Fed on household scraps such as vegetable peelings, leftovers, and stale bread, the omnivorous hogs would be fattened all year for the November pig-slaughter. The blood from the neck artery, severed when the animal is killed, must be caught in a pail and stirred so that it does not coagulate before it cools (this is usually the housewife's job). Then the dark red liquid is thickened with bread-crumbs and a small proportion of chopped pork and pork fat. The flavouring is garlic and cloves. The mixture is then stuffed into well-washed intestines, and the sausages are boiled and stored. To serve, cut it into lengths, fry in butter or lard in company with slices of apples and onions. Beer or milk curds to wash it down — and a clean napkin tucked under your chin to give you courage. A section of the blood sausage can be poached in a thick vegetable soup to give substance to a main meal soup-stew.

Bratwurst   The basic German sausage, made of finely minced pork flavoured with herbs — usually a mixture of thyme, rosemary, and sage. It is an all-meat sausage made without bread or rusk, designed to be eaten fresh, fried in lard or butter.

3 lb/1·5 kg lean pork (leg *or* shoulder)	4 tablespoons chopped herbs (rosemary, thyme, sage)
1 lb/500 g fat pork (belly)	a hank of intestines
2 tablespoons salt	
3 tablespoons freshly ground black pepper	

Mince all together very finely, putting the meat through the mincer twice. Stuff the mixture into well-washed intestines — a butcher who makes his own sausages will be able to sell you a hank of these, usually preserved in a great deal of salt, so that they need to be soaked. Failing the casing, the *bratwurst* meat can be rolled into short cylinders, lightly floured and then fried. When working with sausage mixtures, have a basin of cold water beside you so that you can rinse your hands frequently — this prevents the fat from sticking to your fingers and making you clumsy.

SPANISH EMBUTIDOS

Butifarra   A Catalan sausage made from lean and fat pork, chopped together and seasoned with garlic and oregano, cloves, cinnamon, and hot cayenne pepper. The nearest to the uncooked British banger.

Chorizo   Chopped pork, equal quantities of fat and lean, flavoured with garlic, oregano, and a little chilli pepper, and coloured with paprika and red wine. Coriander and cumin are also sometimes included. Peasant households prepare their own at the autumn *matanza* or pig-killing. Sold both dried and fresh for use fried or in stews, where it is an essential flavouring. Saltpetre is included in small quantities in all these pork preparations.

Morcilla   The Spanish black pudding, made with fresh pig's blood, chopped pork fat, flavoured with paprika (named, in Spain, *pimentón*), salt, and pepper. In rice-growing areas, cooked rice is often included. The casing can be the long thin intestines, washed thoroughly in running water, or the mixture can be packed into the large intestine to make a single large, fat sausage. To be cooked on the day it is made until, as the country people say, it 'sings' — that is, the little holes in the intestines expand in the heat and breathe out a faint whistle. To be eaten cold in slices with bread, or fried, or included in a bean stew.

Longaniza   My own favourite Spanish sausage, this looks like a long loop of *chorizo* and is made with lean pork flavoured with paprika, rosemary, and pepper. It is excellent fried with eggs or used in any recipe that needs *chorizo*. It can easily be prepared at home. Fill sausage skins with 1 lb/500 g pork minced and mixed with 2 teaspoons salt, 2 teaspoons paprika, a pinch of saltpetre, and a teaspoon of freshly ground pepper. Tie the sausage in a loop and hang it in a dry draught for a day. Keep in the refrigerator or a cool larder.

Salchicha   Fresh sausage made with minced fresh pork, both fat and lean, lightly spiced with salt, pepper, and paprika. Eaten fresh, fried crisp.

Sobrasada   A Mallorcan mixture of *chorizo* pounded with chopped fresh pork fat, used as a spread on bread — can be grilled.

PRESERVED PORK
Carne en manteca (Spain)

A product of the autumn *matanza* or pig-killing, this is the standard kitchen standby in rural districts. Town-dwellers buy it from the pig-products stall in the market, where the meat preserved in it is often short lengths of *chorizo*. Both the well-flavoured lard and the meat itself are used to flavour stews. The bright orange *manteca* (butter, as this dripping is named) is often spread on a thick slice of fresh bread — bread and dripping — as a sturdy morning meal. The meat can be refried in its own fat and served with plenty of bread as an instant supper. It is a most useful storecupboard item for those who cannot get Spanish *chorizo* and sausages, since it can substitute for them in any recipe, particularly in chickpea and haricot bean stews.

Quantity Enough for a small family's winter stores
Time Start the day before
Preparation: 1 hour

8 lb/4 kg pork fat (kidney fat is best) *or* 4 lb/2 kg clarified lard
4 lb/2 kg lean pork
4 dried red peppers *or* 2 extra tablespoons paprika
6 fat cloves garlic
1 tablespoon dried oregano *or* marjoram

2 oz/50 g salt
2 tablespoons vinegar
2 lemons
2 tablespoons paprika pepper

Utensils A pestle and wooden mortar or bowl, a roomy bowl, a deep frying pan, and an earthenware pot

Open the peppers and remove the seeds (they will be too fiery if included). Tear the shells of the peppers into small pieces, peel the garlic, and pound the peppers, garlic, oregano or marjoram, and salt together in the mortar or bowl. Mix the pounded spices with the vinegar. Cut the lemons into thick wedges.

Chop the pork into 1 in/2·5 cm cubes, put them into the roomy bowl, and turn them with the chopped lemons and the vinegar and spice mixture until well impregnated. Leave overnight to marinate.

The following morning cube the pork fat (called *pringe,* and sold in sheets in Spanish markets) and put it a few pieces at a time to render slowly in its own grease in the deep frying pan. Gently does it — the fat itself must not brown but remain pure white and clear. Remove and drain the crisp golden fried solids. They make delicious little titbits, lightly salted.

Meanwhile brush the marinade off the cubed pork. Fry the pork gently in the lard for 25 to 30 minutes. It should be very thoroughly cooked. At the end of the cooking time, when the meat is well browned, take the pan off the stove and stir in the paprika. Pour all, meat and bright orange lard, into an earthenware pot and allow to cool.

Make sure all the pieces of meat are submerged and store the pot in a cool place — the refrigerator is best of all. It will keep for a long time, although take care (if you do keep it for more than a week or two) when you remove some of the meat, to melt all down so that the rest of the meat remains sealed.

SUGGESTIONS
● *Chorizos* (the little red spiced dried sausages) are often prepared in this way for keeping.

SPANISH MOUNTAIN HAM
Jamón serrano (Spain)

The lean red half-wild pigs which forage for acorns in the cork oak forests of Andalusia make the best dried hams. Those who live near the sea, where the breezes are damp with spray and the air is warm all year, send their pig's haunches up into the sierras to be cured. The Spanish salt and dry their hams in the cold air of their high hills — they do not smoke them. The best hams are cured at Jabugo up in the Sierra Morena (*serrano* means 'of the mountains') which walls the west bank of the mighty river Guadalquivir. This is the river which rises in the foothills of the Sierra Nevada and waters all the rich *vega* or plains of Andalusia. The salt flats of Cadiz provide plenty of good quality salt, an important trade item bartered long before the Romans took advantage of the rich deposits.

In Jabugo there are commercial salters as well as the small private farmhouse barns. Even the little sheds at the end of the village houses take in the hams from relations who live in less favourable climes. In the big salteries the haunches hang by the trotter in serried ranks. It takes between four and six months to cure them in the snow-cold air, and the price of patience is as always high. Up here the pigs glean beneath the chestnut trees as well as in the oak forests, and the best of all are black. There are long low attics above the salting sheds where metal braziers glow scarlet on the endless loops of carmine sausages. The *chorizos*, paprika and garlic-spiced sausages, which are used extensively in many recipes, are sometimes very lightly smoked, although the ham is never subjected to heat of any kind.

Jamón serrano is not only appreciated as ham — to be cut in long, thin slices from the haunch as it hangs — but every bit of fat and bone has its recipe. As the ham dries out and less choice morsels are available, the cook will chop up the scraps and cook them with eggs, with vegetables, in soups, to give flavour to any and all dishes. The fat is carefully saved and used to enrich the *cocido* or bean stew. The bones are sawn into lengths and included in any dish which requires long slow simmering. The Spanish cook needs her *jamón*, and until recently most rural households kept one or two pigs for the year's supply of products of the *matanza*. In urban communities, there is always at least one stall in the market which sells pig products.

BACON AND HAM
(England)

In the days when each household had its pig, tradition dictated that the animal be killed when the moon had just begun to wane: not such an old wives' tale since free-range pigs graze by moonlight, and would be heavier after a week's feeding in the light of the full moon. The slow ritual process of countryside curing would then begin.

There are still old-fashioned firms who cure good York hams. These are brined, dried, and then aged in sawdust for three months. (Legend has it that the first sawdust to be used came from the oak beams which went into the building of one of the glories of medieval English church architecture, York Minster.)

The York method is certainly very ancient. There is a Roman recipe, recorded in Italy in the second century BC, which is very similar to the technique used today. It advises the good citizens to cover their ham with salt and allow it to steep in its own brine for seventeen days. Then it advises hanging the well-salted joint in a draught for two days to dry and in the chimney for a further two days to take the smoke. In Britain the Romans would have had no difficulty with supplies of salt, the essential agent in the preserving process for hams and bacon, since the valuable commodity had been worked around the coasts from the Celtic Iron Age onwards.

Over the centuries many different breeds of pig evolved from stock which variously fattened in the orchard, on moorland, on wheatland, and by foraging in woodland. In England, Gloucestershire and Buckinghamshire pigs were much prized — they foraged and fattened on beech nuts. Diverse curing techniques also developed, from dry salting to brine cures, combined or not in either case with smoking, and including such flavourings as honey, sugar, treacle, and juniper.

Suffolk hams are characteristically cured in a sweet molasses pickle, which includes juniper berries — the cure gives them a black skin. Suffolk flitch is sweet-cured and then smoked.

DRY SALT CURE FOR A 14 lb/7 kg HAM
(England)

The same method of cure may be used for bacon. A leg of pork severed from the whole side is called a ham. When the leg is left attached to the side, and only severed after the cure, it is called a gammon.

Time   3 weeks

1 ham (English hams weigh
   roughly 14–20 lb/7–10 kg)
½ oz/12 g saltpetre
1 oz/25 g brown sugar
2 lb/1 kg rough salt

Equipment   A salting trough

Leave the joint unskinned. Rub in the sugar and the saltpetre first, paying particular attention to the bone ends. Then rub in 1 lb/500 g of the salt and put the ham to rest on slats in a salting trough (best if it has a channel for the brine to drain out). Rub in the rest of the salt at the end of a week. Leave the ham to take the salt for a total of 3 weeks (depending on the size of the ham), turning regularly. Then hang the joint to dry in a draught of warm air for a day or two. If you would like to smoke your own, follow the method given for smoking salmon (see page 98) — 24 hours in the smoke should suffice for a ham, 6 hours is enough for a side of bacon. York hams are then hung to mature for 2 to 3 months in a temperature- and humidity-controlled room.

HONEY-CURE FOR HAM
(England)

1 ham
1 lb/500 g rough salt
½ oz/12 g saltpetre
1 oz/25 g ground black pepper
1 lb/500 g honey

Utensils   A salting pan

Rub the ham all over with the salt, saltpetre, and pepper. Put it in the salting pan. Turn and rub it well with the mixture every day for 4 days. Then pour the honey over the ham and rub it in. Rub the ham with the pickle twice a week for a month before you hang it up to dry.

TO BOIL A HAM
(England)

A plain salted ham is excellent boiled. A sweet-cured and smoked ham is even better.

Quantity   Enough for a dozen at least
Time   Start the day before
Preparation: 30 minutes
Cooking: 5 hours

1 whole ham (weighing around 14 lb/7 kg)
2 lb/1 kg root vegetables (including onions with their skins on)
½ pint/300 ml cider vinegar *plus* ½ pint/300 ml cider *or* 1 pint/ 600 ml sour cider
1 lb/500 g black treacle
1 teaspoon peppercorns
small bunch of herbs (thyme, sage, bayleaf, parsley, chervil)
1 lb/500 g whole apples

Utensils   A very large stewpot

Wash and scrub the salt-cured ham thoroughly. Put it to soak for 24 hours in at least 2 changes of water.

Find a stewpot which is large enough to take the whole ham comfortably. Wash but do not peel the vegetables and then chop them roughly. In fact, well-washed vegetable peelings would do as well. Put a bed of vegetables in the bottom of the pot. Lay the well-soaked ham on top. Add the cider vinegar and cider or sour cider, treacle, peppercorns, herbs, and enough water to cover. Chop the apples and put them on top (once again, the peelings and cores would be quite enough). Bring to the boil and then turn the heat down. Simmer for 4 to 5 hours.

To eat hot, drain the ham and then let it rest for 20 minutes. Skin it and serve it with apple sauce (see page 153), broad beans, and a parsley sauce (see white sauce, page 378). Or with a pease pudding (see page 255), sauced with the liquor from the cooking if it is not too salty. Cider to drink, of course.

To eat cold, allow the ham to cool in the liquid so that it re-imbibes its own juices. This is a very important procedure if the ham is to be succulent when cold. The following day take out the ham and remove its rind. Either dredge it with brown sugar and stick it with cloves, and then glaze it in a hot oven, or cover it with dried breadcrumbs and put in a hot oven at 425°F/220°C/Gas 7 for 20 minutes to blister and gild the crust.

TO BAKE A HAM
(England)

Quantity   Enough for a dozen servings
Time   Start the day before
         Preparation: 25–30 minutes
         Cooking: 5 hours

1 whole ham (weighing around
   14 lb/7 kg)
3 lb/1·5 kg plain strong flour
1½ pints/1 litre water
cloves (*optional* — traditionally for
   those with money for such
   luxuries)
½ lb/250 g treacle *or* honey

Utensils   A rolling pin and a large baking tray

Scrub the ham and then soak it for 24 hours, changing the water at least twice.

Make a 'huff crust' with the flour and water by working the two ingredients together into a dough. You may well need less water, as this protective paste should be quite stiff. Roll out one-third of the dough into a circle large enough to accommodate the base of the ham, and then roll out the remaining two-thirds into a circle twice the size. Put the smaller circle on an ample floured baking tray.

Preheat the oven to 300°F/150°C/Gas 2.

Skin the ham and put it flesh-side down on the smaller circle of dough on the tray. Stick the fat of the ham with cloves (if you are using them — they are one of the most expensive spices in the world and an early subject of restrictive trade practices). Baste with the treacle or honey. Drape the second circle of dough over the top, arranging it so that the edges of the circles meet. Damp the edges and pinch them together. Fold over the edges for added security. Cut a steam hole in the top.

Bake for 4 to 5 hours in the oven. The crust is not to be eaten, so it does not matter if it gets too dark. Some of this crust would, in medieval times, have been grated and sprinkled over the ham (the origin of breadcrumbing hams today). The rest of the huff crust, rich with the melted fat and ham juices, was the beggar's portion at the medieval table.

Serve with baked potatoes and leeks in a white sauce (see page 378). Cider goes best with ham: the pig himself was very partial to an apple in his time.

PICKLED HAM FOR CHRISTMAS
Julskinka (Sweden)

In Sweden Christmas Eve is 'Dipping Day'. An account of the ceremony was given by the traveller in Scandinavia, L. Lloyd, in 1870:

> The family and guests then assemble at dinner time in the kitchen, which is swept and garnished for the occasion; when, instead of sitting down to a regular meal, each one dips his 'jul-bread' into an immense pan, containing pig in some shape, that is boiling over the fire, considered the more palatable from the quantity of fat floating on the surface.

Mr Lloyd didn't take to the dish, but it none the less continues to be the mainstay of a very popular Christmas family occasion in modern Scandinavia. Light-salting meat is a useful half-way method which develops flavour without the process taking half a year. The result is succulent and well flavoured.

Quantity   Enough for 8–10 Christmas revellers
Time   Start 10–14 days before
Preparation: 10–15 minutes
Cooking: 3½ hours

1 leg of pork (weighing approximately 10 lb/5 kg)
1 lb/500 g salt
½ lb/250 g dark brown sugar
2 pints/1·2 litres light beer

2 pints/1·2 litres dark beer
4 pints/2·5 litres water
peppercorns
bayleaf

Utensils   A large pickling crock, a weight, a large stewpot, and a perforated spoon

Rub the leg of pork all over with 2 tablespoons of salt and 1 of sugar. Leave overnight to take the pickle.

Boil up the beer, water, and remaining salt and sugar together, and then allow to cool. This is the marinade.

Put the leg into the pickling crock and pour the marinade over it. Make sure it is submerged by weighting the top. Leave for 10 to 14 days in a cool place. If the leg is larger, leave it for longer.

When you are ready to cook it, take it out and put it in the large stewpot. Cover with cold water, bring to the boil, and then skim. Throw in the peppercorns and bayleaf, and turn down the heat to simmer. Leave to cook for at least 3 hours, until tender.

Strip off the skin. You can paint the fat of the ham with egg white mixed with sugar and mustard, and then sprinkle toasted breadcrumbs over all. Put it in a medium oven at 350°F/180°C/Gas 4 for 20 minutes to glaze it. Eat the ham hot with sauerkraut on Christmas Eve. Or cold at any time.

Strain the soup and serve it on Christmas Eve with thick slices of bread to dip in the fatty juices on the surface — this is called *Dopp i grytan*, or dip-in-the-pan. The meal then has a very jolly family atmosphere, rather like a fondue party.

SUGGESTIONS

● The ham looks very dramatic with its fat slashed into squares, sprinkled with brown sugar, and glazed in the oven. Stick the golden squares with cloves.

● Sometimes the ham is smoked before being cooked.

● To bake, wrap the joint securely in foil. Bake it for 20 minutes per 1 lb/ 500 g, plus an extra 20 minutes (10 lb/5 kg will take around 3½ hours).

SALT-CURED LEG OF LAMB
Spekemat (Norway)

Mutton was the meat traditionally used for this storehouse staple. Failing a fine three-year-old wether, a leg of lamb will cure well enough in its place. The meat is chewy and well flavoured, much like a dark-fleshed Parma ham or *jamón serrano*. Its preparation was a job for the shepherd's wife during the short cold days of October and November, after the flocks had to be thinned out for the winter. *Spekemat* was expected to last through the winter and provide many a delicious meal into the following summer. At harvest time in particular it came into its own as a mainstay of the midday meal. If there was urgency to get the crops in, it could be eaten on foot in the meadows wrapped in a soft flatbread or *lefse* pancake.

Quantity   Allow 4 oz/100 g dried meat per person
Time   Start 3 months before you need it
Preparation: 20 minutes

  8 lb/4 kg leg of lamb
  3 lb/1·5 kg salt
  8 pints/5 litres water (less if the leg
     is smaller)
  1 tablespoon sugar

Utensils   A large earthenware crock, a weight, and cheesecloth or muslin

Dissolve the salt in the water to make a brine. Add the sugar. Put the leg of lamb in the large crock and pour enough brine over it to cover completely. Put a weight on top to keep it underwater. Leave it to take the salt in a cool larder (not below 32°F/10°C or the salting process comes to a halt) for 2 weeks for a leg weighing 8 lb/4 kg (roughly 2 days per 1 lb/500 g weight of meat).

Take the leg out after the allotted time and rinse thoroughly so that you do not get too salty a rind. Hang it out to dry in a well-aired cool larder, wrapped in a loose bag of cheesecloth or muslin to protect it from flies. It will be dry, delicious, and ready to eat in 2 to 3 months.

Serve, sliced very thin with a sharp knife, as part of an indoor picnic meal, with unsalted butter, fresh hard-boiled eggs, a sliver of *geitost* (the Norwegian sweet brown cheese) and flatbread or potato pancakes to wrap round each morsel. A bowl of soured cream and some fresh raspberries to follow as a replacement for Norwegian cloudberries.

SUGGESTIONS
● Serve thin slivers as a first course with unsalted butter, or with fresh pears or a juicy southern fig, as for Parma ham.

SALT BEEF AND TONGUE
(England)

Silverside and brisket are the best cuts. Ox tongue goes in as it is, well wiped and trimmed. You will not be able to remove all the bits of bone and gristle from the tongue, or skin it, until it has been cooked. The saltpetre (much reduced in modern cures) acts as a preservative, and gives the meat its characteristic pinkish colour.

For salting
8 pints/5 litres water
1 lb/500 g salt
½ oz/12 g saltpetre (chemists do not
    often stock this nowadays, but
    a good butcher will have a
    supply)

Equipment   A brining crock or plastic bucket with a lid, a heavy plate

Scrub the crock or bucket very thoroughly with household soda and rinse out with boiling water. At the same time sterilize a heavy plate in the same way.

Bring the water to the boil with the salt and saltpetre, and then let it cool. Pack the joints to be salted in the tub and put the heavy plate on top. Cover all with the brine and lid the crock or bucket.

Ox tongue needs about 5 days in brine. A 5–8 lb/2·5–4 kg joint of brisket or silverside should be in brine for 6 to 8 days before it is taken out to be cooked. If you wish to leave it longer, it will come to no harm.

SUGGESTIONS

• Brown sugar, juniper berries, peppercorns, bayleaf, and cloves are all excellent additions to the brine: each household would take pride in its own mix. The brine would be topped up with salt and water, and go on from year to year: once the brine is made and kept well topped up with salt, it is as sterile as possible and much less likely to grow harmful bacteria than a new one. For a topping-up mix, make a double strength solution to replace the salt absorbed by the joint you have removed: 1 pint/600 ml water to 4 oz/100 g salt. If white spots of mould appear on the surface, drain out the brine, re-scrub and scald the container, and start again with new brine.

Use the same brine mix to cure pork. A leg or shoulder, trotters, ears, tail, or head can all be pickled to advantage in a salt brine. The larger the piece, the longer the salting it will need.

You can also brine meat which is to be roasted. An overnight sojourn in the brine tub will greatly improve its flavour.

BOILED SALT BEEF AND DUMPLINGS
(England)

One of the oldest traditional English dishes. Salted meats carried many a poor household through the winter.

Quantity   At least 4 lb/2 kg for 6–8
Time   Around 3 hours

1 joint salt beef — your own *or* the butcher's	3 carrots
	parsley stalks
1 onion	2 bayleaves
6 cloves	1 teaspoon peppercorns

For the dumplings

2 oz/50 g flour	1 tablespoon chopped parsley
2 oz/50 g fresh breadcrumbs	½ teaspoon salt
2 oz/50 g suet *or* the equivalent quantity of fat skimmed from the beef	2–3 tablespoons cold water

Utensils   A large stewpot or casserole, a perforated spoon, and a strainer

Wipe the salt beef and put it in a stewpot which will accommodate it comfortably. Cover the meat with fresh water and bring it to the boil. Turn down to simmer for 10 minutes.

Meanwhile stick the onion with the cloves, peel the carrots and reserve the peel. Strip out the stalks from the parsley and set the heads aside for the dumplings.

Taste the beef water which has now been simmering for 10 minutes. If it is very salty, throw it away, re-cover with fresh water, and bring it back to the boil. If it is not too salty, just skim off the foam and continue with the recipe.

Add to the pot the clove-stuck onion, the carrot peelings (save the carrots for later), parsley stalks, bayleaves, and peppercorns. Leave to simmer, so that gentle bubbles are produced, rather than a rolling boil which would toughen the meat. Leave to cook on a low heat. A 4 lb/2 kg joint will take 2½ hours. Add 20 minutes per 1 lb/500 g thereafter.

Half an hour before you are ready to serve, put a large, oval serving dish, preferably of white china, to warm.

When the meat is tender, draw it to the side of the fire and strain off half the stock. Ladle off the yellow fat floating on the surface — you can use this to mix the dumplings instead of the suet, but it must be allowed to cool first. Leave the meat to settle down in its liquid while you cook the sliced carrots in the strained stock. They will take about 20 minutes. Drain and put them into the serving dish to keep warm.

Meanwhile make the dumplings. Knead together all the ingredients into a soft dough with light fingers — that and the air in the bread-crumbs are the only raising agents. You can include a teaspoon of baking powder if you wish. Roll the dough into marble-sized balls with well-floured hands. Poach them in the simmering hot stock in which you have cooked the carrots. They will take 10 to 15 minutes to cook. Take them out with a perforated spoon, and give them a quick splash under cold water to stop them sticking together. Give the stock a final boil to concentrate the flavour while you carve the beef into thick slices.

Serve all on the white china dish: slices of deep crimson meat surrounded by the carrots and green-speckled dumplings. Best beer to drink with it — the Englishman's diet survived many a crisis when he had enough beer to make up for its deficiencies.

SUGGESTIONS

• If you have put an ox tongue in the brine, soak it well before you put it to cook as for the salt beef. It will be ready in 4 hours. Remove the little bones at the root end, and peel off the thick skin — if the tongue is well cooked, it will come off easily. Serve the tongue hot, cut in slices and bathed in a caper sauce made with its own liquor — concentrated by boiling and thickened with flour kneaded with butter, the capers stirred in at the end with a little grated fresh horseradish and a spoonful of mustard. Or serve with a sauce made with some of the stock as before, and flavoured with a glass of Madeira, reduced to half its volume by boiling. If you want to serve the meat cold, pack the peeled and boned cooked tongue into a round bowl or cake tin, neatly curled and pressed under a weight. Leave it to jelly at least overnight.

LEFTOVERS
● Serve the salt beef or the cold tongue cut in thin slices. Accompany with baked potatoes (see page 332), or with the leftover carrots sliced and reheated in a white sauce (see page 378). Or with a French gratin of potatoes (see page 336).

SALT PORK BELLY
Petit salé (France)

A most useful storecupboard item now that good store-bought bacon is so hard to come by. It can be kept for months in the salad compartment of the refrigerator. Ideal for soups, stews, and, cut into fine slivers, as a baster for roast meats. Mme Escrieu, my neighbour in the Languedoc, salted the sides from her annual pig in this fashion, and used it in her fortnightly cassoulet. Maria, my neighbour in the Andalusian valley where I lived before moving to the Languedoc, did not include the aromatics: her pork for salting was simply buried in a heaped mound of salt from the Cadiz flats. She kept her salted meats all through the winter in a drawer in a cool corner of her little kitchen. She did not put in saltpetre, but she would usually include the pig's ear, tail, and trotters in the pile — a kind of culinary lucky-dip.

Quantity Enough for 4 for 4 meals
Time Start the week before
Preparation: 30 minutes

8 lb/4 kg side of belly pork (make sure it has not been frozen)	small bunch dried thyme
	4–5 bayleaves
1 tablespoon peppercorns	2 lb/1 kg salt
1 tablespoon juniper berries	1 oz/25 g saltpetre

Utensils A pestle and mortar, a large salting tray or plastic container, a very clean board or plate, and a weight

Dry the meat thoroughly. Pound the peppercorns and the juniper berries together with the thyme and bayleaves. Mix the aromatics with the salt and saltpetre, which helps to preserve the meat and turns it pink. Rub the salt vigorously but carefully into the skin side of the meat. Turn it over and rub salt into the flesh side. Reverse it again and rub more salt into the skin side. Put the meat on a layer of salt in the well-scrubbed and scalded salting tray. Heap the rest of the salt around and on it. Weight it down with a well-scalded and scrubbed board, with a 2 lb/1 kg weight on top. These can be removed after 2 to 3 days.

Leave the meat in a cool place and turn it in the salt every few days. It will be ready to use in a week. It will keep for a long time, and becomes saltier as it is kept. If it is very salty, throw away the first water in which you cook it. Boil a piece for an hour and it will be very tender. Serve with *choucroute* (sauerkraut) or cold with a salad, as well as using it as an ingredient in dishes such as Mme Escrieu's *cassoulet* (see page 257).

POTTED BEEF
Lou pastis en pott (France)

An unusual potted meat prepared only in the Languedoc. My youngest daughter brought news of it when she stayed with a schoolfriend from the primary she attended near Toulouse. There were many such surprises for her in that particular farmhouse, including a nest of ducklings on the hearth and a pair of lambs who had the freedom of the bedroom.

Quantity   Larder-stores for a small family
Time   Start at least 2 weeks ahead
      Preparation: 30 minutes plus more later
      Cooking: 2 hours plus more later

First cooking
2 lb/1 kg lean beef
2 lb/1 kg lean pork
½ lb/250 g lard
3 bayleaves
a few sprigs thyme and rosemary
1 teaspoon juniper berries
salt and pepper

½ bottle red wine (the near-black wine of Cahors *or* a deep red Medoc for preference)

Second and third cooking
The same ingredients again each time

Utensils   A large straight-sided earthenware pot, greaseproof paper, and a shelf in a cool larder

Scald the earthenware pot and grease it thoroughly with a little of the lard (you can line the base with a few fig or walnut leaves if you have them). Cut the beef and pork into slices, trimming the gristle and sinews as you do so. Put the bayleaves on the bottom of the pot. Lay in the meat slices, seasoning with herbs, salt, and freshly ground pepper as you do

183

so. Pour in the wine — it should just cover the meat.

Simmer the pot uncovered over a very low heat, or in a low oven — 250°F/130°C/Gas 1 — for 1½ to 2 hours, until the volume of the contents is reduced by half. Allow to cool. Seal with a layer of lard, melted and poured over the cool meats. Cover with greaseproof paper tied down with string. Leave the pot on the shelf for a week. Then remove the lard seal and add in another 2 lb/1 kg pork and 2 lb/1 kg beef, the whole covered with wine, seasoned and cooked as before. Repeat the operation at the end of another week. You will now have a delicious dark jelly-meat, which you can eat either hot or cold. If you continue to replace the volume you have removed, the pot can go on for ever.

STOREHOUSE LEFTOVERS: OFFAL AND VARIETY MEATS

These were eaten fresh in peasant communities after the autumn slaughter of livestock. They were the portion of those preparing and salting down the winter's larder stores, providing a quick feast at the end of the long day.

Sweetbreads   The 2 varieties are the pancreas (elongated in shape and found near the stomach) and the thymus glands (rounded and to be found in the animal's throat). Put the sweetbreads in a bowl and cover them with salted water. Leave for 2 hours to soak out any traces of blood. Clean and wipe. Then put them into boiling water with a few peppercorns and a tablespoon of vinegar. Bring back to the boil and simmer for 15 minutes. Drain and remove all traces of skin and sinew. Press between 2 weighted plates until cold and firm. Cut into squares. They are now ready to be stewed in butter and sauced with mushrooms and cream, or egg-and-breadcrumbed and fried — the choice is yours.

Brains   Soak them first in salted water (from 2 to 4 hours depending on the size of the brain). Remove the covering membrane and wipe the meats carefully. Soak them for another hour to get rid of any remaining blood. Finish as for sweetbreads — brains will need an extra 10 minutes' simmering. Store them in their cooking liquid or use at once.

Fry   The testicles of male animals, these are reckoned the most delicious morsel of all by those who appreciate such things. Pour boiling water over the fry, skin them, and leave them to soak in cold water with a teaspoon of vinegar for a couple of hours. Then slice them and sauté them gently in butter or oil. Delicious treated in the French manner, with a few sliced mushrooms (wild would be best of all) and cream tossed into the frying pan as the *animelles* cook. In Spain I have had an excellent dish of goat's fry sliced and cooked in oil and garlic, served with quartered lemons, salt, bread, and fried green peppers.

CHAPTER 5

Lamb, Mutton, and Mincemeat

Many peasant communities were shepherding: the poorest pastures, not required for any more demanding agricultural use, could often support their flocks well. While pork was favoured by sedentary farmers, mutton and lamb became the meat most readily available to nomadic peoples.

Mutton hams were salted for peasant larders in Scandinavia, Scotland, and Wales. The Scots and the English had their mutton specialities such as Jump-short-pie, made from those animals unable to clear the ravine, and Braxy — Highland mutton from the flock's casualties, which needed to be soaked in water overnight and then well salted. Sheep's head broth was a staple of many a poor shepherd's diet, and the head would often be the piece given to an employee by the landlord.

Harvest-home in the remote Cairngorm hills of central Scotland, as Elizabeth Grant of Rothiemurchus recorded in the early nineteenth century, featured plenty of mutton on the menu:

> At the Dell . . . there was always broth, mutton broiled and roasted, fowls, muir-fowl [red grouse], three or four pair on a dish — apple pie and rice pudding, such jugs upon jugs of cream, cheese, oatcakes and butter; thick bannocks of flour instead of wheaten bread. . . . In the kitchen was all the remains of the sheep, more broth, haggis, head and feet singed, puddings black and white, a pile of oaten cakes, a kit [a wooden pail] of butter, two whole cheeses, one tub of sowans, another of curd, whey and whisky in plenty.

Lamb was usually the celebration meat of pastoral communities — above all at the important Easter celebrations throughout Greece and the Balkans, a habit which has since spread across Europe. Surplus members of the flock would also fall prey to the autumn slaughter, and had other uses apart from providing meat-stores. L. Lloyd recorded one such event in Sweden in 1870:

> When they kill cattle, the wealthier peasants generally slaughter one, two or three sheep, and one or more pigs, in the fall of the year, and they tan the whole or greater part of the skins, and about twice during that period they are visited by an itinerant shoemaker, who remains with them for several days for the purpose of converting the leather into shoes and boots for the whole of the household.

Mutton is also a preferred meat in southern Italy. The young American, Eliza Putnam Heaton, travelling in Sicily for her health in 1908, stopped for refreshment in a taverna roofed, she recalled, with the flowering branches of oleander and walled with screens of split and plaited cane:

> These tavernas are furnished with rough tables and benches, and the

keepers sell little but the necessaries of life — wine, peasant bread, raw onions, garlic, Sicilian cheese; but it is understood that the patrons will for the most part bring roast sheep and will buy only bread and wine to complete the Homeric feast. How they eat meat, these Sicilians, when they do eat it, storing up flesh food for months when they do not see it!

LAMB STEW WITH OREGANO
Arni ladorigani (Greece)

A simple and adaptable oven-cooked stew. The flavourings of oregano and lemon are the essence of Greek cooking. This dish can also be made with the internal organs of the lamb — the liver, lights, heart, and all the rest. Cut into bite-sized pieces, they will need no more than 30 to 40 minutes cooking. It is also very good made with a jointed rabbit soaked overnight in vinegar and water.

Quantity   Enough for 6–8
Time   Preparation: 15–20 minutes
          Cooking: 1½ hours

3 lb/1·5 kg stewing lamb including
   some bone (well-trimmed breast
   of lamb is good for this dish)
4 tablespoons olive oil
juice 2 lemons
salt and pepper
1 glass warm water
1 tablespoon chopped oregano
   and/or rosemary

Utensils   A heavy casserole with a well-fitting lid

Wipe the meat and put it in the casserole with the oil, lemon juice, and seasonings. Cover tightly and cook in the oven at 325°F/170°C/Gas 3, or on a gentle heat on top of the stove, for 20 to 25 minutes. At the end of that time, open the casserole — the meat will be delicately brown and sizzling. Add the glass of warm water and the oregano, and stir to incorporate the juices. Cover tightly again. Cook for another hour. At the end all the juices should be absorbed, and only the oil and lemon remain.

Serve with plenty of bread, a plate of crisp-fried chips, a bowl of black Calamata olives sprinkled with oregano, and a bottle of Greek white wine — not all the Greek wines are resinated. Choose two of the refreshing Greek salads (see page 395) to start the meal.

SHEPHERD'S STEW
Tokana (Romania)

In the Carpathian mountains of Transylvania, shepherds move their thousand-strong flocks between their winter and summer pastures, protecting them against the wolf packs and bears that still patrol the upland forests. During the long treks they sleep out beside the sheep and the dogs they use to herd them. In the evenings they will make a thick soup-stew over a blazing fire, its embers glowing all night to ward off the fierce cold. Wrapped like their charges in heavy fleeces, the hardy and stubbornly independent shepherds — their lean Mongolian-cheekboned faces betraying their Slav ancestry — lack for little. Unlike the rest of modern Romania their larders are always well stocked, and there is no shortage of meat in their pots whether simmering beneath the chill stars or in the warmth of their mountain homes.

Quantity   Enough for 4 shepherds after a long day, or 6 more delicate diners

Time   Preparation: 20 minutes

Cooking: 1½ hours

2 lb/1 kg lamb off the bone	2–3 bayleaves
1 lb/500 g onions	2 lb/1 kg potatoes
1½ pints/1 litre water	¼ pint/150 ml soured cream
salt and black pepper	1 tablespoon vinegar

Utensils   A heavy casserole or saucepan with a lid

Cube the meat and trim off the fat. Save the fat. Peel and slice the onions. Put the fat trimmings to render in the casserole or saucepan. Take out the scratchings and add the meat and the onions. Fry until well browned. Add the water, the salt and pepper, and the bayleaves. Bring to the boil and then turn down the heat. Simmer, covered, for 1 hour.

Peel and slice the potatoes and add them to the stew. Simmer the stew for another 30 minutes. Take the lid off towards the end to allow the gravy to thicken by evaporation. When the potatoes are soft, stir in the cream and the vinegar, and take the stew off the heat. Hand round the *tuica* bottle. Serve the *tokana* hot, with plenty of good bread.

SUGGESTIONS

● This recipe can be found in many different versions in both Hungary and Romania. Paprika has crept into the recipe recently on the Hungarian side of the Transylvanian border. Garlic, bacon, and the Hungarian vegetable stew, *letcho*, beef and mushrooms, summer savory and red wine, mustard and beer, all have their place in various household recipes.

LAMB STEW
Kapama (Bulgaria)

The spring version of this dish uses baby onions and fresh garlic, which is pure white, has a very mild flavour, and has not yet developed its cloves. The autumn version is particularly good made with a selection of those wild mushrooms which stand up well to the long cooking — use *cèpes* or chanterelles, both of which grow in profusion in the Bulgarian woods in the autumn. Morel mushrooms could be added in the spring, if you were so fortunate as to find some.

Quantity   Enough for 4–5
Time   Preparation: 20 minutes
          Cooking: 1 hour

For spring kapama	*For autumn kapama*
2 lb/1 kg lamb off the bone (shoulder *or* neck fillets)	2 lb/1 kg lamb off the bone
1 lb/500 g spring onions with green leaves	1 lb/500 g mature onions
2 fresh spring garlics *or* 3 cloves mature garlic *plus* a few chives	½ lb/250 g mushrooms, if not wild, then the large flat black ones
½ pint/300 ml boiling water	½ pint/300 ml boiling water
salt and pepper	salt and pepper

Utensils   A medium-sized, shallow casserole with a lid

Trim off excess fat from the meat and cut it into fairly large pieces. Peel off the papery outside of the onions and garlics (not the green leaves — they are one of the chief beauties of this simple dish). Chop the onions and garlics roughly into lengths. If you have only mature bulbs without their greenery, include a handful of chopped chives. If you are making the autumn version, wipe and slice the mushrooms and fry them first in a little of the trimmed fat from the meat.

Put the onions, garlics, mushrooms, meat, and water in the casserole. Add half a teaspoon of salt. Stew gently on top of the stove or in a moderate oven — 325°F/170°C/Gas 3 — for an hour at least, until the onions and garlics have melted into the sauce and the meat is soft. Taste and add more salt if you need it, and sprinkle in plenty of fresh black pepper. Serve in small earthenware bowls, one each, with black bread and boiled potatoes.

A glass of *slivova* to start the meal.

SUGGESTIONS
● Mint or dill finely chopped can be added right at the end of the cooking.

BAKED LAMB, VEGETABLES AND RICE
Djuvedj (Yugoslavia)

If the six regions which make up Yugoslavia would admit to a national dish, *djuvedj* is probably it. This dish, a recipe shared with the rest of the Balkans, might even reconcile feuding factions from Slovenia, Croatia, Montenegro, Serbia, Bosnia, and Macedonia. Vegetables and meat are variable, but it is particularly good made with well-trimmed breast of lamb.

Quantity   Enough for any 6 of the above nationals
Time   Preparation: 20–25 minutes
         Cooking: 1½ hours

2 lb/1 kg lamb off the bone
2 onions
3–4 garlic cloves
2 lb/1 kg mixed vegetables
    (aubergines, courgettes,
    peppers, green beans)
½ lb/250 g tomatoes *or* 1 medium
    tin

¼ pint/150 ml olive oil
salt
½ teaspoon powdered chilli
4 oz/100 g dry weight rice *or* 1½ lb/
    750 g potatoes, peeled and
    sliced

Utensils   A frying pan and a shallow earthenware dish with a lid

Preheat the oven to 350°F/180°C/Gas 4.
   Cube the meat into small pieces. Peel and slice the onions and garlic. Hull and slice the vegetables. Scald the tomatoes to loosen the skins, then peel and slice them.
   Warm the olive oil in the frying pan. Put in the onions and garlic and fry them until they turn a pale gold, then push them to one side and add the meat. Fry gently for a moment and then season with salt and chilli. Transfer the meat and onion mixture with its oil to the baking dish — earthenware is best. Cover the meat with a layer of the vegetables. Season again. Sprinkle in a layer of rice or potatoes. Finish with a layer of the sliced tomatoes (sprinkle on a little sugar if the tomatoes are the hothouse variety).
   Pour in enough water to reach the level of the rice or potatoes, and trickle on the rest of the oil. Cover the dish, and put it to bake in the oven for 1½ hours.
   Take off the lid for the final 20 minutes. The kitchen will fill with the enticing scent, and the cooking liquid will be concentrated into a rich sauce. Plenty of bread to accompany, and a bottle of the excellent Yugoslavian red wine — just as good as the country's better-known white.

SUGGESTIONS

• Make the dish without meat but with some strong white cheese, such as feta or grated Cheddar, sprinkled over when you take off the lid at the end of the cooking time. Adjust the quantities: 3 people can manage 2 lb/1 kg vegetables as a main dish.

IRISH STEW
(Ireland)

The traditional Irish stew is a white stew of potatoes, mutton (today usually replaced by stewing lamb), and onion. Potatoes are such an important element that they should equal twice the weight of the meat. After the long cooking the potatoes and onions will be reduced by half to a thick creamy mash, but Irish stew should never be watery.

Quantity   Enough for 6 as a hearty dish
Time   Preparation: 20–25 minutes
          Cooking: 2 hours

2 lb/1 kg mutton *or* neck of lamb
4 lb/2 kg potatoes
1 lb/500 g onions
salt and pepper
1½ pints/1 litre water *or* lamb-bone
   stock made with the trimmings

Utensils   A large casserole with a well-fitting lid

Have the mutton or lamb cut into chops no more than 1 in/2·5 cm thick. Peel and slice the potatoes and onions. Reserve 1 lb/500 g of the potatoes (leave them in salted cold water). Arrange in the casserole a layer of potatoes, then meat, then onion, then potatoes, then more meat, then onion, and finally a layer of potato, seasoning as you go. Pour in the boiling water or stock. Cover as tightly as possible. Cook the stew gently on top of the stove or in a slow oven at 250°F/130°C/Gas 1 for 2 hours. Half an hour before the end of the cooking time, add the remaining slices of potato.

Serve hot in deep soup dishes. A good dark stout to accompany and a slice of Irish cheese to finish.

SUGGESTIONS

• An Irish stew can be converted into an Irish hot-pot by including the lamb's kidneys, and removing the lid for the last half hour of cooking to allow the top to brown.

BARLEY OR SCOTCH BROTH
(Scotland)

Dr Samuel Johnson, a demanding gourmet, enjoyed this most traditional of soups on his way to the Hebrides in the 1780s. His biographer, Boswell, recorded the event: 'At dinner Dr Johnson ate several plate-fulls of Scotch broth, with barley and peas in it, and seemed very fond of the dish. I said, "You never ate it before." Johnson: "No, sir; but I don't care how soon I eat it again." ' The soup is simple enough and as variable as your ingredients will allow. Mutton or lamb, and barley should always be present.

Quantity   Enough for 6
Time   Preparation: 20 minutes
       Cooking: 1½ hours

2 lb/1 kg mutton *or* stewing lamb (neck is excellent)	salt and peppercorns
4 oz/100 g barley (pearl *or* pot)	2 bayleaves
4 pints/2·5 litres water	sprig parsley
2 lb/1 kg root vegetables (leeks, onions, carrots, turnips)	extra parsley for garnish

Utensils   A large stewpot and a perforated spoon

Have the meat cut into convenient pieces. Put into the stewpot with the barley. Cover with the cold water, bring to the boil, skim and simmer for half an hour. Meanwhile peel and chop the vegetables into short lengths. Add them at the end of the half hour, together with a few peppercorns, 2 teaspoons of salt, and the bayleaves and parsley.

Bring all back to the boil and simmer for another hour. Sprinkle on a generous handful of chopped parsley and a few finely sliced circles of raw leek.

Serve with Pieces (see page 512) and fresh butter, and follow with a cup of hot milky tea or a dram of Scotch whisky and a slice of rich dark gingerbread.

SUGGESTIONS
● Include 2 oz/50 g dried peas, soaked overnight and added at the beginning of the cooking. If you use freeze-dried, add them 20 minutes before the end, or add fresh ones 5 to 10 minutes before the end. There are households that like to include cabbage or potatoes — there are no strict rules.

LAMB STEW
Cawl (Wales)

The earliest version of this vegetable and meat soup-stew contained a selection of vegetables, pot herbs from the wild as well as from the kitchen patch, and a piece of bacon. Sedentary households could manage to rear at least one pig. *Cawl* is still a popular recipe in rural Wales, and even today there remain those who still sup this ancient dish with a special carved spoon from a wooden or pottery bowl.

Quantity   Plenty for a family of 8 — there should be some left for tomorrow

Time   Preparation: 30 minutes
Cooking: Up to 2½ hours

3 lb/1·5 kg neck of lamb *or* mutton *or* well-soaked gammon hock *or* a piece of each *or* a piece of beef as well if you come from South Wales
4 pints/2·5 litres cold water
salt and peppercorns

1 lb/500 g leeks
1 lb/500 g root vegetables (swedes, carrots, turnips, parsnips)
1 lb/500 g small potatoes
bunch pot herbs (parsley, chervil, chives)

Utensils   A large stewpot and a perforated spoon

Put the meat on to boil in the stewpot with the water (the meat should be in one large piece). If you are using lamb or mutton, add 1 teaspoon of salt and a dozen peppercorns. If you are using gammon hock, only add peppercorns. Bring to the boil and skim. Turn down the heat and simmer for 1 hour. (If the meat is a tender young joint of lamb, you will not need to cook it for this first hour.) Meanwhile scrub and chop the vegetables into chunks. Scrub and cut the potatoes in half, leaving their skins on.

At the end of the first hour, add the pot herbs (saving a tablespoon for garnish) and the vegetables (keeping back the potatoes and one of the leeks). Simmer for a second hour. Add the potatoes and simmer for another 20 to 30 minutes, until the potatoes are soft. Skim as much of the fat off the top as you can (save it for dripping to fry bread). Chop the reserved leek into fine rings and sprinkle them, with the tablespoon of fresh pot herbs, chopped fine, over the surface just before you are ready to dish up.

Some like to sup the clear broth as a first course, from a wooden bowl with a wooden spoon — the better to drink it piping hot on a cold day. Serve the meat and vegetables afterwards in the same bowl. A lovely innocent dish of spoonfood.

SUGGESTIONS
- Make a *Cawl ffa* or summer cawl with broad beans, salt bacon, potatoes, swedes, and leeks, thickened with a handful of oatmeal.
- *Harvest cawl* is celebration cawl made with a best bit of gammon, a whole white cabbage, new potatoes, all flavoured with parsley, savory, leek, and onion tops.

LEFTOVERS
- Should you be but a family of 4, make *Cawl ail dwym* or *Cawl twymo* with the leftovers. When the broth is cold, lift off the layer of fat on the top (save it for frying or pie making), and add a fresh lot of vegetables to the broth. Reboil the soup until the new vegetables are cooked.

ROAST LAMB WITH MINT SAUCE
(England)

The eating of roast lamb with bitter herbs is traditional Easter fare all over Europe. The English have taken the ceremony a stage further and always accompany their roast lamb with mint sauce or jelly, or rowan jelly. The butcher will break the shank off for you to make stock for the gravy. Saddle, leg, or shoulder are the best joints for roasting. In Wales a small succulent leg of marsh lamb comes ready-wrapped in a net of cawl fat so that it needs no basting.

Quantity   Enough for 5–6
Time   Preparation: 20 minutes
          Cooking: 1¼ hours

For the lamb	*For the sauce*
4 lb/2 kg joint of lamb, with the shank for the stock	a generous handful mint leaves
dripping *or* lard	¼ pint/150 ml boiling water
flour for dredging	1 teaspoon sugar
sprig thyme	¼ pint/150 ml vinegar
salt and pepper	
1 onion	

Utensils   A roasting tin, a small jug, and a small saucepan

Preheat the oven to 425°F/220°C/Gas 7.
   If the joint has little fat, spread it well with the dripping or lard and then dredge with flour mixed with thyme, a little salt and plenty of ground pepper. Put the lamb on a grid in the roasting tin in the hot oven for a few minutes to let the fat run. Dredge it again to give the tender

meat a protective crust. Put it back in the hot oven to seal the crust. After 10 minutes reduce the heat to 375°F/190°C/Gas 5 and continue cooking. Allowing 20 minutes for the first 1 lb/500 g and 15 minutes per 1 lb/ 500 g thereafter, the joint will take 1¼ hours. Lamb should not be overcooked. Baste it regularly. Turn up the heat again at the end of the cooking time to finish it crisply.

As soon as you have settled the meat in the oven, chop the mint leaves finely and cover them with the boiling water. Allow to steep for an hour. Stir in the teaspoon of sugar and the vinegar. Serve in a jug to accompany the roast lamb.

Meanwhile make a little stock with the shank bone, the onion cut in half, but with its skin still on to colour the liquid, and ½ pint/300 ml water. When the joint is cooked, mix the stock in with the lamb juices in the pan, scraping well to mix in all the little brown bits. Season.

Serve the lamb and mint sauce with plain boiled potatoes and a tender vegetable — young peas, beans, or carrots.

SUGGESTIONS
● Serve the roast lamb with laverbread (see page 411).

LEFTOVERS
● Make a shepherd's pie, exactly as for the Cottage pie (see page 212), but using lamb instead of beef. A recipe much favoured by the shepherd wives of Cumberland and the Lake District, mincing being a particularly good trick for tenderizing tough mutton.
● Or make a hot-pot with slices of the leftover lamb (as in the recipe which follows).

LANCASHIRE HOT-POT
(England)

This hot-pot was always made with mutton and cooked in a straight-sided earthenware pot — a small version of the chimney pots which forest the skyline of urban industrial Lancashire.

Quantity Enough for 4
Time Preparation: 20–25 minutes
Cooking: 2–3 hours

2 lb/1 kg neck of lamb on the bone	1 lb/500 g onions
or 1 lb/500 g leftover lamb	1 pint/600 ml water *or* stock
lamb's kidneys *(optional)*	salt and pepper
2 lb/1 kg potatoes	butter

Utensils A deep earthenware casserole with a tight-fitting lid

Slice the meat if it is left over from a roast or boiled joint. Neck of lamb should be sliced into chops. If you are using kidneys, skin and slice them. Peel and slice the potatoes. Peel and slice the onions. Layer all into the earthenware casserole, seasoning as you go and finishing with a layer of potatoes. Dot with butter and cover tightly.

Cook for 2 to 3 hours on a very low heat — 250°F/130°C/Gas 1. Take the lid off for the last hour so that the crust can brown.

Serve with fresh green peas.

BOILED MUTTON OR LAMB WITH CAPER SAUCE
(England)

Modern tastes dictate that this dish be made with lamb — mutton, a well-flavoured 3–4 year old wether, being a rare visitor to the butcher's slab. A shame for it was an excellent meat, particularly the little Welsh mutton which fed on the sweet marsh grasses, wild thyme, and scented herbs of the Cambrian mountains.

Quantity Enough for 6–8
Time Preparation: 30 minutes
Cooking: 2–2½ hours

4–5 lb/2–2·5 kg leg of mutton *or* lamb	3 lb/1·5 kg root vegetables (carrots, turnips, leeks, parsnips, onions)
1 teaspoon peppercorns	1½ oz/40 g flour
1 teaspoon salt	1 small jar capers
large bunch herbs (mint, thyme, parsley, bayleaves)	a little butter

Utensils A large stewpot, a perforated spoon, a saucepan, and a whisk

Wipe the meat and put it in the stewpot. Cover with cold water and bring to the boil. Skim off the grey foam which rises. Add the peppercorns, salt, and herbs.

Meanwhile peel the vegetables. Set aside the peeled vegetables, wash all the trimmings and add them to the pot. Simmer the meat for 2 hours if you have mutton, 1 hour for lamb, and then remove the vegetable peelings and herbs. Cut the vegetables into chunks and add them to the pot. Simmer for another half hour, until the vegetables are soft and the meat tender. Remove as much as you can of the fat which is floating on the top of the stock.

Remove 1 pint/600 ml stock from the cooking liquor 10 minutes before the end. Fry the flour with 2 tablespoons of the lamb dripping from the stew in the saucepan. Stir in the hot stock, whisking well so that there are no lumps, and then add 2 tablespoons of drained capers. Taste and adjust the seasoning. Stir in a nugget of cold butter just before you hand it round in a jug to accompany the mutton.

Little fresh peas or green or broad beans, and boiled potatoes to accompany. Mild beer to drink.

LEFTOVERS
• Slice the leftover meat off the bone and layer it with sliced potatoes and the rest of the caper sauce, plenty of parsley, and freshly milled pepper. Cook as for the frico recipe which follows the roast beef (see page 213).

HAGGIS — MUTTON LIGHTS AND OATMEAL
(Scotland)

The haggis is a most romantic dish, enjoyed in Scotland by laird and peasant equally. Queen Victoria declared herself pleased by it. It is not open to complication or delicate amendment, being quite simply a large boiling sausage stuffed with oatmeal and a variety of meats, flavoured with onion. The meats need not be mutton offal: there are recipes which replace it with lean mutton, and others which use venison offal. It can also be made without the stomach bag — cook the mixture gently in a pan for the 3 hours, stirring regularly so that it does not stick. It will be excellent, but not so authentically barbaric.

T. F. Henderson in *Old World Scotland*, published in 1893, explains how the haggis was served in the croft: 'In the peasant's home it was set in the centre of the table, all gathering round with their horn spoons, and it was "de'il tak' the hindmost." '

Quantity   Enough for 6–8
Time   Preparation: 1 hour
        Cooking: 3–4 hours

1 sheep's *or* lamb's stomach bag, well rinsed and fresh
1 sheep's *or* lamb's 'pluck' (the heart, liver, and lungs — if you cannot get the lungs, the kidneys and tongue will do)
6 oz/175 g coarse *or* pin-head oatmeal (not porridge or rolled oats, or you will have a soup mixture and not the light grainy texture of a good haggis)

1 lb/500 g suet (the fat which surrounds the kidneys — can be lamb *or* beef)
1 lb/500 g onions
plenty of pepper
salt

Utensils   Plenty of elbow room, a baking tray, a saucepan, a perforated spoon, a saucer, and a large stewpot

Tackle the stomach bag first. Turn it inside out, then scrub and scrape it in several changes of cold water. Scald it and leave it to soak for a few hours in water and salt. Spread the oatmeal out on the baking tray and toast it golden brown in a hot oven — 400°F/200°C/Gas 6 — for 10 minutes.

Wash the 'pluck'. Drain the liver and heart of its blood (your butcher will probably have done this already). Put the pluck into cold salted water and bring to the boil. Skim and then simmer for at least an hour.

Drain the pluck and check it over, removing the black bits and veins. Grate the liver and chop the rest of the meat. (You will not need all the liver — half is enough.) Chop the suet if it is not already prepared, and rub out the membrane scraps with well-floured hands. Mince the onions finely. Mix the meats, suet, and onions together, and spread them out on the table. Sprinkle the oatmeal over the top. Season well with the salt and a heavy hand on the peppermill. Some cooks include lemon juice, cayenne pepper, and a selection of herbs. The secret lies in the proportions and you will soon establish your own preference. Mix the whole lot together and stuff it into the clean stomach bag. It should be a little over half-full to allow room for the oatmeal to swell. Moisten with good stock — enough to make the mixture look juicy. Press out the air and sew up the bag. Put the haggis on an upturned saucer in a pan of boiling water or stock. Prick the bag with a needle when it first swells. Simmer for 3 hours if the haggis is a large one. To reheat it, simmer it for an hour.

Serve the haggis with Clapshot, which is a well-seasoned and buttered purée of mashed Swedish turnips (bashed neeps) and potatoes (tatties). Keep the fire blazing in the hearth and restrain yourself from pouring whisky on the haggis — drink it yourself as reward for your efforts.

SUGGESTIONS
• If you cannot get the offal, use mutton or stewing lamb. The suet should not really be omitted, but can be replaced by well-minced beef or pig kidney fat if necessary.

LEFTOVERS
• Haggis reheats beautifully — just decant it into a pan, add a little extra water, and heat it up gently.

LAMB GIBLET SOUP
Mageritsa (Greece)

A soup made of lamb's lights, sometimes including the head, split and blanched (although this was more frequently split and roasted on the fire, to be served sprinkled with lemon juice and oregano). This soup is traditionally prepared to be eaten at the beginning of the Easter feast, to break the Lenten fast after midnight on Easter Saturday. The Eastern Church regards Easter celebrations as rather more important than Christmas festivities.

Quantity   Enough for 10–12
Time   Put on the stock a few hours before
Preparation: 40–50 minutes to prepare the meat
Cooking: 1 hour

4 lb/2 kg lamb's lights (liver, lungs, and heart)	6 pints/3·5 litres stock made with 2 lb/1 kg stewing lamb *or* bones
1 lb/500 g spring onions	salt and pepper
4–6 cloves garlic	6 oz/175 g rice
4 tablespoons oil	3 eggs
big bunch dill — you need lots	juice 2 lemons

Utensils   A large stewpot, a perforated spoon, and a whisk

Wash the meats thoroughly, cutting out veins and gristle. Chop all the meat into small pieces. Peel and chop the spring onions and the garlic. Heat the oil in the large stewpot. Add the onions and garlic, and sauté them gently. Add the meats and turn them in the hot fat. Add the dill and pour in the stock. Bring to the boil, skim and season, then simmer for half an hour. Sprinkle in the rice and bring to the boil again. Simmer for another 20 to 30 minutes.

Meanwhile beat the eggs with the lemon juice until thick and white. Just before you are ready to serve, add a ladleful of the hot soup to the egg mixture and whisk it well in. Add another ladleful and whisk that in. Draw the soup to the side of the flame, and whisk the egg and soup mixture back into the rest. It will not need further cooking. Serve warm.

SUGGESTIONS
• Make the soup with breast of lamb and lamb's liver if you cannot get the rest of the meats.

SPIT ROASTED LAMB
Arni bouti sto furno (Greece)

The Easter celebration meal, now prepared in urban Greece by specialist cooks who usually hail from the rural villages. In the villages, each family roasted its own in the open air, the cook having to rise at four in the morning to prepare the lamb, the fire, and the spit. One whole lamb takes 6 to 8 hours to cook. The meal was (and still is today), a great community festival banquet, with the whole village visiting their neighbours' barbecues to taste and compare each cook's skill. A more modern roast can still capture the flavour of the celebration.

Quantity   Enough for 6–8
Time   20 minutes per 1 lb/500 g to roast the joint plus 15 minutes

  5 lb/2·5 kg joint of lamb on the
      bone — leg, shoulder, *or* loin
  4–5 cloves garlic
  1 tablespoon olive oil
  salt, pepper and aromatic herbs
      (rosemary, thyme, oregano)

Utensils   A large roasting tin

Wipe the joint of meat and make slits near the bone in the joint. Peel the cloves of garlic and slip them into the slits. Rub the joint well with the oil, and sprinkle with the chopped or powdered herbs, salt, and pepper. Roast at a high heat — 400°F/200°C/Gas 6 — for the first 15 minutes, then turn the heat down to 350°F/180°C/Gas 4 either in the oven or on a spit.

A fresh salad to follow, with a jug of *retsina* and a basket of country bread. There might even be a dish of the year's first strawberries if Easter is late.

GRILLED LAMB'S LIGHTS
Kokoretsi (Greece)

An Easter speciality served with the roasted lamb — to keep hunger at bay while the delicious scents of roasting meat assail your nostrils. The Italians and the Spanish have similar recipes — the Spanish sometimes use olive twigs as skewers. The Italians also roast pig's intestines in the same fashion. A most delicious dish made on the same lines as the French pork *andouilles* and *andouillettes*.

Quantity Enough for a party
Time Preparation: 40–50 minutes to clean the meats
Cooking: 50–60 minutes

lights from one lamb — liver,
  heart, kidneys, lungs,
  sweetbreads, spleen, stomach,
  and intestines
salt and pepper
plenty of oregano

Utensils A colander and several long skewers

Wipe carefully and cut all the meats into pieces the size of a large walnut. Season with salt and pepper and oregano, and put aside in a colander to drain. Turn the stomach inside out and scrub it thoroughly. Cut into pieces. Turn the intestines inside out by pushing them down a stick, like turning a sock inside out, and wash them very thoroughly.

Push alternate pieces of the different meats on to long metal skewers and then wrap pieces of the large intestines round them to give a good covering. Wrap the smaller intestines over the top. Season with salt and pepper, and put the packed skewers aside to drain for 20 to 30 minutes.

When the *kokoretsi* have drained, grill them gently over a low fire for 30 minutes or so, until they are crisp. They will take longer to cook than most such grills, because their beauty depends on being well roasted and crisp on the outside and cooked but still succulent on the inside.

Cut in slices, sprinkle with extra salt and freshly ground black pepper, and serve hot with quarters of lemon and plenty of bread as a delicious *mezedes*, as a snack or first course is called in Greece.

ROASTED KID
Cabrito asado (Spain)

Haunch of kid is the preferred roast meat of rural southern Spain, where the re-education of the Andalusian population after the departure of the Moors extended to the kitchen. Lamb was the favourite meat of the Muslim Moors, and lamb eating became a sign of pro-Muslim feeling, which led the offender into the arms of the Inquisition and the alternative (somewhat more personalized) barbecue afforded by an *Auto da Fé*. Kid meat is well flavoured and pale in colour — it has a rather gluey texture, which responds well to barbecuing. Insert a clove or two of garlic near the bone, salt the meat well, and baste the joint while it cooks with a rosemary branch dipped in olive oil. Serve with chunks of coarse-textured country bread and a salad. This is the meal for celebrating the roofing-out of a new dwelling.

SUGGESTIONS
● Stew the rest of the kid-meat with olive oil, tomatoes, onions, and garlic, moistened with a glass or two of dry white wine and spiced with bayleaves and pepper. It will need longer than the same dish made with lamb.

MEATBALLS IN EGG AND LEMON SAUCE
Youvarlakia avgolemono (Greece)

Although the Greeks have the oldest written gastronomic records in Europe, Greek life in post-ancient times has been so heavily influenced by the Turks to the east and the Bulgarians and Albanians to the north that the country's own culinary identity is almost impossible to disentangle. On the whole Greek country food is lighter than the Turkish equivalent.

In Turkey *Youvarlakia avgolemono* is called *Terbiyeli kofta* — *terbiyeli* means 'to behave' in Turkish — not something the sauce is naturally inclined to do. Egg-and-lemon sauce is of venerable ancestry. It was made in the kitchens of ancient Egypt, Byzantium, and Rome.

Quantity   Enough for 4–5
Time   Preparation: 25–30 minutes
　　　　Cooking: 30 minutes

1 lb/500 g minced beef	2 tablespoons chopped parsley,
1 onion	oregano, and mint
3 eggs	salt and black pepper
2 tablespoons uncooked rice	juice 2 small lemons

Utensils A mincer or food processor, a large frying pan with a lid, a bowl, and a whisk

The meat should be well minced — twice is best — or thoroughly chopped in the food processor. Peel and finely chop the onion and garlic. Separate the eggs and reserve the yolks. Mix together the minced beef, the herbs, the onions, the garlic, the egg whites, the rice, and the salt and pepper. Knead the mixture into a firm paste with wet hands and form it into walnut-sized balls. This quantity yields about two dozen. Leave the meatballs to rest for 20 to 30 minutes.

Lay the meatballs neatly in a single layer in a frying pan that they just fit. Pour in enough water to cover them. Cover and simmer for 30 minutes over a low heat until the meatballs are well cooked. They will take 25 to 30 minutes, depending on their size. Remove the lid for the last 10 minutes to allow the liquid to reduce to about 1 pint/600 ml. Shake the pan occasionally to turn the balls over and help them keep their shape.

When the meatballs are ready, beat the egg yolks in a bowl with the lemon juice until frothy and thick. Ladle in a couple of tablespoons of the hot reduced stock, whisking energetically. Pour the egg mixture into the pan. Warm the meatballs gently in the sauce, shaking the pan over a low heat until the sauce thickens. Take off the heat as soon as the sauce has thickened. Serve with bread and quartered lemons. A salad to begin the meal.

SUGGESTIONS
- Breadcrumbs can be used instead of rice. The meatballs will then take only about 20 minutes to cook.
- If you make the mixture with breadcrumbs, the meatballs can be fried

rather than stewed. Hot red wine is then poured over them. Serve with bread and a salad.

• Or make the mixture (with breadcrumbs) into rather larger but slightly flattened balls, oiling your hands well before you roll them. Grill these little hamburgers — preferably over charcoal. Serve with lemon quarters and a Greek salad (see page 398).

MEATBALLS
Köttbullar (Sweden)

Made with the basic forcemeat of the Swedish kitchen, these meatballs are a favourite *smörgåsbord* dish. They are served either hot or cold. It is probable that the recipe arrived in Sweden from Turkey, via the offices of the adventuring Swedish king, Charles XII, whose exploits are chronicled in the stuffed cabbage leaves recipe on page 392.

Quantity   Enough for 4 as a main dish
Time   Preparation: 30 minutes

1 lb/500 g minced meat	2 oz/50 g butter for frying
4 oz/100 g fresh breadcrumbs	½ pint/300 ml soured cream
¼ pint/150 ml milk *or* cream	1 teaspoon flour
1 small onion	salt and pepper
1 egg to make a firmer mix *(optional)*	

Utensils   A roomy bowl and a large frying pan

Put the minced meat into the bowl. Put the breadcrumbs to soak in the milk or cream.

Peel and chop the onion finely. Add the crumbs (and the egg, if used, lightly beaten) and the onion to the meat. Mix all together and knead thoroughly. Shape the mixture into 12 to 15 little balls. The easiest way to do this is with hands dipped in cold water.

Melt the butter in the frying pan. When it is foaming, put in the meatballs and fry them gently, shaking the pan to keep them a round shape, for 5 minutes until nicely browned. Splash a tablespoon of water into the frying pan and scrape all the well-flavoured little brown bits into the liquid. Mix the teaspoon of flour with a little of the cream, and then stir it back into the rest of the cream. This will stabilize the soured cream so that it does not split when heated. Pour the cream into the pan, and bubble all together for a few minutes, before tasting and adjusting the seasoning.

Serve as a main dish with boiled potatoes, red cabbage, and a dish of stewed cranberries. Or as part of a *smörgåsbord* table.

MOUSSAKA
(Greece and neighbours)

Moussaka is an Arabic name given in Greece to an oven-baked pie made of layers of minced meat and vegetables, which can be aubergines, courgettes, tomatoes, pumpkin, or potatoes, topped with a white sauce. A dish for the family Sunday lunch which is still carried through the streets of country villages to be put into the baker's bread oven to cook. The recipe derives from a medieval Arab dish, *muhklabah*, which is made with rice and sometimes nuts as well as aubergines and minced meat. Very popular all over the Middle East, as well as being the dish most often identified as typical Greek food.

Quantity   Enough for 6 as a main course
Time   All morning

For the vegetables
1 lb/500 g aubergines
½ lb/250 g courgettes
½ lb/250 g peppers

1 lb/500 g potatoes
¼ pint/150 ml olive oil
1 teaspoon salt

For the meat
1 lb/500 g minced beef
½ lb/250 g onions
2 cloves garlic
1 lb/500 g tomatoes *or* 2 medium tins

2 tablespoons olive oil
½ teaspoon chopped sage
1 bayleaf
salt and pepper

For the white sauce
2 oz/50 g butter (clarified is used in Greece)
1½ oz/40 g flour
1 pint/600 ml milk

2 oz/50 g grated *graviera* or *kefalo* cheese (parmesan or any strong cheese can be used instead)
salt and pepper

Utensils   2 frying pans, a food processor if you have one, a small saucepan, and a wide, shallow baking dish, preferably earthenware

Prepare the vegetables first. Hull the aubergines and cut them in half lengthwise. It is customary to salt the slices so that some of the juice drains out before you fry them. This is thought to make them less bitter and less absorbent of oil — anyway, it's a pleasant and time-honoured ritual. Hull and slice the courgettes. Slice the peppers. Peel, rinse, and slice the potatoes.

Heat the oil in the frying pan and cook the aubergines gently in it, turning once, until soft. Drain off any excess oil when you take them out. Do the same with the courgettes and the peppers. Fry the potato slices gently until they are soft but have not taken colour.

Meanwhile prepare the meat. If it is not already minced, mince it using a sharp knife — this is much the best instrument for mincing, because all the juices are not squeezed out by the machinery. A food processor with a chopping attachment is the next best thing. Peel and chop the onions and garlic. Chop the tomatoes (peel them and de-seed them too if you like). Put the oil to heat in another frying pan and turn the onions and garlic in it until they take colour. Push to one side and put in the minced beef. Fry gently until the meat is no longer pink. Add the tomatoes, sage, and bayleaf and cook for a moment to reduce to a sauce. Adjust the seasoning.

Preheat the oven to 350°F/180°C/Gas 4.

To make the sauce, melt the butter in the small saucepan and scatter in the flour. Cook until the mixture looks sandy. Beat in the milk gradually, heat and stir until it thickens. Simmer for 5 minutes to cook the flour. Save the cheese to sprinkle over the top. Season to taste.

Start assembling the *moussaka* by lining the baking dish with one-third of the fried vegetables. Spread half the meat mixture over. Lay on another third of the vegetables, and then the second half of the meat. Put the rest of the vegetables in next. Pour the white sauce over the top so that it completely covers the surface. Sprinkle with the grated cheese.

Put the *moussaka* to bake in the oven for 20 to 30 minutes, until the top is golden. Allow to settle and cool, and serve, as with most Greek food, warm rather than hot. Plenty of bread and *retsina*, and a dish of fresh fruit to follow. Perhaps a little Greek salad (see page 398) to whet the appetite first, with a glass of aniseed flavoured *raki*.

SUGGESTIONS

• There is a Macedonian–Turkish version of *moussaka* which is made with rice (8 oz/250 g dry weight for 6 people), and baked with a pre-cooked sauce of tomatoes, peppers, onions, garlic, and minced lamb (1 lb/500 g for 6 people). Bake until the rice is soft and the top golden — about an hour at 350°F/180°C/Gas 4. Twenty minutes before the end of the cooking time, cover with a layer of egg custard made with 2 eggs beaten into 1 pint/600 ml milk.

CHAPTER 6

Beef, Reindeer, and Grilled Meat

Throughout Europe, whenever there is a choice, beef is the preferred meat. The prejudice seems to be more than a matter of taste: somehow beef eating confers social status. It is not just that beef is a rich man's meat, it is also a feeling, particularly in relatively primitive peasant societies such as those of eastern Europe, that the warriors and over-lords eat beef, and that beef eating reflects favourably on the prowess of the consumer. Even predominantly shepherding communities such as those of Greece will always choose beef in preference to the much more readily available lamb and mutton. Beef eating reaches its apotheosis in England.

Whatever their means the English have always preferred meat to any other food. Best of all they love roast meat, well seasoned with 'the taste of the fire'. Necessity brings other victuals, and the labourer had frequently to do without, but the plainest of English cooks could always turn out a beautiful roast, flanked by its traditional accompaniments. Beef was available to the countryman after the annual autumn slaughter of cattle that were too costly to over-winter. The less delicate cuts went to pies and stews, while the roasting meat would be taken to the village baker's oven or to the manor-house oven by those who did not have their own. These oven-rights were often an important element in the landlord-peasant relationship in the Middle Ages.

ROAST BEEF WITH YORKSHIRE PUDDING AND HORSERADISH SAUCE
(England)

Per Kalm, a Swedish diplomat on a visit to England in the 1690s, observed the English at table:

> Roast meat is the Englishman's 'delice' and principal dish. The English roasts are particularly remarkable for two things. All English meat, whether it is of ox, calf, sheep, or swine, has a fatness and a delicious taste, either because of the excellent pasture, which consists of such nourishing and sweet-scented kinds of hay as there are in this country, where the cultivation of meadows has been brought to such high perfection, or some way of fattening the cattle known to the butchers alone, or for some other reason.
>
> The Englishmen understand almost better than any other people the art of properly roasting a joint, which also is not to be wondered at; because the art of cooking as practised by most Englishmen does not extend much beyond roast beef and plum pudding. Pudding in the same way is much eaten by Englishmen, yet not so often as butchers' meat, for there are many meals without pudding. I do not believe that any Englishman who is his own master has ever eaten a dinner without meat.

At its best when cooked by the fierce heat of the coal fires of the Black Country, batter pudding is one of the most ancient made-up dishes to be found in the cook's repertoire. In the old manor-house kitchen, it was the portion of the spit-boy and a reward for long hours of turning the roasting spit.

Quantity   Enough to feed a family of 8 for a Sunday dinner
Time   Preparation: In the kitchen for 1½ hours

For the beef
5 lb/2·5 kg joint of sirloin of beef   2 oz/50 g lard *or* dripping
  on the bone *or* the same weight   1 tablespoon flour
  of rib   salt
pepper

For the Yorkshire pudding
8 oz/250 g plain flour   salt
2 eggs   2 oz/50 g dripping *or* lard
1 pint/600 ml milk

For the horseradish sauce
¼ pint/150 ml double cream   1 teaspoon strong English mustard
1 oz/25 g freshly grated   mixed with vinegar
  horseradish

Utensils   2 roasting tins, 2 large bowls, a whisk, and a sauce boat

Preheat the oven to 425°F/220°C/Gas 7.
Wipe, skewer, and tie the meat into a neat joint and season with plenty of pepper but no salt until the end of the cooking. Put the beef spread with lard or dripping in a roasting pan. To roast beef rare, allow 15 minutes per 1 lb/500 g. Roast it in a hot oven at 425°F/220°C/Gas 7 for the first 20 minutes, then down to 400°F/300°C/Gas 6 for the rest of the time. If you like it less rare, add on 15 minutes. Baste the meat throughout with its own juices and drippings, and towards the end of the cooking time dredge it with a sprinkling of flour and salt. This will give the meat a delicious crisp crust and provide a good basis for a gravy. (If you are serving roast potatoes, start them at the same time as the beef.)
Meanwhile make the pudding. Put the flour and salt in a bowl and make a well in the centre. Beat the eggs with half the milk and pour the mixture into the well. Work this in with a wooden spoon and beat it well until it is smooth. Whisk in the rest of the milk. The mixture should be like a pouring custard. Beat it some more. Leave it to rest for half an hour. Then beat it again.

Put the dripping or lard into a roasting tin and heat it in the oven. When the fat is smoking hot, pour in the batter. Everything should be very hot — the fat, the tin, and the oven. Twenty-five minutes should see it well puffed and brown.

Next make the horseradish sauce. Whip the cream and fold in the horseradish and the mustard. Add a little more vinegar if you like the sauce runny.

Serve the roast beef with the sauce, roast potatoes, and either roast or plain boiled vegetables. (No more than two. The English are overly fond of the loaded plate.) Some like a thickened gravy, although the meat juices deglazed with a little more water in the pan make an excellent gravy without further embellishment.

SUGGESTIONS for the Yorkshire pudding
● Some households serve the Yorkshire pudding first, to take the edge off the appetite for the meat.
● Yorkshire pudding does not depend on roast beef to accompany it. It can be enjoyed on its own, with a good gravy.
● In Yorkshire it is sometimes served with cream and treacle, or with a couple of cooking apples, sour and sharp-flavoured, peeled, sliced, and stirred in before the baking.
● There are those who always use water instead of milk, and much less of it at that, and swear it makes a far lighter pudding.
● Make the pudding into Toad-in-the-hole by dropping well-pricked Yorkshire beef sausages or pork sausages in the batter, after it has been poured into the roasting dish. Serve with gravy.

MEAT GRAVY
(England)

This flour-thickened brown sauce based on meat juices is a peculiarly English taste. The word comes from the old French *grané* which in turn derives from the Latin *granatus* meaning 'made with grain' and was applied to a meat stew with a flour-thickened juice — not so far removed from the modern recipe. The French dropped both the word and the substance, and the only modern gravy in French cookery is the *jus*, or juice of the meat — not the same thing at all. Englishmen like gravy to pour on sausages, with batter pudding, and with plain boiled potatoes — it acts, it appears, as a kind of meat substitute.

Quantity Makes 1 pint/600 ml gravy
Time Preparation: 10 minutes

1 oz/25 g lard *or* dripping
1 onion (*optional*)
1 oz/25 g flour
gravy browning and a nugget of
    butter (*optional*)

1 pint/600 ml strong stock (made
    with bacon rind, ham
    trimmings, vegetable trimmings,
    bones, and a few onion skins to
    give it colour)

Utensils   A frying pan

Melt the lard in the pan. If you are using the onion, chop it vertically into fine crescents, add it to the lard and sauté it lightly — do not allow it to burn or the taste will not be pleasant. Add the flour and fry until it turns lightly golden — again, do not allow it to burn. Stir in the stock gradually, beating to avoid lumps. Bring all to the boil and add, if you like, a few drops of gravy browning and a nugget of cold butter.

Serve either with a roast joint of meat, or on its own with Yorkshire pudding, mashed potatoes and/or sausages.

SUGGESTIONS
Gravy browning   Good gravy should be a deep mahogany. To produce the right colour is the hardest part of gravy making. A useful colouring can be made by melting 4 oz/100 g sugar in a heavy preserving pan on a low fire. Continue to heat gently and stir until it caramelizes to a good rich brown. Throw in a glass of cold water and simmer to make a deep rich brown syrup. Bottle and keep for use.

MARROW BONES
(England)

A delicacy from England's beautiful beef and a treat for high tea, or as a savoury after the meal instead of a pudding. The marrow bones used in this dish are the femur or the thigh-bone of beef-cattle. Marrow was used in medieval cookery in sweet dishes and puddings. One of these, made with barley, oats, or whole wheat soaked in milk and sweetened with honey, was the forerunner of our modern rice pudding.

Quantity   Enough for 4, allowing 2 lengths of bone each
Time   Preparation: 5–10 minutes
          Cooking: 1½ hours

2 marrow bones cut into lengths
flour and water paste
bread for toasting

Utensils   A large saucepan and a clean linen cloth, or a roasting tin

Have the bones sawn into 3 in/7 cm lengths, and seal the cut ends with a stiff paste of flour and water. Wrap the bones tightly in a floured cloth and put them to simmer in plenty of salted water for an hour. Or bake them slowly at 300°F/150°C/Gas 2 in the oven for an hour. Serve the bones as they are, with a knife or a long thin spoon to scoop out the delicious marrow on to fresh hot toast.

SUGGESTIONS
● Don't throw away the cooking water — it makes good stock.
● If you have no marrow, dripping from roast beef spread on bread or toast and sprinkled with rough salt is a pleasant alternative.

COTTAGE PIE
(England)

A recipe for the tough cuts of meat which were likely to come the way of the cottager or farm labourer. Equally useful for any bits which might be left over from the Sunday joint. The dish can be made with any meat, cooked or raw, well chopped or minced. Salted meats are not suitable.

Quantity   Enough for 4–5
Time   Preparation: 30–40 minutes
         Cooking: 30 minutes

1 lb/500 g meat (left over *or*
   minced fresh)
1 large onion
1 tablespoon meat dripping *or* lard
1 tablespoon flour
½ pint/600 ml stock *or* meat gravy
gravy browning and a few drops
   Worcestershire sauce (*optional*)

parsley
salt and pepper
2 lb/1 kg old potatoes
large nugget butter
2–3 tablespoons milk

Utensils   1 large and 1 medium saucepan and a gratin dish

Put a large pan of salted water on to boil.
   Meanwhile mince or chop the meat thoroughly. Peel and chop the onion. Put the dripping or lard to melt in the medium saucepan. Add the onion and fry until golden. Stir in the flour (unless you are using leftover, thickened gravy, when no flour is needed) and the meat if it is raw, and cook it until it takes a little colour. Add the stock or gravy and allow it to bubble up. Stir in the meat now if it is already cooked. A little gravy browning will not come amiss, and a shake of Worcestershire sauce. Chop the parsley and stir in a tablespoonful. Bubble all until the

gravy is quite thick. Taste and adjust the seasoning. Pour the mixture into the gratin dish to cool. If you put hot potato on hot gravy, it will sink through the surface and the appearance of your pie will suffer.

Peel the potatoes, cut them into quarters, and plunge them into the water as soon as it boils. Cook them until they are soft, which will take 20 to 25 minutes. Drain them immediately and shake them over the heat to dry. Mash well, beat in the butter and milk, and season with salt and pepper.

Preheat the oven to 350°F/180°C/Gas 4.

Pile the mashed potato on to the cooled meat mixture, doming it, and mark in ploughlines with a fork. Dot with butter and put in the oven for 20 minutes until the top is gilded.

Any lightly cooked green vegetable can accompany, but it is nicest of all with a dish of old carrots, well scraped, sliced fine and cooked in a tightly lidded pan with a tablespoon of water, a knob of salty butter, half a teaspoon of sugar and plenty of freshly milled pepper. There is something particularly reminiscent of the cottage garden about a bunch of freshly dug, well-grown carrots.

SUGGESTIONS
• Chopped mushrooms can be fried in the butter before the flour is added, preferably the delicious field mushrooms which miraculously appear overnight wherever cattle are pastured.

FRICO
(Italy)

This dish from the north-eastern corner of Italy is made with the last of the winter's store of cheese, once known as 'white meat'. In the mountains of Carnia, where there is no oil for frittering it is cooked on a dry pan, but down on the plain around Udine, the grated cheese is deep fried in a shallow pan. Here are both methods.

Makes 3–4 pancakes
Quantity For 3–4 people
Time Active: 20 minutes
Inactive: Overnight

1 lb/500 g hard cheese, grated the day before and left to air overnight

For Carnia's upland frico, you will need a small fryingpan – a small non-stick omelette pan is perfect. Sprinkle a layer of grated cheese into the hot pan. Squish it down with a fork as it melts and crisps. When you have a nice brown lacy pancake, flick it out (don't turn it to cook the other side). Serve with a dollop of polenta and pickled vegetables – salted turnips preserved in cider-vinegar are considered appropriate.

For the lowland frico of Udine, where this is a popular feast-day snack, you need a shallow pan in which you have heated olive oil to chip-frying temperature. Pick up a handful of grated cheese and throw it into the hot oil. Stir it with a fork so that the grated strips melt together into a crisp disk. Don't let it burn. Remove and drain on kitchen paper. Serve with slabs of grilled polenta.

Accompany either version with a salad of spring leaves – spinach, sorrel, young turnip tops, rockette. Wild leaves on sale in those parts include young poppy leaves, lady's smock and bladder campion – *silene vulgaris*.

YORKSHIRE BEEF SAUSAGES
(England)

In the beef-loving countryside of Yorkshire, sausages were made with the parts of the animal that could not be roasted. The breadcrumbs balance the heaviness of the suet.

Quantity Enough for 6–8
Time Preparation: 1 hour

2 lb/1 kg lean beef	salt
1 lb/500 g suet	sausage skins
8 oz/250 g fresh breadcrumbs	dripping for frying
plenty of black pepper	

Utensils A funnel for filling the sausages (a mincer with a sausage attachment makes the job easier) and a frying pan

Mince the meat and pound all the ingredients together. Stuff into sausage skins as for pork sausages (see page 162) but make the sausages rather longer than usual. Their colour should be a strong red.

Fry them in a little dripping until crisp. Serve with mashed potatoes and a jug of gravy, as for pork sausages.

Or drop half a dozen of them into a Yorkshire pudding batter (see page 208) to make a toad-in-the-hole for 4 Yorkshire appetites. A glass of best Yorkshire bitter to keep the dish proper company.

ONE-POT STEW
Pichelsteiner (Germany and neighbours)

The German version of this universal staple.

Quantity   Enough for 6–8
Time   Preparation: 30 minutes
Cooking: 1 hour

1½ lb/750 g beef, veal *or* pork, cut from the shoulder (any or all three can be used)
2 onions
1 oz/25 g lard
1 lb/500 g mixed root vegetables (carrots, turnips, kohlrabi, celeriac, leeks)
1 marrow bone, chopped into lengths (*optional*)

2 pints/1·2 litres stock *or* water
salt and pepper
2 lb/1 kg potatoes
1 lb/500 g white cabbage *or* green beans
fresh herbs — any or all of lovage, basil, savory

Utensils   A large stewpot or casserole with a lid

Cube the meat and slice the onions. Melt the fat in the stewpot and fry the meat to take colour, then add the onions. Put on the lid and leave to stew gently while you prepare the rest of the vegetables.

Peel and cube the root vegetables. Add these to the meat. Add the marrow bone if you have it, and then the stock or water. Season with salt and pepper. Put the lid on tightly again and bring all to the boil. Turn the heat down to simmer. Total stewing time will be about 60 minutes. You may need to add a little more liquid.

Meanwhile peel and slice the potatoes into thick wedges. Add them 20 minutes before the end of the cooking time (give the stew a stir at the same time). Wash and shred the cabbage or top-and-tail the beans. Put them on top of the stew to cook in the steam for the last 10 minutes.

If you are using a casserole, the dish can be cooked in the oven at 375°F/190°C/Gas 5 for the full 40 minutes.

When the meat is soft, remove the marrow bones and scrape out the marrow into the sauce. Mash in the vegetables a little to thicken the sauce. Finely chop the fresh herbs and stir them in just before you serve. The dish is complete in itself and needs no accompaniment except a slice of good bread to mop up the gravy.

SUGGESTIONS
• This dish reheats beautifully.
• The leftovers make an excellent pasty filling.

BRAISED PICKLED BEEF
Sauerbraten (Germany)

Beef, pork, and poultry provide comfortable farmers' fare all over Europe. In the German kitchen these come supported by dumplings, noodles, or potatoes. Large forest game is normally the bag of the rich landowner. Rabbit, hare, and perhaps a partridge or two from the fields and hedgerows fall to the poor man. Country stews are often soured with vinegar or a sharp young wine. Pickled cabbage and a variety of sturdy cheeses complete the meal. Favourite flavouring herbs include caraway, fennel, lovage, savory, horseradish, and juniper.

Sauerbraten is a farmer's dish for a special treat in the winter — particularly for family gatherings at Christmas. It has a succulent rich flavour, much like venison. In Germany, stewed meat is usually cooked in one whole piece.

Quantity   Enough for 6–8
Time   Start 3–5 days before
Preparation: 20–30 minutes
Cooking: 1½–2 hours

2 lb/1 kg beef brisket *or* shoulder	2 bayleaves
½ pint/300 ml wine vinegar	4 oz/100 g streaky bacon
½ pint/300 ml red wine	1 oz/25 g lard
½ pint/300 ml water	1 large onion
1 teaspoon salt	2 lb/1 kg root vegetables (celeriac,
½ teaspoon peppercorns	celery, carrot, parsnip)
1 teaspoon juniper berries	¼ pint/150 ml soured cream

Utensils   A deep dish for marinating, and a roomy casserole with a lid

Trim the meat and lay it in the deep dish. Pour over it the vinegar, wine, water, salt, peppercorns, juniper berries, and bayleaves. Leave in a cool larder for at least 3 days, but no longer than 5.

At the end of the marinating period, take the beef out of the marinade, dry it, roll it up and tie it neatly. Save the marinade. Cut the bacon into cubes and sweat the cubes in the lard in the casserole until the fat runs. Add the beef to the hot fat and turn it to brown it (this is not done to seal in the juices, but to caramelize the outside, which gives colour and a rich roasted flavour to the gravy).

Peel and slice the onion and add it to the browning meat. Peel or scrape the root vegetables and cut them into chunks. Add the vegetables and allow everything to fry together gently for 5 minutes with the lid on. Add the reserved marinade. Cover the casserole tightly.

Either simmer the dish slowly on top of the stove, or bake in a moderate oven — 350°F/180°C/Gas 4 — for 1½ to 2 hours. Turn the meat every now and again. You may need to add some extra water.

When the meat is tender, stir the soured cream into the gravy. Simmer a few moments longer. Slice the meat and serve it with its vegetables and juices. Dumplings, noodles, or *spätzle* to accompany, or potatoes boiled in their jackets.

SUGGESTIONS
• Make this dish with a tough cut of venison. Put a few dried mushrooms (*cèpes* or chanterelles) in the stew and serve it with cranberry sauce and *rösti* (see page 338).

LEFTOVERS
• This dish reheats well — just warm the sliced meat up in its gravy. Serve with refried potatoes or dumplings.

BOILED BEEF
Rindsuppe (Austria)

The broth from this dish is the favourite clear soup of Austria. It is traditional innkeeper's fare, served for the second breakfast between 9·30 and midday.

Quantity   Makes enough for 6 at one meal, soup for the same meal, with enough left for a second soup meal
Time   Preparation: 20–30 minutes
         Cooking: 2 hours

2 lb/1 kg beef for boiling (shin,
   plus a piece of flank *or* brisket)
1 shin bone cut up, with its
   marrow, *plus* a chopped rib
   bone
1 large onion
2 lb/1 kg root vegetables (carrots,
   celery, leeks, turnips)

peppercorns
lovage to flavour
½ lb/250 g beef liver (*optional*)
4 pints/2·5 litres water
salt

Utensils   The largest stewpot you can find

Tie up the beef neatly with string. If you like your soup well coloured, put the bones to roast in a medium oven until they brown.

Cut the onion in half, but leave the golden skin on to contribute its colour to the soup. Peel and roughly chop the vegetables.

Put all the ingredients into the large stewpot, and cover them with the water.

Simmer all gently for 2 hours, topping up with water if necessary. The meat will be much juicier and more delicious if it is cooked slowly.

When the meat is soft, remove it and keep it warm. Strain out the vegetables — they will be very good for the household pig, but will not have any more to contribute to your own meal. Keep the liver to make dumplings (see below).

Serve the rich beef soup first (now you may add salt), with some noodle barley (see page 304) poached in it.

Serve the boiled beef sliced with a spoonful of the broth poured over it. Accompany with pickled cucumbers, mild mustard, and grated horseradish (grate the root on the slope so that you get long thin strips). If you want to serve vegetables with the beef, then poach them plainly in a little of the soup.

LEFTOVERS
● Serve any leftovers as a salad, dressed with oil and vinegar and plenty of finely sliced onions. This salad is particularly good made with pumpkin oil.

SUGGESTIONS
Tafelspitz   This is the Viennese version of *Rindsuppe*: slices of boiled beef served in its own juice, with freshly grated horseradish mixed with grated raw apple (make and serve it when you are ready to eat or the apple will go brown). The usual accompaniment is *rösti* potatoes (see page 338) and creamed spinach with a little sauce of light oil, egg yolk, and plenty of chopped chives.

● In Austria liver dumplings (*leberknödel*) are cooked and served in this clear broth. In Germany they are more likely to appear as a main course with a dish of sauerkraut. Chop $\frac{1}{2}$ lb/250 g liver very fine. Put $\frac{1}{2}$ lb/250 g fresh breadcrumbs to soak in $\frac{1}{2}$ pint/300 ml milk. Beat 2 eggs together. Chop a few sprigs of lovage or parsley and peel and mince 1 clove of garlic finely. Mix all together lightly with the tips of your fingers. Form the mixture into dumplings with wet hands — the dumplings should be the size of large marbles and should puff up to the size of ping-pong balls. Poach them in broth in the saucepan for 15 to 20 minutes.

Serve hot in clear soup. Or with a dish of cabbage, sour or fresh, and a bowl of soured cream handed separately.

Egg custard for Rindsuppe   You need the same volume of eggs as liquid (clear soup or water), beaten together, seasoned with salt and pepper, and cooked as a baked custard — standing in a tray of water in the oven or on top of the stove. Allow to cool. Cut into strips or cubes. Add to clear soup when you serve it.

VEAL STEW
Osso buco (Italy)

This is the classic Italian stew. Veal is the favourite celebration meat and expensive, so it is a special dish to be prepared with care. The method of slow stewing in a *ragù* is also used for game and beef dishes — the long slow braising tenderizes the toughest of meat cuts and most venerable of wild game.

Quantity   Enough for 4–6
Time   Preparation: 30 minutes
　　　　Cooking: 2½–3 hours

1½ lb/750 g veal shin with marrow
　bone
2 cloves garlic
1 lb/500 g tomatoes
2 tablespoons olive oil
2 glasses white wine

small bunch fresh herbs (thyme,
　rosemary, sage, parsley)
salt and pepper
1 stick celery
2 old carrots

Utensils   A large stewpot or casserole with a lid

Have the butcher saw through the shin bones so that you have short lengths. If you try chopping them, the fresh bones will splinter. Wipe the bone sawdust off the neat little round joints — three concentric circles of meat, bone and marrow.

Peel and slice the garlic. Peel and chop the tomatoes.

Warm the oil in the stewpot. Put in the sliced garlic and fry it for a moment, then add the meat, and the celery and carrot chopped.

Lay the meat joints in the hot oil and fry them gently on both sides. Add the tomatoes. Stew uncovered for 3 to 4 minutes, long enough to melt the tomatoes into a sauce. Pour in the wine and add the little bunch of herbs. Adjust the seasoning. A tablespoon of sugar makes a good addition if the wine is dry and the tomatoes have not been ripened in the Mediterranean sun.

Cover the pot tightly and cook for 2½ to 3 hours either on a gentle heat on top of the stove, or in a low oven at 300°F/150°C/Gas 2. This may sound a long time, but shin of veal is full of sinews and if these are allowed to melt through long cooking, they will turn to jelly and the dish will yield a rich, thick sauce surrounding a delicious tender meat joint encasing the marrow. You may need to top up the liquid with a little more wine or tomato juice.

Serve steaming and perfect in its own dish, with quartered lemons and a risotto (see page 268) — the only stew the Italians serve with a risotto — or with a dish of polenta (see page 271).

SUGGESTIONS

● This recipe can be used for any variety of game: partridge, pigeon, hare, rabbit, even a tough cut of venison. Or with a mixture of all or any of them. It is also very good made with beef. If you have a red meat, it is better to use red rather than white wine.

● Dilute ½ pint/300 ml *ragù* (see page 283) with a glass of white wine, and use it as a stewing liquid after you have fried the garlic and meat in the oil. It will yield an excellent dish.

LEFTOVERS

● *Osso buco* heats up wonderfully well. It will be even better second time around. Accompany it with a potato purée or some plain buttered noodles, and a sharp little salad of chicory or watercress.

OXTAIL SOUP
(England)

This recipe comes from the household book of the Luard family, Huguenot refugees who fled to England from France in 1685 to escape the religious persecution which followed the revocation of the Edict of Nantes. The family settled, along with many other refugee families, in the London suburb of Bermondsey, an area which soon became known as 'Petty Burgundy'.

The locals had long specialized in tanning the ox hides available from the markets which supplied the capital with its beef. The refugees, rich and distinguished citizens in their own country but now impoverished, found they had access to plentiful and cheap meat in the ox tails which were sold to the tanners along with the hides. The fame of the soup that the Huguenot families made with this tough but succulent meat spread throughout the land. The household book of Charlotte du Cane, who married William Garnham Luard in 1845, gives her family's preferred version of the dish. Here is an adapted version.

Quantity　Enough for 6–8 Huguenots
Time　Start 1 hour before
　　　　Preparation: 30 minutes
　　　　Cooking: 3 hours

1 large *or* 2 small ox tails
4 pints/2·5 litres cold water
1 pint/600 ml dark beer (porter *or* Guinness)
1 tablespoon salt
8 oz/250 g streaky bacon
3 large old carrots

3 onions
3 small turnips
small head celery
bayleaf, parsley, thyme
½ teaspoon peppercorns
6 cloves

Utensils A large stewpot with a lid, a perforated spoon, and a strainer or liquidizer

Have the ox tail cut into joints, and put it to soak in warm water for an hour. Then drain it and put it in the stewpot. Cover it with the cold water, add the beer and salt and bring to the boil while you prepare the rest of the ingredients. Cube the bacon with its rind. Scrape and chop the carrots into lengths. Peel and slice the onions. Peel and cube the turnips. Wash thoroughly and chop up the celery. Tie the herbs into a bunch.

Skim off the grey foam that has risen on the surface of the boiling ox tail. Add the vegetables, herbs, bacon, peppercorns, and cloves. Bring to the boil, cover, and turn down the heat to simmer.

Stew slowly for 3 hours. Do not, says Mistress Luard, stew them any longer, or they will be ragged and not fit to serve up. Take out the pieces of ox tail, skim off as much of the fat as you can, and push the rest of the soup through a strainer (a liquidizer would do the job more easily). Put back the ox tail and serve hot.

SUGGESTIONS

• If you like your ox tail soup darker, stir in a tablespoon of tomato purée or a shake of the ketchup bottle as you finish the cooking.

PAPRIKAS
(Hungary)

Hungarian paprika is the ground spice made from the dried ripe fruit of *Capsicum annuum*. The sweet capsicum pepper was one of the vegetables brought back to Europe after Columbus returned from his epic voyage. Plenty of alternative theories on its travel route have been on offer ever since: in Victorian times, the missionary-explorer Dr Livingstone assured his readers that the plant had long grown wild all over Africa. However, there is no evidence that *Capsicum annuum* appeared on the dinner tables of Europe until fifteenth-century Spain took to the elegant import.

The plant grew well in the sunny Iberian climate and was soon to be found in every stewpot in the land, of lord and peasant alike. Its fame quickly spread, ultimately as far north as the great plain of Hungary. Nowhere was it received with more delight. The seeds of their great culinary passion reached the Hungarians by a circuitous route. The taste for the strange new vegetable travelled from Spain to Italy, from where the good news was passed on to Italy's trading partners, the Turks. The Ottoman Turks in their turn took the seeds to their own colonials, the gifted gardeners of Bulgaria, for cultivation. Those Bulgarians who fled from the Turks planted new gardens in the fertile Danube basin of Hungary — and so it was that the paprika pepper arrived in its spiritual home.

A *paprikas* is made much like other paprika stews, usually with white meat such as chicken or veal or sometimes fish. The recipe for a *paprikas* calls for fewer onions and less paprika than the *porkolt*, and the most obvious difference is that sweet or soured cream is stirred into the gravy just before serving. This is the recipe which produces the dish most frequently referred to as a goulash.

Quantity   Enough for 6
Time   Preparation: 15–20 minutes
        Cooking: 1¼ hours

2 lb/1 kg veal (a glutinous piece   salt
    from the shoulder *or* leg is best)   1 wine glass water
½ lb/250 g onions   ½ pint/300 ml soured cream and
1 oz/25 g lard   double cream mixed
1 level tablespoon paprika (Noble
    Rose *or* sweet)

Utensils   A heavy stewpot with a lid

Cube the veal into bite-sized pieces. Peel and chop the onions. Melt the lard in the stewpot. Put the onions to fry gently. When they are soft and golden, push them to one side and add the veal. Fry together for 10 minutes. Remove from the heat, and stir in the paprika and the salt.

Replace the pan on the heat and add the water. Not soup or stock-cube liquid, which makes everything taste the same, but pure, clear water.

Bring to the boil, cover tightly, and simmer for an hour. Keep an eye on the pot so that the liquid does not dry out, and only add a splash of water at a time.

When the meat is tender, remove the lid of the pan and boil fiercely to evaporate all but the last of the liquid. Stir in all but 2 tablespoons of the cream immediately.

Serve in a deep dish, with the last of the cream spooned over the top. Flat noodles or *tarhonya* noodles to accompany. A light flowery Hungarian white wine would be perfect with the dish. A handful of apricots and a glass of Hungary's own special apricot brandy, *Barak-palinka*, to complete the meal.

SUGGESTIONS

● Use soured cream only, or double cream only with a tablespoon of vinegar.

LEFTOVERS

● Stir in an equal quantity of fresh, cooked noodles to the leftover stew. Spoon more cream, or a white sauce, over all, dot the surface with butter, and sprinkle with cheese. Bake in the oven for 20 minutes at 350°F/180°C/Gas 4, to heat it through and gild the top. You'll wish you had made double the quantity.

PORKOLT
(Hungary)

The most popular dish of the old Austro-Hungarian Empire, *porkolt* should not be confused with the Hungarian *gulyas*, which is a soup. Strings of the essential ingredient of the *gulyas*, the brilliant crimson sweet paprika pepper, light up the marketplaces of the elegant towns of the old Empire each autumn. This recipe is for beef but the dish can be made with veal, and can be served with sauerkraut or soured cream. It can also be served at midday, in the evening, or even, in Austria, for a 'second breakfast' taken around eleven in the morning. An adaptable and very popular recipe.

Quantity Enough for 6
Time Preparation: 30 minutes
        Cooking: 1 hour

2 lb/1 kg beef	1 wine glass water
2 lb/1 kg onions	salt
2 oz/50 g lard	marjoram and caraway seeds
1 oz/25 g fresh ground paprika (in Austria *Kotanyi edelsvess*)	1 tablespoon wine vinegar

Utensils A stewpot with a lid

Cube the beef. Peel and slice the onions finely. Melt the lard in the stewpot and fry the onions in it until golden. Add the paprika and stir it into the hot fat. Throw in a little water — the paprika burns easily. Add the meat. Stir over the heat until the water has evaporated. Add the salt, herbs, and wine vinegar. Cover tightly and continue to cook over a very low heat or in the oven at 350°F/180°C/Gas 4.

Check the progress of the stew occasionally, give it a stir, and add the minimum amount of water necessary. The meat will be soft in an hour or so, depending on the cut chosen. It is this slow dry stewing which gives the *porkolt* its unique flavour.

Serve with dumplings or boiled potatoes.

AUSTRIAN SUGGESTIONS

● The Austrians make various additions to this stew, which they call a *gulyas* — thus giving rise to the confusion over the soup of the same name.

● A spoonful of tomato purée is stirred in sometimes to darken the stew, or a crushed clove of garlic, or strips of fresh red or green pepper.

Paprikahendl This is simply joints of chicken cooked by the goulash method. If you have an old fowl that you have used to make a clear soup, it will be delicious if jointed and finished in this way (cut the cooking time in half if the bird has already been cooked).

Wurstelbraten The method of cooking is as for the *porkolt* but instead of cubes of meat use a whole joint of one of the tougher cuts of meat. For a 2 lb/1 kg joint to feed 8 people, make 4 holes the length of the joint with a skewer, and push a frankfurter into each hole. Pot roast as for the *porkolt*. Serve the meat sliced vertically across the sausages. Very pretty.

Kartoffel gulyas The same slow pot-roasting method can be adapted for potatoes. For a more substantial meal, slices of frankfurter sausage can be included.

LEFTOVERS

● Best of all as a leftover to begin with — that is, made the day before.

● Make little pastry strudels filled with the leftovers — a delicious Viennese pasty.

PAPRIKA SOUP WITH DUMPLINGS
Bogracsgulyas (Hungary)

There are wet and dry versions of this ancient dish. A *gulyasleves* is a soup and is made with more liquid, and *gulyashus* is a stew, so it is drier. The version I give here ranks as a soup. This most famous of all Hungarian dishes has its origin with the Magyar nomads, who cooked and then dried their meat on a sheepskin in the sun, bundling it up and carrying it tied to the saddle. Such habits made the Magyars highly mobile and very successful marauders. The horsemen had but to pitch camp, and reconstitute their dried meat by stewing it in water in a soup-kettle, a *bogracs*, until all the liquid evaporated. Small wonder they took over the Danube basin.

Once they had settled down the Magyars kept their cooking pot, but added those ingredients that only cultivation and settled habits could provide: the domestic pig for the bacon and the kitchen patch for the rest. The primitive stew evolved into a rich aromatic feast whose ingredients always include beef (both meats and innards), paprika, lard or bacon, and onions. There are plenty of optional additions of which caraway seeds is the most usual. Never add any flour: if you want your *gulyas* gravy thicker, take the lid off the pot and let the liquid reduce. Nor add any spice other than caraway. A *gulyas* has no cream, soured or otherwise. If you want a creamy stew, make a *paprikas* or a *tokany*.

Quantity   Enough for 6 huddled over a blazing campfire on the Anatolian plain

Time   Preparation: 40 minutes
            Cooking: 1 hour

1½ lb/750 g shin *or* flank of beef for stewing
½ lb/250 g onions
2 cloves garlic
2 oz/50 g fat bacon *or* 2 tablespoons lard

½ lb/250 g root vegetables (carrots, turnips, parsnips)
2 tablespoons paprika
3 pints/2 litres water
salt and pepper
1½ lb/750 g potatoes

For the dumplings
1 egg
4 oz/100 g flour
½ teaspoon salt

Utensils   A heavy stewpot with lid or, better still, a soup-kettle or *bogracs*

Cut the beef into neat little cubes — this is spoon-food to be eaten from a bowl and you should not need a knife. Peel and chop the onions and garlic. Cube the bacon if you are using it, then put it or the lard to melt in the stewpot.

   Put the onions and garlic to fry gently in the bacon fat or lard. When they are golden, push them to one side and add the beef. Continue frying until the meat takes colour. Meanwhile peel and chop the root vegetables. Take the pot off the stove and stir in the paprika. Pour in the water and add the vegetables. Bring all to the boil, add salt and pepper, then put on the lid, turn the heat down, and simmer the stew for an hour, by which time the meat should be quite soft.

   Meanwhile peel and chop the potatoes into chunks the same size as your meat cubes. Add them to the stew after the first hour of cooking. Bring to the boil again and simmer for half an hour until the potatoes are soft. Check the seasoning and adjust if necessary.

   Prepare the dumpling dough by mixing the egg into the flour and salt. Knead into a smooth dough and put aside.

   When you are ready to serve the stew, pinch small pea-sized pieces off the dough between your thumb and forefinger, and throw the little dumplings into the simmering stew. They are called *csipetke* and will only need 2 or 3 minutes to be done to perfection.

An excellent dish for campfire cooks.

Lay out your sheepskin and settle down to the feast. The wolf will be far from the door tonight. Finish the meal with a cup of coffee topped with thick cream if you wish to keep proper company: Hungarians were particularly fond of buffalo milk with their coffee, in the days when the buffalo was the workhorse of the country. Buffalo milk is rich and delicious. Neighbouring Romania still has some buffalo employed as beasts of burden on its provincial farms.

SUGGESTIONS
• Possible extra ingredients are chopped green peppers, chopped tomatoes, and chilli peppers — particularly the small, fresh green ones, sliced into little rings, and added right at the end of the cooking.
• Make a *gulyas* with lamb or, better still, mutton and hot paprika. Then it will be an *Urugulyas*. All other rules apply.

GREEK STEW
Stifado (Greece)

The traditional winter stew of country villagers all over Greece and Macedonia. There are, naturally, as many recipes for this ancient dish as there are cooks. Young beef is the preferred meat when available. The small mountain sheep are for milking and their flesh is not prized.

Describing Struga, north of Lake Ohrid, Brian Aldiss wrote in 1966:

> The cattle market is on the whole rather more fun, though less colourful; most of the patrons are male, scruffy, and dressed in working brown. Their white woollen skull caps indicate that most of them are Siptars, or Albanians; it is in this language or in Macedonian that the leisurely morning's disagreement over prices is carried out. Ponies, donkeys, mules, water buffaloes, bullocks were in the market, as well as cows and pigs, the latter the endearing black Serbian porker, often snuggled into the bottom of a wicker basket. . . . A water buffalo is a valuable animal, worth two horses in the villages, since it is the less choosy eater and the stronger beast. Particularly in Macedonia and Kosmet, buffalo are frequently seen, adding an eastern touch to the landscape. They are not an indigenous animal. Probably the Turks brought them in; for a race whose religion forbids them to eat pig, buffalo meat provides plenty of valuable fat.

Quantity Enough for 5–6
Time Preparation: 30 minutes
      Cooking: 2 hours

1½ lb/750 g meat (beef *or* pork)
1 lb/500 g small onions *or* shallots
3 cloves garlic
1 lb/500 g tomatoes *or* 2 medium tins
4 tablespoons olive oil

1 glass wine vinegar *or* young red wine
1 glass water
salt and pepper
bunch of herbs (bayleaf, oregano, rosemary)

Utensils A stewpot with a lid

Cut the meat into 1½ in/3·5 cm cubes. Peel the small onions and put them aside. Peel the garlic. Chop the tomatoes roughly. Put the meat, garlic, oil, tomatoes, vinegar or wine, water, seasonings, and herbs into the stewpot. Bring all to the boil, and then turn down the heat and leave to stew gently for half an hour.

After this time, add the onions. Cover tightly and do not take the lid off again for at least 1½ hours. After the cooking time, remove the lid to evaporate any remaining liquid. The dish should have nearly boiled dry by now. Let it cool a little before you serve.

Put a dish of Greek salad on the table as a first course, and serve the *stifado* with a plate of crisp, golden chipped potatoes. Wash it down with *retsina*, the pine sap scented wine so beloved of the Greeks. *Retsina* is very strongly flavoured and needs a robust dish such as a *stifado* to stand up to it.

SUGGESTIONS
● Game birds, hare, or rabbit can be used instead of domestic meat. If you use rabbit, soak it overnight in water acidulated with vinegar.

BEEF STEW
Boeuf en daube (France)

Winter in the Languedoc is long and hard. Month after month the ground freezes. Flocks of lapwings peck disconsolately at the icy furrows of the farmers' fallow fields, and it seems as if spring will never break through. The days are short and the country people do not leave their stone houses unless there is good reason. Occasionally the wine-rich scent of a slow-cooking *daube* escapes through a gap in the tight-shuttered window of a village house.

The little village of St. Fereol crouches under the dark cliffs of the Montagne Noire, the aptly named 'Black Mountain', near the medieval town of Castres. There each Saturday from early November through March, M Joinel cooks the best *daube* in the Languedoc for his small but devoted local clientele. He swears it is the near-black wine of Cahors which he uses in the dish that makes the difference. All his clients have good appetites and M Joinel allows at least ½ lb/250 g meat per person.

Quantity   Enough for 6–8
Time   If possible start the day before
            Preparation: 1 hour
            Cooking: 4 hours

For the marinade

3 lb/1·5 kg beef (top rump *or* any piece of lean stewing beef)
sprig thyme
2 bayleaves

½ teaspoon juniper berries
½ bottle strong red wine (the darker the better)

For the stew

2 oz/50 g lard
3 onions
3 cloves garlic
3 large carrots
3 large tomatoes
1 medium-sized potato
4 oz/100 g unsmoked bacon *or* back pork fat
4 oz/100 g black olives, pitted and chopped

3 tablespoons oil
2 sprigs thyme
2 sprigs savory
2 bayleaves
6 juniper berries
4 cloves
a curl of orange peel (dried is best)
1 bottle strong red wine
salt and freshly ground pepper

Utensils   A bowl, a frying pan, and an earthenware casserole with a lid

If possible marinate the meat the day before, otherwise an hour or two will suffice. Cut the meat into 2 in/5 cm cubes and put it into a bowl with the marinade herbs. Pour on the red wine, cover, and leave all in a cool place overnight or for a couple of hours. Turn the beef in the marinade a few times.

Next day take the meat out of the marinade and pat it dry (strain the marinade and save it). Rub the casserole with a cut clove of garlic. Put the casserole on a gentle heat and melt the lard in it. When it is hot, put in the pieces of meat. Leave the meat to brown gently while you prepare the rest of the ingredients.

Peel and chop the onions and garlic. Scrape and slice the carrots finely. Scald the tomatoes to loosen the skins, and then peel and chop them. Peel and cube the potato. Cube the bacon small.

Put the bacon to melt in the oil in the frying pan over a low heat. When the fat is running, add the chopped onions and crushed garlic. Cook them gently until they soften and gild. Add the carrots and fry them until they soften. Add the chopped tomato, cubed potato, olives, and the reserved wine marinade. Bubble fiercely for 5 to 10 minutes until all is reduced to a thick sauce. Add the sauce to the meat in the casserole with the herbs and spices. Pour in the bottle of wine and cover tightly.

Put the *daube* to cook in a low oven 250°F/130°C/Gas 1 for 4 hours at least. This can be done on the top of the stove if you wish. The meat will then be so soft you can eat it with a spoon, which is as it should be, and the sauce rich and thick. Taste and adjust the seasoning, and mash the sauce a little before you serve the *daube*.

A plain *gratin de pommes de terre* to follow, or a creamy purée of potatoes and celeriac to accompany and soak up the juices. A delicate salad of *mache*, and a piece of salty Roquefort from the chalk uplands behind the Montagne Noire to complete the meal.

M Joinel would offer his guests a small glass of the local fruit brandy, the special *Eau de vie de prunelles sauvages de la Montagne Noire*, made from the bitter little plums which grow wild in the copses. The distiller of the brandy, a cheerful old gentleman long past retiring age but who still wore the blue working overalls he had worn all his life, was often to be seen sipping his product in one corner of the bar. He had inherited his right to make it from his father, who in turn had inherited it from his father. But the old man was childless. Once he was put to rest under the blackthorn, he would explain happily, there would be no more fire-water from the Black Mountain and the world would be a poorer place.

POT-AU-FEU
(France)

The Guilhermat family, parents, grandparents, two daughters, and a son, farmed the small acreage beside the little house where I lived in the remote region of the Languedoc in southern France. They looked after us well. French peasant farmers are notoriously individual and independent folk, but my four small children quickly learned there would be an open door and a *pain-au-chocolat* or a piece of hot bread and honey waiting for them when the school bus dropped them off outside the farmhouse on a cold winter's evening.

The Guilhermats, who spoke to us in French but used a thick Catalan patois among themselves, ran their affairs in true peasant fashion as their parents and grandparents had done before them. The farm comprised about 50 acres, 30 of which were given over to a cash crop — often sorghum. The rest was a happy combination of those things that the Guilhermats considered necessary for their comfortable survival.

M Guilhermat had a long strip planted with vines, whose wine stocked the family's cellar. In spring he would collect a small army of snails from the wild, and place them in his vineyard so that the creatures could fatten on the young sweet leaves. *Mme Mère* made an excellent *ragoût* with them. At the foot of the vine patch there were two hives whose bees provided honey for the household. The family grew all their own vegetables in a small field near the stream, and left clumps of woodland where red-legged partridges could breed. They knew where morel mushrooms grew in the spring, the best places for wild asparagus, and where truffles might be found under the oaks.

As well as its human occupants the farmhouse sheltered two pigs, a yard-full of chickens and guineafowl, several hutches of rabbits, a cow, and a loft with its quota of pigeons. An old mulberry tree and a walnut tree shaded the walls. Mme Guilhermat's larder was well re-stocked each autumn with her own hams and sausages.

Each year, when the cash crop was sold, the family would buy good beef for a celebration meal of *pot-au-feu*. This is a classic peasant dish — it is prepared in various forms all over France. The aim is to get a good strong broth, which is eaten first, followed by a well-flavoured boiled dinner, plain and wholesome, accompanied by a spicy tomato sauce, capers and other sharp little pickles, or a glorious garlic mayonnaise, the *aioli* beloved of all southerners.

The Guilhermat *pot-au-feu* was cooked in an earthenware casserole with a tight-fitting lid. In the grandmother's day, before the family had a kitchen range, the casserole would have been on a tripod by the open fire and fuelled by vine trimmings. The ingredients were variable — lamb, bacon, a home-made pork sausage or a chicken might be used, and the vegetables depended on the season. White haricot beans could replace the potatoes. Sometimes a clove or two went in. Whatever the ingredients, the only hard and fast rule was that the cooking must be very gentle and slow. Here is the family recipe for a celebration. Mme Guilhermat considered that beef, a real luxury because it had to be acquired with money, made the best dish of all.

Quantity   Enough for 6–8
Time   Preparation: 30 minutes
     Cooking: 4 hours

2 lb/1 kg rib of beef (on the bone, for flavour)

1 lb/500 g shin of beef (off the bone, for strength in the broth)

1 knucklebone *or* marrow bone *or* a length of ham bone

4 pints/2·5 litres cold water
2 onions
1 lb/500 g carrots
1 head celery
1 lb/500 g leeks
2 small turnips

peppercorns, bayleaf, salt
1 lb/500 g potatoes
½ small head green cabbage

Utensils A large stewpot or earthenware casserole with a tight-fitting lid and a perforated spoon

Put the beef, tied in a bundle with string, and the bones, cut into lengths, into the large stewpot. Cover with the cold water. Bring to the boil and skim off the foam.

Cut the onions in half, leaving their skins on to give a little golden colour to the broth. Now wash and peel or trim the carrots, celery, leeks, and turnips. Put all the washed trimmings from these vegetables, with the onions, a few peppercorns, a bayleaf, and a little salt into the pot with the meat.

Bring the soup back to the boil and then simmer (no large bubbles should break the surface) for 3 hours, by which time the meat should be tender. The time might be shorter if the meat is high quality.

Take out the vegetable trimmings. (In the Guilhermat household they would be a treat for the pig.) Leave the meat to cool in its broth. When it is cold, you will be able to lift off the layer of well-flavoured fat (Mme Guilhermat saved it to sauté potatoes or to make dumplings). Alternatively the *pot-au-feu* can be skimmed of its fat with a spoon while it is still hot. The dish can then be finished when you wish as it will reheat superbly.

Cut the prepared vegetables into chunks. Any combination of root vegetables is acceptable, but try and use at least 3 different ones. Peel the potatoes and cut them to the same size as the rest of the vegetables. Slice the cabbage fanshape into the stalk, so that the pieces hold together.

Put all the vegetables, except the potatoes and cabbage, into the broth with the meat. Bring back to the boil. Turn down the heat and simmer. After 10 minutes add the potatoes, and 10 minutes later, the cabbage. Simmer for 15 minutes more, until the vegetables are ready.

On a cold winter's day Mme Guilhermat would serve the broth first, with a handful of noodles cooked in it. Then the meat and vegetables would be placed on the table in a wide flat dish, accompanied by a generous bowl of *aioli* (see page 444), deep yellow and so thick it could be cut with a knife. Plenty of good bread, naturally, and young red wine from the family's own vines to accompany the meal.

SUGGESTIONS
● The same dish can be made with a chicken and a piece of shin beef or 2 pig's trotters.

BEEF AND BEER STEW
Carbonade à la flamande (Belgium)

There can be no more typically Flemish combination. The Belgians use their excellent lager beer as a cooking medium with the same pleasure and ingenuity as the Mediterraneans use wine. Beer is the national drink and comes in many varieties, including the famous *gueuze*, a spontaneously fermented beer. It is usually flavoured with hops — a habit exported to Britain during the early part of the sixteenth century, when Flemish settlers arrived in southern England and planted the Kentish hop fields, which are still cultivated today. The hops have a dual function in beer: they both fine it and help to preserve it. In Belgium, and in Kent too, the young hop shoots in season are lightly boiled and served with fried bread and poached eggs.

Quantity   Enough for 5–6
Time   Preparation: 20–25 minutes
        Cooking: 2 hours

2 lb/1 kg chuck steak *or* skirt of
    beef (lean stewing steak)
salt and pepper
1 lb/500 g onions
2 oz/50 g beef lard
thyme and bayleaf
1 pint/600 ml strong beer
1 teaspoon sugar

Utensils   A deep casserole with a lid

Cut the beef into 1 in/2·5 cm cubes and pepper them well. Peel and slice the onions.

Put the lard to melt in the casserole. Fry the onions until they soften and turn golden. Push them to one side and put in the seasoned meat. Fry until lightly browned. Add the herbs and pour the beer over. Sprinkle in the sugar and a little salt.

Cook either on a low heat on top of the stove or in a moderate oven — 325°F/170°C/Gas 3 — for 2 hours. Mash the onions into the juice to thicken it a little before you serve it. Plenty of plain boiled floury potatoes or a dish of creamy mashed potatoes to accompany. Beer to drink, naturally.

SUGGESTIONS
• Some households add a chunk or two of gammon to the stew.
• Garlic and vinegar are often included.

BELGIAN HOT-POT
Le hoche-pot (Belgium)

Undoubtedly one of the oldest dishes in the Belgian repertoire, even the French class it as *hoche-pot à la flamande*. This is the Belgian boiled dinner and is served in two courses, first the soup and then the meat. Cook it on top of the stove, preferably in your grandmother's old enamel stewpot. The pig's ears and trotters give a gelatinous richness to the soup, and should not be omitted.

Quantity   Enough for 8 hungry people
Time   Preparation: 30 minutes
Cooking: 3–4 hours

1 lb/500 g brisket of beef
1 lb/500 g shoulder of lamb
½ lb/250 g breast of lamb
2 salted pig's ears *or* 4 oz/100 g
  salt pork belly
2 pig's trotters, split and blanched
5 pints/3 litres water

1 teaspoon salt
2 lb/1 kg mixed vegetables (onions,
  leeks, turnips, celery, carrots)
1 lb/500 g potatoes
a small head cabbage
1 lb/500 g small pork sausages
  (chipolatas)

Utensils   A large stewpot with a lid and a perforated spoon

Cut the meats into fairly large chunks — 2½ in/6 cm cubes. Put them with the pig's ears or belly and the trotters in the stewpot. Cover with the salted water, bring all to the boil, skim and then turn the heat down to simmer for 2 to 3 hours, tightly covered until all the meats are soft and you have a rich strong soup.

Meanwhile peel and slice all the vegetables. Add them to the 'hotchpot' stewpot in succession, starting with the carrots and root vegetables half an hour before the end of cooking, then the leeks and onions, then the potatoes, and last of all the cabbage. Simmer for another hour, until all is cooked. Take out all the solid meat and vegetables and put them on a large platter. Keep them warm. Bring the soup back to the boil and poach the sausages in it for 5 to 6 minutes. Drain them and put them with the rest of the meat.

Serve the soup and a few vegetables first. Then bring on the steaming *hoche-pot*. Serve with plenty of mild mustard and a dish of fresh horseradish grated into whipped cream.

SUGGESTIONS
● Instead of the horseradish, serve with a sharp little sauce of chopped pickled vegetables marinated in vinegar, with a handful of chopped parsley and chives stirred in.

LEFTOVERS
- You might like to save the pig's trotters for another meal. Let them cool and then remove all their little bones — pig's trotters have as many bones in them as human hands. Brush the trotters with butter, roll them in breadcrumbs, and put them under a hot grill to gild. Serve with creamy mashed potatoes and a sharp sauce made with ½ pint/300 ml stock thickened with 1 tablespoon of flour mashed with 1 tablespoon of butter, and flavoured with a dash of vinegar, a teaspoon of strong mustard, and a teaspoon of capers.
- Any leftover meat makes an excellent salad if dressed with a mustardy vinaigrette and served with lettuce.
- Put leftover vegetables into the liquidizer with as much of the broth as you need to make an excellent vegetable soup. Serve with sizzling hot *croûtons*. Allow ½ pint/300 ml soup per person.

STUFFED BREAST OF VEAL
Gefülltes Kalbsbrust (Austria)

Veal from veal calves is not such a luxury in dairy-herd country, and is often found on the Austrian table. Before the days of refrigeration, veal would have been available in the late autumn and early winter, when the young male calves had to be slaughtered before the cold weather covered the ground with snow and deprived them of fodder. Country people would only have had enough hay to feed the stabled milk cows throughout the winter.

Quantity   Enough for 8
Time   Preparation: 40 minutes
Cooking: 1¼ hours

1 boned breast veal (weighing about 2½ lb/1·2 kg)	1 egg
	¼ pint/150 ml milk
salt and pepper	3 oz/75 g flour
4 oz/100 g dry bread	1 tablespoon chopped fresh herbs
4 oz/100 g butter	(parsley, chervil, marjoram)

Utensils   A frying pan, a bowl, and a casserole with a tight-fitting lid, just large enough to take the rolled veal

Lay the breast of veal flat on the table and sprinkle it with salt and pepper. Dice the bread and fry it lightly in 2 oz/50 g of the butter. Meanwhile mix the egg and the milk. Tip the contents of the frying pan into a bowl and pour the egg and milk over all. Stir in the flour and the herbs, and season with salt and pepper. You may need more milk to make the mixture damp enough. Allow it to stand for half an hour.

Preheat the oven to 350°F/180°C/Gas 4.

Spread the stuffing mixture over the meat, and then roll it up and tie securely with string. Melt the remaining butter in the casserole and sear the roll, turning it to brown on all sides. Sprinkle it with salt and pepper and cover tightly.

Cook in the oven for 1¼ hours. Remove the lid of the casserole for the last 10 minutes.

Serve with *rösti* (see page 338) and creamed spinach. Good Austrian white wine to accompany.

SUGGESTIONS
• The recipe is very good prepared with a roasting chicken.

TRIPE AND CHICKPEAS
Callos a la valenciana (Spain)

Carne de lidia is the name given to the meat on sale after the bullfight. The morning after the *corrida*, a regular event in my local town of Algeciras, a line would form early in the market for the meat from the *toros bravos*, muscular four-year-olds, six of whom had met their fate in the ring on the previous day. The meat was sold by weight in indiscriminate hacked-off chunks. Since each cut would be on offer at the same knockdown price, early birds caught the best bargains. The liver and lights would go last for a few pesetas to the poorest.

The Spanish way with tripe makes the best of this somewhat awkward, rather slithery meat. Esperanza, one of my neighbours in southern Spain, would walk up the goat track to the main road to catch the bus early on the morning when the *carne de lidia* went on sale. She liked the tripe best, and the local butcher would save a bucketful of the grey honey-comb patterned stomach-meat especially for her. By the early afternoon I would see her with her blue bucket bobbing on her arm, plodding back down the hillside to her whitewashed cottage.

Later, as the sun dipped towards the horizon, she would make her way down to the mill-stream which threaded the valley's floor. There, in the little bay where she always did her washing, she scrubbed the tripe on the stones — rubbing, rinsing, and beating it in the clear running water until it was as white and clean as new linen. Everything else that was needed for the recipe she grew in her own kitchen *huerta*, the fertile vegetable patch beside her cottage, or came from the annual pig-killing.

Quantity Enough for 5–6
Time Start the day before
Preparation: 30–40 minutes if the tripe is ready-cooked
Cooking: 1–4 hours depending on the raw materials

1 lb/500 g tripe	6 cloves garlic
1 salted *or* fresh pig's foot *or* ear *plus* 1 piece dried ham bone (*optional*)	2 onions
	1 fresh red pepper
	6 tablespoons olive oil
½ lb/250 g dried chickpeas *or* 3 medium tins	2 dried red peppers *or* 1 tablespoon sweet paprika
4 oz/100 g bacon *or* gammon with skin	3–4 links dried *chorizo or* 4 oz/100 g dried spicy sausage
2 bayleaves	1–2 tiny red chilli peppers
½ teaspoon black peppercorns	1 glass white wine
1 lb/500 g tomatoes *or* 2 medium tins	salt

Utensils 2 saucepans, a heavy casserole with a lid, and a frying pan

In non-Mediterranean countries, tripe is usually sold not only cleaned but ready-cooked, steam-blanched, and soft so that it looks like white honeycomb. If it is still in the raw state, wash it thoroughly and put it to soak overnight in salt water acidulated with vinegar or lemon juice. At the same time split the pig's trotter and, if it is a fresh one, leave it in salt overnight too. If you are using dried chickpeas, put them to soak in cold water for a few hours.

If your tripe is ready-cooked, omit the following preliminary preparations. Unbleached tripe must be blanched. Put the sheets of tripe in a saucepan, cover with cold water, and bring to the boil. Drain and rinse immediately. Cut into 1 in/2·5 cm squares and put them into the casserole. Rinse the pig's trotter and put that in, together with the ham bone if you have it. Pour in 2 glasses of water, cover tightly, and leave to simmer for 3 to 4 hours, by which time all the meats should be soft. Take out the trotter and pick out the bones. Return the gelatinous meat, chopped into cubes, to the pan.

If your chickpeas are out of a tin, omit the following procedure. After the tripe has been simmering for 2 hours, put the soaked chickpeas in a separate pan and cover them with water to a depth of 2 fingers. Cut the rind off the bacon or gammon, cut it into small squares, and add to the pan with the bayleaves and peppercorns. Cover the pan and bring the contents to the boil. Cook steadily for 1 to 2 hours, until the chickpeas are soft. Some chickpeas take much longer than others. If you need to add water, use boiling water. When they are cooked, drain the chickpeas and add them to the tripe.

If you have tinned chickpeas and pre-cooked tripe, drain the chick-peas and put them in the casserole. Cut the home or shop-prepared tripe into 1 in/2·5 cm squares and add to the chickpeas. Your stew will lack most of the characteristic glueiness, to my mind necessary, imparted by the tripe juices and the bacon rind, but it will be a great deal shorter in the preparation.

Meanwhile pour boiling water over the tomatoes to loosen the skins. Peel and chop them. Chop the rindless bacon or gammon. Peel the garlic cloves and crush them with a little salt. Peel and chop the onions. Hull, de-seed, and chop the red pepper. Warm the olive oil in the frying pan, and put in the garlic, the onions, the red pepper, and the dried red peppers or paprika. Fry gently until the vegetables soften. Chop up the *chorizo* or sausage and add it, followed by the chopped tomatoes. De-seed the chillis (don't rub your eyes) and add them and the wine. Cook uncovered for 20 to 25 minutes, until you have a spicy sauce. Adjust the seasoning.

Tip the sauce into the casserole with the tripe and chickpeas, and stir well. Cook all together gently for 15 minutes to marry the flavours.

Serve with plenty of bread and wine. My neighbour down the valley would serve the dish with a salad of cos lettuce, freshly picked from her *huerta*, sliced and dressed with chopped onion, vinegar, oil, and salt to clear the palate for a piece of her special goat's cheese. The cheese was her cash crop, and she made it 2 or 3 times a week throughout the summer, selling it fresh, or rubbing it with olive oil and paprika and maturing it for a few months on a beam in her lean-to dairy.

Reindeer

The adventurous traveller Paul du Chaillu, fresh from his explorations in West Africa, observed Laplanders milking their reindeer in 1871:

I watched the milking with great interest. The women knew every animal around the tent, and if one had been missing they would have been able to designate it at once. Those which were to be milked were approached carefully, and a lasso was thrown gently over the horns, and knotted over the muzzle, to prevent the deer from running away; but they made no effort to escape. Sometimes one would hold the deer while another was milking. . . . The process was peculiar: the women held in one hand a wooden scoop, frequently pressing hard with the other, for the thick fluid seemed to come with difficulty; it was poured from the scoop into a keg-like vessel closed by a sliding cover, and so contrived that it could be carried on the back of an animal . . . skin bladders were filled, to be used

by the Lapps who were to remain the whole day with the herds. I was surprised at the small yield — some not giving enough to fill a small coffee-cup; but it was very thick and rich — so much so that water had to be added before drinking . . . not unlike goat's milk. The milk of the reindeer forms a very important item in the food of the Lapps . . . butter made from it is like tallow, so they make very little.

In the making of cheese, the milk is first heated, and the scum rising to the top is put in a wooden bowl, while the greater part is then placed in an empty bladder, which is afterwards hung up for its contents to dry; this dried scum, which they call kappa [cream], is considered a great dainty, and is always given to distinguished guests. Then rennet is added to the milk. The cheese is pressed by hand, and is packed in round wooden boxes, or put in forms made of plated spruce roots; after it is dried it is hung up in the smoke in the kata; it is white inside, and tastes of the milk, a great deal of which is kept for winter use. The Lapps are very fond of thick milk, but, on account of the climate, they have to hasten the coagulation by adding fresh butterwort [*Pinguicula vulgaris*].

While the men were enjoying their pipes the women busied themselves with cooking. A porridge was made of the dry skimmed milk, stirred into water with a wooden spoon — a palatable and very nutritious dish. Each person had a little bag from which a spoon was taken for table use . . . forks are not used among the Lapps, but some of their silver-ware is very old. . . . The Laplanders are very fond of dried powdered blood, which is cooked in a kind of porridge mixed with flour, or diluted with warm water and made into a pancake.

And again on another day:

After the meat was cooked it was put on a wooden platter and the father, as is the custom, divided it into portions for each member of the family. The fattest parts are considered the best, and I noticed that these were set aside for us. Then we began our meal, using our fingers as forks. The fire was kept blazing, for it was 40 degrees below zero; and besides, we wanted the light . . . the men and women smoked their pipes. . . . Singing hymns in praise of God, they dressed themselves for the night, putting over their garments a long reindeer gown, extending below the feet — almost a bag. No matter how severe the weather may be, one does not feel cold in such a garb.

REINDEER STEW
Kokt rensdyrkjott (Lapland)

Reindeer are still herded, like cattle in the south, for meat and skins by the Lapp population of northern Scandinavia. The usual cooking method of the nomadic, tent-dwelling Lapps was a heavy iron cauldron suspended over the hearth-fire from the crossbar of the tent. The boiling pot could be let up and down on a sophisticated hook and pulley system. The tents and implements of the *Same*, as the Lapps call their nation, were always impeccably designed and made. The Lapps were (and still are) accomplished craftsmen — so clever were they at boat-building that the Vikings used to employ them to build their long-ships. Lapp-carved bone implements, together with their birch bowls and cups, their horn-handled knives, and their moulded bark storage containers, are always exquisitely carved and often inlaid with bone medallions and other decorations.

This recipe comes from a Forest-Lapp family in Kautokeino, northern Norway, and it was always prepared by the father. In the likely absence of reindeer (or even the alternative, moose), the recipe can be made with beef. The aromatics, with the exception of one trade item, peppercorns, are in plentiful supply in Lapland.

Quantity   Enough for 6 for 2 meals
Time   Preparation: 10 minutes
          Cooking: 3–4 hours

4 lb/2 kg meat *plus* bones
4 pints/2·5 litres water
1 teaspoon juniper berries
1 teaspoon peppercorns
1 tablespoon dried ligonberries

1 tablespoon dried rowanberries
a few young fir needles *or* a
  handful dill
1 tablespoon salt

Utensils   A heavy stewpot and a perforated spoon

Crack the bones. Put the bones and the meat, rolled and tied, into the stewpot, cover with the water, and bring all to the boil. Skim off the froth which rises. Add the aromatics and the salt, and then turn the heat down to simmer for 3 to 4 hours, when the meat should be tender.

Scoop the marrow from the bones into the stew before slicing the meat and serving it with its soup in individual bowls. Dark rye bread to accompany. In *Same* (Lapland), the accompaniment might be little cakes, thin as dollar-pancakes, made from rye flour mixed with blood. Blueberries or wild strawberries to finish the meal.

SUGGESTIONS

● The berries and fir needles can be substituted with twice the quantity of fresh cranberries, and a few sprigs of rosemary or thyme.

● Cook root vegetables, such as potato, turnip, and swede, in the soup to serve with the meat. Nomadic peoples like the *Same* did not have time to plant vegetables, so this would be a modern addition.

HOT-POT
Karjalanpaisti (Finland)

The brick bread ovens which are still to be found in the country districts of Finland were used no more than once every two or three months. Wood fires were lit inside and then the ashes were brushed out, leaving the walls red-hot for batches of bread to be baked. Fuel is always precious in such a climate. The residual heat of the oven was used to prepare slow-stewed dishes. In the north the meat might well be reindeer or moose venison. Beef and pork were more common in the south. Meat baked in the residual heat of the bread oven is a great wedding or celebration dish — the casseroles were put in after the egg-enriched party breads and sugar biscuits had been baked.

Quantity   Enough for 8–10
Time   Preparation: 20 minutes
Cooking: 4 hours or overnight

4 lb/2 kg mixed meats (a combination of reindeer, venison, pork, lamb, beef, veal, whatever can be obtained)	3 lb/1·5 kg onions 1 teaspoon juniper berries salt and pepper 1 pint/600 ml water

Utensils   A heavy casserole with a lid

Preheat the oven to 250°F/130°C/Gas 1.

Slice the meat. Slice the onions. Lay the meat and onions in alternate layers, seasoned well with crushed juniper, salt and pepper, in the casserole. Pour in the water. Cover tightly, sealing with a paste of flour and water if the lid does not fit very snugly. Bake for at least 4 hours. Overnight at the lowest possible temperature is not too long.

Grilled Meats

GRILLED MEATS
(Hungary)

The Hungarian fondness for the nomadic Magyar diet of milk, fresh or soured, and grilled meats (fast food for nomads) reflects the taste for fermented mare's milk and steaks of their hunting ancestors. Dishes called Bandit's roast, *Zsivanypecsenye*, Robber's meat, *Rablohus*, and Gypsy roast, *Ciganypecsenye*, testify to ancient carnivorous leanings. As soon as the Magyars settled down, they took to pig-keeping with enthusiasm. The meat stews also are throw-backs to the nomadic horsemen, as they were originally prepared with dried meat and cooked over an open fire in a *bogracs*, a large copper bucket which is still sometimes used in the modern Hungarian kitchen.

Today itinerant food sellers in the market of Gyor in Transdanubia, as in other markets throughout modern Hungary, continue to offer the public what it has enjoyed for so long: meat fast-grilled and accompanied by good country bread. Hungarian street food is served from portable kiosk shelters equipped with bar-height tables for the customers. On offer are grilled paprika sausage and black pudding, fried liver and pork, sold by weight straight from the fire and wrapped in sugar paper. A screw of mustard, a thick slice of pale dense-crumbed bread (also sold by weight), and pickled yellow hot peppers come with it. A mixture of meats is typically Hungarian. Here are three mixed-meat dishes — make them all together and serve them on a big wooden platter as a rather unusual mixed grill. Finish with the alternative street food — doughnuts hot from the frying vat.

HUNGARIAN SAUSAGES
Rachegi (Hungary)

Quantity   Enough for 4
Time   Preparation: 40 minutes

1 lb/500 g minced veal	salt
1 lb/500 g minced pork	1 tablespoon paprika
2 eggs	1 tablespoon chopped marjoram
1 clove garlic	1 tablespoon chopped parsley

Utensils   A bowl and a grill or a frying pan

Mix the meats and the eggs together well. Crush the garlic in the salt. Add it to the meat mixture, along with the paprika and the herbs. Knead all into a firm paste. If you have a friendly butcher who will let you have sausage casings, stuff the mixture through a funnel into the well-soaked casings, to make a single long sausage. If you have no casings, shape the mixture by hand (a wet hand works best) into sausages about 1 in/ 2·5 cm thick. Grill the sausages or fry them in butter. Serve with spiced vegetable pickles (use the Bulgarian recipe on page 410), good bread, and a bowl of mild mustard. Beer or white wine to quench your thirst.

STUFFED PORK CHOPS
Baranya (Hungary)

Quantity   Enough for 4
Time   Preparation: 20–30 minutes

8 thin slices pork fillet (the chop without the bone)	2 oz/50 g smoked bacon
salt and pepper	1 oz/25 g lard
marjoram	4 oz/100 g liver
1 clove garlic	1 tablespoon paprika
	1 egg

Utensils   A hot grill and a frying pan

Lay the slices of pork fillet out on the table. Sprinkle them with salt, pepper, and some marjoram. Crush the clove of garlic with a little salt. Mince the bacon and put it to fry gently in the lard. Add the garlic. Chop the liver small and put it to fry with the bacon. Cook gently until the liver stiffens and takes colour. Off the fire, stir in the paprika and some more majoram. Allow the liver mixture to cool a little, then season it, and mix in the egg to bind the mixture into a stuffing. Sandwich the pork rounds together in pairs with a mound of the mixture, rather like large ravioli. Fry or grill them until well browned and cooked through.
   Serve with bread, hot pickles, and mild mustard.

FRIED LIVER
(Hungary)

Quantity Enough for 4
Time Preparation: 20–30 minutes

1 lb/500 g calf's *or* pig's liver
2 onions
½ lb/250 g tomatoes *or* 1 medium
  tin

2 oz/50 g lard
1 tablespoon paprika
1 tablespoon chopped marjoram
salt

Utensils A frying pan

Trim the liver of any veins, and then slice it into strips about ½ in/1 cm wide by 3 in/7 cm long. Peel and finely slice the onions. Pour boiling water on the tomatoes to loosen the skins, and then peel and chop them.

Melt the lard in a frying pan. Add the onions and fry them golden. Push to one side and stir in the strips of liver. Cook them until they stiffen and take colour. Sprinkle in the paprika and chopped marjoram. Add the tomatoes and raise the heat to melt them into a thick sauce. Taste and adjust the seasoning.

SUGGESTIONS
● Serve with a ladleful of *letcho* (see page 362) stirred in instead of the tomatoes.

STUFFED STEAK
Kapuvar (Hungary)

Quantity Enough for 4
Time Preparation: 30 minutes

8 thin fillets of beef (of the kind
  sold as beef-olives)
salt and pepper

mild mustard
4 thin fillets pork
4 slices smoked streaky bacon

Utensils A hot grill or a frying pan

Sprinkle the slices of beef with salt and pepper, and spread one side of each with mustard. Sandwich a fillet of pork between each 2 fillets of beef. Cut the bacon into larding strips. Make 2 pairs of slits in the beef and pork sandwiches, and thread strips of bacon through to hold the sandwiches together.

Fry or grill the sandwich steaks — they will have to be well done because the pork in the middle must be thoroughly cooked. Serve with pleasure, pickles, and bread. A big tankard of beer to refresh you.

GRILLED MARINATED MEAT OR FISH
Kebabs (Turkey)

This is food for nomads and was probably man's first taste of the fire. 'Kebab' is an ancient Indian word meaning 'cooked meat' — a modest beginning for a dish which has inspired so many cooks. The secret of good kebabs lies in the marinade. Lamb or kid is the usual (and the best) meat: it is delicate enough to respond well to the spices, and tender enough not to harden under the fierce heat of the grill. Liver and lights and other offal also make good kebabs (see *Kokoretsi* page 201). Pork is another suitable meat, but it must be thoroughly cooked through. Beef is not so suitable, being usually a lean meat and better grilled in larger pieces. Peeled prawns and monkfish make good kebabs, but need a shorter time to marinate.

Quantity   Allow 4–5 oz/100–150 g meat per person
Time   Start several hours or the night before
        Preparation: 20–25 minutes

These marinades are for 2 lb/1 kg meat cut into 1 in/2·5 cm cubes, which is enough for 6 to 8 people. Make the marinade and turn the cubed meat very thoroughly in it. Leave to absorb the flavours overnight, or for several hours at least. Brush off the larger bits of the marinade before you thread the meat on fine skewers (damp wooden skewers first so that they do not burn).

The best cooking medium is a charcoal fire, but the grill of the cooker will do well enough. Turn the kebabs once or twice. They will be ready in 10 to 12 minutes over or under not too fierce a heat.

Serve the kebabs with rough chunks of bread, or with a pilav rice. Accompany with lemon quarters and a few cool refreshing salads, including a cucumber and yoghurt salad (see page 395).

Greek marinade   Mix 4 tablespoons olive oil, 1 lemon cut into chunks or squeezed or ¼ pint/150 ml white wine, 2 bayleaves, 2 tablespoons marjoram and oregano, black pepper.

Turkish marinade   Mix 4 tablespoons olive oil, juice 1 lemon, 2 chopped onions, 1 oz/25 g crushed dried mint, 1 teaspoon cinnamon powder or crushed cinnamon sticks, and ½ teaspoon freshly milled pepper.

Alternatively make up your own marinade with your favourite spices. You should have oil plus a sharp element, and such other spices and flavourings as suit your palate. Yoghurt and onion are suitable ingredients (the yoghurt already has both fatty and sour elements). Cumin, coriander, allspice, turmeric, and ground chilli are all good seasonings.

SUGGESTIONS
• While the kebabs are in the marinade, make a batch of pitta bread (see page 502) to accompany them.

GRILLED SKEWERED MEAT
Souvlakia (Greece)

These unspiced kebabs can be delicious if the meat is good and the charcoal grill hot and clear. Cubes of beef or pork can be alternated with cubes of fat bacon, with squares of a strong hard cheese alternated with cubes of bread, or with chunks of tomato, onion, and green pepper.

Quantity   Allow 4–5 oz/100–150 g meat per person
Time   Preparation: 30 minutes

Thread cubes of beef and any other ingredients you are using on skewers, brush them with oil, sprinkle with pepper, and grill them over hot charcoal or under a blazing hot grill.

When they are ready, sprinkle them with rough salt and serve with quartered lemons, a bowl of *tzatziki* (see page 395), and plenty of bread. Accompany them with a dish of vegetables, such as *Koukia* (see page 401).

GRILLED SAUSAGES WITH PEPPERS
Mititei (Romania)

Grills for the cooking of these little sausages are traditionally set up first thing in the morning on market day in town squares all over Romania. They are usually within range of a portable beer counter, installed by another travelling salesman, who would provide little chairs and tables. The sausages can be made from virtually any part of any animal, an undemanding recipe whose ingredients can still be acquired despite the shortages that plague modern Romania.

Quantity   Enough for 4–5 after market day
Time   Start the peppers the day before, the sausages 2–3 hours before
        Preparation: 25–30 minutes

1 lb/500 g green *or* red peppers	salt and pepper
1 lb/500 g finely minced meat (beef is usual, other meat will do fine)	1 tablespoon summer savory
	$\frac{1}{2}$ teaspoon freshly ground allspice (a favourite spice in Romania)
2 cloves garlic	

The day before you need them, blacken the peppers under or on the grill until all the skin blisters and you can peel them easily. Take off the skin, de-seed and cut the peppers into strips. Dress with 3 parts of oil to 1 of wine vinegar, and sprinkle with a little salt and pepper and a pinch of sugar. Marinate them overnight.

Pound the garlic with half a teaspoon of salt. Mix it thoroughly with the minced meat, the pepper, the finely chopped savory, and the allspice. Leave the mixture for an hour or two for the flavours to blend.

When you are ready to cook them make sure that the grill, whether charcoal, gas, or electric, is good and hot. With wet hands, form the meat paste into stubby little skinless sausages about 1 in/2·5 cm thick. Brush the hot grill with oil, and put the *mititei* to cook about a hand's width away from the heat (that is, not too near). They will take about 7 to 8 minutes, turned once.

To be eaten straight from the grill with a side dish of marinated grilled peppers and plenty of bread.

SUGGESTIONS
● Scatter the peppers with a few black olives, little cubes of white cheese, and the chopped green leaves of an onion (chives will do duty instead).

MINCEMEAT SKEWERS
Raznici (Yugoslavia)

The Yugoslavs pride themselves on their grilled meats. These delicious little kebabs are sold on street corners in the markets and from little snack bars all over the towns and villages. Small paprika-flavoured sausages are often grilled alongside them. The scent fills the air on warm days during the evening promenade when the population turns out to chat, flirt, or gossip as the mood and age takes them. Brian Aldiss described the atmosphere in which *raznici* were eaten in 1966.

> The town of Mali Losinj clusters round an oblong harbour, looking marvellously pretty. Behind the houses a low ridge rises. There the parasol-shaped Mediterranean pine grows and breathes, while behind the ridge is the lovely beach of Citak with its warm water and sand. You can climb out after a long swim and eat tasty *raznici* with onion and mighty tomatoes, grilled by peasants over a charcoal grill under the trees. Losinj was my favourite resort — you may even be lucky enough to find the tasty Jugoslav version of *calamari* or *frito misto* on the menu, a mixed sea food dish that includes baby octopuses . . .
>
> Titovo had all the appearance of a frontier town. . . . The market was on the same primitive level. Great men and hard boys drove before them

black pigs with ropes tied to their hind legs, or wore live lambs like cloaks about their necks, or endeavoured to ride on pony-back through the thick of the crowd. The women had equipped themselves for the parade with hens or cockerels or piglets tucked under their arms or dangling from a meaty fist. . . . There were gypsies too; one group led a performing bear in their midst, all chained and stained and disgraced, and hairy as a Cetnik.

Quantity   Enough for 4–5
Time   Preparation: 30–40 minutes

1 lb/500 g minced meat (pork and beef is the street mix)
½ teaspoon salt
plenty of freshly ground black pepper

½ lb/250 g grated *or* finely chopped onions
1–2 deseeded and chopped green chilli peppers

Utensils   Small wooden skewers and a hot grill or barbecue

Pound the meat up with the salt and pepper. Knead it thoroughly until you have a soft paste. Form the paste into small sausage shapes with wet hands and push a wooden skewer through the middle of each. Wet the ends of the wooden skewers so that they do not burn over the coals.

Cook over a little charcoal brazier or under a hot grill. Serve with a dish of grated onions, the chilli peppers, and a thick slab of country bread. That's all. Simplicity itself — street food at its best.

For a main meal, serve with a salad of roughly chunked onions, tomatoes, and cucumber dressed with a sprinkling of crumbled strong white cheese, and a sliced green chilli pepper. Quartered lemons to accompany.

SUGGESTIONS
• Further varieties of grilled meat in Yugoslavia include cubes of pork and veal, *pljeskavia*, spiced hamburgers, and *sis cevap*, cubes of lamb.

GRILLED CALF'S HEAD
Tête de veau grillée (Switzerland)

The Swiss are particularly fond of veal — a spin-off from their excellent dairy farming and widely available in country districts as well as town markets.

Quantity   Enough for 4
Time   Preparation: 20 minutes
Cooking: 3 hours plus 15 minutes

half a calf's head (weighing
   approximately 2 lb/1 kg)
1 heaped tablespoon flour
small bunch of parsley, thyme,
   and bayleaf
1 onion
2 carrots

1 teaspoon salt
6 peppercorns
2 more heaped tablespoons flour
1 egg
4 heaped tablespoons home-made
   dried breadcrumbs
4 oz/100 g butter

Utensils   A lidded saucepan into which the calf's head will fit comfortably, a perforated spoon, a flat heatproof dish, and a hot grill

Have the butcher soak, bone, and tie the calf's head for you. (A calf's head needs plenty of soaking to rid itself of blood.) The tongue and brains should be prepared separately for another dish.

Put the joint in the saucepan, cover with water, and bring all to a rolling boil. Skim and then add the tablespoon of flour, the bunch of herbs, the onion peeled and cut in half, the carrots scraped and chopped, and the salt and peppercorns. Bring back to the boil, and then turn the heat down to simmer. Cover and cook gently for 3 hours. When the meat is quite soft, take it out of its broth (save this for the basis for a good bean soup) and leave it aside to cool.

Meanwhile beat the egg lightly on the flat plate. Spread the flour on another plate and season it with salt and pepper. Spread the breadcrumbs on a third plate.

Untie the joint and cut it into 4 to 8 pieces. Roll each piece first in flour, then in egg, then in breadcrumbs. Butter the flat dish and lay the pieces in it. Dot with the rest of the butter. Grill for 5 minutes each side, until the breadcrumbs are crisp and golden. Hand round a jug of browned butter separately.

SUGGESTIONS
● This dish can be made with pig's or sheep's head, or the feet or trotters of any of these.
● Stir a splash of vinegar and a few capers into the browned butter. Make a little mustard-flavoured white sauce (use some of the broth as the liquid) to hand round with the grilled calf's head.

CHAPTER 7

Pulses and Grains

Beans-and-bones dishes are classic and staple peasant food in all Mediterranean countries. Recipes range from the simple *cocidos* and *ollas* of Spain to the stupendous *cassoulet* of southern France. Small farmers grew, and in many countries still grow, their own preferred variety of beans and chickpeas which would be dried and stored for the winter. A peasant family in Spain rarely has a meal that does not include these vegetables in one form or another. The flavouring bones and bacon often came from home-cured pork. Before the discovery of the New World, dried broad beans were used for these dishes.

Ritual surrounded the planting of all such important staples, as an Andalusian smallholder, Jesus Peinado, pointed out to Ronald Fraser in 1958:

> There are plenty of crops you can't plant when the moon is waning. The May moon is bad, for example; if you plant beans then they make a mass of stalks and no fruit. You have to plant seedbeds of onions, lettuce, melon and pumpkins with the waning moon as you do vetch and alfalfa. If the latter is planted at any other time the livestock swell up and die when they eat it. That's the truth. I don't know why it is, but everyone here knows it.

Pulse vegetables can provide treats as well as staple meals. Eliza Putnam Heaton observed the roasting of chickpeas at the fair of Sant' Alfio in Sicily in 1908:

> On the other side of the narrow way there bally-hooed three or four vendors of roasted 'ciceri', the chick-peas of Cicero's family name, and squash seeds, peanuts, dried chestnuts and roasted beans. . . . On a circle of lava stones rested a deep iron pan over a fire of vine cuttings. In the pan was sand, which she stirred with a wooden shovel until it came to the right heat; then she turned in her peas, stirred briskly till they began to pop, and then with bundles of rags lifted the pan — it was patched, for I counted, with nine pieces of iron nailed on — and turned the sand through a sieve into another big pan, delivering the hot peas to her husband, who acted as salesman.

BEAN STEW
Cocido (Spain)

A *cocido* is an 'all-in' boiled dinner, Spanish style. It is the most popular everyday dish to be found in the Iberian peninsula. Each region has its variations, dictated by available local ingredients and preferences. In Andalusia, vegetables are usually included, particularly greens such as Swiss chard, spinach, carrots, and small artichokes. The Madrid version

is the grandest, and includes a large piece of beef and a good selection of everyone else's ingredients as well. It is served in two parts: first the broth, with a handful of breadcrumbs or fine noodles poached in it, and then the meats. Meatballs, similar to the Swedish variety (see page 204) but including garlic, are stewed, in the Galician *pote gallego*. Catalonia calls it an *escudella* and incorporates the region's white sausage.

The simplest peasant recipe uses the widely available products of the pig *matanza*, together with a few vegetables. The pulse vegetables can be chickpeas or white beans — this is essentially a pale stew. Many rural communities cultivate and dry their own pulses. The dish is so widespread that it has a variety of names, which makes its true identity somewhat confusing to determine. It often appears as *Olla podrida*, meaning a 'rotting' or 'powerful' dish — a name which occurs in early English cookbooks influenced, no doubt, by the Spanish princesses imported as royal wives at the time. In Andalusia it is sometimes called a *pringa* or *puchero*.

The list of designations, and the variations in its making, could be extended almost indefinitely. What follows is the *cocido* as prepared in the tiny *venta*, or inn, of the Guadalmesi, the little village at the foot of the Andalusian valley that was my home for many years. The few dozen inhabitants of the Guadalmesi settlement managed to make a living out of the fertile alluvial flat which had formed at the mouth of the river where it flowed into the sea. All the ingredients were home-grown and the recipe is, I think, as old and true as any in the patchwork quilt of ancient kingdoms that make up modern Spain.

Quantity Enough for a family of 6–8
Time Start a few hours before
Preparation: 30 minutes
Cooking: 1½–3 hours

1 lb/500 g chickpeas *or* white beans
4 oz/100 g *morcilla* — black pudding (*optional*)
4 oz/100 g salted pork belly *or* green bacon
2 dried red peppers (not the hot variety — you can use a tablespoon sweet paprika *or* 1 fresh red pepper instead)
1 head garlic
3 tablespoons olive oil
4 pints/2·5 litres water (excluding soaking water)

1 length of ham bone (*optional*)
2 small *chorizos or* 4 oz/100 g dried spicy sausage
½ lb/250 g meat (pork, chicken, beef, rabbit)
a choice of ingredients, no more than 1 lb/500 g weight in all, from: green peppers, onions, leeks, tomatoes, potatoes
salt

251

Utensils   A large heavy stewpot with a lid

Put the chickpeas or beans to soak in fresh water for a few hours.

At the end of the soaking time, slice the *morcilla* into short lengths. Cut off the rind from the pork belly or bacon and cut the rind into squares. Cube the pork or bacon meat and de-seed the red peppers. Do not peel the garlic, but hold it in a flame to char the papery skin and roast the cloves a little. This releases and enhances its flavour.

Heat the oil in the stewpot. Fry the salt pork gently in the oil for a few minutes. Add the water, the chickpeas or beans (the beans should be well submerged), the ham bone, the whole garlic head, and the peppers or paprika (or fresh red pepper, hulled, de-seeded, and sliced). Bring all to the boil and then turn down the heat to simmer. You may need to add extra boiling water during the course of the cooking.

Pulse vegetables vary in the length of time they take to soften — they can take anything from $1\frac{1}{2}$ to 3 hours to cook. When they are soft but still firm — this should take about an hour — put in the *chorizos* or dried sausage, well pricked, along with the piece of meat. Add the black pudding and the optional vegetable ingredients towards the end of the cooking time — the *morcilla* and peeled chopped potatoes should be added 30 minutes before the end, and the green vegetables about 20 minutes before.

To finish, taste and add salt (the salt pork will have contributed to the saltiness), and stir in a spoonful of olive oil and a crushed clove of garlic.

Serve the *cocido* in deep plates with plenty of fresh bread. Accompany with a salad of sliced tomatoes, or a crisp green lettuce dressed with olive oil, wine vinegar, and salt.

SUGGESTIONS
● Sometimes the good lady of the Guadalmesi *venta* would stir in, at the end, a ladleful of ready-boiled cabbage fried with garlic.

LEFTOVERS
● Fry steadily in a little oil until all the liquid evaporates and the base forms a hard crisp crust. Stir the crust in several times and continue to fry until the mixture is dry and crumbly. This trick works with all pulse vegetable stews, and the result is quite delicious, particularly if served with a fried egg (see page 458) per person, and a simple fresh tomato sauce spiked with a little chilli.

LENTIL SOUP-STEW
Sopa de lentejas (Spain)

Daily life in the little hill villages of Andalusia today is remarkably little changed from the centuries-old pattern. On a fine cold October evening in the mountains above Ronda, black cliffs soar over white villages; eagles patrol the crags; the last blooms of the rock roses and late scillas glow in the pearl-grey boulders under the olive trees. In the narrow main street of the village of El Gastor the women set up in the open air their cooking braziers, shallow metal bowls balanced on slender tripods.

They cook the evening meal in the scrubbed street outside their shadowed doorways. The fuel is walnut shells, fired with dried olive pits ground to a mush between the millstones — debris of the harvest. Such fuel burns with a clean strong glow and keeps its heat like charcoal. The cooking pots are copper pans — tarred black as pitch outside, mirror-bright within. Their handles are long, made of beaten iron welded on with iron rivets — identical to the pots the Romans used two thousand years ago. The scent of cooking drifts down the narrow street, past the scrubbed doorsteps and iron balconies strung round with pots of scarlet geraniums. The stews bubble with lentils, garlic, dried mountain ham, wild greens, peppers, and olive oil. To ward off the chill of autumn in the hills of the Spanish sierras, it will be a *sopa de lentejas* for supper.

Quantity   Enough for 6
Time   Preparation: 20 minutes
Cooking: 70 minutes

- 1 lb/500 g brown lentils
- 4 cloves garlic
- 4 oz/100 g piece of pork (belly *or* lean)
- 1 lb/500 g greens (Swiss chard, spinach, spring greens)
- ½ lb/250 g potatoes
- 4 tablespoons olive oil
- 3½ pints/2·3 litres water
- 2 short lengths of raw ham bone with meat still on it (*optional*)
- 4 oz/100 g *morcilla* black pudding (*optional*)
- 1 dried *or* fresh red pepper (de-seeded and torn into pieces)
- salt

Utensils   A large stewpot

Lentils happily do not need soaking — they are the fast-food of the pulse vegetable tribe and only take an hour to cook. Pick them over and remove any tiny tooth-breaking stones (which can look exactly like lentils).

Peel the garlic and leave the cloves whole. Cube the meat. Chop the greens. Peel the potatoes and cut them into bite-sized chunks.

Fry the garlic and meats gently in the olive oil. Add the lentils and cover all with the water. Put in the ham bone, the *morcilla*, and the dried or fresh red peppers.

Stew gently for 40 minutes. Add the potatoes to the stew and continue to cook for 20 minutes. Add the vegetables and cook for 10 minutes more. When the vegetables are ready, add salt and stir in an extra spoonful of oil before serving.

SUGGESTIONS
● The ham bone can be replaced by a piece of smoked bacon.
● This is a very variable recipe, depending largely on the products and fortune of those preparing it. Green peppers can be included. Tomatoes are sometimes added, as are onions, carrots, or young tender artichokes. There are several wild greens — in particular the leaf-stems of a thistle *Scolymus hispanicus* or *tagarnina* — that are particularly appreciated in this sturdy soup.
● A fresh red pepper or 1 teaspoon paprika can substitute for the dried red peppers so easily available in Spain, where strings of them hang beside the garlic-plait from every kitchen beam.

YELLOW PEA SOUP
Ertesuppe (Norway)

A meal in itself, this is a delicately flavoured thick golden soup. If you feel those at the table may still be hungry afterwards, serve a filling desert such as pancakes or waffles.

Quantity   Enough for 6
Time   Preparation: 15 minutes
            Cooking: 1½ hours

1 lb/500 g dried yellow split peas
3 pints/2 litres water
1 length of salt lamb *or* ham bone
    (soak it for a few hours if it is
    very salty) *or* 8 oz/250 g piece of
    breast of lamb *or* bacon

herbs (leek top, celery top,
    parsley)

Utensils   A large saucepan

Put the peas into the pan with the water. Add the bone or meat and the flavouring herbs, well chopped, and bring to the boil. Turn down the heat and simmer the soup gently until the peas are soft, which will take around 1½ hours, depending on the peas. Add more boiling water if necessary.

Serve piping hot, with flatbread (see page 508).

SUGGESTIONS

- A piece of salt bacon can substitute for the ham. The bone from a roast shoulder or leg of lamb also gives good results. Root vegetables (carrots, turnips, leeks, potatoes) can be added to the dish. Each household has its preferred recipe.
- The Danes and the Swedes also love this soup. In Denmark it is called *Gule Aerter* and the pork is likely to be simmered separately, with the same herbs, until tender. The stock is then used to cook the peas.

PEASE PUDDING
(England)

One of the oldest dishes in the English culinary repertoire, originally made from dried peas with their skins still on, rather than split peas or old fresh peas. A double handful of these was tied in a clean floured cloth and hung in the pot in which the ham or bacon was boiling. They would swell into a green floury ball, which would be served at the same time as the meat.

Quantity Enough for 6
Time Start a few hours before
Preparation: 15 minutes
Cooking: 2 hours

1 lb/500 g dried peas *or* split peas *or* 1½ lb/750 g old fresh peas, which will not need soaking
water *or* stock from a ham boiling (if not too salty)

bunch of herbs (mint, thyme, marjoram, parsley)
2 oz/50 g butter
salt and pepper

Utensils A saucepan, a pudding basin, some foil, and a liquidizer if you have one

Soak the peas in clean cold water for a few hours. Then drain off the surplus soaking water, put the peas in the saucepan and cover them either with the water or stock. Add the herbs tied together in a bunch. Cook gently until the peas are soft and the skins loosen — about an hour. Remove the herbs, drain the peas thoroughly, and then mash or liquidize them with the butter. Add salt and pepper, put the mixture into a pudding basin, and cover with buttered foil. Either put the basin in a saucepan of water so that the water comes two-thirds of the way up the basin and steam steadily for an hour, or bake the pudding in the oven for an hour at 325°F/170°C/Gas 3, set in a bain-marie.

Serve with sausages or with ham done any way you please. Also good with roast pork. Or eat the pudding plain with a jug of melted butter.

SUGGESTIONS

● Beat an egg and ¼ pint/150 ml cream into the mixture before you bake it to make a richer pudding.

BEAN SOUP
Ciorba de fasole (Romania)

A favourite Romanian one-pot meal. Thick and nourishing in the cold winter months. Vegetable flavourings such as carrot, tomato, garlic, savory, tarragon, and thyme can replace the bacon. It is really a matter of making the best use of what you have.

Quantity   Enough for 6
Time   Start a few hours before
  Preparation: 10 minutes
  Cooking: 1½–2 hours

½ lb/250 g haricot, pinto, *or* butter
  beans
4 oz/100 g piece of smoked bacon
  or bacon bones
3 pints/2 litres water
1 cos lettuce *or* green beans *or*
  Swiss chard

2 egg yolks
¼ pint/150 ml soured cream
1 tablespoon vinegar
salt and pepper
small bunch of dill

Utensils   A roomy saucepan and a perforated spoon

Put the beans to soak in cold water for 3 to 4 hours.

At the end of the soaking time, cube the bacon. Drain the beans and put them into the saucepan with the bacon. The saucepan needs to be large because beans need plenty of room to expand. Pour the water over. Bring to the boil, skim, and then turn the heat down. Simmer the beans for 1½ to 2 hours until they are soft. You may need a little more water — it depends on the beans.

Shred the lettuce and stir it into the soup when the beans are soft. Cook for another 10 to 15 minutes.

Mash the beans a little to thicken the soup. Mix the egg yolks, the cream, and the vinegar together, and stir into the boiling hot soup. Season. Chop the dill finely and scatter it over the surface.

Serve the soup with good dark bread and a bottle or two of Romanian red wine. Fresh fruit to follow — plums, apples, or pears, or a dish of apricots. Or, if you and your diners are still hungry, a plate of *Papanasi* (see page 560).

CASSOULET DE CASTELNAUDARY
(France)

Mme Escrieu, sturdy mother of four strapping sons, lived with her family, two pigs, a dozen rabbits, a cow, three bird-dogs, a yardful of chickens and guineafowl, and a loftful of plump pigeons, in one of the farmhouses near my cottage in the Languedoc. Madame, a massively built matriarch, told me she made a *cassoulet* every fortnight in the winter months for her family's Sunday luncheon — never for the evening dinner as at least six hours were needed to digest it. More often would have been too much even for their gargantuan appetites. Her method begins with the preparation of her own *confit d'oie* made from goose or duck fattened for *foie gras*, but from which the precious liver has been removed and potted. The down from the birds has already been sterilized in the oven and used to re-stuff the matrimonial feather-bed. I watched her construct her mighty masterpiece.

The *cassoulet*, the archetypal peasant meal, is a controversial dish. Cookery writers, culinary scholars, and restaurant chefs have been plucking and worrying at it for years. The *cassoulet*, quite simply, is the creature of its maker: a balance of habit, necessity, and availability and as with all the best peasant cooking, the special genius of the cook. The *cassoulet* is unusual in that most of its ingredients are home-prepared, storecupboard items which demonstrate the cook's abilities in depth. The perfect *cassoulet* can only spring from the perfect larder. Even the cook's good night's sleep on her well-stuffed goosefeather bed can make all the difference.

Toulouse, where the subject has entered the more rarified air of *gastronomie*, insists on the addition of a length of fresh Toulouse sausage and leg of mutton to the stew. Carcassonne adds both mutton and partridges — and brooks no deviation. Others add what they judge to be their essentials. I put my money on Mme Escrieu.

Quantity Enough for 10 of respectable appetite
Time Start a few hours before
Preparation: 30–40 minutes
Cooking: 4 hours

For the first cooking

2 lb/1 kg white haricot beans (those from Soissons are held to be best)
½ lb/250 g bacon rind rolled up and tied
½ lb/250 g cubed salt pork belly
2 carrots, scraped and sliced

1 onion, peeled and stuck with 6 cloves
3 cloves garlic, peeled
bunch of fresh herbs (parsley, thyme, rosemary, fennel, bayleaf) tied together
6 black peppercorns, crushed

For the second cooking

1 leg joint preserved goose *or*
½ duck, with its dripping *and/or*
1 lb/500 g boned, rolled, and
tied shoulder of lamb
1 lb/500 g lean pork cut in large
pieces
3 cloves garlic, crushed

2 onions, chopped
2 large tomatoes, skinned and
chopped *or* 1 medium tin
½ lb/250 g dried spicy garlic
sausage
1 lb/500 g fresh all-meat pork
sausage (*Saucisson de Toulouse*)
salt and pepper

Utensils A large saucepan, a *cassole* or *toupin* (an earthenware casserole) or your favourite large stewpot with a lid, a perforated spoon, and a frying pan

Check the beans over for little bits of gravel, and then put them to soak for a few hours in cold water.

At the end of the soaking time, drain the beans and put them into the large saucepan with the rest of the 'First cooking' ingredients. Cover all with fresh water, bring to the boil, and skim off the grey foam that rises. Turn down the heat and simmer the beans for an hour, until they are soft but still whole, adding more boiling water if necessary.

Meanwhile prepare the meats in the 'Second cooking' group. Put the preserved leg of goose or the duck into a frying pan and melt off the dripping. Take out and reserve the leg itself. Fry the lamb, if you are using it, in the drippings until browned. Take out and reserve the lamb. Fry the pork with the garlic in the drippings, until all are browned. Remove and reserve them. Fry the onions. Drain off the fat that remains and save it for the finishing.

When the beans are ready, take out the onion stuck with cloves and the bunch of herbs. Untie and lay the bacon rind over the base of the *toupin* or stewpot with the fat side upwards.

Layer the beans with the meats, onions, chopped tomatoes, garlic sausage, and pork sausage into the stewpot, finishing with a layer of beans. From now on it is only a matter of oven time: long slow cooking is the trick. Cover the pot and put it in a gentle oven — 250°F/130°C/Gas 1 — for 2 hours. (If the beans get too dry, pour in a little boiling water — the beans will harden if you use cold water.)

At the end of the 2 hours, take the lid off the stewpot for the final stage, which will take another hour, completing the 4 hours.

Pour a tablespoon of the melted goose fat over the surface. Increase the oven heat to 325°F/170°C/Gas 3 and return the dish uncovered to the oven. It will take half an hour to form a beautiful crust. Break this with a spoon and stir it into the beans. Mme Escrieu maintains it is this operation that gives the *cassoulet* authenticity. On the final stirring, taste and adjust the seasoning. Leave for the final half hour. Now you reap the reward of your patience — beneath the golden crust the meats will be tender and fragrant and the beans melted into a delicious creamy mass.

Serve the *cassoulet* with the strong red wine of Cahors. M Escrieu still held licence, from his father and his father before him, to distil his own walnut leaf flavoured *eau-de-vie* — which made a fine *digestif* after his good lady's masterpiece. A green salad to complete the meal and perhaps a small piece of a pungent goat cheese from the nearby Montagne Noire.

SUGGESTIONS

• The *cassoulet* can be made the day before, but give it an hour and a half in a gentle oven to reheat and crisp the crust.
• If you have no preserved goose, omit it. Mme Escrieu did not always include it either. Double the quantity of lamb instead. Use good lard instead of the goose dripping.
• If you like a particularly crisp crust, scatter freshly made breadcrumbs over the surface of the beans for the final crisping.
• Stir 1 tablespoon of chopped fresh herbs (parsley, chives, tarragon) into the stew when you stir in the crust for the last time.
• Pork can replace lamb, or both fresh meats can be omitted, or replaced by fresh all-meat pork sausage. Madame would only add (and indeed only had) the fresh sausage just after the annual pig-killing.
• Mme Escrieu would sometimes replace the fresh meat with a scrag-end of one of her home-dried hams, particularly towards the end of the winter when stores were running down.

BROWN BEANS AND BACON
Bruine bonen (Holland)

A good sturdy meal for hungry countrymen. Sometimes served with honey or golden syrup — the Dutch, long a maritime and colonial nation, had early access to eastern spices and plentiful sugar. They re-exported these valuable goods to Norway, and for many years a profitable triangular trade in Scandinavian berries and fish, English wool, and Dutch sugar and spices operated.

Quantity Enough for 6
Time   Start a few hours before
      Preparation: 15 minutes
      Cooking: 1½–2 hours

1 lb/500 g brown beans	1 lb/500 g leeks
water	2 large potatoes
½ lb/250 g smoked streaky bacon	pepper

Utensils A large saucepan and a frying pan

Put the beans in cold water to cover. Leave them a few hours to soak.

When the beans are ready, cook them in enough water to cover to a depth of 2 fingers, for 1½ to 2 hours, until soft. The water should be mostly absorbed. Drain or evaporate by quick boiling any that is left.

Meanwhile dice the bacon, slice the onions, wash and slice the leeks, peel and slice the potatoes. Put the bacon to sweat in a hot frying pan until its fat runs. When the bacon is golden, add the potatoes and fry them gently. Then add the leeks and fry them too. You may need a little extra lard — it depends on the fatness of the bacon. Finally add the drained beans. Turn all together until well mixed. Fry gently until the beans have absorbed all the bacon dripping and are well flavoured. Taste and add pepper (the bacon should have added enough salt already). Delicious served with a jug of warm syrup or honey.

SUGGESTIONS
Brown bean soup The same mixture makes an excellent soup. Cube the bacon, slice the leeks and potatoes, and cook all the ingredients together with 2½ pints/1·5 litres water for 1½ to 2 hours, until the beans are tender. Mash together to thicken the soup.

LEFTOVERS
• Refry the beans and serve with fried eggs and a bowl of fresh tomato sauce with chilli. A wonderful lunch dish — or, best of all, a late breakfast.

CHICKPEA PORRIDGE
Socca (France)

A preparation much like *mamaliga* and *polenta*, this was the staple of many a peasant diet in poor districts of south-eastern France. Chickpeas grow easily and need little room. They are harvested in the late summer and dried on trays for storage throughout the winter. Today *socca* is most often found on market day. A wood-fired oven and copper dishes are the required instruments.

Quantity Enough for 4
Time Preparation: 10 minutes
Cooking: 20 minutes

6 oz/175 g chickpea flour
1 pint/600 ml cold water

2 tablespoons olive oil
1 tablespoon salt

Utensils   A large baking tray

Preheat the oven to 475°F/240°C/Gas 9.

Mix the chickpea flour with the water in a bowl. Stir in the oil and the salt, beating well to eliminate lumps. Pour the mixture into an oiled baking tray so that it lies in a layer no more than 1 in/2·5 cm thick.

Bake in a very hot oven for 20 minutes. You are aiming to achieve the black blisters on the surface that would be produced by a charcoal fired oven working at full temperature. Cut into squares and serve hot. A dish of stewed tomatoes and a fried egg to accompany perhaps, although *socca* is usually appreciated on its own.

SUGGESTIONS
• Beat a large piece of butter into it and plenty of black pepper. Your neighbours in the south of France would certainly not approve of such deviations.

CHICKPEA FRITTERS
Panisses (France)

There is a complicated ritual for pouring the cooked *socca* into a line of saucers, but this recipe is basically a solution to your leftover *socca*.

Quantity   Enough for 4–5
Time   Preparation: 25–30 minutes

6 oz/175 g chickpea flour
1 pint/600 ml cold water
2 tablespoons olive oil

1 teaspoon salt
oil for frying

Utensils   A large saucepan, a shallow dish, a frying pan, and a perforated spoon

Mix the flour, the water, the olive oil, and the salt thoroughly in the saucepan. Put the pan on the heat and bring the mixture slowly to the boil, stirring vigorously. Those practised in the art of *socca*-making will stir with one hand and rain in handfuls of the *socca* with the other — this takes years of practice if it is not to be lumpy.

Cook the mixture steadily, still stirring vigorously. It will thicken slowly, and be ready in about 10 minutes from the time it comes to the boil. Pour it on to an oiled dish in a thin layer. Leave it to cool. It will set rapidly as it does so.

You can continue when you wish. When you are ready, put a deep pan of oil on to heat. Cut the *socca* into fingers about 3×1 in/7×2·5 cm.

When the oil is smoking, put in the *panisses* and fry them rapidly until they are golden and crisp. Remove them with a perforated spoon and put them on paper to drain.

Serve the *panisses* hot. Hand round a fresh tomato sauce spiked with a little chilli. Finish with a fennel and chicory salad and a little heart-shaped Broussa cheese, marinated to a fine flavour in brine.

SUGGESTIONS
● You can also serve the *panisses* cold, sprinkled with sugar. Try them with fresh strawberries in the summer.

WHITE BEAN SALAD
Fasoul jahnia (Bulgaria)

The Turkish and Greek influence is so strong in Bulgaria, after five centuries of conquest and domination, that it is difficult to unplait the threads of the national origins of this dish. Culinary variations often depend on preferred and local ingredients. In Bulgaria sunflower is the favoured oil and the favourite herbs are mint, dill, savory, thyme, and tarragon. Lentils, peas, and broad beans were all listed by the Ottoman tax collectors in fifteenth-century Bulgarian markets. Lemon is preferred to vinegar as a sour flavouring.

Quantity Enough for 6
Time Start a few hours before
Preparation: 20 minutes
Cooking: 2 hours

1 lb/500 g dried white beans	¼ pint/150 ml sunflower oil
4 cloves garlic	juice 1 lemon
½ lb/250 g onions	mint, dill, thyme, tarragon, savory
½ lb/250 g carrots	salt and pepper

Utensils A roomy saucepan

Pick over the beans and remove any little bits of grit. Put them to soak for a few hours.

Drain the beans and put them in the saucepan. Cover them to a depth of 2 fingers with fresh water. Bring them to the boil and cook them for an hour. Peel and crush the garlic and peel and dice the onions and carrots. Add the garlic and vegetables, and the salt, bring all back to the boil, and cook for another hour. Stir in the oil, lemon juice, and plenty of freshly ground black pepper, and allow to cool. Serve in a shallow dish, sprinkled with chopped mint and herbs. Garnish if you please with a few slices of hard-boiled egg and a scattering of black olives. Follow this little salad with some freshly caught grilled fish, served with bread and quartered lemons, for a perfect light lunch.

FLAGEOLET SALAD
Salade de flageolets (France)

A little salad to be served as an entrée. Flageolets are the most delicate of the dried bean tribe. Pale green in colour, they are the dried seeds of a variety of dwarf green bean.

Quantity   Enough for 6
Time   Start a few hours before
Preparation: 10–15 minutes
Cooking: 2 hours

1 lb/500 g flageolets
salt and peppercorns
6 tablespoons olive oil

1 tablespoon wine vinegar
2 cloves garlic
small bunch of parsley

Utensils   A roomy saucepan

Put the beans to soak in water for a few hours.

At the end of the soaking time, drain them, put them in the saucepan, and cover them to a depth of a finger with new water, preferably soft rainwater. Cook them with salt and peppercorns for 1 hour, until they are soft. Don't let the water come off the boil, and top up if necessary with boiling water.

Drain them. Mix them with the oil and vinegar. Toss in the peeled and finely chopped garlic and the parsley — at least a tablespoon. Sprinkle with freshly ground pepper and salt. Leave for half an hour to cool.

SUGGESTIONS
• This salad can be made with chickpeas, haricots, or any other dried beans.

SAFFRON RICE
(Spain)

Valencia is the home of Spanish rice. Ernest Hemingway, on his way to a bullfight in 1960, made a fine meal of it:

Dinner at Pepica's was wonderful. It was a big, clean, open-air place and everything was cooked in plain sight. You could pick out what you wanted to have grilled or broiled and the seafood and the Valencian rice dishes were the best on the beach. Everyone felt good after the fight and we were all hungry and ate well. The place was run by a family and everyone knew everyone else. You could hear the sea breaking on the beach and the light shone on the wet sand. We drank *sangria*, red wine with fresh orange and lemon juice in it, served in big pitchers and ate local sausages to start with, fresh tuna, fresh prawns, and crisp fried octopus tentacles that tasted like lobster. Then some ate steaks and others roasted or grilled chicken with saffron yellow rice with pimento.

Spain loves its rice dishes and has grown its own supplies since Roman times. *Un arroz*, a rice, is an essential dish in rural celebrations, and for those who can afford it, for the midday meal. It appears as a course on its own after the soup and before the main meat dish. It is not always flavoured and coloured with saffron, but it is always turned in oil before the cooking liquid is added.

Quantity Enough for 4
Time Preparation: 15 minutes
Cooking: 30–35 minutes

6 threads saffron
1 lb/500 g round 'pudding' rice (not long grain)
2 tablespoons olive oil
2 cloves garlic
1 onion
1 green pepper

1¾ pints/1·1 litres well-flavoured stock (water will do, but then a little extra flavouring such as some chopped dried ham or *chorizo* should be added)
salt

Utensils A wide shallow pan (I use a heavy frying pan)

Put the saffron threads to soak in a little boiling water.
Pick over the rice for tiny little pebbles and errant seeds. Warm the oil in the pan. Fry the garlic, peeled and crushed, the onion, peeled and chopped, and the green pepper, chopped and de-seeded (plus any extra bits and pieces — even a bit of chopped smoked bacon helps the flavour). Add the rice and turn it in the oil to fry a little. Pour on the stock

or water and strain in the saffron water, pressing well to extract all the colour and flavour. Add salt if necessary. Cook uncovered for 20 minutes. Rice cooked in the Spanish fashion should always be taken off the heat before it is quite soft. Leave for 10–15 minutes for the rice to finish swelling.

Serve with a crisp fried egg (see page 458) for each diner, and a sauce made with a few fresh tomatoes stewed quickly with a little olive oil and garlic.

SUGGESTIONS

• This rice dish is the basis for a great many regional variations. There is *Moros y cristianos*, when the white rice is served in the company of a dish of stewed black beans — a dish that records the Moorish occupation.
• *Arroz negro*, black rice, is dyed with squid ink: buy 1 lb/500 g squid and carefully remove the ink sacs — break them open into a glass of red wine. Make the rice as above, including the chopped body of the squid with the rest of the ingredients. Strain the inky black wine into the rice 10 minutes before the end of cooking time (you will need less of the other liquids).
• Make a seafood rice, *arroz a la marinera*, with shrimps, prawns, shellfish, clams — anything your fisherman's net hauls in that is fresh and edible.
• Colonial-period Spain transplanted the banana from the Canaries to their New World possessions in Mexico and Central America. Today one of the most popular dishes in the mother country is Cuban Rice — *arroz a la cubana* — which includes a fried banana per person with the rice, egg, and tomato sauce. Delicious. (Add a little chilli to the tomato, too. The Cubans like it hot.)

LEFTOVERS

• Leftover rice or *paella* makes excellent little *croquetas*, one of the favourites of the *tapa* table. Bind the leftover rice with egg, shape into little cylinders, roll them in flour, coat with egg and breadcrubs, and deep-fry.

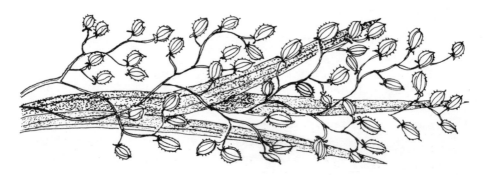

PAELLA
(Spain)

Paella has its origin in the Roman word for a pan, *patella*. Perfectly proper naming since it was the Romans who first imported rice for cultivation in the wetlands around Valencia, from whose rice fields and shores springs the great seafood rice dish *paella valenciana*. Snails, eels, green vegetables, and all manner of *mariscos*, seafood, brought in by Valencia's fishing boats will make their way into the local *paella*.

A rural *paella* — a *paella de campo* — is best cooked in one of those purpose-made, shallow, double-handled iron pans, about 15–17 in/35–40 cm in diameter, in the open air over a wood fire. A wide shallow pan allows the proper degree of evaporation of liquid, and the wood fire, when reduced to a wide circle of charcoal, gives a steady heat all over the base of the pan. The key ingredient is the round absorbent pudding rice, and its preliminary turning in good olive oil. The rest of the ingredients are as variable as the produce of the neighbourhood can make them. This is a dish which those who do not normally cook rather enjoy preparing. It is both dramatic and very easy.

Quantity Enough for 8–10 hearty appetites
Time Preparation: 30 minutes
           Cooking: 30 minutes

two dozen water crayfish *or* large
   snails (prepared in advance —
   see page 79 for crayfish and
   page 122 for snails)
5–6 threads saffron
1 lb/500 g peppers, both red and
   green
4 cloves garlic
1 chicken, jointed into 16 pieces
1 small wild rabbit, jointed into 16
   pieces
¼ pint/150 ml olive oil

1½ lb/750 g round pudding rice
1 lb/500 g tomatoes
salt
a handful peas and a few little
   clams *or* mussels (*optional*)

Utensils A wide shallow iron pan or a Spanish *paellera* or a flat-bottomed wok, and a saucepan

Bring the crayfish to the boil in a panful of lightly salted water. (The snails would of course take longer had they not been ready-prepared.) The crayfish will immediately turn a wonderful scarlet. Boil them for 2 minutes only. Save the water, using a cupful to soak the saffron. De-seed and slice the peppers into strips. Peel and chop the garlic. Lay out your joints of meat within easy reach.

Heat the *paellera* on the fire and pour in the oil. When it is lightly smoke-hazed, put in the chicken and rabbit pieces, turning and frying them on all sides. Then add the garlic and the peppers, and fry them until soft. Add the rice and turn it in the oil until all the grains are coated and transparent. Add a little salt. Finally, add the tomatoes, and pour on the cupful of saffron water and as much crayfish liquor as will cover the layer of rice and meats.

The circle of charcoal should provide a gentle even heat which will allow the rice to cook without being disturbed. Pour on more hot liquid as the moisture evaporates. Leave to cook for 20 minutes. Five minutes before the end, arrange the cooked crayfish over the top, and also the optional ingredients — clams and mussels (which will open in the steam), and peas. The *paella* should still be moist when you take it off the fire. Let it rest (covered in newspaper or a cloth) for at least 10 minutes — this gives the rice time to finish swelling and the grains to separate. The rice should never be dry, but stay moist and succulent.

The traditional way to eat a *paella de campo*, usually a Sunday-outing family affair, with the father in charge of hunting the rabbit and the children taking care of the crayfish, is out of the communal cooking pan itself. When you are ready to serve, see that everyone has a fork and a large hunk of fresh bread, and is sitting round the *paellera* in a circle. Put an inverted plate in the middle, and balance a dish of salad on top (chopped crisp cos lettuce, with sliced tomatoes and onions, salted and dressed with lemon juice and olive oil). Everyone then eats the section nearest to them. The *paella* under the plate keeps hot for second helpings.

SUGGESTIONS

• If you're obliged to cook on a gas or electric stove, you will have to keep the rice moving as it cooks. Then you do not need to give it the resting period at the end.

• In the absence of a *paellera* or a Chinese wok, a large frying pan can be used instead, and almost any combination of shellfish and meat will be good. I have had *paellas* made with prawns, squid, mussels, pork, smoked ham, even black pudding and *chorizo* sausage, all delicious.

• In Valencia the rice is sometimes left deliberately to stick and fry lightly on the base, giving a lovely crisp crust.

LEFTOVERS

• Use to make *croquetas* as for Saffron rice (see page 264), or simply mix with a beaten egg or two, drop into hot oil, and fry crisp. Excellent fritters, particularly served *a la cubana* — with fried bananas, fried eggs, and fresh tomato sauce spiced up with a chilli.

RISOTTO
(Italy)

The rice recipes of Spain, Portugal, and Italy are all Arabian in inspiration. The grain was probably introduced to Europe by Alexander the Great around 300 BC. It was not cultivated in Europe in any quantity until the Moors brought it to the wetlands of southern Spain. European rice recipes are characterized by a preliminary turning in hot oil, often with relatively small quantities of meat, fish, and/or vegetables for added flavouring, and then cooking in good broth. The rice is not white-cooked in plain water or until dry, as is customary in India and China. The Italians like their rice as chewy and *al dente* as their pasta.

Quantity   Enough for 4–6
Time   Preparation: 15 minutes
      Cooking: 20 minutes

1 lb/500 g short grain rice	salt
1 onion	butter, parmesan *or* pecorino
2 tablespoons olive oil	cheese, and pepper to finish
good stock *or* well-flavoured	
zamponi broth to cover (or	
failing either, plain pure water	
will do)	

Utensils   A wide heavy saucepan

Pick over the rice, removing any alien grains. Mince the onion finely. Put the oil to heat in the saucepan. Fry the onion in the hot oil until it turns golden — do not overheat the oil or it will turn bitter. Add the rice and fry it gently until it becomes transparent. Pour over it enough stock, *zamponi* broth, or water to cover it to the depth of a finger. Sprinkle in the salt. Cover the pan tightly and leave to simmer for 20 minutes. The Italians like their rice well-moistened and soupy, with the grains separate but still slightly nutty in the centre.

Meanwhile put a large flat serving dish to warm. At the end of the cooking time, turn the risotto out on to the hot dish. Scatter with small pieces of butter, freshly milled black pepper, and a generous grating of hard strong cheese.

The only stew with which the Italians serve rice is *osso buco* (see page 219). Otherwise it is always served on its own, prepared in any one of hundreds of regional variations.

SUGGESTIONS
• Hand a fresh tomato sauce separately along with extra cheese.

- Risotto can be cooked with chopped chicken livers, little cubes of *prosciutto* ham or *pancetta*, fresh green peas (a popular dish called *risi e bisi*) or broad beans, diced wild mushrooms, baby artichokes, snails, or, perhaps most delicious of all, the prawns, shrimps, or little clams available to those who live close to the sea.
- A risotto is also sometimes cooked with saffron threads to colour and flavour it, particularly around Milan, when white wine or Marsala may be included with the stock.

PILAV RICE
(Turkey and neighbours)

Rice has been cultivated around the Middle East for at least three thousand years. The water-loving grain was apparently first planted by Indo-Iranian tribes who had migrated from their homes. The basic rice dish of the Middle East is never served plain boiled. The variety used for pilav is long grain — Basmati or Patna is best. None of the cooking liquid is thrown away, but is all absorbed by the rice, which makes it the perfect base for a wide variety of flavourings and embellishments. It can be coloured with saffron or scented with spices. A pilav can be cooked with virtually any meat, chicken, vegetables, or fish. The first 8 oz/250 g rice will need just under 1 pint/600 ml liquid to cook it soft. The second 8 oz/250 g rice will only need ¾ pint/450 ml water added.

Turkish rice is not served as wet as the Italian risotto or the Spanish *paella* — both of which are made with the round pudding grains. Rice pilav is wedding and circumcision-feast cooking. The common filler in Turkish food is wheat. Bulgur or cracked wheat is the usual pilav grain in Asian Turkey.

Quantity Enough for 4
Time Preparation: 10 minutes
          Cooking: 30 minutes

2 oz/50 g clarified butter *or*
   3 tablespoons olive oil
8 oz/250 g long grain rice

1 pint/600 ml water
1 teaspoon salt

Utensils A large shallow pan with a lid

Heat the butter or oil in the pan. Add the rice and stir it around until it is transparent. Add the water and the salt, bring to the boil, and allow it to bubble fiercely for a couple of minutes. Turn down the heat, cover the pan, and simmer gently for 20 minutes, until the liquid has all been absorbed and the surface is pitted with little craters.

When the rice is soft, turn off the heat and draw the pan to the side of the stove. Replace the lid with a cloth, and leave the rice to stand for 10 minutes to steam itself dry.

This is a plain pilav, to be served with a skewer of grilled fish or meat — or with a fish, meat, or game stew made with plenty of sauce.

SUGGESTIONS
● Fry a chopped onion in the oil before you stir in the rice.
● Or infuse some of the cooking liquid with a dozen strands of saffron before including it in the cooking liquid.

LEFTOVERS
● Use to make *dolmades* (see page 390) or in a stuffing for vegetables (see page 380).

CHRISTMAS PORRIDGE
Risgrynsgröt (Sweden)

L. Lloyd described the *Brollop* or wedding feast in his *Peasant Life in Sweden*, published in London, 1870:

> At the banquet on the day of the nuptials, nothing is eaten excepting what the larder of the 'Brollop-house' affords; but on the subsequent days, the 'Forning' furnished by the guests is placed on the table, and that in the order in which the matrons, the contributors, stand in regard to relationship to the bride and bridegroom. It consists of many large cakes of both sweet and sour rye-bread, as also are made of wheaten flour, and of several kinds of meat, of which a couple of roast pigs commonly form a part, that are piled one on another, on an immense dish — above this store of good things, again, is a wreath of cakes strung together; as also butter, sugar-cakes, almonds, etc. Another equally capacious dish contains rice pudding.

Scandinavians love imported rice as much as they love the teas which were trekked from China over the trans-Asian trade routes. *Risgrynsgrot* is a special Christmas treat, served before the goose on Christmas Eve. There is always an almond hidden in it, for the children to find for luck.

Quantity Enough for 6–8
Time Preparation intermittently: 1 hour

8 oz/250 g round pudding rice	2 oz/50 g butter
½ pint/300 ml water	2 pints/1·2 litres milk

Utensils A roomy heavy-bottomed saucepan

Bring the water to the boil and put in the rice. Cook at a gentle simmer for 15 minutes or so until the water is absorbed. Beat in 1 oz/25 g of the butter. Add the milk and heat up again until boiling. Turn down the heat and simmer gently (stirring every now and then) for another 45 minutes, until the rice is tender and the liquid virtually absorbed. Stir in the rest of the butter.

Serve the porridge with cold thin cream and a sprinkling of powdered cinnamon — the spice chest can be unlocked for Christmas.

LEFTOVERS

• Beat an egg or two into the leftover porridge and pour it into a baking dish. Smooth down the top and dot with butter. Bake for 30 minutes in a medium oven at 350°F/180°C/Gas 4. Serve with a bowl of double or soured cream.

Risgrynoläter (rice fritters) Beat 1 egg (for each 4 oz/100 g dry weight of rice) into the leftover porridge. Melt 1 oz/25 g butter in a frying pan and drop in spoonfuls of the mixture. Fry the fritters on each side until golden brown. Sprinkle with sugar and serve with a spoonful of jam.

Polenta and Corn Meal

CORN MUSH
Polenta (Italy)

The original *polenta* was made of chestnut flour, a product of the ancient plantations of chestnut trees that flourish in the hills of Italy. When the maize of the New World was introduced into Europe it took so well to the climate of northern Italy — and it was so easy to harvest and store — that it quickly replaced the chestnut as a staple of the poor, in particular among share-cropping peasants.

The new miracle food did however have its drawbacks. When it became the single item of diet, its dependents were liable to *pellagra*, a protein deficiency disease. In the Americas maize has been under cultivation since 3,500 BC. Needing on average only a day's work a week per man, cornmeal provided the dietary powerhouse behind the cultural explosions of the Mayan, Inca, and Aztec civilizations. Recipes for cornmeal porridges are to be found all over eastern Europe. Corn-meal for *polenta* is best when freshly ground.

Quantity   Enough for 6
Time   Preparation: 40 minutes

8 oz/250 g coarse-ground yellow
    maizemeal (the coarse-ground is
    suitable for a mush, the fine-
    ground will give a harder paste
    better suited to cakes for
    grilling)
1½ pints/1 litre water
1 tablespoon salt

Utensils   A heavy saucepan

Bring the water to the boil in the saucepan. Trickle in the maizemeal
from your hand, stirring constantly with a wooden spoon with the other
hand. Make sure the mixture is smooth and press out any lumps with
the back of the spoon. The process is much like making porridge. Add
the salt. Bring to the boil and then simmer on a low heat for 30 minutes
or so. When the mixture is well thickened and comes away from the
sides of the pan, it is done. The *polenta* may need a little more or less
water.

Serve with your favourite well-flavoured sauce for pasta (one with a
mushroom base is particularly suitable). Hand a bowl of grated
parmesan or pecorino round separately.

SUGGESTIONS
• Serve with grilled meat or a rich game stew.

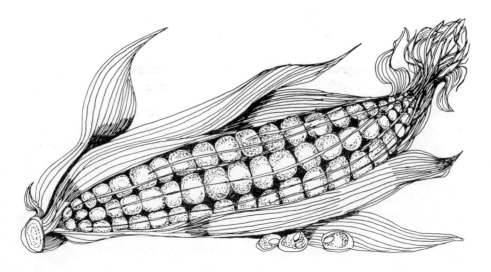

POLENTA CAKES
(Italy)

Make the *polenta* as in the preceding recipe, but using fine-ground meal instead of the coarse-ground. When the mush is cooked, pour it out into a shallow dish to a depth of about ½ in/1 cm and allow it to cool.

When cold this paste can be cut with a wet knife or moulded with floured fingers into any shape you wish.

SUGGESTIONS
● Cut the cold mush into squares, top each square with a slice of mozzarella or Bel Paese and a sprinkle of oil, then arrange the pieces in a lightly oiled, flat ovenproof dish. Bake in a hot oven — 400°F/200°C/Gas 6 — until the cheese is melted and golden. This can be done very effectively under a grill, but the base *polenta* will have to be warmed first. Serve on its own or with a tomato sauce. Or with grilled meat and a salad.

To make *polenta al sugo* for 4, you will need ½ pint/300 ml *ragù* (see page 283) or tomato sauce and 4 oz/100 g grated parmesan or pecorino. Roll the *polenta* into small balls with well-floured hands, or slice into squares with a wet knife. Pour a tablespoon of oil into the bottom of an ovenproof dish, and put in half the *polenta* balls in a single layer. Cover with half the *ragù* sauce and half the grated cheese. Repeat with the other half of the *polenta*, sauce, and cheese. Bake in a hot oven — 425°F/ 220°C/Gas 7 — for 20 minutes, until it is hot and bubbling and the cheese is gilded.

The Basques make a dish called *Broyo*, which is cornmeal mush served with *Boeuf en daube* (see page 227).

CORN MUSH
Mamaliga (Romania)

Teresa Stratilesco appreciated the niceties of *mamaliga* preparation in her travels described in *From Carpathian to Pindus*, around the year 1900:

Roumanian cookery is very elaborate, and there is a number of dishes a Roumanian peasant woman can cook if she only can afford it, but as a matter of fact, want will come to the rescue and make things ever so much easier. The plainest kind of food, the real national dish, is the mamaliga with branza [sheep cheese]. The mamaliga takes the place of bread, which is considered a luxury in a peasant's house; cold mamaliga can be eaten too, but if a fire is at hand, it is cut into slices and fried on the embers. Also a baked bread can be made of Indian meal, called malai, very tasty and sweet. Dishes of herbs and vegetables, and of fowl and fish, are very numerous; meat is rarely used.

In summer the meals are mostly taken in the field, beside the work. After the husband's departure for the field, the wife will put the prepared food in pots, earthen pans, and clean napkins . . . and thus loaded she will walk to the field where the husband is long since at work, and they break their fast, working afterwards, with food for the following meal at midday. At home the meals are taken on a round low table on three legs, which usually stands against the wall in the tinda, and is spread in the middle of the room only for the meals. The family sits around on small stools or where it can, on a log or kneeling on one knee. In well-to-do razadashi the table would be on the bed. . . .

No table cloth except on festive occasions. The table is scrubbed till it shines milk-white. The mamaliga is turned out into the middle of it from the ciaun [iron round kettle for *mamaliga*] and stands like a golden cupola smoking there until everybody has sat down round the bale. In the meanwhile the wife is careful to take off the fire the prostii [iron tripod] or she might burn in hell's flames. If the mamaliga is furrowed with cracks, this means an unexpected journey is at hand for someone of the household. They all make the sign of the cross. Then the mamaliga is cut into slices, with a thread, carefully from upside down, and not the other way, as then the maize grows ear, and divided among the members of the family. The courses then come in, in a porridger [strachina] put in the middle of the table, from which everyone helps himself with his own wooden spoon. . . . The bill of fare will be as varied as means will permit: a chicken bors, a soup, wholesome and tasty — made with fermented meal in water, producing a somewhat sour clear liquid, to be used for cooking the whole week round — more stewed fowl also, meat being very scarce in villages.

Quantity   Enough for 6
Time   Preparation: 40 minutes

8 oz/250 g yellow cornmeal	1 tablespoon salt
1½ pints/1 litre water	2 oz/50 g butter

Utensils   A roomy saucepan

Bring the water to the boil with the salt. If you wish to be authentic, sprinkle the cornmeal over in handfuls, beating constantly to avoid lumps. Stir vigorously until the mush thickens. It is however easier to mix the meal with a little cold water first, and then stir the liquid into the rest of the cold water in the saucepan. Proceed as before. Beat in the butter. Bubble the mixture for a few moments, and then turn the heat down. Stir over a low heat for 30 minutes, until the cornmeal is well cooked.

Serve it on its own or with soured cream. Or like a sorbet, between courses. Or as Yorkshire pudding, to fill up before the meat course. Served authentically it is always a dish on its own.

SUGGESTIONS
• To make the *mamaliga* special, pour it into a buttered gratin dish, spoon soured cream over it, and bake in a hot oven — 425°F/220°C/Gas 7 — for 10 minutes. Cut it into squares while it is still hot.
• Serve it with fresh cream, cinnamon, and sugar, as a sweet dish after a thick soup.
• Or turn spoonfuls of *mamaliga* in poppy seeds and honey, and eat with cream.
• Or serve it as above and accompanied by a dish of stewed plums or apples.
• Or fry breadcrumbs in butter and drop spoonfuls of the *mamaliga* in, shaking them around to coat them in the fragrant crisp crumbs.
• Spread a third of the *mamaliga* into a buttered casserole. Cover with a layer of grated cheese. Continue alternate layers until all is used up, finishing with cornmeal. Dot with butter and put into a moderate oven — 350°F/180°C/Gas 4 — for 20 to 25 minutes, until the dish is piping hot and the crust is golden.

LEFTOVERS
• Allow the *mamaliga* to cool down, then cut into slices, dip into a beaten egg, and roll in grated cheese. Fry quickly on both sides in hot butter. Wonderful as a light lunch with a bowl of soured cream or yoghurt and a fresh little salad.

SWEET CORNMEAL PUDDING
Milhassou (Spain)

This cake was originally made with millet flour and is a great favourite on the French side of the Pyrenees.

Quantity   Makes 1 large cake or 12 small ones
Time   Preparation: 30 minutes
　　　　　Cooking: 20 minutes

1 pint/600 ml milk	grated rind 1 lemon
3 oz/75 g semolina (coarse-ground)	4 eggs
cornmeal	1 oz/25 g butter
½ lb/250 g honey	

Utensils   A heavy saucepan, a mixing bowl, and some cake moulds

Bring the milk to the boil in a saucepan. (Milk burns easily — if you rinse the pan out with cold water first, the milk is less likely to stick.)

Preheat the oven to 425°F/220°C/Gas 7.

Mix the semolina, the honey, and the grated lemon rind together. Beat in the eggs. Add the hot milk slowly, beating to prevent lumps from forming. Butter a large cake mould, or choose little moulds to make small cakes for children or more delicate cakes for grown-ups. Pour the mixture into the moulds.

Bake in the hot oven for 20 minutes for a large cake, or half the time for the little ones. Delicious on a wintry evening, with a glass of sweet white wine made from grapes that have been left on the vine so long they have shrivelled in the frost.

Porridge

Porridge, a thick gruel which could be made with barley or rye as well as oats, was always the great staple dish of the northern peasantry, particularly in Scandinavia and Scotland, which share many culinary preferences as well as climate. During their military scurries with the Scots, the English sometimes attributed their opponents' success to their excessively simple and easily prepared diet. Porridge needs minimum preparation in exchange for maximum food value.

The traveller Paul du Chaillu, touring Scandinavia in 1871, reported on the popularity of porridge inside the Arctic Circle:

> Gröd, porridge, is the daily dish of the Norwegian peasant. It is made from barley-meal, although oat-meal and sometimes also rye-meal are used. After the gröd taken from the fire has ceased boiling, more meal is sometimes added to give it greater consistency; it is then called noever-

graut, and is used on journeys, or when the peasants are at work at some distance from the farm. The gröd is generally eaten with skimmed milk, which is preferred after it has become sour.

OATMEAL PORRIDGE
(Scotland)

The shepherds of Glen Feshie lived on porridge, reported Elizabeth Grant in 1898:

> The shepherds lived in bothies on the hill, miles from any other habitation, often quite alone, their collie dog their only companion, and with no provisions beyond a bag of meal. This they generally ate uncooked, mixed with either milk or water as happened to suit, the milk or water being mostly cold, few of these hardy mountaineers troubling themselves to keep a fire lighted in fine weather. This simple food, called brose, is rather relished by the Highlanders; made with but water or with good milk they think it excellent fare; made with beef broo — the fat skimmings of the broth pot — it is considered quite a treat. Beef brose is entertainment for anyone. The water brose must be wholesome; no men looked better in health than the masons, who ate it regularly, and the shepherds. These last came down from their high ground to attend the kirk sometimes, in such looks as put to shame the luxurious dwellers in the smoky huts with their hot porridge and other delicacies.

1 breakfast cupful (just under $\frac{1}{2}$
  pint/300 ml) water per person
1 handful (a little over 1 oz/25 g)
  coarsely milled oatmeal per
  person (Midlothian oats are
  reputedly the best, but some
  reckon the small Highland ones
  are better)
$\frac{1}{2}$ teaspoon salt

Utensils A large saucepan

Bring the water to the boil in the pan — preferably one kept just for porridge, which picks up alien scents very easily. Sprinkle the oats in loose handfuls over the surface of the boiling water, stirring the while with a flat wooden stick — a 'spurtle'. When the porridge is well boiling, turn the heat right down and cover the saucepan. Simmer very gently, stirring regularly (porridge is terrible for sticking) for 20 to 30 minutes, until the porridge is cooked. Add the salt halfway through the cooking

— it is thought (and my Scots grandmother agreed) that the oats will not soften properly if salt is added at the beginning. Well-cooked porridge should be so stiff that the wooden spoon will stand up in it.

The Scots like their porridge sprinkled with salt. Pour the porridge into cold plates and trickle plenty of cold fresh milk around the edge to make a moat. The milk should remain cold, and each spoonful of hot porridge may then be dipped into the cold liquid. Southerners and some northerners like their porridge with treacle or brown sugar.

SUGGESTIONS
● Some Scots add pinches of dry meal throughout the cooking process, thereby achieving a much more grainy and variable texture. You must find your own preferences. There are even those (particularly children) who love their porridge lumpy.
● Others like a piece of unsalted butter melted into a creamy pool in the middle of their bowl of porridge.
● In northern England porridge is also much appreciated. At the end of the eighteenth century in Westmoreland, a labourer's family of a wife and 4 children had per week: 8½ lb potatoes, ¾ lb butter, 2 lb sugar, 2 oz tea, ¼ lb meat, 1½ lb oatmeal, 30 pints of milk, and a small quantity of treacle, kept in a special treacle jar, to trickle on the oatmeal porridge. In northern England porridge has a wide variety of affectionate nick-names, 'stirabout', 'pandewaff', 'thick 'uns', and many more. 'Lumpydicks' could be made by stirring in squashed fistfuls of oats and then letting the porridge stew in great lumps. There were many who liked that best.
● Today porridge is usually made from prepared rolled oats and can be ready in a few minutes. But the old way gives a rich hay-sweet dish that's a different kettle altogether. Either way it makes the best winter breakfast a northerner could wish for.

BROSE
(Scotland)

A version of porridge that is not boiled, but mixed with hot water or boiling milk. Proportions are a little different as the oatmeal is not given time to swell: allow 2 handfuls (2 oz/50 g) of oats to 1 cup (½ pint/300 ml) of liquid. A little salt should be sprinkled in. Pour the scalding liquid straight on to the oatmeal in the bowl. Stir, preferably with a horn spoon, allowing the mixture to form lumps, called 'knots'. The lumps should be raw and powdery inside. Eat with butter melted into it, or cold milk.

OATMEAL JELLY
Sughan and Sowans (Wales and Scotland)

In the days of local mills, when the oats that had been winnowed and threshed had been returned as meal, the miller always sent it with a bag of 'sids' — the inner husks of the oat grain — to which adheres some of the finest and most nutritive substances of the meal. This was made into a kind of smooth pudding or gruel called Sowans (in Gaelic, Sughan), an ancient dish of Celtic origin. It has a slightly sour taste which some find unpalatable at first, but which usually 'grows on' one. It is a very wholesome and sustaining food, and is said to be an ideal diet for invalids, especially dyspeptics. (*The Scots Kitchen*, F. Marian McNeill, Edinburgh, 1929.)

The 'sids' must be steeped in cold water for 4 to 5 days. The resulting liquid is then pressed through a sieve, and allowed to stand for another 2 days so that the sediment can sink to the bottom. The clear liquid at the top — the 'swats' — is then poured off, and the residue cooked like porridge. Serve like porridge, with plenty of thin cream.

FOOTNOTE

Preparations of oatmeal were so important to the northern Europeans that nineteenth-century Norwegians were treated to a battle between scientists and traditional cookery experts, which the bemused spectators christened the Porridge Feud. 'One single problem became the bone of contention,' say Riddervold and Ropeid in the review *Ethnologia Scandinavica* of 1984, 'the traditional way of making porridge, practised by Norwegian farmers' wives by adding a certain amount of flour to the porridge when it was cooked and ready to eat. This extra flour was in this way eaten uncooked. This method is attacked by Asbjornsen [a much loved author of books of fairy tales] in his book, *Sensible Cookery*, referring to natural sciences and stating that the uncooked flour goes right through the body without being used, and represents as such a heavy economic loss to the individual family and to the country as well.' The Porridge Feud brought Norway's intelligensia to a rolling boil. Scandinavia was at the time struggling to adjust to the changing order of post-revolution Europe. The Porridge Feud became a useful vehicle for debate — a wide range of subjects was covered, including the role of women, the reliability of tradition against the discoveries of science, problems of poverty, the desirability of universal education, and the acceptance of foreign philosophies. A tall order for a pot of porridge.

OATMEAL SOUP
Potage à l'avoine (France)

Oats are much favoured as feed for domestic animals, including poultry and cattle. A storehouse staple among the peasantry of France.

Quantity   Enough for 4
Time   Preparation: 5 minutes
             Cooking: 30 minutes

2 pints/1 litre good chicken *or*
    meat stock
4 heaped tablespoons oatmeal

salt
2 oz/50 g butter

Utensils   A large saucepan with a lid

Put the stock in the saucepan and stir in the oatmeal. Bring all to the boil and then turn the heat down to simmer. Cook gently for half an hour, until the soup is thick and rich. Taste and add salt if necessary. Stir in the butter just before serving.

WHITE PUDDINGS
(Ireland)

Quantity   Enough for 4

Time   Preparation: 30–40 minutes
             Cooking: 40 minutes

½ lb/250 g pinhead oatmeal
4 oz/100 g suet *or* lard
2 onions

thyme, sage, parsley, penny royal
salt and pepper
sausage skins (*optional*)

Utensils   A baking tray and a medium saucepan

Spread the oatmeal out on the baking tray and put it to roast in a low oven — 300°F/150°C/Gas 2 — until it is lightly toasted.

Meanwhile put the sausage skins to soak if they have been in salt. Peel and chop the onion finely. Chop the herbs.

Mix all well with the toasted oatmeal, add salt and pepper and then stuff the mixture into the sausage skins, tying the skins with thread at 3 in/7·5 cm intervals, but leaving at least one-third of the skins empty for the sausages to swell. Two knots spaced ½ in/1 cm apart is best of all — the sausages will then not burst when you divide them.

If you have no sausage skins, cook the mixture in the saucepan with enough water to wet it — start with ½ pint/300 ml and add more as it is absorbed. You will have to keep stirring to avoid sticking.

CHAPTER 8

Pasta, Savoury Puddings, and Pies

The pasta dishes of Italy are the most sophisticated and highly developed of this most ancient group of grain-food recipes. Popular mythology credits that energetic traveller, Marco Polo, who visited the noodle-making Chinese in 1271, with the introduction of pasta to Italy. However, Italian literature of the time seems to indicate that macaroni and ravioli were already well established in the Italian kitchen. The poet Iacopone da Todi, a contemporary of Marco Polo, cites the dominance of a single tiny peppercorn over a lasagna as evidence of the deceptiveness of relative size to strength. While in the *Decameron* Boccaccio, born in 1313, spins a tale of peasant gluttons dreaming of limitless macaroni and ravioli cooked in capon broth.

Whatever its national origins noodle paste is a primitive unleavened dough, and a natural way of preparing grains for cooking. The manufacture of pasta is an even simpler process than bread making, so it seems likely that the technique evolved simultaneously in several different places as well as China — including India, the Middle East, and central Europe. The earliest European pastas were variations on *trahana* (see page 306), a tiny noodle, which looks and cooks like rice. The early forms of Italian pasta seem to have been rather dumpling-like, closer to *gnocchi*, and only began to assume their recognizable modern shapes during the eighteenth century, when machines for moulding and cutting the pasta appeared in Naples. The bourgeoisie took to the new machine-extruded pastas with enthusiasm. The peasantry continued to roll its own and it was not until the 1930s that country people began to accept the change. Today the average Italian eats around 65 lb/30 kg of pasta a year.

As for Marco Polo, he might even have reversed the accepted theory and been teacher rather than pupil in fourteenth-century China's kitchens. Certainly the Chinese were rolling noodles with their customary skill by the first century AD. But one of their early writers on food suggests that after the Chinese peasants invented noodles, they learned how to make them delicious from foreigners.

The basic Italian pasta dough is best made with fine-milled durum semolina (the *semola* being the hard seed at the centre of the wheat grain) or, at a pinch, strong bread flour. Soft-wheat flours that are used in cake and bread making have a weaker gluten content in order to allow the dough to stretch and rise when leavened.

Pasta is a comparatively stiff dough, made with only 25% liquid, whereas bread has a water content around 35%. The machine-extruded varieties of pasta usually sold dried, such as spaghetti, macaroni, and a multitude of bows and shells and shapes, are moulded from a semolina dough made with hard durum wheat, of which the Mediterranean strain is an appetizing natural yellow. Semolina absorbs less water in the making, is very strong so that it can stand up to machine pressure, and dries out without cracking. Eggs are usually included for flavouring and colour. The rolled pastas such as the many varieties of tagliatelle, lasagne, cannelloni, and the rest, are at their best when you make them yourself and prepare them fresh.

You will have to experiment to find your own preferred mix if you are making your pasta in-house. You may need less liquid if the weather is damp, the flour is very rough-ground, or the eggs are very large. Home-made dough that can be rolled on a little hand machine needs to be wetter than that rolled out in the heavy commercial rollers.

The Italian nobles who accompanied their mistress Catherine de Medici, bride of Henri II, to Paris in 1553, gave the French court chefs their grounding in the sophisticated art of saucing. A taste for sauces which are independent of that which they are saucing — that is, those mixtures that are not based on the juices of the food they accompany (such as a *jus* or a gravy) but rather serve to alter and mask its flavour — was fully developed in Italy many centuries earlier by the arch-priests of the kitchen, the Romans. The first century author Apicius details a large repertoire of fragrant sauces common in the Roman kitchen of the day — milky baths of pounded nuts, pungent garnishes based on fermented salted fish, herb sauces, reductions of wine, and delicate honey and herb-scented relishes for anything and everything. Italian country cooks make use of the fresh ingredients from their vegetable gardens and the wild larder available on the hillside, as well as their own good sausages and hams, cheeses, and oils, to embellish their pasta dishes.

Perhaps it was a natural skill as sauce-makers that led Italian cooks to develop so perfect a vehicle as pasta for their talents. No other substance can provide such a magnificent foil.

LASAGNE
Lasagne al forno (Italy)

The little village of Fiesole twenty years ago wound up one side of a narrow olive-tree clad ravine in the hills above Florence in northern Italy. Vines and lettuces, spinach and onions, tomatoes and carrots, grew in all the little gardens. Clay pots cascaded geraniums and sweet basil round the village porches. The roofs and tiles of the houses were of baked terracotta, golden as apricots, nestling among rosemary-scented rocks. Here lived Michaela, the cook who worked for the family in whose little *pensione* I was billeted.

Michaela cooked for us all every evening — wonderful broths, thick minestrone, and clear beef soups with noodles. Her real speciality was the pasta she would always make herself, hanging long delicate yellow and green strings to dry on a laundry line strung up across the current of air from the balconied window. How she sauced her beautiful dishes would depend on what was fresh in the market that day. I would help her in the kitchen whenever I could, chopping the garlic and herbs, slicing purple aubergines into creamy rings for her to fry and layer into a dish with meat and cheese sauce for baking, much as she made her lasagne, and almost exactly like a *moussaka*.

Michaela would sometimes take me, on her one day off a week, back to her little house in Fiesole to spend Sunday with her family. There I would be allowed to help her make the best lasagne in the village. Her children were grown and had babies of their own, but it was always Michaela who cooked the family's Sunday lunch, to be laid out on the wooden table under the back porch, shaded by a vine from the early afternoon sun. The lasagne was preceded, since it was the feast day, by an antipasto — sometimes a few slices of raw Parma ham and salami sausage sliced and served with a pat of butter, sometimes a few chicken livers fried in a little butter, and then spread on slices of crisp toasted bread. There was always a bowl of olives, a big basket of fresh bread, and plenty of wine for the adults. The children came and went from the table at will, and ate as they pleased.

The meat sauce or *ragù* Michaela made for the dish is one of the basic sauces of Italy. Down in the kitchen of the *pensione*, she made a large pan of it once a week (the meat was replaced with a couple of finely chopped carrots and celery sticks for this purpose), and then kept it on the back of the stove, conveniently to hand with a ladle in it ready to add its richness to a sauce or stew.

The Italians rarely put water into a sauce — they appreciate strong concentrated flavours that give character and piquancy to their simple background dishes of pasta, *polenta*, and rice. It is this pleasure in surprise and balance — bland and spiced, cold and hot, sweet and sour, cooked and raw — that makes ordinary Italian cooking so sophisticated. Add to this a natural understanding of texture and form, such as that seen in the dozens of different shapes into which pasta is cut the better to absorb its sauces, and it is no wonder that the Italians taught the rest of Europe how to cook.

Quantity   Enough for 8 as a main dish
Time   Preparation: 1½–2 hours
           Cooking: 20–25 minutes

For the pasta
1 lb/500 g strong flour (preferably durum wheatflour)
1 teaspoon salt
4–5 eggs

3–4 tablespoons water *or* another egg
polenta or semolina flour for sprinkling (*or* ordinary flour)

For the tomato sauce or *ragù*

1 large onion
2 cloves garlic
4 oz/100 g raw ham *or* bacon
2 carrots and 1 stick celery
small bunch of oregano *or* parsley
4 tablespoons olive oil
4 oz/100 g minced meat (*optional*)
1½ lb/750 g ripe tomatoes *or* 3
    medium tins plum tomatoes
1 tablespoon concentrated tomato
    purée
½ pint/300 ml stock *or* wine
salt and pepper

For the cheese sauce and *spinach
    layer*

½ lb/250 g spinach (fresh *or* frozen)
3 oz/75 g butter
3 oz/75 g flour
1½ pints/1 litre milk
2 tablespoons fresh cream cheese
    or double cream
4 oz/100 g grated pecorino *or*
    fontina (a Gruyère-like cheese)
    and parmesan mixed
salt and pepper

Utensils   A rolling pin or a pasta roller, 2 small saucepans, 1 large saucepan, a large shallow gratin dish, and clean tea towels

Make the pasta first. Pour the flour and salt together directly on to the clean scrubbed surface of the kitchen table. You will need plenty of elbow room. Mix the eggs with the water. Make a dip in the flour and pour in the eggs. Work them into the dough with your hand using a circular motion to draw in the flour at the edges. Add an extra tablespoon of water if you need it to make a soft pliable dough. This process can be started in your mixer and finished by hand, but you should knead steadily for 10 minutes.

You will soon develop your own method. Michaela used the flat of one hand to turn the ball of dough, while she knuckled the edges into the middle with the other (an action she also used to knead her bread-dough for pizza). When the dough is smooth and elastic, oil the outside lightly, cover it with a cloth, and leave it to rest for 20 to 30 minutes while you make the first sauce.

Start the tomato sauce by peeling and chopping the onion. The neatest way of chopping an onion is to make close, parallel cuts from the top to the bottom without cutting right through, which you then cross at right angles with another set of parallel cuts. Now you can slice the onion across as if for rings, and it will yield fine squares.

Peel and crush the garlic. Chop the ham or bacon very finely. Chop the herbs. Peel and chop the celery and carrots finely.

Heat the oil gently in a saucepan. Fry the onion and the garlic first until transparent — they should not be allowed to caramelize or the sauce will taste bitter. Add the ham and the meat and fry for a moment, until the meat stiffens and loses its pink colour.

Meanwhile pour boiling water over the tomatoes to loosen the skins if you are using fresh ones. Peel, de-seed, and chop them. Add the tomatoes and tomato purée (and a teaspoon of sugar if you are using the non-Mediterranean variety of tomato). Stir in the stock or wine. Put the sauce, covered, on the back burner to simmer until you are ready to use it — an hour is not too long. Adjust the seasoning at the very end.

Turn your attention back to the pasta. Divide the dough into 6 pieces. Flour the board or table, and roll each piece out so fine you can see the wood of the board faintly through it. Sprinkle the rolled out dough with a handful of *polenta* or semolina flour and leave it for another 10 to 15 minutes to rest.

The easiest method of rolling the pasta is with a pasta roller. If you like pasta it is well worth acquiring one. The roller is an implement which bolts on to the kitchen table like a tiny mangle, and operates on the same principle. Make 6 long sausages of dough and feed them through the mangle. Roll the dough thin enough by progressively decreasing the gaps between the rollers. (You will not need the cutter slots for lasagne). While the pasta is resting, make the second sauce.

For the cheese sauce and the spinach layer, strip out and discard the tough stalks of the spinach and wash the leaves thoroughly — fresh spinach is inclined to be gritty. Fresh or frozen, cook the spinach in a covered saucepan, in the water which clings to its leaves after washing, for 10 minutes if fresh, less if frozen. Drain the spinach and then chop it finely.

Melt the butter in a small saucepan. Stir in the flour and cook it gently until it is sandy, but has not taken colour. Gradually whisk in the milk, beating to avoid any lumps. Simmer the sauce for 5 minutes. Beat in the cream cheese or double cream and half the grated cheese. Put aside half the sauce. Stir the chopped spinach into the other half. Taste and season with salt and pepper. Put aside.

Preheat the oven to 375°F/190°C/Gas 5 and set a large pan of salted water on to boil.

Back to the rested pasta. Cut the sheets into 4 in/10 cm squares. Throw them into the boiling water in small batches. Give the water a stir to keep the leaves separate. Make sure the water reboils fast, and cook each batch for 1 minute only. As the sheets come out of the water, pass them through a bowl of cold water. Drain.

Finally assemble the lasagne. Spread a ladleful of the plain cheese sauce over the base of your gratin dish. Lay a single layer of lasagne over it. Ladle a generous layer of tomato sauce over. Then another layer of lasagne. Then a thick layer of the spinach sauce. Spread another layer of overlapping sheets of lasagne over the spinach. Then another of the tomato sauce. Then another layer of pasta. Finish with a layer of plain cheese sauce. You can make as many layers as your dish dictates, but always finish with cheese sauce. Sprinkle more grated cheese and a few flakes of butter over the top.

Bake the lasagne in the hot oven for 20 to 25 minutes, until the top is brown and bubbling.

Serve a salad after the dish — perhaps fennel dressed with lemon juice and the thick fresh first-pressing olive oil of Tuscany, or a crisp salad of curly endive. Red wine and plenty of bread to accompany. Michaela would be proud of you.

SUGGESTIONS

• This makes plenty of pasta. If you think you have too much (and it is up to you how many layers you use) cut the rest into noodles for another meal. Slice the leftover raw sheets of pasta into strips (see the tagliatelle recipe which follows) or feed them through the cutter of the pasta-roller. Drop them in handfuls from a height on to a floured board. They will keep in a plastic bag in the refrigerator for a week, for far longer in the freezer. Or they can be dried for storage — try looping them over a string hung in a current of air, and leaving them to dry out for a day or two. Or turn them occasionally as they lie in their handfuls on the board and let them dry out in hanks.

• Replace the meat in the *ragù* with 4 oz/100 g chopped mushrooms. Or use both.

• To make a dish of *cannelloni al forno*, follow the same recipe as for the lasagne, but roll the squares of cooked pasta round a line of *ragù* filling, pack the rolls into an oiled gratin dish, and cover with white sauce. Sprinkle with grated parmesan and bake as for the lasagne.

• Make the lasagne recipe using layers of fine pancakes (see page 554, omitting the sugar) rather than pasta.

SPINACH PASTA WITH ANCHOVY SAUCE
Tagliatelle verde (Italy)

Ribbon pasta or tagliatelle are the most usual home-made type of pasta. They are good sauced simply with fresh butter and black pepper, with cream simmered with mushrooms, with a pesto, with a tomato-based *ragù*. Michaela, my friend the cook at the *pensione* in Florence, would make this instant sauce on the days she had made a big batch of pasta for drying and was late with the rest of the cooking. It takes no time at all.

Quantity Enough for 6
Time Preparation: 1 hour to make the pasta, 5 minutes for the sauce

For the pasta
½ lb/250 g spinach (fresh *or* frozen)
1 lb/500 g strong flour
1 teaspoon salt
4–5 eggs
3–4 tablespoons water
    or another egg

For the sauce
1 small tin anchovies (8–10 fillets)
2 cloves garlic
1 large handful parsley
¼ pint/150 ml good olive oil
pepper

Utensils   A rolling pin or pasta roller, a pestle and mortar, 1 or 2 roomy saucepans, a large bowl for serving, and a liquidizer if you have one

First make the pasta. Strip out and discard the tough stalks of the spinach and wash the leaves thoroughly if you are using fresh spinach. Cook the spinach in a covered saucepan, in the water which clings to its leaves after washing, for 10 minutes if fresh, less if frozen. Drain the spinach and then chop it very finely — the liquidizer does this well.

Pour the flour and salt into a pile on a clean table — one with a marble top is best of all as it keeps the dough cool. Make a well in the middle of the flour. Mix the eggs together with the water and pour them into the well. Work the flour and the liquid together with your hands. You may need a little less liquid — it depends on the flour and the size of the eggs. Knead thoroughly for 10 minutes to develop and stretch the flour. At the end of this pummelling, the dough will be smooth and elastic. Put it aside to rest for 15 to 20 minutes while you make the sauce.

Start the sauce by putting the anchovies to soak in a little water for 10 minutes if they are from the barrel. Tinned ones will not need this attention. Peel the garlic. Don't use a garlic press — it does horrible things to the taste. Wash and chop the parsley. Put the anchovies, garlic, and parsley into a mortar and pound them to a paste. Trickle in the oil. This is very easy to do in a liquidizer. Finish with plenty of freshly milled black pepper.

Back to the pasta. Cut the dough into 6 pieces and roll each piece out on a floured board with a floured rolling pin, until the paste is nearly thin enough to read a newspaper through it. Sprinkle the rolled out dough with a handful of *polenta* or semolina flour, and then leave it to rest again for another 15 to 20 minutes.

Roll each piece of pasta up loosely as you would a carpet for storage, and slice across into strips of the width you require — about ¼ in/5 mm is right for tagliatelle, narrower for linguine. Loosen the strips and drop them in handfuls on to a board well dusted with *polenta* or semolina. The pasta is now ready for cooking.

Alternatively use a pasta-rolling machine (see the notes in the lasagne recipe on page 283). As you are making ribbon noodles, roll the flattened dough through one of the slots equipped with cutters. There is a choice of 2 ribbon widths: use the wider one for tagliatelle and the narrow one for linguine. Dust the paste regularly with plenty of *polenta* or semolina flour to stop it sticking to itself. After you have cut it, it is wise to hang the long ribbons over a washing line or the back of a chair to dry their surface a little so the strings do not stick. The pasta is now ready for cooking.

Put the serving dish in the oven to warm.

Put on a large pan of salted water to boil. You will need at least 10 pints/6 litres to cook this quantity of tagliatelle. When the water reaches a rolling boil, drop in the tagliatelle by the loose handful. Try not to let the water go off the boil. Give the pasta a quick stir with a wooden fork to make sure it has not stuck together. Cook the pasta for 1 to 2 minutes — test by nibbling a length before you take it out. Drain it well.

Transfer it to the warm dish and sprinkle on the *salsa verde*. Toss it and take it to table. Make sure there's a pepper grinder and a bowl of grated parmesan cheese to accompany.

Follow the pasta, if you are hungry, with a lamb steak cut straight across the leg bone, or a pair of lamb chops, grilled over charcoal or under a high grill, basted with olive oil, garlic, and rosemary, served with young green beans or a fennel salad. The Italians like their grilled lamb crusty on the outside and succulent inside, but not pink as the French prefer it. Plenty of bread always.

SUGGESTIONS
• Made fresh, egg pasta will keep in a sealed bag in the refrigerator for a week. Pasta freezes very well for at least 3 months and can be cooked straight from the freezer.
• If you want to dry the tagliatelle for keeping, drop it in handfuls on to a clean cloth so that it settles loosely. Leave to dry and then store in an airtight jar or tin.

LEFTOVERS
Toss the cold pasta in more olive oil, crushed and chopped garlic and plenty of chopped parsley. It will make a delicious little salad.

STUFFED PASTA WITH BUTTER
Tortellini al burro (Italy)

These are plump crescents of fresh pasta, filled with a very delicate stuffing. The stuffing can be used to fill other shapes as well, but it is at its best in these seductively curved envelopes — the romantic Italians declare them to have been inspired by the navel of Venus. There are a great many more regional and household variations on these fillings, but the principle is the same: the stuffing is pre-cooked and the envelopes are poached in hot liquid for 4 to 5 minutes. Most Italian country cooks make their own, taking great pride in the dish and serving it for very special celebration meals. These are sophisticated little morsels, depending for their excellence on a fresh-tasting well-flavoured stuffing and they do not need heavy saucing.

Quantity Enough for 6
Time Preparation: 1¼ hours

For the pasta
1 lb/500 g strong flour
4–5 eggs

3 tablespoons water *or* another egg
1 teaspoon salt

For the filling
2 fillets chicken breast
a bayleaf
salt and peppercorns
2 oz/50 g grated parmesan *or*
   pecorino cheese
1 clove garlic

1 teaspoon fresh herbs
1 egg
butter and fresh herbs to finish —
   basil *or* a bunch of parsley and
   a leaf or two of sage (no more
   — sage is a very strong herb)

Utensils A rolling pin or a pasta roller, 1 small and 1 large saucepan, and a pretty serving dish

Make the pasta dough as for the tagliatelle (see page 287). While the dough is resting, make the stuffing.

Poach the chicken breasts very gently for 5 minutes in a very little water flavoured with a bayleaf, some peppercorns, and a little salt. Drain the chicken and strain and save the liquid. Mince or chop the chicken very finely indeed with the cheese, the peeled garlic, and the teaspoon of herbs. Bind into a stiff paste with the egg. Add a spoonful or two of the chicken liquor to moisten the mixture. Salt and pepper to taste. Simple. Put the stuffing aside while you finish making the pasta.

Cut the dough in half and roll it out on a well-floured board with a well-floured rolling pin. It must be fine enough for you to see the woodgrain through it. Cut out circles of the dough with a wine glass. Put a little pile of filling on one side of each circle, wet the edge, and then double the circle over to make a semicircle. Join the two little wings to make a ring, pinching them lightly together with damp fingers. Now you can see what they mean about the navel of Venus.

Put on a large pan of well-salted water to boil — 5 pints/3 litres for this quantity. Stuffed pastas are as perishable as their contents and are at their best cooked on the day they are made. Put the serving dish in the oven to warm. Chop the herbs.

Poach the tortellini in 2 or 3 batches for 5 minutes per batch — timed after the water comes back to a rolling boil. Drain them thoroughly — they must not be soggy. Put them in the warm dish and scatter small pieces of butter over them. Toss them delicately. Sprinkle with the chopped herbs. Serve with extra butter and a bowl of grated parmesan.

Follow with a rich *ragù*-based stew — and don't forget to drink a toast to the goddess of beauty whose navel inspired the dish.

LEFTOVERS
• Heat gently in a little cream.

SPINACH AND RICOTTA RAVIOLI
Ravioli alla fiorentina (Italy)

The classic and favourite stuffing for fresh pasta, this can be used to stuff other shapes as well. Cannelloni are delicious stuffed with this mixture.

Quantity   Enough for 6
Time   Preparation: 1 hour

For the pasta

½ lb/250 g fresh *or* frozen spinach	3–4 tablespoons water
1 lb/500 g strong flour	*or* another egg
4–5 eggs	1 teaspoon salt

For the filling

6 oz/175 g ricotta (or any white soft fresh cheese)	2 tablespoons grated parmesan
	salt and pepper
1 lb/500 g fresh *or* frozen spinach	butter to finish

Utensils   A rolling pin or a pasta roller, 1 medium and 1 large saucepan, a dish for serving, preferably a beautiful white one to complement the green pasta, a zig-zag pastry-cutter to make neat ravioli if you have one, and a perforated spoon

Make the spinach pasta as in the *Tagliatelle verde* recipe (see page 287) not forgetting to cook the extra spinach for the stuffing at the same time as you prepare the spinach for the pasta. While the dough is resting, make the stuffing.

Mix the ricotta, the chopped cooked spinach, and the parmesan together very thoroughly. Season them with salt and pepper (ricotta will not need much salt).

To make ravioli mark one half of the pasta sheet into squares without cutting through. Pile little heaps of filling in the centre of each square. Damp the pastry between the piles, and then fold the other side of the dough over the top. Cut through both layers with a zig-zag pastry cutter if you have one, to give you little sealed square envelopes.

Put the serving dish to warm in a low oven, and put on a large pan of salted water to boil.

When the water comes to a rolling boil, throw in the ravioli and cook them for 4 to 5 mintues, until the pasta is tender. The stuffing is already cooked so only needs to be heated. Fish them out with a perforated spoon and drop them on to a clean cloth, and then transfer them to the warm serving dish. Scatter the ravioli with slivers of butter and perhaps a few torn leaves of basil (Michaela, who taught me to make these, would never chop a basil leaf. She said it brought bad luck). Serve with a bowl of grated parmesan.

Follow with a roasted chicken, or, for a light supper, a salad of curly endive or slices of fennel dressed with the thick fresh olive oil of Tuscany.

LEFTOVERS
● Heat gently with a little cream. Sprinkle with chopped fresh basil or parsley.

RAVIOLI WITH MEAT
Ravioli alla calabrese (Italy)

A stuffing from the harsh mountain landscape south of Rome. Calabria is one of the most isolated provinces of Italy. If fresh meat was not available, it would be omitted and the weight of sausage doubled.

For the pasta
1 lb/500 g strong flour
4–5 eggs

3 tablespoons water *or* another egg
1 teaspoon salt

For the filling
4 oz/100 g Italian sausage
  (*mortadella or bologna* will do
  well)
4 oz/100 g finely minced veal *or*
  pork
½ pint/300 ml stock *or* water

2 oz/50 g grated parmesan *or*
  another strong cheese
1 teaspoon finely chopped herbs
  (parsley, oregano, marjoram)
1 egg
salt and pepper

Utensils   A rolling pin or a pasta roller, 2 large saucepans and a deep serving dish

The ravioli are made as in the previous recipe, omitting the spinach.

Simmer the meat in the stock or water until it loses its pink colour. Empty the sausage meat out of its skin and pound it up with the cooked minced meat, immersed in a little water or stock. Mix in the cheese and the herbs. Bind with the egg. Don't forget the salt and pepper — in moderation if the sausage is spicy.

Put a serving dish to warm and a large pan full of plenty of salted water to boil. When it boils, throw in the ravioli — they will take no more than 4 to 5 minutes. Serve with a cream sauce ($\frac{1}{2}$ pint/300 ml double cream simmered until thick with a teaspoon of flour), or the tomato sauce from the recipe which follows. Put plenty of grated cheese and black pepper on the table. You will need no more than a plain grilled chop or a dish of vegetables to follow.

LEFTOVERS
- Heat the leftovers gently in a fresh tomato sauce.

TAGLIATELLE WITH TOMATO SAUCE
Tagliatelle al pomodoro (Italy)

Mediterranean tomatoes — golden apples — are inevitably sweeter and meatier than the northern-grown varieties. Their arrival in the Italian kitchen garden during the course of the sixteenth century — they are a New World vegetable — had a dramatic effect on the Italian culinary repertoire. Italian food today without the tomato would be a shadow of itself. This very basic tomato sauce is best made with the large sweet Mediterranean tomatoes.

Quantity Enough for 5–6
Time Preparation: $1\frac{1}{4}$ hours

For the pasta
1 lb/500 g strong flour
4–5 eggs

3 tablespoons water *or* another egg
1 teaspoon salt

For the sauce
$1\frac{1}{2}$ lb/750 g tomatoes *or* 2 medium tins
2 cloves garlic
$\frac{1}{2}$ teaspoon salt

4 tablespoons olive oil
1 teaspoon sugar
1 tablespoon tomato purée
pepper

Utensils A rolling pin or a pasta roller, 2 large saucepans, a liquidizer if you have one, and a deep serving dish

Make the fresh pasta as for the *Tagliatelle verde* recipe on page 287, but without the spinach. The scarlet sauce is prettiest on plain pasta.

Start the sauce by scalding the tomatoes with boiling water to loosen the skins. Peel them and chop very thoroughly — this is easily done in the liquidizer. If you have to use tinned tomatoes, stew the sauce a little longer. Peel and crush the garlic with the salt (a single blow with the flat of your heaviest kitchen knife will do the trick nicely). Warm the olive oil in the saucepan and add the garlic. Stew gently for a moment without allowing it to take colour. Add the tomatoes, the sugar, and the tomato purée. Simmer the sauce for 20 minutes or so, uncovered so that the flavours can be concentrated.

Put the serving dish to warm and a large pan of salted water on to boil.

When the water comes to a rolling boil, throw in the fresh pasta. Cook it for no more than a minute or two. Drain the tagliatelle thoroughly. Rub the warmed dish with garlic, trickle in a little oil, and tip in the tagliatelle. Pour the sauce on to the hot pasta, turning it over gently once or twice to mix it in. Serve with a bowl of grated parmesan cheese.

Follow with something simple — fresh fish grilled with herbs, or perhaps a plain roasted chicken. Or serve as an antipasto a plate of sliced Parma ham and dried sausage with a pat of butter and plenty of bread, and to follow the scarlet sauce, a green salad or a dish of fresh green vegetables, lightly cooked and tossed in butter and chopped herbs.

SUGGESTIONS
• In hot weather and with sweet juicy tomatoes still warm from the sun, such as you might expect to find in Tuscany in July, the sauce does not need to be cooked at all, nor does it need sugar and tomato purée. It can just be allowed to stand on the kitchen table for an hour or so to infuse. The tomato sauce is delicious spooned over an egg fried crisp in olive oil and set on a slice of home-made bread rubbed with garlic. Also good served as a sauce for boiled meat.

LEFTOVERS
• Put the tagliatelle mixed with the sauce into a shallow ovenproof dish. Cover all with a well-flavoured cheese sauce (see the *Lasagne al forno* recipe on page 283). Sprinkle with plenty of grated cheese and reheat in the oven at 350°F/180°C/Gas 4 for 15 minutes.

FETTUCINE WITH BASIL SAUCE
Fettucine al pesto (Italy)

Genoa claims the miraculous *pesto* for its own, although the mixture is known and appreciated throughout Italy. The paste will keep all winter if sealed and kept in a cool larder or the refrigerator. Delicious stirred into a pasta dish, into a soup, or into a sauce for grilled fish. An invaluable 'secret ingredient' for winter dishes. Make a supply for your larder at the end of the autumn, stripping the summer's crop of basil plants before the first frosts nip the tender leaves.

Quantity Enough for 5–6
Time Preparation: 1 hour to make the pasta
15 minutes to make the sauce

For the pasta
1 lb/500 g strong flour
4–5 eggs

3 tablespoons water *or* another egg
1 teaspoon salt

For the sauce
2 cloves garlic
1 handful basil leaves stripped
from their stalks
1 oz/25 g pine kernels *or* walnuts
½ teaspoon salt

4 oz/100 g grated parmesan *or*
pecorino cheese *or* the Sardinian
sardo
6 tablespoons olive oil

Utensils A rolling pin or pasta roller, a pestle and mortar or liquidizer, a large saucepan, and a serving dish

Make the pasta as for the *Tagliatelle verde* recipe on page 287, omitting the spinach and making the ribbons finer to give you fettucine. The sauce is particularly suited to these fine strings.

Chop the garlic and tear the basil leaves into shreds. Pound the garlic, the basil, the nuts, and the salt together in a mortar.

Add the cheese and the oil gradually until you have a thick creamy paste. This job can be done in the liquidizer if you prefer. There is a superstition in Italy about cutting basil leaves with knives, and even many of those Italian households equipped with modern gadgets continue to use the old pestle and mortar method to make their *pesto*.

Put the serving dish to warm in the oven, bring a capacious panful of salted water to the boil, and throw the fresh noodles in. Try not to let the water go off the boil, and cook them for 1 minute only. Drain them and toss them with the basil sauce in a warm bowl. A very light and delicious dish. Serve game or a rich stew afterwards.

1 Spaghetti   2 Conchiglie   3 Fiochetti   4 Fusilli   5 Diamanti   6 Capellitti
7 Farfalle/Farfalline   8 Ruoti   9 Vermicelli   10 Maccheroni   11 Tubetti Lunghi
12 Ditali   13 Rigatoni   14 Elicoidali   15 Penne   16 Lasagne   17 Tagliatelle
18 Linguine   19 Fettucine   20 Tortellini   21 Ravioli   22 Gnocchi   23 Cannelloni

SUGGESTIONS
● If you want to store the *pesto*, make it rather thicker, and pack it into small sterilized pots. Cover with a layer of pure oil before you seal down the lids. Store in a cool dark larder or at the back of the refrigerator.

DRIED PASTA
Pasta asciutta (Italy)

There are almost as many shapes of dried pasta as there are varieties of fish in the Mediterranean. The basic dough is the same — the pastas differ from each other only in the variety of their lengths and widths, their curves and folds, all of which accept and adapt in different ways to the sauces in which they are bathed.

You will certainly be spoiled for choice in any good pasta shop. There you will find the familiar bundles of spaghetti ('little strings') and a multitude of little shapes, each of which is perfect for someone's special sauce.

Conchiglie are graceful shells, *fiochetti* are elegant little bows and knots, *fusilli* come in the shape of corkscrews, *diamanti* explain themselves, *capellitti* are shaped like tiny hard-hats with zig-zag edges (very useful for cupping a cream and mushroom sauce), *farfalle* and *farfalline* are, as their names suggest, butterflies both great and small, *ruoti*, shaped like old-fashioned cartwheels. *Vermicelli* ('little worms') are used in soup or sometimes as an ordinary pasta. They take very little time to cook — 2 to 3 minutes is usually quite enough from dry to *al dente*.

Then there are the various *maccheroni* (not to be confused with *macaroni*, which in Italy are potato dumplings), hollow tube shapes, perfect for fresh tomato and cream sauces, the *tubetti lunghi* like little bent elbows, *ditali* and *ditalini* thimbles for the old grandmother at her darning, and mouse-sized thimbles for soup, striped *rigatoni* and spiralled, striped *elicoidali*, and a variety of *penne*, quill pen nibs cut on the cross to give a sharp point. Here are all the images of domestic life.

Allow 1 lb/500 g pasta for 6 healthy appetites. Short dried pasta of good quality will be *al dente* in 5 minutes. Long pasta such as spaghetti will take a little longer, as indeed will old pasta, or pasta of an inferior quality. Accompany all pasta with a bowl of grated parmesan or pecorino cheese. It is very important to serve any pasta dish piping hot and as soon as it is ready.

SPAGHETTI WITH HAM AND EGGS
Spaghetti alla carbonara (Italy)

Charlotte Gower Chapman, a young American sociologist studying the village of Milocca in Sicily in 1928, chronicles the arrival of commercially prepared pasta in a peasant community:

At present most of the families in Milocca manage to afford to buy the spaghetti manufactured at the mill. In former days this was a luxury and pasta was used only on festive occasions. Some women still make their own at home, in the form of a sort of noodle. A few possess small presses for making spaghetti. Almost everyone makes home-made pasta occasionally for a change, although as a general rule they prefer the mill variety. The pasta is served in a variety of ways: with the conventional tomato sauce, with the juices from meat which has been cooked in a casserole, or with vegetables. The last fashion is the cheapest and the most common. People are very particular as to the degree to which their pasta is cooked and the form of pasta used, and some can detect the almost imperceptible difference between the Milocchese pasta and that purchased in other towns. (Since the Milocchese mill is owned by the Angilellas, some of the most violent of the Cipolla partisans insist on buying pasta which is imported.)

Most of the foods that are used to accompany and dress these farinaceous staples are likewise of local production. All the milk is supplied by local goats, and the flocks of sheep furnish enough cheese for the community and a small quantity for export. The increase of these flocks provides the meat, with the occasional and rare addition of pork or beef when one of the two dozen pigs is slaughtered, or a draught animal meets an accidental death. Chickens are raised in large numbers and their flesh adorns the table at high feasts. However, their most important contribution to the diet and to the local economy is their eggs. These serve as legal tender in the local stores and are also bought up by peddlers from other towns.

This dish is known as the 'charcoal-burner's pasta' — perhaps since most of the ingredients can very easily be transported in a satchel. Charcoal burners were accustomed to living rough in the woods for a week or two at a time.

Quantity Enough for 4–5
Time Preparation: 20 minutes

1 lb/500 g spaghetti	3 oz/75 g Parma ham *or* Italian
2 cloves garlic	*pancetta or* any dried ham
4 tablespoons olive oil	3 egg yolks and 1 egg white
1 lemon	salt and pepper

Utensils   1 large and 1 small saucepan and a serving bowl

Fill a large pan with plenty of salted water, and put it on to boil while you prepare the rest of the ingredients.

Peel and chop the garlic, put it in a little saucepan with the oil, and leave it to infuse by the fire. If you like your flavours tamed, stew it on a low heat. Grate the rind of the lemon. Chop the ham small. Beat the egg yolks and the white together in the serving bowl. Grind in some pepper and a pinch of salt.

When the water comes to a rolling boil, hold the spaghetti in a bundle and lower it in, pushing it down as it softens. Give it a turn with a wooden fork to keep the strands separate. Bring the water back to the boil as quickly as possible. Wait for the water to return to the boil before timing the cooking — 5 to 7 minutes should be enough. Keep tasting for the right moment to take it off. Spaghetti is as variable as vegetables — it depends on grain and age. *Al dente* is the Italian way to serve pasta, as with their rice dishes, and requires that pasta in general and spaghetti in particular still retains a slight chewiness, a resistance to the teeth, at the centre.

Drain the spaghetti thoroughly and tip it into the bowl with the eggs. Turn the strands to coat them with sauce. The egg will cook in the heat from the pasta. Sprinkle with the grated lemon rind, the chopped ham and pour over all the infused oil and garlic. Fold all together.

Make sure that your diners are to hand so that you may serve the dish immediately. Hand round a bowl of grated parmesan and the pepper grinder. A dish of sliced tomatoes dressed with a sprinkle of salt and a few slices of sweet raw onion. Fruit and a piece of good Italian cheese to follow — a slice of the delicious smoked *Provolone* to give you a breath of the charcoal-burners' habitat.

LEFTOVERS
● Put in a baking dish and cover with a well-flavoured white sauce. Sprinkle with grated cheese and heat in the oven at 375°F/190°C/Gas 5, for 15 to 20 minutes to heat the dish through and gild the top.

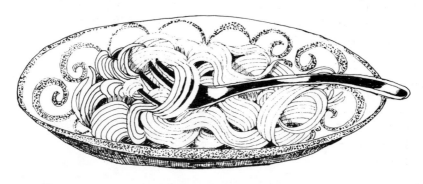

FARFALLE WITH CHICKEN LIVERS
Farfalle con fegatini (Italy)

Butterfly bows tossed with sliced lightly cooked chicken livers — the shapes complement each other perfectly.

Quantity Enough for 4–5
Time Preparation: 25–30 minutes

1 lb/500 g dried farfalle
8 oz/250 g chicken livers
2 cloves garlic
2 oz/50 g butter *or* 4 tablespoons
  oil

salt and pepper
1 tablespoon chopped herbs
  (thyme, marjoram, oregano)

Utensils A large saucepan, a small frying pan, and a pretty serving dish

Put on a large saucepan of salted water to boil. Put the serving dish to warm in the oven.

Pick over the chicken livers, remove any strings and bitter green bits, and then slice them. Peel and chop the garlic. Put the oil or butter to warm in the frying pan. Add the garlic and then the chicken livers. Cook gently until the livers are stiff but still pink. Mash them a little. Season with salt and pepper.

When the water is boiling, throw in the pasta. Cook at a rapid boil for 5 minutes, then nibble one to test. It should retain a slight bite. Drain the pasta and transfer it to the warm dish.

Toss in the livers, garlic, the cooking juices, and the herbs. Plenty of pepper to season. Accompany with a bowl of grated parmesan. Serve as a main dish for a light luncheon, with a green salad and a tomato salad dressed with sliced spring onions and a handful of black olives.

LEFTOVERS
● Moisten the farfalle with a little cream, put them back in the saucepan, and reheat for a moment on top of the stove with a little chopped ham. Sprinkle with more chopped fresh herbs. Serve small portions as a light first course.

PENNE WITH HAM AND MUSHROOMS
Penne alla paesana (Italy)

An everyday pasta dish made with ingredients always to hand in the Italian peasant larder — a ham from the autumn pig-slaughter, and mushrooms fresh or dried from the woods and fields. The shape of the little quill-pen pasta accepts the garnish well, particularly good with dried *boletus* — *porcini*, which are sold in many Italian delicatessens. They will need to be soaked first. Save the soaking water to use in a soup or stew.

Quantity   Enough for 4–5
Time   Preparation: 20–25 minutes

1 lb/500 g dried penne	2 cloves garlic
4 oz/100 g raw Parma ham *or* lean bacon	4 tablespoons olive oil
4 oz/100 g mushrooms	salt and pepper

Utensils   A large saucepan, a small frying pan, and a pretty serving dish

Put on a large pan of salted water to boil and the serving dish to warm in the oven.

Chop the ham. Wipe and chop the mushrooms. Peel and slice the garlic. Put the oil to warm in the frying pan and add the garlic and mushrooms. Fry for a moment.

When the water is boiling, throw in the penne. Cook them for 5 minutes and test to see if they are ready. They should still have a slight bite to them.

Drain and transfer them to the warm serving dish. Toss in the garlic and mushrooms and their oil, and then add the chopped ham. Mix all well together. Sprinkle with salt and pepper. Hand a bowl of grated parmesan separately. Follow with a tomato and fennel salad if you are eating lightly, or a rich stew if this is your main meal of the day.

LEFTOVERS
• Toss with oil and vinegar and more pepper. Mix in an equal quantity of chopped fennel bulb and chopped spring onion. Makes a delicious little salad.

FUSILLI WITH CHILLI
Fusilli alla molisana (Italy)

Spiral pasta to hold the tomato sauce in its curves. The southern Italians like hot chilli in their food.

Quantity   Enough for 4–5
Time   Preparation: 25 minutes

1 lb/500 g dried fusilli	2 cloves garlic
1½ lb/750 g tomatoes *or* 2 medium tins	4 tablespoons olive oil
	1 tablespoon tomato purée
1 small scarlet chilli	salt and pepper

Utensils   1 large and 1 small saucepan and a liquidizer if you have one

Put the serving dish to warm in the oven.

Scald the tomatoes with boiling water to loosen the skins. Peel and chop them finely (use the liquidizer if you like). Tinned tomatoes can also be liquidized. De-seed and chop finely the chilli (don't rub your eyes afterwards — chilli gets in everywhere). Peel and chop the garlic. Warm the olive oil in the small pan, and add the garlic and the chilli. Stew all gently for a moment without allowing it to take colour. Add the tomatoes, the tomato purée, and salt and pepper. Simmer gently for 15 to 20 minutes.

Put on a large pan of salted water to boil 10 minutes before the sauce is ready. When the water comes to boil, throw in the fusilli. Cook them for 5 minutes at a rolling boil. Test to see if they are done — they should still offer a slight resistance to the teeth.

Drain the pasta spirals, and toss them with the sauce. Hand a bowl of grated parmesan separately. Follow with a dish of aubergines, cut into rounds, dipped in milk and seasoned flour, and then fried crisp in smoking hot oil. Aubergines are a great favourite in the south of Italy.

LEFTOVERS
● Add a little more tomato sauce — a tablespoon of tomato purée diluted in half a cup of water is fine — and spread the leftovers in a gratin dish. Sprinkle with plenty of cheese, and put the dish in the oven to reheat the pasta and melt the cheese. Bake for 15 minutes at 375°F/190°C/Gas 5.

CONCHIGLIE WITH MUSHROOMS
Conchiglie con funghi (Italy)

The delicate shell-shape of this pasta complements wild mushrooms perfectly. The *boletus* species the Italians call *porcini*, 'little pigs', have the right nutty flavour and gluey texture. They can be bought dried from Italian delicatessens, and will then need soaking to plump them out — 30 minutes in warm water should be sufficient. If using fresh wild or cultivated mushrooms, then wipe them and chop them. Put them to stew gently in a few tablespoons of sweet green olive oil, spiked with a crushed clove of garlic and a handful of chopped parsley. Toss the contents of the pan with the fresh cooked pasta. Pasta is the perfect vehicle for fresh *funghi*. Try it with slices of raw truffle scattered over a dish of plain buttered home-made egg tagliatelle; or sauced with a few of the curly patterned dark morels of spring time, stewed in fresh cream with plenty of freshly ground pepper to bring out their subtle flavour.

MACARONI WITH CHEESE AND HAM
Maccheroni alla pastora (Italy)

Eliza Putnam Heaton reports on primitive macaroni-making in Sicily in 1908:

> Let those criticise Vana's housekeeping who have themselves kept house and reared live stock in one room. Beside the cold fireplace were heaped brambles and roots of cactus fig for the cooking fire. . . . While she talked Vanna (the local witch-wise woman, elf locks hanging to the floor) did not neglect the macaroni. Rocca held on her knees a board carrying a lump of dough, from which from minute to minute she pinched off bits. Rolling these between her hands, she passed the rolls one by one to Vanna, who sank into each a knitting needle and re-rolled the paste on the board to form the hole. Each short piece as she slipped it off the needle she hung to dry over the edge of a sieve that balanced the rolled up mattress at the foot of the bed. When enough for supper was ready she tied the rest of the dough in a kerchief and shut it in the chest, throwing the crumbs to the cock with a 'chi-chi! cu-cu-rucu!'

Quantity   Enough for 4–5 shepherds down from the hill
Time   Preparation: 15–20 minutes

1 lb/500 g macaroni	4 tablespoons olive oil
6 oz/175 g fresh ricotta cheese	salt and pepper
4 oz/100 g raw ham *or* bacon	

303

Utensils   A frying pan if you are using bacon, a large saucepan, and a serving dish

Put on a large pan with plenty of salted water to boil. Put the serving dish to warm in the oven. This is fast food.

Crumble the cheese. Chop the ham or chop and fry the bacon. As soon as the water boils, throw in the pasta. Cook at a rolling boil for 5 minutes and then test it by biting a piece. It should be slightly firm to the teeth — *al dente*. Drain and transfer to the warm dish. Toss with the rest of the ingredients, sprinkle with plenty of pepper. Hand a bowl of grated parmesan separately. A salad to follow, dressed with oil, vinegar and salt.

LEFTOVERS
● Dress with oil and vinegar, chopped fennel and plenty of freshly milled pepper. Serve with a dish of ripe tomatoes, sliced and dressed with finely chopped garlic and a trickle of olive oil.

NOODLE BARLEY
Tarhonya (Hungary)

This is probably the most primitive noodle-dough in the world, the ancient solution to the problem of how to make milled grain palatable, storable, and portable. Recipes for the dough, sometimes mixed with yoghurt, with plain water, with sour milk, or with anything which will improve its flavour and nutritional value, are to be found all over Europe and Asia. In Hungary today these barley-shaped noodles are made by kneading flour and eggs into a dough, breaking or grating it into little pellets, and then drying them (sometimes in the post-harvest sunshine) until they are quite hard. *Tarhonya* are still popular in modern Hungary. They can be plain boiled to accompany a *gulyas*, thrown at the last minute into a soup or a stew to add protein and body, or fried with onions and paprika and cooked like a risotto to be served on their own. A useful little staple and very easy to make.

> There were other stalls too, heaped with big black loaves, balls of cheese, strings of sausages, strips of paprikas bacon, inedible looking pieces of dried pigmeat, huge jars of pickled gherkins, of salted eggs, of boiled butter, pots of honey, sacks of dried pastry, called tarhonya, heaps of almond biscuits made in all sorts of shapes lay side by side with gilded gingerbreads, honey cakes and walnut rolls. . . .
>
> Ellen Browning, *A Girl's Wanderings in Hungary*

Quantity   Makes 4 oz/100 g dry weight — enough for 2–3
Time   Preparation: 25–30 minutes

4 large eggs
1 lb/500 g flour
1 teaspoon salt

Utensils   A grater and a large tray

Mix the eggs slowly into the flour by hand and salt until you have a few pieces of very stiff dough. Work them well. If you need more liquid, add a little water. If the mixture is too soft, add more flour. Leave the dough, covered with a cloth, to rest and dry out a little. If you want to use the dough right away as tiny dumplings in a soup, grate the paste straight into the hot liquid. The little grains will take only a moment to cook.

If you want to dry *tarhonya* for storage, spread a clean cloth over the tray. Rub the dough through the large holes of a grater on to the cloth, allowing the gratings to fall loosely in a single layer like grains of barley. Leave them on their cloth, tossing them lightly every now and again to keep the grains separate and to allow them to dry evenly, for 3 days in a warm dry kitchen, by which time they should be as hard as catapult pellets.

Tarhonya noodles can be stored in an airtight tin virtually for ever.

To boil: toss the noodle barley into plenty of boiling salted water for 1 minute after the water reboils if they are fresh and for 5 to 10 minutes if they are dried. When they are cooked, drain and toss them with chopped streaky bacon frying gently in its own lard, or with butter or soured cream. Or cook the little scraps in a clear soup. They are excellent in a plain chicken soup made with an old hen, past her laying days, boiled with an onion and a carrot for flavour.

To fry: brown the *tarhonya* in hot lard or butter, tossing frequently, for 3 to 4 minutes, until the grains take a little colour. Take the pan off the heat and stir in a sprinkling of paprika and a little salt. Add enough water to cover the *tarhonya*, and simmer either in a moderate oven — 350°F/180°C/Gas 4 — for 40 minutes or so, until all the water is absorbed, or on top of the stove, where they will only take about 20 minutes, but you will have to keep checking that the water has not boiled away. Sprinkle with plenty of pepper. You can stir in cream if you want to serve them as a light supper dish.

Tarhonya can be served instead of rice or potatoes with any eastern European stews, or with a dish of *letcho*, the vegetable stew which does duty both as a dish in itself and as a basis for other dishes.

MILK NOODLES
Trahana (Bulgaria)

The Bulgarian way with the universal staple of the Balkans.

Quantity Enough for 5–6
Time Preparation: 25 minutes
　　　　Cooking: 10 minutes

1 lb/500 g flour	1 pint/600 ml water
4 large eggs	2 oz/50 g butter
1 teaspoon salt	4 oz/100 g grated cheese
1 pint/600 ml milk	

Utensils A grater, a large saucepan, and a gratin dish

Make the little noodles as for the Hungarian *tarhonya* in the previous recipe. Preheat the oven to 450°F/230°C/Gas 8 and put in the gratin dish to warm.

Bring the milk and water to the boil and throw in the noodles. Cook them for 3 minutes. They will absorb all the liquid. Toss with butter and put them in the warmed gratin dish. Sprinkle with grated *kashkaval* cheese, or any strong cheese such as Cheddar or Gruyère.

Bake them in the hot oven for 10 minutes. Hand more cheese with the dish. Follow with one of the excellent Bulgarian vegetable dishes (see Chapter 10).

PORRIDGE NOODLES
Trahana (Greece)

The Greek version of this ancient universal staple. Sweet and sour varieties are sold in most Greek grocers. The sour version is made with yoghurt or sour milk. The Balkans, Greece, and Turkey have shared each other's territory and habits for so long it is not surprising they have so many culinary tricks in common.

Quantity Enough for 6. Make double or treble the quantity if you wish to store some as a most useful staple to throw in soups. It cooks in the blinking of an eye. Very good in a minestrone.
Time Preparation: 20 minutes

2 large eggs	4–5 tablespoons yoghurt *or* sour
1 lb/500 g flour	milk

Utensils A grater

Make exactly as for the Hungarian *tarhonya* (see page 304). This noodle paste is still made by hand in the more isolated communities, particularly on the islands, where it is rolled into egg-sized balls which are turned daily until they dry, and then crumbled into small bits and finished off on cotton sheets in the sun. Greek fishermen much appreciate *trahana* cooked in soup as an instant nourishing breakfast. The result is a sort of southern version of porridge.

NOODLE DOUGH TURNOVERS
Schlick Krapfen (Austria)

Reminiscent of Italian ravioli, these little envelopes are cooked in a clear chicken or beef broth, or served with melted butter and grated strong cheese (in Austria this would be a Gruyère-like cheese from the mountains).

Quantity   Enough for 4
Time   Preparation: 1 hour

For the dough

8 oz/250 g flour	2 eggs
$\frac{1}{2}$ teaspoon salt	2 tablespoons water

For the filling

6 oz/175 g chopped cooked meat	1 tablespoon chopped parsley
2 tablespoons meat gravy	1 egg

Utensils   A rolling pin or a pasta roller, a pastry brush, and an electric mixer if you have one

Make the dough first. Sift the flour and salt together directly on to the kitchen table. You need plenty of elbow room. Make a dip in the middle and crack the eggs into it. Work them into the dough with your hand. Add water, kneading as you go, until you have a soft pliable ball of dough. (This can be started in your mixer and finished by hand.)

Roll out the noodle dough into a flat sheet. Make the filling next. Moisten the chopped cooked meat with the gravy, mix in the parsley, and the egg lightly beaten. Mark a line down the centre of the dough sheet without cutting through. Put small teaspoons of the meat mixture well spaced out on one half of the dough. Brush between the piles of filling with water and then fold the empty half of dough over. Cut into squares. Poach gently in clear soup for 10 to 15 minutes.

SUGGESTIONS

• Cut the rolled-out dough into fine noodles and use to make one of the following recipes.

Baked noodles and fruit (Suessen Nudelauf)   Butter a deep casserole and layer cooked noodles into it, alternating with sliced apples and pears, sprinkling each layer with sugar and a few currants. Finish with a layer of apple and top off with breadcrumbs fried in butter. A powdering of cinnamon makes this particularly delicious. Bake at 350°F/180°C/ Gas 4 for 20 to 30 minutes. Serve the noodles hot with thick cream. The same dish can be made with stewed plums.

Mohn Nudeln   Toss cooked broad-cut noodles in melted unsalted butter and scatter them with poppyseeds and sugar. Serve piping hot after a nourishing soup.

• Or make *Fleckerl*, which is the noodle dough cut into squares. It is used in the same way as thin noodles.

Savoury Puddings and Dumplings

The divorce of salt and sweet came late to Europe. For centuries meat puddings and dumplings were as likely to be flavoured with plums and raisins, nuts and honey, as they were with herbs and salt. Roman recipes mix their flavourings with abandon. In Germany and Austria the division is less marked than it has become in Britain, and fruit or curd dumplings made with yeast-leavened dough still often actually replace the meat course. The English, as befits their culinary expertise and raw materials, specialized in suet pastry dumplings, from which grew their acknowledged skill as pastry and cake-makers.

STEAK AND KIDNEY PUDDING
(England)

Boiled puddings made with a suet crust are of very ancient date and have fed many generations of Englishmen. The original boiled puddings were solid affairs made with flour and suet mixtures — preferably suet from the Englishman's favourite meat animal, beef cattle. The dough was rolled into a ball and tied up in a clean floured cloth. The traditional round Christmas Pudding belongs to this group. These 'cloutie dumplings' were boiled along with a joint of meat or a bit of bacon, and a net of vegetables, all of which hung suspended in boiling water in a cauldron hanging over the hearth fire. There was no distinction between sweet and savoury and it was this taste for unusual combinations, such as mutton or pork with apples, game with wild berries, which fathered the modern English predilection for sweet sauces with meat.

The cauldron-broth provided a savoury soup as well as a plate of dinner. Later, as cooks became more expert, the puddings were made hollow, the crust being supported by a pudding bowl, and then stuffed with a filling — most often a mixture of savoury and sweet. Boiling and roasting remain the techniques best understood in the English kitchen, along with a considerable skill, shared by the rest of the British Isles, in baking pies and cakes. Thickened stews and ragouts took a long time to establish themselves in the British culinary tradition.

Quantity   Enough for 6
Time   Preparation: 1 hour
          Cooking: 3 hours

For the suet pastry
6 oz/175 g suet
12 oz/350 g self-raising flour (if
   you have a wonderfully light
   hand with pastry, you can use
   plain flour)

1 teaspoon salt
¼ pint/150 ml cold water

For the filling
8 oz/250 g beef kidney
1 lb/500 g stewing steak
1 tablespoon vinegar
8 oz/250 g mushrooms (*optional* —
   field mushrooms are the best
   for this)
1 onion

1 tablespoon chopped fresh herbs
   (parsley, thyme, sage)
salt and pepper
½ glass water *or* claret *or* port

Utensils A small bowl, a large bowl, a 3-pint/2-litre pudding bowl, a rolling pin, a large saucepan, a heatproof saucer or metal ring, greaseproof paper, string, and a clean pudding cloth or some foil

Skin, wash, and cube the kidney into 1 in/2·5 cm squares. Put it in to the small bowl and cover it with water acidulated with the tablespoon of vinegar. Set aside.

Next make the suet pastry. Suet is the fat which encases a beef kidney. To be properly prepared it must be shredded, freed from its fibres, and flaked. Chop the suet thoroughly if you have prepared your own. The bought kind in a packet needs no such attention.

Sift the flour into a bowl with the salt, and then stir in the suet. Add cold water slowly (you may need more or less liquid) to make a smooth soft dough that leaves the sides of the bowl clean.

Grease the pudding bowl. Cut off two-thirds of the pastry and roll it out on a well-floured board with the rolling pin, until you have a big enough circle to line the bowl. Line the pudding bowl, easing the pastry well down so that it does not shrink too much in the cooking. Roll out the rest to make a lid and put it aside.

Put on to boil a large pan of water which will accommodate your basin. On the base put a metal ring or heatproof saucer to keep the base of the pudding bowl away from direct heat. Let it come to the boil while you start the filling. Cut the meat into fillets not more than $\frac{1}{2}$ in/1 cm thick. Sprinkle each piece with salt and freshly milled black pepper. Drain and dry the kidneys, and roll each piece up in a steak fillet. Wipe and slice the mushrooms and peel and chop the onion. Pack the meat rolls with the chopped onion and the mushrooms into the lined pudding bowl, sprinkling all with more pepper and salt and the herbs. Pour in the half glass of water. Claret or port would be even better. Damp the edges of the pastry and fit on the lid. Mark the lip with a fork to seal the edges. Cut a small hole in the centre for the steam to escape.

Traditional recipes give very long cooking times — from 7 to 14 hours. Modern meat does not need such drastic treatment — just as well since the pastry has little chance of surviving without getting soggy.

Cover either with a round of greaseproof paper and a clean white cloth or a sheet of foil, both pleated in the middle to allow room for the pastry to rise. If you use a cloth, tie it on with string below the lip of the bowl. Stretch a string handle across the bowl for lifting it in and out of the boiling water, which should reach no more than two-thirds of the way up the sides. The water must be boiling when you put the pudding in. Add boiling water when necessary and make sure it never boils dry. The pudding must not be allowed to come off the boil at any time, or the pastry will be as heavy and grey as a school dinner. Boil for 3 hours.

Serve still in its basin but with its top wrappings removed, swathed in a clean white napkin. To accompany, finely shredded cabbage cooked lightly in no more than half a glass of water and a generous knob of butter, or finely sliced carrots cooked in the same manner. Best bitter to wash it down, unless you can lay your hands on the Englishman's favourite imported claret. A syllabub (see page 477) to round off the repast.

SUGGESTIONS
- This recipe gives you the basic suet pastry. It can be baked as a pie-crust, or bits can be twisted off for dumplings as well as being the traditional pudding crust.
- If you would rather make a steak and kidney pie, use the same pastry and filling, but flour the meat and fry it with the onions and mushrooms first, then add enough water to cover and stew it until tender before you make the pie. Allow it to cool before you cover it with the crust (half the recipe should be enough — use the rest to make a rhubarb dumpling for another day).
- Or put a cover of suet pastry over a top-heat simmered stew such as Lancashire hot-pot, cover tightly and then cook as usual. A speciality of the English Midlands.

For stuffings   Cut any of the following into even-sized cubes: gammon or pork with apples; small game birds, such as woodcock or neatly jointed partridges; pigeons with bacon; a jointed rabbit and a handful of field mushrooms; joints of chicken with cubes of salt-cured gammon. Rook pies, made with the skinned breasts and legs of young rooks with bacon to add flavour, was an old country favourite. There is no shortage of the raw materials still (a single rook is always a crow, a flock of crows are always rooks).

SEMOLINA GNOCCHI
Gnocchi de semolino (Italy)

These little dumplings are probably the original pasta of Italy. Today there are three main varieties made, using three different starch bases. All are poached and then either grilled with cheese or sauced. Semolina is the coarse-milled grain of a particularly hard species of wheat, *Triticum durum* (distinct from the bread-wheat, *Triticum aestivum*). Durum wheat flour is used to make pasta.

Quantity   Enough for 4
Time   Start 1–2 hours before
Preparation: 40–50 minutes
Cooking: 20 minutes

311

8 oz/250 g semolina	2 oz/50 g butter
1 pint/600 ml stock *or* milk	2 eggs
½ onion	salt and pepper
1 bayleaf	butter and grated cheese to finish

Utensils   A saucepan, a shallow dish, and a gratin dish

Bring the stock or milk to the boil with the onion and bayleaf to flavour it. Just before it boils, remove the onion and bayleaf, and sprinkle the semolina, stirring constantly, in handfuls into the hot liquid. Cook gently until thick and smooth — about 20 minutes in all. Remove from the heat and beat in the butter. Allow to cool a little and then beat in the eggs. Pour into a flat dish to a depth of a finger.

When the mixture is cold, cut it into squares, or circles, or crescents, or whatever you please.

Preheat the oven to 350°F/180°C/Gas 4. Butter the gratin dish and scatter grated cheese over the base of it.

Arrange the gnocchi discs like lines of leaning dominoes in the gratin dish. Dot with butter and sprinkle more grated cheese over the top. Bake in the oven for 20 minutes until the top is well browned. (Do not underdo it — a gratin should be flecked with little burnt bits and nicely crisp.)

Serve hot with a salad of young vegetables, such as green beans, lightly cooked in salted boiling water and then tossed in oil and vinegar.

POTATO GNOCCHI
Gnocchi de patate (Italy)

The Italian response to the easily grown import from the New World. Potatoes replace semolina, but the recipe is in all other ways unaltered.

Quantity   Enough for 4–5 servings
Time   Preparation: 1 hour
           Cooking: 30 minutes

2 lb/1 kg potatoes (the dry mealy varieties are best)	2 eggs
	salt and pepper
4 oz/100 g flour	butter and grated cheese to finish

Utensils   A saucepan, a grater or sieve, and a gratin dish

Scrub the potatoes and boil them in their skins until tender — this will take about 20 minutes.

Scrub a corner of the kitchen table and sprinkle it with flour. Put the flour ready in a pile beside you and beat the eggs. Peel the hot potatoes as soon as you can handle them and then grate them on to the floury table. Knead them lightly together with the flour and the beaten eggs — you may need extra water, but the dough should be soft and light and not overworked. Roll the paste into sausages, then cut them into discs with a knife. Make a little dent in each disc. Bring a large pan of salted water to the boil and slide in the little discs. Poach in simmering water until they float to the top — about 5 to 6 minutes.

Preheat the oven to 325°F/170°C/Gas 3. Butter the gratin dish and scatter some grated cheese over the base.

Drain the gnocchi and prop them like leaning dominoes against each other in the gratin dish. Dot the top with butter and sprinkle on more grated cheese. Bake in the oven for 25 to 30 minutes. Serve piping hot, with a salad to accompany, more grated cheese and a bowl of fresh tomato sauce.

SUGGESTIONS
- Yesterday's cold potatoes can be used.
- Sauce the gnocchi with a *ragù* (see page 283) before you bake them. Finish with grated cheese.
- Instead of baking in the oven, butter the poached gnocchi and serve.

CHOUX PASTRY GNOCCHI
Gnocchi di Parigi (Italy)

Catherine de Medici, betrothed to Henri II of France, took her retinue of Florentine nobles to Paris to instruct the chefs of the French court in the Italian culinary arts. Sixteenth-century Florence had the most accomplished cooks in Europe. The visiting Italians also accepted instruction from their talented pupils. This is one of the recipes that emerged from the collaboration.

Quantity   Enough for 4
Time   Preparation: 1 hour
        Cooking: 30 minutes

For the gnocchi
½ pint/300 ml milk
6 oz/175 g flour
2 oz/50 g butter
3 eggs
salt
a pinch of cayenne pepper
4 oz/100 g grated parmesan *or* pecorino

For the cheese sauce
4 oz/100 g parmesan *or* pecorino
2 oz/50 g butter
2 oz/50 g flour
1 pint/600 ml fresh creamy milk
salt and a pinch of cayenne pepper (black pepper will do — lock up the spice box again)
1 oz/25 g butter to finish

Utensils   2 or 3 saucepans, a perforated spoon, a whisk, a gratin dish, and a food processor if you have one for beating in the eggs

Bring the milk to the boil in a roomy saucepan with the butter. When it has boiled and the butter is melted, beat in the flour. Beat the mixture over the heat until the dough comes away from the sides of the pan. Take the pan off the heat to cool for a moment and then beat in the eggs one by one. This is easy to do in a food processor. The paste goes dull when it has accepted all the egg. If it looks like becoming too liquid, stop adding egg — it is merely that the eggs are larger than usual. Hens lay such monsters these days. Add salt and cayenne and grate in the cheese. There you have *choux gnocchi*: much easier than the ones made with potato.

Bring a large pan of salted water to the boil. Using 2 teaspoons dipped in cold water, drop in small dumplings of the *chou* mixture. Poach the gnocchi gently for 15 minutes, until they bob to the surface, puff and firm up. Remove and drain carefully with a perforated spoon.

Meanwhile make the cheese sauce. Grate the cheese. Melt the butter in a small saucepan and stir in the flour. When the mixture is sandy, whisk in the milk, beating to avoid any lumps. Stir in the grated cheese, salt, and cayenne pepper. Or put all the ingredients into the food processor to blend them. The sauce can then be brought to the boil and simmered for 5 minutes. It still needs to be beaten as it cooks.

Preheat the oven to 325°F/170°C/Gas 3.

Spread half the sauce in the base of the gratin dish. Put in the *choux gnocchi* as they come out of the water. Cover with the rest of the sauce. Dot with butter and sprinkle with cheese. Bake for 20 to 30 minutes in the oven. Serve hot — a gratin should be bubbling when it comes to table. A dish of wild mushrooms stewed in butter or oil with garlic and herbs, and a salad to accompany.

BREAD DUMPLINGS
Knockerl (Austria)

The favourite dumpling for poaching in soups, stews, anywhere where potatoes might otherwise be used. A great standby if you have more mouths to feed than anticipated. They are the work of a moment.

Quantity   Enough for 12 dumplings
Time   Preparation intermittently: 1 hour

4 oz/100 g dry bread
½ oz/12 g butter *or* lard
1 egg
¼ pint/150 ml milk
3 oz/75 g flour

salt and pepper
1 tablespoon chopped fresh herbs
(parsley, chervil, marjoram —
optional, but a great
improvement)

Utensils   A frying pan, a bowl, and a saucepan

Dice the bread and fry it lightly in the fat in the frying pan. Meanwhile mix the egg and the milk. Tip the contents of the frying pan into a bowl, and pour the egg and milk over all. Stir in the flour and season with salt and pepper. You may need more milk. Allow it to stand for half an hour.

Roll the mixture with hands dipped into cold water into a dozen small balls. Put a pan of salted water on to boil, if you do not already have a simmering soup-pot waiting. Drop little balls from a teaspoon into the boiling salted water. Poach them for 10 to 15 minutes, until they are light and firm and well risen.

SUGGESTIONS
• Include chopped fried bacon in the mixture, or cubed pork crackling.
• A lighter dumpling can be made if the flour is left out. Less liquid will then be needed.
• The mixture can be used to make a *Cloth* or *Clootie Dumpling*, which used to be popular in both Britain and Germany. It is made as follows. Line a colander with a clean, floured cloth and put the dumpling mix into it. Tie up the corners. Put the handle of a wooden spoon through the handles thus made, and, using the spoon as a crossbar, suspend the dumpling in a pan of boiling water to cook for 30 minutes. Often cooked in the stewpot with a piece of meat, and very good with a game stew. stew.

LEFTOVERS
• Scrambled egg and dumplings. Slice the dumplings and fry them in a little lard or bacon fat. Add beaten egg to the pan, and proceed as for scrambled eggs. Delicious as a late breakfast, or a light lunch with a green salad.

Savoury Pastries and Pies

VENISON PASTY
(England)

The favourite picnic of Robin Hood's jolly companion, Friar Tuck. The pies and pasties of England developed from the bag puddings of pre-oven days. With the advent of bread ovens, the same mixtures were often stewed first, then put into a pie dish and covered with pastry, which could then be baked to a crisp savoury perfection while the oven was lit for the bread baking. Local peasantry had access to the village or manorial oven. A complicated system of rights and duties governed this privilege, usually to the disadvantage of the peasant. These gave rise to frequent feuds, as in this quarrel, quoted in the medieval law records of the Seldon Society:

> It fell out that on Monday next after St. Andrew that M. wife of the hayward and E. wife of a neighbour were baking at an oven, to wit that of N., and a dispute arose between them about the loss of a loaf taken from the oven, and the said old crones took to their fists and each other's hair and raised the hue; and their husbands hearing this ran up and made a great rout. Therefore by award of the court the said women who made the rout and raised the hue are in mercy. And so on with other cases as they arise.

Quantity   Plenty for 6 diners
Time   Start if possible the day before
Preparation intermittently: 1½ hours
Cooking: 30–35 minutes

For the rough puff pastry
6 oz/175 g cold butter
6 oz/175 g cold lard
1 lb/500 g plain flour
1 teaspoon salt
6–7 tablespoons cold water

For the filling
2 lb/1 kg venison off the bone
4 oz/100 g streaky bacon
8 oz/250 g mushrooms — the
   large, dark ones are best
1 onion
6 peppercorns
1 teaspoon juniper and allspice
   berries
1 oz/25 g lard
½ pint/300 ml water
salt

Utensils   A large bowl, a baking tray, a saucepan, and a rolling pin

Trim and cut the venison into 1 in/2·5 cm cubes. It will do no harm to prepare the venison the day before and marinate it overnight in a glass of wine, or half vinegar and water, with a bayleaf and spices. Cube the bacon, slice the mushrooms, peel and chop the onion. Crush the peppercorns with the juniper and allspice berries.

Put the bacon to melt gently in the saucepan. When enough fat has run to grease the pan thoroughly, put in the onions and sauté them lightly. Push them aside and add the lard and then the venison. Fry to allow it to take colour. Add the mushrooms and the spices and fry them for a moment. Pour in the water. No salt yet. Stew all gently until the meat is soft — an hour should be sufficient, unless the meat is very tough. Keep an eye on the pan so that it does not cook dry. There should be only enough well-flavoured gravy left at the end to moisten the stew. Leave it to cool. Taste and adjust the seasoning.

Meanwhile make the pastry. Chop the butter and lard together. Put the flour and the salt into a roomy bowl and rub in half the fat, crumbling lightly with your fingers until the mixture looks like fine breadcrumbs. Sprinkle in the water and press the dough together. Knead the dough lightly into a soft ball of pastry.

Roll out the pastry into a long rectangle, and spread the rest of the butter and lard over two-thirds of it. Fold the unbuttered third into the middle, and then the last third over that, to give you a triple-decker layered with fat. Turn the pastry through a quarter circle and roll it out again. Refold in three. Turn and give it another roll. Refold. Put the pastry to rest in a cool place until you are ready for it.

When the stew is cooked and cooled, preheat the oven to 400°F/200°C/Gas 6.

Cut the pastry in half and roll out two large circles. One should be slightly bigger than the other. Put the smaller circle on the baking tray and pile the cooled venison stew on to it. Wet the edges of the pastry and cover with the other circle. Press the edges together lightly with a fork. Rough up the cut sides with a knife so that it looks like horizontal flaking. Cut a hole in the top for the steam to escape.

Bake in the oven for 30 to 35 minutes until the pastry is golden and well risen.

Serve with new peas or beans and English mustard.

SUGGESTIONS
● Steak and kidney, steak and onion, chicken and mushroom, all manner of furred and feathered game, fish — haddock in particular — in white sauce with hard-boiled eggs, all make good pie fillings. There are many purely regional pies which make use of local specialities.
● The pasty can be baked as a pie, but you will only need half the quantity of pastry to cover it.

CHEESE PIE
Kajmak (Yugoslavia and neighbours)

Big trays of this *filo*-based pie are sold from special kiosks in the marketplaces of Yugoslavia. These little shops also sell *baklava* (see page 542) and *kataife*, another honey and nut sweet pastry, a very finely shredded pastry made by forcing a noodle paste through pinholes punched in a tin sheet. This cheese pie prepared with good ingredients is one of the most delicious dishes imaginable, not unlike a French quiche. The difference is that the crisp *filo* makes the dish wonderfully light. The filling is fresh, clean, and a perfect match for the delicate pastry.

Quantity   Enough for 6 depending on appetites
Time   Preparation: 30 minutes, longer if you make your own *filo*
        Cooking: 40–50 minutes

½ lb/250 g *filo* pastry
6 oz/175 g melted clarified butter
1 lb/500 g *kajmak* cheese *or* 8 oz/
    250 g *feta or* other strong cheese
    mixed with 8 oz/250 g cream *or*
    cottage cheese

4 eggs
2 tablespoons cream
salt and pepper

Utensils   A bowl, a 12×8 in/20×30 cm deep-sided baking tray and a liquidizer if you have one

Take care to keep the *filo* pastry covered while you work — it dries out and cracks very easily.

Clarified butter is ordinary butter, melted and then allowed to cool so that the whey, salt, and colouring matter settle on the bottom of the bowl. Pure clarified butter can then be lifted off. This butter has a far higher burning point than ordinary butter so it is very good for frying. It will also keep sweet for a very long time.

Beat the cheese, the eggs, and the cream together in a bowl. Add salt in accordance with the saltiness of the cheese you are using. Be generous with the pepper. This whole operation can be done to perfection in the liquidizer.

Butter the baking tray and line it with 2 thicknesses of *filo* pastry, leaving an edge which can be tucked up and over the filling. Sprinkle the top sheet with the clarified butter, then put on another 2 and sprinkle the top one generously with butter, and so on until you have 8 thicknesses of *filo*.

Spread on the layer of filling — lightly so that you do not press the air out of the layers. Cover with 6 to 8 more sheets of *filo* pastry, buttering alternate layers as before. Pour any butter which remains (if you have a lot, next time be more generous with the layers) over the top. Mark into diamonds, and sprinkle with water. Bake at 350°F/180°C/Gas 4 for 40 to 50 minutes, until well risen and golden. It puffs up like magic and will stay puffed and crisp even when cold.

Serve as an appetizer, or as a main course with a salad of sliced peppers, tomatoes, and onions dressed with lemon juice and salt.

SUGGESTIONS
• Chop a handful of parsley finely and stir it in to the filling mixture.

BOREK
(Turkey, Greece, and neighbours)

Borek are a great treat: these small triangular stuffed pastries are made with strips of *filo*, neatly folded zig-zag fashion to keep the filling in. The Turks have brought the preparation and the fillings to a fine art. In the Middle East, where these little pastries are very popular, the *filo* dough is sometimes made with lemon juice or yoghurt — its composition is a matter of passionate debate and each region or even family has its own theories. Find a mix which suits you and form an equally passionate break-away group. The filling is very variable, but should be delicate and well minced, and can range from a simple handful of chopped spinach to the most complicated and intricately spiced palace mixtures. Here are a few on which to get started.

Quantity   Make several different fillings for a party — yields 40–50 *borek*
Time   Active: 1–1½ hours

For the dough

1 lb/500 g plain strong flour	*Or* use ready-made *filo* pastry (one
½ teaspoon salt	packet of bought *filo* pastry
3 eggs	usually yields around 24 sheets)
small glass water	oil for frying
1 tablespoon melted butter	

Utensils   Clingfilm, a deep pan for frying, and a perforated spoon

First make the *filo*. Pour the flour directly on to a clean table top. Make a well in the flour, and put in the salt and eggs. Work all together thoroughly, adding enough water to give a soft pliable dough. Work in the butter. Cut the dough into 40 walnut-sized pieces and roll each out until it is as fine as paper. Or stretch it on your fists as in the Strudel recipe on page 532.

The following fillings are given in quantities to stuff pastries made from a dozen 12 in/30 cm sheets, yielding 40 to 50 little *borek*. If you want a choice of fillings, adjust the quantities. Keep the *filo* pastry rolled up and covered with clingfilm while you work — it dries out in no time and becomes too brittle to roll. You will also need oil or clarified butter to brush the pastry.

Cheese filling 1 lb/500 g grated cheese beaten with 2 eggs. Use Greek *halumi*, or substitute Cheddar, Gruyère or mozzarella plus a spoonful of grated parmesan. Salt and pepper.

Curd cheese filling 1 lb/500 g soft white cheese mashed with chopped mint, dill, or parsley. Use Greek *feta*, or any soft white cheese, plus plenty of salt and pepper and a spoonful of grated parmesan.

Spinach filling 1 lb/500 g fresh spinach or other greens plus 4 oz/ 100 g grated hard cheese (*halumi* or Cheddar). Cook the spinach in the water which clings to its leaves after washing — 5 to 10 minutes will be enough. Mince it very finely and put it back into the pan with 1 oz/25 g butter and sweat it until it is as soft and dry as possible. Allow the mixture to cool. Beat in 1 egg and the grated cheese and freshly milled pepper — only add salt if the cheese is not already salty enough. Nutmeg is a good spice for this mixture.

Aubergine filling 1 lb/500 g aubergines, cubed and fried gently in 2 tablespoons of oil, with 1 finely chopped onion. When the vegetables are well browned, add 2 chopped, peeled, and seeded tomatoes. Simmer until all are soft. A minced clove of garlic or a tablespoon of lightly fried pine kernels makes a good addition. Mash well before using.

Meat filling 1 lb/500 g lean minced meat stiffened in a spoonful of olive oil with 1 finely chopped onion. Moisten with $\frac{1}{4}$ pint/150 ml water, add salt and pepper and any seasonings you like. Cook gently for 10 to 15 minutes. Lamb is the best meat for this and a tablespoon of pine kernels, fried with the meat, is a good addition. Allow the mixture to cool before using. Cinnamon or allspice are good spices to include.

Sweetbread filling 1 lb/500 g calf's or lamb's brains or sweetbreads. Prepare the meats by soaking them first for an hour in water with a tablespoon of lemon juice. Drain them, peel off the outer membrane, and clean away any traces of blood. Simmer the meats in water with a little salt and a tablespoon of lemon juice, for 10 to 15 minutes. Drain them carefully and then mash them up with a tablespoon of chopped herbs (dill, parsley, chervil, fresh oregano), salt, and pepper. A particularly good stuffing. A dish for the urban poor, who could, in times of plenty, buy quite cheaply the offal which the rich man foolishly rejected.

Now assemble the *borek*. Lay out the *filo* pastry and cut it into strips 2½ in/6 cm wide by the full length of the pastry. Brush each strip as you work through the layers with oil or melted butter. Put a teaspoon of your chosen filling on the near corner of the strip. Fold it over to make a triangle, and then fold again to make another triangle, and so on up the strip, always rolling away from you, until you have a well-wrapped little *borek* covered in half a dozen thicknesses of pastry.

Put a deep pan of oil on to heat.

Deep fry the *borek* in batches in hot oil for 5 minutes, until the pastry is well puffed and golden. Drain the *borek* on kitchen paper.

They should be served warm — particularly delicious with a tiny glass of *raki* or *ouzo*, the anis-flavoured liquor of Turkey and Greece. You will not regret making the necessary effort.

CORNISH PASTY
(England)

The best of lunch-pail food, versions of this pasty are to be found all over Europe, although nowhere was it taken to its logical perfection as it was in Cornwall. The Cornish pasty is as easily transportable down the mine as it is into the fishing boat or out into the fields at harvest time. It is a satisfying, well-balanced meal contained in a pastry crust. The pasty was sometimes stuffed with a sweet filling (jam or apple sauce) at one end, a savoury one at the other, with a solid disposable 'handle' at one extremity of the half-moon to accommodate the miner's or field-worker's blackened thumb. When it was exported with the Cornish miners to the New World, the immigrant Finns adopted and adapted it and washed it down with their favourite sour milk. The immigrant Italians spiced it with peppers, tomatoes, and a chopped chilli or two and also claimed it as their own.

Quantity   Makes 4 large pasties
Time   Preparation: 1 hour
            Cooking: 50–60 minutes

For the filling
1 lb/500 g steak
1 lb/500 g potatoes
1 small onion
salt and pepper

For the pastry
1 lb/500 g flour
½ teaspoon salt
¼ pint/150 ml water
½ lb/250 g prepared grated suet *or* butter *and/or* lard

Utensils   A bowl, a rolling pin, a large saucepan, and a baking sheet

Prepare the filling first. Slice the meat and chop it into small squares. Peel and dice the potatoes small. Peel and chop the onion. Mix all together in a bowl and season with salt and pepper.

For the pastry, sift the flour with the salt. Bring the water to the boil in a large pan with the suet, and boil until the suet melts (if you are using butter or lard this will happen more quickly). Beat in the flour and cook until the paste comes away from the sides of the pan. This is hot water paste and at this point it will look slightly transparent. Tip it out on to a well-floured board, knead into a ball and cut into quarters. Work quickly because the pastry will crack if it is allowed to cool. Roll each quarter into a circle $\frac{1}{4}$ in/6 mm thick.

Preheat the oven to 350°F/180°C/Gas 4.

Divide the meat mixture between each circle, piling the mixture up in the middle. Damp the edges of the pastry and pull them over the filling to meet in the middle. Pinch the edges together to make a wavy line, known as the Cornish crimp. Leave a little hole in the middle for escaping steam. Glaze with egg if you like a shiny crust. Bake in the oven for 50 to 60 minutes.

SUGGESTIONS

• Variations in Cornwall are many, including mutton and leeks (sometimes raisins), chopped egg and bacon, lamb and parsley, fish and potato, pork and apples, turnip and carrot, fruit and jam. Mark with the recipient's initials and stuff and season the pasty to his or her particular taste.

• Shortcrust pastry (see page 530) can be used instead of the hot water crust.

CHAPTER 9
Potato Dishes

The potato, a relative newcomer to the European peasant larder, has none the less had a prodigious influence on European life. The first potato plants arrived in Spain in the baggage of the Conquistadores returning from Peru in 1540. The Incas had cultivated the potato for centuries to supply their mountain fortresses high in the Andes mountains, where their usual crop of maize could not survive. Just as Amsterdam was built on herring bones, so were Manchu Pichu and Quito built on the potato. The Spanish court failed to see the tuber's culinary potential, but they found the pale mauve blooms very pretty and bedded the plants in flowerpots. The English received their first plants when Francis Drake brought some back from North America. Elizabeth I was not at all sure what to make of them, and she too planted them in her ornamental flower beds.

For the next two centuries the potato as a food source was treated with suspicion. A few brave souls took a chance and planted potatoes on the stony hillsides of Galicia, in the vegetable gardens of Lyons (even then the good burgers of Lyons were in the gastronomic vanguard), and in the flat fields of the Low Countries. Over in England some progress was being made. A dish of potatoes is recorded as appearing on King James's dinner table in 1619. Even with royal patronage the poisonous looking roots were widely considered untrustworthy, and in 1630 the Parliament of Besançon, in south-west France, outlawed the tuber, declaring it responsible for a particularly virulent outbreak of leprosy. Nevertheless, the potato patch spread slowly across the fertile fields of Europe throughout the next century. From the sunlit valleys of Spain to the frozen mountains of Scandinavia the miraculously adaptable food-plant flourished.

Nowhere was it more successful than in the soft climate of Ireland. It was Elizabeth I's favourite sailor, Sir Walter Raleigh, who took the first potato plants to the green hills of the Emerald Isle. A mere century and a half later, virtually all other crops had been abandoned in its favour. A single damp Irish acre put down to potatoes by one Irish peasant, equipped with a spade and a hoe, yielded enough food to fill his family's black iron cooking pot all year — with some left over for the family pig. The population of Ireland tripled — from three million in 1750 to nearly nine million a century later. In 1841 the blight struck the potato. By 1846 a million and a half Irish men, women, and children had died of starvation. Of those who survived thousands emigrated to the New World.

Between 1750 and 1850 not only the Irish but the whole population of Europe exploded — victualled increasingly by the ever-adaptable jack-of-all-foods. An English traveller in Westphalia in 1780 reports the change in diet:

Peasants tire of oatbread eaten dry with salt and water. I can heartily recommend the potato boiled and then moistened with a little milk, roasted in the ashes and eaten with a little butter, or eaten cold as a salad. Grated and mixed with eggs, oats and sugar it makes an excellent rissole. On this diet the peasants of Sauerland endure hard heavy work, and yet live as healthily as fish in the sea.

Whether boiled or baked, eaten as potato bread or in soup, used for animal fodder or fermented and distilled into alcohol, there was virtually no culinary need the potato could not supply. Just as the potato had been essential to the supremacy of the Incas in Peru, so it now dominated the politics of Europe. Revolution, war, the growth of empires — all were fuelled by the pressures of an expanding population. That curious basket of sprouting tubers in Francisco Pizzaro's luggage has proved as powerful as any of Alfred Nobel's explosive mixtures.

The best potatoes are those freshly dug from your own garden — the finest I have ever tasted grew in the stone-strewn, sheep-manured 'tattie patch' beside a shepherd's farmhouse on the rocky Atlantic coast of a Hebridean island. They were always freshly dug and scented the kitchen with smells of peat and bracken. The soft mists seem to make Scottish potatoes particularly delicious — feathery pillows, plump and sweet. Their skins are pale gold and translucent, and stretched so tightly over the snowy flesh that they pop when you bite into them. Hebridean potatoes are scrubbed, never peeled, and cooked in boiling water with salt. They are eaten scalding hot, straight from the pot, with cold unsalted butter and salt, washed down with the Scots' favourite strong tea. Better than the finest caviar to an appetite sharpened by a long day walking the heather in search of a lost new-born lamb.

IRISH POTATOES

An article in *Frazer's Magazine* dated April 1847, just after the potato blight, explains the significance of the loss of so important a crop to the Irish peasant: 'Easily boiled in an iron pot, served in a turf-basket or rolled on a table, peeled with the fingers, and palatable in its own sweet moisture, the Irish peasant could better spare a far better nutriment.'

Quantity   Enough for 4 (An Irish working man of the last century would have managed a daily quota of 10–14 lb of boiled tatties.)
Time   Preparation: 10 minutes
        Cooking: 30 minutes

2 lb/1 kg large old floury potatoes
salt
unsalted butter

Utensils   A heavy saucepan

Choose evenly sized potatoes and scrub them thoroughly, but don't leave them to soak in the water. Put them in the saucepan and just cover them with fresh cold water. Add a teaspoon of rough salt. Bring the water to the boil quickly, and then turn the heat down to a steady simmer. Potatoes will take 20 minutes (up to 30 if large) to cook. When the potatoes are soft right through, drain them and toss them over the heat to dry them. Their skins should burst a little, like roast chestnuts, to show the snowy flesh inside. Serve with salt and a pat of cold fresh butter. (The Irish turned to dairy farming after the disaster of the Potato Famine — Irish butter and cream are now excellent.)

SUGGESTIONS
● Potatoes baked in the oven in an unglazed earthenware pot will be light, floury, and have their vitamins intact.
● Dress boiled, skinned potatoes with breadcrumbs fried crisp and golden in butter.
● Do not use potatoes which have green parts, or which have sprouted, as these will have developed a harmful substance called 'solanin'. Should you keep a household pig, cut out and discard the green pieces from the spoiled ones, boil up the good bits, and put them in the pigmash.

BOXTY
(Ireland)

A special potato bread for serving at Hallowe'en, when the restless spirits of witches are abroad. This celebration reaches back into pre-Christian harvest festivals, although the potato did not feature until at least the eighteenth century. Country memories are long and bonfires are still traditionally lit as part of Hallowe'en, which in turn has its roots in thanksgiving to the Sun God — a custom shared with the Scandinavians, who have more cause than most to be anxious for the god's patronage.

> Boxty on the griddle, Boxty in the pan,
> If you don't eat Boxty you'll never get a man.

2 lb/1 kg potatoes

1 lb/500 g flour

2 teaspoons salt

¼ pint/150 ml milk

butter

Utensils A grater (food processors have a useful attachment for this job), a large bowl, and a baking tray

Peel the potatoes and grate them raw. Mix in the flour and the salt and leave the mixture to stand for an hour. Add the milk and knead the mixture well on a floured board.

Preheat the oven to 350°F/180°C/Gas 4. Butter the baking tray.

Divide the dough into 4. Roll each piece out into a cake, roughly 6 in/15 cm in diameter. Put the cakes on to the buttered baking tray. Mark the cakes into quarters with a cross.

Bake in the oven for 40 minutes, until they are cooked through and lightly browned. Serve hot with plenty of butter. Not a dish for anyone on a diet.

SUGGESTIONS

• A lighter mixture can be made by boiling half the quantity of potatoes and then mashing them with 4 oz/100 g butter or bacon dripping. The mashed potato is then kneaded into the raw mixture.

• The Boxty batter can be softened to a dropping consistency with extra milk, and then cooked on a lightly greased griddle or heavy frying pan, as for drop-scones. These are served with butter, and sometimes with treacle or sugar.

COLCANNON
(Ireland)

A Hallowe'en food like Boxty. There used to be a ritual attached to the supping of Colcannon. Four favours would be hidden in the dish: a gold marriage ring, a piece of money, an old maid's thimble, and a bachelor's button. Those who got them in their portion had their fates decided for the coming year.

Quantity Enough for 6

Time Preparation: 40 minutes

2 lb/1 kg potatoes

2 lb/1 kg curly kale *or* dark green cabbage

½ lb/250 g leeks

½ pint/300 ml cream (milk will do at a pinch)

6 oz/175 g butter

salt and pepper

Utensils   3 large and 1 small saucepans

Peel and quarter the potatoes, and put them to cook in boiling salted water for 20 minutes until cooked through. Drain well.

Meanwhile rinse, slice, and cook separately the kale or cabbage in a very little water for 15 to 20 minutes (you need the vegetable soft for this dish). Drain well and chop fine.

Wash and slice the leeks into thin rings, and put them to stew in yet another pan with the cream or milk until soft — about 6 to 7 minutes should be enough.

Put the butter to melt in the small pan on the side of the stove. Put a deep serving dish to warm.

Mash the potatoes with the leeks and the cream. Then beat in the kale/cabbage. Beat it some more over a low heat until it is pale green and fluffy. Salt and pepper to taste.

Put the hot mixture into the well-warmed serving dish. Make a well in the centre (and don't forget to bury the favours). Pour the melted butter into the well. Put the dish in the middle of the table. Each person takes a helping with a spoonful of butter.

SUGGESTIONS
● Omit the kale/cabbage and you have a dish of Champ.

LEFTOVERS
● Colcannon and Champ will refry beautifully in the leftover butter. Excellent too with a few slices of good bacon and refried in the bacon fat.

FISH AND POTATO FRY
Fischlabskaus (Germany)

A dish from the seacoast of Schleswig Holstein, where the fishermen's wives can make it with any of the fish in the catch. The same dish is made with meat or fish in all the Atlantic ports of Europe, from Tromso to Liverpool to Lisbon.

Quantity   Enough for 4 hungry fishermen
Time   Preparation intermittently: 40 minutes

2 lb/1 kg potatoes	2 oz/50 g lard *or*, better still, bacon
1 lb/500 g skinned and filleted fish	fat
1 lb/500 g onions	salt and pepper

Utensils   A heavy frying pan with a lid

Peel the potatoes and slice them thickly. Check the fish for bones. Peel and slice the onions.

Melt the lard or bacon fat in the frying pan. Fry the onions golden. Lay the potatoes on top and cover with water. Add a little salt and put the lid on the pan. Simmer gently until the potatoes are soft and most of the water has evaporated. Lay the filleted fish on top. Continue to cook. The base will dry out and begin to fry again. Continue until there is a golden crust underneath. Do not mix up the ingredients too much — it should not be a mush. Adjust the seasoning. Serve with a dish of pickled cucumbers (see page 410).

SUGGESTIONS
- Butter or vegetable oil can substitute for the lard — in which case include a bit of bacon, chopped fine.
- *Labskaus* is also delicious made with salted or smoked fish.
- Sometimes salt pork or salt beef replaces the fish to make a good simple hash.

LEFTOVERS
- Bind the mixture with an egg and fry spoonfuls to make excellent fish cakes.

POTATO PANCAKE-BREAD
Lompe (Norway)

An excellent soft pancake-wrapper, easily made at home, eaten in Norway with butter and *geitost* cheese, or used to wrap delicious little morsels of smoked ham, *fenalår*, dried and salted leg of mutton, or a spoonful of berry conserve.

Quantity Makes 10–12 small pancakes
Time Preparation intermittently: 1 hour

2 lb/1 kg old potatoes (the older
   the better)
½ teaspoon salt
4 oz/100 g flour

Utensils A saucepan, a rolling pin, and a griddle or heavy iron frying pan

Peel, quarter, and boil the potatoes in plenty of salted water. Drain them thoroughly and mash them. Mix with the flour and knead vigorously into a dough. (Less or more flour may be needed — potatoes are very variable. The less flour you use the better.) Roll the dough into a long sausage and chop it into 10–12 in/25–30 cm lengths. Roll these pieces out on a well-floured board into pancakes no more than ⅛ in/3 mm thick.

Bake the *lompe* on a very lightly greased griddle or heavy frying pan until they blister. Turn once.

SUGGESTIONS

• Potato *lompe* have entered the fast-food repertoire of Norway and are sold on street corners as a wrapper for hot dogs — a great improvement on the usual soft white bun.

POTATO AND BACON DUMPLINGS
Kroppkakor (Sweden)

Quantity Enough for 5–6
Time Start the day before
Preparation: 40 minutes

8 large potatoes	½ teaspoon salt
4 oz/100 g streaky bacon	4 oz/100 g flour
1 onion	1 large egg

Utensils A large saucepan, a small frying pan, a large bowl, and a grater

Scrub the potatoes and put them on to boil in their skins — this will take 20 to 30 minutes depending on size. Drain them and leave them overnight.

The next day dice the bacon. Peel and chop the onion finely. Put the bacon in the small pan to melt gently. As soon as there is enough fat from the bacon to fry them, add the onions. Cook all gently until soft.

Peel and then grate the potatoes into a large bowl. Mix in the salt, the flour, and the egg. Swift fingers make light dumplings. Roll out the dough in a sausage shape, and chop into 20 short lengths. Roll each length into a small ball and push a nest in it with your finger. Fill the nest with a little of the bacon and onion mixture, and then close up the hole. Continue until all the potatoes and bacon are used up.

Meanwhile set a pan of salted water to boil on the stove. When all the dumplings are made — there should be 15 to 20 — put them to poach in the simmering water until they are light and well risen.

Serve with a jug of melted bacon dripping with little pieces of bacon in it. Or with melted butter.

SUGGESTIONS

• You can use yesterday's leftover boiled potatoes.

ANCHOVIES AND POTATOES
Janssons Frestelse (Sweden)

This dish was re-christened 'Jansson's Temptation' in the eighteenth century after a deeply religious Swede, Erik Janson (whose name was apparently misspelt during the long Atlantic crossing). Janson, the tempted one, was forbidden any enjoyment by his devout church. This simple but delicious dish from his native land was his one transgression. The Swedish tinned anchovies are usually billed as Marinated Sprats.

Quantity   Enough for 4
Time   Preparation: 20 minutes
        Cooking: 1¼ hours

20 salted anchovy fillets (2 small tins)	½ lb/250 g onions
	pepper
2 lb/1 kg potatoes	1 pint/600 ml single cream

Utensils   A deep gratin dish and some foil

Peel and slice the potatoes finely. Peel and slice the onions finely. Open the tins of anchovies. Save the oil — if you buy the anchovies from a barrel, you will need to soak them for 10 minutes in milk to de-salt them a little, and you will need 1 oz/25 g butter.

Preheat the oven to 400°F/200°C/Gas 6.

Layer the potatoes with the onions and the anchovies into the gratin dish. Sprinkle with freshly ground pepper as you go. There should be enough salt in the anchovies. Finish with a layer of potatoes. Pour in half the cream. Trickle the anchovy oil over the surface, or dot with butter. Cover with foil.

Put in the hot oven to bake for 15 minutes. Then pour in the rest of the cream and turn the heat down to 300°F/150°C/Gas 2. Leave to cook gently. The potatoes will take another hour to soften. Ready when they yield to a knife. Remove the lid for the last 20 minutes to allow the top to gild.

That's all. Simple perfection. No wonder Erik was tempted. A blueberry pie to finish in celebration of the American connection.

BAKED POTATOES
(England)

The embers of a wood fire are the best place to cook the last old potatoes of the year. I remember the bonfire my grandfather would light at dusk on a cold November evening — my grandmother knew it was to burn up the dry leaves and debris of summer, but we children knew differently. When the fire burnt down we were allowed to tuck potatoes into the hot ash at the edge. It was our reward for a day's raking fallen leaves and dead branches in the garden. We would crouch, scarlet faces turned to the flames, icy winter night wind cold on the back of our necks, until long past supper time. At last we would poke out our very own tattie, charred and crisp outside, soft and sweet within. My grandmother looked the other way when we thieved a pat of butter and a paper of salt from the larder. An unbeatable dish.

Time   Preparation: 5 minutes
           Cooking: 60 minutes

1 or 2 large potatoes per person
salt (*optional*)

Scrub large potatoes very thoroughly and puncture the skins with a fork. You can rub the skins with salt if you like a salty crust. They will take 60 minutes in a moderate oven — 350°F/180°C/Gas 4. (Don't wrap them in foil or the skins will be soft.) Eat the potatoes as soon as they are ready, when they are at their crispest and most succulent, with cold butter and salt.

The skins are the best part, and the most nutritious.

POTATO NOODLES
Krumpli nudli (Hungary)

Undergraduate Miss Ellen Browning, niece of the poet Robert, travelled through Hungary in 1895. She greatly approved the supper she was offered in a peasant farmhouse:

Presently the good woman began to set about her preparations for supper. We were to have 'krumpli nudli'. I begged permission to assist in preparing them, which was readily granted. A large pot of potatoes had been boiling in their jackets. These were now strained off, skinned, mashed with salt and flour into a paste and rolled into 'worms', then dropped into a pan of boiling lard and thrown into a hot colander to drain as soon as they were cooked, then turned into a big dish, sprinkled with breadcrumbs and popped into a hot oven for ten minutes. These are excellent, I can assure you, and Madame Irma made them to perfection. She seemed to be a very capable plain cook. For my dinner she had given me roast chicken with pickled-plum compote, followed by 'jam-bags' [dumplings stuffed with jam].

HEAVEN AND EARTH
Himmel und Erde (Germany)

The German kitchen has some particularly good potato recipes, including delicious pancakes made with raw grated potatoes and served with apples or stewed fruit; and this excellent dish known as 'Heaven and Earth', which mixes boiled potatoes with apples and crisp fried bacon. This mixture of fruit and vegetables, sweet and sour, is characteristic of northern country cooking — Holland, Belgium, Alsace, Poland, Czechoslovakia, and Scandinavia all have similar mixtures. Immigrants to America, particularly the German and Dutch settlers in Pennsylvania, took their sweet-salt dishes with them and adapted the recipes to local ingredients. The resident Indians already used sweet maple syrup to dress their meat. Thence developed those peculiarly American dishes such as pumpkin and marshmallow pie to eat with the Thanksgiving turkey. Waffles with maple syrup and bacon, even the peanut butter and jelly sandwich, belong to the same tradition.

This makes an excellent supper or light luncheon dish.

Quantity Enough for 3–4 as a main course
Time Preparation intermittently: 40 minutes

2 lb/1 kg potatoes	salt
2 lb/1 kg apples	8 oz/250 g streaky bacon

Utensils A large saucepan and a small frying pan

If the potatoes are new and small, you merely need to wash them. If they are old, peel them closely and quarter them. Put them to boil in plenty of salted water. Peel and cut the apples into chunks the size of the potato pieces. Add them to the potatoes after 10 minutes. Finish cooking both together. By the time the potatoes are cooked the apples will be soft but still holding their shape.

Put a serving dish to heat in the oven.

Meanwhile dice the bacon and fry it in its own fat (if possible — modern vacuum-packed bacon is so wet you may need a little extra lard. Spanish and Italian delicatessens, as well as German ones, sometimes have good bacon — look for it hanging on a hook from the ceiling. It is sold sliced from the piece in the thickness you want — in this case, 3 or 4 thick slices.)

Drain the cooked apples and potatoes. Pile them into the hot serving dish and sprinkle the crisp bacon, with its cooking juices, over all. Serve immediately.

SUGGESTIONS
● Cook 1 lb/500 g fresh sausages (*bratwurst* would be most appropriate) with the bacon. Serve all together.
● Fry 1 oz/25 g fresh breadcrumbs in the bacon fat until crisp and golden. Scatter over the potatoes.

POTATO PANCAKES
Kartoffelpuffer (Germany)

One of the most delicious ways of preparing potatoes. A classic peasant recipe which is simplicity itself.

Quantity   Enough for 4
Time   Preparation intermittently: 30 minutes

 2 lb/1 kg potatoes
 ½ teaspoon salt
 lard *or* butter for frying

Utensils   A grater or a food processor if you have one, and a frying pan

Wash and then peel the potatoes. Grate them through the largest holes of the grater to give noodle-like strips. Do not wash them again — they need the natural starchy juice to hold them together. Mix in the salt.

Heat the lard or butter in the frying pan. If you only have cooking oil, fry a small piece of bacon in it first to scent the oil. Drop spoonfuls of the potato mixture into the hot fat, pressing the mounds flat with the back of a wooden spoon. Fry the patties gently and steadily until they are crisp and golden underneath and soft right through — they will only unstick from the pan when the bottom is cooked. Then turn them over and fry the other side.

A delicious innocent dish to be served straight from the pan. Excellent with fried apple quarters or apple sauce (see page 153).

SUGGESTIONS
● Put the peeled potatoes to soak for 10 minutes in water acidulated with vinegar (1 tablespoon vinegar to 1 pint/600 ml water). This will help them stay white — grated raw potato quickly turns a foggy grey. Then rinse them and grate as above.

● In Franconia a more substantial dish is made by mixing the grated potato with an egg or two at the start, together with a large boiled potato well mashed. Served with a dish of stewed cranberries instead of the apple.

POTATO SOUP
Kartoffelsuppe (Germany)

Soups are staple fare all over Germany. In the colder climate of the north, the preference is for thick rib-sticking potages — potato, pumpkin, root vegetable, perhaps flavoured with a piece of smoked meat or a slice of sausage. There is a repertoire of wine soups and beer soups (particularly around Munich, whose brewers are held in high esteem) which make their appearance at the beginning of the meal. Hamburg specializes in fruit soups. The lowland farmer likes his broth clear and strong, fortified with little dumplings, slices of egg custard, and semolina or noodles.

This is one of those thick soups designed to precede not a meat course, but the housewife's best strudel or fruit pie. The favourite Friday soup.

Quantity Enough for 6 sturdy Bavarian farmers or 8 more delicate appetites

Time Preparation: 20 minutes
Cooking: 30 minutes

3 lb/1·5 kg potatoes
3 lb/1·5 kg root vegetables (carrots, turnips, swedes, celery, parsnips)
1 lb/500 g onions

1 oz/25 g butter *or* lard
3 pints/2 litres water *or* stock
salt and pepper
fresh herbs for flavouring (lovage, basil, parsley, marjoram)

Utensils A large stewpot with a lid

Peel and chop the potatoes into 1 in/2·5 cm cubes. If they are new, just scrub them and cut them in half. Wash and scrape the vegetables and cut them into similar chunks. Peel and slice the onions.

Heat the butter or lard in the stewpot, and fry the onions gently until transparent. Add the potatoes and vegetables. Pour in the water or stock, bring to the boil, cover the pan, and simmer the soup for half an hour. Mash lightly to thicken the broth.

Season with salt and pepper. Chop the herbs finely and stir them into the soup just before you serve it. If you are using dried herbs, they should be added at the start.

Enjoy your strudel to finish.

SUGGESTIONS

● Add 1 oz/25 g dried mushrooms (*cèpes* are best — they have a delicious gluey texture). Soak them in a little warm water before adding them, with their liquor, to the soup. Raw cultivated mushrooms can be used, but they are not so well flavoured.

● The Franconians would include a crust of dark rye bread to be stewed with the vegetables. This gives a slightly nutty flavour. Only marjoram to flavour.

● Dice and fry 4 oz/100 g fat bacon and sprinkle it on the soup as you serve it. (This would naturally not have been permitted on a Friday fast-day.) Once again only marjoram to flavour.

● For another non-fast-day meal, cook a few slices of smoked sausage in the soup.

● Serve the soup with a bowl of soured cream or grated cheese.

POTATO GRATIN
(France)

There are many regional variations of this dish, all floodlit with passionate controversy, raging mainly over the inclusion of eggs, cheese, onions, cream, and nutmeg. I give here one of the simplest Provençal versions. It will be just as delicious as the more complicated recipes.

Quantity   Enough for 6
Time   Preparation: 20 minutes
    Cooking: 1 hour

3 lb/1·5 kg potatoes
1 onion
4 oz/100 g strong cheese
    (parmesan is best)
1 pint/600 ml strong meat *or*
    chicken *bouillon*
olive oil
salt and pepper

Utensils   A shallow gratin dish, some foil, and a food processor with a slicing attachment if you have one

Peel, rinse, and slice the potatoes thinly. To assist them in this job, the French housewives have an instrument called a *mandoline* — a neat wooden board which has 2 slanted razor-sharp blades embedded in it. Peel and slice the onion finely. Grate the cheese. Heat up the stock.
    Preheat the oven to 350°F/180°C/Gas 4.
    Pour 2 tablespoons of olive oil into the bottom of the gratin dish. Put in a layer of potato, then a layer of the sliced onion, then half the grated cheese, then the rest of the potatoes. Season as you go. Pour in the hot stock. Trickle a little oil over the surface, and cover the dish with foil.

Put all to cook gently in the oven for 50 to 60 minutes in all. Keep the dish covered for the first half hour, then take off the cover and sprinkle on the rest of the grated cheese. Allow to finish cooking and gild a rich brown.

Serve the gratin in its own dish, bubbling hot and accompanied by a plain grilled chop, or a chicken roasted with a little olive oil and rosemary or thyme.

A *salade de mesclun* (see page 403) or a beautiful Provençal vegetable dish to follow. A meal for a long leisurely Sunday lunch, to be taken in good company, preferably on the back porch of a whitewashed Provençal farmhouse. A meal to be eaten off glazed pottery plates, terracotta and cream, laid on a comfortable, scrubbed wooden table in the shade of a wisteria-twined trellis. Wisteria thrives in the sunshine of Provence — there, cascades of pale blue blossom starred with nectar-sipping swallowtail butterflies tumble down old stone walls in every village.

GRATIN DAUPHINOIS
(France)

This most simple and perfect of all potato dishes undergoes many unnecessary embellishments in the course of its travels from the Alps of the Dauphiné. Cheese is added to it, and eggs — all too frequently scrambled slowly to a grainy water — nutmeg is sprinkled in, the potatoes are parboiled before being sliced, flour is added to the cream. This gratin is a mountain dish, as befits the hardy potato. Made carefully and cooked slowly, it will be as you would expect to find it in its home country. The quantity of cream is lavish — but you will serve nothing else rich in the meal, and it will be much more delicious than if you had stuffed the same amount of cream into a cake.

Quantity   Enough for 4
Time   Preparation: 20–30 minutes
            Cooking: 1½ hours

2 lb/1 kg old potatoes	salt and pepper
1 clove garlic	1 oz/25 g butter
1 pint/600 ml double cream	

Utensils   A round earthenware dish, which is considered proper to the *Gratin Dauphinois*, some foil, and a *mandoline* or a food processor with a slicing attachment to make the dish easier

Peel and slice the potatoes as fine as gold florins. Peel and finely slice the garlic.

Preheat the oven to 300°F/150°C/Gas 2.

Layer the potatoes into the gratin dish, sprinkling with salt, plenty of pepper, and sliced garlic as you go. Pour in the cream. Dot the surface with little bits of butter, and cover all loosely with foil.

Put the gratin to bake in the low oven for 1½ hours. Uncover it and turn the oven up to 350°F/180°C/Gas 4 for the last 10 minutes to brown the crust.

Accompany with a perfect steak plain grilled with plenty of pepper, or a pair of plump baby lamb chops, lightly grilled so that they are still pink and juicy within, and served in their innocence garlanded with no more than a small bunch of watercress.

A bowl of fresh strawberries dressed with orange juice, or raspberries sprinkled with sugar, to follow. No cream — perish the thought.

GRATED POTATO CAKE
Rösti (Switzerland)

The favourite Swiss way with potatoes. It is a requirement of those who wish to become Swiss citizens that they 'eat Swiss', and government inspectors are liable to arrive unannounced at the backdoor of those seeking citizenship to check on the dish of the day. Tax exiles would do well to start cooking a dish of *rösti*.

Quantity Enough for 5–6
Time Preparation: 20 minutes

3 lb/1·5 kg potatoes
4 oz/100 g lard

Utensils A grater or a food processor with a grating attachment and a frying pan

Grate the potatoes coarsely while you put the lard to melt in the frying pan. When the lard foams, spread in the grated potatoes. Fork over the mixture constantly for the first 15 to 20 minutes while the flakes soften and take colour. When they are brown and cooked, flatten the cake out and leave it to crisp on the base. Turn out, crisp side up, on to a plate to serve.

Delicious on a cold night with a mug of mulled wine and a piece of Swiss cheese. Try the Swiss *Vacherin* — somewhat like a very soft brie, it has a hard rind and must be eaten with a spoon. It is only made in the autumn for consumption before spring. It'll satisfy the inspectors, too.

In some households the potatoes are cooked in their jackets the day before and then grated. Fry as in the recipe — they will take half the time.

LABSKOVA AND LOBSCOUSE
(Denmark and neighbours and England)

This dish is universal fare in northern Europe. On the Baltic coast of Germany, it is made with fish and called *Fischlabskaus* (see page 328). In England, Liverpudlians make it with neck of mutton or lamb, and claim it as *Lobscouse* — from where comes their sobriquet 'scouse'. The link appears to be the sea — the dish is a way of making ship's stores palatable. Scouse can be made with fresh raw food or leftovers. It can be cooked in the oven, and it used to be cooked in an old black iron cauldron slowly over the hearth fire. For the rest of us, a heavy frying pan and a low heat will do well enough.

Quantity   Enough for 4
Time   Preparation: 20 minutes
Cooking: 50 minutes

1 lb/500 g beef (a nice cheap cut such as brisket with plenty of golden fat)
2 lb/1 kg potatoes

2 oz/50 g lard *or* beef dripping
1 pint/600 ml stock *or* water
1 bayleaf
salt and pepper

Utensils   A large frying pan with a tight-fitting lid

Cut the beef into 1 in/2·5 cm cubes. Peel and cut the potatoes into similar size chunks. Melt the lard or dripping in the pan. Brown the meat gently, turning to gild all sides. Add the potatoes, and then pour in the stock or water. The potatoes should not be submerged, but should just steam above the meat. Tuck in the bayleaf and add salt and pepper. Cover tightly and simmer on top of the stove very gently for 50 to 60 minutes. Take the lid off and stir all together. Turn up the heat to allow the remaining liquid to evaporate and the base to brown. Reverse it when you turn it out. Serve with a knob of cold butter on each helping.

SUGGESTIONS
• The dish can be made with leftovers both of meat and potatoes, and it will then need less cooking. If made with green cabbage or spinach instead of the meat, it will become Bubble and Squeak (particularly delicious if cooked in bacon fat, with a runny-yolked fried egg on top).

OLD CLOTHES WITH HOT SAUCE
Roupa velha con salsa Piripiri (Portugal)

Roupa Velha is the Portuguese version of *Lobscouse* and, like that versatile and much-travelled dish, the basic hash can be made with fresh ingredients or with leftovers. Sailors everywhere love it. The Portuguese have a taste for hot chillies, acquired courtesy of the fiery palates of the natives of their former colony of Brazil. *Piripiri* sauce is often used for flavouring or sparking up soups and dishes such as this one, whose taste is essentially bland. Addicts like it on plain grilled fish as well.

Quantity Enough for 4–5
Time Make the sauce a few days before
　　　　　Preparation: 30 minutes

For the old clothes
1 lb/500 g filleted fish, fresh *or* cooked
2 lb/1 kg potatoes (cooked, if the fish is already cooked)
1 large onion
2 cloves garlic

¼ pint/150 ml olive oil
2 bayleaves
½ teaspoon salt
2 tablespoons vinegar
½ pint/300 ml water

For the Piripiri sauce
12 tiny dried chilli peppers
approximately ¼ pint/150 ml olive oil

Utensils A glass jar and a large saucepan with a lid

The tiny fierce Brazilian *malagueta* chilli-pepper is the best one for this wicked little sauce. A few fresh hot green or red chillis will do, although I find the dry ones sweeter. Pack the peppers, whole and still with their stalks, into a glass jar. Cover with the olive oil and seal down. Ready in a day or two, but will keep for a long time. The oil will be well spiked, and the chillies in turn give up some of their fire. Use with discretion.

Skin and remove the bones from the fish. Peel the potatoes and slice them. Peel the onions and the garlic, and slice them too.

Heat the olive oil in the saucepan, and put in a layer of onions and garlic. Fry gently for a moment. Add a layer of the sliced potatoes and the bayleaves, and cover with 2 glasses of water. Sprinkle on the salt and the vinegar. Cover the pan and allow the old clothes to stew steadily for 15 minutes, when the potatoes should be nearly done. (If the potatoes are already cooked, 5 minutes will be enough to warm them through.) Lay the fish on top of the potatoes and put the lid back on. Stew gently for another 5 to 10 minutes until the fish is done. Take the lid off, and turn the heat up to evaporate any extra liquid and allow the base to brown.

Serve warm with a crisp salad of cos lettuce, dressed with lemon juice and salt and a shake of *Piripiri*.

HOT LIGHTNING
Hete bliksem (Holland)

The Dutch were as slow as the rest of Europe to grasp the potential of the potato. Although the tuber had been championed vigorously by the botanist, Carolus Clusius, at the end of the sixteenth century in Vienna, Frankfurt, and Leyden, it was not until the eighteenth century that it began to be planted widely in northern Europe. By the middle of the century, potatoes were being grown in all the United Provinces, and they rapidly replaced grain products and bread in the diet of the poor, particularly after the disastrous grain shortages of 1770–1. At this time the bourgeoisie sometimes ate potatoes, particularly with haddock, although the aristocrats hardly touched them.

Mr Hough, student of peasant life in Holland at the turn of the century, attended a Dutch country wedding:

> When all the invited guests are assembled and have partaken of hot gin mixed with currants, handed round in two-handled pewter cups, kept especially for these occasions, the whole party goes about at eleven o'clock, to the Stadhuis, or Town Hall, where the couple are married before the Burgomeister. . . . On returning home the mid-day meal is ready, and on this festive occasion, consists of ham and potatoes, and salt fish.

Quantity Enough for 4–5
Time Preparation: 20 minutes
  Cooking: 30 minutes

2 lb/1 kg small potatoes
8 oz/250 g lean bacon
2 oz/50 g butter
salt, sugar, and pepper

2 lb/1 kg apples *or* pears (dried and soaked will do well enough, but halve the weight)

Utensils An earthenware heatproof casserole or a heavy iron pot with a lid

Scrub the potatoes. Dice the bacon. Put both into the pot with the butter. Salt, sugar, and pepper to taste. Cover tightly and put to cook on top of the stove, shaking the pan to avoid sticking. Or cook in a moderate oven at 350°F/180°C/Gas 4 if you are worried about the casserole on direct heat.

Meanwhile peel, quarter, and core the apples or wipe, quarter, and core the pears. Add them to the casserole after 15 minutes, when the potatoes are half cooked. Continue to cook until all is soft — about 30 minutes in all.

Take the bacon out, cut it into slices, and serve on top of the potatoes and apples or pears, which should still hold their shape.

SUGGESTIONS
● Instead of bacon, sausages can be cooked with the potatoes.

HOTCHPOTCH OF CARROTS AND POTATOES
(Holland)

Mr Hough has more to say on this subject:

> The Dutch peasant *is* a peasant, and does not mix, or want to mix with the townsman except in the way of business. He brings his garden and farm produce for sale, and as soon as that is effected — generally very much to his own advantage, for he is wonderfully 'slim' — rattles back, drawn by his dogs or little pony, to the farmhouse.
>
> North and South Holland are famous all over the world for their rich pastures. Potatoes and other vegetables are also extensively cultivated, and in Friesland they have begun to cultivate them also.

The hotchpotch is a traditional old recipe, economical and simple.

Quantity   Enough for 4 as main dish, 6 as an accompaniment
Time   Preparation intermittently: 40–60 minutes

2 lb/1 kg old carrots	1 onion
2 lb/1 kg potatoes	2 oz/50 g butter
1 lb/500 g flank of beef, salted for 2 days (*optional*)	salt and pepper

Utensils   2 medium saucepans

Scrape and cut the carrots into chunks. Peel the potatoes and cut them into thick slices. Put the carrots and potatoes to cook in salted water until nearly done (about 15 minutes). If you are using salt flank, cut it into bite-sized squares and lay it over the top of the vegetables.

Meanwhile peel and chop up the onion, and fry it lightly golden in the butter in another pan. Lift out the nearly cooked vegetables and add them to the pan containing the onion and butter, leaving the meat to continue to simmer in the water. Leave the 2 pans to cook gently until all is done. Adjust the seasoning. Serve the meat on a separate plate.

OYSTER SHELL POTATOES
(Holland)

These potatoes were baked, in the days before the installation of kitchen ovens, in a copper kettle on a tripod with the lid reversed to hold hot coals. The heat above had to be very strong to give a crisp brown top, and underneath the pot, the fire was just enough to keep the dish warm.

Quantity   Enough for 6 as a side dish
Time   Preparation: 15 minutes
　　　　　Cooking: 20–25 minutes

2 lb/1 kg potatoes
salt
4 oz/100 g butter

Utensils   A saucepan, 12 oyster shells, empty of their inhabitants, and a grill

Scrub and then boil the potatoes with salt until they are soft — about 20 to 25 minutes. Peel them while still hot. Mash them thoroughly with the butter. Taste and adjust the seasoning. Fill the oyster shells with the mixture, dot with butter, and then brown them well under the grill.

If you have the oysters themselves, serve each oyster wrapped in a fine rasher of smoked bacon and flashed under the grill just long enough to sizzle the bacon and warm the oyster through.

As Sam Weller said in the *Pickwick Papers*: 'Poverty and oysters always seem to go together.'

SPANISH POTATO STEW
Patatas a la riojana (Spain)

The gardeners of Spain were among the first to appreciate the possibilities of the potato. Rioja, the most famous wine-growing district of Spain, skirts the River Ebro about halfway between Pamplona and Burgos, a lush countryside where vegetables grow fat and sweet among the vines. For 4, make a basic stew in a shallow pan by frying in 4 tablespoons olive oil, 1 large Spanish onion and 3 cloves of garlic peeled and chopped, and perhaps a few cubes of bacon or ham. When these have softened, add 1 lb/500 g chopped ripe tomatoes and cook the mixture down a little. Meanwhile peel and slice 2 lb/1 kg old waxy potatoes. Add them to the stew with a glass of water. Cover and cook until the potatoes are soft. Taste and adjust the seasoning. Artichoke hearts, beans, leeks, courgettes, peppers can all be added to make a *pisto manchego*.

Serve on its own, or with a fried egg per person, or with baby lamb chops grilled over vine twigs. To finish the meal, Burgos is famous for its delicious thick yoghurt served with honey. Accompany, naturally, with the good red wine of Rioja.

KILL-HUNGER
Matafaim or *Crique* (France)

Exactly as its name implies, this is fast food from Provence. In early September there are many fields to harvest all at once, and for those who share machinery, as do many in the village cooperatives of smallholders, the harvesting goes on through the night in the light from the headlamps of the combine harvesters, until the morning dew makes reaping impossible. A dish of *matafaim* will be waiting on the farmhouse table as the workers return home in the autumn dawn.

Quantity   1 *matafaim* per 2 workers
Time   Preparation: 10 minutes
         Cooking: 20 minutes

2 lb/1 kg potatoes
2 eggs
salt and pepper
1 clove garlic
3 tablespoons olive oil

Utensils   A heavy frying pan and a grater

Peel and grate the potatoes. Beat the eggs up with the salt, pepper, and the garlic clove crushed with a little salt under the flat of a heavy knife. Stir in the grated potatoes and mix well.

Heat the frying pan before you put in the oil — this stops anything sticking to the pan. When the oil is smoking, pour in the potato and egg mix, and spread it well over the pan, patting it well down with a wooden spoon to make a thin pancake. Leave it to cook gently for 15 minutes, shaking the pan every now and again to discourage sticking. Turn the pancake and cook it for another 5 minutes to brown the other side. While it is cooking, make a salad to serve with it. Turn it out on to a hot plate and serve the Kill-Hunger immediately

CHAPTER 10

Vegetables

Hot Vegetable Soups

MINESTRONE
(Italy)

Minestrone should be so thick with vegetables that a wooden spoon will stand up in it. Signor Bertorelli, the famous London restaurateur, recalls that the diet of his family — his father and four brothers — living on the small family farm near Parma during the first half the twentieth century, was *minestrone* and *polenta*, with one pig slaughtered annually.

The best *minestrone* is made with the stock left over from the boiling of a ham or one of the Italian stuffed sausages such as *zampone*. The vegetable, herb, and pasta content is open to any variation you please, as long as all three elements are present. If the stock you have is uninteresting, or you are using plain water, add a few cubes of *prosciutto* or a little chopped lean bacon to the pot.

Quantity Enough for 4–6
Time Preparation: 1 hour

1 large onion
2 large carrots
2 sticks celery
¼ pint/150 ml olive oil
2 large tomatoes
2 large potatoes

2 pints/1·2 litres stock
small bunch of parsley
2 oz/50 g dried short macaroni *or*
    any medium-sized pasta shape
4 outside leaves green cabbage
salt and pepper

Utensils A large saucepan

Peel and chop the onion. Scrape and slice the carrots, and then dice them if they are large. All the vegetables should be chopped into similar-sized cubes. Wash and chop the celery. Warm the oil in the saucepan, and then add the vegetables you have prepared so far. Leave them to stew gently.

Peel and chop the tomatoes, and then add them to the pan. Mash them in as they melt in the heat. Peel the potatoes and cut them into small cubes. Add the stock to the mixture in the pan and sprinkle in the parsley. Simmer for 10 minutes. Put in the cubed potatoes. Simmer for 10 minutes longer. Add the pasta and the cabbage sliced into strips. Simmer all for another 10 minutes, until the vegetables are soft and the pasta well cooked.

Taste and adjust the seasoning. Mash a few of the vegetables in to thicken the liquid a little before you serve it. Hand round a bowl of grated cheese separately.

Minestrone makes a complete supper dish, as the young American,

Eliza Putnam Heaton, observed when travelling through Sicily early this century: 'Candela never ate meat except at carnival and on holidays. In the morning he had bread and olives; at noon bread and finocchi; salt fish once or twice a week; at night minestrone.'

SUGGESTIONS

- Stir in a spoonful of *pesto* (see page 295) to make *soupe au pistou*.
- 1 small tin of tomatoes can do duty for the fresh variety.
- Use 4 oz/100 g cooked white *cannellini* beans instead of the pasta.
- Or a handful of rice or a few crumbled slices of stale bread.
- Swiss chard and courgettes can be added in season.
- Use *tarhonya* noodles (see page 304) instead of the macaroni.

LEFTOVERS
- Toast a piece of bread and rub it with garlic for each diner. Put a piece of toast into the bottom of each bowl and pour the hot soup over. Trickle on a little fresh olive oil and a scattering of chopped chives or spring onions before serving. Or float the bread on top, then sprinkle it with cheese, and brown it under the grill.

BAVARIAN HERB SOUP
Krautlsuppe (Germany)

Bitter herbs are traditionally eaten at Easter in Christian countries as a sign of penitence. This Bavarian soup is served on Easter Thursday, known as Maundy Thursday. Chervil, easily available in any German market, is usually the dominating flavour. This is a delicate fresh-tasting soup for any time of year.

Quantity   Enough for 4
Time   Preparation: 30 minutes
Cooking: 15 minutes

1 lb/500 g herbs (at least three or all of — chervil, watercress, spinach, sorrel, with dandelion and pimpernel for brave souls. Experiment with your own favourite herbs. Try young nettletops in the early spring using just the top 4 leaves of the spring shoots.)

1 large onion
2 oz/50 g butter
2 pints/1·2 litres water *or* vegetable stock
1 large potato
salt and pepper

Utensils   A large deep saucepan

Pick over and wash the herbs, stripping the leaves from those stalks that are too woody. Chop the rest. Peel and chop the onion.

Melt the butter in the pan and fry the onion gently in it until transparent. Add the herbs and sweat them for a moment before you pour in the water or stock. Peel the potato and cut it into small cubes. Add to the soup. Bring the soup to the boil and then turn down the heat. Simmer for 20 minutes. Mash the potato into the soup to thicken it a little. Taste and add salt and freshly milled pepper.

Serve with *croûtons* fried in butter or bacon fat (goose fat is even better). They should be so hot that they sizzle when they are added to the hot soup at the table.

PUMPKIN SOUP
Kuerbissupe (Germany)

Pumpkin is undemanding in its cultivation. It was a very convenient vegetable for storage and hence for making a winter soup at a time when fresh vegetables were not readily available.

Many peasant communities took advantage of the pumpkin's tractability, as Lady Llanover pointed out in the middle of the last century:

> Perhaps Gower in South Wales it the only part of the United Kingdom where pumpkins are grown as an article of diet by the rural population; and there they are to be seen, as on the Continent, hanging from the ceilings for winter store, and any little spare corner in the field or garden is made use of to place the small mound on which to sow a few pumpkin seeds. . . . In Gower they are added to hashed meat, made into pies with apples, and put into soup. Pumpkins have one peculiar quality in addition to a good deal of natural sweetness: they will absorb and retain the flavour of whatever they are cooked with. If stewed with plums it tastes exactly like them in puddings and tarts; the same with apples, rhubarb or gooseberries; and for savoury cookery it would be difficult to say in what dish it may not be used with advantage as an addition.

Quantity   Enough for 4
Time   Preparation: 20 minutes
            Cooking: 20–30 minutes

2 lb/1 kg piece pumpkin	2 tablespoons wine vinegar
1 pint/600 ml water	2 oz/50 g butter
6 cloves	salt, pepper, sugar
small piece cinnamon stick	

Utensils   A saucepan, a muslin bag, and a liquidizer

Peel the pumpkin and scoop out the seeds and fibrous middle. Cut the flesh into cubes and put them in a saucepan with the water (it looks like too little but the pumpkin itself is full of water). Tie the cloves and the cinnamon in a muslin bag (which is easy to remove) and add to the pan. Stew the pumpkin gently with the spices for 20 to 30 minutes, until soft.

Take out the spices, then purée the pumpkin with its cooking liquid. You can do this in the liquidizer. Stir in the vinegar. Reheat and beat in the butter. Season with salt, plenty of freshly milled black pepper, and a little sugar to bring out the sweetness of the vegetable. This a very delicate, amber-clear soup. (Resist the temptation to stir in cream or it will be cloudy and lose its innocence.)

Complete the meal with a sweet dumpling, a strudel, or a fruit tart.

CABBAGE SOUP WITH BACON
(Romania)

D. J. Hall had a good supper at the village priest's home in pre-Second World War Romania:

The cabin in the yard had two little rooms. In one Stanescu slept and worked, in the other we ate. There was only just space to move, for there were packed in there a dresser, a chest of drawers which was used as the table, and a sheet-iron stove. As we drank our cabbage soup Stanescu told me of his difficulties in getting the cooking to his taste.

'This now, it is delicious.' He pursed his lips. 'But most of the peasants throw in a cabbage, boil it, and call it soup. I pick only the finest of my cabbages, choose only the tender leaves, flavour it with green peppers, put in a little bacon and then. You see . . .' Pressing his forefinger to his thumb he expressed its exquisite delicacy.

So with the fried chicken and the cheese pancakes which followed he told me minutely how they should be cooked. It was certainly a meal such as I had not tasted for a long while.

Quantity   Enough for 6 as a main dish
Time   Preparation: 20 minutes
         Cooking: 50 minutes

1 cabbage	salt and pepper
8 oz/250 g streaky bacon *or* belly pork	3 pints/2 litres water
2 onions	2 egg yolks
2 green peppers	$\frac{1}{4}$ pint/150 ml cream (sweet *or* soured)
small posy dill and savory	1 tablespoon vinegar

Utensils   A large heavy stewpot, a whisk, and a small bowl

Wash and slice the cabbage. Slice the bacon or belly pork and chop one of the slices. Peel and slice the onions. Hull and chop the peppers. Chop the herbs.

Fry the chopped slice of bacon in the stewpot until the fat runs. Fry the onions in the fat until they are golden. Add the peppers and fry them too. Remove the stewpot from the heat, and layer the cabbage and the bacon into it. Season between the layers with salt and pepper and the herbs.

Pour the water over all and bring to the boil. Turn the heat down and simmer the soup for 40 to 50 minutes until all is tender. Remove the soup from the heat.

Beat up the egg yolks with the cream and vinegar in a small bowl. Stir in a ladleful of the hot soup. Whisk well and pour the mixture back into the soup to thicken and enrich it.

Serve in deep bowls accompanied by fresh bread. This soup is a meal in itself, and wants only a piece of cheese and fresh fruit to make it complete.

SIBIU SAXON SOUP
(Romania)

The Sibiu Saxons, formerly citizens of the Austro-Hungarian Empire and today Romanian nationals, are still, after eight centuries, blond and blue-eyed and purely Saxon. The Saxons of Sibiu and its seven sur-rounding villages are very orderly — their children receive Saxon schooling in the shadow of their austere, cavernous Lutheran Church building, newly re-roofed with beautiful glazed viridian tiles made to the old pattern. The Transylvanian plain on which Sibiu stands in the shadow of the Carpathians has never been a peaceful thoroughfare. The Saxons fortified their churches and defended their own throughout the centuries against would-be conquerors and marauders.

Their cooking is as conservative as their religion, reflecting its German origins. An appetite for eastern spices in breads, cakes, and dried sausages was supplied until 1980 by the 'foreigners' market', held on Tuesdays and Saturdays in a corner of the arcade in the market square. Silks and carpets, coffee and tea also came with the Turkish traders in the old days. The most beautiful carpets went to commemor-ate prominent Saxon citizens in the Black Church at Brasov — where they still glow like dark jewels. Sadly, there are no more 'foreigners' markets' in modern Romania, and the Saxons have to manage as best they can.

Quantity Enough for 6 as a main meal
Time Preparation: 40 minutes

1 whole cabbage
½ lb/250 g frankfurter-type boiling sausage
3½ pints/2·3 litres water
1 teaspoon salt
6 slices day-old bread (black *or* white)

1 lb/500 g onions
2 tablespoons oil *or* butter
2–3 egg yolks
¼ pint/150 ml cream
1 tablespoon chopped fresh tarragon and dill

Utensils A deep saucepan, a soup tureen, a frying pan, a small bowl, and a whisk

Rinse and slice the cabbage. Put it in the deep saucepan with the boiling sausage, water, and salt. Bring to the boil, and then turn down the heat. Simmer for 20 minutes, until the cabbage is well cooked and the broth flavoured with the sausage.

While it is cooking, turn your attention to the rest of the operation. Put the slices of bread into the soup tureen. Peel and slice the onions. Heat the oil or butter in the frying pan, and sauté the onions until they are soft and golden. Lay them on the bread. Mix the egg yolks with the cream in a bowl, and whisk in a spoonful of hot broth from the soup.

By now the soup should be ready, so remove it from the heat, take out the sausage, and stir in the egg and cream mixture and the herbs. Cut up the sausage, and lay the slices on top of the bread and onions in the tureen. Pour the cabbage soup over all.

Serve a compote of fruit and a slice of cake after the soup and your meal will be complete.

SIBIU SAXON SALAD SOUP
(Romania)

Frau Klein, wife of the Lutheran Bishop of Sibiu, whose recipe this is, says these soup-stew dishes are typical of the ancient dishes: 'Characteristic of the special meals of Transylvania's Saxon peasants is a kind of soup or *eintopfgericht*, one-pan-meal, which can be eaten with the spoon. The meat is always cut before, and bread is always used.'

Quantity Enough for 5–6 summer workers
Time Preparation: 40 minutes

3 firm lettuces — cos *or* iceberg if possible
3 pints/2 litres water
salt
2 oz/50 g streaky bacon
1 oz/25 g butter

2 oz/50 g flour
¼ pint/150 ml milk
2–3 eggs
1 tablespoon vinegar
salt and pepper
dill and savory

351

Utensils   A large stewpot and a frying pan

Wash and shred the lettuce. Put it to simmer in the stewpot with the water and a teaspoon of salt for 20 minutes.

Cube the bacon. Put it into a hot, dry frying pan with the butter and fry gently. When the cubes are browned, take them out and add them to the lettuce. Meanwhile mix the flour to a thick cream with the milk, and then beat in the eggs. Fry the egg mixture a tablespoon at a time in the hot bacon fat. Cut these little pancakes into strips and add them to the soup.

Bring all to the boil, stir in the vinegar, taste and adjust the seasoning. Sprinkle in the chopped dill and savory. Serve all together very hot, with dark rye bread. Follow with a dish of *mamaliga* and poppy seeds (see page 273).

> The ordinary diet of the Wallachian consists of vegetable soups, eggs, sheep's milk cheese, melons, pickled cucumbers, black bread, fried potatoes, maize porridge, grey salt and raw onions, washed down by a small 'porzion' of palinkas.
>
> Ellen Browning, *A Girl's Wanderings in Hungary*

SPINACH BOUILLABAISSE
Bouillabaisse d'épinards (France)

A very popular country soup and an excellent light lunch. The greens can be varied from Swiss chard through the repertoire of edible green leaves (including cabbage) which the Provençal farmer's wife is likely to grow in her vegetable patch. *Bouillabaisse* is a description of the cooking method rather than the ingredients — the soup is boiled very fast to allow reduction by evaporation.

Quantity   Enough for 4 as a main dish
Time   Preparation: 40 minutes

2 lb/1 kg fresh *or* frozen spinach	1 branch fennel
1 onion	salt
4 medium potatoes (yellow potatoes are preferable to white for this dish)	2 tablespoons oil
	$\frac{1}{2}$ teaspoon saffron
	4 eggs
2 pints/1·2 litres boiling water	4 slices dry bread
2 cloves garlic	

Utensils   A saucepan and a large stewpot (an earthenware *marmite* is the proper utensil)

Wash the spinach if it is fresh and put it in the saucepan with the water which clings to its leaves. Cover and cook it in its own moisture for 5 minutes, until the leaves are wilted. Drain and then chop the spinach finely. If you are using frozen spinach, defrost, drain, and chop it.

Peel and mince the onion. Peel and slice the potatoes. Put the water to boil. Peel and crush the garlic — a blow from the flat blade of a heavy knife will serve the purpose. Chop the fennel into short lengths.

Warm the oil in the stewpot. Add the onion and cook for a moment until it is transparent. Push to one side. Add the spinach and turn it in the oil. Add the sliced potatoes, and then pour in the boiling water. Now add the salt, garlic, fennel, and saffron. Bring all rapidly to the boil. Simmer for 20 minutes, until the potatoes are cooked. When you are ready to serve, slide in one egg per person on to the surface of the simmering soup. Poach the eggs gently for 2 to 3 minutes, so that the white sets into a veil for the soft yolk.

Serve in deep soup plates, with a slice of dry bread in each. Be careful not to break the eggs as you take them from the broth.

SUGGESTIONS
● Make a *bouillabaisse de petits pois* by replacing the spinach with 2 lb/ 1 kg little shelled peas. Possibly even better than the spinach.
● Replace the dry bread with little *croûtons* fried in olive oil perfumed with garlic.

GARLIC SOUP
Sopa de ajo (Italy)

'Gina Ciccia, how often do you bake?'

'Every 12 days.'

'How long does it take to heat the oven?'

'Half an hour in August, but in winter, when the walls are damp perhaps an hour.'

A colonial housewife used to piling wood into her brick oven would have rebelled if expected to bake with no fuel but grape prunings, but in Gina Ciccia's land these are good fuel; the woman who bakes with thorn twigs or brambles is the one to pity.

'And the bread, does it get dry?'

'Hard as a stone to kill a dog. Too hard to eat without grinding teeth. But at night if there is no cooked food one boils water with a little garlic and dips in the bread. That is good.'

Eliza Putnam Heaton, *By-Paths in Sicily*

Quantity Enough for 4
Time Preparation: 10–15 minutes

8 cloves garlic	2½ pints/1·5 litres water
4 tablespoons olive oil	½ teaspoon salt
4 slices stale bread	4 eggs

Utensils An ovenproof casserole or a roomy saucepan

Peel and crush the cloves of garlic with the flat blade of a knife. Put the oil to warm in the casserole or saucepan. Add the crushed garlic and the slices of bread. Fry gently together until they take colour. Add the water and salt and bring all to the boil. Simmer gently for 10 minutes. Slip in the eggs one by one. Allow them to poach gently for 5 minutes. Serve each person with soup and an egg.

SUGGESTIONS
• Those nervous of poaching eggs may prefer to hard boil them first, and add them quartered or sliced to the finished soup.
• A sprinkling of chopped dried ham can be added. Other variations as you please.
• A very similar soup appears in southern France as *Aigo-boulido*. To make the French version, stir the eggs into the soup once you have removed it from the fire, so that they cook immediately in the hot liquid and thicken the broth.

ONION SOUP
Soupe à l'oignon (France)

The soup of the market men of Les Halles in Paris. Very comforting on an icy morning in the French capital, and a universal staple, with minor amendments, throughout the rest of Europe.

Quantity Enough for 4–5
Time Preparation: 20 minutes
　　　　Cooking: 20 minutes

1½ lb/750 g onions	salt and pepper
3 oz/75 g butter	slices day-old bread
2½ pints/1·5 litres cold water	4 oz/100 g grated cheese

Utensils A large saucepan or earthenware *marmite*

Peel and slice the onions very finely. Put the butter to melt in the saucepan and throw in the onions. Cook them gently, stirring every now and then, for 10 minutes or until they are soft and golden. Add the water. Bring all to the boil, and season with salt and pepper. Turn down to simmer. Leave on a low heat for 20 minutes.

Meanwhile put the slices of bread to dry in a low oven. Put each slice in the bottom of a soup bowl. Pour the soup over and serve. Hand the cheese separately. This is a very simple soup, but quite excellent if prepared with care.

SUGGESTIONS
• Thicken the soup with a couple of eggs beaten up first with a tablespoon of vinegar and a ladleful of the hot soup. Don't reboil the soup once the eggs have been stirred in.
• Or stir in a little cream.

GREEN PEA SOUP WITH DUMPLINGS
Gronaertesuppe mit melboller (Denmark)

Although at its best made with tender young peas, this soup can be made with peas late in the season, when they are a little hard for serving unadorned. Either way it is a delightful dish — emerald green in colour and delicately flavoured.

Quantity   Enough for 4–5
Time   Preparation intermittently: 1 hour

For the soup
1 lb/500 g green peas in their pods
2 pints/1·2 litres water
1 large potato
1 large onion
salt and pepper
1 teaspoon sugar
1 oz/25 g butter

For the dumplings
$\frac{1}{4}$ pint/150 ml water
2 oz/50 g butter
2 oz/50 g flour
1 large egg
salt and pepper

Utensils   2 saucepans, a strainer, and a liquidizer if you like a smooth soup

Shell the peas and put them aside. Put the pods into a saucepan with the water. Bring to the boil and stew gently until the pods are soft — about 30 minutes. Strain out the stock, which will add plenty of flavour to the soup. Discard the pods.

Meanwhile peel and cube the potato. Peel and chop the onion finely. Put the shelled peas, potato, onion, and pod stock back into the saucepan, and bring them all to the boil. Turn the heat down and simmer for 20 to 30 minutes until the vegetables are soft.

Meanwhile make the dumplings. Put the water to boil in a roomy saucepan. When it is boiling, add the butter and melt it in. Beat in the flour. Continue to beat out the lumps as the paste cooks. When you have a homogeneous paste which leaves the sides of the pan clean, take it off the heat. Allow to cool a little, then beat in the egg. Season with salt and pepper.

The soup should now be cooked. Mash the vegetables in to thicken it a little, or if you like a very smooth soup, purée it in the liquidizer. Taste and season with the salt, pepper, and sugar, and bring it back to the boil. Drop in dumplings formed with two wet teaspoons. The dumplings will puff up and be ready in a few minutes. Just before you serve the soup, float a nugget of cold butter on the surface.

SUGGESTIONS
• Instead of the dumplings, serve the soup with sizzling hot *croûtons* fried in bacon fat or butter. *Croûtons* are only at their best if they are so hot they hiss when added to the soup.
• The dumplings are made as for a *choux* paste. They can be sweetened and poached in a fruit soup as well as the more usual meat or vegetable soups.

CHESTNUT SOUP
Puchero de castañas (Spain)

The best dried ham in Spain comes from Jabugo, where the incomparable flavour comes from pigs loosed to roam free in the chestnut woods that clothe the surrounding slopes of the Sierra Morena. The nuts are harvested in the autumn by troops of villagers who work from the tops of the slopes to the bottom, shaking the trees so that the prickly balls roll down to where they can be gathered easily by the women and children. This rough-and-ready harvesting technique leaves plenty for the four-legged gleaners. The gathered chestnuts are peeled, dried, and stored for the winter, to be cooked either with chickpeas or beans in a *puchero* or stew, or on their own as a soup, flavoured with ham from the gleaning-fattened porkers.

Quantity Plenty for 6
Time Preparation intermittently: 90 minutes

2 lb/1 kg fresh *or* 1 lb/500 g dried and soaked chestnuts	4 oz/100 g dried ham *or* gammon
	1 carrot
3 pints/2 litres home-made stock *or* water	1 onion
	salt and pepper
bayleaf	1 teaspoon sugar
2 oz/50 g streaky bacon	

Utensils   A saucepan and a frying pan

Roast the chestnuts for half an hour in a low oven. Peel them when they are cool enough to handle. Put them in the saucepan and cover them with the stock or water. Put in the bayleaf. Leave to stew gently for another half an hour.

Meanwhile, cube the bacon and the ham. Scrub and cube the carrot, and peel and cube the onion. Put the bacon in the frying pan and sweat it gently so that the fat runs. Add the ham or gammon and the carrot and onion. Cook for 5 minutes, then add the contents of the pan to the stewing chestnuts. Simmer together for another 15 minutes. Taste and season with salt and freshly ground pepper and a little sugar. Serve in deep bowls, accompanied by good bread and a bottle of dry white wine from the plains of the Guadalquivir below the mountains.

SUGGESTIONS
● An old partridge or a pheasant, roughly jointed and stewed with the chestnuts, improves the dish greatly. The Spanish red-legged partridge is quite common in the area.

Cold Vegetable Soups

TOMATO AND GARLIC SOUP
Gazpacho (Spain)

Gazpacho is a true peasant dish which has become as gentrified as *bouillabaisse*. At its simplest (and probably most ancient), it is a kind of thick bread porridge flavoured with olive oil, vinegar, and garlic (the

357

essential ingredients) with, if possible, a sprinkling of whatever the *huerta*, the vegetable patch, can offer in the way of green peppers, tomatoes, and onions. In winter the dish can be taken hot. In summer it is eaten cold. The bread, garlic, vinegar, and water are either pounded in a mortar, or merely infused together. The vegetables in the simplest version would have been used as a garnish, rather than as an integral part of the liquid. The modern version is nearer to a vegetable soup than the bread soup of earlier days, and increasingly leaves out the bread and oil altogether. A special Sunday *gazpacho* makes the best compromise.

Gil Lopez, a local landowner in Andalusia interviewed by Ronald Fraser in 1968, remembered:

> In our house we ate what everyone in Andalusia eats — bread and tomato soup made with oil and water, fried fish, fried potatoes, pimientos, whatever the land produced. We had money enough to buy meat, but we hardly ever ate it. The Catalans and Basques say they can't understand how the Andalusians have the energy to work eating only 'bread and water'. That's what they call the soups we eat here. But you go to the largest, wealthiest cortijo and that's what you'll find being eaten there.

This was confirmed by Salvador Torres, a day labourer reaping the wheat:

> We had a young boy with us who brought us water in the fields and cooked. He had to get up at two or three in the morning to start preparing a soup. We'd eat that at seven, for by then we had been working two or three hours. At noon a gazpacho — and then back to work until six. By then the boy had prepared a stew of chickpeas and potatoes . . . at the end of the day's work we'd eat more gazpacho.

Quantity   Enough for 6
Time   Preparation: 30 minutes

3–4 slices day-old bread
1 pint/600 ml cold water
2 tablespoons wine vinegar
2 cloves garlic
1 small cucumber *or* half a large one (Spanish cucumbers are the size of the pickling variety)
2 lb/1 kg ripe tomatoes
2 green peppers
1 large Spanish onion (if you need to keep the *gazpacho*, omit the onion — it ferments easily)

2 tablespoons olive oil
½ pint/300 ml tinned tomato juice (unless you are making this in Spain, when you can use extra water because the tomatoes are much better flavoured)
salt

Utensils   A food processor or liquidizer or a pestle and mortar

Put the bread to soak in a few tablespoons of the water, all the vinegar, and the peeled and crushed garlic.

Meanwhile prepare the vegetables. Peel and roughly chop the cucumber. Chop the tomatoes roughly (they may be peeled first if you wish — in which case, scald them in boiling water to loosen the skins). Take the seeds out of the green peppers and chop the flesh roughly. Peel and chop the onion. Put aside a quarter of the chopped vegetables in separate dishes, to be handed round as a garnish.

Either blend the soaked bread and garlic, the rest of the chopped vegetables, and the olive oil in a liquidizer, or pound them in a mortar. Add the tomato juice and then the rest of the water until you have the consistency you like. Adjust the seasoning with salt. Put the soup in a cold larder or the refrigerator for at least an hour. Serve as iced as possible (but not with ice cubes in it — ice cubes always seem to taste odd and will dilute the soup overmuch).

Hand round small bowls of the extra chopped vegetables for each person to sprinkle on their own serving — as in the everyday peasant version. Chopped hard-boiled eggs and little hot *croûtons* fried in olive oil can be included as a special treat. This final garnishing is an integral part of the modern dish.

COLD ALMOND SOUP
Ajo blanco (Spain)

An excellent cold soup of the peasant bread-soup family which is prepared in the rich *vega*, the great fertile plain of Granada. The inclusion of almonds is a refinement introduced by the Moors. The legacy of six centuries of Moorish occupation did not vanish overnight — nor indeed did the extensive plantations of almond trees brought by the Muslims from the Jordan valley. Almonds are still an important cash crop for the small farmers of Andalusia.

Quantity   Enough for 4–5
Time   Preparation: 30 minutes
              Cooking: 1 hour

3–4 slices stale bread	2 pints/1·2 litres cold water
3 oz/75 g blanched almonds	salt
4 cloves garlic	2 tablespoons white wine vinegar
2 tablespoons olive oil	handful small grapes

Utensils   A pestle and mortar or a liquidizer

Put the bread, almonds, garlic, oil, and 1 pint/600 ml of the water into the liquidizer, and blend thoroughly. In the peasant kitchen, this job would have been done with a pestle and mortar, and there are those who say the soup is finest thus made. Add the rest of the water until you have the consistency you like. Season with salt and vinegar. Leave to cool, and infuse in the cold larder or the refrigerator for an hour or so.

Peel and pip the grapes and float them on top of each serving of soup. The patios of rural dwellings in the south are usually shaded by a trellis with a vine which bears grapes long into the winter months, so this ingredient is very much to hand, and is essential to the proper flavouring of the soup.

Little *croûtons* fried golden in olive oil and served sizzling hot, make a delicious addition.

COLD SOUP MADE WITH YOGHURT AND WALNUTS
Tarator (Bulgaria)

This soup is a legacy from the Ottoman Turks, whose officers and governors took pleasure in laying a good table and were more than willing to train up servants from their subject nations. As the Romans before them, the Turks planted their favourite ingredients if they were not available locally. Today walnut, hazelnut, and almond trees shade the foothills of Bulgaria's mountain ranges. The woods blaze scarlet and gold in the autumn, towering over the gilded onion domes left behind in the wake of the retreating Ottoman armies.

Quantity Enough for 5
Time Preparation: 20 minutes
      Cooking: ½ hour

2 pints/1·2 litres yoghurt	½ teaspoon salt
1 cucumber	3 oz/75 g walnuts
2–3 cloves garlic	small bunch of mint and dill

Utensils A grater or a food processor and a colander

Grate or dice the cucumber, salt it and put it to drain in a colander for half an hour. Peel and crush the garlic with the salt. Crush the walnuts. Chop up the herbs.

Rinse the cucumber and stir it into the yoghurt with the garlic and the walnuts. Ladle into bowls, and sprinkle the chopped dill and mint over the top. Deliciously refreshing on a hot day.

Vegetable Stews

VEGETABLE HOT-POT
Xhivetch (Bulgaria)

Vegetable gardens are called 'bulgaridi' in Romania, being always kept by immigrant Bulgarians, who grow all the vegetables for the town's supply, the staple produce being melons, water and sugar melons, cucumbers, pimentos, cabbages, vegetable marrows, tomatoes. Potatoes do not yet enjoy much favour with the Roumanian peasant as regular food, but seem to be gaining ground, nevertheless; they are grown in the 'bulgaridi', but still more they are sown between the maize, where one can see no end of pumpkins creeping among the maize in all directions, and also haricot beans, which are grown in great quantities, being the staple food of the Roumanians in fasting times.

Theresa Stratilesco, *From Carpathian to Pindus*

This stew is called *Yhiveci* in Romania — the etymology is Turkish.

Quantity   Enough for 6 enthusiastic gardeners as a main meal, or 8 if meat is included

Time   Preparation: 25–30 minutes
          Cooking: 1 hour

1 lb/500 g onions
2–3 little hot red chilli peppers (*optional*)
3 lb/1·5 kg vegetables (choose at least 3 varieties: potatoes, aubergines, peppers, okra or ladies' fingers, green beans, broad beans, peas, carrots, leeks, courgettes, spinach, Swiss chard)

¼ pint/150 ml sunflower oil
1 lb/500 g cubed lamb (*optional*)
salt and pepper
1 lb/500 g tomatoes
2 heaped tablespoons chopped parsley, ½ pint/300 ml rich yoghurt, and 2 eggs to finish

Utensils   A large casserole or stewpot with a lid (the ones made in Bulgaria for the purpose are of pale earthenware with a pearly blue glaze) and a frying pan

Peel and chop the onions. De-seed and crush the chillies. Prepare the rest of the vegetables, peeling only when necessary, and cutting them into even-sized cubes.
   Preheat the oven to 300°F/170°C/Gas 2.
   Heat the oil in the casserole if it is flameproof, if not, start in the frying

pan. Fry the onions, then the meat if you are using it, then add the crushed chillies. Add the vegetables and toss all in the hot oil — transfer everything to the casserole once it is sautéed if you are using a frying pan. Season with salt and pepper and then pour in enough water to cover. Lay the tomatoes over the vegetables. Cover and cook very gently in the oven for an hour, or equally gently on top of the stove.

Mix the eggs with the parsley and the yoghurt, and pour into the casserole 10 minutes before the end of the cooking time. Allow to cool a little and serve with plenty of good bread.

Finish the meal with a dish of those particularly succulent large white grapes which the Bulgarians grow so well. Eating-grape vines are often trained over a shed-shaped trellis, which provides dappled shade in the summer and autumn for semi-outdoor activities such as fermenting plums for *slivova*, the Bulgarians' favourite liquor, or yoghurt and cheese making.

SUGGESTIONS
• Instead of the yoghurt and egg topping, scatter a handful of little sharp grapes over the top of the dish 15 minutes before the end of the cooking time.

GREEN PEPPER AND TOMATO STEW
Letcho (Hungary)

The Hungarians rival the Bulgarians (from whom they learned much, including the cultivation of their beloved paprika) as gardeners, and are blessed with the fertile soil of the Danube basin in which to hoe and sow. This very basic and versatile vegetable preparation is Serbian in origin. Hungarian housewives take their vegetables seriously and consider them the central ingredient for main dishes in their own right. No Hungarian cook worth her salt would serve vegetables plain boiled as a garnish for meat. This mixture is used for flavouring and fulfils a similar function to the *ragù* in the Italian kitchen.

½ lb/250 g onions	1 lb/500 g tomatoes *or* 2 medium
1 lb/500 g green peppers	tins
(preferably the thin-skinned	1 oz/25 g lard
frying variety)	1 tablespoon paprika

Utensils   A heavy saucepan

Peel and chop finely the onions. Hull, de-seed, and slice the peppers finely. Chop the peppers — the fatter-fleshed they are, the finer you should chop them. Scald the tomatoes with boiling water to loosen the skins, peel them, and chop them. If the tomatoes are the northern sunless variety, add a tablespoon of tomato purée to the dish, together with a teaspoon of sugar.

Put the lard to melt in the saucepan. Add the onions and stir them round in the hot fat until they are golden. Push to one side and add the chopped peppers. Fry gently. Sprinkle in the paprika and add the tomatoes. Add a little extra liquid if the tomatoes are not very juicy.

Simmer all together for 20 to 30 minutes. Use as you please, on its own or for flavouring other dishes. Make a double quantity and keep it in the refrigerator to add to stews and baked dishes.

Very good served with plain-boiled noodles or *Tarhonya* noodle barley (see page 304), or with fried eggs or a slice of grilled bacon.

SUGGESTIONS
● Add 4 oz/100 g sliced sausage to the *letcho* and then scramble 4 eggs in it. Almost exactly like the Basque *piperade*.

BAKED VEGETABLES
Briam (Greece)

The selection of vegetables varies according to the season and the gardener, so leave out or add to the list as you please. *Briam* is a very popular dish in Greece and often provides a meal in itself. Fresh vegetables are easily available everywhere — sold in the country villages from the backs of local farmers' lorries, the tailgate swung down to provide a sales counter. City-dwellers often buy their vegetables and fruit straight from the producer's roadside stall. Okra (ladies' fingers) is sold dried as well as fresh, strung like beads on thin cotton thread.

Quantity   Enough for 4–5 as a main course, 6–8 to accompany a roast or a kebab

Time   Preparation: 30 minutes
          Cooking: 1½–2 hours

½ lb/250 g potatoes

½ lb/250 g aubergines

½ lb/250 g courgettes

½ lb/250 g okra

½ lb/250 g green peppers

2 onions

4 cloves garlic

2 lb/1 kg ripe tomatoes

½ pint/300 ml olive oil

salt and pepper

Utensils   A wide shallow ovenproof dish

Peel and rinse the potatoes and cut them into thick slices. Wash and slice into rounds the aubergines and the courgettes. Wash the okra and sprinkle it with lemon juice (okra is a good addition if you can get it — the juice gives a nice gluey texture to the dish). De-seed and slice the peppers. Peel and chop the onions and garlic. Slice the tomatoes.

Preheat the oven to 350°F/180°C/Gas 4.

Trickle a thin layer of oil over the bottom of the shallow dish. Lay half the tomato slices over it. Arrange the rest of the vegetables in layers over the tomatoes, sprinkling with salt and pepper and onions and garlic as you go. Lay the second half of the tomato slices on top. Pour the rest of the oil over all.

Bake in the oven for 1½–2 hours. Serve warm or cool. The Greeks never eat their food piping hot. Plenty of bread to accompany — the juices are delicious. A wonderful light summer lunch to be taken in the pearl-grey shade of an olive tree beside the Aegean. It will smell as sweet as the drowsy heat of a Greek summer's day.

BROAD BEANS WITH HAM
Habas con jamón (Spain)

One of my favourite Spanish dishes, this is best made when the broad beans are small and tender and the pods, which are used in the dish, are not stringy. The slightly sticky, velvety texture, not unlike okra in flavour and feel, is surprisingly good. A dish I first had in one of the mountain villages behind Ronda, where the wild sweet pea tangles with the rows of broad bean plants in blossom on the stony terraces. Wild and cultivated crops unite in such primitive fields: round pink heads of the wild garlic, *Allium roseum*, add confusion to the cultivated garlic patch. Wild and domestic animals graze the same meadow flowers. Old men with panniered donkeys collect greens from the road verges — *tagarnina* thistle stems for the evening stew, clover and pea for the rabbits.

Quantity   Enough for 4 as a main dish
Time   Preparation: 30 minutes
Cooking: 1½–2 hours

2 lb/1 kg young broad beans in
their pods
4 oz/100 g dried ham *or* salt bacon
3 cloves garlic
1 onion
small bunch of parsley

¼ pint/150 ml olive oil
small glass dry sherry *or* white
wine
large glass water
salt, pepper, and sugar

Utensils   A large stewpot

Top and tail the beans, and chop them into short lengths — more or less following the swell of each bean. Don't do this in advance as the beans go an odd navy blue colour at the edges. Cube the ham or bacon small. Peel and chop the garlic and the onion. Chop the parsley.

Heat the oil in the stewpot. Put in the onion and garlic and fry for a moment without allowing it to take colour. Add the beans, the ham or bacon, and the parsley. Fry for a moment longer. Add the sherry or wine and the water. Cover and stew gently for 1½ to 2 hours. Add salt and pepper and a little sugar when the beans are tender — they will be bluey-grey and completely soft. Cook the stew uncovered for a moment to evaporate the liquid if there is too much juice. Delicious on its own as a first course of a light supper. It is also good served with cubes of fried bread or *migas*.

SUGGESTIONS

● For a more substantial dish, stir in 2 to 3 eggs beaten together, and scramble them with the juice. Serve with squares of bread fried in olive oil and garlic.

LEFTOVERS

● Stir into a *cocido* (see page 250) or a lentil stew.
● Or reheat with chopped tomatoes and onions which have been stewed together in a little oil.
● Reheat as it is, but stir in a spoonful of fresh herbs chopped with garlic just before you serve it.

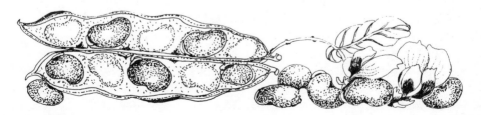

STEWED ARTICHOKES
Ragoût d'artichaut (France)

One of those simple Provençal vegetable dishes at which the country people excel. Reminiscent of the Greek vegetable dishes.

Quantity　Enough for 4
Time　Preparation: 20 minutes
　　　　Cooking: 1½ hours

8–12 small artichokes
1 onion *or* 2 small white new ones
4 tablespoons olive oil
branch of thyme *or* rosemary *or* a
　　bayleaf
juice 1 lemon
glass white wine
salt and pepper

Utensils　A large stewpot with a lid, which will allow you to cook the artichokes in a single layer

Trim the artichokes down to their edible parts with a small sharp knife. Make sure you manage to remove the whole choke and trim the tough outer leaves right down. If the artichokes are on the large side, cut them in quarters. Peel and chop the onion.

Warm the oil in the pan and put in the chopped onions. Let them soften without browning, and then add the artichoke bottoms and the herbs. Cook all together gently until the vegetables are impregnated with the oil. Then add the lemon juice, wine, salt, and pepper. Cover tightly and cook very gently for 1½ hours.

Serve the artichokes on their own — perhaps to follow (or precede) a small shoulder of lamb slowly pot-roasted at the same time. Sprinkle the tender little joint with rosemary, and shove in a clove or two of garlic near the bone before you put it in a covered casserole to roast in its own juices. A glass of white wine poured round it will keep it deliciously moist.

RATATOUILLE
(France)

The vegetable patch of a Provençal family is usually carefully located near the stream so that the young shoots can easily be watered. My neighbours in Mirabel in the Baronnies of Provence grew garlic and onions, haricots and chickpeas, spinach, carrots, potatoes, parsley, cabbage, and chard. Every year in the spring, the father would plant peppers, tomatoes, and aubergines too. The garlic and onions were plaited into skeins and hung in the barn. When the dried beans were gathered at the end of the summer, it was the grandfather who sat on the stoop in the autumn sunshine, stripping and podding the winter's supplies.

The *ratatouille* of Provence is a thorny subject. No family can agree with its neighbour on the correct composition. However, the parameters are well-enough defined: only those vegetables which can readily be found in peak condition simultaneously in the Provençal summer garden will do. To the gardener-cook the slow deliberate choosing of precisely the most scarlet tomatoes, the plumpest peppers, the firmest plum-purple aubergines, the sweetest onions, is the primary ingredient in the recipe. This dish is a marriage of cooked vegetables, not an all-in stew. Make it with care and you will be well rewarded.

Quantity Enough for 4 as a main dish — make double and it will be delicious cold tomorrow

Time Preparation: 1 hour

1 lb/500 g aubergines	1 lb/500 g peppers
2 onions	1 lb/500 g tomatoes *or* 2 medium
2 cloves garlic	tins
$\frac{1}{3}$ pint/200 ml olive oil	salt and pepper

Utensils A frying pan and a casserole

Slice the aubergines finely, salt them, and leave them to drain. Peel and chop the onions and garlic. Fry them gently in some of the oil in the frying pan until they are soft and lightly golden. Transfer them to the casserole, and put it on a very low heat.

Scorch the peppers by turning them in a naked flame. When the skin is charred all over, scrape it off, Hull and de-seed the peppers, and cut them into strips. Cook them gently in the frying pan until they are soft. Transfer them to the casserole.

Rinse and pat the aubergines dry, and fry them gently in more oil until they are soft and golden. They drink oil like blotting paper, so drain them well in a sieve after cooking and before you transfer them to the casserole.

Plunge the tomatoes into boiling water to loosen the skins. Peel them and chop them (you can take out the seeds too if you wish). Put the pulp to melt down to a rich sauce in the rest of the oil, including the oil drained from the aubergines. Transfer the tomato mixture to the casserole.

Heat all together for a few minutes. Do not cook any further.

Serve the *ratatouille* on its own with plenty of fresh bread. Or with eggs fried crisp in hot olive oil so that the yolks remain runny. Or with a plain-grilled steak or chop. Accompany with a bottle of red wine from the Rhône. Finish with fresh walnuts, cheese, and fruit. Or, great luxury, a *tarte au citron* (see page 540).

SUGGESTIONS

● Include 1 lb/500 g courgettes, sliced and fried as the aubergines.

● The dish has a close cousin with which it is frequently confused, the *Bohèmienne*, which confines its vegetables to the tomato and the aubergine. This is also a delicious dish.

● If you cannot obtain good olive oil, include a few stoned chopped black olives and use the best seed oil you can find.

GARLIC PURÉE
Purée d'ail (France)

The first unformed heads of fresh garlic appear in Mediterranean markets in the spring. This delicate dish is best made a few weeks later when the cloves have just formed. Fresh garlics look like very white onions, and it takes a couple of weeks for the cloves to suck the juice from the onion layers and plump themselves out. Garlic cloves are then at their sweetest and best for this dish. Cooked garlic has a mild flavour quite unlike the fierce raw bulb.

Quantity   Enough for 4 as an accompaniment
Time   Preparation: 20 minutes

  10 heads garlic
  ¼ pint/150 ml thick cream
  salt and pepper

Utensils   A small pan with a lid and a sieve or a liquidizer

Peel the garlic cloves and put them to cook in the pan with enough boiling salted water to cover them. Let them simmer for 10 minutes, then drain them. If the garlic is old, cook it a little longer.

Purée the garlic with the cream. (A liquidizer will do the job swiftly.) Season with salt and pepper.

Irresistible with a dish of fried eggs. Or a piece of roast pork, or a leg of spring lamb roasted and basted with oil and a few sprigs of thyme or rosemary. This purée is also very good with roast game.

FARMHOUSE PEAS
Petits pois à la fermière (France)

Peas, new carrots, and wild asparagus were the spring vegetables most appreciated by my neighbours in the Languedoc. All through the winter I would cross the farm's snow-covered courtyard in the early dawn, on the way to leave my children in the local village to catch the school bus. French schools start early and finish late, and there was never a sign from the farmhouse's shuttered windows as we passed. Everything changed as soon as the thaw set in in early March. Then the courtyard came alive long before we came through. Even the rooster and the rabbits had been fed well before dawn, and Madame was out in her garden tending her young vegetables in the first shafts of sunlight. She told me what to do with the basin of peas and herbs she gave me when the plants were at the height of their crop.

Quantity   Enough for 4
Time   Preparation: 30 minutes

2 lb/1 kg peas
1 lettuce
½ lb/250 g baby onions
bunch of parsley and chervil
2 oz/50 g butter
½ tablespoon flour

1 teaspoon sugar
1 pint/600 ml home-made stock *or* plain water (don't use stock cubes)
1 oz/25 g butter to finish
salt and pepper

Utensils   A roomy saucepan or casserole with a lid

Shell the peas. Wash and then shred the lettuce leaves. Peel the baby onions. Chop the parsley and chervil.

Put the peas, the butter, and the flour in the saucepan over a low heat. Cook until the butter melts, stirring all the while. Add the lettuce, the onions, the sugar, and the stock or water. Cover and stew all gently for half an hour. Stir in the herbs and the extra 1 oz/25 g butter. Salt and pepper to taste.

A pork chop or a piece of black pudding fried with apples might start the meal. Serve the peas as a dish on their own, perhaps with a few small triangles of bread fried golden in butter. A good piece of cheese to round off the meal.

LEFTOVERS

● Liquidize into a luscious pale green soup with as much again of creamy milk and a few leaves of parsley and chervil. To be taken hot or cold.

PEAS WITH HAM
Petits pois au jambon (France)

My Languedoc neighbour also had the benefit of a larder full of the products of the autumn pig-killing. Her family liked their Sunday peas cooked with a thick slice of their own ham.

Quantity   Enough for 6
Time   Preparation: ½ hour
            Cooking: 1 hour

1½ lb/750 g peas	½ pint/300 ml clear stock *or* water
1 oz/25 g butter	1 teaspoon sugar
½ lb/250 g gammon *or* raw ham	salt and pepper
2–3 crisp lettuces (cos *or* iceberg)	1 oz/25 g butter to finish

Utensils   A roomy stewpot or casserole with a lid

Shell the peas. Melt the butter in the casserole. Cube the gammon or ham into small squares, and put it to sweat gently in the butter. Wash and chop the lettuces roughly, and add them to the pot. Pour in the stock or water, and cover tightly. Leave to cook over a low heat for half an hour — lettuce requires either no cooking at all or a very long stew.

Add the peas after the half hour of cooking, along with the teaspoon of sugar. You may need to add a little more water. Continue to cook all over a low heat for another half hour. When the peas are ready, stir in the extra butter. Salt and freshly milled pepper to taste.

Serve as a dish on its own. The peas are in no hurry, so you will have plenty of time to make and serve omelettes for everyone first. Madame, my neighbour, made hers with the little spindly wild asparagus for which our neighbourhood was famous.

LEFTOVERS
● Reheat and stir in a couple of well-beaten eggs and a tablespoon of chopped parsley and chives.
● Or drain and put the peas in the bottom of individual earthenware dishes with a teaspoon of cream. Crack an egg or two into each dish. Cook in a hot oven or on direct heat until the egg is set.

CATALAN VEGETABLE STEW
Garbure catalane (France/Spain)

The *garbure* is the classic peasant dish most likely to be found on the countryman's table on his return from a hard day in the fields. It is neither soup nor stew but something in between. Its ingredients are dependent on the means, the habits, and the origin of the cook and vary widely, from the thick green-vegetable stew of Béarn, to the *ratatouille*-like mixtures of Provence. The *garbure* is probably a reference to the chief ingredients of the dish, *garbe* meaning a branch or sheaf of vegetables. The alternative theory is that the word — and the dish — springs from the Spanish *garbias*, a stew. In its simplest form it is a soup-stew of vegetables, sometimes flavoured with a small piece of bacon, and thickened with dry bread. I offer here the version which is native to the Catalan border and so spans the two cuisines.

Quantity   Enough for 6 as a main dish
Time   Preparation: 30 minutes
          Cooking: 1½ hours

small loaf bread
1 lb/500 g tomatoes
1 lb/500 g onions
3 lb/1·5 kg pumpkin
2 cloves garlic
handful of herbs (parsley,
    marjoram, thyme)

¼ pint/150 ml olive oil
salt and pepper
wine glass water

Utensils   A glazed earthenware pot with a lid and a frying pan

Slice the bread and put it to toast crisp in a very low oven. Pour boiling water over the tomatoes, peel and slice them. Peel and slice the onions. Peel and slice the pumpkin. Peel and chop the garlic with the herbs.
    Preheat the oven to 325°F/170°C/Gas 3.
    Put half the olive oil to warm in a frying pan. Add the onions and fry them gently. When they are soft and golden, put a layer of them in the bottom of the earthenware pot, seasoning with herbs, garlic, salt, and pepper as you go, continue with a layer of bread, a layer of pumpkin, a layer of tomatoes, a layer of bread, a layer of pumpkin, another of onions, a layer of pumpkin, a layer of tomatoes, and finish with bread. Or in any other order which appeals to you, as long as you finish with a layer of bread. Pour the water over all, and trickle the rest of the oil over the top.
    Cover and bake in a moderate oven for 1½ hours. Take the lid off for the last 15 minutes of the cooking time and turn up the oven heat to crisp the top.
    Serve with a green salad, a bottle of red wine, and you will need nothing more but the *goudale* — pour a glass of your wine into the last of your soup and drink it straight from the bowl. Finish with a handful of sweet grapes and a small glass of *eau de vie*.

SUGGESTIONS

Garbure provençale Aubergines, peppers, onions, tomatoes, cour-gettes, and a little garlic are layered with toasted bread and olive oil in a deep casserole, with a layer of bread on top. Pour in a glass or two of water or stock. Cover and cook slowly in the oven for 2 hours — take the lid off for the last 10 minutes and turn up the heat to crisp the top. A few minutes before you serve it flamed, pour over it half a glass of armagnac or brandy. Whisky would do.

Garbure gasconne has turnips, potatoes, cabbage, and onion layered with bread, with a piece of bacon or preserved goose buried in it.

Garbure béarnaise is the classic *garbure*, the glory of Béarn, and includes fresh vegetables (cabbage, potatoes, beans, peas), and, in its grandest form, a piece of preserved goose — the whole finished with a *trebuc* — a slice of salt meat. Chestnuts and dried beans are added in the winter months.

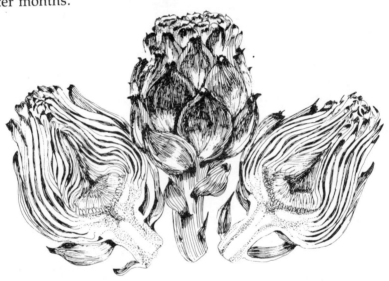

Fried and Roast Vegetables

ROAST ONIONS
(England)

The English appetite for roasting and the taste of the fire extends to vegetables as well as meat. Vegetables with a high sugar content are the ones to roast, best of all round the joint: potatoes, onions, and parsnips respond particularly well. Carrots and turnips tend to dry out. Roast a panful of the mixed vegetables together in a medium oven, and serve them with Yorkshire pudding (see page 208) and gravy (see page 210).

Quantity   Enough for 4
Time   Preparation: 5 minutes
         Cooking: 2 hours

4 large *or* 8 medium onions
salt, pepper, and butter to finish

Utensils   A roasting tin

Leave the onions as they are — neither peel them nor cut off the root end. Put them in the roasting tin, root-side downwards, and put them to roast in a slow oven — 325°F/170°C/Gas 3 — for 2 hours. Serve with plenty of cold butter, salt, and pepper, just as they are, in their own golden skins.

ROAST PARSNIPS
(England)

Quantity   Enough for 4
Time   Preparation: 10–15 minutes

4 large parsnips
salt and pepper
4 tablespoons dripping *or* lard

Utensils   A roasting tin and a saucepan

Peel the parsnips and then boil them for 10 minutes in salted water. Drain and shake them over the heat to dry. Salt and pepper them, and then roast them, well basted with dripping or lard, in a low oven — 325°F/170°C/Gas 3 — for 1½ hours. They can also be cooked round your roasting joint of meat.

ROAST POTATOES
(England)

Quantity   Enough for 4
Time   Preparation: 10–15 minutes
         Cooking: 1¼ hours

2 lb/1 kg old floury potatoes   1 oz/25 g flour
4 oz/100 g good dripping *or* lard   salt

Utensils   A roasting tin and a saucepan

Peel the potatoes and bring them to the boil in a pan of salted water. Cook gently for 15 minutes, until nearly soft. Drain them, shake them over the heat to dry them, and rough up the outsides with a fork. A sprinkling of flour helps them to crisp. Melt some dripping in the roasting tin and turn the potatoes in the very hot fat. Or put them to cook in the hot dripping round the joint as it roasts (cook them on their own if the meat has been frozen, it will give out too much liquid and make the potatoes soggy). Roast the potatoes, turning and basting them occasionally, in a hot oven — 425°F/220°C/Gas 7 — for an hour. They should be brown and crisp outside, and soft and fragrant within.

ROAST GARLIC
Ail au four (France)

The people of Provence like their garlic baked long and slow. The baking process tames the fierce tuber into a sweet, mild vegetable — from Shrew to gentle Kate in half an hour.

Quantity Enough for 4
Time Preparation: 30 minutes

8 whole heads fresh firm garlic	salt and pepper
2 tablespoons olive oil	French bread for toasting

Utensils A bowl, a small casserole, and a toasting fork

Do not peel or separate out the heads of garlic. Put them in a bowl and pour boiling water over them. Leave them for 1 minute and then drain them.

Pour the oil over the bottom of a small casserole, and put in the whole heads of garlic. Sprinkle them with salt and pepper, and then put the dish to bake uncovered in a hot oven — 400°F/200°C/Gas 6 — for half an hour. Open the oven occasionally and sprinkle the garlic with a little water from your fingers.

Meanwhile cut the bread into 1 in/2·5 cm thick slices. Toast the slices — if possible on the end of a toasting fork over a direct flame (there are wire grids available in Mediterranean countries which assist this). The bread is then singed rather than dried out, and adds its own peculiar pungency to this simple but delicious dish. To eat, squeeze the aromatic contents of each clove of garlic on to a piece of toast, sprinkle with a little salt and pepper and pop it in your mouth. A quick sip of light rosé from neighbouring Tavel when you burn your mouth. A salad of *mesclun* (see page 403) and a little goat's cheese to complete a light meal. Or you might have room for a *clafoutis* (see page 541).

PROVENÇAL TOMATOES
Tomates à la provençale (France)

Another of the Provençal vegetable dishes that achieves its concentrated sweetness through long slow cooking.

Quantity Enough for 4
Time Preparation: 10 minutes
 Cooking: 1¼ hours

8 large tomatoes (only fresh will do)
3 tablespoons olive oil

salt
2 cloves garlic
handful of parsley

Utensils A heavy frying pan

Cut the tomatoes in half and remove the seeds. Warm the oil in the frying pan. Put in the tomatoes, cut side down. Fry them over the gentlest of heat for 40 to 45 minutes, shaking the pan from time to time so that the tomatoes do not stick and burn. It is this slow patient cooking that gives the dish its unique flavour.

Peel the garlic, crush it, and then mince it very finely with the parsley.

Turn the tomatoes over, and sprinkle them with salt and the minced garlic and parsley. Let them continue to cook very, very gently on the other side — another half hour is not too long.

Serve the tomatoes after a dish of little fried fish, or a *loup de mer grillé au fenouille*, sea bass, roasted over a fire made aromatic with dried stalks of fennel. Or after a dish of fresh sardines, grilled for no more than 3 minutes a side over hot charcoal and served with a knob of butter pounded with garlic and parsley. There is nothing that can recall more vividly the scents of Provence.

BAKED SPINACH
Tian d'épinards (France)

The *tian* is a wide earthenware baking dish which has given its name to that which is baked in it. The prepared dish would have been taken to cook slowly in the local baker's cooling oven. The Provençaux often serve their beautiful vegetables as the main dish of the meal.

Quantity Enough for 4 as a light main dish
Time Preparation: 20 minutes
         Cooking: 1 hour

2 lb/1 kg fresh *or* frozen spinach   salt and pepper
1 clove garlic   2 tablespoons olive oil
8 eggs
2 oz/50 g grated strong cheese
   (parmesan or mature Cheddar)

Utensils A saucepan with a lid, a bowl, and a *tian* or gratin dish

Wash and strip off the stalks of the spinach if it is fresh. Put the leaves in a tightly covered saucepan to cook in the moisture which clings to them. When they are wilted — which will only take a few minutes — drain them, squeezing hard to extract all the liquid. Mince the spinach with a sharp knife.
   Preheat the oven to 300°F/150°C/Gas 2.
   Crush the garlic with a little salt and chop it in with the spinach. Beat the eggs in a bowl with the cheese, the salt, and the pepper. Stir the spinach and garlic into the eggs.
   Oil the *tian* or gratin dish and fill it with the mixture. Bake in the oven for 1 hour.
   Plenty of fresh bread and red wine to accompany. While you are waiting for the *tian*, serve a few slices of one of the delicious rosy dried sausages, a *saucisson d'Arles*, any *saucisson sec*, or raw salted *jambon cru*. Follow the *tian* with a green salad — *mâche* or chicory would be good — dressed with olive oil and wine vinegar in a proportion of 4:1, salt, and pepper.
   If you are cooking the dish in its native territory, you might finish the meal with a ewe's milk cheese which comes from the hills behind Nice, La Brousse, eaten with sugar and *grappa* or orange-flower water.

SUGGESTIONS
• Make a *tian de printemps* with spring vegetables replacing the spinach. Choose among young broad beans (pods and all), new carrots, baby green beans, courgettes, and baby artichokes. Best of all, see if you can

find the young shoots of wild asparagus, native throughout central and southern Europe, which appear overnight beneath the parent plant. Like mushrooms, they are a gypsy crop, sold in the spring by dark-eyed girls with wicker baskets over their arms, in the markets of the Mediterranean.

RE-FRIED CAULIFLOWER
Cavolfiore stracciato (Italy)

My favourite way with both cauliflower and cabbage, this makes an excellent light supper dish if you serve it with plenty of bread, and a cheese, and some fruit to follow.

Quantity   Enough for 4–6
Time   Preparation: ½ hour

  1 large cauliflower
  salt
  2 cloves garlic
  4 tablespoons olive oil

Utensils   A large saucepan and a roomy frying pan

Trim and then cook the cauliflower until soft in boiling salted water — 15 to 20 minutes. Drain thoroughly and break it up into florets.
    Meanwhile peel and chop the garlic. Put the olive oil to heat in the frying pan, and when it is hot put in the garlic. Fry for a moment to perfume the oil and gild the garlic, then throw in the cauliflower. Turn up the heat and fry it until it is a little crisp and well impregnated with garlic and oil. Salt and pepper with a generous hand. Serve hot. Best as a course on its own.

SUGGESTIONS
• Fry a handful of breadcrumbs in with the garlic before you add the cauliflower. Drain them and sprinkle them over the vegetable after it has been fried.
•   Make the recipe with finely shredded, cooked cabbage.

Boiled Vegetables

BOILED VEGETABLES WITH WHITE SAUCE
(England)

Vegetables to be sauced in the English style should be well cooked and soft to the fork. If they are crisp, the ingredients will not marry properly. This particular white sauce is referred to in Victorian cookery books as 'French White Sauce', perhaps to distinguish it from the English 'Butter Sauce'. This last is the notorious sauce of which Francesco Caraccioli, travelling in England at the end of the eighteenth century, complained: 'There are in England sixty different religions, but only one sauce.'

In Caraccioli's day butter was not only used to sauce, but, as the most widely available fat in dairy country, it was also often employed as a deep-frying medium. E. S. Dallas, author of *Kettner's Book of the Table*, cast a cold eye over the subject in 1877:

> English Sauce — the so-called melted butter, said to be the one English sauce. We might expect the one English sauce to be always made in perfection, and especially as nothing can be more simple. On the contrary, it is proverbial for its villainy and its resemblance to bill-stickers' paste, which is the result not only of carelessness but very often of stinginess. . . . The sauce is the result of two processes which are quite distinct; and all the many failures of it are due, even where there is no stint of butter, to the fact that as commonly made it is the result of but one process.
>
> Act First. Knead an ounce of fresh butter into a paste with an equal

quantity of sifted flour, some salt, nutmeg and mignonette pepper; dilute it with a gill, or even a gill and a half, of warm water; stir it on the fire till it boils; let it boil for three minutes — that is, till the flour is cooked — and then pass it through the pointed strainer. This is what many people call melted butter: they think that with the first act there is an end of the business. But even if four times the quantity of butter were used it would not produce a good sauce, for butter cooked in this way loses much of its flavour. The first act makes no melted butter; it only makes a vehicle for the melted butter which is to come.

Act second. The vehicle being boiling hot, mix in at the last, when the sauce is to be served, three more ounces of butter, stirring it quickly with a wire whisk. This butter is not to be cooked — only melted, as its name indicates; and in order to melt it quickly without cooking it, the butter, which should be of the best, is often divided into small pieces before being thrown in. Take it off the fire in the moment of melting, add to it a few drops of lemon juice, and serve it at once. Act First may be performed at any time, hours before the sauce, which may be kept hot in the bain marie, is wanted. Act Second is to be deferred to the last moment.

When this sauce is served with asparagus or cauliflower add a tablespoonful of cream to it, and either increase the lemon juice or use a tablespoon of white wine vinegar.

Quantity Enough for 4 as a side dish
Time Preparation: 40 minutes

For the vegetables
1 lb/500 g carrots, scraped and sliced into rings
or 1 lb/500 g leeks, washed thoroughly, topped and tailed and cut into 2 in/5 cm lengths
or 1 lb/500 g medium onions, peeled and left whole
or 1 cauliflower divided into florets
or 1 lb/500 g shelled broad beans
or 1 lb/500 g beetroot, to be cooked whole and then peeled and cubed

or 1 lb/500 g spinach stripped of its stalks and chopped after cooking
or 1 lb/500 g Swiss chard, washed and sliced
or 1 lb/500 g broccoli, washed and separated into florets
or a large head celery, thoroughly washed

For the white sauce
2 oz/50 g butter
2 oz/50 g flour

1 pint/600 ml creamy milk
salt and pepper

Utensils A large and a small saucepan

Bring plenty of salted water to the boil in the large saucepan. When it is boiling, throw in the chosen vegetable. Cook for 15 to 20 minutes until the vegetable is soft. Beetroot and onions will take longer, spinach and chard less time.

Melt the butter in the small pan and stir in the flour. Cook the flour (the sauce will taste of raw flour if you omit this step). Fry gently until the mixture is sandy but has not yet taken colour. Whisk in the milk gradually over the heat, beating to keep it smooth (you can heat the milk first to ensure minimum lumps).

Simmer the sauce gently for 5 to 6 minutes to thicken it. Add salt and pepper to taste. A sprinkle of nutmeg and a spoonful of cream, or a nugget of butter stirred in just before you sauce the vegetables, will do wonders for the flavour.

SUGGESTIONS
• To convert the dish into a gratin of vegetables, stir into the sauce 2 oz/ 50 g grated cheese, spread all in a shallow gratin dish, and sprinkle 2 oz/ 50 g more cheese over the top. Slip it under a hot grill for a few minutes to melt and brown the cheese. This quantity will be enough for 2 as a main dish.

Stuffed Vegetables

MIXED STUFFED VEGETABLES
Gemista (Greece)

Vegetables are a very important item of diet among Greek peasants and mountain people. They are eaten fresh in season and are dried in the autumn sun for use throughout the winter even today. Big flat earthenware dishes of these stuffed vegetables, rich with oil and scented with herbs, would be cooked in the cooling bread oven after the day's baking. They can be eaten warm or cold. If eaten warm, it is as the main dish of the meal. Served cold they are a snack or appetizer.

Prepare any selection from the following list for stuffing.

Tomatoes The big meaty Mediterranean ones called 'beef' tomatoes are best. Wash them but do not peel. Cut off a lid from the round end, and scoop out the seeds and central pulp. Chop up the pulp and reserve it for inclusion in the stuffing. Save the lid to put back after stuffing.

Aubergines Choose firm fruits. Wash and hull and cut them in half. Scoop out the central pulp, and mince it for inclusion in the stuffing. Salt the flesh and put the aubergine upside down to drain out some of its juice. This is not an essential ritual but it is rather soothing to do things which everyone has done for centuries. A Greek friend of mine says that imported aubergines are soft and dry, and not a patch on those found in Mediterranean markets.

Artichokes Rinse them and cut off the stalk at the base of the leaves. Peel the stalk and chop it up for inclusion in the stuffing. Blanch the artichokes in boiling salted water for 10 minutes. Drain them, and then slice off the top part of the leaves. Dig out the hairy choke in the middle with the point of your knife. Rub the wound with a cut lemon to prevent it turning black.

Courgettes The little round variety are the only ones worth stuffing. Hull them, wash them, and cut them in half round the equator, or top and tail them so that they can sit on their bottoms. Scoop out the seeds and pulp in the middle, and chop it to include in the stuffing.

Onions Choose large firm onions, preferably the Spanish variety. Peel them, and then blanch them in boiling water for 10 to 15 minutes. Cut a lid off the top and take out the middle sections, leaving 3 to 4 layers of flesh to form the cup to be filled. Reserve the top for a lid.

Peppers Hull the peppers and cut a lid from the stalk end. Remove the seeds. Since there is no flesh to be scooped out, use one of the peppers chopped up in the stuffing. Reserve the lid so that you can put it back after stuffing.

In the peasant kitchen the vegetables are likely to be fried in oil before being stuffed. This makes a rather heavy dish — so unless you intend a long day building a stone wall or harrowing a field by hand, it is probably wise to omit this preliminary and just sprinkle the hollowed-out vegetables with a little oil before you stuff them.

The best stuffings are made with plain and fresh ingredients.

Quantity   Enough for 3 lb/1½ kg vegetables for 6
Time   Preparation: 1 hour
      Cooking: 1 hour

1 onion *plus* the pulp from the vegetables	wine glass water
¼ pint/150 ml olive oil	3 tablespoons chopped herbs (oregano, marjoram, parsley)
4 oz/100 g rice	salt and pepper
2 oz/50 g pine nuts	juice 1 lemon
2 oz/50 g raisins	

Utensils   A frying pan with a lid and a wide shallow gratin dish (preferably earthenware) with a lid

Peel and mince the onion finely. Heat 4 tablespoons of oil in the frying pan, stir in the chopped onion, and fry it for a moment. Put in the rice and turn it in the hot oil until it is transparent. Add the nuts and cook for a moment longer. Put in the vegetable pulp, the raisins, and the water. Cover and leave all to simmer together for 10 to 15 minutes, until the rice is nearly cooked. Stir in the herbs, and season with salt and pepper.

Preheat the oven to 350°F/180°C/Gas 4.

Stuff the vegetables with the rice and vegetable mixture. Put the lids back on those of the vegetables which have them.

Pour the rest of the oil into the gratin dish — it must be large enough to accommodate all the vegetables in a single layer. Put the dish in the oven to heat the oil. When it is smoking, take the dish out, put in the vegetables, and replace the dish in the oven. Let all cook in the oil for 10 minutes. Then pour in the lemon juice mixed with an equal volume of water, and cover the dish.

Cook for 40 minutes, then uncover the dish and allow another 20 minutes. The oil will splutter as the juice is concentrated. The total cooking time is 1 hour 10 minutes, by which time the vegetables should be soft and the juice concentrated to a few tablespoons of well-flavoured oil. All this can be done on top of the heat if you prefer.

Have patience and allow the dish to cool down before you serve it — with accompaniments of bread, a side-dish of Greek yoghurt and cucumber salad (see page 395), quartered lemons, and a jug of *retsina*.

STUFFED POTATOES
Pommes de terre farcis (France)

The southern French farming communities prefer to live in or close to villages, even the smallest of which has a local baker who bakes the village's bread. Until quite recently many of his customers required the provision of a hot oven, and the housewives themselves would make their own bread from their own flour. So well organized was this in the larger villages that a crier would go round the streets very early in the morning crying '*Mesdames, faites vos pains!* ' to warn the good wives it was time to put their loaves to rise. He would wake different streets in rotation according to the baker's list of who was due to bake.

Mlle Morell, the sister of the curé of Mirabel in the Baronnies of Provence, remembers the crier well. She also remembers that her mother would rise at two o'clock of a baking morning to set her yeast to work to be ready for the first shift. Later in the day, great round shallow earthenware dishes of vegetables, stuffed and herbed and shiny with olive oil, would be taken down to the bakery to take advantage of the cooling oven. Joints of meat, a special treat usually reserved for a Sunday or a day of celebration, would go in at the same time. The food would be ready in time for the early evening meal, eaten in the warm kitchen after the day's work in the fields was done. Many of the beautiful slow-baked vegetable dishes of Provence originated with this ritual.

Quantity   Enough for 4 as a main dish with 2 other stuffed vegetables
Time   Preparation: 30 minutes
　　　　　Cooking: 1 hour

4 large baking potatoes	small bunch of parsley
1 onion	2 sage leaves
2 oz/50 g streaky bacon *or petit salé*	1 egg
5 tablespoons oil	salt and pepper
4 oz/100 g chopped cooked meat *or* dried pork sausage	glass water *or* stock

Utensils   A saucepan, a perforated spoon, an earthenware gratin dish, a frying pan, and a small bowl

Peel the potatoes, and cut them into 2 lengthwise to give a thin lid and a thick base. Scoop out the centres to leave a hollow shell for stuffing. Scoop a teaspoon of flesh out of the lid. Chop up the scraped out potato. Put the hollowed-out potatoes into a pan of cold salted water, and bring it to the boil. Add the lids and simmer for 5 minutes. Remove all carefully with the perforated spoon, and arrange the bases in a gratin dish which will just accommodate them.

Peel and chop the onion very fine. Chop the bacon or *petit salé* small and put it to melt in a tablespoon of the oil in the frying pan. Add the onion and fry for a moment. Add the chopped potato and the meat. If you are using dried sausage, split the skin and empty out the contents into the pan. Cook until the potato pulp is soft. Tip all into a bowl.

Preheat the oven to 350°F/180°C/Gas 4.

Chop up the herbs — the sage is very pungent. Mix them into the contents of the frying pan, and add the chopped meat and the egg lightly beaten. Season with freshly ground pepper. No salt if you are using dried sausage. Work all well together, and divide the stuffing between the hollowed-out bottom shells of the potatoes. Put on their lids. Trickle the rest of the oil over them, and pour in the water or stock to come halfway up the lower shells.

Bake the stuffed potatoes in the oven for 40 to 50 minutes.

Serve them piping hot, with at least one other baked stuffed vegetable. Two would be twice as good.

SUGGESTIONS

• If you have fresh *cèpes*, replace the minced meat or sausage with the mushrooms well cleaned and then chopped, stalks and all. *Cèpes* have a lovely gluey texture which goes well with potatoes. Dried *cèpes* can be bought in most Italian delicatessens, and are a very acceptable substitute after they have been soaked.

• Any variety of dried sausage can be used.

STUFFED TOMATOES
Tomates farcies (France)

Quantity   Enough for 4 as part of a main meal
Time   Preparation: 30 minutes
Cooking: 1 hour

4 large firm beef tomatoes	4 oz/100 g fresh peas, shelled
1 clove garlic	1 egg
1 small onion	small bunch of fresh basil and
4 tablespoons olive oil	parsley
3 oz/75 g rice	salt and pepper

Utensils   A small frying pan, a bowl, and a shallow baking dish

Cut lids off the round ends of the tomatoes. Save the lids and scoop out the seeds and pulp from the tomatoes. Salt the shells, and up-end them to drain on a plate while you prepare the stuffing.

Peel and chop the garlic and the onion. Warm 2 tablespoons of oil in the frying pan. Throw in the garlic and onion, and let them soften. Then stir in the rice. Fry all gently together until the rice turns transparent. Add the tomato pulp and a tablespoon of water. Leave to cook on a low heat for 15 minutes — the water should be all absorbed and the rice *al dente*. If the mixture looks a little liquid, turn up the heat for a moment to evaporate it. Stir in the peas, and transfer the mixture to a bowl.

Preheat the oven to 350°F/180°C/Gas 4.

Beat the egg lightly, and then mix it into the rice. Sprinkle in 2 tablespoons of the chopped herbs, and season with salt and freshly milled pepper. Pile the stuffing into the tomatoes. Put back the lids.

Arrange the stuffed tomatoes in the baking dish — round brown earthenware is prettiest against their scarlet skins. Pour the rest of the oil over them. Bake in the oven for 30 to 40 minutes.

Serve in their own dish, accompanied by another stuffed vegetable or two.

STUFFED AUBERGINES WITH ANCHOVIES
Aubergines farcies aux anchoies (France)

A stuffing from the littoral of Provence. Many households salted their own fish, so all these ingredients would be ready to hand in the larder.

Quantity   Enough for 4 as part of a main course
Time   Preparation: 40 minutes
   Cooking: 40 minutes

4 large aubergines	1 small onion
salt and pepper	½ lb/250 g tomatoes *or* 1 medium
6–8 anchovy fillets *or* 1 small tin	tin
2 oz/50 g black olives	parsley and thyme
2 slices day-old bread	1 egg
2 cloves garlic	¼ pint/150 ml olive oil

Utensils   A small frying pan, a colander, and a wide shallow baking dish

Hull the aubergines and cut them in half. Hollow them out and sprinkle the insides with salt. Put them to drain while you prepare the rest of the ingredients.

Chop up the scooped-out aubergine flesh. Chop up the anchovies finely. Stone and chop the olives finely. Soak the bread in a little water and squeeze out excess moisture. Peel and chop the garlic and the onion. If you are using fresh tomatoes, cover them with boiling water to loosen the skins and then peel and chop them roughly. Chop the herbs. Beat the egg lightly.

Rinse away all the salt from the aubergine shells. Heat the oil in the frying pan and fry the aubergines, flesh-side down, for 5 minutes to soften them. Take them out and put them into a colander to drain. Save the oil. Put some more oil in the pan and fry the chopped garlic, onion, and the rest of the aubergine pulp gently for a moment — the vegetables should soften, not take colour. Add the tomatoes, the olives, and the anchovies. Simmer gently uncovered for 5 to 10 minutes, until the sauce thickens. Allow it to cool for a moment.

Preheat the oven to 350°F/180°C/Gas 4.

Mix in the soaked bread, the egg, the herbs, and a good sprinkling of freshly ground pepper. Arrange the aubergine shells in a single layer in the baking dish. Divide the stuffing mixture between them. Trickle the oil which drained from the fried aubergines over the top.

Bake in the oven for 45 minutes.

Serve with plenty of bread — this is a very rich dish. A *salade de mesclun* (see page 403) would be good with it. A *vin gris* from the salty flatlands of the Camargue to accompany.

SUGGESTIONS

• Anchovies from the barrel need 10 minutes soaking in milk to rid them of excess salt. The ones in a tin can go in as they are, although the mixture should not be further salted.

STUFFED COURGETTES
Courgettes farcies aux grisettes (France)

Mediterranean courgettes for stuffing are short and fat like little oval melons. They are really the only kind worth stuffing. Failing these, slices of a larger vegetable marrow are a better alternative than the long, thin courgettes. Their companion in the dish, *grisettes,* are one of the most sought-after mushrooms in the markets of France. Their Latin name is *Amanita vaginata*. To be found in beech woods in autumn where their pale grey caps are easily visible among drifts of bronzed leaves.

Quantity Enough for 4 as part of a main dish
Time Preparation: 30 minutes
          Cooking: 40 minutes

4 round courgettes

4 *grisettes or* 4 oz/100 g cultivated mushrooms

2 cloves garlic

6 tablespoons olive oil

2 oz/50 g fat bacon

2 oz/50 g diced ham *or* cooked chopped meat

2 slices day-old bread

1 egg

parsley and thyme

salt and pepper

Utensils A large saucepan, a colander, a small frying pan, and a shallow baking dish

Wipe and cut the courgettes in half. Hollow them out. Chop up the scooped-out flesh, sprinkle it with a little salt, and put it aside to drain. Put on a pan of salted water, bring it to the boil and plunge in the courgette shells. Bring the water back to the boil, and simmer the vegetables for 5 minutes. Put them hollow-side-down in a colander and leave them to drain thoroughly.

Wipe the mushrooms and trim the stalk-ends off. Chop them. Peel and chop the garlic. Warm 3 to 4 tablespoons of the oil in the frying pan and put in the bacon and ham, well chopped. Add the garlic and chopped mushrooms. Stew gently for 5 to 10 minutes, until the mushrooms are tender.

Preheat the oven to 350°F/180°C/Gas 4.

Tear up the bread, soak it in a little water, and then squeeze it dry. Lightly beat the egg. Chop the herbs. Add the bread to the mushroom/bacon mixture, along with the herbs, a teaspoon of salt, freshly milled pepper and the beaten egg. Mix all well together. Stuff the courgettes with the mixture.

Arrange the courgette shells in a single layer in the baking dish. Fill them with the stuffing and trickle the rest of the oil over the top. Cook in the oven for 40 to 45 minutes.

SUGGESTIONS

• Courgette flowers, which appear at the tip of the baby marrow or as the male flower, can be picked without affecting the rest of the plant, and stuffed with the same mixture.

• Any other wild or cultivated mushroom (known as *champignons de Paris* — the location of the caves where they were first successfully cultivated) can replace the *grisettes* in the recipe — try cultivated mushrooms plus one of the Chinese dried mushrooms such as Wood Ears, *Auricularia polytricha*, well soaked and chopped (use the soaking liquid to dampen the breadcrumbs).

STUFFED PEPPERS WITH PINE KERNELS
Poivrons farcis (France)

Pine kernels are the little kernels of the nuts which drop out of pine cones. They need plenty of patience to prepare as they are small and well protected by stone-hard shells. An ideal harvest, since time is more available than money in the peasant community. The task of cracking the shells often fell to the children. Pine kernels are sold from open sacks by the spice-vendor in Mediterranean markets, along with toasted salted sunflower seeds, pumpkin seeds, and melon pips which mothers give their children instead of sweets.

Quantity Enough for 4 as part of a main dish
Time Preparation: 30–40 minutes
             Cooking: 40–45 minutes

5 peppers	large glass water
2 oz/50 g streaky bacon *or petit salé*	1 egg
1 clove garlic	4 oz/100 g grated cheese
1 small onion	small bunch of parsley
4 tablespoons olive oil	2 oz/50 g pine kernels
4 oz/100 g rice	salt and pepper

Utensils A small frying pan, a bowl, and a wide shallow baking dish

Cut a lid off the stalk end of 4 of the peppers and remove the seeds. Put these aside to await the stuffing. Hull, de-seed, and finely chop the other pepper.

Peel and chop the bacon, the garlic, and the onion. Warm 2 tablespoons of the oil in the frying pan. Add the bacon, garlic and onion, and fry for a moment. Stir in the rice and fry it gently until it turns transparent. Add the chopped pepper. Pour in the water. Leave all to simmer for 15 minutes — the water should be well absorbed and the rice *al dente*. If you have any liquid left, give a fierce boil at the end to evaporate it. Leave it to cool a little.

Preheat the oven to 350°F/180°C/Gas 4.

Beat the egg lightly with half the cheese, and then mix it into the now-cooled rice, along with a tablespoon of chopped parsley and the pine kernels. Season with salt and freshly milled pepper.

Arrange the peppers in a single layer in the baking dish. Fill them with the stuffing, sprinkle some more cheese over, and trickle over the rest of the oil. Cook in the oven for 40 to 45 minutes.

Stuffed Leaves

The travels of the Turkish *dolma* are quite remarkable. It would seem that the Ottoman Turks are responsible for the whole gamut of regional stuffed leaf dishes, ranging from the *avgolemono*-sauced vine leaves of Greece to the braised stuffed cabbage of the Swedish table. The progress of the *dolma* can be traced in the baggage train of the Ottoman Empire, which in its heyday during the sixteenth century under Suleiman the Magnificent stretched across Persia, Egypt, and Arabia, took in most of Greece and the Balkans, and reached as far north as the borders of Austria. Not until the early part of this century did the Empire finally shrink within the confines of today's Turkey.

Although *dolma* is a Turkish word meaning 'stuffed', wrapped vine leaves feature in both Ancient Greek and Persian writings. The Ottoman Turks started with a rather poor kitchen themselves, being nomadic Mongolians in origin. Affluence and stability brought new habits, and a natural appetite for pleasure made them very receptive to new ideas. *Dolmas* were originally palace cuisine — they need skill and patience. The Sultan's kitchens in Topkapi Palace in Istanbul were entirely staffed by professional male chefs, and although many of the utensils they used were of the mass-catering variety — huge cauldrons and pans — there is a small collection of implements such as Chinese steamers, whisks, and small mixing bowls which indicates a more sophisticated and elegant approach to the royal table.

RICE-STUFFED VINE LEAVES
Dolmades (Greece, Turkey, and neighbours)

The Revd W. Denton, writing home to his wife from his travels through eastern Europe in the 1860s, came across the *dolma*, in company with that other standby of the Greek table, *avgolemono*:

> The traveller then, whether on a visit to a family in Servia or staying at an inn, will almost to a certainty be served with sour soup — that is, with soup flavoured with lemon juice — and perhaps thickened, as was the case at Swilainatz, with champillons shred into it. Then will come forced meats, or rissoles, dressed in vine leaves or mixed with raisins, followed by a more substantial dish either of lamb or mutton, according to the season. The bread will be of the same dark and sour description to which he has been accustomed in Germany, unless he be fortunate enough to meet with maize bread, which is sweet and agreeable, but is generally rejected as being of too heating a nature to be wholesome. Should a ham make its appearance, he will find it well flavoured, and partaking of all the excellency of wild boar.
>
> By the side of one dish or another, but most likely with a plate of soft cheese, will be laid two or three very strong green onions; and the whole meal will invariably close with two eggs, just warmed — and barely warmed though, in fact, raw — which, if careful to follow the practice of the country, he should suck. Good Negotin or some similar wine, of a bright rose-colour, will be placed on the table in decanters holding half a gallon, to be taken — as indeed the size would indicate — ad libitum, and with this a small glass or two of raki or slivovitza.

Quantity Enough for 4–5
Time Preparation: 40 minutes
    Cooking: 1 hour

½ lb/250 g vine leaves	2 oz/50 g pine nuts
1 lb/500 g onions	2 oz/50 g raisins
¼ pint/150 ml olive oil	salt and pepper
8 oz/250 g rice	juice 2 lemons

Utensils A large saucepan, a frying pan, and a shallow heatproof dish

If the vine leaves are fresh, clip off their stalks and lay them in a saucepan. Cover with boiling water and simmer them for 5 minutes. Drain and use when cool enough to handle. If the leaves are tinned, they will probably need no extra preparation.

Peel and mince the onions finely. Put 4 tablespoons of the oil in a frying pan and heat until a faint blue haze rises. Fry the onions lightly and then add the rice. Turn it in the oil to coat the grains and then add the pine nuts, the raisins, the seasonings, and a glass of water. Cook for 10 minutes or so, until the rice has absorbed all the water.

Pick up one vine leaf at a time in the palm of your hand, shiny-side down. Put a teaspoon of the filling at one end of the leaf. Fold over the two sides and roll it up into a little bolster — not too tightly as the rice still has to swell a little. Repeat until all the filling is used up. Pack the leaf parcels as close together as possible in the shallow pan — they must not roll around or the filling will fall out. Pour in the rest of the oil, the lemon juice, and another glass of water. Cover and cook them on a low heat for an hour. Or in the oven at 300°F/150°C/Gas 2 for an hour.

SUGGESTIONS
● This rice mixture can be used for the Greek stuffed vegetables (see page 380).

LEFTOVERS
● Serve the little parcels when cool as a snack or appetizer.

STUFFED CABBAGE
Gefüllter Kohl (Germany)

One of the most universal northern dishes. Variations on this recipe are found all round the Baltic, including Scandinavia, and also in Hungary, Bulgaria, Romania, Yugoslavia, and northern France.

Quantity Enough for 4–5
Time Preparation: 40 minutes
Cooking: 40 minutes (plus $\frac{1}{2}$ hour if you use sauerkraut)

1 fresh white cabbage *or* 12–15 leaves salted (sauerkraut) cabbage	1 egg
	1 lb/500 g minced meat (pork, beef, veal — *or* all three mixed)
4 oz/100 g breadcrumbs	salt and pepper
$\frac{1}{4}$ pint/150 ml milk, stock *or* water	$\frac{1}{2}$ pint/300 ml thick soured cream
1 onion	2 oz/50 g butter
1 teaspoon marjoram (*optional*)	1 teaspoon flour

Utensils 2 bowls, a large saucepan, and a shallow casserole with a lid

Soak the breadcrumbs in the liquid. Peel and chop the onion finely. Chop the marjoram. Beat the egg.

Squeeze excess liquid from the breadcrumbs, and then mix all the stuffing ingredients — the breadcrumbs, onion, marjoram, egg, and minced meat — together and work them into a soft dough. Have a bowl of cold water beside you so that you can dip your hands in to stop the mixture sticking to them.

If you are using fresh cabbage, bring a large pan of salted water to the boil. Trim off any damaged outside leaves, and then plunge the whole head into the boiling water to blanch. Bring the water back to the boil, and then drain the cabbage. This will allow you to separate out the leaves.

If you have chosen to use sauerkraut cabbage, rinse it well and then stew it gently for half an hour before draining and stuffing.

Cut off the larger cabbage leaves and spread them out on the table — you may need to flatten the stalks with the back of a knife. (Shred the rest of the leaves to cook lightly in a little boiling salted water and serve in a separate dish to accompany the stuffed rolls.) Fill each leaf with a teaspoon of stuffing, and then roll it up into a little parcel. Continue until all are finished.

Preheat the oven to 350°F/180°C/Gas 4.

Butter the casserole and pack the stuffed leaves into it in a single layer. Dot with the rest of the butter and trickle in a tablespoon or two of water. Sprinkle with salt and pepper, and cover the dish tightly.

Cook in the oven for 40 minutes. Ten minutes before the end of the cooking time, stabilize the soured cream with the teaspoon of flour, and pour it into the gaps between the rolls. Cook uncovered for the remaining 10 minutes.

Serve hot in its own dish. The shredded lightly cooked cabbage dressed with more soured cream can be handed separately. Alternatively serve with potatoes mashed with cream. Wonderfully comforting on a cold day.

STUFFED CABBAGE LEAVES
Kaldomar (Sweden)

This is the northern version of the Turkish/Greek stuffed vine-leaf dish, *dolmades*. Cabbage replaces the southerly vine leaf. It seems likely that the dish arrived in Sweden with the creditors of the warrior-king, Charles XII. His Majesty had been roundly defeated in 1709 by Tsar Peter the Great at the Battle of Poltava, and the great military-adventurer had escaped by the skin of his teeth and without his army. He took refuge in Turkey, where he attempted without success to persuade the Sultan to take up arms on his behalf. When, some five years later, Charles set off to ride home, his Turkish creditors and their obligatory retinue of cooks followed. Although Charles (who managed to start another Nordic war on his return) died in 1718, the Turks stayed around for a further fifteen years to collect what they were owed. The first recipe for their favourite dish, Nordicized into *Kaldomar*, is to be found in Kajsa Warg's 1765 book on household management.

Quantity   Enough for 6 as a main dish
Time   Preparation: 30–40 minutes
          Cooking: 20–30 minutes

1 large white cabbage	1 lb/500 g minced meat
4 oz/100 g fresh breadcrumbs	1 egg
¼ pint/150 ml milk *or* cream	salt and pepper
1 small onion	4 oz/100 g butter to sauce the dish

Utensils   A bowl, a saucepan, and a shallow pan with a lid

Put the breadcrumbs to soak in the milk or cream. Peel and chop the onion finely. Put the minced meat into a bowl with the egg, a teaspoon of salt, and fresh pepper. Squeeze excess moisture out of the bread and add it to the meat, along with the chopped onion. Mix all together and knead thoroughly.

Break off 16 to 20 outside leaves from the cabbage, and blanch them for a moment in boiling salted water. Place a sausage of the forcemeat in each leaf, tuck over the sides, roll the leaf up with its stuffing inside, and lay the rolls in a single layer in the shallow pan. Cover with boiling salted water and poach them gently for 20 to 30 minutes.

These rolls can be served as they are, or browned quickly in butter and then served with a jug of more melted butter.

SUGGESTIONS
• Cooked rice often replaces the breadcrumbs in the mixture: echoes of the Mediterranean *dolmades*. All the Scandinavian nations love rice.
• Use young beech or hazlenut leaves instead of cabbage as the wrapper.

STUFFED LEAVES
Sarmale (Romania)

The favourite dish of rural Romania, here the Turkish/Greek *dolmades* are at their most adaptable and it is truly a dish of the crossroads of Europe. The variability of its composition reveals Romania as a kind of culinary Galapagos Islands. In the late spring and early summer vine leaves are the preferred wrapping for the stuffing. The late summer and autumn sees cabbage leaves employed for the purpose. By the winter, the *dolma* is well on its way north and appears wrapped in sauerkraut leaves. The Turks established paddy fields to grow their favourite crop, rice, in the fertile Danube delta.

Quantity Enough for 4

Time If you salt your own cabbage, start 1 week before
Preparation: 30 minutes
Cooking: 30–40 minutes

16–20 vine leaves *or* 1 fresh *or* salt
   cabbage
8 oz/250 g long grain rice
2–3 spring onions with their green
   leaves

3 tablespoons oil
½ pint/300 ml water
salt, pepper, savory, tarragon,
   thyme to flavour
½ lb/250 g minced meat

Utensils A saucepan, a frying pan, a bowl, and a shallow casserole
with a lid

To salt a whole cabbage, make a brine with 1 oz/25 g salt to 1 pint/600 ml
water. Put the cabbage in a deep dish and cover it with brine. Weight it
to keep it well under. Cover and leave to ferment in a cool larder. Ready
in a week — rinse well before using.

If you are using a fresh cabbage, blanch it for 5 minutes in boiling
water. Separate and trim the leaves if you are using vine. Remove any
particularly thick ribs from the cabbage, whether salt or fresh. Pick over
the rice. Peel and chop the onions finely, leaves and all.

Put the oil to heat in the frying pan. Toss the chopped onions in the oil
and push them to one side. Turn the rice in the oil until it is transparent.
Add the water, a little salt, pepper, and chopped herbs. Bring to the boil
and simmer for 10 minutes, when the rice will still be chewy. Tip all in to
a bowl with the meat and turn it with your hand, squeezing to make a
firm mixture. Clean hands are the most versatile implements in the
kitchen and this is a lovely tranquil job.

Lay out the leaves. Place a small ball of stuffing (about a tablespoon a
time) on each leaf, and roll it up neatly, tucking the sides over first to
enclose the mixture. Put each little parcel into the casserole as you make
it, seam downwards, all the rolls tucked neatly together. Pour enough
water in to cover the base of the dish to the depth of a finger. Cover and
cook either gently on top of the stove, or in a medium oven — 350°F/
180°C/Gas 4 — for 30 to 40 minutes.

Serve Romania's favourite dish with *mamaliga* (see page 273) and a
bowl of thick soured cream.

SUGGESTIONS

● Minced bacon, finely chopped vegetables, wild or cultivated mushrooms chopped, or a few chopped fresh herbs can replace the meat. At
the Cernice Monastery just outside Bucharest, whose inmates are
condemned to a perpetual fast of superb fish, they make excellent
sarmale with a fish stuffing.

Vegetable Salads

CUCUMBER AND YOGHURT SALAD
Tzatziki (Greece and neighbours)

A refreshing salad for a hot day which makes use of the excellent Greek yoghurt — the most delicious of which is made from sheep's milk. In Greece a special drained yoghurt is prepared for this dish — it can be achieved by leaving ordinary yoghurt to drain overnight through a jelly cloth. The guiding principle is the thicker the yoghurt the better. The Turkish name for this dish is *Cacik*.

Quantity   Enough for 5–6 as a side salad
Time   Preparation: 25 minutes

1 large cucumber
½ teaspoon salt

1 pint/600 ml yoghurt
2–3 garlic cloves

Utensils   A grater, a sieve, and 2 bowls

Grate or chop the cucumber finely, then put it into a sieve or colander and sprinkle it with salt. Leave it to drain for 20 minutes or so, while you prepare the rest of the ingredients.

Put the yoghurt into a deep bowl. Peel and crush the garlic and stir a little of the yoghurt into it. Mix well, and then add it to the rest of the yoghurt. Fold in the rinsed, drained cucumber. Serve the salad cool from the larder, with a dish of black olives and plenty of bread. As a first course, another salad or two should accompany — say the *taramasalata* (see page 89) and the *melitzanosalata* (see below).

SUGGESTIONS
• In Turkey and the Middle East chopped mint is often added.

AUBERGINE SALAD
Melitzanosalata (Greece)

One of a range of purées which are eaten with bread. More of a dip than a salad, aubergines thus prepared have a peculiarly addictive slightly bitter, smoky flavour. Similar recipes appear all round the Middle East.

Quantity   Enough for 5–6 as a side salad
Time   Preparation: 20 minutes
      Cooking: 40 minutes

1½ lb/750 g aubergines
1–2 cloves garlic
⅓ pint/200 ml olive oil

juice 1 lemon
salt and pepper

Utensils   A food processor or a liquidizer or a pestle and mortar

Wipe the aubergines, and put them to roast in the oven at 400°F/200°C/ Gas 6 until they are soft and the skin has blistered. This will take about 40 minutes. It can also be done on top of a charcoal brazier.

Peel the aubergines and pound the pulp to a paste with the garlic, peeled and crushed. Beat in the oil and lemon juice until you have a thick pale purée. This can be done very successfully in the processor or liquidizer — add the oil and lemon in a thin stream. Add more salt and pepper to taste. Serve the purée at room temperature. Garnish with a few black olives — Calamata for preference. Accompany with one or two other salads, perhaps a *taramasalata* (see page 89) and a *horiatiki* (see page 398). Plenty of good Greek bread to scoop up the purée.

SUGGESTIONS
• In Bulgaria the dish is named *zelen haviar*, and is usually spiked with a little chilli and some chopped tomato.

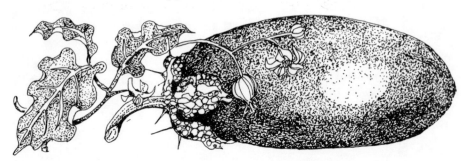

GREEK GARLIC SAUCE
Skordalia (Greece)

There is no other garlic sauce which approaches this in drama and pungency. Only for committed garlic lovers. In Greece where the sauce is much loved, it is pounded in a *goudi* — a special pestle and mortar. Served with fried fish (particularly salt cod fritters and fried mussels), fritters of aubergines and courgettes, or fried potatoes. It is also served with the beetroot salad (see page 399). *Skordalia* can be made without either nuts or bread to thicken: it is then spooned directly on to the food rather than being handed separately.

Quantity   Enough to sauce 6–8 plates
Time   Preparation: 20 minutes

1 whole garlic bulb (10–12 fat
  cloves)
2 slices bread
4 tablespoons hot water

1 teaspoon salt
½ pint/300 ml olive oil
juice 1–2 lemons

Utensils   A food processor or a liquidizer, or a pestle and mortar

Peel all the garlic cloves. Tear up the bread and mash it thoroughly in the hot water. Put in the garlic cloves and the salt, and mash all to a pulp. A pestle and mortar are the best instruments for this. Gradually trickle in the oil, adding the lemon juice as you go, as if making a mayonnaise, beating vigorously.

   The result should be a thick paste which can be used as a dip as well as a sauce. The whole job can be done most effectively in a liquidizer or food processor.

SUGGESTIONS
● If it separates, take the easy way out and start again, this time with an egg yolk, as for a mayonnaise.
● Include 4 oz/100 g ground almonds to make a more elegant sauce. In Turkey, where the sauce is called *tarator*, walnuts replace the almonds. Pine kernels are also used where they are more readily available.

GREEK SALAD
Salata horiatiki (Greece)

These simple salads appear on the countryman's board almost automatically, to be eaten with bread as a sop to the appetite while the hot dish is made ready. The salad itself can be as elegant or as simple as the habit and means of the housewife dictates, but it is always freshly made from the best ingredients available.

In a household that lives near the sea, there might be a dish of crisp-fried fish to follow, or a plate of chipped potatoes topped by a couple of eggs, the whites fried crisp in olive oil. All accompanied by a glass of *retsina* for pleasure and water for thirst.

Quantity   Enough for 5–6 as a side salad
Time   Preparation: 20 minutes

4–5 large tomatoes
1 cucumber
3–5 green peppers
1 bundle little spring onions *or* 2
  sweet Spanish onions
8 oz/250 g feta cheese (a salty
  white goat's cheese —
  Caerphilly or white Stilton can
  substitute)

2 teaspoons salt
1 tablespoon vinegar
4 tablespoons olive oil
oregano
olives

Utensils   A large flat serving dish

Wash the vegetables and quarter the tomatoes — cut them into chunks if they are the large Mediterranean variety. All the vegetables should be cut into approximately the same size chunks. Cut the cucumber into generous cubes. De-seed the peppers and cut them into squares. Peel the onions and either slice them or chop them roughly. Mix the vegetables and spread them decoratively over a flat plate.

Slice the cheese and cut it into squares. Lay the cheese slices over the top of the salad — they are the most important ingredient, and generous quantities indicate a generous host. Mix the salt and vinegar together until the salt has dissolved — this makes all the difference to the result — and then mix in the oil. Sprinkle the salad with chopped oregano and a few black olives. The country people might have a dish of fried eggs and chips after this to complete the midday meal: plenty of eggs and plenty of chips.

BEETROOT SALAD
Patzaria salata (Greece)

This beetroot salad makes use of both the root and the leaves of the beetroot. Wide use is made in Greece of wild greens such as *radiki*, dandelion greens, which are particularly important in the early spring. They are the Lenten bitter herbs, most welcome after the winter's shortages. Wild greens are always gathered by the women. *Radiki* leaves are mild in flavour when young, and are even gathered in the cities. They must always be washed very thoroughly. Another of this range of green salads is *vlita*, mustard greens, which are lightly boiled and dressed while still warm with olive oil and chopped raw garlic.

Quantity   Enough for 6 as a side salad
Time   Preparation: 10 minutes
       Cooking: 45 minutes

2 lb/1 kg beetroot, young, uncooked, and still crowned with their fresh leaves	salt
	2 tablespoons wine vinegar
	6 tablespoons olive oil

Utensils   A large saucepan

Cut off the green leaves and wash both the roots and the tops. Cook the roots, without peeling them, in the saucepan in plenty of boiling water for 30 minutes. Then add the leaves and stems. Cook for another 15 minutes. Drain.

Peel the beetroots, keeping them separate, and then slice them. Chop the leaves and stems. Pile the greens in the middle of a flat dish, and surround them with an overlapping circle of the deep crimson slices of beetroot. Mix the salt and vinegar together until the salt crystals dissolve, then stir in the oil. Dress the salad with this, preferably while the beetroot is still warm.

Best of all served with its favoured accompaniment, a bowl of *skordalia* (see page 397). To follow, a dish of plain grilled meat or fish, served with lemon quarters, salt, and good Greek bread.

SUGGESTIONS
• If you cannot buy raw beetroot, make the dish with 2 lb/1 kg ready cooked beetroots and a few stalks of Swiss chard — which you will have to boil for 15 minutes before you drain and dress them.

VEGETABLE SALAD
Salata (Bulgaria)

The Ottoman yoke came down on the Bulgarian ox in 1393 when the ancient capital, Turnovo, was captured and destroyed. Today in Bulgaria, the best gardeners in eastern Europe have plenty of New World vegetables in their kitchen plots, supplied initially by the gourmet Turks anxious for new flavours. The change was chronicled by the meticulous Turkish tax collectors. The vegetables readily available in fifteenth-century Bulgarian markets were sturdy peasant crops: cabbages, cucumbers, spinach, turnips, radishes, broad beans, peas, lentils, melons, onions, and garlic. The Turks were responsible for the introduction of rice, the Damask rose (attar for Turkish beauties and sybaritic sweetmeats), Egyptian maize ('Turkish Wheat'), and finally from America came the haricot bean, the tomato, the capsicum pepper, the potato, and the pumpkin. The Bulgarians planted and tended them all with enthusiasm. Their reward ever since has been an excellent vegetable store.

Quantity   Enough for 6 as a side dish
Time   Start 1 hour before
Preparation: 15 minutes

2 green and 2 red peppers	juice half a lemon
2 lb/1 kg tomatoes	4 tablespoons sunflower oil
½ lb/500 g sweet onions	1 tablespoon each chopped parsley
2 oz/50 g pine kernels	and dill
salt	

Hull, de-seed, and chop the peppers very fine. Wipe the tomatoes and chop them very fine. Peel and mince the onions. Pound up the pine kernels (almonds will do as well, as will walnuts). Mix all the ingredients together and leave them for an hour or two for the flavours to develop.

Serve with plenty of rough black bread on which to pile spoonfuls of the salad. In Bulgaria it might come accompanied by a few slices of *sirene*, the local fresh white goat's cheese, for which feta, or any strong salty goat's cheese can substitute. Or some *kashkaval*, the local cured yellow cheese.

SUGGESTIONS
● Excellent with a little grilled lamb cutlet or lightly spiced kebab. The Bulgarians make their own variety of minced meat kebabs called *kebapcheta*.

BROAD BEAN SALAD
Koukia (Greece)

Broad or horse beans have been grown in Greece since neolithic times. One of the most ancient of the European cultivars.

Quantity   Enough for 4
Time   Preparation: 15–20 minutes
   Cooking: 1½ hours

1 lb/500 g young broad beans in the pod	1 lemon
6 tablespoons olive oil	1 sweet onion
1 glass water	parsley and dill
	salt and pepper

Utensils   A saucepan or heatproof casserole

String the beans and then chop them into lengths, pod and all. Later in the year you may have to shell them, later still use them dried.

Put the oil to warm in the pan or casserole. Add the beans and stew them in the oil for a moment before pouring in the water. Cover tightly and simmer very gently for 1½ hours until the beans are mushy, the juices evaporated, and only oil remains. Take the lid off towards the end of the cooking to assist the evaporation process.

Squeeze the lemon and stir the juice into the beans. Peel and chop the onion finely — hold it in the palm of your hand and make downward cuts into it in a close noughts-and-crosses pattern. Now you have but to slice across the cuts and you will have perfectly minced onion. Chop the herbs. Scatter the onion and the herbs over the warm beans. Season with salt and pepper. Serve cool.

Accompany with plenty of good bread and serve with grilled fish or *souvlakia*, cubes of meat threaded on skewers and grilled simply, brushed with oil and lemon juice. Finish the meal with a short glass of *ouzo*, a long glass of water, and a tiny cup of thick sweet Turkish coffee.

SUGGESTIONS

• This dish can be made with almost any Mediterranean-grown vegetable: green beans, Swiss chard, spinach, baby artichokes, potatoes, peppers.

• Chopped tomatoes (if you use these, leave the water out of the recipe), whole olives, and garlic can be included — and you have a *plaki*.

LEFTOVERS

• Liquidize the plain mix (with no *plaki* additions) with stock or milk to make a light and delicious soup. Sprinkle with chopped onion and mint. Serve hot or cold.

ASPARAGUS VINAIGRETTE
(France)

After the terrible winter of 1956, when two-thirds of the olive trees in Provence had the sap frozen in their taproots, only a few farmers had the courage to replant. The rest spread the risk: apricots, cherries, more vines, asparagus. The asparagus is the most demanding — seasonal labour must be employed, and they must be up at five to look in the heaped beds under plastic strip blankets. Mlle Morell, my octogenarian neighbour, found the fast-growing asparagus magical:

> "You wouldn't believe it. At night there is nothing there, and in the morning, marvellous, a row of little points, ready to be plucked with the special knife that can nip them off down under the earth. Then the sticks must be graded and bundled for market. People today are very demanding. They must have their points just so. Two months only the season lasts, but all that time you must be in the fields with the dew before dawn, every day, and then all day picking and grading, picking and grading."

The fruit of the olive trees that survived the terrible cold of that year still blesses the vegetables that replaced them. Good Provençal olive oil is as sweet and thick as half-melted butter.

Quantity Enough for 4
Time   Preparation: 15–20 minutes
         Cooking: 15–20 minutes

2 lb/1 kg large white asparagus	¼ pint/150 ml first pressing olive oil
salt	3 tablespoons wine vinegar

Utensils A very large deep saucepan or an asparagus boiler

Wash and trim the asparagus stalks and tie them into a bundle. Bring a large pan of salted water to a rolling boil and lower the bundles in, feet first. Prop them up so that the stalks are submerged but the tips are above the level of the water and cook in the steam. Bring the water back to the boil, turn the heat down, and boil gently for 15 to 20 minutes, until the stalks are soft. Lift them out, drain them thoroughly, and serve them piping hot on a white napkin.

Accompany with a jug of the best olive oil you can find, mixed with the wine vinegar. Put a dish of rough salt and a peppermill on the table, and plenty of bread. Few French countrymen would enjoy a meal without bread to mop up the juices.

A pork or lamb chop, grilled with rosemary and accompanied by a potato gratin (see page 336) to follow. Cheese and fruit or a fresh fruit tart (see page 538) to complete a perfect Sunday lunch.

SUGGESTIONS

• Serve the stalks of the Swiss chard which you have used to make a *trouchia* in the same manner. The hot vegetable and the light vinaigrette are delicious together. The oil must be of the best. Lemon juice can be used instead of the vinegar — citrus and vines grow side by side in the fertile Rhône basin.

MIXED LEAF SALAD
Salade de mesclun (France)

This is the mixture of herbs, named from the Latin word *miscellanea*, long appreciated as a special salad mixture around Nice and lately the darling of *nouvelle cuisine*. Packets of assorted *mesclun* seeds can be bought from the seedsmen and spice merchants who set up their stalls in the market squares of the villages of Provence. The salad leaves used to be cultivated in the monastery garden of the Franciscan friars at Cimiez in the hills behind Nice, and fetched in special baskets to be presented by children to favoured adults. Dandelion, rocket, purslane, and chervil provide the small leaves; red Treviso chicory, white bitter chicory, oak leaf, and cos lettuce the larger. Rub the salad bowl around with a cut clove of garlic, or toss it with a *chapon* — a nugget of bread rubbed with garlic — and dress the salad lightly with olive oil, a few drops of vinegar, and salt.

A nut oil makes a delicious dressing, but a blessing of olive oil is more likely in the home territory of this salad. At its delicate best after a dish of plain grilled fish or a beautiful fish soup. Follow with a sharp salty, dark-rinded little goat's cheese, or a *tarte au citron* (see page 540).

FIELD SALAD
Salade des champs (France)

Food for the road, to be taken into the fields by harvesters for their midday breakfast. The fish mixture would be made *in situ* with a salted fish (ramrod straight and known as a *gendarme*) from the barrel in the local shop. The salad would always be easily gathered from the kitchen garden — corn salad grows anywhere, all year round if the climate is mild.

Quantity   Enough for 4
Time   Preparation: 10 minutes

1 smoked herring (preferably with roe)
4 tablespoons olive oil
1 tablespoon wine vinegar

½ lb/250 g corn salad (also called in Provence *mâche, doucette, lachuguetto*)

Utensils   A pestle and mortar or a food processor

Skin the herring and grill it lightly. Fillet it and pound it in a mortar or in the processor with the oil and vinegar. Toss the salad in this fishy dressing.

Plenty of bread, a handful of olives, a bottle of red wine, a piece of ripe salty Roquefort from the neighbouring Causses, and you will be well satisfied.

SALADE NIÇOISE
(France)

This is one of the most abused salads ever devised. Cooked vegetables, including potatoes, are often quite wrongly included. On the other hand, prepared correctly with good fresh ingredients and absolutely no cooked vegetables, it provides the most refreshing of light summer lunches, or a delicious entrée to a meal. All the ingredients, with the exception of the comparatively expensive tunny fish, are easily come by in the Mediterranean kitchen garden and storecupboard.

Quantity   Enough for 4 as a main dish
Time   Preparation: 30 minutes

4–5 fresh eggs
2 lb/1 kg tomatoes (plump, firm, and ripe)
salt
1 cucumber (not too large)
1 small tin anchovies *or* 12 anchovy fillets from the barrel, soaked in milk to remove excess saltiness
1 tin tunny fish, but only for very special occasions (*optional*)

2 green peppers
1 small bundle spring onions *or* 1 sweet onion
½ lb/500 g shelled young raw broad beans *or* raw baby artichokes
1 clove garlic
handful black olives
few leaves fresh basil
olive oil

Utensils   A small saucepan to boil the eggs and a large shallow bowl or dish

Hard-boil the eggs, but do not overboil them or they will go grey at the edges and smell of sulphur — bring fresh eggs to the boil, simmer for 6 minutes, and then take them out and plunge them into cold water. When they are cool enough to handle, peel them and quarter them lengthwise.

Quarter the tomatoes, sprinkle them with salt, and put them to drain while you prepare the rest of the ingredients. Wipe and then slice the cucumber (not too finely). Cut the anchovy fillets in half and flake the tunny fish roughly. Wipe, top, and de-seed the peppers. Cut them into rings. Peel and trim the onions and cut them into rings. Slice the broad beans or, if you are using baby artichokes, trim off the hard leaf tops, scoop out the tiny choke, and slice the rest finely.

Rub thoroughly the large, shallow bowl, preferably made of olive wood, with the cut clove of garlic. Arrange all the salad ingredients carefully in the bowl. Sprinkle the olives and a few torn leaves of basil over the top. Sprinkle with olive oil and salt. That's all. Serve immediately.

Accompany with the best fresh bread in the neighbourhood and a bottle or two of strong young wine — red or white. Serve a potato gratin (see page 336) after the salad. Finish the meal with a piece of cheese and a bowl of fresh southern fruit — sweet orange-fleshed cantaloup, ripe peaches, apricots, or grapes. Or take the opportunity to make a fruit tart (see page 538).

LEFTOVERS
• Make a *pan bagnat* or 'wet bread' — there is a special little round loaf baked in the Nice area for this favourite 'second breakfast' which is taken to the fields or the place of work. Bread rolls or a long French bread will do. Cut the rolls in half horizontally and scoop out most of the inside crumb. Rub the inside with a cut clove of garlic. Trickle in some olive oil, a few drops of vinegar, and sprinkle some salt and pepper. Fill the hollows with *salade niçoise* or a few slices of tomato and sweet onion, and sandwich the bread together again. Put a cloth over the filled rolls and a board on top, and leave it weighted for an hour or so for the flavours to mingle. It makes a splendid picnic lunch.

POTATO SALAD
Salade de pommes de terre (France)

An excellent salad from the olive groves of Provence. Potatoes grow well, waxy and yellow and perfect for the purpose, in the sandy soil of the coast.

Quantity   Enough for 6 as a side dish
Time   Preparation: 20 minutes

2 lb/1 kg small new potatoes
salt
2 tablespoons mild French
    mustard
2 tablespoons wine vinegar
4 tablespoons olive oil

2 slices day-old bread
1 garlic clove
1 small bunch spring onions
1 glass white wine *or* meat stock
black pepper

Utensils   A roomy saucepan and a wide shallow earthenware dish

Bring a pan of salted water to the boil. Scrub the potatoes, and then plunge them into the boiling water. Boil them for 15 to 20 minutes, until they are soft.

Meanwhile mix the mustard, vinegar, and oil with the bread cut into small cubes and the garlic, peeled and crushed with a little salt. Trim and chop the spring onions, and mix them in. Put all into the shallow dish.

Drain the potatoes when they are ready. Slice them roughly into the sauce. Pour in the wine and add freshly milled black pepper, and turn all over together. The potatoes will drink all the liquid as they cool. Serve with a plate of charcuterie — sliced dried sausages and raw dried ham, *Jambon de Bayonne* or Parma, with a pat of unsalted butter and plenty of crusty French bread.

DEVILLED PEPPERS
Piments à la diable (France)

Part of the Provençal table, a simple and delicious salad. Red peppers grow plump and sweet in the Mediterranean sun.

Quantity   Enough for 4
Time   Start the day before
          Preparation: 20–25 minutes

6 large red peppers
small glass olive oil
small bunch of fresh basil

Grill the peppers until their skins turn black. This can be done either under a very hot grill, or by turning them, speared on a knife, over a direct flame. The blackened peppers will peel cleanly back to their soft scarlet flesh. Hull and de-seed them, and cut them lengthwise into strips. Put them on a plate and film them over with the oil. Sprinkle with the basil, well chopped. Leave them overnight in a cool place, but not in the refrigerator. The next day they will provide a delicious hors d'oeuvre.

Storehouse Vegetables

SAUERKRAUT
(Germany and neighbours)

Sauerkraut — salted and fermented or 'barrel cabbage' — is an important national dish. It can be served with sausages, with pork, with anything and everything, or on its own with a sprinkling of caraway seeds, a spoonful of soured cream, and a thick slice of black rye bread to mop up the juices. During the summer if may be replaced in the recipes with fresh cabbage — as with all peasant cooking, ingredients are dictated by season.

Sauerkraut substitutes for the fresh cabbage available in the summer, and is made from firm heads of cabbage (Savoy, Drumhead, or Flat Dutch) cut after the first frosts of autumn. The new sauerkraut traditionally used to be eaten with fresh pork after the autumn pig-killing. It was eaten again on New Year's Day as an oblation for the year's renewal; with goose for the Christmas festivities; with salt pork and smoked sausages all winter; and then with fresh fish when the spring thaw released the fishing boats. It should be all finished up by the time the young spring cabbage is ready for gathering — the salt content is too low to conserve the pickle in the heat of summer (with today's central heating it must be stored in a cool larder).

Sauerkraut can be eaten raw as a salad. It should be thoroughly rinsed in cold water to get rid of excess salt. Then mix it with raw chopped onion and perhaps a little chopped apple. Dress with oil and black pepper.

In Transylvania (now a province of Romania) I have eaten sauerkraut salad dressed with pumpkin oil. This is a very dark oil with a light nutty flavour which is prepared in the autumn by farmer's wives all over eastern Europe. The women sit out in their fields in the middle of the pumpkin patch in early October, slashing the over-ripe fruit open with heavy knives, and scooping out seeds into big wire-meshed trays. The pulp goes for winter cattle fodder and the seeds are pressed for their oil in a hand mill. Pumpkin oil must be stored, tightly corked, in a cool larder — in common with all vegetable oils, it is really a fruit juice and is volatile and goes rancid after it has been exposed to air.

Sauerkraut is best made in quantity. I give the recipe as much for interest as in expectation of a practical application. You can always take the easy way out and buy your supplies ready-made.

Quantity   30 cabbages would have kept a small family going all winter
Time   Preparation: 2 hours
            To take salt: 3 weeks

50 lb/25 kg cabbage
2 lb/1 kg salt

Equipment   A large wooden barrel with a lid and a weight

Scrub the barrel very thoroughly. Set it on boards so that the air can circulate — a cool larder or dry cellar is ideal.

Pick off the outer leaves of the cabbage and save the perfect ones. Line the bottom of the barrel with 10 of these large leaves.

Slice each cabbage head in 2 and cut out the solid stalk. Put aside 3 or 4 heads so that you have some large leaves for stuffing (replace fresh cabbage with sauerkraut in stuffed cabbage recipes). Shred the rest of the cabbage with a very sharp knife. It should look like a mountain of very fine-cut noodles. Mix the salt with the shredded cabbage, and thoroughly salt the whole half-heads.

Pack into the barrel, pressing each layer well down. (Country women used to tread it down with clean bare feet). Cover with 20 perfect outside leaves, well salted. Top with a lid whose diameter is slightly smaller than the barrel top. Weight it down heavily. After a week check to see if the brine is forming well. It should cover the cabbage after 10 days. If not, top up with a brine made with 1 oz/25 g salt to 1 pint/600 ml water. Replace the lid and weight because sauerkraut, like all pickles, must not be allowed to come into contact with air. The cabbage will now begin to ferment and be ready to eat in 3 weeks from the start of the operation. Quite apart from its excellence as food, many blood-cleansing, digestion-aiding properties are ascribed to fermented cabbage.

Check your barrel every week throughout the winter, skim off the foam of the fermentation, and give the sauerkraut a stir every few days.

At the same time, rinse off and wipe down the sides and lip of the barrel and the weighted lid. The sauerkraut should then keep sweet and fresh until next season's greens are sprouting.

SUGGESTIONS
• Buy your sauerkraut straight from the barrel in the delicatessen or in tins from the supermarket shelves.

TO COOK SAUERKRAUT

Quantity   Enough for 4
Time   Preparation: 10 minutes
        Cooking: anything from 30 minutes to 3 hours

1 lb/500 g sauerkraut (your own or shop-bought. The tinned variety, unless pre-cooked, takes the same time. Check the instructions on the tin.)

½ pint/600 ml water *or* stock
1 potato (*optional*)
1 teaspoon caraway seeds (*optional*)
freshly ground pepper

Utensils   A deep saucepan with a lid

Drain the sauerkraut, rinse it, and put it in a deep saucepan. Cover with boiling water or strong clear stock, and cook for an hour, tightly lidded. Some households cook their sauerkraut for as long as 3 hours. Others for only half an hour. I prefer it not too soft. A potato can be grated into it half an hour into the cooking to give a richer sauce. Uncover the dish and turn up the heat for the final 10 minutes to evaporate the remaining liquid. Season with the caraway seeds, if you are using them, and freshly ground black pepper. If you prefer, cook the sauerkraut in a moderate oven for an hour at 350°F/180°C/Gas 4.

SUGGESTIONS
Sauerkraut cooked with white wine   Substitute half a bottle of white wine for the liquid in the plain sauerkraut recipe.
   Sauerkraut cooked with lard   Melt 2 oz/50 g pork or goose fat (nicest of all) in a roomy saucepan. Add a piece of pork bone or fat bacon if you have it. Drain and rinse the sauerkraut and put it in the pan. Cover with stock and simmer as usual.
   Sauerkraut with apples   Add 1 lb/500 g sharp green apples, cored and sliced, to the sauerkraut with lard recipe.
• Season the sauerkraut with fennel seeds or crushed juniper berries instead of the caraway.

PICKLED VEGETABLES
Torshi (Bulgaria)

These pickles are made all over eastern Europe. The Bulgarians, being the best gardeners in the region, make the best pickles. The vegetables should retain a crisp bite, and are often eaten on their own as a salad meal with bread.

Quantity   Enough to make 8 pints/5 litres pickles
Time   Start 6 weeks ahead
Preparation: 40 minutes

For the brine
3 pints/2 litres water
1 pint/600 ml white wine vinegar

4 oz/100 g salt

For the vegetables
a selection of 6–7 lb/3–3·5 kg
mixed vegetables from: carrots,
cauliflower, young turnips,
small pickling cucumbers, red,
yellow, and green peppers, and
green beans

1 head dill
3 cloves garlic
3 small red chilli peppers

Utensils   Pickling jars and a large saucepan

First prepare the vegetables. Peel and cut the carrots lengthways into quarters, chopping them in half if they are long. Divide the cauliflower into florets. Peel and quarter the turnips. Wipe and leave whole the small pickling cucumbers (if you have only large cucumbers, quarter them lengthways and cut them into convenient pieces). Seed and quarter the peppers. Top and tail the beans. Separate the dill into short branches. Peel and halve the garlic cloves. Wipe and leave the chillis whole.

Pack the vegetables neatly into sterilized jars — sterilize them either in a hot oven for 10 minutes, or by rinsing them out with scalding water.

For the brine, bring the water, vinegar and salt to the boil in the saucepan. Pour the hot brine over the vegetables, and prod the pieces well with a skewer to shake off the air bubbles, which might make the pickle go bad. Air is the arch-enemy of pickles and preserves. Seal the jars down tightly and store.

Ready to eat in 6 weeks, just as the cold wind begins to sweep the plain. Very good with fresh bread and a slice of cheese.

SUGGESTIONS
• If you want your pickles to last longer than a few months, use only vinegar and salt as the brine mixture.

Seaweed

LAVERBREAD
Bara lawr (Wales)

Laverbread is not so much a bread, but more of a vegetable purée. The vegetable is a seaweed, *Porphyra umbilicalis*, and green laver, *Ulva lattissima*, which is common on the shores of Britain, particularly on the west coast. It is there for the taking although most of its devotees, of which there are many in Wales, buy it in its cooked form as laverbread since its preparation is somewhat lengthy and laborious. The seaweed itself has thin purple fronds and grows on rocks and stones at the edge of the water. Its use is by no means confined to Wales. The Japanese semi-cultivate it and use it as a food wrapper. Like all seaweeds it is rich in minerals and vitamins. Laverbread is called *Sloke* in Ireland and Scotland.

Wash the laver well. Then stew it gently in water to cover for 5 to 6 hours, until it is like a mush of well-cooked spinach. Drain. It can be stored thus in a jar for several days, and it is this purée which is generally sold as laverbread. It refrigerates and freezes successfully.

Let it cool to a stiff jelly and toss spoonfuls into a plateful of fine or medium oatmeal — wholemeal flour can substitute for the oatmeal. Fry the spoonfuls like fritters in bacon fat for a delicious Welsh breakfast. Accompany with a glass of new or skimmed milk.

It can be bought ready-rolled in oatmeal, but this is inclined to sour it.

SUGGESTIONS
● Laverbread keeps good company, if used fresh and beaten up with 1–2 oz/25–50 g butter and a squeeze of lemon, with a roast haunch of the small sweet Welsh marsh mutton.

CARRAGHEEN PUDDING
(Ireland)

The brown-purple fan fronds of *Chondrus crispus* fringe the Atlantic shores of Britain and Ireland. This seaweed is highly gelatinous and can even be processed into fine sheets for sausage casings. It is usually used to set jellies. It is best gathered from a clean mid-tide line during the months of April and May. Wash it well and remove the dark stems. Then lay it out to dry on the rocks in the salt breeze before you store it. Sun to dry and showers to rinse is the best weather for this. Leave the carragheen out for several days to bleach to a creamy white — if there are no showers, you will have to sprinkle it with water intermittently yourself. Store in paper bags. There are ·those knowledgeable in the matter who say the bleaching process is unnecessary, and removes some of the goodness and flavour.

Quantity   Enough for 4–5
Time   Start the day before
                  Preparation: 10–15 minutes

½ oz/12 g dried carragheen moss	1 tablespoon sugar
1¾ pints/1·1 litres milk	knifepoint salt

Utensils   A saucepan, a strainer, and a jelly mould

Bring all the ingredients to the boil together. Allow to boil until the moss has dissolved and setting point is reached. This will only take a couple of minutes, and it will then coat the back of your wooden spoon. Pour the liquid through the strainer into the mould to set. Leave it overnight.
    Serve it with a jug of yellow cream and a bowl of the tiny sweet strawberries which grow wild in the woods and the heather. It makes a delicious pudding, or a light supper dish with home-made scones.

SUGGESTIONS
● Put in a piece of lemon peel for flavouring.
● Stir in an egg yolk as the mixture cools, and then fold in the well-beaten white. Allow to set as usual.
● If you are using the seaweed fresh, wash it thoroughly, and simmer it in proportions of 1 cup of seaweed to 3 cups of milk or water, until the weed has practically dissolved. Add sugar and pour through a sieve into a mould to set.

CHAPTER 11

Herbs and Fungi

THE MINT OR LABIATAE FAMILY

1 Basil 2 Marjoram 3 Oregano 4 Spearmint 5 Rosemary 6 Sage 7 Savory 8 Thyme

Herbs and wild plants gathered from field and wood have always been a valuable source of both food and medicine to the peasant community. The herb-seller occupies to this day a special corner in all Mediterranean and central European marketplaces.

My favourite herb market is held every week in Buis-les-Baronnies in the mountains behind Provence. (Many of its raw materials are gathered from the rocky slopes which surround it, and today the little town boasts a factory for the drying and packaging of its own products.) There, under the medieval arches of the market square, wooden trestles are loaded with sacks of dried aromatic leaves, invitingly open for inspection. Among them are five varieties of thyme, and rosemary, bay, sage, and juniper berries gathered wild in the *garrigue* scrub. There is lime tea, green tea, vervane, lemon balm, dried mint, rose petals, marigolds, three varieties of camomile, cherry stalks, and a hundred different roots and herbs for infusions, each with a special property. The people demand — as they have always done — great variety. This one for sleep, this for sloth, this for a bad stomach, this for women's ills. Then there are the imported cloves and peppercorns, cinnamon and bundles of liquorice root for the children to chew, and bundles of lavendar, grown in rows as a crop for the perfume industry.

Herbs for flavouring

These are grouped in their botanical families, which I hope will encourage the cook to look for a substitute within the family if a given herb in a recipe is unavailable. There are four main groups in the European wild larder: the Mint family, the Carrot family, the Onion family, and the Cabbage family.

THE MINT OR LABIATAE FAMILY

All the herbs in this family except sweet basil, which is a native of tropical Africa and Asia, are indigenous to the Mediterranean. Their use was spread throughout Europe by the Roman colonists. If you cannot obtain a specified herb, reach for another in the same group. The results are generally perfectly satisfactory and would be as expected in the peasant kitchen, where the cook would use whichever herb came most easily to hand.

Basil (*Ocimum basilicum*) A native of India and tropical Africa but imported into the Mediterranean many centuries ago, basil was used as a charm against the Basilisk or dragon in ancient Italy, while to the early Greeks it was a royal (basilikon) herb. A favourite flavouring in Greece, Italy, and France, it is the dominant herb in the making of Chartreuse. Nip the top leaves of a growing plant to encourage branching. Dry and store after flowering. Or keep the leaves steeped in vinegar for use in salad dressings. Or store as *pesto* (see page 295).

Sweet marjoram (*Origanum majorana*) A native of the Mediterranean and used interchangeably with oregano, or indeed to replace basil in the winter, it is rather more subtle in flavour. In medieval times it was gathered as a strewing herb for the floor. Pick for drying just when it comes into flower — its flavour is strongest when the herb is dried.

Wild marjoram or **Oregano (*Origanum vulgare*)** Another native of the Mediterranean, oregano was named 'mountain joy' by the Greeks. It is very often used with tomatoes in Italy, particularly in pizzas. Bees love its little white flowers. Dry sprigs of it when it is in flower. There is a Mexican oregano much used in the United States, which has a similar flavour but it is a member of the Verbena family.

Spearmint (*Mentha spicata*) Growing wild throughout central and southern Europe, spearmint is the best mint for drying and has been in use for thousands of years. Peppermint (*Mentha piperata officinalis*) is a stronger variety and is used for oil. Dry mint for storing by tying in bunches and hanging in a dry current of air. Then strip and crumble the leaves to keep, like all stored herbs, in an airtight jar out of the light. In pre-refrigeration days mint was believed to prevent milk from turning sour in warm weather. An excellent herb for the digestion, the French use the dried leaves to make an infusion. In England fresh mint is used to sauce lamb and flavour peas. In eastern Europe and the Middle East it is infused fresh to make a delicious sugar-sweetened tea.

Rosemary (*Rosmarinus officinalis*) The deliciously named 'dew-of-the-sea', *rugiado di mare*, does indeed grow best near the seashore. The French burnt branches as incense, and believed that the flowers were an aphrodisiac. It was used throughout Europe as a protection against the spells of witches. In warm climates its delicate blue flowers blossom all year round, and are much loved by bees. It can be picked for drying at any time, although its oil is strongest in August and September.

Sage (*Salvia officinalis*) A herb used initially as a medicine, sage was planted throughout Europe by the Romans. It was incorporated in the peasant diet for its health-giving properties. The best time to dry it is in the spring, before the plant flowers and its stalks begin to lengthen.

Summer and **Winter savory (*Satureia hortensis* and *S. montana*)** Two very similar species, of which the summer variety is a more gently flavoured annual, and the winter a woody perennial. The flavour of both is somewhere between sage and rosemary. Savory was so popular in medieval England that it was one of the herbs taken by the settlers to be seeded in the New World. Medicinally it was used as an antihystamine to relieve the pain of insect stings. Savory dries well, is an excellent flavouring for meat and fish dishes, particularly trout, and in England has the same affinity with beans as mint has with peas.

Thyme (*Thymus vulgaris* plus a great many other varieties) Its name derives from the Greek for 'burnt offering'. Thyme has long been used medicinally, both burnt as a fumigant and through its oil as an antiseptic, particularly against fungoid and bacterial infections. Bees love it and collect its delicately perfumed nectar to make the most delicious honey of all. The flavour is strongest when the leaves are dried. Thyme is the principal herb used in the flavouring of Benedictine.

THE CARROT OR UMBELLIFERAE FAMILY

The parts of these plants most usually employed for flavouring are the complete fruits rather than the seeds. The varieties used in Europe are, as with the mint family, native to the Mediterranean. All varieties taste of aniseed in varying degrees.

Aniseed (*Pimpinella anisum*) A white-flowered eastern Mediterranean annual, aniseed was used as a liquorice-like flavouring by the Greeks, the Hebrews, and the Romans, who baked it in cakes which they ate at the end of their gargantuan meals to assist digestion. Anise is still used today as a *digestif*, although more usually now as an ingredient in various strong liquors: Spanish *anis*, French Pernod and *anisette*, and the Greek *ouzo*. Anise shares with its close relation, fennel, and with the star-anise, which is a fruit of the magnolia family, an essential oil, anethole. Aniseeds can be bought from any Mediterranean spice stall and are generally used to flavour sweet biscuits. The seeds are also used in Greece and Turkey to spice stuffed vine leaves and vegetable dishes. They have a particularly natural affinity with their cousin, the carrot.

Caraway (*Carum carvi*) A biennial Mediterranean native, the roots of the plant are sometimes eaten as a vegetable as well as the fruit seeds being used for flavouring. Caraway is one of the most ancient spices known to man — it has been found in 10,000-year-old lakeside dwellings in Switzerland. Much liked in central Europe as a universal flavouring, it is used for meat, fish, cheese, pickles, bread (particularly rye bread), and also for liqueurs like the German *Kümmel*. Caraway has a reputation as a *digestif* and has given its name to seed cake.

Chervil (*Anthriscus cerefolium*) A native of eastern Europe and needing the winter sun to flourish, fresh leaves of chervil were used by the Romans. Chervil continues to be popular in France and Germany as a flavouring for soups, stews, and eggs, often in conjunction with other

THE CARROT OR UMBELLIFERAE FAMILY

1 Aniseed   2 Caraway   3 Chervil   4 Coriander   5 Cumin   6 Dill   7 Fennel   8 Parsley

fresh herbs such as parsley and tarragon. The leaves also appear in the delicious little salads of semi-wild greens at which the French are so adept.

Coriander (*Coriandrum sativum*) A pink-flowered native of southern Europe, coriander is used either as dried seeds (the fresh ones have an unpleasant taste rather like the smell of crushed bugs), or in the form of its fresh parsley-like leaves. Another of the most ancient and widespread culinary herbs, it has been employed since at least 5,000 BC when it appears in Egyptian and Sanskrit records. The seeds are also mentioned in the Old Testament as comparable to manna. Today it is come across most often in Europe in southern Mediterranean recipes. The herb is also used extensively in India and China, and is frequently known by the name 'Chinese parsley'. Coriander was successfully transplanted to the New World, where the fresh leaves and the seeds alike are now a dominant flavouring in Mexican and South American dishes. The seed is good in soups and stews.

Cumin (*Cuminum cyminum*) A native of Egypt, it is the dried fruit of the little annual pink-flowered herb that is used in cooking. Another ancient spice, mentioned in both the Old and New Testaments, cumin is much used in Moorish-influenced Spain and in Mediterranean eastern Europe. In England it was an important item in the medieval spice chest.

Dill (*Anethum graveolens*) A delicate feathery annual with a flavour much like caraway, dill's popular name derives from the Norse word *dilla*, to soothe. Dill was originally a native of southern Europe, and was transplanted over the centuries to northern climes where it has long been a great favourite, and in particular a staple of the German and Scandinavian kitchens.

Fruit seeds and leaves are both used, particularly in the flavouring of pickles and the famous Scandinavian *gravlaks*, where it superseded the ancient flavouring of young pine needles. The seeds are widely employed in dried form to flavour cabbage, pork, and potato dishes.

Sweet fennel and **Florentine fennel (*Foeniculum vulgare* and *F. vulgare dulce*)** The first is a tall feathery annual native to southern Europe and today to be found growing on every road verge. The second is the annual variety, and is grown for its juicy edible celery-like bulb, which is eaten raw in salads or cooked as for celery. Both types of fennel can be used as herbs, fresh or in the form of the dried fruit. The dried stems of the wild variety are gathered in France as an aromatic fuel over which to grill fish. In Spain the same dry branches are used as a flavouring for pickled green olives.

Parsley (*Petroselinum crispum*) *Petroselinum crispum* is the well-known curly-leafed variety, followed in popularity by the flat or fern-leaved parsley. A biennial from Sardinia, many varieties of parsley are

419

THE ONION OR LILIACEAE FAMILY

1 Onion 2 Leek 3 Chive 4 Garlic 5 Shallot

now cultivated. Grown as a medicinal plant by the Greeks, it is the most widely available herb in today's kitchen and much liked as decoration.

The Greeks, from whose word meaning 'rock celery' its name derives, used it to adorn their athletics heroes. The plant was introduced, like so much else, to northern Europe by the Romans. Parsley had many virtues ascribed to it as a medicinal plant and was used to treat several diseases, in particular kidney and liver complaints. It is rich in vitamins and a spoonful will make up for a deficiency in fresh vegetables. Best used fresh, although it can be dried. Take care to pinch out the flowering stems if you want the plant to continue in leaf.

THE ONION OR LILIACEAE FAMILY

The family includes the genus *Allium*, all of whose members (around 90 species in Europe) share a similar, familiar pungent odour — many of the wild varieties were used as flavouring by the country people.

Onion (*Allium cepa*) In cultivation since pre-classical times and used both as a vegetable and as a flavouring. The onion family has a chemical element in its composition which, when cooked, can become at least 50 times sweeter than granulated sugar. The sugar caramelizes on a high heat, as in frying, and is very useful in giving colour as well as flavouring to stews and sauces.

Leek (*Allium porrum*) A particularly hardy member of the family, leeks are usually employed as a vegetable. They can also substitute quite satisfactorily in any recipe which calls for either raw or cooked onion. The tender part of the green tops finely sliced can do duty for chives.

Chives (*Allium schoenoprasum*) A miniature onion that forms a compound bulb, each of which has within it a bud. It is the green shoots from these buds that are used as flavouring and decoration.

Garlic (*Allium sativum*) The bulb was cultivated at least as far back as the Greeks and Romans. When first harvested in the spring the plant looks like a juicy white onion. It is not until it has been allowed to dry out (either in the larder or in the ground) that the seeds develop into garlic cloves by absorbing the moisture from the onion-like layers which enclose them. When the process is complete, which will take 2 to 3 weeks, the seed will have grown into a juicy fat clove, and the moisture-filled layers will have been reduced to a fine white protective papery covering. Used in Mediterranean countries as a vegetable as well as a flavouring, garlic when cooked on a gentle heat loses its ferocious strength.

THE CABBAGE OR CRUCIFERAE FAMILY

All the brassicas, including cabbage, cauliflower, turnip, swede, and radish belong to this family, which has the distinction of including no members poisonous to humans. The family also includes such garden flowers as candytuft, alyssum, and wallflowers — pretty cousins to the fierce horseradish.

Mustard (*Brassica alba*)   A native of Europe and Asia, this is a very widespread plant. The flavour only develops when the seed is crushed and then wetted. Its name comes from the Latin *mustum*, grape juice, with which the Romans were wont to mix it into a paste. Its ancient use as a medicinal plant, in poultices, plasters, and baths, was based on its ability to irritate the skin and thus draw blood to the surface.

Horseradish (*Amoracia rusticana*)   A naturalized introduction from the East, horseradish now flourishes in the wild, particularly in waste places. A very popular and pungent seasoning in central Europe, Austria, and Germany, horseradish is at its best used fresh and grated on the diagonal to produce long thin strips — particularly good when stirred into thick or whipped cream in company with its near relation, mustard. Horseradish secretes a volatile oil which is enough of an irritant to be poisonous to livestock.

MISCELLANEOUS HERBS AND SPICES

Bay laurel (*Laurus nobilis*)   An evergreen native of Asia Minor now widely cultivated throughout Europe, the leaves of this tree are used both fresh and dried as a flavouring, particularly in many Mediterranean dishes. Wreaths of bay laurel were awarded as trophies in classical times — hence the modern use of the word 'laureate'.

Caper shrub (*Capparis spinosa*)   The flower buds of this native Mediterranean shrub are blanched and pickled in vinegar for use as a seasoning. In Britain, nasturtium buds are sometimes substituted.

Poppy (*Papaver rhoeas*)   The corn poppy was originally a native of Asia, but is so ancient and accustomed an immigrant in Europe that it grows wild everywhere. Its seeds are used in cakes and pastries and sprinkled whole on breads and rolls, particularly in eastern Europe, where tall mounds of the slate-blue seeds are to be seen on sale in all the autumn markets. The seeds are rich in minerals and, pounded into a paste with eggs and sugar, make a delicious filling for strudel pastries and dumplings. They are also ground down into flour and used, mixed with eggs, to make a nourishing wheat-free and fat-free cake. Today, Holland, gardener to Europe, is the major exporter. The opium poppy is also used for seeds: it is *P. somniferum* whose unripe seed pods are cut to yield the famous narcotic-loaded juice.

Capsicum pepper (*Capsicum annuum* and *C. frutescens*)   These are the two main species: *C. frutescens* is the smaller, hotter variety.

Two principal varieties of paprika are grown in Hungary today: those for drying and powdering, and those to be eaten fresh. 'Green paprika' means the fresh vegetable known as a green pepper (if it is red and ripe, it is called a 'tomato paprika'). In both its forms it can be 'hot' or mild. The hotness lies in the filaments which attach the seeds to the flesh.

The peppers for grinding were traditionally dried in the autumn sunshine, as in many country districts they still are today, hanging in garlands under the eaves of the houses until they are so brittle they click and rustle in the breeze. Then they would be further dried in outdoor ovens. In the old days the peppers would be crushed to a fine powder by being trodden with bare feet over a huge sieve or stone mortar, much as grapes are trodden in a wine press. Later the millers of flour took over the job. Towards the end of the nineteenth century a milling device was invented which could leave out, or control the inclusion of, the 'hot' element of the paprika, capsaicin, and produce the 'noble sweet rose', mild paprika. Thirty years ago a new strain of *Capsicum annuum* was produced which is not naturally fiery, and can be ground up, seeds, filaments, flesh, and all.

Six categories of varying fierceness are available from the paprika merchants of Budapest today, all ground from *Capsicum annuum var.*

lingum Szegedense. They are *Kulonleges*, the most mild; *Edesnemes*, mild; *Feledes*, half mild; *Rozsa*, rose paprika, mild and sweet; and *Eros*, hot paprika.

Fresh ripe peppers contain up to 6 times as much vitamin C per drop of juice as lemons and oranges. They are also plentifully endowed with other good things including vitamin A, the source of carotene — which makes flamingo feathers pink, shrimps blush scarlet, gives the carrot its orange hue, and enables good children who eat up all their vegetables to see in the dark.

Paprika is considered a cure-all by the peasantry, who cultivate it tenderly and prepare it with immense care. It has come in fact to be accorded the same reverence in the European kitchen as it is given in its homeland of Central America. The most effective antidote to the cold winds of the Anatolian plain has long been a shot of brandy with a pinch of hot paprika. Chilli paprika is even sometimes sprinkled on wounds to assist in the healing process.

Peppers contain, by weight, between 6 and 9 times the amount of vitamin C found in tomatoes. Their pepperiness derives from the alkaloid capsaicin, which is to be found mainly in the white tissues to which the seeds are attached. It appears that the substance encourages the secretion of gastric juices. It may also perhaps have an antibacterial effect. The Mexicans believe it essential to a healthy diet in their own country where even the most resilient stomach is notoriously vulnerable — a chilli a day keeps the doctor away.

The almost-universal popularity of chilli is a very odd phenomenon: it is now consumed by more people and in larger quantities than any other spice in history, and it has taken only 4 centuries to reach this preeminence. Recent research suggests that the roots of our passion may lie in the chilli's capacity to trigger the body's warning signals. Reactions such as a running nose, watery eyes, and painful sensations in the mouth would normally tell a human not to eat a particular food. Yet this very warning of danger, albeit denied by the intellect, may well encourage the brain to manufacture endorphins, its own natural (and naturally addictive) opiates. Chilli-devotees may share that lust for excitement which bonds racing drivers, mountaineers, and addicts of all dangerous sports.

Pepper (*Piper nigrum*) Pepper, although a native of India, has been prized in Europe since pre-Roman times. It is the dried fruit of a vine. The black variety is picked unripe, and then fermented and dried in the sun. The white variety is produced by allowing the fruit to ripen to scarlet, and then soaking them in water to loosen the skins, which are rubbed off and the seeds dried. Pepper accounts for one quarter of the world's spice trade.

Saffron (*Crocus sativus*) A native of Asia Minor, saffron has been used certainly since Old Testament days as a dye, food-colourant, and medicine. Today it is still widely employed in Mediterranean cooking particularly with rice. Because 13,000 stigmas go to make 1 oz/25 g saffron, and each crocus can only produce 3 stigmas, the spice, wherever labour is the chief cost, is very expensive indeed and turmeric often replaces it (under the name 'Indian saffron' or, as I saw it recently in Istanbul's spice market, made from marigold petals and labelled 'Mexican saffron'). Saffron was very popular in medieval England, where the aristocracy had a passion for highly coloured food. Great fields of *Crocus sativus* blossomed annually, particularly in East Anglia around the eponymous town of Saffron Walden. In Britain it survives in a cake, and sometimes in recipes for sweet buns. In France it is used to colour and spice fish soups including the famous *bouillabaisse*.

Mushrooms and Fungi

Not all of Europe makes use of its cornucopia of edible fungi. The British are somewhat suspicious of all but the common field mushroom (the variety which is now cultivated). The French, on the other hand, consume a wide variety of theirs, as do the Italians and the Swiss. Yet the real European experts are to be found in the markets of central Europe. A shopping trip for edible fungi on sale by licensed vendors in the markets of Romania and Hungary during the autumn of 1985 yielded the varieties listed below, all of which are native throughout Europe, including the British Isles.

Take great care when collecting your own. As a general rule gather only the ones which are familiar to you. Use a good field guide to make a preliminary identification of new species, but always double-check by taking expert advice before you add them to your basket. The variations caused by sun, rain, temperature, and age can be so wide that the best colour photograph — let alone the usually more accurate painting — is often misleading. The penalties for mistakes can be very heavy. Markets in mushroom-gathering areas, like Budapest's superb food market, normally have an expert on hand to check those which are offered for sale, and to give advice to the buyer. In France pharmacies are a common source of guidance during the mushroom-harvesting season.

Horse mushroom (*Agaricus arvensis*)* Very good eating. Stains yellow and smells of aniseed. Found in pastures from August to November.

Field mushroom (*Agaricus campestris*) Very good eating, this is the original cultivated mushroom. Found in pastures and meadows away

1 Agaricus   2 Boletus   3 Armillaria   4 Cantharellus   5 Craterellus   6 Flammulina
7 Lactarius   8 Lepiota   9 Tricholoma (Lepista)   10 Lycoperdon   11 Marasmium
12 Morchella 13 Pleurotus

from trees from August to November.

Cèpe or **'Penny bun'** (*Boletus edulis*)* Excellent eating. Mostly found in leafy woods, particularly beech. Looks like a shiny brown bun when damp. Found from late July to November.

Honey or **Bootlace fungus** (*Armillaria mellea*)* Good eating, with very rich flavour. This fungus is parasitic on rotten or dead trees — either frondose or conifer. Can be gathered from July to December.

Chanterelle (*Cantharellus cibarius*)* Absolutely delicious. Beautiful apricot-yellow fungi which thrive, half-hidden in fallen leaves and moss, in thick skeins under frondose woods. To be found from July to December.

Horn of Plenty (*Craterellus cornucopioides*)* Excellent eating and dries particularly well. From the same family as the chanterelle whose habitat it shares. This very dark (near black) fungus particularly likes beechwoods. Can be found from August to November.

Winter fungus (*Flammulina velutipes*) Good eating as long as you discard the stems, which are tough. This may explain why they can survive the winter cold and so are available when supplies of the others have finished. Pale yellow gills, with a sticky-looking red-brown cap, winter fungus grows in clumps on the stumps of frondose trees. To be found from September to March.

Saffron milk cap (*Lactarius deliciosus*) Good eating, although not quite as delicious as its name implies. The cap is a bright orange-brown, as are the stipes. It will weep orange tears, so wash its face well before cooking. Can be gathered in conifer woods from August to November.

Parasol mushroom (*Lepiota procera*)* Excellent eating, this mushroom looks not unlike the cultivated field mushroom, but is taller, has a pronounced double ring round the stipe, and a darker shaggy cap and white gills. Find it at the edges and clearings of frondose woods from July to November.

Wood bluett (*Tricholoma nuda*) Both wonderful eating and beautiful to see, this mushroom is tinted a delicate violet. Grows in woods and gardens. Gather from late September to the end of December.

Giant puffball (*Lycoperdon giganteum*) A very large puffball (it can measure 12 in/30 cm in diameter) which makes good eating when young and white. When older its insides disintegrate into dark powdery spores. Find it almost anywhere, in field, garden, or wood, from August to November.

Fairy ring mushroom (*Marasmium oreades*)* Delicate small mushrooms which grow in a ring in short grass — particularly on garden lawns. Can be found from June to November.

Morel (*Morchella esculenta*)* To my mind the most delicious morsel of all. This mushroom has a distinctive wrinkled dark cap attached to a pale stipe. Can be found all over the place, often as solitary specimens.

It likes rich soil — meadows, hedgerows, and grassy banks. Its equally delicious cousin, *M. vulgaris*, grows in woods and gardens. To be gathered in the spring from March to May.

Oyster fungus (*Pleurotus ostreatus*) Excellent eating when young and tender, this fungus grows on decaying wood, particularly beech and sometimes conifers. It has pearly gills and a dark grey-blue cap — which makes it look rather like an inverted oyster shell. Grows all year round.

* These fungi can be dried successfully.

1 lb/500 g fresh mushrooms can always be replaced by 2 oz/50 g dried. dried.

MUSHROOM RICE
(Romania)

Wild mushrooms are used in Romania to flavour soups and stews, and in particular as an addition to a rice pilaf.

Quantity Enough for 4
Time Preparation: 30–40 minutes

8 oz/250 g rice	scant pint/600 ml water
2 oz/50 g streaky bacon	2 oz/50 g butter *or* bacon fat
1 onion with green top *or* without, and with a little bunch of chives	salt and pepper
1 lb/500 g wild *or* failing that, cultivated mushrooms	

Utensils A frying pan and a small saucepan

Pick over the rice. Cube the bacon small. Peel and chop the onion, putting aside the green top with the mushrooms. Fry the bacon in a hot dry frying pan. If you heat the pan first, good bacon (which has not been pumped full of water and saturated with chemicals) will not stick to it. Push the bacon to one side, and turn the onions and the rice in the bacon fat until both are transparent (you may need a little extra fat). Add the water, bring to the boil, and simmer the rice, uncovered, for 20 minutes until all the moisture is absorbed and the rice is tender.

Meanwhile pick over and wipe your treasure-trove of wild mushrooms. A pleasure that will fully occupy the 20 minutes which it takes the rice to become tender if you have a mound of beautiful wild fungi piled on your kitchen table — fresh from the woods, the green moss and autumn leaves still lightly pressed into their scented flesh. The inky-dark Horn of Plenty goes particularly well in this dish. Or its cousin the apricot-scented golden-fleshed chanterelle — don't forget to turn it over and admire the delicate cathedral-vault fluting of its gills. Or make the dish in the spring with the most delicious of all mushrooms, the morel, when its dark wrinkled cap and white stipe share the fields with the first speckled purple orchids of the year — little stubby Beasts among so many Beauties.

Slice your crop of mushrooms and chop the onion leaves which you have saved. Melt the butter in the small pan. Fry the mushrooms in the butter until they are tender. At the last moment, stir in the onion tops or the chives, well chopped. Salt and pepper in moderation.

Mix the mushroom ragout into the warm rice. Heaven will have nothing more to offer.

MUSHROOMS IN OIL AND GARLIC
Champignons à la bordelaise (France)

Use, if you can, the big flat black-gilled field mushrooms. *Cèpes*, penny buns or *Boletus edulis*, are even better. Baskets of *cèpes* are on sale in the markets of Bordeaux from July onwards, and this is the most delicious way of preparing them.

Quantity   Enough for 3 or 4 as a first course
Time   Preparation: 30 minutes

1 lb/500 g flat mushrooms	2 cloves garlic
4–5 tablespoons olive oil	salt and pepper
1 handful parsley	2 oz/50 g fresh breadcrumbs

Utensils   A frying pan

Wipe and slice the mushrooms. Sprinkle them with a tablespoon of olive oil and put them aside. Mince the parsley and crush the garlic. You need plenty of parsley — 4 heaped tablespoons is not too much.

Put the oil to heat in the frying pan. When the oil is warm but not smoking, put in the mushrooms. Cook them gently for a few minutes. Add the garlic and parsley, and allow all to cook together gently for 5 minutes. Season with salt and pepper, and then throw in the bread-crumbs — enough to absorb all the juices. Turn the heat up for a moment. They are done.

Serve the mushrooms piping hot with bread and a red wine from the Loire. Follow on with a plain grilled steak, flanked by thick-cut chips fried golden (in half olive oil, half seed oil, fried twice and drained in between — once to cook the potatoes, once to fry them crisp); and a green salad — a delicate one of *mesclun* leaves (see page 403).

HORN OF PLENTY MUSHROOMS ON TOAST
Croûte aux trompettes de la mort (Switzerland)

The mountains and forests of Switzerland provide fertile territory for fungi, and Swiss mushroom markets are in full swing throughout the autumn. Most farmers have dairy herds to provide the rest of the ingredients. The sinisterly named *trompettes de la mort*, 'last trump', are among the most prized of the crop. The same recipe is equally good with their cousin the chanterelle — and in fact with any of the edible mushrooms, including the fresh morels of springtime.

Quantity   Enough for 4
Time   Preparation: 30 minutes

1 lb/500 g Horn of Plenty *or*
    ordinary mushrooms
3 oz/75 g unsalted butter

salt and pepper
½ pint/300 ml double cream
4 slices day-old bread

Utensils   A frying pan

Wipe the mushrooms and slice off the hard earth tip of the stalk. If they are very large, slice them into strips. Put the butter to heat in the frying pan. When it is frothing (do not allow it to brown), lay in the mushrooms. Season with salt and pepper. Put a large serving dish to warm.

Trompettes and chanterelles need a little longer to cook than the cultivated variety of mushroom. Let them stew gently in their own juices for 10 minutes. Stir in the cream. Allow all to bubble up while you make a large slice of toast for each person.

Put the toast *croûtes* on the warm dish. Pour the bubbling mushrooms and sauce over them and serve immediately. You can sprinkle parsley over, but a good twist of the pepper grinder is more than enough embellishment.

SUGGESTIONS
• Next time, serve them with scrambled eggs. If you make the dish with chanterelles collected in Scotland — say you have been scouring the woods of the Western Isles — then stir in the flesh of a smoked haddock which you have poached in the cream first. Or stir in a few pieces of smoked salmon.

CHANTERELLES WITH BACON
Girolles au lard (France)

This dish comes from the wooded hills below Provence's Mount Ventoux, whose cold peak broods over the fertile Rhône basin and is still covered in snow in high summer. The woods provide plenty of the leaf-mould needed by these beautiful apricot-yellow fungi.

Quantity   Enough for 4 from the autumn woods
Time   Preparation: 30 minutes

1 lb/500 g fresh chanterelles *or*
   ordinary mushrooms
4 oz/100 g smoked streaky bacon
2 oz/50 g butter

1 small onion *or* shallot
small handful parsley
salt and pepper
1 glass white wine

Utensils   A frying pan

Trim and wipe the chanterelles, and slice them if they are large. Cube the bacon small, and melt it gently with the butter in the frying pan.
   Peel and finely chop the onion or shallot. Chop the parsley.
   Add the chanterelles to the pan when the bacon has taken colour and its fat has run. Stir over a gentle heat for a moment. Add the onion and the parsley, salt, pepper, and the wine. Raise the heat and cook fast for 5 minutes. Then turn the heat down and continue the cooking for another 20 minutes, shaking the pan occasionally and checking that it does not boil dry. Serve with fresh crusty bread and a green salad.

STUFFED MILK CAPS
Lactaires delicieux farcis (France)

Good mushrooms for stuffing, these have a rather alarming habit of crying orange tears. The stuffing puts an end to all that. A recipe from the wooded slopes behind the Roman town of Vaison-La-Romaine.

Quantity   Enough for 4
Time   Preparation: 25 minutes
      Cooking: 20 minutes

12 saffron milk cap *or* ordinary
   mushrooms
¼ pint/150 ml olive oil
2 oz/50 g fresh breadcrumbs
4 oz/100 g minced pork *or* chopped
   bacon
1 egg

1 tablespoon chopped parsley
1 clove garlic
1 teaspoon juniper berries
½ teaspoon black peppercorns
freshly milled pepper
4 very fine-cut rashers streaky
   bacon

Utensils   A pestle and mortar and a shallow baking dish

Wipe well and remove the stalks from the milk caps. Leave them to soak in the olive oil while you prepare the stuffing.

Soak the breadcrumbs in a little water and then squeeze them dry. Mash them up with the minced pork, the egg, and the parsley. Crush the peeled garlic with salt, the juniper berries, and peppercorns in a mortar, and then add them to the stuffing. Sprinkle with pepper and mix all well together. Cut each bacon rasher into 3 pieces.

Arrange the milk caps, gills upwards, in the baking dish. Divide the stuffing among them. Lay a square of bacon on each mound of stuffing. Pour the remaining oil over them.

Either cook under the grill, or bake them in a hot oven — 425°F/220°C/ Gas 7 for 20 minutes. Best grilled over a fire of juniper twigs in the open.

Truffles

There are three edible and esteemed European truffles. These tubers are more localized in their distribution than other fungi.

The Perigord truffle, *Tuber melanosporum*, is the true and legendary black truffle, whose price approaches its weight in gold. The tinned version is as ghostly an echo of the fresh tuber as the tinned mushroom of its alter-ego plucked fresh and scented from the field in the morning dew. There is no help for it — if you want to taste the true flavour you will have to find yourself an accommodating pig or a well-trained truffle hound and search out your own in the oak woods of southern France, an activity which would almost certainly bring you into violent conflict with rival hunter-gatherers.

The estimable M Farnoux, hereditary oil-presser to the Provençal village of Mirabelle aux Baronnies and in whose olive mill I have often been a guest, told me that he collected baskets of Perigord truffles as a child in the 1940s. Not to sell, you understand. The family ate the treasure themselves, it being wartime in occupied France, and such isolated communities had to survive on very short commons. He faced no problems with oak trees and truffle-hounds: he had but to walk down the avenue of limes that skirted the olive tree plantations which led from the village to the neighbouring château. There, when his sharp child's eyes spotted a little mound of cracked earth by the tree roots, he would stop. If the mounds had a few little flies attending them, that was the place to dig for the truffle. It would take only a morning for him and his brother to fill their basket. (At today's prices they would swiftly have become Provence's youngest millionaires.)

No fancy cooking was necessary, M Farnoux explained. You had only to roll the truffles, the earth still fresh upon them, into the glowing embers of the wood fire. There they would roast to perfection and need no dressing but a sprinkle of salt. The problem, of course, in those days, he added, was not how to find the black gold — it was how to get the wherewithal to bake a loaf of bread to go with the truffles.

To cook a Perigord truffle — if you are fortunate, knowledgeable, or rich enough for one to come your way — clean off the earth with a little brush. Wipe the truffle, then chop it and scramble it delicately with fine fresh eggs from your own or your neighbour's hens — that is, free-range hens of good pedigree whose eggs have been laid in a country garden. (There is no false mystique about eggs from free-range chickens. Like the grapes of the vine — as every experienced wine-taster knows — eggs pick up the flavours, colours, and scents of the surroundings which produce them.)

Or leave the truffle in the egg basket overnight to perfume the eggs. Then soft-boil the eggs, slice the raw truffle on the cucumber-slicer of the grater, and serve the two together with your best fresh bread.

The creamy-pale Piedmont truffle, *Tuber magnatum*, whose flavour is second only to the black gold of Perigord, should be eaten as nearly raw as possible. Brush off the earth, and then wipe the beech-leaf brown nugget clean with a damp cloth. The truffle does not need to be peeled. Scatter a careless magnificence of fine slivers over home-made pasta or a dish of Italian rice (see page 268), or — best of all — a *fonduta* (see page 483). The truffle season opens in September, and by mid-October it is in full swing. November is the best month of all — by January it is all over.

The cook's truffle, *Tuber aestivum*, which is found in calcareous soil, usually under beech trees, is the commonest species and the variety native to the British Isles. Although it is not as highly esteemed as the others, the seventeenth-century diarist and epicure, John Evelyn, speaks of it warmly and lists Northamptonshire as fertile soil for truffle-hounds. To be cooked in any way suitable for ordinary mushrooms.

TRUFFLE SALAD
Salade aux truffes (France)

A windfall of truffles requires the best of ingredients and simplest of treatments. This recipe is from the olive oil country up the Rhône valley behind Avignon, seat in medieval times of the magnificent Popes-in-exile. The olive growers had their own liquid gold on their trees and black gold in their woods.

Quantity Enough for 6
Time Preparation: 5 minutes

6 black truffles, weighing about
   1 oz/25 g each
3 egg yolks

salt and pepper
juice 1 lemon
1 tablespoon olive oil

Utensils A bowl

Wash and brush the truffles, and slice them finely. Cut the slices across again into matchsticks. Lightly beat together the egg yolks, salt, freshly milled pepper, lemon juice, and olive oil. Turn the truffle matchsticks in this little sauce. Serve with plenty of fresh bread and the best bottle of wine in the house. Perhaps a bottle from the Avignon Pope's own summer stronghold, Châteauneuf du Pape, where the vines grow mysteriously soil-less in fields of golden pebbles.

TRUFFLE AND WALNUT SALAD
Truffes et cernaux (France)

The year's crop of walnuts are still fresh and milky when the truffle season begins. This excellent salad takes advantage of the happy coincidence.

Quantity Enough for 4
Time Preparation: 5 minutes

4 black truffles, weighing 1 oz/25 g
   each
4 lettuce hearts
hazelnut *or* walnut oil

wine vinegar
salt and white pepper
16 fresh walnuts

Utensils A serving dish

Brush, wipe, and finely slice the truffles. Mix with an equal quantity of the palest of lettuce hearts, dressed with a trickle of hazelnut or walnut oil, a few drops of wine vinegar, salt, freshly milled white pepper, and the green walnuts (that is very fresh, still dripping sweet milk when they are cut), scooped from their shells.

Serve with fresh bread.

TRUFFLES WITH POTATOES
Pommes de terre aux truffes (France)

A fine way to make the most of a single truffle.

2 lb/1 kg potatoes
1 small truffle, weighing about
   1 oz/25 g

¼ pint/150 ml double cream
salt and pepper
olive oil

Utensils   A large saucepan, a frying pan, and an earthenware casserole

Scrub and cook the potatoes in their skins in salted water until they are soft, 20 to 25 minutes boiling. Drain them and peel them as soon as they are cool enough to handle. Cut them into thick slices.

Brush and rinse the truffle. Cut it into fine slices.

Preheat the oven to 350°F/180°C/Gas 4.

Put a layer of sliced potatoes in the bottom of the casserole. Pour in some of the cream, and sprinkle with salt and pepper. Lay on a layer of truffle slices, then a layer of potatoes. Continue until all is used up, finishing with a layer of potatoes. Trickle a little olive oil over the top along with the last of the cream.

Cook in the oven for half an hour.

Serve with a light salad and a bottle of white wine from the Rhône valley.

TRUFFLES IN THE ASHES
Truffes sous les cendres (France)

My neighbour in Provence had an easy time-honoured way with his private truffle harvest. He would brush the truffles clean, and then wrap each up in a piece of dough made with flour, water, and a little salt. These nuggets he would put in the warm ashes at the edge of the kitchen fire. Little hot embers would be piled on top. There they would roast for 20 to 30 minutes, until the outside was blackened like an overdone chestnut. A quick turn with his countryman's knife would free the truffle, steaming and fragrant and perfectly cooked, to be eaten with its gritty covering. Here is a more sophisticated version of this ancient dish which, although less innocent, does not take the same risks with the precious ingredients.

Time   Preparation: 10–15 minutes
Cooking: 20–25 minutes

1 black truffle, weighing 1 oz/25 g, per person
salt and pepper
1 thin slice pork fat per truffle

1 oz/25 g pastry (yeast, flaky, short *or* puff) per truffle
1 egg

Utensils   A baking tray

Wipe and brush and rinse the truffles as necessary. Sprinkle each with salt and freshly milled pepper. Wrap each one in a jacket of pork fat.

Preheat the oven to 400°F/200°C/Gas 6.

Roll out a round of pastry for each truffle..You can use a plain bread dough if you beat a little butter into it. Place the jacketed truffle on one side of its pastry circle. Damp the edges of the pastry, and fold the other side over to make a semicircle enclosing the truffle. Put them on the baking tray. Brush with beaten egg.

Bake in the hot oven for 20 to 25 minutes. Serve hot on a clean white napkin. Paradise calls for champagne.

CHAPTER 12

Olive and
Vegetable Oils

Olive Oil

In Tuscany and Provence olives are harvested when almost ripe, throughout November and December. They are taken to be ground (whole — stones and all) into a paste at the local press. Oil is then extracted by centrifugal force to give 'First Pressing, cold pressed' oil. The rest of the pulp is then often sold to a factory, which processes it with heat — to give a more fatty oil with a higher acidity, called the 'Second Pressing'. This oil goes rancid more quickly when exposed to air. The old un-mechanized mills had no facilities for this, and would use the olive pulp as fertilizer or fuel.

Gradings of Italian olive oils are defined by law. The best oil is classified as Extra Virgin and must be below 1% acidity. Second is Soprafino Virgin which is allowed up to 1.5% acidity. Next is Fine Virgin — below 3%. Last is Virgin which can have up to 4%. These oils can be either Cold Pressed, or Hot Pressed and factory rectified.

Olives ripen from green to black, and the first oil of the year is always greener than the last-harvested because the early oil has more vegetable matter which has not had time to settle. If you want to use up this *fondo* of vegetable matter, give the bottle a shake before you pour the oil. Olives are still largely picked by hand — there being no machinery which can cope with the eccentricities of the trees and the crop. Olive oil will keep for many years if sealed in a container of glass, steel, or tin — plastic is no good for long storage — and kept in a cool dark larder. It is reckoned at its best in the first year, and at its healthiest when eaten uncooked, being rich in vitamin A, D, and F, low in saturated fats and high in unsaturated. Many of the recipes of the eastern Mediterranean used olive oil more as a rich juice than as a frying medium.

The olives and oils of different Mediterranean countries are harvested and prepared according to ancient traditions. The Italians make a range of individual *'mis en bouteille au château'* oils, with more leaf, late or early picked olives, and many other factors to differentiate appearance and flavour, specialities which reflect the ancient independence of the Italian farmer. French olive oil is generally of a very high quality, but tends to owe allegiance to cooperative and district rather than individual growers. Spanish olives have a harder soil and a poorer peasantry who often were obliged to sharecrop and turn in their fruits to a central buyer. The Portuguese like their olive oil stronger than the rest of Europe, and allow the fruit to ferment (a matter of hours) before pressing.

Re-seal olive oil carefully after opening, and do not leave it too long before using it up. All fruit juices, and olive oil is exactly that, deteriorate on exposure to air. Small containers are more convenient for this reason.

Other Oils

Corn oil   The staple oil of northern Europe and an introduction from the New World. Good for frying although rather strong flavoured. Somewhat heavy on salads.

Nut oils   Almond oil is produced mainly in Italy and used in sweet making. Walnut and hazelnut are very delicately flavoured oils produced in the central districts of France, usually above the olive-growing line, and used today mainly as salad dressings. In those districts such as Berry in central France, where nut oils were locally produced, they were used for both cooking and industrial purposes. Lid and keep in the refrigerator once opened — these delicious oils do not stay fresh for long.

Poppyseed oil An oil used in eastern Europe, where poppy seeds are used in cooking and flavouring. A good salad and cooking oil.

Pumpkin oil A dark, delicate oil mostly home-milled all over eastern Europe. The pumpkins are allowed to ripen to near-rottenness so that the seeds are fully developed. Then in early September, local peasant housewives will spend all day out in the fields cutting the fruit open and scooping the seeds into trays for drying in the late sun. The pumpkin flesh is then carted back to the steading, mashed, stored, and used as cattle fodder throughout the winter. The oil is much prized for salads and cake making.

Rapeseed oil Various members of the colza or rape plant, a member of the cabbage family. The familiar sunshine yellow plants of *Brassica napus* spread bright sheets of colour across the fields of Europe.

Sunflower oil The favourite oil of Romania and Bulgaria, this oil is made from the seeds of the beautiful giant sunflower. An excellent all-purpose oil.

SALAD DRESSING
Vinaigrette (France)

This is the universal classic oil and vinegar dressing for salads. Mix 3 tablespoons of olive oil with 1 tablespoon wine vinegar, and add salt and freshly ground pepper to taste. This proportion can be varied in many ways: replace the vinegar with lemon juice; include chopped fresh herbs in the mix; mash in the yolks of 2 hard-boiled eggs. Add the oil gradually to a tablespoon of mild French mustard mixed with the vinegar, much as if making a mayonnaise, to produce a thick emulsified sauce — good for a marinated salad such as the one made with fine strips of celeriac which is to be bought in all French charcuteries.

MAYONNAISE/MAYONESA
(France/Spain)

The origins of the classic cold sauce of south-western Europe are shrouded in the usual swirls of mist and controversy. Carême made a strong case for its derivation from the word *manier*, to work by hand. Others suggest it may have come from the ancient Languedoc verb *mahonner* meaning to tire, precisely as in the modern French use of *fatiguer*, to tire a salad. The residents of Mahon, Menorca's chief port, offer the theory that the recipe made its way into the kitchens of France after the Duc de Richelieu captured the strategically important

Menorcan port of Mahon from the English. Whatever the origins of the 'butter of the south', mayonnaise is very simple to make, and the ingredients are immediately to hand in all Mediterranean countries, available to rich and poor alike.

Quantity   Makes enough for 4
Time   Preparation: 20 minutes

  2 egg yolks
  ½ pint/300 ml olive oil
  2 tablespoons white wine vinegar
      or the juice ½ lemon
  salt

Utensils   A bowl, a small jug, a fork or whisk, and a wooden spoon

Make sure both the egg yolks and the olive oil are at room temperature. The mixture will not emulsify if the 2 major ingredients are not agreeable to each other. Pour the oil into a small jug, and pour the egg yolks, the vinegar or lemon, and the salt into the bowl. Beat them together thoroughly with a fork or a whisk. Whisking constantly, trickle the oil drop by drop into the egg. The oil is added to the yolk, rather than the other way round, because the yolk is the emulsifier which needs to coat each particle of oil — an easier job if it starts out as the dominant ingredient. Continue thus until a quarter of the oil has been absorbed, then change to a wooden spoon and speed up the rate of flow. At this stage you should not beat too hard, and as the mixture thickens, so you may pour the oil in faster. When the mayonnaise is beautifully shiny and stiff enough for your purposes, it is ready. If you keep it in the refrigerator, the oil will leak. The same thing happens if you put it on hot food. Should the emulsion separate and go liquid again, start with a new egg yolk in a fresh bowl, and add the curdled mixture to it as slowly as at the beginning.

   This sauce is one of the few which is far better done by hand. Mayonnaise made in a liquidizer will not be the same — it will be good, but it is a different sauce. This is because the action of the blades is too rapid and consistent for the oil to emulsify properly with the egg yolks alone, so the sauce has to be made with whole eggs or it will not stabilize. This inclusion of the whites gives a lighter, pale sauce, without the rich heaviness of the true mayonnaise, which can be thickened so solid that it will cut like soft butter.

SUGGESTIONS

● *Salsa mayonesa* is used in Spain to sauce their excellent grilled or baked fish — particularly the larger white-fleshed species such as the

Spaniard's favourite *merluza*, hake, which is sold whole or chopped into thick steaks, and a speciality claimed by the fishermen of the Straits of Gibraltar, *urta*, a large and delicious member of the bream family.

● Potato salads and salads of chopped vegetables (*picadilla* or *ensalada rusa*), both generously blanketed with *salsa mayonesa*, have their place in every *tapa* bar.

● In France *mayonnaise* is the glory of Provençal cuisine, and is used almost as if it were butter.

AIOLI GARNI
(France)

This dish is really an excuse to eat the *aioli* sauce itself. It is interesting to compare the recipe with the Greek *skordalia*, bearing in mind the early Greek presence on the Mediterranean seaboard of France. The first pressings of the year's olives are available by early December in Provence, when the oil is fresh and strong and green, just in time for the Christmas Eve fasting dish of *aioli garni*. Although not complicated to prepare, it is at its best with a wide selection of ingredients — and it is this which makes it festive.

Quantity   Enough for 8
Time   Start 48 hours before if you are using salt cod
Preparation: 1½–2 hours

The garnish   Prepare the accompaniments first. You will then be clear-minded and relaxed for the preparation of the sauce. The *aioli* mayonnaise (see following recipe) is so rich that its background must be as simple as possible. The constrasting colours of the pale creamy fish, and the green, red, and gold of the vegetables and eggs look their best on a handsome white serving dish. Include 4 elements in the *aioli* garnish (weights are very approximate, since you can include more or less of each).

All are to be plainly and perfectly cooked. Here's how to prepare them, in descending order of cooking time (if you are using salt cod, see the fish entry and remember you will have to put it to soak at least the day before you need it).

The meat   (Omit if it is to be a fast-day dish.) A small shoulder of lamb (the best and sweetest joint for this dish) to be cooked in its own juices. Wipe the joint and sprinkle it with salt, pepper, and a few sprigs of rosemary and thyme. Wrap it thoroughly in foil. Put it to cook in a medium oven — 350°F/180°C/Gas 4 — for 1 to 1½ hours (allow 20 minutes per 1 lb/500 g).

The vegetables Choose 4 lb/2 kg mixed vegetables. Small potatoes, scrubbed but not peeled, will take 20 minutes in boiling salted water. If you can only find old potatoes, scrub them even more thoroughly and then boil them in their skins in plenty of salted water — start them in cold water, and time the cooking from the moment the water boils. They will take 20 to 30 minutes to be quite soft (depending on the size of the tubers, which should be more or less even in size). Drain the potatoes as soon as they are ready, and then shake them over the heat for a moment to dry them.

Sweet potatoes, peeled and cut in slices and poached in salted water for 30 minutes.

Artichokes, trimmed and washed and cooked in boiling salted water acidulated with a squeeze of lemon. They will take 20 to 30 minutes, depending on size. They are done when a leaf pulls away easily from the base.

Young carrots and turnips, topped and tailed and scrubbed. They will take 15 to 20 minutes in boiling salted water. If you can only find old vegetables, peel them and quarter them lengthwise before you put them to cook.

Cauliflower, divided into florets. Cook briefly, so that the stalks stay slightly crisp, in boiling salted water for 5 minutes maximum.

Green beans, topped and tailed and plunged into boiling salted water for 3 to 4 minutes only.

Raw tomatoes, cut into quarters.

The fish Choose 2 lb/1 kg fish. Cod is usually included in an *aioli garni* — if fresh, it is cut in thick steaks or fillets. Poach the fish in a simmering pan of half-milk, half-water, flavoured with a slice of onion, a bayleaf, half a teaspoon salt and some peppercorns. It will only need 5 to 6 minutes to be perfectly cooked. Drain carefully.

You can use well-soaked dried cod if you wish, in which case cut it into neat portions and put it to soak for 48 hours, changing the water frequently. Poach the soaked fish in half-milk, half-water, perfumed with a bayleaf and a few peppercorns for 10 minutes. Drain.

The sea snails Put them to soak in clear water with a handful of salt for an hour or two, so that they spit out as much as possible of their sand. Simmer them in boiling water with salt, peppercorns, and a spoonful of vinegar for 20 minutes.

The eggs Allow 1 egg per person, and an extra one for the unexpected visitor (a Provençal family expects a stranger on Christmas Eve). Boil the eggs for 8 minutes exactly if they are large — less if they are small. As soon as they are ready plunge them immediately into cold water. Peel the shell off as soon as the eggs are cool enough to handle. Use the best eggs you can find — the brighter the yolks and the snowier the whites the better.

AIOLI
(France)

This garlic mayonnaise is the glory of Provence. All the ingredients should be at room temperature to allow them to emulsify properly.

Quantity   1 pint/600 ml oil will sauce 8 servings
Time   Preparation: 15 minutes

1 pint/600 ml olive oil
10 cloves garlic
½ teaspoon salt
1–2 egg yolks (depending on the
    size of the eggs)

juice 1 lemon
1 tablespoon warm water

Utensils   A jug, a bowl, and a pestle and mortar

Pour the oil into the jug. Peel the cloves of garlic and put them into the bowl with the salt. Pound the garlic and salt together with the pestle until you have a thick paste. Pound in the egg yolk. In Provence you would have a small marble mortar for this job.

Never ceasing to work the mixture, drip in the oil quite slowly. When you have added about 4 spoonfuls of oil, stir in the lemon juice and the water. Trickle in the rest of the oil, beating without pause. Watch carefully as the sauce thickens and add a little more water if the emulsion shows signs of separating. The egg and the vegetable matter both act as emulsifiers of the oil — the making of a mayonnaise is a magical process.

Should such a disaster as the sauce splitting befall you, don't worry. It happens so frequently the French have a special phrase for its redress — *relever l'aioli*, 'revive the *aioli'*. Empty the split mixture out of the bowl, and put in another egg yolk and a few drops of lemon juice. Slowly add the split mixture to the fresh yolk. As surely as night follows day, it will thicken.

SUGGESTIONS

• Of course you can reduce the quantity of garlic if you wish. However, bear in mind that J.-B. Reboule, the great French authority on Provençal cooking, suggests 2 cloves per person, which would bring the tally up to 16 for this particular party.

• The egg yolk can be replaced or supplemented by a boiled mashed potato or a crust of dry bread. Some authorities suggest replacing one of the yolks in a 2 pint/1.2 litre *aioli* with one hard-boiled egg yolk.

• The garlic mayonnaise can be made in the liquidizer — then you will have to use a whole egg, and the mixture will be paler and lighter.

• My household has a passion for garlic and will stir this beautiful sauce into any and all broth-soups whether of fish, vegetable, or chicken, and eat it in sandwiches or with fresh raw vegetables. All the ingredients should be at room temperature to allow them to emulsify successfully.

• The sauce is delicious served with *crudités* as prepared for *Bagna caouda*.

VEGETABLE FONDUE
Bagna Caouda (Italy)

This is a very ancient recipe which has long been popular both in Piedmont, and around Nice in Provence, where the Italian influence is strong. It is basically a fondue of vegetables. The combination of ingredients has its roots in a far older tradition of a pocket-meal, to be taken out into the fields as a midday break of bread basted with olive oil, a pickled fish, and a few fresh raw vegetables.

Quantity　Enough for 6 for a light meal
Time　Preparation: 20–30 minutes

For the fondue
2 small tins salted anchovies *or* 12 fresh fillets
2 slices dry bread
2 tablespoons milk *or* cream *or* water
2–3 cloves garlic
½ teaspoon salt
2 pints/1.2 litres olive oil

For the vegetables
12 oz/350 g vegetables per person, chosen from:
bulb fennel — washed and separated into bite-sized segments
celery — washed and cut into short lengths
chicory — quartered just before you put it out
lettuce — more or less separated into leaves (if the heart is tight, cut
　　the whole lettuce into eights just before serving)
radishes — scrubbed and quartered
tiny artichokes — quartered
young carrots — scrubbed and topped (older ones will have to be
　　peeled and quartered lengthwise)
cauliflower and broccoli — separated into florets
baby turnips — rinsed and quartered
very fresh cultivated mushrooms

Utensils   A small saucepan and a stand with a spirit lamp or night light in it — a fondue arrangement, in fact, and a pestle and mortar or food processor

Drain the anchovies. You can buy them loose from a barrel in the delicatessen, but then they will need a preliminary soaking of half an hour in milk to get rid of excess salt. Crumble the bread and put it to soak in the milk, cream, or water for a few minutes. Squeeze out the excess liquid.

Peel and crush the garlic with the salt in the mortar. Add the anchovies and the bread, and pound them thoroughly with the garlic. Easy to do if you have a food processor.

Prepare a large flat plate of the raw vegetables. Arrange them as carefully as you would a bowl of flowers. Set it out on the table. Provide each guest with a plate, a large napkin, and two forks, one to stir the vegetables in the hot oil, and the other to eat with, for fear they will burn their lips with the hot fork used for frying.

Put the fondue and the olive oil into the small saucepan, which you can put on the table and keep hot on the stand over the tiny spirit lamp or night lamp. The Italians can buy a purpose-built neat little earthenware casserole which has a space for a candle beneath rather like a fondue set.

Bring the oil and fondue to the boil, stirring thoroughly. When it is hot but not smoking, call your guests and put the saucepan over its flame on the table. Each guest then spears a piece of vegetable and swirls it around in the hot bath.

Flank the dishes with plenty of fresh bread, and perhaps a plate of raw ham or salami and a fine piece of cheese for those who hanker after something more substantial. Make sure there is plenty of wine to cool throats after the hot salty sauce.

BRINED GREEN OLIVES
Aceitunas en escabeche (Spain)

The dry pale unfortified sherry wines of Jerez and Montilla are at their best partnered by the roughly cracked, garlic-scented green olives prepared in the little *cortijos* or farmhouses of Andalusia. A pleasure to be savoured under the silvery leaves of an ancient grove, the twisted roots of the olive trees lapped by the red earth of the Serranía de Ronda. The first fresh olives, freckled bright emerald, begin to appear in the markets in October, ready to be pickled for Christmas. Later in the harvest they ripen and darken to a full soft plum. The first bitter green ones are the most appreciated in sherry country.

Quantity   Enough for a small family's storecupboard
Time   Start 3–4 weeks before
         Preparation: 30–40 minutes

4 lb/2 kg green olives	1 tablespoon dried oregano
8 oz/250 g salt	1 small bunch dried thyme
8 pints/5 litres water	1 tablespoon fennel stalks
2 lemons	2 whole heads garlic

Utensils   A deep earthenware crock and a wooden board

Spread the olives out on the kitchen table, and pick out any shrivelled ones and odd bits of leaf and stalk. Hit each one with a small hammer or heavy rolling pin, so that the flesh cracks although the olive remains intact. Put all the crushed olives into the deep crock and cover them with fresh water. Leave them to soak for a week, changing the water every 2 days. These little green olives are very bitter — if you taste the water, you will find it gets progressively milder as it is changed.

At the end of a week, drain out all the water. Make a brine by dissolving the salt in the water and pour it over the olives. They should be completely submerged. Add the herbs and the lemons chopped into chunks. Hold the whole head of garlic over a flame and char it (the scent is wonderfully evocative of Spanish peasant kitchens). Put the garlic in with the olives. Cover with a wooden board.

Ready to use in 2 to 3 weeks. The olives become progressively less bitter as the year wears on. If they begin to ferment a little (the olive, after all, is a fruit), change the brine — they will not keep indefinitely.

SUGGESTIONS
● In Seville, very bitter little oranges, unpeeled but quartered, are used to flavour the olives.
● If you cannot obtain fresh olives, drain a tin or two of brined green ones and put them to marinate for a few days in a jar with fresh olive oil, a clove of garlic sliced, a few sprigs of thyme, and a chopped whole lemon. But look out for the fresh ones — they are much more interesting than the bland commercially prepared variety.

PICKLED BLACK OLIVES
Olives noires piquées (France)

The Farnoux household, millers to the olive growers of Nyons in the Baronnies of Provence, pickle only the largest and most perfect of the fully mature black olives. M Farnoux' position as proprietor of the most ancient olive press in the Baronnies allows him to be very selective in these matters. The olives are put to soak out the bitterness in a brine made with a handful of salt — about 4 oz/100 g — to each 2 pints/1.2 litres water. Each household in the area had such a brine pot, topped up annually so that it covered the new olives, with a few bayleaves added when needed, but the liquid itself was not changed from year to year. That water, say the locals, was sometimes a hundred years old, dark and oily and rich, and it pickled the olives as sweetly as honey.

There were those who liked their olives green. Such olives would need to be layered first in wood ash to draw the bitterness. In the old days whole families would turn out for the olive harvest, and the women would climb up the trees to pick the ripe fruit, with a basket slung round their neck and a shawl over their heads and backs to protect them from the dark ripe juice. It was always the largest olives, either unripe and green, or ripe and black, which were kept for pickling. The burghers of Nyons offer instructions for the preparation of their treasure.

4 lb/2 kg black olives	3 bayleaves
salt	3 cloves garlic
2 tablespoons olive oil	

Olives picked in the fullness of their maturity must be left in a basket on the windowsill to take the frost for 3 to 4 nights. When they have been well frozen, take them indoors and prick them all over with a fork or with a cork set with pins. Rub them with fine salt and toss them in a basket 3 or 4 times a day for a week. After that mix them with a little pure olive oil and some peeled cloves of garlic roughly chopped. Pack them into an earthenware jar for storage. Tuck in the bayleaves.

CAPER AND OLIVE PASTE
Tapenade (France)

An olive paste from the kitchens of Provence, today made in quantity by millers such as M Farnoux. J.-B. Reboule, writing at the end of the nineteenth century, records *tapenade* as a restaurant invention from the Maison Dorée at Marseilles. It did, however, catch the imagination of the Provençaux who now use it as their own. Salted capers, anchovies, and tuna were all sold straight from the barrel by weight in M Reboule's day. The tuna was a far greater luxury than the anchovies. The capers are the nominate ingredient: *tapeno* means caper in the patois, although the modern version relies more heavily on the olives than did the original.

Quantity Makes about 1 lb/500 g *tapenade*
Time Preparation: 20 minutes

8 oz/250 g black olives
2 oz/50 g (1 small tin) anchovy fillets
2 oz/50 g (1 small tin) brined tuna fish
2 oz/50 g (2 small jars) capers

¼ pint/150 ml good olive oil
1 teaspoon brandy
a good powdering freshly milled black pepper
1 teaspoon strong English mustard

Utensils A pestle and mortar or a food processor and a pot with a lid

Drain and store the olives. Drain the anchovy fillets (salted ones from a barrel will have to be soaked in milk for 30 minutes first). Drain the tuna and the capers.

Pound all the solid ingredients together to a fine paste in the mortar. Trickle in the olive oil, beating as for a mayonnaise. Stir in the brandy. Or conserve your strength and put the whole lot in the food processor. Pot and cover tightly.

SUGGESTIONS
• Serve the paste as a garnish with hard-boiled eggs cut in half lengthwise, with a little of the *tapenade* mashed into the egg yolks which are then replaced in their whites. Trickle olive oil over all, and serve with a green salad and a tomato salad and plenty of hot fresh bread. This is a light lunch which will leave room for a fruit tart (see page 538).

OLIVE SAUCE
Riste (France)

A sauce from Vaison-La-Romaine in the hills above the Rhône valley. The town was an elegant spa resort in Roman times and this preparation dates back to then. The Romans liked it with fried fish.

Quantity Enough for 4 (this is a pungent little sauce which goes a long way)
Time   Preparation: 20 minutes
        Cooking: 20 minutes

2 oz/50 g black olives
1 onion
3 cloves garlic
1 large tomato *or* 2 small ones
2 tablespoons olive oil

1 tablespoon flour
1 glass red wine
1 glass water
thyme, parsley, and a bayleaf
1 tablespoon capers

Utensils A small saucepan

Pit the olives and chop them roughly. Peel and chop the onion. Peel and crush the garlic. Pour boiling water over the tomato to loosen the skin, then peel and chop the flesh.

Put the oil to warm on a low heat and then throw in the onion and garlic. Sprinkle in the flour and fry all gently until it takes a little colour. Put in the tomato and then the water and wine. Add the aromatics. Leave it all over a gentle heat to simmer until it reduces to half its volume.

Stir in the olives and capers. You should need no extra salt. Serve with fried fish. It goes well with lightly boiled vegetables too.

POOR MAN'S POLENTA
Polenta povera (Italy)

A delicious and simple dish from Italy which takes advantage of those ingredients most easily available to the poorer peasant. The flavour is best if the stones are left in the olives — but beware not to crack your teeth on them.

Quantity   Enough for 4
Time   Start a few hours before
     Preparation and cooking: 30 minutes

2 oz/50 g black olives	1½ pints/1 litre water
2 oz/50 g green olives	1 tablespoon olive oil
8 oz/250 g *polenta* (roughly ground cornmeal)	

Utensils   A saucepan, a wooden spoon, a deepish mould, and a frying pan if you wish to fry the *polenta* at the end

Rinse excess salt off the olives and set them aside. Put the *polenta* in the saucepan with the water. Bring all to the boil and then turn down the heat. Simmer gently for 30 minutes, stirring all the while with a wooden spoon. *Polenta* is a terrible sticker. At the end of the cooking time, stir in the olives. Mix well, taste, and add salt only if necessary.

Oil the mould and pour in the *polenta*. Allow it to cool before turning it out. Serve either as it is, cut in slices, with a tomato and fennel salad, or fry the slices in a little olive oil, and serve with a green salad. Delicious with a tomato sauce spiked with chilli pepper, or the olive sauce (see above).

CHAPTER 13

Eggs, Dairy, and Cheese

Savoury Egg Dishes

SOFT-BOILED EGGS
Oeufs à la coque and *Oeufs mollets* (France)

The French way to boil eggs. Do not refrigerate eggs — it is not necessary for their freshness, and it makes them not only liable to crack when you put them into boiling water but it also lowers the temperature of the water too much. If the eggs have been refrigerated, allow them to come up to room temperature before you start. A perfectly soft-boiled egg is a nice-run thing.

Quantity   Allow 2 eggs per person

Bring a large pan of water to the boil. When it is boiling slip in the eggs. Cover the pan and leave the eggs to simmer for 3 to $3\frac{1}{2}$ minutes, depending on the size of the eggs. This will give you a soft-set white and a runny yolk.

If you leave the eggs in for $1\frac{1}{2}$ minutes longer, this will give you *oeufs mollets*. Plunge them immediately into cold water and then peel them — the whites will be firm and the yolks still soft. Serve with a cheese sauce, creamed vegetables or with a vegetable stew. There are a great many dishes which require *oeufs mollets* — nicest served with the Hollandaise sauce which follows.

SUGGESTIONS
- Hard-boiled eggs will need 8 to 10 minutes, depending on size. Do not leave them longer or the whites will be leathery and the yolk will turn grey-green at the edges.
- Successful truffle hunters in France sometimes leave a black Perigord truffle in a basket of fresh eggs overnight. The scent of the fresh truffle is pungent enough to perfume the eggs. These are then soft-boiled or scrambled the following day, allowing the frugal folk to eat their truffle and sell it in the market too.

HOLLANDAISE SAUCE
(Huguenot Dutch)

Sauce hollandaise, or Dutch sauce, appears first in the household books of Huguenot refugees who fled to Holland in 1685 to escape religious persecution in the wake of the revocation of the Edict of Nantes. Many of the refugee families came from the south of France, from the

Protestant strongholds of the Languedoc and Provence, olive oil country, where Huguenot housewives were used to preparing egg-and-oil sauces such as *aioli* and mayonnaise.

Holland, flat land of fertile pastures and dairy herds, had only good sweet butter to offer in place of the oil. The resourceful Huguenots needed to make but minor adaptations to their recipe to produce the delicious *sauce hollandaise*. A recipe for 'Dutch Sauce: An Easy Way', appears in the household book of Charlotte du Cane, who married William Garnham Luard in 1845. The family lived in Essex, within easy access of their relations who had settled in Holland. Contemporary English versions incidentally usually begin with a white sauce.

> Put two tablespoons of boiling water with pepper and salt into a small saucepan. Stir into it four ounces of fresh butter melted, and whisk in the yolks of two eggs. Place this first saucepan into a second saucepan which is half filled with cold water. Put it on a moderate fire, stirring the contents of the inner saucepan without cease. When the water in the outer saucepan boils, the sauce will be thickened enough. Finish with lemon juice.

If you make your *sauce hollandaise* in the liquidizer, replace the 2 egg yolks with 1 whole egg. Egg yolks will split. Serve with a dish of *oeufs mollets*.

SCRAMBLED EGGS
(England)

The earliest cooked eggs were probably simply roasted in the embers of the fire. Perhaps some enterprising Ancient Briton one day solved the problem of a cracked shell by mixing up the contents with a twig and cooking the result.

Quantity Enough for 4, allowing 2 eggs per person
Time Preparation: 10 minutes

8 eggs	2 tablespoons milk
salt and pepper	2 oz/50 g butter

Utensils A bowl and a small saucepan

Break the eggs into the bowl and beat them to a froth with salt and freshly milled black pepper. Add the milk and beat the mixture some more.

Melt the butter gently in the small pan — the butter should only melt, not take colour. Roll it round the pan. Tip in the egg mixture. Stir constantly with a wooden spoon over a low heat while the eggs thicken. They will form soft curds on the bottom of the pan, and this is what you must scrape into the rest of the liquid. When they are on the point of setting but still runny, take them off the heat. Give a final stir.

They must be served at once, accompanied by hot toast or fresh bread. At their best in the company of crisp-fried thin rashers of smoked streaked bacon, or smoked haddock cooked in milk.

SUGGESTIONS
● If you have managed to acquire a truffle (only the cook's truffle, *Tuber aestivum*, is native to Britain), clean it and chop it and fry it in the butter before you add the eggs.

OMELETTE
(France)

The French omelette is served *baveuse* — a wonderfully onomatopoeic adjective to describe the juicy froth which remains enfolded at its tender heart. Make each omelette individually.

Quantity   Enough for 1 omelette

2 eggs
salt and pepper
a nugget of butter

Utensils   A small, iron omelette pan — cheap thin ones are the best. If they are made of raw iron such as those available in the marketplaces of the Mediterranean, they will need to be tempered first. Do this by overheating a tablespoon of oil in the new pan until it is smoking. Throw in a handful of salt and heat the pan again. When it is smoking some more, take a pad of newspaper and polish the surface well with the hot salt. Wipe out the salt and polish the pan with fresh paper.

Put the plates to warm before you begin. They should not be too hot or the omelette will start to cook again.

Whisk the eggs together vigorously with a pinch of salt and a few turns of the peppermill. When they are well mixed and frothy, put a small nugget of butter in the omelette pan to melt. Move it round the pan as it does so. When it is good and hot and foamy but has not changed colour, tip in the eggs. Hold the handle with one hand and the fork with the other. Move the eggs as they cook, pulling them away from the base of the pan in soft creamy curds, much as if you were scrambling them.

When the curds are forming but still frothy stop moving it so that a skin can form on the base. Drop an extra piece of cold butter on the froth. Fold one third of the omelette over the middle third. Tip the omelette on to the waiting warm plate, folding it over the open third as you do so, to give a plump oblong bolster, set and slightly browned on the outside, and *baveuse* within. The cooking should take no more than 2 to 3 minutes.

SUGGESTIONS

● Mix some chopped fresh herbs in to the eggs before you start the cooking for an *omelette fines herbes*.
● Or sprinkle the soft surface of a plain omelette with chopped ham or grated cheese just before you fold it.
● Or fill it with a tablespoon of something delicious in a creamy sauce — French cookery books have plenty of suggestions. Mushrooms in cream are particularly good.
● A plain mushroom omelette can be made by stirring into the beaten eggs a few chopped mushrooms which have been sautéed first in butter. The fillings in a French omelette are always cooked before they are folded in.
● Try a spoonful of fresh tomato sauce laid on to the *baveuse* centre before you fold the omelette over and serve it.

ITALIAN CHEESE OMELETTE
Frittata con pecorino (Italy)

The Italians make their omelettes flat, cooked through, not juicy or *baveuse* as the French omelette should be. The filling is usually fried in the pan first and then the egg is poured round it into the hot oil. This version made with cheese is particularly delicious.

Quantity Enough for 2
Time Preparation: 20 minutes

2 tablespoons olive oil	4 eggs
4 slices fresh pecorino cheese	salt and pepper

Utensils A small frying pan — one used just for omelettes is best

Heat the olive oil in the pan. Lay the slices of cheese in the oil when it is smoking lightly. Fry them swiftly to melt them, turning once.

Meanwhile beat the eggs up with the salt and pepper. When the cheese is melted and beginning to crisp at the edges, pour the eggs round the slices. Turn up the heat and cook till set on top. Slide the *frittata* out on to a plate and reverse it back into the hot pan. Cook the other side for a moment or two. Serve immediately, with fresh bread and cold white wine. Accompany with a green salad, dressed with olive oil and a squeeze of lemon.

SUGGESTIONS
- A strong cheese which melts well — such as Gruyère or a mature Cheddar can be used instead of the pecorino.
- Make the *frittata* with tiny green artichokes, sliced vertically across the 'choke' in thin slivers. Cook them quickly in the hot oil before the eggs are poured round.
- Make the *frittata* with sliced rings of salami, or *prosciutto*, or black pudding, all fried until crisp in the oil before you add the eggs.
- Or make it with slices of onion or fresh garlic.
- Very good served with a fresh tomato sauce.

PEASANT OMELETTE
Bauernomelett (Germany)

A particularly good breakfast or light supper dish.

Quantity   Enough for 4–6
Time   Preparation: 20 minutes
          Cooking: 20–30 minutes

2 lb/1 kg old potatoes	6 eggs
1 lb/500 g onions	salt and pepper
4 oz/100 g streaky bacon	chives

Utensils   A saucepan and a frying pan

Boil the potatoes in their skins in plenty of boiling salted water. This will take 20 to 30 minutes depending on size. Peel them as soon as they are cool enough to handle and slice them. Slice the onions and chop the bacon.

Fry the bacon gently in its own fat (you may need a little extra lard). Add the onions and potatoes and fry until golden.

Meanwhile lightly beat the eggs together and season them. When the potatoes are ready, pour the egg over and around them. Cook until set.

Serve the omelette without turning it out, in its pan, sprinkled with chives. Complete a light supper with a salad of lettuce, and a glass of milk curds.

SPANISH POTATO OMELETTE
Tortilla española (Spain)

Eggs are the great standby of the Spanish kitchen. Hard-boiled eggs with mayonnaise (a Spanish invention, it appears, from the island of Menorca) do duty on the *tapa* counter, but the Spaniards love their potato omelette, a thick, juicy, fragrant egg-cake, best of all. Other folded omelettes are designated 'French'. Whatever other culinary skills she may lack, every Spanish country girl makes a beautiful *tortilla*. It is served hot, cold, or just warm (the best temperature for it), at any meal. It is good provender for the field worker; schoolchildren take a portion, wrapped carefully in a square of sugar-paper for their lunch, toothless old grannies live on it; it is served, cut into small neat squares speared with a toothpick, as a *tapa* in every bar from Cadiz to Bilbao.

Quantity   Enough for 4 as a main course
Time   Preparation: 30 minutes

2 lb/1 kg potatoes (1 large potato per egg)	¼ pint/150 ml olive oil
	6 eggs
1 large Spanish onion (*or* 2 smaller ones)	salt

Utensils   An 8 in/20 cm frying pan (in Spain, a thin iron pan is kept well oiled for this duty), a bowl, a perforated spoon, and a metal spatula

Peel and cut the potatoes into slices or fat chips. Peel and chop the onion. Put the oil to heat in the pan. Fry the potatoes and the onion gently in the oil. They should soften, but not take colour. Transfer the potatoes and onion to the bowl.

Beat the eggs lightly with a little salt and add them to the potato and onion mixture. Pour most of the oil out of the pan, leaving only a tablespoon or two, heat it again and tip in the egg mixture. Fry gently until the eggs begin to look set. The heat should be low or the base will burn before the eggs are ready. As it cooks, neaten the sides with the spatula to build up a deep straight edge to the *tortilla*. When it looks firm, slide it out on to a plate. A little more oil in the pan may be necessary. Invert the *tortilla* back into the pan to cook the other side. Drain well.

Serve warm, cut in wedges for a main meal, or into squares for *tapas*. If it is to be for a light supper, accompany it with a salad of chopped cos lettuce, chunks of tomato and cucumber, and slices of mild purple Spanish onions, all dressed with olive oil, wine vinegar, and salt.

SUGGESTIONS
• Add chopped raw Spanish ham, *jamón serrano*, a little chopped *chorizo* or dried sausage, and a handful of cooked green beans, peas and chopped green peppers to the mixture (leave out one of the potatoes) to make a juicy *tortilla paisana* or peasant omelette.

FRIED EGGS
Huevos fritos (Spain)

This very simple meal can be excellent if made with fresh free-range eggs and pure olive oil. The better the ingredients, the better the dish.

Quantity   2 eggs per person
Time   2–3 minutes per egg

olive oil
rough salt

Utensils   A small shallow frying pan and a perforated spoon

Make one fried egg at a time. Crack one egg into a cup. Pour enough oil into the frying pan to give a depth of one finger. Heat the oil until a faint blue smoke rises. Tip the pan to one side on the heat, so that you have a deep pool of oil. Slide the egg into the hot oil and fry swiftly, spooning hot oil over the top and tucking the edges over to make a little round cake. The edges should crisp into a light golden frill, the white set just firm, and the yolk still runny. Sprinkle with rough salt and serve immediately.

Accompany with a dish of the large sweet Spanish tomatoes (imported as 'beef' tomatoes) fried with a little garlic, and a plate of fried green peppers. The green peppers sold in Spain for this purpose are a long green variety with thin flesh — they cook quickly and are best when slightly charred.

SUGGESTIONS
• Also delicious served with *migas*, diced dry bread soaked and fried with or without bacon.
• Serve with rice (cooked in the Spanish manner, where the rice grains are first lightly fried in oil before liquid is added), a sauce made of fresh tomatoes stewed with a little oil and garlic and then puréed. A little sugar helps imported tomatoes which have been picked before their time.
• The Italians use double quantities of oil to deep fry their eggs, turning them over halfway through to produce a neat crisp patty.

EGGS WITH HAM
Huevos al plato con jamón (Spain)

A favourite instant meal or a first course for the heavy midday meal, which is usually taken around two in the afternoon and is followed by the famous *siesta*. Spaniards lunch prodigiously well if they can, and have a relatively light supper.

Quantity Enough for 4
Time Preparation: 10 minutes

8 eggs
olive oil
4 rashers raw Spanish ham *or* back
  bacon
black pepper

Utensils 4 small earthenware fireproof dishes

Pour a film of olive oil into each individual dish and put them straight on to direct heat. When the oil is smoking hot, lay in a slice of ham in each dish and top each slice with 2 eggs (crack them into a cup first). Fry for 3 to 4 minutes to set the white. Give each dish a turn of the peppermill and then serve. The eggs will continue to cook in their dish.

Serve with fresh bread and a green salad if you are serving this as a light supper.

SUGGESTIONS
• A couple of slices of *chorizo*, *morcilla*, or any spiced dry sausage can replace the ham. A few peas, green beans, and chopped peppers can be added.

SWISS CHARD OMELETTE
Trouchia (France)

Equally good cold as hot, this is food for the picnic-pocket in the area around Nice, where the Italian influence is very strong. The Niçois have such a passion for *blea* or Swiss chard that they have earned the rude nickname of *caga-blea* or cack-chard. For the *trouchia* use only the tops of the chard — the stalks are too juicy and make the omelette grey and damp if it is to be eaten cold.

Quantity Enough for 4 as a light lunch
Time Preparation: 30–40 minutes

1 lb/500 g Swiss chard leaves (save
    the stalks to cook like
    asparagus)
4 oz/100 g strong cheese
    (parmesan is often used)

6 eggs
salt and pepper
bunch of chervil (basil can be
    included, parsley can substitute)
4 tablespoons olive oil

Utensils A roomy frying pan

Wash and dry the chard leaves. Slice them into strips. Grate the cheese and beat it into the eggs in a bowl. Season with salt and pepper. Chop the herbs — you will need plenty, 3 to 4 heaped tablespoons is about right — and then mix them in with the eggs.

Put 3 tablespoons of the oil to warm in the frying pan. Throw in the chard. Turn the strips of leaf quickly in the oil till they wilt (don't allow the chard to burn or it will taste bitter). Tip the contents of the pan into the eggs and stir all together.

Put the last tablespoon of oil into the frying pan. When it is quite hot but not burning, pour in the egg-chard mixture. Cover the pan and cook over a gentle heat until the eggs are set — 15 to 20 minutes should do the trick. The method is then the same as for the Spanish *tortilla*. Turn the now-firm pancake out, reversing it as you do so, so that the cooked side is uppermost, on to a plate. Add a trickle more oil to the pan if necessary, and slide it gently back into the hot pan. Finish cooking it, uncovered now, on the other side. The *trouchia* will be ready in about another 15 minutes. Notice that the cooking is very gentle — this is the southern way with eggs, and has little in common with the fast butter-cooked French omelette which is soft inside and rolled before serving.

For a main meal serve the *trouchia* as an entrée to a dish of grilled sardines or some other fresh fish simply prepared, or after a plate of charcuterie accompanied by radishes and fresh butter.

SUGGESTIONS
- This mixture can also be baked in the oven as a *tian* (see page 376).

EGGS AND VEGETABLES
Piperade (Basque country)

The Basque nation is highly individualistic. Their language owes nothing at all to their Latin neighbours and has no readily identifiable relatives. Recent research has come up with a possible link with the Finnish and Hungarian languages — themselves both orphans in the linguistic storm. It is a lovely onomatopoeic tongue which is a delight to the ears — how could the dancing butterfly be better served than with *papalanpausa* for a given name? The Basques share at least one culinary passion with the Hungarians, of rather more recent date than the language: the cooks of both nations took enthusiastically to the New World import, the capsicum pepper. The Hungarians refined the vegetable into their universal seasoning, paprika. The Basque national egg dish, the delectable *piperade*, is named after the same vegetable.

Quantity   Enough for 4 as a light meal
Time   Preparation: 20–25 minutes

    6–8 eggs
    salt and pepper
    1 large sweet onion
    2 cloves garlic
    1 red and 1 green pepper
    1 lb/500 g ripe tomatoes
    2 tablespoons olive oil *or* goose fat

Utensils   A frying pan or shallow casserole

Beat the eggs lightly together with a little salt and pepper. Peel and chop the onion and the garlic. De-seed the peppers and cut them into short strips. Peel the tomatoes — the skin will slip off easily enough if you pour boiling water over them first — then chop them well. Sprinkle on a little sugar if they have had no Mediterranean sun to sweeten their flesh.

Put the oil or fat to melt in the frying pan or casserole. The Basques share their neighbours' fondness for beautiful glazed earthenware dishes that can withstand direct flame. Add the chopped onions and garlic to the hot fat, and fry them gently until they turn golden. Push them to one side and add the peppers. Fry them for a moment or two, and then put in the tomatoes. Stew all together gently so that the tomatoes reduce to a thick sauce. This should take about 10 minutes. The peppers must remain visibly whole chunks.

Meanwhile cut some slices of country bread to be served either fresh, or fried in a little olive oil or goose fat. Put 4 plates to warm in the oven.

Now that the tomato and pepper mixture is thick and rich and its water has evaporated, tell your diners to take their places.

Stir in the eggs over the heat, turning the mixture as it thickens. As soon as it is creamy, take the dish off the heat. You don't want a watery grainy mess instead of a soft smooth scramble — and there is only a minute or two of difference between. Spoon the *piperade* on to the warm plates, accompanied by the bread you have already prepared. A light red wine from the slopes of the Pyrenees to serve with it.

SUGGESTIONS
● Add a slice of raw ham per person (the delectable *jambon de bayonne*) or lean bacon, fried and served atop each portion of *piperade*.
● Or chop 4 oz/100 g raw ham or bacon and fry it in with the onion at the beginning. Every Basque farmhouse has hams and good bacon: the pig is a versatile and much travelled beast.

EGGS WITH YOGHURT
(Bulgaria)

A delicious sharp-flavoured main dish prepared with Bulgaria's favourite product.

Quantity   Enough for 2 as a light lunch
Time   Preparation: 10 minutes
　　　　Cooking: 30–35 minutes

½ pint/300 ml yoghurt
4 eggs
4 oz/100 g fresh white cheese
　　(*labna*, perhaps)
2 oz/50 g fresh breadcrumbs
salt and pepper
butter

Utensils   A shallow baking dish, and a liquidizer or a whisk and bowl

Beat all the ingredients except the butter together until creamy — in the liquidizer if you have one.
　　Butter the baking dish and pour in the mixture. Put it to cook in a medium oven — 350°F/180°C/Gas 4 for 30 to 35 minutes until firm and gilded.
　　Serve with thick slices of brown bread and a Bulgarian salad.

SUGGESTIONS
● To make a more substantial dish, line the baking dish first with 6 layers of buttered *filo* pastry.

Sweet Egg Dishes

EGG NOG
Zabaglione (Italy)

Although this dish frequently appears today as either a sweet dish on its own, or to sauce other puddings, it was customarily made by Italian housewives as a restorative for the old and the sick. And a very good restorative it makes too — a most superior egg nog.

Quantity   Enough for 4 glasses
Time   15–20 minutes

  6 eggs
  6 tablespoons sugar
  6 dessertspoons Marsala *or* sweet
    white wine

Utensils   A saucepan, a bowl which can rest comfortably over it, and a whisk

Put a pan of water on to boil. In the bowl, beat the eggs, yolks and whites together, with the sugar until they are light and fluffy. This will take twice as long as you think. Beat in the Marsala.

Rest the bowl over the boiling water. Beat until the mixture is firm and holds the mark of the whisk. Serve in glasses with a long spoon, just like an egg nog.

SUGGESTIONS
• If the *zabaglione* is to be eaten immediately, you need not cook it. Freeze it (cooked) to make a delicious ice-cream.

EGG CUSTARD or HEAVENLY BACON
Tocino del cielo (Spain)

The Moors introduced sugarcane sugar to Europe both directly via their occupation of Spain, and indirectly via the returning Crusaders. Sugarcane was planted both in Andalusia and in the Algarve to supply the Arab taste for sweetmeats and syrups. By the time Ferdinand and Isabella finally took Granada and the Moorish occupation was over, the imported taste was centuries old — and centuries-old habits die hard.

The Spanish and Portuguese convents in particular continued with the tradition of sweet making. Confections made with egg yolks (left over from wine clarification, where only the whites are used) and sugar became specialities of various religious festivals. The nun-confectioners gave their products deliciously erotic names: 'nun's bellies', 'virgin's dew', 'angel hair'. Recipes for Portuguese egg yolk and sugar sweetmeats soon began to appear in the cookbooks of Europe, including those of England — whose links with Portugal in particular were strong. Sir Kenelm Digby's 'Closet Open'd' of 1669 has several recipes for egg yolk and sugar custards. Meanwhile Portugal was rapidly becoming a successful colonizer, and had acquired a clutch of new and sun-drenched territories where her sugarcane could be planted. Limitless supplies of the previously expensive ingredient further encouraged the confectioners. Rum, spin-off from the sugarcane industry, was added to their cellars (and the rural breakfast table as well).

Quantity   Enough for 8–10 portions (it is very rich)
Time   Preparation: 30–40 minutes
            Cooking: 30 minutes

caramel made with 2 oz/50 g sugar, 2 teaspoons water, juice ½ lemon	piece lemon peel
	½ pint/300 ml cold water
12 oz/350 g granulated sugar	12 large egg yolks (another 2 if the eggs are small)

Utensils   An 8 in/20 cm square baking tin, a roasting tin larger than the baking tin to act as a *bain-marie*, a heavy saucepan, and some foil

Make the caramel in the baking pan you will use for the *tocino*. Melt the ingredients together in the pan, turning it over a high flame until the sugar caramelizes a rich golden brown. This will take only a moment or two. Tip to coat the base. Set aside to cool.

Preheat the oven to 350°F/180°C/Gas 4.

Put the sugar with the lemon peel and the water in the heavy pan, and heat over a medium flame until the sugar is dissolved. Boil for about 20 minutes. Stir with a wooden spoon: if the syrup trails a transparent string when you lift the spoon out, it is cooked enough. Remove the lemon peel.

Meanwhile whisk the egg yolks thoroughly. Pour the hot syrup into the eggs, beating as you do so. This will begin the thickening process. Pour the mixture into the caramel-lined baking tin. Cover with foil. Set the baking tin in the roasting tin and pour boiling water all around. Put in the oven and bake for 30 minutes. It should be firm and solid when it is done.

Allow to cool. Cut into squares: sticky, rich, and golden as the sun of heaven — the Moors named Granada the antechamber of paradise. You will need to take a glass of water, Moorish style, with it.

CUSTARD PUDDING
Flan (Belgium)

Egg and milk puddings are common all over Europe in dairy-farming lands such as the rich Belgian countryside. *Flan* also appears under the same name as the most universal sweet dish in Spain — where dairy products are by no means widely available. Possibly the recipe travelled south during the sixteenth century, when Spain and the Netherlands were united under the Hapsburg Holy Roman Emperor, Charles V. In modern Spain, however, it is simply a baked caramel custard much like the *tocino del cielo* above.

Quantity   Enough for 4
Time   Preparation: 15 minutes

 5 eggs
 2 pints/1.2 litres creamy milk
 5 oz/150 g flour
 4 oz/100 g sugar

Utensils   A bowl, an oval pudding dish, and a saucepan

Beat the eggs together with 1 tablespoon of the milk. Put the flour into the pudding dish, and beat it to a thick paste with the egg mixture.

Bring the rest of the milk and sugar to the boil in the saucepan. Pour the hot sweetened milk into the dish, over and round the egg-flour paste.

Bake in a medium oven — 375°F/190°C/Gas 5 — for 20 to 25 minutes.

SUGGESTIONS
• Flavour the pudding with vanilla or cinnamon.

BUTTERMILK EGG SOUP
Kaernemaelkssuppe (Denmark)

A dish from the same stable as the Swedish Christmas Porridge. A lovely dish for a simple evening meal. I have a friend who always has it as a light supper when he is alone. In Denmark it is eaten before the meat.

Quantity   Enough for 4–6
Time   Preparation: 20–25 minutes

  2 oz/50 g ground rice
  2 pints/1.2 litres buttermilk
  2 eggs
  1 tablespoon sugar

Utensils   2 bowls, a heavy saucepan, a wooden spoon, and a whisk

Mix the ground rice to a paste with some of the milk. Put the rest of the milk in the saucepan. Whisk in the paste, and then stir over a gentle heat until the soup thickens and the ground rice loses its raw taste. Keep stirring — milk burns rather easily.

When the soup is ready, mix the eggs with the sugar in a separate bowl. Slowly pour on the hot liquid, whisking steadily. In winter, serve the soup hot sprinkled with chopped almonds.

SUGGESTIONS
● A tablespoon of raisins (soaked for a few minutes in boiling water first) can be added, along with a small stick of cinnamon or a piece of lemon peel for flavouring.
● On a cold winter's evening stir in small glass of strong liqueur along with the eggs (whisky will do as well as *schnapps*).
● On a hot summer's day, serve it ice-cold, with slices of lemon and a plate of sweet biscuits.

Milk and Dairy Produce

FRESH MILK CURDS
(Germany and Northern Neighbours)

Specially soured milk has always been much appreciated in the dairy-producing regions of northern Europe. It is credited as very healthy fare. To be supped with a spoon from small bowls, accompanied by fresh berries or sugar and cinnamon, or eaten plain with a slice of black bread.

Quantity Allow ½ pint/300 ml per person
Time Setting: 4–5 hours

1 pint/600 ml fresh raw milk
2 tablespoons buttermilk *or* soured
  milk

Mix the 2 ingredients together in a bowl and set in a warm (not hot) place for a few hours. It will be best if it sets rapidly. Serve cool.

YOGHURT
Kisselo mleka (Bulgaria)

Yoghurt is eaten with meals or as a snack and praised as the 'milk of eternal life'. Bulgarian yoghurt is the original and only begetter of *Lactobacillus bulgaricus*, the little organism now used worldwide, in company with *Streptococcus thermophilus*, to turn milk into the delicious healthy curds which appear on so many modern breakfast tables.

Yoghurt is very easy to make, and needs no complicated apparatus. You will need a tablespoon of 'starter' yoghurt per 1 pint/600 ml milk — any plain unsweetened yoghurt will do, but Bulgarian is best. There are those devotees who insist on bringing their very own 'starter' from its home territory. Once you have made the first batch, a spoonful of the home-made yoghurt can be used in the next batch. The Bulgars have lost none of their ancient enthusiasm for their national delicacy: refillable glass jars of yoghurt are on sale in the State distribution centres all over modern Bulgaria. Sheep's milk makes the best yoghurt, but whatever you do, native Bulgarian *baccillus* notwithstanding, there will still be a few unidentified and elusive organisms native to Balkan wooden troughs, pails, and spoons that produce the perfect sweet-sour thick curd only on home territory. However, your own home-made yoghurt will undoubtedly be an excellent runner-up.

The very best Bulgarian yoghurt is to be bought at the top of the Shipka pass where the Russians fought with the Turks to throw off the Ottoman yoke. This is the pass which stands at the head of the Valley of the Roses — where the flowers are harvested to provide most of the world's attar.

Quantity   Makes 2 pints/1.2 litres yoghurt
Time   Start at least the day before
          Preparation: 15 minutes

  2 pints/1.2 litres milk ('long life'
     homogenized milk makes a
     thick rich yoghurt)
  1 tablespoon fresh yoghurt

Utensils   A heavy saucepan, a thermos if you have one or a large glass bowl, a perforated spoon, and a rug or small blanket to keep the culture coddled

Bring the milk to the boil in the saucepan. If you do not boil the milk first, it will not make a smooth yoghurt. Turn down the heat as soon as the milk froths up, and simmer it for a minute or two. Remove from the heat. Leave it to cool down to 110°F/45°C. The traditional indicator of this temperature is when you can manage to hold your index finger in the liquid while you count to 10. Skim the milk of any skin which has formed. Beat the tablespoon of yoghurt 'starter' with a little of the warm milk in the bottom of the large bowl, and beat in the rest of the milk.

Pour the mixture into the thermos and seal it. Or cover the bowl with a plate or lid, and then wrap it up tenderly in the blanket and put it in a warm place overnight to curdle. It will keep well in the refrigerator for a week, but if you want to use a spoonful to start a new batch, do not leave it longer than 3 or 4 days or the new yoghurt will not turn into a thick enough curd.

SUGGESTIONS
● The original yoghurt was made with goat's or sheep's milk — a strong rich milk which, if well salted, does not curdle easily when boiled. Cow's milk yoghurt *does* curdle, so must be stabilized first if it is to be used in a hot sauce without separating. For 2 pints/1.2 litres yoghurt, beat in a tablespoon of flour mixed first with 2 tablespoons of water; or beat an egg into the yoghurt before you heat it.

YOGHURT CHEESE
Labna (Central Europe)

A fresh cheese made by draining the whey out of yoghurt, which is very popular throughout the Middle East where it is named *labna*. Stir in a little salt — a scant teaspoon per 1 pint/600 ml yoghurt. Pour the mixture into a clean linen or cotton cloth, which can be tied over an up-ended stool as if it was a jelly cloth, or used to line a colander. Allow the whey to drip away overnight, and the following morning you will have a pure white curd cheese. Roll it into little balls and sprinkle with fresh herbs or olive oil and paprika. Or use in any recipe which calls for curd cheese.

If you are able to make the *labna* with goat's milk yoghurt, you can prepare the fresh cheese for keeping (it won't work with cow's milk — the curds are too soft and will disintegrate). Dry the little balls of cheese on a clean cloth in a cool larder for 2 days, and then pack them into a large glass jar. Cover with olive oil. They will keep for months if stored in the refrigerator, and are excellent with fresh bread or used as a stuffing for *borek*.

BREAD CHEESE
Uunijuustoa (Finland)

A very unusual preparation. The result is a wheel of creamy yellow curds with a consistency rather like dry cottage cheese — squeaky when you bite into it. Particularly good with summer berries, although the Finns treat it as a staple storehouse food.

Quantity   Makes about ½ lb/250 g
Time   1–2 hours to simmer

5 pints/3 litres fresh milk
1 teaspoon rennet
1 teaspoon salt

Utensils   A large saucepan and a very large flat baking tin or a wide frying pan

Bring the milk to blood heat and then stir in the rennet. Leave to set into junket — this will take about an hour in a warm place. Heat the junket gently on the stove until the curd separates and you can lift the clots of curd out with your hands. Squeeze out the liquid as you do so.

Pat the curd into the baking tin or frying pan to give a cartwheel of cheese about ½ in/1 cm thick. Cook either on top of the stove or in the oven at 350°F/180°C/Gas 4 for 1 to 2 hours, until the outside is golden brown. Eat with coffee or milk, or fry slices in butter and sprinkle them with sugar. The Finns treat it as if it were bread.

LEFTOVERS
• Use the whey to make bread and scones.

SOUR MILK
Piimä (Finland)

In the 1890s at the *majatalo* of the rich Finnish peasant who could afford tenant farmers who paid their rent in labour:

What a scene met our eyes! An enormous kitchen, a wooden-floored, ceilinged and walled room about thirty feet square, boasting five windows — large and airy, I was about to say, but it just missed being airy because no fresh breeze was ever allowed to enter except by the door. At one end was the usual enormous fireplace, with its large chimney and small cooking stove, into which wood had continually to be piled, coal being as unknown to the inland Finn as the sea-serpent itself. At the other end of the room, opposite the fireplace, was a large wooden table with benches arranged along two sides, at which the labourers were feeding, for the one o'clock bell hanging above the roof had just been rung by the farmer and they had all come in for their midday meal. It was really a wonderful scene; five men wearing coloured shirts, and four women, with white handkerchiefs over their heads, were sitting round the table, and between each couple was a small wooden, long handled pail from which the pair, each duly provided with a wooden spoon, were helping themselves. Finnish peasants . . . all feed from one pot and drink from one bowl in truly Eastern fashion. The small wooden receptacle, which really served as a basin, contained 'pimmea' or skimmed milk that had gone sour, a composition somewhat allied to skyr, on which peasants lived in Iceland, only that skyr is sheep's milk often months old, and 'pimmea' is cow's milk fairly fresh.'

Ethel B. Tweedie, *Through Finland in Carts*

CURD CHEESE
Skyr (Iceland)

Skyr is soft white cheese made in Iceland in former days from ewe's milk, today from cow's. Eaten on its own, mixed with porridge and served with milk, or as a luxury (and most delicious of all) with sugar and cream and perhaps a spoonful of bilberries. In former times *skyr* was a peasant year-round staple and a very important element of a healthy diet. The soft curds, bland and sweet when made by the best cooks, used to be stored in big wooden barrels sealed with tallow — an expertise apparently brought with the first settlers when they landed in Iceland during the ninth century. The rennet to turn the milk was made by taking the stomach of the year's last new-born lamb or calf, killed before it took grass. The tiny bag full of strong curd and powerful enzymes was then hung in a corner to dry. The next season, the stomach would be soaked in salted water and the liquid would be used to turn the new year's *skyr*.

This method is common to many cheese-preparing communities, particularly in poor areas, where a small cash crop is needed for items which cannot be home-grown. I have seen goat's cheese made in this fashion in Spain as recently as 1980, although there the little stomach is prepared from the first kid of the year and tiny pieces of the actual curd are used rather than an infusion. In Iceland, chemically made rennet began to replace the old technique during the course of the nineteenth century. Today *skyr* is prepared in large quantities in commercial dairies and is a very popular part of the modern Icelandic diet. Modern methods of refrigeration and pasteurization have also replaced the barrel-and-tallow ritual.

Quantity   Makes ½ lb/250 g *skyr*
Time   Start the day before

6 pints/3.5 litres skimmed milk
1 drop rennet
1 tablespoon previous batch of
   skyr or soured raw milk *or* fresh
   raw yoghurt

Utensils A large saucepan, a wooden bowl, a large thermos if you have one, a rug or blanket for coddling, and a linen cloth for straining

Commercially prepared skimmed milk will not need boiling to kill the bacteria — the home-made variety will. Bring the skimmed milk to the boil and then pour it into the deep bowl — wooden ones are best. Allow the milk to cool down to 70°F/37°C — that is, until it feels bearable to the tip of your finger.

Whip up the spoonful of sour milk or *skyr* until smooth and unctuous. Stir it into the milk very thoroughly. Leave for half an hour. Then stir in the rennet slowly and with care. Cover the bowl with a blanket, or pour all into a thermos. Put aside in a warm place.

Be warned: Icelanders say it takes a few small experimental batches before the *skyr* is not too sour but yet well set. When this has been achieved, a spoonful of the perfect batch is used to turn the *skyr* all summer long. The bacteria will then reproduce themselves impeccably every time. Wonderful enzymes to help the digestive system, say the Icelanders.

The milk should have curdled within 2 hours. Pour the curds through a linen cloth, as if straining jelly, to allow the whey to drain out. Save the whey — the Icelanders would have put their straining cloth over a wooden barrel in order to catch it. For how to use it see the entry on whey which follows.

The *skyr* will be ready to eat in 2 hours. Kept in a cool place it will stay fresh for around a week. After that it begins to go sour. Serve with sugar, cream, and fresh berries — blueberries are best of all. Sugar has only been in general use in Iceland since the end of the nineteenth century.

SUGGESTIONS

• A bowl of *skyr*, plus a bowl of oatmeal porridge, milk and a slice of blood sausage or liver and a small dish of fresh berries or fruit, makes an unbeatably well-balanced meal for a healthy adult.

• For breakfast, take a helping of *skyr*, beat in a raw egg and top with a spoonful of honey. Accompany with a glass of skimmed milk.

• Or mix with chopped onion, chopped herbs, or paprika and salt, and eat as a fresh cream cheese.

WHEY
(Iceland)

After the making of *skyr* in Iceland, there would be large quantities of whey to be stored in barrels. Sometimes these had a practical non-culinary use, when they were used to extinguish the fires to which wooden houses with no fire-protection devices were always prone. A broom-handle and a barrel of whey were always to hand in the old days beside the front door of the wooden dwellings. In the Icelandic sagas a heroic chieftain once hid in a barrel of whey to escape his enemies. Not only did this provide him with nourishment and shelter in a single container, but it saved him from incineration when the building was burnt down around him. A heroic substance indeed.

In a less demanding role, whey provided a healthy drink which was taken by fishermen on long sea voyages. Rich in proteins, salt and vitamins, no sailor would starve if he had a barrel aboard, and if his catch was inadequate, the whey could be used as a trade item. Whey as a drink was held to be at its best after two years maturing in an oak-barrel — not unlike whisky. It was also valued as a preservative pickle for meat, particularly such vulnerable delicacies as blood sausage and liver sausage, the products of the autumn slaughter of domestic animals which could not be overwintered.

In modern times this miracle substance has been redefined as a toxic waste. It was discovered that when the waste whey from modern cheese factories is poured into the local rivers it acts as a highly efficient fertilizer for algae, whose growth explosion depletes the supply of oxygen in the water with the inevitable catastrophic effect on aquatic life. The Icelanders are now marketing a fruit-flavoured whey drink which they hope will take the place of soft drinks, and will certainly be a great deal healthier for its consumers.

CURDS
Filbunke (Finland)

As she journeyed through Finland in the 1890s, the intrepid Mrs Ethel Tweedie worked up a fine appetite for her meal in the farmer's kitchen:

> The housewife had two huge soup tureens before her, soup or filbunke, a very favourite summer dish. This is made from fresh milk which has stood in a tureen until it turns sour and forms a sort of curds, when it is eaten with sugar and powdered ginger. It appears at every meal in the summer, and is excellent on a hot day. It must be made of fresh milk left 24 hours in a warm kitchen for the cream to rise, and 24 hours in the cellar to cool afterwards.

FRESH BUTTERMILK CHEESE
Hangop (Holland)

Hangop means 'hanged' — the name comes from the old practice of hanging up a pillowcase on a convenient branch for the buttermilk inside to drip out its whey. The dish is very ancient but still enjoyed today — particularly during the strawberry season.

Quantity Enough for 4
Time Start in the morning to be ready for the afternoon

4 pints/2 litres buttermilk
8 oz/500 g Dutch rusks (these are
   usually made with egg — a
   bread dough with an egg or
   two beaten into it, baked in a
   long thin loaf, which is then
   sliced and dried)

brown sugar
fresh strawberries (*optional*)

Utensils A linen towel, a large colander, and 2 roomy bowls

Take a fresh clean linen towel and use it to line the colander. Put the colander in the bowl, large enough to allow the whey to collect beneath. Pour the buttermilk into the lined colander, and leave for several hours so that the whey drips through. Stir it from time to time. When you have a thick creamy yoghurt-like curd, scrape it into another bowl.

Serve each person with a bowl of the *hangop*. Crumble an egg-rusk on to each portion and sprinkle with brown sugar. Hand the strawberries separately.

JUNKET AND CURD CHEESE
(Northern Europe)

Rennet is the curdling medium used for this milk product. It is a very ancient culinary process which makes use of a natural enzyme present in the fourth or 'true' stomach of dairy animals.

Quantity Enough for 4–6 as a junket
Time Start a few hours or the day before

2 pints/1.2 litres milk
2 teaspoons rennet (can be bought
   at good grocer's and chemist's)
1 tablespoon sugar (for junket)

Utensils A large bowl and a colander and linen cloth if you are making curd cheese

Warm the milk to blood temperature — test with your finger as for a baby's bottle. Stir in the rennet. If you are serving it as junket, sweeten it when it is warm with a tablespoon of sugar. Cover and leave to set — this will take at least 2 hours. Overnight is best.

Serve with nutmeg sprinkled over. A very light and delicious nursery pudding served with stewed fruit and cream.

If you wish to proceed to make curd cheese, do not add any sugar. When the junket has set, pour the curd into a colander lined with a clean cloth. Leave overnight for the whey to drip through. This quantity will only yield a small amount of cheese.

SOURED MILK AND CREAM
(Northern Europe)

Take as much fresh milk or cream as you require. To turn it, use a buttermilk starter, stirred into the milk or cream and left to develop for 24 hours in a cool larder. Or stir in a teaspoon of vinegar or lemon juice, and allow the mixture to stand for an hour or two. If this soured cream is dripped through a jelly cloth as for the junket, it will make good cream cheese. Leave it wrapped in a cloth under a weight for a day or two.

CLOTTED CREAM
(England)

Pour fresh un-homogenized milk into a shallow pan, and leave it overnight on a very low heat: the warm ashes of a fire were the preferred place. In Devon the pans used to be of earthenware, a material which holds its heat comfortably, but enamel and metal are used today. The following morning you will find a thick creamy skin has formed. The depth and colour of the cream will depend on the pasture, the breed of cow, and the time of year. Spring grass is lusher, summer grass is sweeter. Good hay in winter can be best of all.

Cut the creamy skin carefully into squares and roll each up into a little carpet-roll. Let the cream rise again — there will be a little more to collect. Clotted cream is wonderful with fresh scones and strawberry jam for tea. Keep it in the refrigerator, but not for more than a week.

COTTAGE CHEESE
Topfen **(Austria)** *Quark* **(Germany)**

Quantity   Yields around 8 oz/250 g cheese
Time   Start the day before

6 pints/3.5 litres whole milk
4 tablespoons buttermilk *or* plain
   yoghurt

Utensils   A heatproof basin, a baking tin to act as a *bain marie*, a sieve, and a linen cloth

Mix the milk with the yoghurt or buttermilk in the basin. Put it in a warm place for 4 to 5 hours to set as solid as yoghurt. Put the bowl into a pan of water to reach halfway up, and heat to a temperature into which you can just dip your finger — 120°F/50°C. At this point the curd separates from the whey. Cut the curd with a knife and heat again briefly, stirring with a wooden spoon. Pour the hot mixture into a sieve lined with a clean linen cloth. Put a plate on top to weight and encourage the whey to drip through. The curds in the cloth are the cheese. Cover and store in a cool larder. It will keep for about a week. Drink the whey for your health.

BUTTER
(Central and Northern Europe)

All the farming communities of central and northern Europe made their own butter in-house until recently. Ethel B. Tweedie reported on the dairy farmers of Finland towards the end of the last century:

> We got excellent butter of course — the smallest home had good butter and milk in Finland, where the little native cows can be bought for 60 or 100 marks. They live on what they can find in the summer, and dried birch leaves, moss. . . . We had also deliciously cold fresh milk, and coffee [barley] being the only drinks procurable, as a rule, and a small fish with a pink skin like a mullet, fresh out of the water, was served nicely fried in butter, the farmer having sent a man to catch it on our arrival.

Dorothy Hartley chronicled butter-making procedures still being used in England during the first half of the twentieth century:

> In all England I hardly know a craft that varies more than making butter. It was made from milk cooled in round flat milk pans, the cream taken off with a skimmer of porcelain or a shell. Some block-tin milk pans are in use

now, there are a few earthenware ones and glass ones may be found with luck; and there's many a bird-bath in a country garden that was once a square, built-in marble milk-cooler, and the pride of the dairy. Of the old tall plunge churns there is nothing left but their shape and name in the present-day iron milk 'churns' of railway and lorry. . . . There is much 'traditional' usage involved with the 'practical' in dairy work. Wool and cloth must not come into the dairy; old linen for the wood; and scouring sack [hempen] for the floor. White sand from the brook to scour the floor with, and lime 'set' with skim milk to whiten the walls. . . . A dairy-woman's hands should be smooth as butter, white as milk, and cool as spring water.

SYLLABUB AND HATTED KIT
(England and Scotland)

Syllabub is an ancient recipe for a milk pudding made by milking the cow straight on to the bowl containing *Sill*, a wine which used to be made in the district of Champagne. Hatted Kit is a similar poor man's version. The following recipe was contributed by a Scottish reader to *Farmer's Weekly* in 1940: she explained it was her grandmother's recipe, and *her* grandmother's before her.

Warm slightly over the fire 2 pints of buttermilk. Pour it into a dish and carry it to the side of a cow. Milk into it about 1 pint of milk, having previously put into the dish sufficient rennet for the whole.

After allowing it to stand for a while, lift the curd, place it on a sieve, and press the whey through until the curd is quite stiff. Season with sugar and nutmeg before serving. Whip some thick cream, season it also with a little grated nutmeg and sugar, and mix gently with the curd. This dish can quite well be made without milking the cow into it, although direct milking puts a better 'hat' on the Kit.

Make a modern syllabub with ½ pint/300 ml double cream well whipped and sweetened with a tablespoon of sugar. Remember that cream whips better when it is cold. Fold into the whipped cream the juice of a lemon, a glass of dry sherry, and a tablespoon of brandy. The old wives will tell you that a syllabub without brandy is like kissing a man without a moustache.

BUFFALO MILK
(Hungary)

Ellen Browning, a clever young university graduate and kinswoman of Robert Browning, travelled alone through late nineteenth-century Hungary, trying to restore her health while recovering from her father's death. She admitted fear of nothing except mice and wore long cloth knickers under her gown as an anti-mouse device. She had constant trouble with fleas, but was a very observant traveller:

If a man is rich enough to keep a buffalo or two, he and his family drink some of the warm milk for breakfast and supper, but cow's milk is considered only as a food for pigs and calves, or to mix with other milk for making cheese. You can't expect human beings to drink such poor stuff as that! they argue gravely. Even the household at 'the big house' would have jibbed had they been required to drink cow's milk with their daily coffee. For my palate buffalo milk was too rich in quality and flavour, but we used to have it boiled and sent to the table half and half. Even then it tasted like cream. By the way, 'brigand's coffee' is a beverage not to be despised. You roast the berries in the wood-ashes of your fire, wrapped in a maize leaf, bruise them whilst hot between two stones, drop them into the iron pot of boiling water, and cover it up for five minutes over the fire; then you pour if off into an earthenware pitcher on to a large lump of wild bees' honey (there are scores of nests about in the forest) and stir it with a wooden spoon. It must be drunk either out of the mug, turn about, or in wooden bowls. We always drank our onion soup with the wooden spoons out of the same bowls, therefore we were never able to indulge ourselves with soup and coffee on the same day.

The dairy of the rich peasant was a funny-looking place. A wooden shelf ran round it to hold the brown earthenware pitchers of milk 'till the cream rose'. On the earthen floor stood a multiplicity of articles, including garden implements, washing tubs, baskets, and jars of wine, besides a tall upright churn and the wooden accessories for butter-making. The cream was churned fresh every morning during the summer, and the butter, after standing in water for a few hours, was beaten and then boiled down into pans and sent off weekly to Kolozsvar market. Butter in this form keeps well, and is used for culinary purposes all over Hungary. Once a week it was made into long rolls and taken in fresh to be sold as 'breakfast butter'. No salt is ever put into this, and you buy it by the kilogramme fresh every day. It is generally delicious; so are the tiny cream-cheeses, done up in a scrap of muslin; some of them are flavoured with sage. Before leaving we were regaled with slices of kolaczid and glasses of pale yellow wine. The latter was a present from their doctor-son, who owned a vineyard near Maros-Vasarhely and came to see them every year.

Cheese

Cheese is one of the great staples of European peasant larders. It has the advantage of being easily made and stored, needing nothing but the ingredients easily to hand in any peasant community. Curd-making agents vary from the simple or complex preparations which take advantage of the natural curdling enzyme, rennet, to be found in the digestive lining of dairy animals, to infusions of plants such as butterwort.

Curd cheese has long been a valuable source of protein in Scandinavia as noted by Henry de Windt travelling in Finland in 1900:

> Dairy-farming is found to be more profitable and less risky than the raising of wheat and barley in a land where one night of frost sometimes destroys the result of a whole year's patient care and labour. . . .
>
> The chief occupation of the peasantry is agriculture — shovel and hoe prevail — cattle breeding and dairy farming in natural meadows, good pasturage and plenty of water.

Sheep's cheese is no less valuable in southern Europe. Travelling through Sicily for her health early this century the young American, Eliza Putnam Heaton, visited the shepherds who lived in caves supplied by bubbles in the lava of Etna:

> 'Ricotta? Sure! What says the Signora?'
> 'Zu Puddu!' he shouted — as, in a yard where steaming kettles spoke of cheese-making, there stood up a dwarfish old man.
> Agile as a lizard the shepherd came towards us, his little black eyes

lively with curiosity. Behind him raced swart children and from a hovel peeped a bare-legged woman.

'Ricotta?' she echoed. 'I myself strained the milk through fern leaves and stirred it with wild olive twigs!' Her great earrings shook as she trotted to the carriage side, fetching a wooden bowl full of curds made from 're-cooked' whey. . . .

There was bread from wheat grown on Sambastiano's land, and ground by his mother in a hand-mill. There was no butter, but 'ricotta', buttermilk curd dried in the sun and baked, food for Sicilian gods. There were fresh figs, bought at the fair, the early summer figs, sweeter and bigger than later cullings. There was wine pressed from Sambastiano's grapes, not more than a year old, pure and delicious.

Brian Aldiss tried sheep's cheese in 1966 when travelling through the Macedonian mountains:

> We visited two little Zadrugas where the famous cheese, *kackavalj*, is made. The process is not elaborate. When the milk arrives from the mountain top, it is already sour, as we had found. At the Zadruga it is boiled until it reaches a doughy consistency. This dough is worked and salted and rolled until a shine forms on it, when it is bundled into a wide wooden hoop to set and assume its round shape. Left in cold store for a fortnight, it sweats and matures and becomes ready to sell. In one of the two stores we looked round, some eleven thousand kilograms of cheese were coming up to standard. We were given hot rubbery chunks of *kackavalj* straight out of the boiling pan, as well as slices in its final state, when it is as cool and mature as James Bond. In the latter state, we found it not much inferior to a good Cheddar. In the former, it tasted like hot rubbery sheep's cheese.

CHEESES OFTEN USED IN COOKING

Bel Paese (**Italy**) A modern commercially prepared cheese first marketed in the 1920s, this cheese is white and mild, melts smoothly, and is used in cooking as a substitute for mozzarella.

Cantal and *La Fourme de Cantal* (**France**) A cow's milk cheese, first made in Roman times, from the mountains behind Marseilles. A good matured cheese for melting, somewhere between a Cheddar and a Gruyère.

Caerphilly (**Wales**) A crumbly white cheese, matured for only 3 weeks. Known as the most digestible of cheeses, it is difficult to grate but melts well.

Cheddar (**England**) A matured Cheddar made from unpasteurized milk is one of the finest cheeses for cooking available anywhere. It is elastic enough to be easily grated and melts down beautifully smoothly. Farmhouse Cheddar is still made in many dairies in the neighbourhood of Wells in Somerset.

Cheshire (**England**) Probably the most ancient cheese made in Britain. Its crumbly quality makes it difficult to grate, but it melts well and can be used in cooking to good effect.

Dunlop (**Scotland**) The Scottish variety of Cheddar, which it closely resembles and for which it can substitute in cooking. A very good cheese for melting.

Edam (**Holland**) The familiar round ball of cheese encased in red wax. Its imitators are many. A bland cheese, a little soft for grating, but none the less a very popular cooking cheese.

Emmentaler (**Switzerland**) One of Switzerland's two great cheeses for melting, this is the one with the holes (the bacteria *Propionibacterim stermanii* is responsible for them). Made in huge wheels which weigh at least 145 lb in the valley of Emmental in the canton of Berne, and known since the sixteenth century. It grates suberbly, and melts in characteristic long strings.

Feta (**Greece**) A soft, salty, strong-flavoured cheese, white and crumbly, much used in salads in Greece and the Balkans. Originally made by shepherds from sheep's milk.

Fontina (**Italy**) The cheese from the Val d'Aosta which is used to make a *fonduta* (see page 483). A very good cheese for melting, which can substitute for Gruyère.

Geitost (**Norway**) The dark brown *geitost* is made from the whey remaining from the common cheese, boiled until the water is evaporated and then shaped into square cakes weighing from 2 to 5 lb/1 to 2·5 kg. As Paul du Chaillu noted in the middle of the last century:

> It must stand at least a day before it is fit to be eaten and is made only at the saeters, where wood is plentiful, for it requires a great deal of fuel. It is eaten in thin slices, and with bread and butter — women and children are especially fond of it. The best is from goat's milk. It can hardly be called a cheese, as it consists chiefly of sugar of milk.

Geitost is sold in square bricks and can only be sliced effectively with a Scandinavian cheese slicer — a spatula-shaped instrument with a sharp blade embedded in the middle. *Geitost* melts smoothly and is sometimes eaten thus with *lompe* or *lefse*, one of Norway's soft unleavened pancake breads.

Gruyère (**Switzerland**) The second of the two great Swiss cheeses for melting, this is a cow's milk cheese which dates from the eighteenth century. It is made in a smaller wheel (weight only around 80 lb), has only a few small holes, and contains a higher fat content that the Emmentaler. The best Swiss fondue is made with a mixture of these two cheeses. Both melt in characteristic long strings.

Kefalotiri **(Greece)**   The Greek cheese most used for grating and cooking. A hard, strong, well-flavoured goat's milk cheese. Used as a seasoning as much as a food, it is sprinkled on salads, on grilled meat, on rice, and even over a plate of chips. One of the cheeses which are used for toasting, a group which includes Raclette, Caerphilly, and Cheddar.

Laguiole **(France)**   Made near Bordeaux and belonging to the Gruyère-Cantal family, this is excellent for melting.

Manchego **(Spain)**   A hard, salty matured cheese, not unlike a pale Cheddar, with a straw-patterned dark rind. It grates well and cooks tolerably. A shepherd's cheese made with sheep's milk from the central plateau of La Mancha — from where comes its name.

Mozzarella **(Italy)**   The true mozzarella is made from buffalo milk and for cooking is usually used fresh. It is also eaten when dry and matured. This cheese cooks in an interesting fashion: it melts into a delicious rubbery sauce which pulls into characteristic long strings. It provides the best topping for pizzas.

Parmesan **(Italy)**   The Italian's favourite cheese for grating, parmesan is used as an important flavouring agent as well as a food. This universally popular, hard pungent cheese is supposed to have originated in the environs of Parma. The large wheels are coated with lamp black and burnt umber mixed with wine when it is six months old. After that, the older it is the better, within reason. *Vecchio*, old, has two years to come to maturity. *Stravecchio*, extra old, is fully three years in store. The oldest is *Stravecchione* which takes four years before it is ready.

Pecorino **(Italy)**   Made from ewe's milk, this cheese is used for grating when it is matured. Often employed instead of parmesan.

Valais Raclette **(Switzerland)**   This cheese, made only in the canton of Valais, is used for toasting. A large piece of cheese is speared on a knife and held over an open fire (special little single-bar fires now substitute for this in restaurants), and the crisp sizzling crust is sliced straight on to freshly toasted bread. Eat immediately of course, with good white wine from neighbouring Neuchâtel.

Roncal **(Spain)**   A hard cheese matured and used for grating and cooking. Made in the northern province of Navarre from cow's milk.

Ricotta **(Italy)**   A whey cheese which can be eaten as wet white curds, not unlike cottage cheese, or dry, in which case it can be grated like parmesan. Particularly used when fresh mixed with chopped spinach as a stuffing for pasta, and to make a delicious cheesecake for special occasions. Sometimes taken stirred into strong black coffee.

Sardo **(Italy)**   The Sardinian version of pecorino. Now made with ewe's and cow's milk mixed.

CHEESE DIP
Liptauer (Hungary)

A mixture made in the northern province of Liptow in Hungary. The earlier versions were made without paprika, an arrival from the New World. The mixture is now popular all over central Europe, from Macedonia to Austria.

8 oz/250 g fresh cream cheese
1 small tin anchovies (8–10 fillets)
1 tablespoon capers
1 tablespoon mild mustard

1 tablespoon paprika (as hot or mild as you please)
salt and pepper

Mash up the cream cheese. Pound together the anchovies and the capers. Stir all into the cheese with the mustard and the paprika. Taste and adjust the seasoning.

Serve with pickled vegetables (see page 410) and rye bread.

SUGGESTIONS
• In olive territory, very finely chopped black olives might replace the capers.

CHEESE AND EGGS
Fonduta (Italy)

The *fonduta*, an Italian fondue-like dish, is at its most sublime in the company of a Piedmont truffle or two. If you can lay your hands on a fresh tuber, ask your three best friends to share the feast. As with a pound of caviar, four is the maximum number to one good-sized truffle.

Quantity   Enough for 4 favoured friends
Time   Preparation: 1 hour 10 minutes

8 oz/250 g fontina cheese
   (Gruyère, Emmentaler, Cantal,
   or Cheddar can substitute
½ pint/300 ml rich milk

4 egg yolks
1 firm, touch-dry, sweet-scented
   truffle (*optional*)

Utensils   A basin, a large saucepan, a clean cloth, and a food processor if you have one

Chop the cheese with a sharp knife into tiny pieces. This is supposed to produce a smoother, less stringy melted cheese than if you grate. A food processor will do the job in no time.

Put the cheese into the basin with the milk warmed to blood heat. Stand the basin over a saucepan of boiling water. Cover it with a clean cloth. The milk and cheese must be kept warm on the side of the stove for an hour, so that the cheese melts very gently into the milk.

While you are waiting make a plain risotto (see page 268), or prepare thick slices of fresh bread for each of your guests. Put 4 plates to warm.

If you have a truffle, brush and wipe it delicately. If it's very sandy you may have to rinse it.

At the end of the hour whisk the egg yolks in to the cheese and milk. Put the saucepan on the heat and bring its water to the boil. Turn it down to simmer. Carry on whisking while the *fonduta* thickens over the simmering water. Don't hurry it. You want a thick cream, not scrambled eggs.

When the mixture has thickened so that it can comfortably blanket the back of a wooden spoon, take it off the heat.

Make sure your friends are all at table, each with a warm plate in front of them on which you have placed a thick slice of bread scattered with little pieces of fresh butter, or a mound of risotto.

Pour the *fonduta* over the bread or rice.

Sliver the truffle over each portion in front of your guests, using the cucumber-slicer on your grater. You can get special truffle graters for this if you anticipate many such banquets.

MELTED CHEESE
Fondue (Switzerland)

When I lived in the Languedoc in south-western France, among my acquaintances was a family who kept a small flock of goats on an isolated farm in the hills. The family had a daughter known as *La Petite Pascale*, who went to school with my own children in the neighbouring town.

Unusually for the Languedoc, where the dark Catalan Spanish colouring is the norm, Pascale had blonde hair and blue eyes. Pascale was soon befriended by my middle daughter, whose colouring matched her own, and the two little blonde girls became inseparable. The Languedoc winter was bitter that year and my own farmhouse was sometimes cut off by snow and floods, but the rough track to Pascale's remote home was even more often blocked. When it happened Pascale would spend the night with us. On one of those dark and snow-bound evenings she offered to make me a real Swiss fondue — revealing, as she did so, the origins of her blonde hair and blue eyes.

Pascale, I learnt, had a Swiss grandmother who she visited each year, and from whom she had both her colouring and her skill in the art of fondue making. This is her grandmother's recipe from Neuchâtel, the heart of Switzerland's fondue country.

Quantity Enough for 4
Time Preparation: 30–40 minutes

½ lb/250 g Gruyère cheese (this is
the one with only a few small
holes)

½ lb/250 g Emmentaler cheese (the
one with the large holes)

1 teaspoon cornflour *or* potato
starch

1 tiny glass kirsch
1 loaf day-old bread
half a bottle dry white wine
1 clove garlic

Utensils A small heatproof glazed earthenware casserole with a spirit lamp or night light stand to keep the fondue warm (the Swiss use a *caclon* and keep it specially to make this dish), and a wire whisk

Chop the 2 cheeses into tiny pieces. Pascale was very particular about this and explained that grating the cheese produces a tough, stringy fondue. Mix the cornflour into the kirsch. Cut the loaf into bite-sized cubes. Lay the table — you will need a fork each, a plate of bread cubes, a large napkin apiece, and plenty more white wine.

Rub the *caclon* with the garlic to scent it. Pour the wine into the pot and stir in the cheese. Heat the mixture gently, stirring with a wire whisk, until it bubbles. Stir in the cornflour and kirsch mixture. Cook very gently until the mixture thickens and it no longer smells of alcohol. Take the fondue to those waiting at the table and put it on the lit spirit lamp to keep warm. Give it one more stir.

Each diner now spears a cube of bread on their fork and stirs it once round the pot to cover it with cheese. Anyone who drops bread into the fondue has to fetch another bottle of wine. At the end a beautiful brown crust of toasted cheese is waiting to be discovered on the bottom of the caclon. This is the *dentelle* (lace) and is the best part of all.

Many Swiss housewives consider a mixture of at least 3 cheeses desirable — Jura or Gruyère, Bagues or de Courbier, and Vacherin fribourgeois. Cider sometimes replaces the wine.

WELSH RAREBIT
Caws pobi (Wales)

Lady Llanover tells the true story of the Rabbit from the distance of 1871:

Welsh toasted cheese and the melted cheese of England are as different in the mode of preparation as the cheese itself; the one being only adapted to strong digestions, and the other being so easily digested that the Hermit frequently gave it to his invalid patients when they were recovering from

485

illness. Cut a slice of the real Welsh cheese, made of sheep and cow's milk; toast it at the fire on both sides, but not so much as to drop; toast a piece of bread less than a quarter of an inch thick, to be quite crisp, and spread it very thinly with fresh cold butter on one side (it must not be saturated with butter); then lay the toasted cheese on the bread, and serve immediately on a very hot plate. The butter on the toast can of course be omitted if not liked, and it is more frequently eaten without butter.

SUGGESTIONS
● Use Caerphilly if you can find it. A well matured Cheddar or Cheshire cheese otherwise.
● The Swiss serve their special raclette cheese thus.
● The Greeks have a similar trick with $\frac{1}{2}$ in/1 cm thick slabs of kefalotiri cheese, grilled to a crisp brown crust on a flat iron sheet over the fire. The melted cheese is served immediately, piping hot, with a lemon quarter to squeeze over it. Bread and a couple of the excellent Greek salads to accompany.

CHEESE PASTRY
Gougère (Northern France)

This dish — basically a cheese flavoured *choux* pastry — provides the perfect partner for the wonderful wines of Burgundy. There are indeed those who say the dish was invented precisely with that purpose in mind. Take the cork out of the best bottle of Burgundy available — there is just time for it to breathe while you cook the *gougère*. You will never have a better excuse for drinking it.

Quantity Enough for 4-5
Time Preparation: 30 minutes
       Cooking: 35 minutes

$\frac{1}{2}$ pint/300 ml water	4–5 eggs
4 oz/100 g butter	salt and pepper
8 oz/250 g flour	
8 oz/250 g strong cheese (Gruyère is best, Cheddar will do)	

Utensils A saucepan, a baking tray, and an electric mixer to save you trouble

Put the water to boil with the butter chopped up. When all has melted together and come to a rolling boil, take it off the heat and beat in the flour. Put it back on the heat and beat the mixture until it leaves the sides of the pan — which it will swiftly do.

Remove from the heat, and allow the dough to cool for a moment while you chop finely two-thirds of the cheese, or grate it through the rough grater. Cut the remaining piece of cheese into fine slivers. The dough will by now have cooled down enough to beat in the eggs one by one. This is easiest to do in the mixer — the dough is at first somewhat reluctant to accept the eggs. Persist: the dough will soon be easier to work, rather as a mayonnaise becomes more manageable. Judge how many eggs you put in by the appearance of the mixture — when finished it should be light, shiny, and firm but soft, so that it holds its shape but drops from a spoon. Beat the chopped or grated cheese into the dough. Add a teaspoon of salt and plenty of freshly ground black pepper.

Preheat the oven to 350°F/180°C/Gas 4.

Butter the baking tray, and use 2 tablespoons to drop egg-shaped and sized dollops of the pastry on to it in a circle, each dollop to overlap the other. Smooth the top so that you have a round ring. Sprinkle with the slivers of cheese. Put the pastry to bake in the moderate oven for 35 to 40 minutes.

Serve the *gougère* warm. Accompany with a plate of charcuterie: a few slices of raw ham cut quite thick, rosy slivers of garlic-flavoured sausage, perhaps a slice of rough pâté; and a bowl of well-washed, scarlet-skinned radishes, still tied into a bridesmaid's posy; and a salad dressed with walnut oil and salt. No vinegar in the salad to spoil that beautiful bottle of Burgundy.

CHEESE PASTRIES
Tiropiti (Greece)

The Greeks love to use cheese in their cooking. These little fried pastries are often served to favoured visitors, accompanied by a tumbler of water, a glass of *raki*, and a little cup of strong black Greek coffee.

Quantity Makes enough for 6
Time Preparation: 40 minutes

4 oz/100 g kefalotiri (or another strong cheese such as parmesan *or* Cheddar)
8 oz/250 g feta cheese (use a white curd cheese such as Cheshire *or* Caerphilly to substitute)
2 eggs

2 oz/50 g clarified butter
1 packet *filo* dough, or your own made with 8 oz/250 g flour, 4 tablespoons olive oil, and 2 eggs (see page 532)
oil for frying

Utensils A bowl and a deep frying pan

Grate the kefalotiri. Mash it with the feta and the eggs. Put the butter to melt.

Make the *filo* dough, or lay out a dozen sheets if you are using ready-prepared dough — be careful to keep them covered so that they do not dry out and become unmanageably brittle. Cut the dough into long strips, about 3 in/7 cm wide and the full length of the pastry. Brush each strip as you come to it with melted butter. Put a little mound of filling in one corner, and fold it over to make a triangle. Fold over and over diagonally until you have a neat little triangular cushion. Continue thus until you have finished up the rest of the filling and the pastry.

Put on a deep pan of oil to heat. When a faint blue haze rises, test it by throwing in a cube of bread — if it turns golden immediately, the oil is hot enough.

Slip the pastries a few at a time into hot oil. Alternatively brush them with more melted butter, and bake them in the oven at 400°F/200°C/Gas 6 for 15 to 20 minutes until they are puffed up and golden.

Delicious with a little glass of *ouzo* and a plate of salad as a light lunch. You might even finish with a bowl of strawberries dressed with a squeeze of lemon. Followed by a tiny cup of Greek coffee and a piece of Turkish delight from the Greeks' least-favourite neighbours.

SUGGESTIONS
• The Turks make a similar cheese pastry which is made like a small strudel — just tuck the sides over the stuffing and roll it up. Fry or bake as for the *tiropiti*.

CHAPTER 14

Bread and Yeast Pastries

The sight and scent of a newly baked loaf has a romantic appeal that transcends all other culinary achievements. William Cobbett, chronicler of things English and rural *circa* 1830, expressed the traditional view of the English Victorian male:

> Give me for a beautiful sight, a neat and smart woman, heating her oven and setting in her bread! And, if the bustle does make the sign of labour glisten on her brow, where is the man that would not kiss that off, rather than lick the plaster from the cheek of a duchess?

Stirring stuff! However, Mme Suzanne Llewelyn (an unlikely Welsh name to find in a hill village in the Languedoc, but acquired through the passion for the game of rugby which she, a good daughter of south-western France, shared with her husband, a son of the distant Rhondda valley), remembers her own family's pre-1914 baking day somewhat more realistically.

> "Our own wheat from our own fields was taken to the miller to be ground into flour, and the miller kept a proportion for his services. More of the flour went to the baker as payment for the use of the oven.
>
> "Bread was made at home, once a week, and it never went bad. Never. It went dry of course, but it had a wonderful rough texture that did you good. The oven was communal, a small brick building, no longer used, but still there, on one side of the square. Our mother rose at two in the morning to start the leaven. At five, while the oven was being heated with a fire of wood and sage-brush, a crier would go round the neighbouring streets calling: 'Ladies, time to make your bread.' All the ladies would knead and pummel. When the oven was good and hot and the fire had burned down, the master baker scraped out the ashes and hot embers so that the floor would be clean for the bread.
>
> "By then the ladies were ready with their big family loaves, oval or round, plump and well risen and ready for the heat. Such bread. For a special treat on baking day, you could cut off a hot fresh slice, rub it once with a clove of garlic and then trickle a little olive oil over it. Fresh oil was the best — from that same year, and still cloudy from the press. At winter work in the fields, there was nothing better at midday than a slice off the ham, a piece of cheese and a thick wedge of that bread. Such a meal with a flask of wine and a handful of olives were all anyone could desire."

Charlotte Gower Chapman, young American sociologist studying rural life in the village of Milocca in Sicily in 1928, observed the local housewives at their baking:

> Miloochese diet centres round bread and its close relative, spaghetti, which in its various forms is known as pasta. In most families the baking is done by the women of the household. A sufficient quantity of wheat is taken from the bin under the floor, cleaned with care, and sent to the mill

for grinding. When the flour returns, it is sifted several times to remove the bran, and then mixed with warm water, salt, and a bit of the fermented dough from the previous week, to form a stiff dough. This is worked on a special wooden platform by means of a thick bar attached to one end of the board with a hinge. It is strenuous work and requires at least two people, one of whom turns the heavy mass of dough. Neighbours may drop in to help in this process or exchange gossip with the workers. Kneading by hand succeeds the heavier manipulation, and loaves are made. These may take various forms, depending on the whim and the skill of the housewife. The simplest form is a round loaf, with a long semicircular gash on the top. More elaborate forms which almost anyone can make are the 'fish' and the 'pistol'. The top of the loaf may be left plain, glazed with white of egg or covered with poppy seeds or sesame.

As soon as they are made, the loaves are put to bed, literally, and covered with all the available blankets and shawls. While they are rising, the oven is heated by a fire of straw and twigs built inside it. When both it and the bread are ready, the oven is swept out, and the loaves put in with a long wooden shovel kept for this purpose. A flat stone door closes the oven and is sealed in place with wet ashes. The sign of the cross is made over the door, and the bread is left for an hour or so to take care of itself. The finished bread is dusted and kept in a basket. It is of a yellowish colour and close texture. Butter is not eaten with it, but hot bread may be seasoned with olive oil, salt, pepper, and grated cheese, as a treat for the children or for visitors. Every woman is convinced of the superiority of her bread to that of any other woman in the community and of the excellence of the bread of Milocca over that of any other town. Bread is never lightly treated. Before a new loaf is cut the sign of the cross is made on it with the knife and the knife is kissed. No loaf is ever put down bottom-side up. It is the 'providence of God' and so to be respected.

Northern bakers had somewhat less tractable raw materials to hand. Mrs Tweedie, travelling through Finland with her sister and a Finnish friend in 1898, recorded her own observations of local bread making:

A servant girl — for well-to-do farmers have servants — made black bread in a huge tub, the dough being so heavy and solid that she could not turn it over at all, and only managed to knead it by doubling her fists and regularly plunging them to the bottom with all her strength. Her sunburnt arms disappeared far above her elbow, and judging by the way the meal stuck to her she found bread making very hard work. Finlanders only bake every few weeks, so the bread is often made with a hole and hung up in rows from the ceiling, or, if not, is placed on the kitchen rafters till wanted. This bread is invariably sour — the natives like it so — and to get it rightly flavoured they always leave a little in the tub, that it may taste the next batch, as sour cream turns the new cream for butter.

COUNTRY BREAD
Pan de campo (Spain)

The Romans held Spanish bakers in high esteem. Spanish bread was delicately white, they wrote home, fine textured, a miracle of flavour and aroma. The Spanish have still not lost their skill, at least in the country districts. All over the Iberian peninsula each little *pueblo* takes passionate pride in its own master breadmaker, whose loaves are highly individual, easily recognizable to his customers, and whose merits are fiercely contested with the neighbouring bakeries. This difference is not in shape — which varies from area to area, although usually not within the area: in Andalusia, for instance, convention decrees shape should be either perfectly round and smooth, or oblong and slashed down the top to give a specially crisp crust. Nor is it in weight — which ranges from half-kilo loaves suitable for the old grandmother who lives with her unmarried daughter in a Catalan mountain village, to five-kilo special orders to be taken by the southern cork tree strippers on their two-week work spells in the forests of Andalusia.

Rather, the difference comes from the bread's texture and taste. Spanish country bread is made with a sourdough starter — which also depends for its efficacy on the bacteria in the kneading trough and other factors difficult to provide in the modern kitchen. A few isolated rural Spanish bakeries (particularly in the undeveloped south) still use the old brick and adobe bread oven, and light a brushwood and log fire inside to burn until the walls are hot enough for baking. The fire is then raked out and the bread put to bake — such loaves are easy to identify since they have minute bits of charcoal and a light dusting of wood ash left sticking to their bases. Some bakeries add a trowel of lime to the mix to whiten the dough.

Even so, Eugenio Lopez, an Andalusian landowner interviewed by Ronald Fraser, was nostalgic in 1958 for the old ways:

> Sometimes I go out into the countryside with a loaf and some lard and a penknife to slice the bread the way the people used to. It reminds me of my childhood and the way everyone lived. How well I remember it! The barley coffee and buñuelos [doughnuts] before going to school when the men and women took down the aguardiente bottle from the dresser to drink a copita to start the day off. The 'viva Jesus' I always called it.

Quantity   Makes 2 large loaves
Time   Start 2–3 hours ahead
　　　　Preparation: 40 minutes
　　　　Baking: 40 minutes

3 lb/1·5 kg plain strong flour	1½ pints/1 litre water
1 oz/25 g fresh yeast *or* half the quantity if dried	2 tablespoons milk
	1 flat tablespoon salt

Utensils A large warm bowl, a baking tray, and an electric mixer with a dough hook would be useful

Sieve the flour into the bowl. All your utensils and ingredients should be around blood temperature to allow the yeast to thrive and work properly. Anything that would scald you will do the same to the little organisms. Mix the yeast into a cup of warm milk and water to liquify it and start it working. Dried yeast takes an extra 20 minutes. Make a well in the warm flour and pour in the yeast liquid. Sprinkle a handful of the flour over it for the yeast to feed on. Cover and leave in a warm place for half an hour to 'set the sponge'. This allows the yeast to start working initially on a small quantity of dough, a step which should not be omitted as it will speed up the process of fermentation.

The mixture is now ready for kneading. Sprinkle in the salt. Have beside you the rest of the warm water. Draw the dry flour into the now-bubbling well with your hand, adding more water as you need it to slake the flour, until it all sticks together in a soft thick mass. If the dough is too hard, it cannot expand properly. Tip it out on to the floured table top, and push and pummel it with your fingers and the heel of your hand. Give it a thorough working until it is elastic. When the dough is smooth and the glutein in the flour well stretched, fold it into a cushion with the tucks underneath and replace it in the bowl. Cover with a clean damp cloth and put in a warm place for an hour to double in size. Experience will tell you where and how long — I put mine in an unlit oven with a tray of boiling water beneath. The dough is ready when it will hold the mark of a finger pushed into it.

Knock it down again by kneading well with clenched fists. This to distribute the carbon dioxide manufactured by the yeast evenly through the dough. Knead well and cut the dough in half. Knuckle each piece into a firm plump cushion. Grease a baking sheet and dust it well with flour. Turn the round loaves over so that the creases are underneath.

Put the loaves to double in size in a warm, damp, draught-free place — back in the unlit oven with fresh boiling water. It should only take 20 to 30 minutes this time.

Preheat the oven to 425°F/220°C/Gas 7.

Sprinkle the loaf with flour and bake in the oven for 35 to 40 minutes. When the bread is cooked, it will be well risen, crusty, and golden, and the base will sound hollow when you tap it. Dry the loaf upside-down in the turned-off oven for 5 minutes.

SUGGESTIONS

● This dough can be made in a tin, or moulded into any shape you please — in the north of Spain it would be twisted into a tear drop, other regions have their preferred shapes. Country bakers often prick their loaves with the sign of the cross and their own initials.

LEFTOVERS

● Use the stale bread to make soups such as *gazpacho* (see page 357).
● Make *migas* with the leftovers. Chop or tear the bread into rough small squares and sprinkle them with water or wine. Leave the cubes to soak up the liquid, wrapped in a damp cloth. Heat olive oil in a frying pan with a clove or two of garlic. Chopped onion, cubes of salt pork, bacon, or little pieces of raw ham can be included, together with a pinch of paprika and that very Moorish spice, cumin. Fry the wet bread very gently for half an hour with the flavourings until it is crisp but not brown. A kind of fried *gazpacho*. Delicious with fried eggs (see page 458).
● Or cut stale bread in slices and dry in the oven to make *biscottes* for storing in an airtight tin. Very good with cheese.
● Or dry the slices in the oven until crisp, and grate or put them in the liquidizer to make breadcrumbs for *croquetas*.
● Or follow Thomas Carlyle's recipe, as recorded in *Sartor Resartus*:

> On fine evenings I was wont to carry forth my supper (bread-crumb boiled in milk), and eat it out-of-doors. On the coping of the Orchard-wall, which I could reach by climbing, or still more easily if Father Andreas would set up the pruning-ladder, my porringer was placed: there, many a sunset, have I, looking at the distant western Mountains, consumed, not without relish, my evening meal.

SOURDOUGH RYE BREAD
(Northern Europe)

This is the classic northern peasant rye bread. Rye is a very hardy early ripening cereal, which can be cropped successfully where the more delicate wheats cannot survive. It has enough glutein for the making of bread. Oats and barley although hardy, have a low glutein content and the dough simply will not stick together. A mix of barley and wheat flour is sometimes used — although barley-wheat bread is overly heavy and rather indigestible. Each household would take its own mixture of grain to be milled. Both this highly individual flour, and the wooden troughs used for the proving, gave a recognizably different flavour and texture to the products of each housewife. A peasant family took great pride in its own household bread.

Rye has a very low glutein content, which makes it exceptionally hard to work. It is characteristic of the eastern European peasant board, and worth making for its very distinctive flavour and texture. It will never be light, so don't expect miracles. A semi-sourdough seems to work best. If you would like to make it easier for yourself, use half wheat flour — it will give you a much lighter loaf, but it will be a pale ghost of the real thing.

Quantity Makes 1 large loaf
Time Start the sourdough 2 days ahead, on baking day 2 hours ahead
Preparation: 30 minutes
Baking: 2 hours

For the sourdough starter
a small nugget of yeast
4 oz/100 g rye flour
2 tablespoons warm milk

For the bread
1 oz/50 g yeast (half the quantity if
the yeast is dry) dissolved in 1
tablespoon warm milk
1 pint/600 ml warm water
2 lb/1 kg rye flour
1 teaspoon salt

Utensils A large warm bowl, an oblong loaf tin, and an electric mixer would be very helpful

Mix and leave the starter to sour in a warm place for 48 hours. This, plus the extra yeast and enough warm water to make a really wet dough, will raise 2 lb/1 kg rye flour.

Put the flour and salt into a warm bowl. Mix the yeast-and-milk with the water. Pour it into a well in the middle of the flour and add the sourdough starter. Beat well with an electric beater's dough hook for 5 minutes. If you do it by hand, beat with a wooden spoon — rye dough sticks to the fingers like no other. I wish you power to your elbow — it's a tough job.

Leave to prove and double in size — this will take about 1 hour. Knock the dough down and knead it in the mixer again, or with a wooden spoon. Grease the loaf tin. Preheat the oven to 375°F/190°C/Gas 5. Roll the dough out into an oblong the length of the tin, and then roll it up like a carpet. Settle the dough roll in the loaf tin. Leave it to rise again for another 30 minutes.

Bake the loaf for 30 minutes at 375°F/190°C/Gas 5 for half an hour, then give it 1½ hours at 325°F/170°C/Gas 3. At the end of this time, take it out and tap the base to see if it rings hollow — the sign that it is ready. Rye bread can take an unconscionable length of time to cook. If your starting mixture was very wet, it will take longer.

Do not cut the bread until the day after you make it, to allow the crumb to settle down. Black bread is dark and sticky and eastern. Eat with a slice of sheep's cheese, soft white *brinza* or firm yellow *kashkaval*, and a plate of fresh raw vegetables: cucumbers, radishes, peppers, sliced onions, quartered tomatoes. Or accompany with pickles and a bowl of thick yoghurt. You may then look forward to a long and healthy life. This is the favourite meal of the Georgians, and they are practically immortal.

RYE BREAD
Røgbröd (Sweden)

The traditional breads of both the Finns and the Swedes are often leavened, in contrast to their neighbours in Norway. This mix includes molasses, a much prized trade item supplied through the Baltic ports.

Ragbrod, or rye bread, is the ordinary black bread of the country, made in large flat loaves. Halkaka, the peasants' only food in some parts, is baked two or three times a year, so they put the bread away in a loft or up on the kitchen rafters; consequently by the time the next baking day comes round it is as hard as a brick. A knife often cannot cut it. It is invariably sour, some of the last mixing being always left in the tub or bucket, so that the necessary acidity may be ensured. Knackebrod is a thin kind of cake, made of rye and corn together, something like Scotch oatcake, with a hole in the middle, so that it may be strung up in rows like onions on a stick in the kitchen. When thin and fresh it is excellent, but when thick and stale a dog biscuit would be about equally palatable.

Wiborgs kringla, called in Finnish Wiipurin rinkeli, is a great speciality, its real home and origin being Wiborg itself. It is a sort of cake, but its peculiarity is that it is baked on straw, some of the straw always adhering to the bottom. It is made in the form of a true lover's knot, of the less fantastic kind, and a golden sign of this shape hangs outside to determine a baker's shop.

Ethel B. Tweedie, *Through Finland in Carts*

Quantity For 6 rings of *rågbröd* or 3 loaves
Time Start 2 hours ahead
Preparation: 30 minutes
Baking: 20–40 minutes

1½ lb/750 g rye flour
½ lb/250 g plain flour
1 oz yeast/25 g (*or* 1 recipe
sourdough starter as for
sourdough rye bread)

1 pint/600 ml warm water *or* milk
and water
1 tablespoon salt
6 oz/175 g black molasses
2 oz/50 g lard

Utensils   A large bowl, a baking tray, and an electric mixer would be helpful.

Mix the 2 flours and put them into a warm bowl. Make a well in the middle. Liquidize the yeast with a little warm milk, and mix it with a cup of the warm water. Or mix the sourdough starter with some warm water. Pour this raising liquid into the well in the flour. Sprinkle the surface with a handful of flour, and put the basin in a warm place for 30 minutes to set the sponge.

Hand beat the sponge into the rest of the flour with the warm water, salt, molasses, and melted fat. You may need more or less water — dampness in the air or peculiarities of the mix can influence this. You should have a soft dough which is easy to handle, not so wet that it sticks to your fingers, nor so dry that it cracks when you work it. Knead the dough thoroughly, pulling and knuckling it with warm hands and a closed fist until the dough is smooth and elastic. Knuckle it into a large smooth bun.

Leave until the dough is well risen and has doubled in bulk — do not leave it too long — 30 minutes should be sufficient. Putting the dough into a turned-off oven with a baking tray of boiling water on the base speeds up the process.

When the dough is ready, knuckle it down again and divide it into 6 pieces. Roll out each piece into a flat round loaf. Cut a hole in the middle (in the old days, this would allow you to hang the breads by a rope looped across the kitchen rafters for storage). Put them on a greased baking tray to rise again for 30 minutes.

Preheat the oven to 400°F/200°C/Gas 6.

Bake the bread in the hot oven for 20 to 30 minutes, until the buns sound hollow when you tap them underneath.

Or shape the dough into 3 round flat loaves, lay them on a greased baking tray, prick them firmly all over with a fork, and put to rise again for 30 to 40 minutes. Bake in a medium oven — 375°F/190°C/Gas 6 for about 40 minutes. Check after half an hour and turn the heat down if the crust is browning too fast.

This bread will keep well.

SUGGESTIONS

• Keep a cupful of the uncooked bread-dough, covered with water, in the larder until the next baking day. It will keep for 8 days. A greater proportion of white flour can be used to make the bread lighter.
• Add 2 teaspoons of whole caraway seeds at the kneading stage.

OAT BREAD
(Wales)

An excellent and light mixed-cereal bread, easily made when you are baking a batch of ordinary bread. Welsh baking ovens were, in the old days, often brick-built and peat-fired. There are still a few of these ovens in working order today, and those who use them say they cook a Christmas turkey to perfection. To be of the correct temperature to bake bread, the cook must be able to just bear to put her hand in and out 8 times. If she cannot do this, or can manage a ninth thrust, the heat must be adjusted. A heavy fruit cake for a wedding will take 2 days to bake in such an oven, when it is cooling after the weekly bread making. The bricks bleach in the heat to a pale ivory, and it takes days before they lose all their warmth.

Quantity Enough for 1 loaf
Time Start 2–3 hours ahead
　　　　Preparation: 30 minutes
　　　　Baking: 30 minutes

8 oz/250 g flour	1 tablespoon warm milk
¼ pint/150 ml water	4 oz/100 g fine oatmeal
½ oz/12 g yeast	2 oz/50 g bacon dripping *or* lard

Utensils A large bowl, a baking tray, and an electric mixer to save elbow-grease

Make the bread dough as in the recipe for country bread (see page 492).

Melt the fat, and beat it and the oatmeal into the dough after the first rising. Knead well.

Preheat the oven to 350°F/180°C/Gas 4.

Roll the dough out very thin and lay it on the well-greased and flour-dusted baking tray. Mark it into squares and prick it with a fork. Do not put it to rise again. Bake for 25 to 30 minutes, until the cakes are crisp. Delicious eaten hot, spread with butter and heather honey.

OLIVE BREAD
Elioti (Cyprus)

This bread was originally prepared during Lent by members of the Eastern Orthodox Church. Neither flesh nor eggs nor milk can be consumed during this time, so it was a complete meal in itself. Lord Byron, expert after all in everything Greek, laments the future absence of such delights in his epic poem *Don Juan*:

The simple olives, best allies of wine
Must I pass over in my bill of fare?
I must, although a favourite plat of mine
In Spain, and Lucca, Athens, everywhere:
On them and bread twas oft my luck to dine,
The grass my tablecloth, in open air

Quantity   Makes 1 medium loaf
Time   Start 2–3 hours before
         Preparation: 30 minutes
         Baking: 1 hour

1 lb/500 g flour
½ pint/300 ml water
½ oz/12 g yeast (half the quantity if
   dried)
1 teaspoon salt
1 tablespoon olive oil
1 onion
8 oz/250 g black olives

Utensils   A large bowl, a baking tray, and an electric mixer would be a
help

Make the bread dough according to the recipe for country bread (see
page 492). When you knock the dough down after the first rising, work
in the following onion and olive mixture.

Peel the onion and chop it finely. Pit and chop the olives. Fry the
onions in the oil until they are transparent. Add the olives to the pan
and then tip the contents on to the bread dough. Work it well in — it will
take the full quantity. Shape the dough into a round loaf, and then put it
to double its bulk in a warm damp corner (inside a plastic bag produces
the necessary greenhouse effect), for 40 to 60 minutes.

Bake the loaf at 375°F/190°C/Gas 4 for 30 to 40 minutes, until well risen
and golden.

To be eaten fresh. Or toasted over an olive wood fire, a trickle of oil to
moisten the hot crisp crumbs. With such a feast and a bottle of wine, you
will be tranquil as the scholar-monks of Mount Athos.

SUGGESTIONS
● Serve slices of this bread with a dish of *plaki*, the Greek stew made
with olive oil, tomatoes, onions, garlic, and olives to which fish or meat
may be added. The whole to be simmered until most of the juices have
evaporated and the vegetable, meat, or fish is cooked.

PIZZA
(Italy)

A speciality of the resourceful bakers of Naples — a very simple dish, invented as a filling fast meal for the poor of the teeming city. The true pizza oven is a beehive-shaped brick-built village bread-oven. It is fuelled with wood in the old-fashioned way when the fire is built inside the oven itself, and the embers are raked out after the walls are thoroughly hot. Pizza baked in such an oven will have a few tiny tell-tale cinders stuck to its base where a scattering of embers have escaped the sweeping. The dish sprang from less commercial and more ancient stock — peasant cooks would enrich their ordinary bread dough for special occasions with olive oil and a spoonful of sweet tomato purée, plus a few onion rings, spread over the top of a rolled out pancake. This would be baked on a special flat clay pan which could be raised to white heat on the cooking fire. These pans can still be bought in rural Italy, but today they are made of concrete. Special breads stuffed with olives, or a bit of *prosciutto* chopped and fried crisp, or merely sprinkled with olive oil and a few leaves of fresh rosemary or sage, are still very popular in country districts.

> The loaves were still abed, literally in the family bed. Many times I have watched Gina Ciccia knead her dough, spread a dark bread blanket on the bed, set her round loaves in rows and cover them with another blanket. Once, when her husband had been driven home from work by rain, I saw him roused from a nap to give place to the batch. . . .
>
> This is the charm to be said over bread: 'Crisci, crisci, pastuni, Como crisciu Gesuzzu 'u fasciuni.' ['Grow grow dough, as grew little Jesus in his swaddling clothes.']
>
> Eliza Putnam Heaton, *By-Paths in Sicily*

Quantity Pizzas for 4
Time Start 90 minutes ahead
Preparation: 1 hour
Baking: 15–20 minutes

For the dough
½ lb/250 g plain flour
½ oz/12 g fresh yeast (half the quantity if dried)
1 tablespoon warm milk
¼ pint/150 ml warm water
1 teaspoon salt

For the topping
2 lb/1 kg ripe tomatoes *or* 3 medium tins
2 onions
4 tablespoons olive oil
4 oz/100 g mozzarella cheese, cut in fine slices
oregano

Utensils A large bowl, a frying pan, a baking tray, and an electric mixer with a dough hook would be useful

Make the dough as in the country bread recipe (see page 492).

Roll the dough, after its first rising and knocking down, into a long sausage shape and cut off short sections each about the size of a golf ball. To make individual pizzas, roll each ball out into a thin circle of dough about 8 in/20 cm across. Press down the middle to give a depth of about $\frac{1}{4}$ in/6 mm, leaving a slightly thicker rim round the outside. If you are making a single large pizza, roll out the whole piece, but it should still be only $\frac{1}{4}$ in/6 mm thick. Put the dough to rise inside a large, loosely tied plastic bag for 10 to 15 minutes.

Preheat the oven to 450°F/230°C/Gas 8.

Meanwhile scald and then peel and chop the tomatoes. Peel and chop the onion. Heat the oil gently in the frying pan. Put in the chopped onions and fry lightly until transparent. Add the tomatoes with a pinch of sugar if the tomatoes have not ripened to sweet perfection in the Mediterranean sun. Simmer uncovered until the tomatoes melt into a rich thick sauce — this will take no longer than it takes the dough to rise.

When the oven is good and hot, spread the tomato and onion mixture over the dough. Arrange on top of this any extra ingredients of your most discriminating choice. I confess to liking my pizza plain, or at most with a few anchovies and black olives. Lay the slices of mozzarella on the top and sprinkle a little olive oil over all. Grated Gruyère or mature Cheddar or Bel Paese are all possible alternatives if you cannot get fresh mozzarella. Scatter a little chopped oregano over all.

Bake in the very hot oven for 15 to 20 minutes, until the bread dough is crisp and the cheese bubbling.

Eat it while it's hot. If you were a ragged customer in a backstreet of Naples, you would eat your pizza, straight from the oven, sitting on a doorstep in the sun or jogging along the street, under balconies strung with lines of faded washing.

SUGGESTIONS
● Arrange the extra ingredients of your choice over the layer of tomato (the cheese should still top the lot): salted anchovies, black olives, chopped salami, cubed raw ham, mushrooms, sweet peppers, capers, even shellfish are all included in various regions. However, a good pizza should not be an overladen table. Try and restrain your enthusiasm to no more than 3 additional ingredients.

Calzone is made by spreading the filling thickly over half the dough, wetting the edge, and then folding the other semicircle over the top, pressing down lightly to seal the 2 edges together. This arrangement, being twice as thick, will take about half as long again to cook.

Pissaladière, the great favourite of Italy's near-neighbours in Provence, is made in the same fashion. For this quantity of bread dough, peel and slice 6 lb/2·5 kg onions, fry them gently in olive oil until soft and golden but not brown, and pre-cook the bread dough in a shallow baking tin in a medium oven for 10 minutes. When its surface is well risen and dry, spread on a layer of onion as thick as the dough itself. Scatter with black olives, anchovies, and cheese, and a trickle of olive oil. Finish the cooking in a hot oven — 450°F/230°C/Gas 8 for 15 minutes. Keeps well.

PITTA BREAD
(Turkey)

A yeast-raised flat bread made all over the Middle East and now popular as a sandwich container in Europe and America. Cut in half or slit down one side, it provides a pocket for stuffing with fillings. Good particularly for kebabs and salads.

A very ancient recipe, as the nineteenth-century traveller A. W. Kinglake pointed out in *Eothen*, his account of his travels in the Near East in 1844:

> The Arabs adhere to those ancestral principles of bread baking which have been sanctioned by the experience of ages. The very first baker of bread that ever lived must have done his work exactly as the Arab does to this day. He takes some meal and holds it out in the hollow of his hands, whilst his comrade pours over it a few drops of water; he then mashes up the moistened flour into a paste, which he pulls into small pieces, and thrusts into the embers. His way of baking exactly resembles the craft or mystery of roasting chestnuts as practised by children; there is the same prudence or circumspection in choosing a good berth for the morsel, the same enterprise and self-sacrificing valour in pulling it out with the fingers.

Quantity Makes 20 pittas
Time Start 2–3 hours ahead
　　　　 Preparation: 30 minutes
　　　　 Baking: 15 minutes

2 lb/1 kg plain flour	2 teaspoons salt
1 oz/25 g fresh yeast (half the quantity if dried)	1 pint/600 ml warm water
3 tablespoons warm milk	oil

Utensils A basin, 2 baking sheets, and a mixer with a dough hook to save energy

Make the dough as for country bread (see page 492) — it should be a little on the soft side. Work in 2 tablespoons of olive oil.

Cut the dough into 20 pieces, knead each into a ball, and then roll each one out into an oval about 8 in/20 cm long. Put the pittas to rise for half an hour.

Preheat the oven to its maximum temperature — 475°F/240°C/Gas 9.

Flour the baking sheets and put them to heat. Slap the pittas on to the hot baking sheets and put them into the oven for about 5 minutes. Take them out while they are still soft. Wrap them in a cloth so that they do not harden, and bake the next batch.

PITCHY BREAD
Bara pyglyd (Wales)

This ancient Welsh recipe for yeast-raised pancakes made the journey across the hills to England, where they are known as 'pikelets'.

Quantity   Enough for 6 for tea
Time   Start 1 hour ahead
          Preparation: 40 minutes

½ oz/12 g fresh yeast (half quantity   1¼ pints/600 ml milk
   if dried)   2 eggs
1 teaspoon caster sugar   1 teaspoon salt
1 lb/500 g flour   lard for greasing

Utensils   A large bowl, a whisk, and a griddle or heavy iron frying pan

Liquify the yeast by mixing it with the sugar. Put the flour in the warmed bowl, make a well in the middle and pour in the milk, beaten up with the egg, and the yeast, mixing as you do so. Whisk the batter for 10 minutes, until all is light and frothy. Leave in a warm place for an hour to prove.

Put the griddle (a *planc* in Wales) or frying pan to heat. When it is good and hot, grease the surface with a piece of lard held in a rag. Or heat a well-greased baking tray in the oven. Pour spoonfuls of the batter on to the hot surface. Cook on not too fierce a heat on top, or in a moderate oven for 20 minutes at 375°F/190°C/Gas 5. Turn the pitchy bread once, when holes have formed on the upper surface and it looks dry.

Serve hot, well spread with plenty of Welsh salted butter, piled in a hot dish so that the buttery juices run right through the pyramid.

LEFTOVERS
• Delicious toasted.

PLANC BREAD
(Wales)

The bakestone or griddle (in Gaelic, *greadeal*), a flat piece of iron to be rested over the heat source, sometimes equipped with tripod legs, sometimes with a handle for hanging it up, a *planc* in some parts of Wales.

Quantity Makes 1 loaf
Time Start 1½ hours ahead
　　　　　Preparation: 20 minutes
　　　　　Baking: 40 minutes

2 lb/1 kg flour	1 teaspoon sugar
1 teaspoon salt	½ pint/300 ml milk and water
1 oz/25 g yeast (half the quantity if dried)	1 oz/25 g lard *or* butter

Utensils A large bowl, a griddle or a heavy iron frying pan, or (best of all) a Welsh *planc*

Sieve the flour with the salt into the warmed bowl. Mix the yeast to a liquid with the sugar and the milk and water, warmed to blood heat. Rub the lard or butter into the flour, make a well in the centre, and pour in the yeast liquid. Knead into a soft dough and put aside in a warm place for an hour to double in bulk.

Knock the dough down, knuckling well with your fists to distribute the working yeast. Mould the dough into a flat round loaf 1 in/2·5 cm thick. Leave it to rise again for 15 to 20 minutes. Put on the moderately heated, lightly greased *planc* or heavy iron frying pan. Bake gently for 20 minutes on one side, then turn and bake for 20 minutes on the other side. If the *planc* is too hot, the crust will burn before the crumb is cooked.

Split and eat hot with butter. Do not make in quantity — it is much better eaten fresh.

SODA BREAD
(Ireland)

The daily bread of Ireland, soda bread can be made with white or brown flour and is baked fresh as required, much as the Scots make their scones and pieces. In the days before ovens were usual (that is, until well into this century), the bread would have been baked in a pot with burning turfs on the inverted lid to give all-round heat. The chemical raising agents are a late nineteenth-century innovation, but without them the bread is rather heavy. Use the scone mix (see page 512) for a soda bread without baking soda.

Quantity Makes 1–2 loaves
Time Preparation: 20–25 minutes
        Baking: 45 minutes

1½ lb/750 g plain flour
1 teaspoon bicarbonate of soda
1 teaspoon salt

½ pint/300 ml sour *or* buttermilk (if you cannot get either, fresh milk and a teaspoon of cream of tartar will have to do)

Utensils A large bowl and a baking tray

Mix the flour with the soda and salt in the bowl, and make a well in the middle. Pour in the liquid in one stream, and knead it swiftly and lightly into a ball. The dough should be on the soft side. Flatten the ball with well-floured hands. Grease the baking sheet and put the dough-cake on it. Make a cross on the top. Bake at 400°F/200°C/Gas 5 for 45 minutes.

Eat the soda bread hot or cold with butter. Treacle is good with it too.

SUGGESTIONS
• This quantity will make 2 smaller breads which will not need more than 30 to 35 minutes baking.

LEFTOVERS
• Store the bread wrapped in a clean tea towel to keep it soft.

SAVOURY TOASTS
Crostini (Italy)

Slices of good leftover bread (French-type bread sticks are good for this) are toasted in the oven, and then either used fresh or stored until needed as the basis for an antipasto, the dish served before the pasta. *Crostini* also make an excellent breakfast dish. Either way they should be warmed, and then spread with a savoury mixture, which can be as simple as a rub of garlic and a trickle of olive oil.

Spread the *crostini* with chicken livers sautéed in butter, or olive oil and garlic and mashed together with salt and pepper.

Trickle good raw olive oil over the *crostini*, and then top with a slice of cheese, or a salted anchovy, chopped olive paste, and a slice of fresh ripe tomato sprinkled with a few leaves of basil.

Or a combination of any or all of these. Other variations include chopped hard-boiled eggs pounded to a paste with anchovies, or butter and a slice of *prosciutto* ham or salami sausage.

BREAD AND BEER SOUP
Ollebrød (Denmark)

The Danes make particularly good beer and they use it in this beer porridge. A private supper to be enjoyed on a cold winter's night.

Quantity For 2 people to share
Time Start 2–3 hours before
           Preparation: 15 minutes
           Cooking: 30 minutes

1 lb/500 g stale rye bread   thick cream
¼ pint/150 ml water   brown sugar
1 pint/600 ml light Danish beer

Utensils A saucepan and a bowl

Crumble the bread and soak it for a few hours in the bowl in the water mixed with half the beer.

Put the bread in a saucepan when it is properly soaked, and simmer the mixture until it is a soft, thick mass. Stir in the rest of the beer. Bring back to the boil and simmer gently for half an hour uncovered. It should reduce to half the quantity. Eat hot with plenty of thick cream and brown sugar.

SUGGESTIONS
• A little grated lemon rind to flavour.

OPEN SANDWICHES
Smørrebrød (Denmark)

Smørrebrød, literally 'buttered bread', is the Dane's favourite meal and prefectly suited to a dairy farming community. It can be a simple lunch time sandwich, or served in an infinite variety of ways, a banquet of different flavours and ingredients, for a party. Danish rye is the basic bread used. Otherwise, any good brown bread. Do not use German pumpernickel though, its flavour is too overwhelming and it is best kept for cheese.

At home in Denmark for everyday fare, the topping would be simple and wholesome: fish, eggs, or meat spread on top of the buttered rye bread, the meal washed down with beer or milk. There might be spiced herring, or fillet of cold fried plaice, or slices of hard-boiled egg, or liver sausage with pickled cucumber, cheese and radish, shrimps, sardines, smoked eel with scrambled eggs. Again, there might be sliced meat, cold roast pork flanked by a strip of its crackling and a stoned prune, or beef and fried onions. Resist the temptation to garnish with sticky things like tinned peaches, pineapple, or glacé cherries. Shavings of fresh horseradish or a slice of beetroot are just as pretty and much more appropriate.

POOR KNIGHTS
Wentelteefjes (Holland)

A delicious way of making use of stale bread, this recipe appears all over Europe under different guises. In France it is called *pain perdu*, 'lost bread'. Children love it.

Quantity 2 pieces each for 4
Time 25–30 minutes

8 slices old bread	4 oz/100 g sugar
½ pint/300 ml milk	2 oz/50 g butter
2 eggs	

Utensils A soup plate and a frying pan

Beat together the milk, the eggs, and the sugar in a soup plate. Melt a nut of the butter in the frying pan. Soak one piece of bread in the egg-and-milk mixture and fry it golden in the butter, turning once to brown the other side. Continue until bread and batter are all used up.

Serve the Poor Knights immediately, sprinkled with more sugar.

SUGGESTIONS
● Sprinkle the slices with cinnamon as well, or serve with a spoonful of jam. Syrup — either Golden or maple — is also delicious with Poor Knights, as are fresh strawberries and cream.

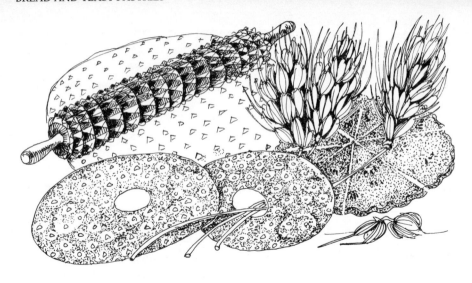

Unleavened Bread

FLATBREAD
Flatbrød (Norway)

Probably the oldest and commonest form of bread in pre-modern Norway, this is a fine, paper-thin unleavened oatbread which used to be baked in the farmhouse kitchen only twice a year, so fine and dry and indestructible that it could remain fresh stored on a beam in the kitchen for six months at a time. There are still countrywomen around who make their own *flatbrød*. Since oats, rye, and barley are the cereals which can be successfully grown in the cold of northern Scandinavia, these are the grains which are used. The inclusion of wheat in this recipe makes the dough much easier to work. The wide round discs of flatbread are usually factory-baked today. For convenience they are often cut into neat rectangles and packaged in paper to be sold widely in supermarkets as 'extra-thin crispbread'.

> Fladbrod is made from an unfermented dough of barley and oatmeal, often mixed with pea-flour. The dough is rolled into large circular loaves, having a diameter of two to three feet, and of a thickness of heavy paper or thin pasteboard, and is then baked over a slow fire on an iron plate. In the dough are often kneaded boiled potatoes. This bread will keep for a year or more. It is much thinner than the Swedish bread, and is brittle.

Each farming household had its own special *flatbrød* mix, depending on the cereals it could produce. The following is a basic modern recipe.

Quantity   Enough for 12–15 flatbreads
Time   Preparation: 1 hour

8 oz/250 g oat *or* barley flour   1 flat teaspoon salt
8 oz/250 g rye flour   1 pint/600 ml skimmed milk
8 oz/250 g wheat flour

Utensils   A griddle or heavy frying pan, or, best of all a *takke*, and a
rolling pin, grooved if possible

Mix the different flours together with the salt. Pour the skimmed milk
into a well into the middle and knead into an elastic dough. Work it well
to develop the gluten. Cut into pieces and roll each one out, preferably
with the grooved rolling pin, into the widest, thinnest sheets possible
(you should aim to achieve a diameter of 18 in/45 cm).

Bake on an ungreased metal sheet (a *takke*) on top of your heat source
until the *flatbrøds* are quite crisp and dry. Store in airtight tin. (In the cold
dry air of winter Norway this would not be necessary.)

SUGGESTIONS
- Thin flatbread was eaten crumbled into small pieces very much like
cornflakes, with fresh or soured milk or, for special occasions, cream
poured over it.
- A part of Christmas celebrations is *mølje* — flatbread crumbled into
the broth from the boiling of the special Christmas meats.
- In certain parts of Norway, dry-baked *flatbrød* used to be (and still is
in those places where the old traditions hold) the central ingredient of
the harvest meal. Damped to make it as pliable as a pancake, the bread is
quartered, spread with fresh unsalted butter, and used to wrap up
titbits such as dried mutton, slices of fresh, deep-orange-yolked hard-
boiled egg, a fine slice of the dark brown sweet cheese, *geitost*, so
beloved of the Norwegians, salted herring, and finally a spoonful of
cloudberry jam to round off the meal.

POTATO PANCAKE BREAD
Lompe (Norway)

An excellent soft pancake-wrapper, easily made at home, eaten in
Norway with butter and *geitost* cheese, or used to wrap delicious little
morsels of smoked ham, *fenalår* — dried and salted leg of mutton or a
spoonful of berry conserve.

Quantity   Makes 10–12 small pancakes
Time   Preparation intermittently: 1 hour

2 lb/1 kg old potatoes (the older the better)	1 tablespoon salt
	4 oz/100 g flour

Utensils   A griddle or heavy frying pan, or, best of all, a *takke*

Boil the potatoes in their skins. Peel them as soon as they are cool enough to handle and mash them with the salt immediately. Speed makes light pancakes. Mix with the flour into a dough. (Less or more flour may be needed — potatoes are very variable. The less flour you use the better.) Form into a long sausage and chop off lengths. Roll these pieces out into pancakes about ⅛ in/3 mm thick.

Bake the *lompe* on a hot iron surface.

SUGGESTIONS
• Potato *lompe* have entered the fast-food repertoire of Norway and are sold on street corners as a wrapper for hot dogs: a great improvement on the usual soft white bun.

BREAD PANCAKE
Lefse (Norway)

There are many local variations of this type of *flatbrød*. That of Nordland is thicker, today raised with baking powder and sweetened, but the most traditional *lefse* has neither sugar nor baking powder, but is made from a grain flour and mashed boiled potatoes mixed with milk or water. It is made and stored like *flatbrød* itself.

> Lefse is made in the same manner as the fladbrod, but is only half baked, and is then folded together, generally four times. The fladbrod is kept in the larder in large cylindrical heaps, often for half a year and longer; the lefse, with its convenient form, is used on journeys.
> Paul du Chaillu *Land of the Midnight Sun*

Alette Golden's cookery book (she ran a famous Norwegian cookery school) gives three recipes:
• Equal quantities of oatmeal and rye and boiled mashed potato.
• Equal quantities of barley, oat and rye flour, with equal quantities of boiled mashed potato.
• Three parts of oatmeal to one part of rye.

Whichever mix you prefer, mash the potato as soon as it is cool enough to handle and mix in most of the flour, with enough water to mix to a smooth dough. Leave the dough until the following day. Then roll it out into thin wide pancakes. Bake them on a lightly greased griddle. Store as for *flatbrød*.

510

When you wish to eat your *lefse*, sprinkle both sides with water and sandwich it between clean linen cloths for an hour or so. Then it will be soft, and can be buttered and folded and cut into neat pieces.

Lefse can be eaten as the dampened *flatbrød* in the suggestions at the end of the recipe (see page 509). It can also be layered into a cake with double or soured cream and sugar.

OATCAKES AND BANNOCKS
(Scotland)

The Scots make a wide variety of oatcakes — no surprise since the main ingredient is the grain most compatible with the cold northerly climate. The original oatcake mix was a simple paste of milled oats worked with cold water. The fishermen of Skye used to dip a handful into sea water and then knead it into a cake for immediate consumption — the most portable of fast food. Even so, to many poor crofters, oatcakes were food for special occasions — daily fare was barley-cake. The instruments for making rolled-out oatcakes are four in number: the 'spurtle', a flat stick for stirring the water into the oats; the 'bannock-stick', a rolling pin with a criss-cross pattern on it like that used in Norway for flatbread, which leaves indentations on the upper side of the cake; the 'spathe', a flat iron instrument like a palette knife used to flip the cakes on to the hot griddle; and the 'banna-rack', used for toasting the oatcakes. Northern England preferred a batter oatcake.

The cooks of Yorkshire and Lancashire needed a deft hand to throw and scrape the elongated-egg-shaped batter oatcakes. Their utensils were different as well: there was the riddleboard and throwing board and ungreased bakestone, requiring skills which could only be acquired through long apprenticeship, and a ready supply of unstabilized oats — very difficult to come by today. There are Scots oatcake recipes which are raised with yeast, and some which replace the water and fat with buttermilk and cream, or with whey. Milk used alone makes them hard.

Quantity Makes 1 large oatcake or 3 or 4 small ones
Time Preparation: 40 minutes

4 oz/100 g oatmeal — fine *or* medium, but not the rolled oats sold today to make porridge
1 teaspoon salt

½ tablespoon melted fat — bacon dripping, lard *or* butter
4 tablespoons hot water

Utensils A bowl, a rolling pin, a griddle, and a heavy iron frying pan (the non-stick variety is perfect) or a baking tray

Put the oatmeal into the bowl with salt and pour the fat and hot water into a well in the centre. Mix all the ingredients together as quickly and lightly as possible. Put the ball of dough on an oatmeal-dusted board, and knuckle it swiftly into a smooth, soft dough. Oatmeal is sticky and thoroughly unruly with a tendency to crack.

Roll the dough out very thin — no more than $\frac{1}{8}$ in/3 mm thick. You will need to dust frequently with the extra meal to counter the stickiness, and keep pinching the cracked edges together to keep it whole. Cut the rolled out dough into rounds — either a large one by cutting round an inverted 6 in/15 cm diameter plate, leaving it whole to make bannocks, or cutting them in quarters to make farls. Or make small ones using a biscuit cutter or a fine-rimmed glass. Rub with oatmeal again and put them to bake on the hot ungreased iron griddle or heavy frying pan. Cook until you see the edges curl — this will only take a few minutes. Remove them and put them either in front of the fire or in a medium oven for a few moments to dry the tops.

Or roll the dough out into a square, again about $\frac{1}{8}$ in/3 mm thick and put it on the baking tray. Mark it into squares and prick it all over with a fork. Put it to bake in a medium oven — 350°F/180°C/Gas 4 until the dough is dry and crisp — this will take 10 to 15 minutes.

Oatcakes are delicious with butter, with cheese, or with butter and marmalade for breakfast. Keep them in an airtight tin. They are best if you warm them again before serving. Oatcakes were often stored buried in the meal-chest, where they kept sweet and dry until needed. Robert Burns, Scotland's favourite bard, considered them a delicate relish when eaten warm and washed down with a jug of ale. The West Highlanders liked them with fresh herrings, cold butter, and a sliced raw onion.

SCONES AND PIECES
(Scotland)

The most delicious bread Scotland can offer, the housewives of Scotland have a light hand with the baking which is unrivalled anywhere in the world. Sour milk or buttermilk and very light fingers were the raising agents employed before the appearance of chemical raising agents. Scones are at their best made fresh and served straight from the oven. They appear at any and all meals, although they are particularly good for breakfast and tea, with plenty of cold butter to melt into the tender dough and a strong brew of sweet milky tea to wash them down. A 'piece' can be any small bread, and many highland families used to (and sometimes still do) build all their meals around such 'pieces'.

Quantity Just enough for 4
Time Preparation: 15 minutes
   Baking: 15 minutes

8 oz/250 g plain flour
¼ teaspoon salt
½ teaspoon baking powder
   (*optional*)

2 oz/50 g butter
¼ pint/150 ml sour milk *or* sweet
   milk

Utensils A bowl and a baking tray

Sift the flour, the salt, and the baking powder (if you are using it — as your fingers grow lighter and more skilful you will not need a chemical raising agent) into the bowl. Make a well in the centre and chop in the butter. Rub the butter into the flour with your fingertips. Knead into a soft dough with the milk. A soft dough makes a light scone.

Preheat the oven to 400°F/200°C/Gas 6.

Pat out on a well-floured board and press out small rounds. If you were making scones for tea, you would cut larger triangles instead. Bake them on a hot griddle, although 10 to 15 minutes in the hot oven will do very well instead.

LEFTOVERS
● Split the scones and toast them. Or split them and fry them on the crumb side only. Often served thus at a Highland breakfast.

SHORTBREAD
(Scotland)

A celebration bread which is essentially a rich biscuit paste, originally baked for the New Year Festival of Hogmanay. Only the finest ingredients should be used. Do not skimp on any of them.

Quantity Makes 2 rounds of shortbread
Time Preparation: 20 minutes
   Baking: 1 hour

4 oz/100 g caster sugar
8 oz/250 g butter
12 oz/350 g fine white flour *or*, to
   give even better results, 10 oz/
   275 g fine white *plus* 2 oz/50 g
   ground almonds *or* rice flour

Utensils A pastry board, baking tins, a food processor and a shortbread mould if you have them, and a cooling rack

Cut the sugar and butter together on a wooden board, and then work with your hands, or in the processor until thoroughly blended. Sieve the flour and then mix it in gradually, not working the pastry too hard or it will toughen, until all is incorporated into a soft dough-like shortcrust pastry. The mixture should not look oily or be overworked or it will toughen. Cool hands, or better still, a cold northern kitchen, are best for this job.

Preheat the oven to 325°F/170°C/Gas 3.

Do not roll out the pastry, but cut it in half, mould it into 2 flat cakes, and press each gently either into a greased and floured wooden shortbread mould (there are lovely old ones with thistles or other patterns carved into them), which you then reverse on to a baking sheet, or into two 8 in/20 cm ungreased cake tins. They should be about $\frac{3}{4}$ in/1.5 cm in depth. Linings of kitchen paper are a good safety device to prevent sticking and burning.

Bake the shortbread in the oven for 50 to 60 minutes, turning the oven down a little halfway through the baking time. The biscuit will be soft when you take it out, but will crisp as it cools. Transfer it to the cooling rack as soon as it firms up a little.

SUGGESTIONS
● Store the leftovers when quite cooled, wrapped in paper and kept in an airtight tin. If you keep the shortbread for long, it can be refreshed and crisped if you bake it again in a low oven for 10 minutes.

PLUM TART
Zwetschkenfleck (Austria)

Fine blue plums are gathered and made into prunes or brandy, and others used for those nice large plum tarts or cakes, of half a yard wide, which they bake in tins, with the plums cut in halves and stuck with the split side upwards all over them.

In Austria and Germany it would not be proper to serve a strudel, a fruit tart or a dumpling after a heavy meat dish. German country puddings are solid affairs, designed to be the main dish to follow a meatless vegetable-thickened soup. These main-dish pastries conformed to the Catholic rules of Friday fasting and were called *Fastenspeisen*. They include a wide range of delicious sweet dumplings stuffed with fruit or curds, a variety of strudels, and egg-noodle dishes baked or served with fruit. For special meals German country wives make excellent cakes and pies: fruit breads, yeast cakes, cheesecakes, doughnuts, and apple cakes are all traditional dishes served on festival days. Eggs are used to enrich rather than to lighten dough. Yeast and light fingers are the true peasant raising agents. (Baking powder and chemical raising agents are modern innovations more at home in the bourgeois kitchen.) The use of beaten egg whites as a raising agent was not widely understood even in aristocratic kitchens until the eighteenth century.

One of the best of fruit tarts, this is also one of the simplest. Make it when you bake a batch of bread — it is quite easy to beat in the extra sugar and butter to an already prepared bread dough.

Quantity   Makes 1 large tart
Time   Start 2 hours in advance
           Preparation: 30 minutes
           Baking: 50 minutes

For the dough
1 lb/500 g plain flour
½ teaspoon salt
1 oz/25 g fresh yeast (half the
   quantity if dried)
½ pint/300 ml warm milk
2 oz/50 g butter *or* lard
1 oz/25 g sugar

For the filling
2 lb/1 kg plums
4 oz/100 g sugar (more if the fruit
   is very sour)

Utensils   A large bowl, a small saucepan, a rolling pin, and a baking tray

Put the flour in the warmed bowl and sprinkle in the salt. Make a well in the centre. Mix the yeast to a liquid in half a cupful of the warm milk. Pour the yeast liquid into the well in the flour and sprinkle a handful of flour over the top. Put aside for 15 minutes in a warm, draught-proof corner for the yeast to develop and set the sponge — a process you can watch if you wish. The yeast, activated by warmth and fed by the starch in the milk and the flour, multiplies its cells and makes oxygen until the surface skin of flour is covered with spongy bubbles. This gets the yeast working well and is a step which should not be left out.

When the sponge is set, melt the butter or lard in the small pan over a low heat. Sprinkle the sugar and the salt over the flour. Beat in the liquid butter (it should not be hot, just warm) and as much of the rest of the warm milk as you need to make a smooth elastic dough. The amount of liquid you require will naturally also depend on the liquid additions. Pummel the dough thoroughly to stretch the gluten.

Knead the dough into a soft white cushion with your fists. Put it to rise for about 40 to 50 minutes in a damp, warm, draught-proof place such as an unlit oven with a tray of boiling water on the base, or inside a plastic bag in the airing cupboard.

When the dough has doubled in size knock it down and knead thoroughly to distribute the oxygen bubbles. Roll the dough out in a circle (or a square — a very usual way of presenting this pie) as thin as for a shortcrust pastry. Butter the baking tray and lay the yeast pastry on it. Put it to rise in a warm, draught-free corner (inside a plastic bag is a good place) for 15 to 20 minutes until the dough is quite puffed up again. When the dough has risen, prick it all over with a fork.

Meanwhile preheat the oven to 450°F/230°C/Gas 8 and prepare the filling. Stone the plums neatly without cutting them right through, then place them stalk-end down on the dough — then you can be sure they will be tightly packed. Lay a thick layer of fruit over the whole surface. Sprinkle with sugar.

Put the tart to bake for 25 to 30 minutes in the oven. When you open the oven door, the tart will look distinctly singed. Don't worry — it will be fragrant, juicy and delicious. Slip it out on to a large dish.

Serve the country tart warm. Northern French housewives also make this tart, and accompany it with yellow *crème fraîche*. At its best after nothing but a soup, while you are still hungry

SUGGESTIONS
● Instead of the plums use cherries (the little sour wild ones are best of all) or damsons or apples.
● When the dough has doubled in size and is ready to be knocked down and kneaded into its final shape, this is the basic yeast pastry which can be used in any number of ways: roll it out and use as ordinary pastry for strudels and pies and cheesecakes; break off pieces to poach as dumplings; mould it into balls or rings to fry as doughnuts; mix in nuts and raisins to make fruit bread — whatever you please. The dough can be braided into a plait or put into a baking tin to make a tea bread. When settled into its final shape, the dough should be allowed to double its size again before it is baked. This will take about 20 to 30 minutes — doughnuts are the exception to this, and must not be left so long.

POPPY SEED STRUDEL
Mohnstrudel (Austria)

A very popular pastry in country districts throughout Austria and Germany, offered for sale to travellers from road-side stalls in rural Yugoslavia, and in the markets of Hungary and Romania. As for the ingredients, markets all over central Europe have their special corner for the nut-merchants, on whose stalls mounds of poppyseed, pumice-stone-grey like small volcanoes, are flanked by mountains of shelled walnuts, hazelnuts, sultanas, and raisins.

Time Start 2 hours before
Preparation: 30 minutes
Baking: 45–50 minutes

For the dough
8 oz/250 g plain flour
½ teaspoon salt
1 oz/25 g fresh yeast (half the
quantity if dried)
¼ pint/150 ml warm milk
1 oz/25 g sugar
2 oz/50 g butter *or* lard

For the filling
4 oz/100 g poppy seeds
¼ pint/150 ml milk
1 oz/25 g butter
2 oz/50 g sugar
icing sugar for dusting

Utensils A large bowl, a rolling pin, a liquidizer or pestle and mortar, a
small saucepan, a baking tray, and a cooling rack

Make the dough according to the recipe for plum tart (see page 514). Roll
out the yeast pastry on a well-floured board in an oblong to a thickness
of ⅛ in/3 mm.

Grind the poppy seeds in the liquidizer or crush them in a mortar.
Bring the milk to the boil in the small saucepan and add the ground
poppy seeds. Boil until the mixture thickens. Remove from the heat and
beat in the butter. Add the sugar.

Spread the filling over the pastry. Roll it up like a Swiss roll. Butter the
baking tray and put the strudel on it, curled into a horseshoe shape.
Cover with a damp cloth and put to rise in a warm place for half an hour.
Preheat the oven to 375°F/190°C/Gas 5.

When it has risen, brush the strudel with egg and bake it for 45 to 50
minutes. Take it out and put it on the rack to cool. Dust the top with
icing sugar.

This strudel is best if it is stored in a cool place for a few days before it
is eaten.

SUGGESTIONS

● For a special occasion include 2 oz/50 g raisins, 2 oz/50 g chopped or
ground almonds, grated lemon rind, and cinnamon.
● Enrich the mix with 2 eggs beaten into the cooled poppy seed filling
before it is spread on the dough.
● Replace the poppy seeds with a filling of chopped walnuts or
hazelnuts (wives and walnut trees, goes the old saying, are better for a
good beating — presumably husbands and hazelnut trees are made of
more delicate stuff, so take your pick) mixed with a handful of breadcrumbs, or with sweetened curd cheese.

RING DOUGHNUTS
Kucheln (Germany)

A particular favourite at church fairs in Bavaria — all children love them.

Quantity   Makes 20–25 doughnuts
Time   Start 2 hours before
　　　　Preparation: 60 minutes

1 lb/500 g plain flour
½ teaspoon salt
1 oz/25 g fresh yeast (half the
　quantity if dried)
½ pint/300 ml warm milk

1 oz/25 g sugar
2 oz/50 g butter *or* lard
oil for frying (this would have
　been clarified butter)

Utensils   A large bowl and a deep frying pan

Work the dough as for the plum tart (see page 514).

Doughnut dough must be on the soft side so you may need a little extra liquid. Allow it to rise once. Then knock the dough down, and cut it into 20 to 25 equal pieces. Form these pieces into spherical flat doughnuts with a diameter of about 2 in/5 cm. Brush the tops with melted butter and leave the doughnuts to rise for 10 minutes — they should only be allowed to expand a little.

Pinch each risen doughnut through the middle with your thumb and forefinger. Pinch on round in concentric circles so that a thin circle of dough remains to hold the outside ring together — rather like the hub of a car wheel.

Put the oil on to heat until a faint blue haze rises. Test with a cube of bread — it should quickly fry golden.

Fry the doughnuts in hot, but not smoking, oil, turning them gently once. The thin web in the middle will be kept clear of the oil by the buoyant ring of dough, and remain pale. The doughnuts will rise as they cook. Fry them for 5 to 6 minutes until well risen and bronzed as autumn leaves.

Roll the doughnuts in sugar and serve them warm. Hot chocolate with whipped cream to accompany as a special treat — church fairs come round only once a year.

JAM DOUGHNUTS
Pfannkuchen (Germany)

These doughnuts are party food, particularly in the Berlin area. They are traditionally served at New Year's Eve celebrations, where they accompany a steaming bowl of wine mulled with orange peel, sugar, and cloves — *glühwein*.

Quantity   Makes 20–25 doughnuts
Time   Start 2 hours ahead of time
Preparation: 60 minutes

1 lb/500 g plain flour
½ teaspoon salt
1 oz/25 g fresh yeast (half the
quantity if dried)
½ pint/300 ml warm milk
1 oz/25 g sugar

2 oz/50 g butter *or* lard
1 lb/500 g scarlet jam (raspberry,
strawberry, redcurrant)
oil for frying (this would have
been clarified butter)

Utensils   A large bowl, a rolling pin, a baking tray, and a deep frying pan

Make the yeast pastry dough as for the plum tart (see page 514). This dough should be on the soft side, so use a little extra liquid if necessary.

Knock it down after its first rising and roll it out. Using a glass tumbler, mark one half of the dough with circles without pressing right through. Put a spoonful of jam in the middle of each circle and then fold the other half of the dough over the top. Press out a circle round each hummock of jam. Put the doughnuts on a well-floured baking tray — spaced out to allow them to expand. Leave to rise for 10 minutes.

Put the oil to heat in the pan.

Fry the doughnuts in the oil for rather longer than the ring doughnuts — 7 to 8 minutes depending on the size. They should have a character-istic pale ring round the circumference where the dough has risen in the cooking.

SUGGESTIONS
● Austrian Carnival doughnuts, *Faschinskrapfen*, are made to the same recipe, but are stuffed with apricot jam before they are fried. Finish them with a dusting of powdered sugar.

HONEYED DOUGHNUTS
Loukoumades (Greece)

The Greeks are justifiably proud of their beautiful honey. On the three-pronged peninsula of Thrace, where the tall peak of Mount Athos shelters an autonomous republic of black-robed monks, the summer air is filled with the hum of millions of honey-bees. Their nectar comes from the wild herbs, rosemary, lavendar, and thyme. Each human village has its captive bee-village: long lines of miniature bungalows, numbered like beach chalets, have now mostly replaced the old wattle-and-dung baskets. There is an abandoned village in the foothills of Mount Athos. Its site is marked by cemetery cypresses, its stone rubble walls give shelter to a peregrine falcon and only the bee-village is still busy.

Unhusbanded olive trees, pomegranate and walnut trees and thickets of sloe colonize the ancient foundations. Down below where the village has been re-sited to be more accessible to the road, there is a village bread oven and a small café. Alexandra (called after the conquering king who passed through so many centuries ago), a handsome woman of some forty summers, works behind the café's counter-cum-kitchen. She serves Greek salad with feta cheese, salt-pickled fish cut small and dressed with onion, chips fried in olive oil, and crisp fried eggs. She also sells five-kilo tins of the dark thick honey from the bee-village, and on baking days, when the village bread oven is lit, she makes these doughnuts with some of her own bread dough and honey from the bee-village.

Quantity   Makes 20 doughnuts
Time   Start 2 hours ahead
         Preparation: 60 minutes

1 lb/500 g flour	1 tablespoon warm milk
1 teaspoon salt	½ pint/300 ml warm water
1 oz/25 g fresh yeast (half the	oil for frying
quantity if dried)	1 lb/500 g jar honey

Utensils   A large bowl, a deep frying pan, and a perforated spoon

Make a bread dough as for the country bread (see page 492). The dough should be on the soft side, so you may need an extra tablespoon of liquid. When the bread dough is well risen but still in one piece, put on a pan of oil and heat until a faint blue haze rises.

Put the honey jar in a bowl of hot water to liquify its contents.

This is how Alexandra makes her doughnuts: wet your hand and pick up a handful of dough. Squeeze it gradually through the top of your fist into short lengths. Drop the pieces of dough into the hot oil, slicing them in off your fist with a knife. Allow them to puff up and fry golden. When well risen, take them out and drain them on paper.

Pour the warm honey over the hot doughnuts before you serve them with a tall glass of cold water, a small glass of *raki*, and a tiny cup of Greek coffee.

CAKE BREAD
Kugelhupf (Austria)

The *Kugelhupf* has an unusual claim to inclusion in a book on peasant cookery. This cake was a particular favourite of the unfortunate Queen Marie Antoinette of France — casualty of the guillotine and daughter of Francis I and Maria Theresa of Austria. It was Marie Antoinette's reported suggestion that the peasantry should eat her preferred cake as a solution to the bread famine that lit the torch for the French revolution. Marie Antoinette's *Kugelhupf* might thus be held indirectly responsible for the emancipation of most of Europe's peasantry.

Quantity   Makes 1 large cake
Time   Start 2 hours ahead
Preparation: 30 minutes
Baking: 40–45 minutes

1 lb/500 g flour	4 oz/100 g butter
1 teaspoon salt	3 oz/75 g sugar
1 oz/25 g yeast (half the quantity if dried)	2 eggs
	2 oz/50 g currants
⅓ pint/200 ml warm milk	2 oz/50 g blanched almonds

Utensils   A large bowl and a *kugelhupf* mould, a china or tin mould in the shape of a jelly ring (if you have no mould, improvise one out of a heatproof pudding basin with a heavy jam jar in the centre to make the hole)

Put the flour and salt in the warmed bowl. Make a well in the centre. Mix the yeast to a liquid in half a cupful of the warm milk. Pour the yeast liquid into the well in the flour and sprinkle a handful of flour over the top. Put aside for 15 minutes in a warm, draught-proof corner for the yeast to develop and set the sponge.

Warm the butter to soften it. Sprinkle the sugar over the flour. Beat in the liquid butter, along with the eggs, currants, and almonds, and as much of the rest of the warm milk as you need to make a smooth elastic dough. Pummel the dough thoroughly to stretch the glutein.

Knead the dough into a soft white cushion. Put it to rise for about 30 minutes in a damp, warm, draught-proof place such as on a rack above a tray of boiling water in an unlit oven.

When you have removed the dough from the oven, preheat the oven to 400°F/200°C/Gas 6.

When the dough has doubled in size, knock it down and knead it into its final shape. Roll the dough into a long sausage. Butter the *kugelhupf* mould and sprinkle it with flour (better still, with ground almonds). Curl the dough sausage round the ring mould, pressing it gently down — it should fill the mould to within two-thirds of the top. Cover with a damp cloth and put it to rise in a warm place. It will take about half an hour to rise sufficiently.

Bake the *Kugelhupf* at 400°F/200°C/Gas 6 for 20 minutes, then turn the oven down to 375°F/190°C/Gas 5 and bake it for a further 20 to 25 minutes (check that the crust is not burning — you might have to protect it with paper or foil). The total baking time is 40 to 45 minutes. The *Kugelhupf* should then be perfectly well risen, fragrant and golden. Fit for a queen, if not for a revolution.

SUGGESTIONS

- Some cooks use a mixture of butter and lard.
- For Easter the *Kugelhupf* is baked in a special fish-shaped mould.
- *Stollen* is the Christmas speciality and the mix is as for the *Kugelhupf*, but with double the quantity of butter and a handful of candied fruit. Grated lemon rind, nutmeg, and cinnamon are sometimes included as well. Press the dough out into a flat oval and fold the dough over on itself lengthwise to give the classic *Stollen* form. Put it to rise again until it has doubled its bulk. Brush with melted butter. Bake as the *Kugelhupf*. When cool, dust the top of the cake heavily with icing sugar.

FRUIT BREAD
Kletzenbrot (Austria)

A favourite Austrian treat. Made with dried pears or plums, harvested in the late summer and dried spread out on racks in the autumn sun. The plums are dried whole, and the pears are cut in half first.

Quantity   Enough to make 16–20 little buns
Time   Start 2 hours ahead
Preparation: 30 minutes
Baking: 30–40 minutes

For the dough

1 lb/500 g plain flour
½ teaspoon salt
1 oz/25 g fresh yeast (half the quantity if dried)
½ pint/300 ml warm milk
1 oz/25 g sugar
2 oz/50 g butter *or* lard

For the filling

12 oz/350 g dried pears *or* stoned prunes (dried plums)
8 oz/250 g hazelnuts *and/or* walnuts
4 oz/100 g sugar
1 egg

Utensils A small bowl, a large bowl, a rolling pin, and a baking tray

Put the dried fruit to soak in a little water while you make the dough according to the recipe for plum tart (see page 514). When the dough has risen once, roll it out very thin and cut it into 16 to 20 squares.

Chop the nuts and the fruit together and mix in the sugar and the egg. Put a pile of the nut and fruit filling on to each square of pastry dough. Wet the edges of the pastry and fold over the edges. Turn them so that the joins are underneath. Butter the baking tray and put the buns on it, well spaced out to allow them room to rise. Put the tray of buns somewhere warm and draught-free to rise for half an hour (on a rack above a baking tray full of hot water in an unlit oven is my favourite place).

Preheat the oven to 350°F/180°C/Gas 4.

Bake the little buns for 30 to 40 minutes until they are well risen and golden. When you take them out of the oven and while they are still warm, brush them with a syrup of sugar and water (3 spoonfuls of each melted together). Delicious for tea.

SUGGESTIONS
● Brandy or lemon juice can be used to soak the fruit.

YEAST CAKE
Bara brith (Wales)

Welsh country cooks are particularly skilled bakers and can boast almost as many varieties of oven as there are recipes for bread and cakes to cook in them. At Brynmerheryn near Aberystwyth, the pre-1900 oven was a square brick-built cupboard beside the fire. Its door was of cast iron, and the peat fire which burnt beside it on the floor could be pushed in to heat the oven and then pulled out again. The baker would thrust her hand in eight times, that and no more or less, to test if the heat was enough to bake the bread but not to burn it. The neighbour, Mrs Evans, baked her wedding cake in one of these ovens, but the fire had to be let out for two days before it was cool enough for the rich fruit mixture. There was no chimney — smoke found its way out into the chimney of the main fireplace via the 'mantell' — a wicker-work construction which was jammed through the floor and into the room above.

Bara brith is a rich dough cake and a special treat. Today fashion and speed dictate it is made with chemical raising agents. The yeast-raised version is much more satisfactory. The recipe is to be found all over Europe in various guises and regional variations.

Quantity Makes 1 large cake
Time Start 2 hours ahead
Preparation: 40 minutes
Baking: 1 hour

1 lb/500 g flour	1 egg
1 teaspoon salt	4 oz/100 g lard *or* butter
1 oz/25 g yeast (half the quantity if dried)	8 oz/250 g raisins and currants
	1 tablespoon treacle
1 oz/25 g sugar	1 teaspoon caraway seeds
⅓ pint/200 ml warm milk	

Utensils A large bowl and a small oblong bread tin

Liquify the yeast with a teaspoon of the sugar and half a cup of the milk, warmed. Put the flour and salt in a warm bowl, make a well in the middle and pour in the yeast mixture. Sprinkle with a little flour and put aside in a warm place for 10 to 15 minutes to set the sponge.

Add the rest of the milk, beaten up with the egg, and mix to a firm smooth dough. Put aside for an hour to rise in a warm place — inside a plastic bag in the airing cupboard is a good choice.

Meanwhile melt the lard or butter to a warm cream, and lightly flour the raisins and currants so that they do not sink to the bottom of the cake. Butter the bread tin (if you use butter to grease a cake baking tin, the cake will taste of butter, whatever fat you have used in the mixture itself).

Preheat the oven to 350°F/180°C/Gas 4.

When the dough has doubled in bulk, knock it down, knuckling thoroughly with your fists, and work in the rest of the ingredients — the remaining sugar, the melted fat, the raisins and currants, the treacle, and the caraway. Knead the dough into a fat sausage, and press it into the bread tin. Leave in a warm place for 30 to 40 minutes to double in bulk again.

Bake in the oven for 1 hour. It is done when well risen and golden.

LEFTOVERS
- Delicious toasted and buttered.

DANISH PASTRIES
Wienerbråd (Denmark)

The country population of Denmark today is largely occupied with dairy farming and meat production. Until a century and a half ago Danish farming was comparatively undeveloped. Crops were limited to wheat and cereals, and one-fifth of the total area of the country was wasteland: heath and swamp. During the nineteenth century the bottom dropped out of the cereals market as the prairie farmers of the United States began to export to Europe, and Denmark adapted, importing the cut-price grain herself, and fed it to the livestock. Most Danish farmers today own their own farms, growing cereals and vegetables both for cattle feed and human consumption.

In 1882 the first cooperative was formed, and it is on this system that modern Danish prosperity is founded. There are cooperatives for dairy products, bacon factories, egg exporting societies, and poultry dressing stations. Each group supplies the neighbours — buttermilk is used to feed the pigs, and so on. Although the inspiration of the Danish pastry is acknowledged in its name, never was a marriage more clearly made in Heaven than that between the riches of Denmark's dairy farms and the Ottoman-inspired skills of the Viennese kitchen.

Quantity   Makes about 36 little pastries
Time   Start 2 hours ahead
           Preparation: 1½ hours
           Baking: 20 minutes

For the dough
1 lb/500 g plain flour
1 teaspoon salt
1 oz/25 g fresh yeast (half the
   quantity if dried)

⅓ pint/200 ml warm milk
1 oz/25 g sugar
8 oz/250 g butter
1 egg

For the fillings
Mandelmassa
4 oz/100 g ground almonds
4 oz/100 g icing sugar
1 egg white

Hanekam
2 large cooking apples
½ oz/12 g sugar
2 oz/50 g almonds

Spandau
1 egg yolk
1 oz/25 g sugar
1 oz/25 g flour
½ pint/300 ml milk *or* cream
jam

Utensils A large bowl, some small bowls, a rolling pin, and a baking tray

Sieve the flour into the warmed bowl and sprinkle in the salt. Make a well in the centre. Mix the yeast to a liquid in half a cupful of the warm milk. Pour the yeast liquid into the well in the flour and sprinkle a handful of flour over the top. Put aside for 15 minutes in a warm, draught-proof corner for the yeast to develop and to set the sponge.

When the yeast has bubbled up and begun to work, sprinkle the sugar and 2 oz/50 g of the butter, chopped into little bits over the top. Beat the egg with the rest of the warm milk and pour into the spongy centre of the flour. Work the liquid into the flour with a circular motion until you have a smooth elastic dough. You may need a little extra liquid. Pummel the dough thoroughly with your fists, working the mass up and over itself, to stretch the glutein ready for the next stage. It will take a 5 to 10 minute workout.

Form the dough into a smooth white cushion, tucked ends underneath.

Flour the table or a wooden board. With a floured rolling pin roll out the pastry into a large rectangle about ½ in/1 cm thick. Slice the remaining 6 oz/200 g cool butter over the centre third of the dough (dough and butter should be alike in consistency). Fold the other two-thirds up over it, as for puff pastry. Seal the edges down with the rolling pin. Leave in a cool place for 20 minutes.

Meanwhile prepare the filling. This can be simply a spoonful of jam or a piece of fruit sprinkled with sugar, or a more sophisticated egg custard mix, ground almonds and sugar bound with egg white, a strudel-roll filled with soaked raisins — there are many varieties, of which here are 3 representative versions:

Mandelmassa Mix the ground almonds, the icing sugar, and as much of the egg white as you need to make a thick paste. Put it aside.

Spandau Mix the ingredients together until you have a cream. Put the cream into a small saucepan and heat gently, whisking to avoid lumps, until the custard thickens. Be careful not to overcook the egg. Allow the custard to cool before you use it.

Hanekam Cock's comb. Peel and core the apples and stew them gently with a little sugar and a spoonful of water until they are soft. Mash them to a purée, peel and chop the almonds and mix them in. Put the mixture aside to cool.

Roll and fold the dough again once. Let it rise inside a plastic bag for another 20 minutes. Cut the dough into 3 pieces. Roll each piece into a 12 in/30 cm square and then cut it into 4 in/10 cm squares, to give you 9 pastries per square. Divide them into 3 groups.

Use the first group to make the *Mandelmassa*. Put flattened balls of the marzipan paste into the middle of each small square of pastry, and fold 2 of the opposite edges up to meet over the marzipan.

Use the second group to make *Spandau*. Spread a tablespoon of the cold custard over the centre of a small square of pastry and put a teaspoon of jam in the middle. Fold all 4 corners up and pinch them together.

With the last group of little squares, use the *Hanekam*. Put a sausage-shape of the apple purée down one side of each small square. Fold the other side over to make an oblong sandwich. Notch down the seamed side to make a cock's comb effect, and fan out the notches by curving them into a crescent.

When the pastries are filled, put them on a greased baking tray and leave them to prove for 20 minutes. Not in too warm a place or the butter will oil. This pastry has a split personality, being a combination of cold-worked and warm-worked pastes.

Preheat the oven to 425°F/220°C/Gas 7.

Brush the tops of the pastries with egg white when nicely risen and bake in the oven for 15 to 20 minutes.

SUGGESTIONS

• Don't worry if the pastries don't look very professional the first time — they will still taste delicious and with practice you will soon become more dextrous. The Danes learnt in no time.

• Make a tea-ring by dividing the dough into 3 strands. Brush each strand with melted butter and sprinkled with cinnamon, sugar, and nuts pounded together. Plait the 3 strands together and curl the plait into a ring. Sprinkle more nuts over the top. This will take 30 to 40 minutes to bake.

APPLECAKE
Æblekage (Danish)

In the old days this Danish party treat would have been made with a yeast dough and be much like the Austrian *Zwetschenfleck*. The arrival of chemical raising-agents early in this century gave the Danes an opportunity to lighten the mix.

Quantity   Enough for 6 portions
Time   Preparation: 30 minutes
      Baking: 35–40 minutes

6 oz/175 g butter

6 oz/175 g sugar

3 eggs

6 oz/175 g self-raising flour

1 lb/500 g cooking apples (2–3 large ones)

1 teaspoon powdered cinnamon mixed with 1 tablespoon sugar (*optional*)

1 tablespoon chopped blanched almonds (*optional*)

Utensils   A large mixing bowl, a hinged 10 in/25 cm cake tin, and an electric mixer would be useful

Soften the butter and beat it in the mixing bowl with the sugar until the mixture is light and fluffy (it takes twice as much energy as you think — the mix has to be really white and airy — and is easiest to achieve with an electric mixer). Beat in the eggs, one at a time. Sieve in the flour and fold it in thoroughly (called 'tiring'). The mixture will be quite stiff.

Grease the baking tin and preheat the oven to 350°F/180°C/Gas 4.

Peel the apples and slice them. Spread half the mixture in the bottom of the cake tin and lay half the sliced apples over it. Cover with the rest of the mixture and then arrange the rest of the apple slices in pretty wheels over the top. Sprinkle over all the cinnamon, sugar, and chopped almonds if you have them.

Put the applecake to bake in the oven for 35 to 40 minutes, until well risen and golden.

CHAPTER 15

Sweet Pies, Pancakes, and Puddings

Sweet Pies

APPLE AND BLACKBERRY PIE
(England)

The early English system of annual triple-crop rotation in open strip fields made it impracticable for fruit trees, which take far longer than a year to mature, to be planted in fields. The solution, both in England and in Norman France, was to plant semi-wild trees on the edges of the woods, thus giving free access to a fruit orchard to all including the poorest. Blackberries grew wild in any event, as did raspberries, strawberries, and several other varieties of berry. These were joined in the woodland by pear, plum, quince, cherry, and medlar. The raw materials for fruit pies and dumplings were thus not difficult to come by, even in years of poor harvest.

Quantity   Makes 1 pie
Time   Preparation: 30–40 minutes
         Baking: 40–45 minutes

For the shortcrust pastry
8 oz/250 g plain flour
1 teaspoon salt
1 oz/25 g sugar
3 oz/75 g cold butter
3 oz/75 g lard
4 tablespoons cold water

For the filling
1 lb/500 g sharp cooking apples
½ lb/250 g blackberries
3 oz/75 g sugar (more if the fruit is
   very sour)

Utensils   2 large bowls, a shallow pie dish, and a rolling pin

Make the pastry first. Sieve the flour with the salt into the bowl. Add the sugar. Cut the butter and lard into the flour with a sharp knife. When it is all minced fine, finish rubbing the fat into the flour with your fingertips. The secret of light pastry is keeping it cool — if you use the palms of your hands, the butter will oil and make the pastry tough.

When you have a mix like fine breadcrumbs, work in the water a tablespoon at a time still with the tips of your fingers. Knead into a soft round ball. You may need more or less water — it all depends on the weather and the dryness of the flour.

Leave the dough to rest in a cool place for 10 minutes, while you prepare the fruit. Peel and slice the apples. Pick over and hull the blackberries. Put them into another bowl and mix in the sugar. Leave them aside to form juice.

Preheat the oven to 400°F/200°C/Gas 6.

Roll out two-thirds of the dough into a round base for the pie, and then roll out the remaining third into a lid. Do this on a well-floured board with a rolling-pin, using quick light strokes pushing away from you.

Line the pie dish with the larger round of shortcrust pastry. Pile in the fruit. Sprinkle a little water over it — just fingertips dipped in fresh water, enough to help the juice, but not enough to make the pastry soggy. Damp the edges of the pastry, and lay the lid over the fruit. Crimp the edges together with a fork and cut a steam hole in the top. If you have some scraps of pastry over, make a few pastry leaves with diagonally cut strips. Bake in the preheated oven for 15 minutes to set the pastry. Then turn the oven down to 350°F/180°C/Gas 4 and bake it for another 25 to 30 minutes.

Serve with plenty of thick cream — lovely after a Sunday lunch of roast beef.

SUGGESTIONS
- If you are using a pastry lid only, make half quantities and reduce the cooking time by 10 minutes.

TREACLE TART
(Scotland)

This was by Scottish grandmother's favourite pudding. The Scots have a sweet tooth — and the largest per capita consumption of sugar in the world. Greenock is the sugar centre of Scotland, and has been so ever since the first sugar shipments began to arrive in the 1680s direct from the West Indies. Then the tart would have been made with the dark brown treacle from the bottom of the sugar barrels and would have contained raisins and currants and spices if the cook could afford it. Modern golden syrup is more refined and does not need such disguises.

Quantity   Enough for 6
Time   Preparation: 30 minutes
Baking: 25–30 minutes

For the shortcrust pastry	*For the filling*
6 oz/175 g plain flour	1 lb/500 g Golden syrup
1 teaspoon salt	2 oz/50 g fresh (untoasted)
1 oz/25 g sugar	breadcrumbs
4 oz/100 g cold butter	1 oz/25 g softened butter
3 tablespoons cold water	

Utensils   2 mixing bowls, a rolling pin, a shallow pie dish, and a food processor if you have one

Make the shortcrust pastry as for Blackberry and Apple Pie (see above).

Preheat the oven to 400°F/200°C/Gas 6. Roll out two-thirds of the pastry to line the pie plate. Roll out the other third and cut it into strips.

Mix together the golden syrup with the fresh breadcrumbs and the butter. Spread the mixture over the pie-base and lay a criss-cross lattice of pastry over the top. Bake for 25 to 30 minutes.

My grandmother used to serve the treacle tart hot with thick cream or a dollop of vanilla ice-cream melting into it. Wonderful. She sometimes mixed in the juice of half a lemon to give a little sharpness to the flavour. It was either served after a roast chicken Sunday lunch or on an ordinary winter's day after a thick soup of potatoes and leeks made with the stock from an old boiling hen past its best. My grandmother was very proud of her hen coop full of Rhode Island Red chickens — and I was sometimes allowed to collect the eggs tucked protectively under their soft marmalade-gold breast feathers.

APPLE STRUDEL
Apfelstrudel (Austria)

A 'strudel' is a whirlpool — the recipe is the cook's whirl of pastry. From the high hills of Yugoslavia to the plains villages of Hungary, each housewife has her special recipe. Mountain village housewives make sturdy strudels with yeast dough spread with curds or poppy seeds. The farmers' wives, their larders stocked with fresh butter and fine-ground wheat, may choose to make theirs with a shortcrust pastry stuffed with sour cherries or plums from the orchard. In the old days, before the advent of ready-made strudel dough, the most delicate recipe was reserved for those households blessed with a cook who had learned her trade in the kitchens of the occupying Turks.

The Ottoman Empire, founded in the thirteenth century and not finally dismantled until the early twentieth century, stretched, in its prime, as far as the battlements of Vienna. On the departure of the invaders, their unemployed cooks took the new skills to the kitchens of the aristocrats of the Austro-Hungarian empire — and eventually back home to their own valleys. The old-fashioned, heavy strudel, made with yeast dough or pastry, is still widely popular all over eastern Europe. However, 'strudel' now means two different things — it is applied both to the dish itself, and also to the *filo*-like pastry learnt from the Turks. Strudels made with the fine *filo* pastry need patience and time — today most Austrian housewives buy theirs ready-made.

Strudels were most usually made with yeast pastry in the peasant kitchen as everyday fare, although a skilled cook would always prefer to make a *filo*/strudel pastry for a special occasion. Frozen strudel pastry can be bought in supermarkets and delicatessens — you might have to overlap the sheets to get the width you want. When you make it yourself, remember it must be kept warm to stay flexible.

Apple strudel is the basic and best-loved strudel of all. A marriage of the skill of the Ottoman Turks and the fragrant orchards of the northern valleys.

Quantity Enough for 6 after a good thick soup
Time Preparation: 1 hour
    Baking: 45 minutes

For the pastry (bought frozen *filo* can substitute)
8 oz/250 g plain flour
½ teaspoon salt
2 tablespoons oil

¼ pint/150 ml warm water
1 oz/25 g melted butter

For the filling
3 lb/1·5 kg apples
2 oz/50 g sugar (more if the apples
    are sour)
2 oz/50 g raisins, juice 1 lemon,

and 1 teaspoon powdered
    cinnamon (*optional*)
2 oz/50 g butter
4 oz/100 g breadcrumbs

Utensils A bowl, a rolling pin, a pastry brush, a large, clean linen cloth, and a baking sheet

Pile the flour on to a large pastry board, or, better still straight on to your table top. Sprinkle on the salt. Make a well in the centre of the flour hill and pour in the oil and warm water. Mix thoroughly into the flour, from the centre outwards. You may need a little more water if the flour or the air is very dry. The paste must be on the soft side. Flour your hands and set about kneading the dough very thoroughly. Feel it grow silky and elastic under your hands as the flour granules absorb the water. When it is smooth and shiny, knead the dough into a cushion, brush with the melted butter and set it to rest in a warm place under an upturned bowl for at least 20 minutes — maximum 12 hours. At this stage it is a good-natured dough.

While the dough rests prepare your filling. Peel and core the apples. Slice them finely and sprinkle the sugar over them. Mix in the raisins and sprinkle with the lemon juice and cinnamon if you are using them. Melt the butter and fry the breadcrumbs gently until they turn pale gold. Set aside.

Lay the clean linen cloth out on the table. Flour your hands and the cloth (leave the flour jar out in case you need more). Until you are used to the method, cut the dough in half and make 2 cushions — a smaller strudel is easier to handle. Put one cushion in the middle of the floured cloth and flatten it with the palm of your hand. Roll the dough out with a floured rolling pin until you have a circle about 9 in/22 cm in diameter. That is as far as you go with the rolling pin.

Using the backs of your hands — the fingers loosely bent into a fist, the fists pushed gently under the dough circle until the outer edge of the pastry rests on the knuckles — pull the pastry outwards, stretching it as you go. Pull it in all directions until you have a large transparent pancake through which, should you feel inclined, you could read a page of the family Bible. The edges will be comparatively thick. These you tear off as you make the strudel. If the transparent part tears, patch it with trimmings from the edge. The pancake will lap over the edge of the cloth. Brush with melted butter.

Preheat the oven to 450°F/230°C/Gas 8 and butter the baking sheet.

If you have decided to make 2 smaller strudels, each one will take half the filling. Spread the filling over two-thirds of the dough, leaving a gap round the sides. Tear off the thicker edges of pastry. Fold in the edges of 2 parallel sides of the dough. Pick up the corners of the cloth and roll the strudel gently away from you and over itself to curl into a Swiss roll shape.

Pick up the strudel in its cloth sling and roll it out on to the baking sheet. Brush the pastry with melted butter.

Bake the strudel in the hot oven for 45 minutes. Brush the strudel with melted butter and serve warm, sprinkled with icing sugar. Austrian-Ottoman magic.

SUGGESTIONS
● Leftover strudel paste cannot be used again. Instead, gather up the bits into a flat cake and allow it to dry until firm. Grate the cake on the coarse grater to make little scraped noodles called *Reibgerstl*. Dry them

in a very low oven and store them in a tin. Sprinkle them into boiling soup — they will only take a few minutes to cook.

Bavarian apple strudel   The housewives of Bavaria like to cook their apple strudel bathed in cream, or egg and milk custard, in a deep pan. Settle the strudels side by side in a well-buttered pie dish (if you have made a single large one, curl it round in a hairpin bend), leaving a ½ in/ 1 cm hand-width gap between each strudel. Bake in a hot oven — 475°F/ 240°C/Gas 9 — for 10 minutes to set the dough. Then pour into the gaps between the strudels ½ pint/300 ml cream, or ½ pint/300 ml milk with a little sugar and 2 eggs beaten into it. Turn the heat down to 425°F/220°C/ Gas 7, and cook for a further 45 minutes (total cooking time, 55 minutes). A deliciously juicy and fragrant dish to be served warm. It's very good cold too — but nothing can compare with a freshly baked strudel still warm from the oven.

Cherry, plum, or rhubarb strudel filling   Proceed exactly as for apple strudel, but use stoned cherries, stoned plums, or rhubarb cut into short lengths, instead of the apples. Be careful not to include too much juice — the mixture should not be too wet.

Curd cheese filling   Proceed exactly as for apple strudel (not forgetting the fried breadcrumbs). Beat together 1 lb/500 g curd or white fresh cheese, 2 eggs, a tablespoon of raisins, and a tablespoon of sugar. Use this instead of the apple mixture.

● All these strudels can be made with shortcrust pastry or yeast pastry. They will of course be far more substantial dishes.

APPLE CAKE
Apfelkuchen (Germany)

The everyday version of Mum's apple pie had a basis of yeast pastry and was made as for the plum tart (see page 514). This recipe is for a special occasion. The dish migrated with immigrants to the New World, and early American cookbooks are full of such recipes. There are no less than eight versions in my American grandmother's *Settlement Cook Book* of *circa* 1900. The inclusion of almonds is nice but not essential. Germany is too northerly for almond trees to thrive anyway, although these nuts were always part of the travelling spice merchants stock-in-trade.

Quantity   Enough for 6–8
Time   Preparation: 40 minutes
Baking: 45–55 minutes

For the murbteig pastry
12 oz/350 g flour
2 oz/50 g sugar
½ teaspoon salt
8 oz/250 g butter
2 egg yolks
4 tablespoons cold water
1 tablespoon brandy

For the filling
2 lb/1 kg apples
1 oz/25 g butter
2 oz/50 g raisins
1 tablespoon brandy
1 oz/25 g blanched almonds
 (*optional*)

Utensils   A mixing bowl, a rolling pin, a small saucepan, and a pie dish with hinged sides (this allows the making of a deep pie)

Put the flour, sugar, and salt into the bowl and cut in the butter with a knife. When your mixture is like fine breadcrumbs, mix all to a soft dough with the egg yolks, the water, and the brandy (the alcohol evaporates during the cooking and leaves the pastry short and crisp). Knead the pastry lightly with the tips of your fingers — use more liquid if the mixture is too crumbly. Everything must be kept as cool as possible. The palms of the hands are too warm — using them will oil the dough and make it tough.

Put the pastry aside to rest while you peel, core, and slice the apples. Fry the apples lightly in the butter. Meanwhile put the raisins to swell in the brandy, and then mix them with the apples. Add the almonds if you are using them.

Preheat the oven to 425°F/220°C/Gas 7.

Roll out two-thirds of the pastry and use this to line the pie dish. Roll out the remaining third into a circle to fit over the top. Fill the dish with the apple mixture. Damp the edges of the pastry. Lay on the lid and seal the edges by pressing them together with a fork. Decorate the lid. Make a hole for the steam to escape.

Bake for 45 to 55 minutes until the pastry is crisp and golden. Scatter thickly with caster sugar. Serve warm with whipped cream. Perfection after a good soup.

SUGGESTIONS
• Make the pie in a large ring placed on a baking sheet.

CHEESE CAKE
Kasblotz (Germany)

This recipe made the transatlantic crossing most successfully and a grand total of 6 alternative mixtures is on offer in my turn-of-the-century *Milwaukee Settlement Cook Book*. This version is from Franconia.

Quantity   Makes 8–10 portions
Time   Preparation: 40–50 minutes
           Baking: 30–35 minutes

For the murbteig pastry	*For the filling*
12 oz/350 g flour	1 lb/500 g white curd cheese
2 oz/50 g sugar	¼ pint/150 ml double *or* soured
½ teaspoon salt	cream
8 oz/250 g butter	3 eggs
2 egg yolks	2 oz/50 g sugar
4 tablespoons cold water	grated rind 1 lemon (*optional*)
1 tablespoon brandy	1 egg yolk beaten up with a
	tablespoon cream to glaze

Utensils   2 mixing bowls, a rolling pin, and a deep pie dish, 10 in/ 25 cm in diameter

Put the flour, sugar, and salt into a bowl and cut in the butter with a knife. When the mixture is like fine breadcrumbs, mix all to a soft dough with the egg yolks, the water, and the brandy. Knead the pastry lightly with the tips of your fingers until you have a soft ball.

Roll out the pastry to fit the pie dish. Ease the pastry into it. Put aside to rest while you make the filling.

Preheat the oven to 450°F/230°C/Gas 7.

Beat the cheese into the cream, then beat in the eggs and the sugar. Stir in the grated lemon rind — this improves the flavour but is not essential. The top of the cheesecake remains rather pale and anaemic unless you glaze it before cooking with a spoonful of cream mixed with an egg yolk. Pour the cheese mixture into the pie dish.

Bake the cheesecake for 30 to 35 minutes. It should be well set and brown on the base when it is done.

Serve the cheesecake warm — delicious with fresh berries.

SUGGESTIONS
● Spread the mixture over a yeast-pastry base as for the plum tart (see page 514).

STRAWBERRY TART
Tarte aux fraises (France)

French bakers prepare these pies all year round with whatever fruit is in season. They may use raspberries, strawberries, split and stoned apricots, sharp little mirabelle plums, and, all winter long, cartwheels of sliced apple, the edges caramelized dark by the oven's heat. They also make tarts with dried prunes, soaked, stoned, and glistening rich as a plum pudding during the winter. In my local market-town of Revel they were baked every day and three times on Saturday. When the pies were taken out of the oven, the scented steam curled out into the street and a queue of customers would form immediately: French housewives think it no shame to buy their Sunday treat from the pâtisserie, provided, it goes without saying, the pâtissier is unquestionably the best pastry-cook in the area. In France, wise patronage reflects as well on the customer as it does on the purveyor.

Quantity   Enough for 4
Time   Preparation: 50 minutes
          Baking: 25–30 minutes

For the pastry (a *pâte brisée*)
4 oz/100 g plain flour
½ teaspoon salt
1 oz/25 g caster sugar
3 oz/75 g butter
2–3 tablespoons cold water

For the custard   (*crème pâtissière*)
½ pint/300 ml creamy milk
1 oz/25 g flour
2 egg yolks
1 oz/25 g sugar
1 oz/25 g butter

For the filling
1 lb/500 g fresh strawberries
½ lb/250 g redcurrant *or* raspberry
   jam

Utensils   A mixing bowl, a rolling pin, an 8 in/20 cm round pie tin, preferably one of those with fluted sides and a removable base, a liquidizer if you have one, a saucepan, and a basin larger than the saucepan

Pour the flour into a bowl with the salt, the sugar, and the butter cut into pieces. Chop the cold butter into the flour and sugar with a knife, and finish by rubbing in with the tips of your fingers. Mix in the minimum amount of cold water needed to form a soft dough ball. Flatten the ball lightly with a rolling pin dusted with flour, then drape the pastry over the rolling pin to transfer it to the tin. Press the circle of pastry out until it covers the base and the sides of the tin. This recipe is nearly as rich as shortbread which allows it to be baked blind, or empty, without bubbling. Prick the pastry base all over with a fork, and then put it to rest while you make the filling. You can if you wish, line the pastry with foil and weight it with beans — then you will need to add on 5 minutes to the cooking time.

Preheat the oven to 375°F/190°C/Gas 5.

Meanwhile make the custard cream. Stir 2 tablespoons of the milk into the flour. Whisk in the egg yolks and the sugar. Chop up the butter and stir that in. This job can be done best in the liquidizer. Heat the mixture gently in a pan until it thickens, stirring all the time. The flour must be cooked, or the custard will taste starchy, and the eggs should not be over-cooked or they will scramble (though not as seriously as with an egg-only custard). If the mixture does curdle or go lumpy pour it quickly back in the liquidizer with a little cold milk and beat it up again. When the custard is good and thick, set the bottom of the saucepan in a basin of cold water to cool it down.

Put the empty pastry case to bake for 25 to 30 minutes (adding 5 minutes if you have weighted it with beans and foil), until the pastry is golden and crisp. Slip off the fluted side piece and leave the pastry shell to cool down.

Now prepare the fruit. Wipe, hull, and halve the strawberries. Warm the jam (redcurrant is best, raspberry is good) with a little water to make a thick syrup. If there are masses of pips, pass it through a sieve when you pour it over the fruit.

Assemble the pie just before you are ready to eat it — its flavours are as fugitive as ripe strawberries themselves. Spread the now-cooled pastry shell with the cream. Lay the strawberries on their bed of custard, cut sides upwards, in a single layer of concentric circles. Finally pour over all a glazing of warm jam, which will release the irresistible perfume of warm berries. Serve the tart immediately.

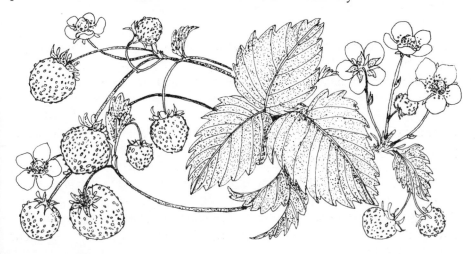

LEMON TART
Tarte au citron (France)

These beautiful sharp-flavoured lemon tarts kept company with the *pissaladière* on the counter of my local pâtisserie in Castelnaudary. The pâtisserie stood on one corner of the town square, next to the charcuterie which supplied the locals with their *cassoulet* — own earthenware pot to be brought, three days' notice required. Tuesday was market day and the scent of citrus oil and warm butter would mingle with that of the blossom on the lime trees which lined the avenue where the stallholders set up shop.

Quantity   Gives 8–10 servings
Time   Preparation: 30–40 minutes
          Baking: 40 minutes

For the pastry
6 oz/175 g flour
1 teaspoon salt
1 oz/25 g sugar
6 oz/175 g cold butter
2 egg yolks
3 tablespoons water

For the filling
4 lemons
4 oz/100 g unsalted butter
5 eggs
5 oz/125 g caster sugar

Utensils   A mixing bowl, a 10 in/25 cm tart tin, preferably one with a removable base, a rolling pin, grater, lemon squeezer, and a whisk or electric mixer

Sift the flour into a bowl with the salt and sugar. Make a well in the middle and grate in the cold butter. Mix it lightly in. Beat the egg yolks with the water and work them into the flour and butter with the tips of your fingers. Gather all into a ball. If you need a little more water to make a soft dough, sprinkle in the minimum. Knead lightly and gently for a short time — this is a very rich pastry and liable to oil. However, the dough should not be too stiff. Flour a board and roll out the pastry dough into a circle to fit the tart tin. Lay the pastry in the tin, easing it into the corners. Cover and put it aside to rest in a cool place.

Preheat the oven to 350°F/180°C/Gas 4.

Grate the rind of one of the lemons and squeeze the juice from all of them. Melt the butter. Beat the eggs and the sugar together (much easier with an electric whisk) until they are light, white, and fluffy. This takes twice as long as you think. Fold in the lemon juice and the butter. Pour the filling into the tart case immediately and put it in the oven to bake for 40 minutes, until the pastry is crisp.

Serve warm, with a bottle of chilled Beaume de Venise from the hills of Provence.

CHERRY BATTER
Clafoutis aux cerises (France)

A recipe from the Limousin district of France and a true peasant dish. A kind of Yorkshire pudding with cherries. I first encountered it in the Andalusian *finca* of a French woman, long resident in Spain. Her orchard had lemon trees, orange trees, medlars, even avocado — strange hermaphrodite tree — and only one cherry. When it finally fruited in its seventh spring, this is the dish she made with its black harvest. She was a marvellous cook, but I have never seen her put a dish on the table with such pleasure and pride.

Quantity   Enough for 6
Time   Preparation: 20 minutes
　　　　Baking: 40 minutes

1 lb/500 g black cherries
1 oz/25 g butter
4 oz/100 g flour
½ teaspoon salt
½ pint/300 ml milk

4 eggs
1 small glass *eau de vie or* fruit
　brandy
sugar for sprinkling

Utensils   A large bowl, a 10 in/25 cm square baking tin, a liquidizer if you have one

Preheat the oven to 350°F/180°C/Gas 4 and put in the baking tin with a knob of butter. Stone the cherries.

Mix the flour, the salt, the milk, and the eggs into a smooth batter. Stir in the *eau de vie* or brandy. All this can be done in a liquidizer.

Take out the hot tin, roll the melted butter around it and pour in the batter. It will sizzle for a moment. Pour in the batter. Scatter the cherries into the batter and then sprinkle all with sugar. Bake for 1 hour.

The *clafoutis* will puff up like a Yorkshire pudding, and sink somewhat as it cools. Eat it warm with the thick, pale sour *crème fraîche* of France. Failing that, Devonshire clotted cream would do well enough. A little glass from the bottle of *eau de vie de fruits* — *framboise* or *Poire William* — to echo the ingredients.

SUGGESTIONS
● Any other fruit suitable for pies — apples, plums, apricots, or pears can substitute for the cherries. But there is something about the rich, dark cherry juice on the golden crust that is particularly special.
● You could always marinate the fruit in brandy.

PASTRY WITH NUTS
Baklava (Turkey and Greece)

The best-loved sweet dish of the Middle East, the original *baklava* is claimed by everyone in the region. Bakers from Sophia to Alexandria sell it from huge shiny golden trays. The Armenians probably have the best title to its modern identity — the pastry was baked as a Lenten dish, *bahk* meaning 'Lent' in Armenian and *halva* being the ancient word for 'sweet'. The ingredients were permitted during the fast, and the layers of pastry were supposed to be forty in number. Not an association the sponsoring Church necessarily condoned, the flock being more eager to adapt its favourite pagan rituals than the shepherd to countenance their pedigree. The dish appears on the menu at the Ottoman Emperor's court no earlier than the end of the fifteenth century. It has made up for its late arrival in popularity ever since.

Quantity   Makes 36–40 pieces
Time   Preparation: 30 minutes (longer if you make your own pastry)
        Baking: 45–50 minutes

1 lb/500 g home-made (see page 532) or bought *filo* pastry
8 oz/250 g chopped almonds *or* walnuts
8 oz/250 g clarified butter, made by melting ordinary butter, allowing it
   to cool and then lifting off the solids at the top. The watery whey
   and salt will remain at the bottom along with any additives and the
   butter will keep sweet and fresh for a long time.
1 lb/500 g honey

Utensils   A baking tray (approximately 12×8 in/30×20 cm), a small saucepan, and a pastry brush

Chop the nuts roughly and put them aside. Melt the clarified butter. Brush the baking tray with butter. Lay 2 layers of *filo* on the tray — with light fingers so that there is plenty of air between. Don't press on the pastry if you can help it — air between the layers is very important. Sprinkle melted butter over the sheets. Lay on another 2 sheets and sprinkle on more butter. Continue until you have 8 sheets in place.
   Preheat the oven to 350°F/190°C/Gas 4.
   Scatter half the nuts over the pastry. Continue with more *filo* sheets and butter until you have added another 8 sheets. Scatter on the rest of the nuts. Finish with a final layer of 8 sheets. Mark into lengthways parallel lines and then cut diagonals across to give you diamonds. Pour the rest of the butter over. Sprinkle with water from wet fingers so that the sheets stay flat.
   Bake for 40 to 45 minutes.
   Meanwhile make a syrup by melting the honey in a little pan with 3 to

4 tablespoons of water. The syrup must be hot when you pour it over the *baklava*.

When the pastry is well risen and golden pour the honey syrup over it, trickling it well into the cuts. Put the pie back into the oven for 5 minutes.

Serve the *baklava* warm or cold, with a glass of water and a little cup of thick black Turkish coffee.

SUGGESTIONS

● Instead of honey, make the syrup with ½ pint/300 ml water, 8 oz/250 g sugar and the juice of a lemon, simmered together for 10 minutes until the syrup thickens. But it is much nicer with the beautiful honey of Greece.

OIL BISCUITS
Tortas de aceite (Spain)

A treat for both children and adults, these biscuits are characteristically marked with black blisters from the hot oven. They are crisp and delicious — not unlike sweet water biscuits.

Quantity   Makes 15–20 biscuits
Time   30 minutes to make and bake

1 lb/500 g flour	1 liqueur glass dry *anis* (aniseed-
6 oz/175 g sugar	flavoured liqueur) *or* 1 glass
½ teaspoon salt	water and 1 teaspoon aniseed
4 tablespoons oil	(sweet cumin)
1 egg	

Utensils   A mixing bowl and a baking sheet

Preheat the oven to 425°F/240°C/Gas 9.

Mix the flour, 4 oz/100 g of the sugar, and the salt together in the bowl. Make a well in the middle and pour in the oil and the egg beaten into the *anis* or water and aniseed. Knead into a pliable dough. Roll into a sausage shape and cut into 15 to 20 short lengths. Roll out each piece into a thin circle. Repeat until all the dough is used. Put the circles on a greased baking sheet.

Bake in the hot oven for 10 minutes. Sprinkle the biscuits with extra sugar a minute or two before you take them out. They will keep very well if wrapped in waxed paper and stored in a tin. Delicious for breakfast or as a tea-time snack. Children in Spain have them as a special treat during the festival *feria*.

WALNUT PIE
(Romania)

The Christmas Eve, the Ajun, the day of the 24th of December, the last of Advent, is a holiday too, and a special dish is eaten in every household, the turte. It is made up of a pile of thin dry leaves of dough, with melted sugar or honey and pounded walnut, the sugar being often replaced by the juice of bruised hemp seed, supposed to be sweet too. These turte are meant to represent the Infant Christ's swaddling clothes. The dough is prepared on the previous evening, and in some places it is used as a means of making the trees bear a rich crop of fruit in the coming summer, a kind of suggestion to Nature by threatenings. The wife, with her fingers full of dough, walks into the garden; the husband, axe in hand, follows close after. They stop at the first tree, and he says,

'Wife, I am going to fell this tree, as it seems to me it bears no fruit.'

'Oh no,' says she. 'Don't for I am sure next summer it will be as full of fruit as my fingers are full of dough.' And so on with every other tree.

Theresa Stratilesco *From Carpathian to Pindus*

Quantity   Yields 6–8 portions
Time   Preparation: 30 minutes
          Baking: 35–40 minutes

For the pastry
8 oz/250 g flour
1 teaspoon salt
1 oz/25 g sugar
4 oz/100 g cold butter
2 egg yolks (the whites go into the filling)

For the filling
8 oz/250 g shelled walnuts
4 oz/100 g sugar
4 egg yolks
6 egg whites
apricot jam
juice 1 lemon

Utensils   A mixing bowl, a rolling pin, a whisk or an electric beater, a pestle and mortar, an 8 in/20 cm baking tin, and a food processor

Sieve the flour and salt into the bowl with the sugar. Cut the butter into the flour and then finish rubbing them together with the tips of your fingers — do not use the palm of your hand as it would oil the butter and make the pastry tough. There are those who freeze the butter and then grate it in and swear this makes the lightest pastry of all. When the mixture is like fine breadcrumbs, work in the egg yolks to make a soft dough — you may need extra liquid, in which case use soured cream or cold water. Roll out the ball of dough with firm light strokes of a rolling pin into a thin circle to fit the baking tin. Ease the pastry into the tin — if you stretch it, it will shrink back in the cooking. Put it in a cool place to rest while you make the filling.

Preheat the oven to 350°F/180°C/Gas 4.

Grind or pulverize the walnuts finely in the mortar. Whip up the egg yolks with the sugar until you have a fluffy pale mixture. This always takes far longer than you expect, and is best done with an electric beater. Fold in the ground walnuts. Beat the egg whites with a little more sugar until they hold soft peaks. Fold them into the egg and walnut mixture. Pile the filling into the pastry case.

Bake in the medium oven for 35 to 40 minutes, until well risen and golden. It should hardly sink at all as it cools.

Serve the pie when cool with hot wine. A pie to be nibbled on a cold winter's night in the Carpathian mountains, by a family huddled round the little crib on Christmas Eve, waiting for the stroke of midnight so that the youngest child of the house can put the tiny figure of Jesus in his hay-lined manger.

PLATE PIES
Teisen lap (Wales)

There is great skill in the making of a plate pie — cooked on the griddle or *planc* over the fire. These are flat pies which have to be neatly flicked over halfway through the cooking to be baked on the other side. A favourite all over Wales. Modern usage adds baking powder to the mix.

Quantity Enough for 5–6 portions
Time   45 minutes to make and bake

6 oz/175 g flour	3 oz/75 g sugar
½ teaspoon salt	3 oz/75 g currants and raisins
1 teaspoon baking powder	1 egg
(*optional*)	¼ pint/150 ml cream *or* milk
4 oz/100 g salty butter	

Utensils A mixing bowl, a rolling pin, an 8 in/20 cm enamel plate or shallow baking tin, and if possible a *planc* or a griddle

Sieve the flour and salt and the optional baking powder into the bowl and then rub in the butter lightly with tips of your fingers. Stir in the sugar and the fruit. Beat the egg with the milk or cream and mix it into the flour. Knead all into a soft dough ball. Roll the dough out into a circle to fit the plate.

Bake the pie on a medium hot *planc* or griddle or on a heavy pan placed directly over the flame, for 15 to 20 minutes. Then turn it over with great skill and Welsh sleight of hand, and cook it on the other side for 15 minutes.

If you prefer, the pie can be baked in the oven at 350°F/180°C/Gas 4 for 45 minutes. Sprinkle the top with plenty of caster sugar.

Sweet Puddings and Dumplings

RHUBARB DUMPLING AND CUSTARD
(England)

Rhubarb, a native of Tibet, was introduced to the English medicinal herb garden in Tudor times, but it was not until the eighteenth century that its scarlet, straw-cosseted early spring shoots became a familiar sight near the manure heap of every English cottage garden. The country poor of northern Europe soon discovered the virtues of a hardy perennial plant which could survive freezing winters, and give plentiful fruit (albeit in an unfamiliar shape) for its pies, and, most importantly in Scandinavia, good material for its cottage wines. This dumpling was originally tied in a cloth and suspended, along with the vegetables and the meat, in the soup pot.

Quantity   Enough for 6
Time   Preparation: 40–50 minutes
         Cooking: 2½ hours

For the suet pastry
8 oz/250 g self-raising flour
½ teaspoon salt
1 oz/25 g sugar

4 oz/100 g suet
¼ pint/150 ml cold water

For the filling
1 lb/500 g rhubarb (weighed after trimming)
3–4 oz/75–100 g sugar
½ wine glass water

For the custard
4 egg yolks
2 oz/50 g sugar
1 pint/600 ml milk
¼ pint/150 ml cream

Utensils   A mixing bowl, a 3 pint/1·5 litre pudding bowl, a rolling pin, greaseproof paper, string, a clean pudding cloth or silver foil, and a large boiling pan

Sieve the flour into the mixing bowl with the salt and sugar and then stir in the suet. Add cold water slowly (you may need more or less liquid) to make a smooth, soft dough which leaves the sides of the bowl clean.

Grease the pudding bowl. Cut off two-thirds of the pastry and roll it out on a well-floured board with a rolling pin, until you have a big enough circle to line the bowl. Line the pudding bowl, easing the pastry well down so that it does not shrink away in the cooking. Roll out the rest to make a lid and put it aside.

Put on to boil a pan of water large enough to accommodate your basin. Put in a metal ring or upturned unbreakable saucer on which to rest the basin. Trim the leaves and stalk end off the sticks of rhubarb — the leaves themselves are toxic. Wash the sticks and chop them into 1 in/2·5 cm lengths. Pack the rhubarb into the lined pudding bowl, sprinkling on the sugar as you go. Pour in the half-glass of water. The filling should come to within a finger's breadth of the top.

Wet the rim of the pastry and lay on the rolled-out lid. Pinch the edges of the pastry together to seal. Cover over with a circle of greaseproof paper and the cloth, pleated in the middle and tied round with string. Make a string handle to lift the bowl in and out. Silver foil can be used instead of the cloth. Steam the pudding for 2 to $2\frac{1}{2}$ hours, checking regularly that it has not boiled dry. Top up with boiling water. Suet puddings are amiable and easy-going: the only damage that can be done is to let them boil dry or come off the boil while they are cooking.

Meanwhile make the custard. Beat the egg yolks with the sugar. Bring the milk nearly to the boil, and pour it over the egg yolk mixture, whisking vigorously. Return it to a gentle heat and stir until the custard thickens enough to coat the back of the spoon. Remove from the heat and stir in the cream. Float a knob of butter to melt over the surface if you are going to keep it waiting to prevent a skin forming. Beat the butter in just before you serve. The custard should be put on the table in a jug for the diners to help themselves.

Serve the suet pudding without delay — it gets heavier as it cools, although an extra half-hour's boiling will do it no harm. The pudding can be made in advance and then reboiled for at least an hour to return it to its former lightness.

Precede a heavy pudding with a dish of plain boiled meat — perhaps beef boiled with carrots, or a piece of boiled bacon served with stewed apples.

SUGGESTIONS
• Fill the dumpling with apples sweetened with honey, or with black-berries, cherries, damsons, or plums. Bury 1–2 oz/25–50 g butter in the fruit to give a delicious flavour. Extra ingredients might include raisins, almonds, lemon peel, curd cheese — there is plenty of room for invention.

• Suggestions for the custard. Custard is served with steamed pud-dings in particular, although it also keeps good company with stewed fruit, baked apples, and fruit pies. Flavoured with vanilla, coffee or chocolate or fresh fruit purées, it can be frozen into an ice-cream. Mix it with a sweetened fruit purée in the proportion of 1:1 and fold in the leftover egg whites well beaten to a froth, for the traditional English fruit fool.

STEAMED JAM PUDDING
(England)

A relatively recent late Victorian recipe, but still the heir to the great English pudding. The inheritors of the peasant tradition in England appear to have retreated to the nursery, and this is where this delicious pudding has been found for many years.

Quantity Enough for 6
Time Preparation: 20–25 minutes
Cooking: 1½ hours

8 oz/250 g flour
1 teaspoon baking powder
½ teaspoon salt
4 oz/100 g butter

4 oz/100 g sugar
2 eggs
¼ pint/150 ml milk
½ lb/250 g jam (damson is best)

Utensils A mixing bowl, a 2 pint/1·2 litre pudding basin, some greaseproof paper, some foil, and a large boiling pan with a lid

Sift the flour with the baking powder and salt. Cut the butter into the flour until the mixture looks like very coarse breadcrumbs. Or cut the butter in with a knife if your hands are too warm. Add the sugar. Beat the eggs and stir them in. Mix to a soft dropping consistency with the milk.

Put the ½ lb/250 g jam into the pudding basin and spread it up the sides and round the base. The basin need not be greased. Tip in the pudding mixture. Top with a circle of buttered greaseproof paper. Cover the basin with a double layer of aluminium foil well-folded over the edges. Place the basin on a piece of wood or an upturned saucer in the large pan with a well-fitting lid. Pour in boiling water to come just under halfway up the basin — any higher and you risk a soggy boiled pudding rather than a light steamed one. Bring the water back to the boil and then turn the heat down.

Keep at a steady simmer for an hour and a half, checking every 20 minutes or so that the pan has not boiled dry. Keep topping up with boiling water. Unmould on to a hot plate just before you are ready to serve the pudding — it is very good-natured and can be kept warm in its simmering water for as long as convenient. Serve with custard as for the Rhubarb Dumpling (see above).

SUGGESTIONS
● Treacle can be substituted for the jam — use plenty to give a sticky, slightly caramelized coating to the pudding (to weigh syrup, scatter a handful of flour in the scales first). Or add chopped ginger and its syrup (a taste acquired in the Colonies).

• The pudding can be baked in the oven in a well-buttered dish for 1 hour. Serve after a simple nursery dish such as Shepherd's Pie or Cottage Pie (see page 212).

SEMOLINA HALVA
(Turkey and the Balkans)

The *halva* made in peasant kitchens all over the Balkans as well as Turkey is a simple affair, made with semolina, baked and sweetened with honey or *pekmekz*, a concentrated grape syrup. Sometimes the balls are spiked with pine kernels. Semolina *halva* remains a favourite votive gift among Turkish women. Promised and delivered in gratitude for favours, it combines the most symbolically valuable and the most enjoyable ingredients available.

Quantity   Makes 20–25 little balls
Time   Preparation: 40–50 minutes

For the syrup
4 oz/100 g sugar
¼ pint/150 ml water
juice 1 lemon

For the paste
2 oz/50 g butter
6 oz/175 g semolina
2 oz/50 g whole nuts (walnuts,
    pine kernels, almonds,
    hazelnuts, whatever grows in
    your wood)

Utensils   A small saucepan and a flat dish

Make the syrup by heating together in the small pan the sugar, water, and lemon juice and simmering them together for 10 minutes. Chop the nuts roughly. Lightly oil the dish.

Melt the butter in a pan and stir in the semolina. Stir it around while it takes a light colour — this is an important step as it gives the finished *halva* a delicious roasted flavour. Add the nuts. Fry lightly for a moment. Pour in the syrup, stirring vigorously. Simmer gently for 5 minutes to allow the semolina to absorb the liquid. Remove from the heat and pour into the lightly oiled dish. Leave to cool a little and then cut the paste into small squares. Roll each one into a ball in clean hands. You can spear each little ball with a nut if you like, or roll the balls in chopped nuts. Serve them warm, with thick cream.

Take a little glass of *raki* with the *halva*, a small cup of Turkish coffee, and a long glass of water. They taste like a particularly nutty marzipan.

SUGGESTIONS
• Stir in 2 oz/50 g raisins when you add the nuts.

SOURED CREAM PORRIDGE
Rømmegrøt (Norway)

Porridge is a favourite time-honoured Norwegian country meal. Taken at any time of the day, ordinary porridge is prepared with coarsely milled grains (oats, barley, rye). Special porridge is made with the best the larder holds — rich cream and fine flour. *Rømmegrøt* is served as festival food, at Christmas and on Midsummer Day. Very good *rømmegrøt* is now made and sold deep-frozen by Norwegian dairies. Some confusion arose when nineteenth-century travellers, and indeed twentieth-century sociologists, questioned the inhabitants of isolated communities on their diet. When the reply was universally *grøt*, it was not appreciated for some time that *grøt* and 'food' were synonymous, and that those questioned did not think it necessary to specify that they also ate fish, berries, milk, and meat.

Quantity   Enough for 6
Time   Preparation: 10–15 minutes (positively fast food)

1 pint/600 ml soured cream
6 oz/175 g flour
1 pint/600 ml soured *or* sweet milk
1 teaspoon salt

Utensils   A roomy saucepan and a perforated spoon

Bring the cream to the boil. Mix half the flour to a liquid with a little cold milk. Stir it into the boiling cream and simmer to allow the butter in the cream to rise. Skim off the butter — it will be served separately. Stir in the rest of the flour and milk.

Simmer for 5 minutes to cook the flour (stirring all the while, it's a devil for sticking and burning). Add salt.

Serve with a jug of the hot skimmed butter and a bowl of sugar. If berries are in season, serve the porridge with strawberries or raspberries. Raspberry or blackcurrant juice to drink with it.

SUGGESTIONS
● Unlock the spice chest for Christmas — sprinkle cinnamon over the porridge.
● The dish can be made with porridge oats, but you will have to increase the cooking time (see page 276 for a porridge recipe).

BAVARIAN CURD DUMPLINGS
Topfennockerl (Germany)

Specially delicate dumplings to follow a good thick soup. Serve them with a dish of stewed fruit.

Quantity   Makes 15–20 little dumplings
Time   Preparation: 30 minutes

½ lb/250 g fresh curd cheese
2 eggs
1 oz/25 g sugar
1 oz/25 g flour

Utensils   A mixing bowl, a saucepan, and a perforated spoon

Beat the curd cheese, eggs, and sugar together. Beat in the flour — you may need more or less to give you a soft firm dough. The less you use, the lighter the dumplings.

Bring a pan of salted water to the boil.

Form into little dumplings with 2 wet teaspoons and drop them into the water. Poach them for 5 to 8 minutes at a gentle simmer. They will bounce up to the top of the water. When they are firm, fish them out with a perforated spoon.

Serve the *Topfennockerl* with a dish of stewed apricots or plums

SUGGESTIONS
● Bury a stoned plum in the middle, or a dark little damson, its stone replaced by a lump of sugar.
● Or poach them and serve them in a fruit soup (see page 565).

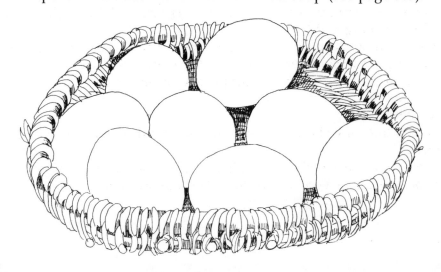

VEILED COUNTRY MAIDEN
Bondepige med slør (Denmark)

A very favourite Danish country dish, served after a thick soup such as the Green Pea Soup on page 355.

Quantity   Enough for 6
Time   Preparation: 30 minutes

  2 lb/1 kg cooking apples
  ¼ pint/150 ml water
  3 oz/75 g sugar
  8 oz/250 g dry rye bread
  2 oz/50 g butter
  ½ lb/250 g raspberry *or* any red jam
    (*optional*)

Utensils   A small saucepan, a small frying pan, a pudding dish, and a food processor if you have one to make the breadcrumbs

Peel, core, and slice the apples. Stew them to a mush in the small pan with the water and a tablespoon of the sugar.

Grate the bread into fine breadcrumbs. Fry them in the butter until they are a nutty golden brown. Mix in the rest of the sugar.

Layer the breadcrumbs when cool with the stewed apples and the raspberry jam (if you are using it) in the pudding dish. Breadcrumbs on the base, then all the apple, then more breadcrumbs, then all the jam, then the rest of the breadcrumbs. Serve cool with plenty of thick cream.

SUGGESTIONS
• The French version is the *Charlotte aux pommes* — a rather grander confection, where a mould is lined with crustless slices of white bread fried golden in butter. The centre of the mould is then filled with apples stewed with sugar and butter, and a lid of more fried bread is put over it. The whole mould is then baked in a moderate oven for 15 to 30 minutes to crisp its exterior. Serve hot or cold. This sophisticated version of the dish is credited to the kitchens of the Emperor Napoleon, who was a great fan of Goethe's heroine Charlotte in the novel *Werther*.
• In England, Apple Charlotte fills the same gap. Some hold Farmer George's Queen Charlotte responsible for its introduction. The pudding is baked as for the French *Charlotte*, and the jam of the Danes is omitted in favour of 2 layers of apples.

BREAD PUDDING
(Wales)

Watkin Williams-Wynne's recipe for bread pudding. The marmalade is optional, although oranges have been traded around the coasts of Britain since Phoenecian times.

Quantity Enough for 5–6
Time Preparation: 15–20 minutes
      Cooking: 2 hours

6 oz/175 g breadcrumbs	1½ tablespoons marmalade
3 oz/75 g suet	(*optional*)
3 oz/75 g sugar	a little milk
2 eggs	

Utensils A mixing bowl, a 2 lb/1 kg pudding basin, greaseproof paper, and a food processor if you have one to make the breadcrumbs

Make the breadcrumbs. Shred and chop the suet finely. Mix the breadcrumbs, suet, and sugar in the bowl. Beat up the eggs and add with the marmalade to the dry ingredients. The mixture should be rather moist, as the breadcrumbs swell. Add milk, therefore, as required. Turn the mixture into the greased pudding bowl, cover with greaseproof paper and steam for 2 hours (see recipe on page 548 for steamed pudding). Turn the pudding on to a hot dish, and pour round it either marmalade or sweet melted butter sauce.

BREAD AND BUTTER PUDDING
(England)

The recipe given in E. S. Dallas' idiosyncratic mid-Victorian cookery manual *Kettner's Book of the Table*, says all that need be said on the matter of this simple dish:

> Bread Pudding: When one is in the humour to eat bread pudding one wants it very simple — therefore the simplest receipt is the best, and the less we say of currants and candied citron the better. The rule is to pour upon fine breadcrumbs about three times the quantity of liquid, in the form of rich milk and butter. Say there are six ounces of bread, on this put two ounces of fresh butter, and then pour boiling hot a pint of the creamiest milk to be obtained. Cover this over, and let it stand until the bread is well soaked — which will take about half an hour. Then mix in three ounces of sugar, the yolks of five eggs, the whites of three, and a little nutmeg. Pour it into a dish and bake it for half an hour.

I would only add that a jug of cream makes the dish sublime.

Pancakes

SMALL PANCAKES
Plättar (Sweden)

A special frying pan is available in Sweden with little hollows in it for cooking several small pancakes at a time.

Quantity   Makes 25–30 pancakes
Time   Preparation intermittently: 1 hour

8 oz/250 g flour	3 eggs
2 tablespoons sugar	1 pint/600 ml milk
pinch salt	butter for frying

Utensils   A bowl, a whisk, a *plättar* pan or small frying pan, and a liquidizer if you have one

Put the flour, sugar, and salt into the bowl. Whisk the eggs and milk and stir them gradually into the flour until you have a thin cream. This is easily done in a liquidizer. Leave the batter to rest for half an hour or longer. A spoonful of snow lightens the mix in winter.

Melt a knob of butter in each of the dips in the special *plättar* pan, or in the small frying pan. When the butter foams, pour in enough pancake mixture to coat the pan in a thin layer, rolling it around so that the coating is as thin as possible. Pancakes are nicest when they are as fine as a lawn handkerchief. Flip it over when one side of the pancake is golden-brown — the sides will peel away from the pan as it cooks. Cook the other side. Continue until all the batter is used up. Serve the pancakes immediately with a spoonful of fresh berries rolled up in each pancake — little wild strawberries, raspberries, blueberries — or best of all in Scandinavia, cloudberries, ripened corn-gold under the midnight sun. Or serve wrapped round a spoonful of berry jam.

SUGGESTIONS
● Serve the pancakes with sugar and lemon — the English treat for Shrove Tuesday designed to use up all the good things in the larder before Lent.

JAM PANCAKES
Palacinke (Yugoslavia)

Sweet pancakes are a favourite treat throughout the Balkans. And also throughout Scandinavia, and the Low Countries, and France, and Britain (where the rich ingredients symbolize a pre-Lenten larder-clearing), and practically everywhere else. Each region has its own way of enjoying them, and great pride is taken in the excellence of the raw materials. No housewife would bother to make them unless these were of the best. The eastern Europeans like their sweets to be sweet and cannot resist stuffing the pancakes with their delicious fruits jams. Buffalo cream would have accompanied — and still does, if you are very fortunate and happen to be passing through Sibiu, or some such town in Romania or points east, where buffalo are still the beasts of burden.

Quantity　Makes 15–20 small pancakes
Time　Preparation intermittently: 1 hour

4 oz/100 g flour	small glass fruit brandy *or* any
¼ teaspoon salt	white alcohol
1 tablespoon sugar	butter for frying
2 eggs	½ lb/250 g jam to stuff the
¾ pint/450 ml milk-and-water	pancakes

Utensils　A bowl, a whisk, a jug, a small frying pan, and a liquidizer if you have one

Put the flour and salt and sugar into the bowl. Stir in the eggs and then gradually beat in the milk-and-water, until you have a thin cream. This is easily done in a liquidizer. Leave the batter to rest for 20 minutes.

When you are ready to make the pancakes, beat the cream again for a few minutes, adding the fruit brandy (the Yugoslavs make an excellent plum brandy — the famous *slivovica*) to lighten the mix. Up in the mountains, a fistful of snow can be used instead. Transfer the batter to a jug.

Heat your smallest frying pan — an omelette pan is very suitable. Throw in a tiny knob of butter (clarified if you have any — it will not splutter and burn). Roll the pan around to spread the melted butter evenly. Pour in a couple of tablespoons of the batter (judged by eye of course — you don't want to be fiddling around with spoons at a moment like this). Roll the batter round the pan — it will coat it in a thin layer. If you have put in too much, just pour it back into the jug. Cook the pancake over a medium-high flame, keeping a careful eye on it. When the edges are lacy, dry, and curl away from the sides of the pan (the work of a few moments), the pancake is ready to be turned. If you are feeling exuberant and the pan is one of those light raw iron ones, flip it over in the air. If not, a spatula will do fine. Turn the pancake and cook the other side. Flip it out on to a reversed saucer — pile the pancakes on top of each other as you make them.

Repeat until all the batter is used. Stuff the pancakes with a spoonful of your best home-made jam. Imagine serving them with little rolls of thick, yellow buffalo cream. Clotted cream will have to do instead.

SUGGESTIONS
- Make double quantities — these pancakes freeze beautifully.
- Or tuck them into a baking dish in rows, bathe them in $\frac{1}{2}$ pint/300 ml double cream, cover the dish with foil and put it to bake in a moderate oven — 350°F/180°C/Gas 4 — for 20 minutes.

Fritters

CINDERS
Cenci (Italy)

Cenci, Cinderella's fritters, are the north Italy country child's favourite treat. Michaela, who cooked in the *pensione* in which I stayed as a student in Florence, would make them to keep her little grandchildren happy while she prepared the family's Sunday lunch. She would simply throw scraps of sweetened pastry, left over from the making of a pie, into deep oil and fry them until golden. Transferred to one of her big earthenware dishes, the piping-hot fritters would be sprinkled with icing sugar. The children never learned to leave them until they were cool enough to handle.

' "The rich strangers who visit our country pick a little of many things, but we eat all we can get of one or two things — bread and

macaroni, or bread and beans. It is only at weddings," he finished confidentially, "that we arrive at sweets." ' Sicilian peasant to Eliza Putnam Heaton. Sugar appeared in the Italian diet relatively early. The Vatican librarian Bartolomeo Sacchi recorded in 1475 that sugar was being grown in Crete and Sicily as well as India and Arabia.

Quantity   Makes 20–25 fritters
Time   Preparation: 30–40 minutes

1 lb/500 g flour	2 eggs
2 oz/50 g sugar	small glass brandy *or* water
2 oz/50 g butter	oil for frying

Utensils   A bowl, a rolling pin, a deep frying pan, and a food processor if you have one to make the pastry in a moment

If you have no food processor to help make the pastry, put the flour and sugar into a bowl. Cut the butter in with a knife. Mix the eggs together and work them in, adding a little brandy or water as you need it to make a soft dough. Roll the dough out and cut the pastry into ribbons. Twist the ribbons into knots.

Heat oil in the pan — use a clear olive, sunflower, or other good vegetable oil. Deep fry the knots until they are light and golden. Drain them on kitchen paper and then pile them up on your best earthenware platter. Sprinkle with sugar and serve hot, just as for the Scandinavian Christmas dish of *hjortetakk* (see below).

Children can have their *cenci* with fresh grape juice. For grown ups, serve the *cenci* with a bottle of cold sweet white, the *vin santo* of Italy.

STAG'S ANTLERS
Hjortetakk (Norway)

Made with luxurious ingredients, these fritters are an absolutely indispensable Christmas treat, as Paul du Chaillu discovered when he visited a Norwegian farmhouse in 1871:

> The larder is well stocked; fish, birds, and venison are kept in reserve; the best spige kjod [dry mutton, or either beef or mutton sausage] is now brought forward. A calf or a sheep is slaughtered, and as the day draws near sweet fritters and cakes are made. The humblest household will live well at Christmas. . . . The little country stores carry on a thriving trade in coffee, sugar, prunes, raisins, and rice for puddings. Oats are specially bought and put out to feed the birds.

Similar special treats — waffles and pancakes peculiar to the different regions — are made all over Scandinavia at Christmas. *Goro* are made for special occasions, particularly for Christmas and Easter, in a beautifully patterned iron. The *goro* maker used to have an extra-long handle which allowed it to be held straight over the fire. Electric versions are now sold.

Quantity   Makes 25–30 fritters
Time   Start if possible the day before
         Preparation: 1 hour in total

3 eggs	grated lemon rind
6 oz/175 g sugar	1 lb/500 g flour
2 oz/50 g butter	fat for frying (pork lard was used
6 tablespoons double cream	in Norway, but vegetable oil
2 tablespoons brandy	usually substitutes today)
crushed cardamom	

Utensils   Several bowls and a pan for deep frying

Beat the eggs thoroughly with the sugar. Melt the butter. Whip the cream. Stir the butter, cream, brandy, and flavourings (if used) into the eggs and sugar. Work in the flour — you made need less or more, depending on the size of the eggs and the absorbent quality of the flour — to give a soft, workable dough. Allow the dough to rest in a cool place, overnight in the refrigerator if possible.

Roll the dough into a sausage and chop off lengths. Roll each length into pencil-thin ropes which you can bend to form a ring. Cut a few notches into each ring to make the horn branches.

Heat a pan of deep fat until a faint blue haze rises. Fry the fritters until puffed and golden. Drain on absorbent paper.

Serve sprinkled with sugar and cinnamon, in a beautiful golden scented pile on your best white dish.

SUGGESTIONS
● These biscuits keep well in an airtight tin. In the clear Arctic sunshine of July, I enjoyed a plateful which had somehow escaped my hostess' children's attentions the previous Christmas.

WAFFLES
Gauffres de Brussels (Belgium)

The Belgians are very fond of their food and take particular pleasure in their waffles. Belgian kitchen equipment nearly always includes one or several of the square-patterened waffle irons, both the thin ones to make *gauffrettes* and the thicker ones for the *gauffres*. There is considerable debate over the inclusion of yeast in the mix. The alternative raising agent is an egg white beaten to a snow. I give a yeast recipe as more likely to be the peasant version — the incorporation of air via beaten egg white is a sophisticated and comparatively modern idea.

Quantity Makes 12–15 waffles
Time Start 2 hours ahead
          Preparation: 40–50 minutes

1 pint/600 ml milk
1 oz/25 g yeast (half the quantity if dried)
1 lb/500 g plain flour
6 eggs
2 oz/50 g sugar
¼ teaspoon salt
1 oz/25 g melted butter

Utensils A large basin and a waffle iron

Warm half a cup of the milk and dissolve the yeast in it.

Beat the eggs with the rest of the milk. Put the flour in the warmed basin, make a well in the centre and pour in the yeast mixture, the eggs, and the milk. Beat until you have a creamy lump-free batter. Put aside in a warm, draught-free cupboard for 2 hours to allow the yeast to develop. Then stir in the sugar, salt, and melted butter.

Cook the waffles in a well-buttered waffle iron. Serve with sugar and butter, or jam, or syrup.

FRESH CHEESE FRITTERS
Papanasi (Romania)

A kind of fried dumpling, these little fritters can be served with meat, or, as here, as a sweet dish after a soup.

Quantity   Makes 20–25 fritters
Time   Preparation intermittently: 40 minutes

8 oz/500 g fresh curd cheese
2 oz/50 g butter
2 whole eggs and 2 egg yolks
4 oz/100 g flour
½ teaspoon salt
grated rind 1 lemon *or* orange
   (*optional*)

1 oz/25 g sugar
oil for frying
soured cream and icing sugar to
   finish

Utensils   A sieve, a food processor if you have one, a bowl, and a deep frying pan

Sieve or process the cheese if it is the lumpy cottage variety, and then beat it into a smooth dough with the butter, egg yolks (save the 2 whites), flour, salt, and grated rind. Leave the mixture to rest for 15 to 20 minutes. When you are ready to proceed, beat the whites with the sugar until they hold peaks. Fold this into the cheese mixture.

Put the oil on to heat. When a faint blue haze rises, drop in tablespoons of the mixture. Fry them gently until puffed up and golden. Drain well on kitchen paper.

Spoon soured cream over the fritters and sprinkle them with icing sugar. Serve them piled in a glorious golden pyramid to be eaten immediately.

SUGGESTIONS
● If you are serving the *papanasi* to accompany a meat dish, leave out the sugar and the grated peel. The soured cream should be spooned over just the same.

CHAPTER 16

Fruits and Nuts

The wild larder of Europe is naturally very rich in fruits and nuts. The Romans were the first to improve on nature and were responsible during their colonial period for the spreading of improved strains of orchard fruit throughout Europe. This free bounty was both available and useful to the peasantry who were able to supplement their diet in a thoroughly healthy fashion. As a result in predominantly meat-eating communities such as Britain, the poor man at the lord's gate, provided he managed to survive the early years, was likely to live longer and stay healthier than his lord in the manor.

Berries have always been important winter stores in northerly countries where the growing season for fruit lasts only two or three months. So short a ripening time allows only small fruit to develop. Sometimes the berries were preserved unsugared. The sourer the better, cranberries, blueberries, and cloudberries could be simply mashed, packed into clean china bowls, covered, and then stored in a cool corner as an excellent source of vitamin C throughout the long dark winters. When the Norwegian Arctic explorers under Roald Amundsen battled their way to the South Pole in 1911, he and his men did not suffer from scurvy as did the unfortunate British under Captain Robert Scott. Fruit syrups still stock Scandinavian country-dwellers' winter larders.

My favourite nineteenth-century traveller, Mrs Ethel Tweedie, appreciated the berry harvest in Finland in 1878:

> From the middle of June till the middle of July we ate wild strawberries three times a day with sugar and cream. They simply abound, and very delicious these little Mansikka are. So plentiful are they, that Suomi is actually known as 'strawberry land'. There are numbers of wild berries in Finland; indeed they are quite a speciality, and greet the traveller daily in soup — sweet soups being very general — or they are made into delicious syrups, are served as compote with meat, or transformed into puddings.
>
> The berries . . . include Vaccinium occycoccus, a small red berry, something like a cranberry. It grows in the autumn under the snow where it ripens, and is ready to be picked in spring when the snow melts. It keeps in a tub for months without any preparation, and is particularly good as a jelly when eaten with cream. Suomuurain, in appearance like a yellow raspberry, grows in the extreme north in the morasses during August. It is a most delicious fruit with a pine tree flavour.

FRUIT SYRUPS
(All Scandinavia and Central Europe)

Blackberries, blackcurrants, blueberries, cherries, raspberries, redcurrants, strawberries, and those special fruits of the far North, cloudberries, ligonberries, and Arctic raspberries are all suitable for the preparation of this staple winter store — absolutely essential to the well-being of those without access to fresh fruit in the frozen landscape of the Arctic winter. There are few sights more cheering in the long night than a larder-cellar well stocked with these jewel-bright syrups and a few bottles of rhubarb wine and *aquavit*. Small wonder that Raoul Amundsen, equipped with the knowledge of centuries, succeeded in reaching the South Pole and survived a journey which proved fatal to so many others. Make a few bottles to light up your own winter.

Quantity   1 lb/500 g fruit yields roughly ¾ pint/450 ml syrup
Time   Preparation: 15–20 minutes
Cooking: 20 minutes but allow time for the straining

the fruit of your choice	6–8 oz/175–250 g sugar per 1 pint/
½ pint/300 ml water per 1 lb/500 g	600 ml liquid
fruit	

Utensils   A preserving pan, a clean linen cloth, an upturned stool, and a large bowl

Pick over the berries and remove any rotten ones. Put the fruit into a large preserving pan and cover them with the appropriate quantity of boiling water. Bring back to the boil and cook the berries for 10 minutes.

Pin or tie the clean cloth on to the legs of an upturned stool and place a bowl beneath to catch the drips. Tip the juice and pulp from the pan into the dip in the cloth. Allow it to drip through as for jelly. This will take a few hours. I leave it overnight.

Measure the juice back into the saucepan, and add the sugar (more if the juice is tart, less if it is sweet). Heat gently to dissolve the sugar, but do not boil again. Bottle and seal and store in a cool larder.

SUGGESTIONS
• Fruit cordial can be made with any other berry which is local and plentiful. The strength and keeping properties of your particular choice is a matter for experiment. Here are a few guidelines:

Cranberry syrup   5 lb/2·5 kg cranberries, ¾ pint/450 ml water, 4 oz/100 g sugar per 1 pint/600 ml juice. Simmer the berries in the water until they burst. Drip them through a tea cloth as if you were making jelly.

Measure the juice and add the sugar. Bring to the boil, stir to dissolve the sugar. Pour into sterilized bottles.

Raspberry syrup 5 lb/2·5 kg raspberries, ¾ pint/450 ml water, 8 oz/250 g sugar per 1 pint/600 ml juice. Cover the raspberries with boiling water. Allow them to infuse in a warm place for a couple of hours. Strain through a tea cloth. Measure the juice and add the sugar. Boil up and bottle.

Strawberry syrup 5 lb/2·5 kg strawberries, juice of 2 lemons, 2 pints/1·2 litres water, 1 lb/500 g sugar per 1 pint/600 ml juice. Put the strawberries and the lemon juice into a bowl. Pour the cold water over. Allow to infuse for 24 hours in a cool place. Strain through a cloth and then measure the juice. Boil up the juice with the sugar. Skim and bottle.

Apple juice 10 lb/5 kg sour apples, 5 pints/3 litres water, 8 oz/250 g sugar per 1 pint/600 ml juice. Cut the apples into chunks, peel, core, and all. Put them into a saucepan with the water and stew them until soft. Strain out the juice and measure it. Add the sugar to the juice and boil, skimming well, until the syrup clears.

Fruit butter Use the leftover fruit pulp from syrup or jelly-making for fruit butter to eat as a pickle with cold meat or in pies. Rub the pulp through a sieve (if it is already cooked — if not stew until soft). Weigh the pulp and then add half the weight in sugar. Simmer slowly for a couple of hours. Pack into sterilized jars.

BLACKCURRANT SYRUP
(Norway)

Scandinavian berries seem to have better keeping properties than southern fruit. In the old days only the more well-to-do used sugar as an additional preservative in jams and syrups. Here is a recipe which makes use of the berries' natural sweetness.

Quantity Yields roughly 3¾ pints/2·5 litres syrup
Time Start 1–3 days before
　　　　Preparation: 20 minutes

5 lb/2·5 kg black *or* redcurrants *or*
　　a mixture
3 pints/2 litres water

Utensils A preserving pan, a perforated spoon, a strainer, and bottles for storage

Put the berries, crushed with their stalks and all, into the preserving pan. Pour boiling water over them. Leave them in a cool place for 1 to 3 days to ferment. Skim off any mildew which forms.

Strain out the juice and put it back in the pan. Bring to a fast boil as quickly as possible and then skim off the scum. Boil rapidly for 5 minutes. Pour into sterilized bottles and store in a cool dark larder.

Dilute with water to make a delicious drink, or use in fruit soups, or as a sharp sauce for winter puddings. Jewelled colours to brighten an Arctic storecupboard.

SLOE SYRUP
(Romania)

Sloes are sold by the gypsies in the markets of central Europe throughout the autumn. Bullaces and sloes are used to make an excellent syrup which is stored and used through the winter. Frau Klein, wife of the Bishop of Sibiu in Transylvania, makes this syrup every year. Her storecupboard also contains green tomatoes pickled in brine, rosehip jelly, damson cordial, and quince paste for Christmas. Here is her recipe:

> Prick the sloes (gathered after the first frost has tenderized their skins) and put them to soak in water to cover for 3 days. Measure the juice and add 1 kilo of sugar to each 1 litre of juice. Boil up, pour into sterilized bottles, and seal the bottles up when they are cool. This is a very good syrup and will last until the following autumn. You can take it hot with a little plum brandy and honey in the winter months.

BERRY COMPOTE
Rødgrød (Denmark)

One of the best loved of the fruit soups, the best version combines three red fruits in equal measures. Naturally a single one will do. Served as a soup before the meat dish.

Quantity Enough for 6
Time 40 minutes

½ lb/250 g redcurrants	2 oz/50 g potato flour, sago flour
½ lb/250 g cherries	*or* cornflour
½ lb/250 g raspberries	2 oz/50 g sugar
2 pints/1·2 litres water	

Utensils A large saucepan, a sieve or jelly cloth, and a serving bowl

Stew the 3 red fruits with the water until the juice has all run out. Press through a fine sieve or jelly cloth. Mix the flour with a little water.

Bring the juice back to the boil and stir in the flour liquid and the sugar. Bring back to the boil again, stirring as it thickens. Pour into a bowl, sprinkle with a little sugar (this stops a skin forming), and allow to cool.

Serve with plenty of thick yellow cream.

SUGGESTIONS
- This makes rather a good summer pudding if accompanied by little hot biscuits.
- Serve as a breakfast dish with soured cream or yoghurt.
- Make the dish with elderberries (at the end of the summer the tiny black berries will be ripe, but do not pick them until the heads turn over to face the ground) and serve with sliced apples floating in it.

LEFTOVERS
- Delicious as a sauce for ice-cream.

REDCURRANT SOUP
(Finland)

The Finns eat their sweet fruit soups and porridges after their meat. The country people do not much like oatmeal — they prefer these wheat and bread-based porridges, or milk preparations such as curds, junkets, and soured cream.

Quantity Enough for 4
Time Preparation: 15 minutes
    Cooking: ½ hour

  4 thick slices stale rye bread
  1 pint/600 ml water
  1 pint/600 ml redcurrant purée
  2 oz/50 g sugar

Utensils A blender or sieve and a saucepan

Tear up the bread and put it to soak in the water for half an hour. Mix it with the fruit purée. Beat all together with the sugar in a blender, or push it through a vegetable sieve. Pour the soup into a saucepan, heat to boiling point and simmer for a few moments to thicken. If you are hungry, serve it with curd dumplngs (see page 551). Otherwise eat with plenty of thick fresh cream and brown sugar.

SUGGESTIONS
- Raspberry, sour apple, or sour cherry are all suitable fruits for this recipe.
- A squeeze of lemon juice will sharpen up a purée which is too bland.
- Delicious for a late Sunday breakfast.

ORANGE PRESERVE
Glyko portokali (Greece and neighbours)

Very sweet sticky fruit preserves are offered to guests as a sign of hospitality all over central Europe — sweetmeats to anticipate sweetness. They were made with honey or, in the eastern Mediterranean, with sugarcane syrup. The lemon juice is to help prevent the sugar crystallizing. These sweetmeats are accompanied always by a glass of water and sometimes by a tiny cup coffee. To be eaten with a spoon.

Quantity   Makes 2–3 pots
Time   Start 2 days before
           Preparation: 1 hour 20 minutes

12 oranges with thick skins
3 lb/1·5 kg sugar
1 pint/600 ml water
juice 1 lemon

Utensils   A heavy saucepan and some storage jars

Pare off the outer and bitter skin (save it to dry in a warm oven and store for use as a flavouring in soups and stews). Boil the oranges in water till they are soft. This may take as long as 2 hours. Drain them and put them to soak in cold water for a day, changing the water 2 or 3 times.

Quarter the oranges and halve the quarters, to give 8 pieces per orange. Make a syrup by simmering the sugar in the water until all the grains dissolve. Pour the syrup over the oranges and leave them to stand overnight. The following day put the syrup and oranges into the heavy pan and bring all to the boil. Continue to boil until the syrup thickens — the oranges dilute the liquid with rather a lot of juice, so this may take half an hour or so. Add the juice of the lemon and boil for a moment longer.

Allow to cool and then store in sealed jars. The preserve will keep well — sugar is a marvellous preservative.

Serve one piece on a little plate with a teaspoon and a glass of water, to your favourite guests. A spoonful of jam has largely replaced these sweets today.

SUGGESTIONS
• Quite delicious served in small quantities with a generous dollop of cream, particularly clotted cream. Consider it a replacement for the rich little roll of buffalo cream which would have accompanied it to welcome you to the Palace of Topkapi. A little cup of bitter Turkish coffee to accompany.

ROSEWATER
(Bulgaria)

In the eighteenth century, when the whole of Bulgaria formed part of the Turkish Empire, a merchant familiar with the rose gardens in Asia passed in a carriage along the main highway that leads over the Balkan Mountains towards Rumania, and when he came into the vicinity of the Wild Rose Pass — the Shipka Pass — he was struck by the extraordinary abundance of the flowers and their extreme fragrance. He immediately perceived that these roses were very similar to the oil-bearing roses on the other side of the Bosphorus . . . so he managed to persuade some of the Turks living in the valley to set out roses and start a little distillery. The results proved very favourable, and for years after this little wild-rose valley gave humanity most of its rose-oil, as it does today. . . .

The flowers belong, I found out on inquiry, to varieties of Rosa damascaena and Rosa alba. They are small and unpretentious and are always picked before they are opened. The gathering time is in the early morning, just as soon as it is light enough to see, and girls — some pretty and some plain — dressed in simple black costumes, go from bush to bush and pluck the blossoms and put them into baskets, from which they are poured into sacks and taken to the distilleries with the dew still upon them. I was told that if these blossoms were exposed to the sun they would give less oil and of an inferior quality.

The old-fashioned distilleries were very simple, easy to make and easy to manage. These facts alone kept the industry in the hands of the peasants, who were well able to tend them without any outside help from the urbanites, engineers, and agriculturalists. Rows of big, upright, closed kettles containing water were placed on bricks over a fire. The roses were dumped into the water and boiled. The steam passed through the head of the kettle and was conducted through long pipes lying in cool, running water. As it distilled, little yellowish green drops appeared on top. This was the rose-oil which, when it cooled, congealed and had the appearance of salve. Many of these primitive distilleries still exist. . . .

This rose-industry fascinated me. . . . The oil is put into tiny bottles shaped like acorns, closed with a metal cap that screws on tightly, since the essence evaporates very easily. One of Bulgaria's best stories is about a peasant called Bai Ganyou, who filled his saddle-bags with these tiny bottles and went to Europe to sell them. The best and I think unrivalled preserve made throughout the country is the 'rose-jam' called sladko, or just 'the sweet'. Everybody eats it and has it at home. It is delicious and tastes just as it smells — of roses. Puddings and pastries are frequently flavoured with rose-water.

George Sava, *Donkey Serenade*

ROSEPETAL PRESERVE
(Bulgaria)

One of the nicest of all preserves. Use petals picked at the beginning of the season — I am told the dark red ones are good, but you will have to experiment with your own. The petals are inclined to be leathery if the rose is not suitable.

Quantity   Makes approximately 6 lb/3 kg preserve
Time   Preparation: 30 minutes
         Cooking: 40–50 minutes

2 lb/1 kg rose petals
4 lb/2 kg sugar
1 pint/600 ml water
juice 2 small lemons

Utensils   A large saucepan with a lid, a perforated spoon, and some storage jars

Wash the petals thoroughly and clip off the white ends. Put them to boil in the covered saucepan with ½ lb/250 g of the sugar and ½ pint/300 ml of the water. Then remove the cover and add all the rest of the sugar and water. Bring to the boil and skim. Simmer until the mixture thickens. Add the lemon juice and boil for a few minutes longer. Allow to cool and seal into small jars.

SUGGESTIONS
• The preserve can be made with a range of different fruits. Use more lemon juice if the fruit has little natural acidity (this helps prevent the sugar crystallizing). Choose from cherries, dates, lemons, pears, apples, pumpkin, marrow, or anything else which you would like to try.

QUINCE PASTE
Dulce de membrillo (Spain)

All Mediterranean countries love this paste. It is a great Christmas treat since it can be stored through the winter. It will last from one year to the next. Quinces, once as popular a cultivar as grapes or apples, have a most delicate flavour and powerful scent when ripe. They are unpalatable raw.

Quantity   Makes 8 lb/4 kg paste
Time   Preparation: 40 minutes
        Cooking: 1 hour

5 lb/2·5 kg ripe quinces
water
4–5 lb/2–2·5 kg granulated sugar

Utensils   A preserving pan or large saucepan with a lid, a sieve or a liquidizer, and a baking sheet

Peel and quarter and core the quinces. Put the pieces in the large pan and pour in a glass of water. Cover tightly and cook on a gentle heat until the fruit is soft. Push the pulp through a sieve or purée it in the liquidizer. Weigh the pulp and add 9 oz/300 g granulated sugar for each 1 lb/500 g fruit. Put the fruit and sugar back in the pan and cook gently for 30 to 40 minutes until the paste is stiff and transparent. Oil the baking sheet. Spread the paste out on the baking sheet and leave it to cool. Store, cut in squares wrapped in waxed paper, in the larder.

SUGGESTIONS
● Peeled sliced fresh quinces are a particularly good addition to apple pie. Marrow or pumpkin is sometimes cooked in the same fashion to give a very popular sweetmeat called *Cabello de Angel*, Angel's Hair.

STORECUPBOARD FRUIT, NUTS, SPICES, AND SWEETS
(Turkey)

For centuries the Bosphorus provided the highway down which the spices of Asia reached the markets of Europe. The steps of the ancient spice market of Istanbul, on the Asian side of the water, lead quite properly straight to the old loading quays. The market itself is still an Aladdin's treasurehouse of delights, as befits the shopping-centre of the former capital of the all-powerful Ottoman Empire. Today the merchants are housed in a vast cavernous building, its roof supported by great sweeping arches through which thread alleyways lined with kiosks. Some of the shops sell gold jewellery, Japanese watches and calculators, hand-made baskets and goods from Taiwan, silks and embroidered slippers, but most of them specialize in the culinary delicacies which have always been the single most valuable item of trade. The overflow spills on to the pavement — there are open sacks of herbs and aromatics: turmeric, cumin, coriander, cinnamon, cloves, nutmeg, aniseed, dried ginger root, tea, mint, fennel, marigold petals (called de-hydrated Mexican saffron), lime blossom, camomile, and vervane. Counters are stacked high with glass jars filled with precious spices: paprika, pepper, saffron, and salep.

Some of the shops are decked with strings of dark dried sausages, necklaces of okra, garlic, onions, and bundles of aubergines dried till they look like the shrivelled soles of leather shoes, all store-vegetables to be soaked and stuffed and cooked. Paper-thin slices are shaved off dried hams of paprika-rubbed beef, like a Parma ham but with a bitter crust. There are backgammon and chess boards for sale, dried flowers, pungent salt fish, barrels of wrinkled, shiny black olives and others full of the dull green ones, plump in brine or stuffed with scarlet peppers. Pickled vegetables are sold by weight, scooped up in perforated draining spoons and weighed in plastic bags.

There are shops which sell dried fruit: fat sweet prunes, golden apricots, and peaches, endless shades of raisins and sultanas, and orange and lemon peel for flavouring. And beside them there are sacks of beautiful nuts — almonds, hazelnuts, chestnuts, sag-bellied sacks of walnuts, jars full of pine kernels, sunflower seeds, salted pumpkin seeds, dried melon pips.

Other kiosks are rich with the scent of fresh coffee — busily milling each customer's own mix. They also sell bags of freshly roasted beans to be ground minutes before the brewing in one of the heavy brass coffee grinders which look like oversize peppermills.

But it is the shops which sell honey — big, irregular combs robbed from the wild bees, neat squares from the domesticated insects, tins of treacle-dark nectar — which draw the biggest audience. The Turks love sweet things — there are queues to buy slices cut off great blocks of sesame seed *halva*, studded with pale green pistachios, swirls of chocolate, walnuts, coconut; and, stored in wooden boxes, squares of transparent *loukum*, Turkish delight, flavoured with rosewater and half-buried in drifts of snowy icing sugar. The same shops also sell country *halva* made with semolina, and great flat discs of noodles fried and then drenched with syrup.

SALEP
(Turkey, formerly all Europe and Britain)

Salep is a powder which can be mixed to make a drink still widely available and popular in Turkey and parts of the Balkans. Sacks of the creamy-white powdered root are on sale in most eastern European markets. It is not cheap, owing to the difficulty of gathering the raw material, usually the tubers of the *Orchis* species, although *Anacamptis pyramidalis* and the lesser butterfly orchid *Plantanthera bifolia* are also considered edible. The tubers themselves have a higher protein content than meat, and were a valuable source of protein (and invalid restorative) among the peasant community because the roots could be gathered from the wild. Its use in Britain was widespread, particularly among the rural poor, for many centuries — the root of *Orchis mascula* was that most commonly used, called 'dogstones'. The arrival of cheap tea and coffee was probably the indirect salvation of our rarest group of wildflowers. However, Hannah Glasse mentions it as obtainable at a shilling an ounce in 1747, Victorian workmen drank it in their 'car men's rests', and Dorothy Hartley records in 1954 that she was grateful for a bowl of 'salop' hot and thick and sugared, in a seaman's cottage after a long wet crossing. The Irish, she records, took theirs in a teacup, thickened with cream and egg yolk. The Scots liked it with whisky in a glass.

Should you find yourself in a Turkish market, with access to the precious powder, here is how to prepare it.

1 pint/600 ml milk *or* water   powdered cinnamon *or* ginger
1 teaspoon salep powder

Stir the powder into the milk in a saucepan. Heat gently and simmer till it thickens into a runny jelly. Flavour with a pinch of powdered cinnamon or ginger.

ALMOND MARZIPAN CREAM
Frangipane (Italy)

Sicily, 1928.   Almonds are raised primarily for exportation and their local consumption is regarded as something of an extravagance. Families in modest circumstances frequently depend on the produce of their few almond trees to provide their supply of ready cash for the year. Other uses are also made for the almond. The outer husk is burned to make a sort of ash soap used in laundering and the hard shell serves as fuel in the braziers.

Charlotte Gower Chapman, *Milocca*

3 eggs
3 oz/75 g flour
1 pint/600 ml milk

4 oz/100 g sugar
6 oz/175 g ground almonds

Utensils   A saucepan and a baking dish

Beat the eggs together. Mix the flour with a little of the milk and then stir it into the rest of the milk and the beaten eggs. Cook the mixture over a low heat like a custard, whisking steadily and adding little by little the sugar and the almonds. When thick, remove and pour into an oiled baking dish. When it is cold, cut it into squares like Turkish delight. A special treat for holidays.

Drink

WINE SOUP
Weinsuppe (Germany)

Sweetened wine, beer, and fruit soups are served before the meat in Germany, in the usual order for soup. In Finland such sweet soups are served at the end of the meal.

Quantity   A light private supper for 2
Time   Preparation intermittently: 20–30 minutes

1 bottle white wine
2 cloves and a small stick
   cinnamon for flavouring
1 tablespoon sugar
2 eggs

Utensils   A saucepan, a roomy bowl, and a whisk

Bring the wine to the boil with the spices and the sugar. Meanwhile beat the eggs in the bowl. Take the pan off the heat and pour the soup from a height into the beaten eggs. A slice of Maria Antionette's *Kugelhupf* (see page 521) to accompany your delicate meal.

SUGGESTIONS
● To make hot beer soup, substitute beer for the wine. Accompany with a slice of Welsh Rarebit (see page 485).

COLD BEER SOUP
Bierkaltschale (Germany)

One of those little meals to be enjoyed on one's own, a pleasure like that of good bread dunked into strong red wine, as with the southern French habit of *faire chabrot*. The dish has its strong supporters.

Quantity   Enough for 1
Time   Preparation: 20 minutes

    2 oz/50 g currants
    4 oz/100 g brown bread, crumbled
    1 pint/600 ml light beer

Utensils   A bowl

Put the currants to swell in the bowl in a warm oven for 10 minutes. Take the bowl out of the oven, put in the breadcrumbs and pour in the beer. Put all in a cool place to soak. Ready to eat in 10 minutes. Sprinkle it with brown sugar and eat it with cream.

OATMEAL CAUDLE
(England)

A good pub drink once very popular in rural England. Digestible and fortifying enough to set a person up for the homeward journey after a long day at market.

Quantity   Enough for 4 homeward bound travellers
Time   Preparation: Minimal
           Cooking: 30 minutes

    2 pints/1 litre light beer
    2 pints/1 litre water
    4 oz/100 g oatmeal
    1 teaspoon grated nutmeg
    1 teaspoon powdered ginger

    4 cloves (a careful housewife
       would take them out and use
       them again)
    4 tablespoons brown sugar *or*
       Golden syrup

Utensils   A heavy-bottomed saucepan and a wooden spoon

Put all the ingredients in the saucepan and mix all well together. Bring to the boil and then turn down the heat immediately. Stir frequently as the caudle simmers for half an hour, until it is good and thick. You may need to add a little extra liquid.

Set out 4 heavy mugs and put a spoonful of sugar or syrup in each. Pour the hot caudle over it. Stir well and serve while piping hot.

PLUM BRANDY
Tuica (Romania)

Strong alcohol can be distilled from any vegetable matter which will rot, a process of fermentation well known to anyone who has ever gone into an apple-loft. The taste for fermented liquor is by no means confined to humans — baboons will feast on rotten fruit which makes them so drunk they lie in helpless heaps; elephants will search out baobab groves where the fruit has fermented on the ground. From the freeze-distilled potato spirits of Finland, to the herb-scented liquors of the monasteries of France and Italy, all Europe distils. The peasant community was more accustomed to using its hard liquor as a morning pick-me-up than as an elegant *digestif*.

In Romania to this day the preferred raw material for fruit brandy is plums. The local village doctor showed D. J. Hall his home-still in 1937:

'Have you seen how tuica is made? Come with me and I will show you.' So we went down together, the doctor knocking the plums from the trees and filling my hands with them. In a barn were eight enormous barrels about three feet high, standing on their ends. A gentle sizzling came from them, the air was filled with the scent of fermenting plums.

'When I make tuica I do not make it straight from the fruit off the trees as the peasants do. I fill these barrels and let the plums lie there fermenting for about six weeks. After that I put them in fabrica. That is in the other shed. There are some there now.' I had no idea that tuica could be made so simply. On a brick furnace stood a large copper, a long pipe from it led through a barrel and from the pipe's end fell drop by drop the tuica into a container.

'It is primitive, is it not? The fermenting plums are put in the copper, the vapour passes through the pipe. In that barrel is water which is always cold because a stream from the hill flows through it. So the vapour is condensed and there is tuica. So simple, eh?'

There can be no better conclusion to a good meal. Bon appétit.

BIBLIOGRAPHY
Principal Sources Consulted

Aldiss, Brian. *Cities and Stones: A Traveller's Jugoslavia*. Faber, London, 1966.

Arensberg, Conrad M. *The Irish Countryman*. Macmillan, USA, 1937.

Ayrton, Elisabeth. *The Cookery of England*. André Deutsch, London, 1974.

Van Bath and B. S. Slicher. *The Agrarian History of Western Europe,* AD *500–1850*. London, 1963.

Beeton, Isabella. *Household Management* (1912 Edition). Ward Lock, London.

Bennett, H. S. *Life on the English Manor, a Study of Peasant Conditions 1150–1400*. Cambridge, England, 1948.

Blum, Jerome. *The End of the Old Order in Rural Europe*. Princeton, USA, 1978.

Blum, Jerome (Ed). *Our Forgotten Past*. Thames & Hudson, London, 1982.

Bonham Carter, V. *The English Village*. London, 1952.

Borrow, George. *The Bible in Spain*. London, 1843.

Borrow, George. *Wild Wales*. London, 1862.

Boswell, James. *Journal of a Tour to the Hebrides*. London, 1785.

de Boulay, Juliet. *Portrait of a Greek Mountain Village (Life in Anbeli in Euboea, 1966–68.)* Clarendon Press, England, 1974.

Brennan, Gerald. *The Face of Spain*. Turnstile Press, London, 1950.

Brennan, Gerald. *South from Granada*. Hamish Hamilton, London, 1957.

Browning, Ellen. *A Girl's Wanderings in Hungary*. London, 1896.

Carlyle, Thomas. *Reminiscences*. London, 1881.

Casas, Penelope. *The Foods and Wines of Spain*. Knopf, USA, 1982.

du Chaillu, Paul. *The Land of the Midnight Sun*. London, 1881.

Chamoux, Simone. *Les Olives dans la Cuisine*. Lys, France, 1985.

Chapman, Charlotte Gower. *Milocca: A Sicilian Village*. Allen & Unwin, London, 1973.

Clair, Colin. *Of Herbs and Spices*. Abelard Schuman, London, 1961.

Cobbett, William. *Rural Rides*. London, 1830.

Dabitesse, M. L. *Révolution Silencieuse*. Paris, 1931.

Dallas, E. S. *Kettner's Book of the Table*. London, 1877.

David, Elizabeth. *French Provincial Cooking*. Michael Joseph, London, 1960.

Davidson, Alan. *North Atlantic Seafood*. Viking, London, 1979.

Davidson Alan. *Mediterranean Seafood*. Allen Lane, London, 1972.

Denton, Revd W. *Servia and the Servians:* (Letters to his wife). London, 1862.

Dickens, Charles. *The Posthumous Papers of the Pickwick Club*. London, 1836.

Fisher, M. F. K. *The Cooking of Provincial France*. Time-Life Books, 1969.

Fitzgibbon, Theodora. *A Taste of Ireland*. Dent, London, 1968.

Franklin, S. H. *The European Peasantry*. London, 1969.

Fraser, Ronald. *The Pueblo (Life in the Village of Tajo, Andalucía in 1958)*. Allen Lane, London, 1973.

Freeman, Bobby. *First Catch Your Peacock*. Gwent, Wales, 1980.

Fytrakis, Eva. *Traditional Greek Cooking*. (Trans. Diana Reid). Athens, 1981.

Gordon, Jan and Cora. *Two Vagabonds in Sweden and Lapland*. London, 1926.

Grant of Rothiemurchus, Elizabeth. *Memoires of a Highland Lady*. Edinburgh, 1830.

Grigson, Jane. *Charcuterie and French Pork Cookery*. Michael Joseph, London, 1967.

Hall, D. J. *Romanian Furrow*. London, 1939.

Hardisty, Jytte. *Scandinavian Cooking*. Hamlyn, London, 1970.

Hartley, Dorothy. *Food in England*. Macdonald, London, 1934.

Heaton, Eliza Putnam. *By-Paths in Sicily*. Dutton, USA, 1920.

Hemingway, Ernest. *The Dangerous Summer*. Hamish Hamilton, London, 1985.

Henderson, T. F. *Old World Scotland*. Edinburgh, 1893.

Hoskins, W. G. *The Midlands Peasant*. London, 1957.

Hough, P. H. *Dutch Life in Town and Country*. London, 1901.

Howitt. *Rural Life of Germany*. London, 1842.

Johnston, Isobel Christian. *The Cook and Housewife's Manual of Mrs Margaret Dods*. 1826.

Kinglake, A. W. *Eothen (Travels in the Near East)*. London, 1844.

Ladurie, E. Le Roy. *Les Paysans du Languedoc*. Paris, 1966.

Lang, George. *The Cuisine of Hungary*. Athenaeum, London, 1971.

Leib, Ollie. *Bayerische Leibspeisen*. Munich, 1979.

Levai, Vera. *Culinary Delights*. Budapest, 1983.

Llanover, Lady. *The First Principles of Good Cookery*. London, 1867.

Llewellyn, Richard. *How Green Was My Valley*. Michael Joseph, London, 1939.

Lloyd, L. *Peasant Life in Sweden*. London, 1870.

Lovell, M. S. *Edible Mollusks of Great Britain and Ireland*. London, 1867.

Luard, Nicholas. *Andalucía*. Century, London, 1984.

Mabey, Richard. *Food for Free*. Collins, London, 1972.

McGee, Harold. *On Food and Cooking*. Scribner, USA, 1985.

McNeill, F. Marian. *The Scots Kitchen*. Blackie, Edinburgh, 1929.

Médécin, Jacques. *Cuisine Niçoise* (Trans. Peter Graham). Penguin, London, 1983.

Montagne, Prosper. *Larousse Gastronomique*. Paris, 1938.

Morton H. V. *In Search of Ireland*. Methuen, London, 1930.

Olsson, Brita. *Baka Matbrod*. Sweden, 1984.

Oxford Symposium Notes. 1981, 1983, and 1985.

Oyler, Philip. *The Generous Earth*. Harmondsworth, London, 1961.

Pagnol, Koscher & Mattern. *Les Recettes de la Table Provençale*. Strasburg, 1982.

Pohren, Donn. *Adventures in Taste: The Wines and Folk Food of Spain*. Seville, 1972.

de Pomiane, Edouard. *Le Code de la Bonne Chère*. Paris, 1930.

de Pomiane, Edouard. *Cooking with Pomiane*. Faber, London, 1962.

Raymont, Ladislas. *The Peasants*. Knopf, USA, 1925.

Reboule, J.-B. *La Cuisinière Provençale*. Marseilles, 1895.

Renell of Rod, Sir James. *Customs and Lore of Modern Greece*. London, 1892.

Riddervold, Astri and Andreas Ropeid. *Popular Diet*. Ethnologia Scandinavica, 1984.

Romer, Elizabeth. *The Tuscan Year*. Weidenfeld, London, 1984.

Root, Waverly. *The Food of France*. Cassell, London, 1958.

Rousseau, Jean-Jacques. *La Nouvelle Heloise*. Paris, 1767.

Spink, Reginald. *Denmark*. A & C Black, London, 1957.

Stratilesco, Theresa. *From Carpathian to Pindus. (Pictures of Roumanian Country Life)*. London, 1906.

Stromstad, Asse. *Eat the Norway*. Oslo, 1984.

Thackeray, W. M. *The Ballad of Bouillabaisse*. Punch, London, 1849.

Turney-High, H. H. *The Life and Times of a Walloon Village*. Columbia, USA, 1958.

Tweedie, Ethel B. *Through Finland in Carts*. London, 1898.

Vidoudez, Michele and Jacqueline Grangier. *A la Mode Chez Nous*. Payot (Ed), Lausanne, 1976.

Warriner, D. *The Economics of Peasant Farming*. London, 1964.

Weaver, William Woys. *Sauerkraut Yankees*. UPP, Philadephia, 1983.

Willson, Revd T. B. *Norway at Home*. London, 1908.

Wilson, C. Anne. *Food and Drink in Britain*. Constable, London, 1973.

de Windt, Henry. *Finland As It Is*. London, 1901.

Woodforde, Revd James. *Diary of a Country Parson 1758–1802*. London, 1924–31.

INDEX